Heritage Futures

Heritage Futures

Comparative Approaches to Natural and Cultural Heritage Practices

Rodney Harrison, Caitlin DeSilvey, Cornelius Holtorf, Sharon Macdonald, Nadia Bartolini, Esther Breithoff, Harald Fredheim, Antony Lyons, Sarah May, Jennie Morgan and Sefryn Penrose

with contributions by Anders Högberg and Gustav Wollentz

First published in 2020 by
UCL Press
University College London
Gower Street
London WC1E 6BT

Available to download free: www.uclpress.co.uk

ISBN: 978-1-78735-602-3 (Hbk.)
ISBN: 978-1-78735-601-6 (Pbk.)
ISBN: 978-1-78735-600-9 (PDF)
ISBN: 978-1-78735-603-0 (epub)
ISBN: 978-1-78735-604-7 (mobi)
DOI: https://doi.org/10.14324/111.9781787356009

Contents

List of figures

Notes on contributors

Rodney Harrison is professor of heritage studies at the UCL Institute of Archaeology. He has experience working in, teaching and researching natural and cultural heritage conservation, management and preservation in the UK, Europe, Australia, North America and South America. His research has been funded by AHRC/UK Research and Innovation, the Global Challenges Research Fund, the British Academy, the Wenner-Gren Foundation, the Australian Research Council, the Australian Institute of Aboriginal and Torres Strait Islander Studies and the European Commission. Rodney was principal investigator and led both the Diversity theme and the Heritage Futures research programme.

Caitlin DeSilvey is professor of cultural geography at the University of Exeter, and associate director of the Environment and Sustainability Institute at Exeter's campus in Penryn, Cornwall. Her research explores the cultural significance of material change and transformation, and she has worked with artists, archaeologists, environmental scientists and heritage practitioners on a range of interdisciplinary projects. Her monograph, *Curated Decay: Heritage Beyond Saving* (UMP, 2017), received the 2018 UMW Historic Preservation Book Prize. Caitlin was a co-investigator and led the Transformation theme of the Heritage Futures research programme.

Cornelius Holtorf is professor of archaeology and holds a UNESCO chair on heritage futures at Linnaeus University in Kalmar, Sweden. He also directs the Graduate School in Contract Archaeology (GRASCA) at his university. Having collaborated for many years with the Swedish Nuclear Fuel and Waste Management Company (SKB) and other major stakeholders in the nuclear waste sector, he is currently directing the project Memory across Generations. His research interests lie in contemporary archaeology, heritage theory and heritage futures. Cornelius was a co-investigator and led the Uncertainty theme of the Heritage Futures research programme.

Sharon Macdonald is Alexander von Humboldt professor of social anthropology and director of the Centre for Anthropological Research on Museums and Heritage (CARMAH) in the Institute of European Ethnology, Humboldt-Universität zu Berlin. She is also an honorary professor in the Department of Sociology, University of York. She is currently a principal investigator on the following projects: Making Differences: Transforming Museums and Heritage in the Twenty-First Century (Alexander von Humboldt Foundation); Matters of Activity: Image, Space, Material (German Research Foundation); and Curating Digital Images (German Research Foundation). Sharon was a co-investigator and led the Profusion theme of the Heritage Futures research programme.

Nadia Bartolini is a consultant researcher and associate of the Environment and Sustainability Institute, University of Exeter, who has worked as a postdoctoral research associate on AHRC-funded research projects based at the University of Exeter and at the Open University. Her research explores the geographies of heritage, ranging from urban cultures and the built environment to transitional and spiritual landscapes. She has a particular interest in mixed qualitative and creative research methods, and in interdisciplinary collaborations that centre on public engagement. Nadia was a postdoctoral research associate on the Transformation theme of the Heritage Futures research programme, based at the University of Exeter.

Esther Breithoff is a UK Research and Innovation Future Leaders fellow and lecturer in contemporary archaeology and heritage at Birkbeck, University of London. She has held postdoctoral research positions at UiT The Arctic University of Norway and UCL. Her research spans the fields of contemporary archaeology and critical heritage studies, and traces a common set of interests in the relationships between conflicts, resources, recycling and rights across the human/non-human divide in the Anthropocene. Esther was a postdoctoral research associate on the Diversity theme of the Heritage Futures research programme, based at UCL.

Harald Fredheim is a postdoctoral research associate at Museum of London Archaeology (MOLA) and the University of Exeter. His research explores heritage values and participatory approaches to heritage practice, with a particular focus on how heritage policies and practitioners view and relate to various publics. Harald was a research associate on the Profusion theme of the Heritage Futures research programme, based at the University of York.

Antony Lyons is an independent artist–researcher whose creative methods include film, photography, sonic works and intermedia installation. With a background in eco/geosciences and landscape studies, his practice is concerned with ecological processes, environmental change and nature–culture relationships. Current work includes projects that explore, and juxtapose, liminal land–water places; social and heritage challenges; and diverse perspectives relating to rewilding and novel land-use futures. Antony was the senior creative fellow on the Heritage Futures research programme and also contributed to the work of the Transformation theme.

Sarah May is a senior lecturer in public history and heritage at Swansea University. She has previously worked as senior archaeologist for English Heritage and as an independent consultant. Sarah was a postdoctoral research associate on the Uncertainty theme of the Heritage Futures research programme, based at UCL.

Jennie Morgan is a lecturer in heritage in the Division of History, Heritage and Politics at the University of Stirling, where she also directs the MSc Heritage programme. Her research focuses on museological change, often by studying museums as organisations and the day-to-day work of museum practitioners. She has a particular interest in sensory, visual and material ethnographic methods, as well as applied, interdisciplinary research. Jennie was a postdoctoral research associate on the Profusion theme of the Heritage Futures research programme, based at the University of York.

Sefryn Penrose is a consultant researcher and archaeologist of the recent past. She has a background in heritage consultancy with Atkins, and is the author of *Assessment of Heritage at Risk from Environmental Threat* (2013), a major Historic England policy project, and editor of *Images of Change: An Archaeology of England's Contemporary Landscape* (English Heritage, 2007). Sefryn was a research associate on the Diversity theme of the Heritage Futures research programme, based at UCL.

Anders Högberg is a professor of archaeology at Linnaeus University and an associated researcher at the University of Johannesburg. He has broad research interests, and is working with projects in heritage futures studies, human migration and cognitive evolution. Anders was an affiliated researcher on the Uncertainty theme of the Heritage Futures research programme.

Gustav Wollentz defended his PhD in summer 2018 at the Graduate School Human Development in Landscapes, Kiel University, Germany, focusing on the relationship between difficult heritage and temporalities. He received his bachelor's and master's degrees in archaeology from Linnaeus University in Sweden. He is working as a project leader/researcher at the Nordic Centre of Heritage Learning and Creativity in Östersund, Sweden. Gustav contributed to work on the Uncertainty theme of the Heritage Futures research programme.

Preface

The Heritage Futures research programme set out to explore how heritage practices, broadly defined, contribute to the making of future worlds. From 2015 to 2019, an interdisciplinary, international team of 16 researchers collaborated with 25 international partner organisations and many others to investigate heritage and heritage-like practices in a broad range of fields and contexts, and to explore the potential for innovation and creative exchange within and across them. This book assembles the research produced by the research programme, which was funded under the UK Arts and Humanities Research Council's (AHRC) Care for the Future theme. The book shares the outcomes of the research programme's distinctively collaborative and comparative approach, which sought to bring heritage conservation practices of various forms into closer dialogue with the management of other material and virtual legacies, and to explore different forms of conservation activities and initiatives as unique and individual future-making practices.

The research programme aimed to:

- Document and analyse practices by which pasts, presents and futures are assembled across a range of different heritage and heritage-like domains, by exploring them through mixed ethnographic and creative visual methods, in comparative perspective;
- Draw on this empirical research to understand and theorise the values that are generated by the work that is undertaken in caring for futures, within each of these heterogeneous domains; and
- Explore, in partnership with its project partners, how those different practices of assembling and caring for the future might be creatively redeployed to generate innovation, foster resilience and encourage sustainability.

This book documents the work of the research programme, presents its main results and points to emerging implications for academic research (particularly in the field of interdisciplinary critical heritage studies) and more generally for an expanded global heritage sector. The book addresses what we set out to do, what we did, and what we learned during the programme of research. We address our original aims and some of the difficulties we faced along the way in attempting to realise these aims, as well as the transformative insights we took away from the research programme as it progressed. In particular, the book explores what a focus on heritage futures means in a variety of specific contexts, and how such a perspective can change the heritage agenda for researchers, practitioners, policymakers and publics.

There are many practitioners outside the academy who work in the broad field of heritage preservation, conservation and legacy management. Although our main audience for this particular book is an academic one, we also hope it can act as a resource for practitioners both inside and outside existing natural and cultural heritage preservation and conservation fields, to encourage them to think about heritage in new ways and how it might be practised 'otherwise' (see Povinelli 2011a; 2012; 2014; 2016).

The research programme was organised around four themes, each of which identified a challenge for the future of heritage. This thematic focus also forms the structure of the book, which is divided into four parts: Diversity, Profusion, Uncertainty and Transformation. Research under each theme was carried out with reference to a specific framing question, respectively: What kinds of futures are realised by the preservation of biological, cultural and linguistic diversity – and what can each of these fields learn from one another? In the face of a profusion of things – especially those mass produced for mass consumption – what gets kept for the future in museums and homes? How does the perceived uncertainty of the long-term future provide opportunities for heritage and conservation practice? What are the future-making processes and practices involved in heritage landscapes that are undergoing significant change and transformation? Researchers on each theme used a range of ethnographic and creative methods to engage with individuals and institutions involved in addressing these challenges in various ways. In this book, we document the research undertaken within each theme and the lessons we learned from our work, both within each theme and collectively. The book aims to communicate the insights we gained from our extensive (although inevitably far from comprehensive) look at future issues in relation to heritage theory and practice.

While the conception, development and writing of the book was a collaborative effort, this necessarily required a division of authorship and editorial responsibilities across the different parts of the volume. We present the book as a co-authored monograph because we acknowledge the collective contributions to the arguments developed within it, and the collaborative nature of the work. This has in itself been an experiment in finding a format in which diverse voices and views could productively speak to one another, while also acknowledging and foregrounding the diversity and range of different views, academic traditions and writing styles of contributors. As principal investigator, Harrison acted as the lead and coordinating author of the book, taking overall responsibilities for its editing and production. The co-investigators (DeSilvey, Holtorf, Macdonald) shared with Harrison editorial responsibilities for the individual thematic parts they each led, and for shaping the intellectual agenda of the book as a whole. However, we also felt it important to indicate the main authors of individual chapters within the book, to make clear specific contributions to the text and its arguments, and to highlight which named individuals were responsible for the empirical work that underpins them. Thus, coordinating and lead authors on individual chapters are listed first in the naming order of each individual chapter, with co-authors listed in alphabetical order where equal inputs have been made, or in relative order of the level of input, except where specifically noted. Some individual chapters within the book also include named contributors who are not listed as authors on the book itself. The difference between authors and contributors recognises a qualitative difference in contributions of authors to the overall framing and intellectual agenda of the book and its underpinning research programme. In most cases, 'contributors' have been involved in making inputs to the individual chapter on which they are named as first or subsequent author, while book 'authors' have additionally contributed by commenting on, and shaping, the broader intellectual agenda of the monograph and the research programme more generally.

Acknowledgements

Heritage Futures (originally known by the longer title Assembling Alternative Futures for Heritage) was funded by an AHRC Care for the Future: Thinking Forward through the Past Theme Large Grant (AH/ M004376/1), awarded to Rodney Harrison (as principal investigator), Caitlin DeSilvey, Cornelius Holtorf, Sharon Macdonald (as co-investigators), Antony Lyons (as senior creative fellow), Martha Fleming (as senior postdoctoral researcher), Nadia Bartolini, Sarah May, Jennie Morgan and Sefryn Penrose (as named postdoctoral researchers). Three PhD students were additionally funded as in-kind support for the research programme by their respective host universities – Kyle Lee-Crossett (UCL), Bryony Prestidge (University of York) and Robyn Raxworthy (University of Exeter). Martha Fleming left to focus on other responsibilities during the research programme's first year. The team of researchers was subsequently joined by Esther Breithoff, as postdoctoral researcher, and by Hannah Williams, as administrative assistant and events coordinator, a role that was in turn later filled by Kyle Lee-Crossett, and, in its final year, by Harald Fredheim, as postdoctoral researcher. Anders Högberg (Linnaeus University) was an associate researcher to the research programme. In addition, the research programme was supported by the work of a series of separate creative commissions with artists Shelley Castle (Encounters Arts), Nancy Campbell and Karen Guthrie, and through collaborations with Henry McGhie, who acted as the curator of the Heritage Futures exhibition, which opened at the Manchester Museum in December 2018. The research programme further benefited from the work of the artist and illustrator, Pernilla Frid.

Our work was helpfully and generously guided by an international and cross-sectoral advisory group, who commented critically on our research and helped us to ensure it engaged our professional audiences. The advisory group members were Gustavo Araoz, then president of the International Council on Monuments and Sites (ICOMOS); Tim Badman, then director of the World Heritage Programme at the International

Union for the Conservation of Nature (IUCN); Francesco Bandarin, then assistant director-general for culture of the United Nations Educational, Scientific and Cultural Organization (UNESCO), and professor of urban planning and conservation at the University IUAV of Venice; Saida Laârouchi Engström, then vice-president for strategy and programmes at SKB, the Swedish Nuclear Fuel and Waste Management Company; Loyd Grossman CBE, then chairman of the Heritage Alliance (UK); John Orna-Ornstein, then director of museums at the Arts Council England (ACE) and later head of collections with the National Trust; and Ingrid Samuel, historic environment director for the National Trust. In addition to formal advisory group meetings with the academic members of the research programme, many of the members also participated in knowledge-exchange workshops and other activities we organised throughout the four-year research programme. We thank all members of the group for their contributions to our work, and their respective organisations for supporting our research and its outcomes by resourcing their involvement.

We acknowledge and thank the partner organisations with whom we have worked as part of the Heritage Futures research programme: ACÔA (Friends of the Côa Museum and Archaeological Park); the Anthropology Institute, Minzu University of China; the Anthropology of Art Research Centre, Chinese National Academy of Arts; Associação Transumância e Natureza (ATN); ACE; the Association of Independent Museums (AIM); Coastal and Intertidal Zone Archaeological Network (CITiZAN); the Endangered Languages Documentation Programme (ELDP); the Frozen Ark Project; Future Terrains; the Heritage Alliance; ICOMOS; IUCN; Manchester Museum; Memory of Mankind (MOM); the Musée d'ethnographie de Genêvre (MEG); the National Trust; the New School House Gallery (York); One Earth: New Horizons Message Project (OEM); NordGen/The Svalbard Global Seed Vault (SGSV); Rewilding Europe; Royal Botanic Gardens Kew; Svensk Kärnbränslehantering AB (SKB, The Swedish Nuclear Fuel and Waste Management Company); Tropcnmuscum/National Museum of World Culture; UNESCO; the University of Gothenburg (UGOT); the Wheal Martyn Trust (and the affiliated China Clay History Society); and York Museums Trust.

We extend particular thanks to the following individuals for their assistance with our work (in no particular order): Ana Berliner and António Monteiro (ATN); Andrea Meanwell; Anna Bohlin and Staffan Appelgren (UGOT); Anna Bunney, Henry McGhie, Nick Merriman and Esme Ward (Manchester Museum); Åsmund Asdal (NordGen); Bárbara Carvalho (ACÔA); Boris Wastiau (MEG); Colin Vallance, Jo Moore and

Sue Ford (Wheal Martyn Trust); Cornwall Council Historic Environment Team; Daniel Lindskog; Duncan Kent, Grant Lohoar, David Mason and Angus Wainwright (National Trust); Edmund Flach (Zoological Society of London); Erik Setzmann and Sofie Tunbrant (SKB); Gill Greaves (ACE); Jacqueline Mackenzie-Dodds (Natural History Museum); Jon Lomberg (OEM); Lara Band (CITiZAN); Mandana Seyfeddinipur (ELDP); Martin Kunze (MOM); Megan von Ackermann; Michael Turnpenny (York Museums Trust); Mike Bruford, Mafalda Costa and staff and students of the Biomedical Research Laboratory at Cardiff University (Frozen Ark); Anne Clarke and Jude Smith (Frozen Ark, Nottingham); Nancy Campbell (artist); Nina Davies, Clare Drinkell and Mark Nesbitt (Kew); Paula Jackson and Robert Teed (the New School House Gallery); Pedro Prata (ATN & Rewilding Portugal); Pete Whitbread-Abrutat (Future Terrains); researchers at the Centre for Anthropological Research on Museums and Heritage (CARMAH), Berlin; Sean Simpson (Imerys Minerals Ltd); Shelley Castle (Encounters Arts); Wayne Modest (Tropenmuseum/ National Museum of World Culture); Zemirah Moffat (Insightful Moves).

During the course of the research programme we presented our work at a number of different academic and professional forums. We particularly wish to acknowledge several of these where we received significant feedback as a result of cross-programme presentations, interventions and workshops. These included the third and fourth biennial Association of Critical Heritage Studies (ACHS) Conferences held in 2016 in Montreal, Canada and 2018 in Hangzhou, China respectively; the eighth World Archaeological Congress (WAC-8) in 2016 held in Kyoto, Japan; the second international Anticipation Conference in 2017 held in London, UK; NESTA's FutureFest in 2018 held in London, UK; the IUCN World Conservation Congress in 2016 held in Hawaii, USA; and the ICOMOS Scientific Symposium held in 2017 in Delhi, India. During the IUCN and ICOMOS events, we helped to formulate, and made contributions to, their shared 'nature–culture journey' theme. We thank the organisers of, and participants in, each of these events for the opportunities to participate and contribute, and for valuable feedback.

Our work also benefited from collaborations with the Manchester Museum on the development of a major exhibition, which was inspired by the Heritage Futures research programme. The exhibition was developed over the period 2017–18 and hosted by the museum from December 2018 to December 2020. The exhibition was curated by Henry McGhie and Rodney Harrison, with contributions from the Heritage Futures research team, and was accompanied by a programme of events hosted as part of the museum's Heritage Futures Studio (see Figures 0.1, 0.2 and

0.3). The development of the exhibition and subsequent engagement with its visitors over the period in which this book was being written and edited contributed significantly to its final shape and form.

Parts of the book draw on material previously published elsewhere, although in all cases this has been substantially edited and revised in the form in which it appears in the present volume. Chapters 1 and 2 draw partially on material previously published as Rodney Harrison (2015), 'Beyond "Natural" and "Cultural" Heritage: Toward an Ontological Politics of Heritage in the Age of Anthropocene', *Heritage and Society* 8 (1): 24–42; Rodney Harrison (2016a), 'Archaeologies of Emergent Presents and Futures', *Historical Archaeology* 50 (3): 165–80; and Rodney Harrison, Nadia Bartolini, Caitlin DeSilvey, Cornelius Holtorf, Antony Lyons, Sharon Macdonald, Sarah May, Jennie Morgan and Sefryn Penrose (2016), 'Heritage Futures', *Archaeology International* 19: 68–72.

Chapters 3 to 7 include some material previously published as Esther Breithoff and Rodney Harrison (2020a), 'From Ark to Bank: Extinction, Proxies and Biocapitals in *Ex-Situ* Biodiversity Conservation Practices', *International Journal of Heritage Studies* 26 (1): 37–55; Esther Breithoff and Rodney Harrison (2020b), 'Making Futures in End Times: Nature Conservation in the Anthropocene', in *Deterritorialising the Future: Heritage in, of and after the Anthropocene,* edited by Rodney Harrison and Colin Sterling, 155–87, London: Open Humanities Press; Rodney

Figure 0.1   A view of the Heritage Futures exhibition, hosted by the Manchester Museum (courtesy of Manchester Museum).

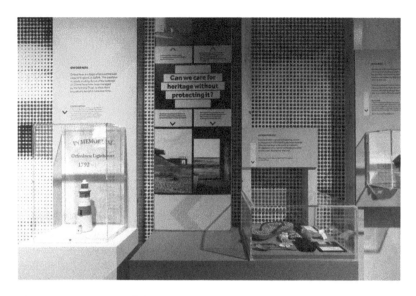

Figure 0.2 A view of the Heritage Futures exhibition, hosted by the Manchester Museum (courtesy of Manchester Museum).

Figure 0.3 A view of the Heritage Futures exhibition, hosted by the Manchester Museum (courtesy of Manchester Museum).

Harrison (2017), 'Freezing Seeds and Making Futures: Endangerment, Hope, Security, and Time in Agrobiodiversity Conservation Practices', *Culture, Agriculture, Food and Environment* 39 (2): 80–9; and Rodney Harrison (2018), 'On Heritage Ontologies: Rethinking the Material Worlds of Heritage', *Anthropological Quarterly* 91 (4): 1365–83.

Chapters 10 to 15 include some material previously published in Harald Fredheim, Sharon Macdonald and Jennie Morgan (2018), *Profusion in Museums: A Report on Contemporary Collecting and Disposal;* Sharon Macdonald and Jennie Morgan (2018a), 'What Not to Collect? Post-Connoiseurial Dystopia and the Profusion of Things', in *Curatopia: Museums and the Future of Curatorship*, edited by Philipp Schorch and Conal McCarthy, 29–43, Manchester: Manchester University Press; Sharon Macdonald and Jennie Morgan (2018b), '"How can we know the future?": Uncertainty, Transformation and Magical Techniques of Significance Assessment in Museum Collecting', in *Assessment of Significance: Deuten – Bedeuten – Umdeuten*, edited by Regine Falkenberg and Thomas Jander, 20–6, Berlin: Deutsches Historisches Museum; and Jennie Morgan and Sharon Macdonald (2020), 'De-Growing Museum Collections for New Heritage Futures', *International Journal of Heritage Studies* 26 (1): 56–70.

Chapters 17 to 22 include material previously published in Cornelius Holtorf and Anders Högberg (2014a), 'Communicating with Future Generations: What Are the Benefits of Preserving Cultural Heritage? Nuclear Power and Beyond', *European Journal of Post-Classical Archaeologies* 4: 343–58; Cornelius Holtorf and Anders Högberg (2014b), 'Nuclear Waste as Cultural Heritage of the Future – 14361', WM2014 Conference Proceedings, 2–6 March 2014, Phoenix, Arizona; Cornelius Holtorf and Anders Högberg (2016), 'The Contemporary Archaeology of Nuclear Waste. Communicating with the Future', *Arkæologisk Forum* 35: 31–7; Cornelius Holtorf and Anders Högberg (forthcoming b), 'Perceptions of the Future in Preservation Strategies', in *Cultural Heritage and the Future*, edited by Cornelius Holtorf and Anders Högberg, London and New York: Routledge; Sarah May (2020), 'Heritage, Endangerment and Participation: Alternative Futures in the Lake District', *International Journal of Heritage Studies* 26 (1): 71–86; Gustav Wollentz, Marko Barišić and Nourah Sammar (2019), 'Youth Activism and Dignity in Post-War Mostar: Envisioning a Shared Future through Heritage', *Space and Polity*, 23 (2): 197–215; Gustav Wollentz (2019), 'Conflicted Memorials and the Need to Look Forward: The Interplay between Remembering and Forgetting in Mostar and on the Kosovo Field', in *Memorials in the Aftermath of Armed Conflict: From*

History to Heritage, edited by Marie Louise Stig Sørensen, Dacia Viejo-Rose and Paola Filippucci, 159–82, Cham: Palgrave Macmillan.

Chapters 24 to 28 include material previously published as Nadia Bartolini and Caitlin DeSilvey (2020a), 'Recording Loss: Film as Method and the Spirit of Orford Ness', *International Journal of Heritage Studies* 26 (1): 19–36; Nadia Bartolini and Caitlin DeSilvey (2020b), 'Rewilding as Heritage-Making: New Natural Heritage and Renewed Memories in Portugal', in *The Routledge Handbook of Memory and Place*, edited by Sarah De Nardi, Hilary Orange, Steven High and Eerika Koskinen-Koivisto, 305–14, London: Routledge; Caitlin DeSilvey and Nadia Bartolini (2019), 'Where Horses Run Free? Autonomy, Temporality and Rewilding in the Côa Valley, Portugal', *Transactions of the Institute of British Geographers* 44 (1): 94–109; Caitlin DeSilvey (2019), 'Rewilding Time in the Vale do Côa', in *Rethinking Historical Time: New Approaches to Presentism*, edited by Marek Tamm and Laurent Olivier, 193–206, Bloomsbury Academic; Caitlin DeSilvey (2020), 'Ruderal Heritage', in *Deterritorialising the Future: Heritage in, of and after the Anthropocene*, edited by Rodney Harrison and Colin Sterling, 289–310, London: Open Humanities Press; and Antony Lyons (2020), 'Côa Valley' in *Konesh* journal, Issue: *TRACE* (online only, www.konesh.space).

Chapter 29 includes material previously published as Caitlin DeSilvey and Rodney Harrison (2020), 'Anticipating Loss: Rethinking Endangerment in Heritage Futures', *International Journal of Heritage Studies* 26 (1): 1–7.

We thank the anonymous reviewers of the book proposal and final manuscript for their suggestions, which helped us to improve the text. Kyle Lee-Crossett provided support in assisting with the administrative aspects of assembling the present volume, for which he is especially thanked. We thank UCL Press for their support and assistance with bringing this volume to publication.

Part I
Heritage futures

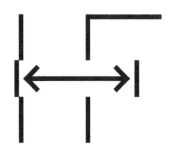

1
'For ever, for everyone ...'

Rodney Harrison, Caitlin DeSilvey, Cornelius Holtorf
and Sharon Macdonald

For ever, for everyone[1]

National Trust motto

... development that meets the needs of the present without comprom-ising the ability of future generations to meet their own needs.

Our Common Future
(Brundtland Commission 1987)

Introduction

It is a widely accepted trope that the conservation or preservation of both natural and cultural heritage is something that is done 'for the future', or on behalf of 'future generations'. Explicit statements to this effect have for some time been common. In cultural heritage fields, they often appear as a justification for a definition of heritage as something that is 'of the past, in the present, for the future' (for example, Agnew and Bridgland 2006). In natural heritage fields, especially following the widely cited defini-tion of sustainable development that was popularised by the Brundtland Report, *Our Common Future* (Brundtland Commission 1987) – which we will discuss in more detail later in this chapter and in the following one – the implication that the future is something which 'we' have responsibil-ities 'to' or 'for' has become particularly widespread. But who is this 'we' (see Adeney Thomas 2016)? Precisely 'what' are we obligated to do, and for 'whom'? And 'when' is this future to which we are obligated? These kinds of statements appear to lend moral weight to the mission of conser-vation practice, but the precise relationship of such practices to the future is less often reflected upon (but see Zetterstrom-Sharp 2015; Stainforth and Graham 2017; Holtorf and Högberg forthcoming a). While it is conventional to think about conservation or preservation as a series of different practical fields oriented towards managing and maintaining what remains of biological and/or cultural diversity from the past, it is surprisingly less often the case that scholars have reflected seriously and critically on the role of preservation practices of different kinds in assembling and making futures, despite ubiquitous claims that the aim of such procedures is the preservation of objects, places and practices *for future generations*. If we begin to probe seriously these future orientations, then it becomes possible to think of heritage as a series of activities that are intimately concerned with assembling, building and designing future worlds. This book aims to comparatively explore the ways in which heritage practices of different kinds assemble and resource different kinds of futures.

The book engages with and compares selected practices within a range of domains that are variously dedicated to perpetuating 'things' – which might include ideas, words, objects, places, species and persons (both human and non-human) – into more or less distant futures. We refer to such practices throughout the book using various terms that may speak to some readers more than others depending on their personal, professional and academic backgrounds – 'conservation' and 'preservation' are the main terms we deploy, often interchangeably, but we acknowledge that other terms are often more dominant in other settings ('keeping'/'disposing', for example, in museums and homes – see Part III, Profusion). In other contexts, the terms 'conservation' and 'preservation' are used more strictly, sometimes even in opposition to one another, as in the late nineteenth- and early twentieth-century debates that characterised the US nature conservation movement, where they were used to delineate specific philosophical approaches concerned with acceptable levels of human intervention in the natural environment. 'Conservation' in this context designated the careful management of the use of natural environments, while 'preservation' was taken to mean the protection of such environments from human use (see Sellars 1997).

As we go on to discuss, however, we see the practices associated with conservation and preservation as sharing fundamental similarities in the sense in which they both aim to resource specific futures by acting on or around certain physical or non-physical objects and subjecting them to particular practices of 'care' – a term that we will also aim to problematise and discuss in more detail, acknowledging that, in some cases, 'care' may also be shown precisely by *not* acting, which is, of course, its own form of action. (We discuss these issues in more detail in Part II, Diversity and Part V, Transformation.) In addition to designating certain levels of intervention in the maintenance of different forms of heritage, these terms ('conservation' and 'preservation') might be used in distinguishing between different kinds of heritage ('natural' or 'cultural', for example). We use these terms in the introductory part of the book more generally to denote activities concerned with sustaining (or not sustaining) anything that might be seen to be vulnerable, and hence both endangered and valuable, which becomes a target for more or less authorised and institutionalised practices of designation, collection, curation, maintenance and care. In doing so, our focus is on the *practices* by which heritage is assembled as an object of knowledge and as field of intervention, the *apparatuses* by which these practices are mediated, and the *organisations and groups* involved in promoting and undertaking such practices, as much as it is on the humans and non-humans, things, places and customs that constitute the *targets* of these conservation practices.

Comparative approaches to heritage

In looking across the range of professional fields that are implicated in undertaking and promoting practices of conservation and preservation, the book seeks to make a contribution to current discussions relating to the value of comparison in the humanities and social and historical sciences, expanding them to the study of human and non-human collectives. We chose this approach because we think that a comparative analysis of different kinds of natural and cultural conservation and preservation practices might develop and open up the notion of heritage in creative and productive ways, and also help us to explore what social and material work is facilitated by the 'doing' of heritage. Through a focus on conservation or preservation as creative, dialogical (Harrison 2013a), 'more-than-human' engagements between persons, objects, places and practices, we aim to explore heritage as a series of distinctive *processes* rather than the 'end products' of such engagements (or, indeed, simply the values associated with those end products). Through a dialogue with recent work on 'sticky', ubiquitous and pervasive forms of inheritance,[2] which may be positively, negatively or even ambiguously valued, we aim to bring the study of heritage into conversation with the study of other hyperobjects (see Morton 2013a) and Anthropocene legacies, such as waste and climate (see also Harrison 2015; Pétursdóttir 2013; 2014; 2017; 2020; Olsen and Pétursdóttir 2016; Harrison and Sterling 2020; Bartolini and DeSilvey, 2020b; DeSilvey and Harrison 2020; Breithoff 2020; further discussion in Chapter 2).

We argue that a reframed notion of heritage as a processual and discursive, as well as material, legacy might reorient heritage studies more explicitly as a study of future-making or worlding practices. In our research, we aimed to show how such 'things', and the practices by which they are realised, form templates for the organisation of new contingent realities and the construction of divergent future worlds. Working across natural and cultural heritage, our work is informed by Chakrabarty's (2009) observations of the ways in which research in what we might call 'the climate change era' forces a dissolution of the distinction between natural and cultural history. Here we intersect with a new critical engagement with nature conservation (for example, Benson 2010) and extinction studies (for example, Rose 2013; Heise 2016; Van Dooren 2016; Bird Rose et al. 2017) in exploring the distinct social and cultural frameworks that produce 'natural heritage' – and the ways in which 'cultural heritage' is not outside of, but integrally a part of, them (for example, Harrison 2015; DeSilvey 2017). Our work also connects both conceptually and empirically with recent anthropological engagements with 'futures' (for example, Appadurai 2013; Salazar et al. 2017), multiple worlds and their associated *worlding practices* (for example, Barad 2007; Stengers 2010; 2011; Povinelli 2012; Latour 2013; De la Cadena and Blaser 2018; Omura et al. 2019), and with current creative academic engagements with global climatological and environmental change (for example, Haraway 2016; Tsing 2015; Tsing et al. 2017).

Conceptually, the book draws on and expands previous work by the authors and others on the application of assemblage and actor–network theory to the critical investigation of heritage and museums (Macdonald 2009; 2013; Harrison 2013a; Bennett et al. 2017), applying these perspectives to a range of other collections and institutional contexts. It is influenced by the comparative perspectives adopted by the *Endangerment and Its Consequences* project (Vidal and Dias 2016b) in our aims to explore a range of different cultural and natural heritage conservation practices collectively, drawing on the perspectives of histories of science, and science and technology studies more generally, in doing so.[3] It is also influenced by the 'ontological turn' in the social sciences (for example, Kohn 2015; Holbraad and Pederson 2017), in particular by Karen Barad's (2007) agential realism. We extend these perspectives to adopt an approach that sees heritage practices of various kinds as enacting new realities through contingent practices of assembling and reassembling bodies, techniques, technologies, materials, values, temporalities and spaces in particular ways. Central here is a notion of plural heritage ontologies – understood as the world-making, future-assembling capacities of heritage practices of different kinds, and attending to the ways in which different heritage practices might be seen to enact different realities, and hence to assemble radically different futures

(Harrison 2015; 2017; Harrison et al. 2016; Breithoff 2020). Drawing on the work of Arturo Escobar (2018) and Marisol de la Cadena and Mario Blaser (2018), we could thus characterise the book as an investigation into the heritage 'pluriverse', or, to borrow from Bruno Latour (2013), an investigation into conservation's varied 'modes of existence'.

In developing a comparative framework for a range of different heritage and heritage-like domains, we found it helpful to designate a series of general processes that can describe heritage and conservation practices in abstract terms across a diverse range of practical fields. These processes are:

- **categorising:** practices concerned with identifying, naming, recovering, documenting
- **curating:** practices concerned with collecting, selecting, nominating, designating, listing, enumerating and attributing value
- **conserving:** practices concerned with caring, preserving, storing, archiving, managing
- **communicating:** practices concerned with using, interpreting, exhibiting, disseminating and expressing values.

These processes operate across *ex-situ* (off-site) and *in-situ* (on-site or in-place) forms of conservation. While the existence of these generic processes has been largely confirmed by our research, we began with this abstract model of heritage processes to help us to identify some other adjacent fields of practice that might be drawn in to our comparative analysis. We wanted to do this not only to attempt to broaden our understanding of heritage practices and the social, material and cultural work that they do, but also to explore the potential for specific heritage domains to do heritage *otherwise*. While the idea of exploring cultural alternatives and possibilities can be seen as fundamental to much social and cultural anthropology, the term 'otherwise' has recently been specifically theorised by Elizabeth Povinelli in what she terms an 'anthropology of the otherwise' (2011a, 10; 2014; 2016), which 'locates itself within forms of life that are at odds with dominant, and dominating, modes of being' (Povinelli 2011b, 1). What are the alternatives to contemporary heritage practices? To what extent can the practices in one domain contribute to the development of creativity and innovation when applied to another? Our work is also more or less explicitly influenced by Povinelli's interests in the role of speculation and emergent potentiality. How can the comparative project we map out for heritage studies help to rethink and actively create alternative future heritages? And in what ways can a focus on heritage practice as contingent, emergent and open lead to the development of new heritage futures (see also CARMAH 2018)?

Empirically, this book draws on the results of comparative research with more than 25 organisations which represent a diverse range of interests in the preservation or conservation of natural and cultural heritage. Our research collaborators included museums and museum professional organisations, endangered language documentation programmes, cultural heritage and protected area site management agencies, frozen zoos, herbaria, seed banks, botanical gardens and landscape rewilding projects, as well as a range of government and non-government organisations tasked with representing the interests of natural and cultural heritage preservation in a number of different ways. We also worked across fields that are not conventionally understood as 'heritage' domains, such as nuclear waste disposal and extraterrestrial communication initiatives, which we think share certain objectives with heritage practices and might be productively brought into conversation with them. We have worked across multiple sites of engagement with these organisations in around a dozen different countries to collect the empirical material on which the book draws.

Themes and structure of the book

The book, and the research programme on which it is based, is organised around four themes, each of which identifies a challenge for the future of heritage. Within each theme, we carried out ethnographic research with a range of institutions to understand how they are engaging with or responding to this particular challenge in their work. These themes provide an organisational device for making comparisons across fields of practice that are rarely, if ever, thought about collectively. The themes also provide an intellectual architecture for beginning to think in new ways about heritage and how it might be done 'otherwise'. Below, we introduce and provide the rationale for each of these themes in the order in which they appear in the book.

Diversity

Conserving endangered 'diversity' is the aim of a range of different contemporary heritage domains, where this term may refer variously to cultural, linguistic or biological diversity. While the potential for innovation in knowledge transfer across some of these domains has recently been acknowledged, such thinking has not been widely pursued across these domains of practice. This is a significant failing, as the links between biological, cultural and linguistic diversity are commonly acknowledged (for example, Maffi 2005). This theme compares ways of valuing and managing biological, cultural and linguistic diversity in biodiversity conservation programmes, endangered language preservation programmes, seed banks and other agrobiodiversity conservation programmes, herbaria and frozen zoos (repositories of genetic materials from endangered animals and plants stored at low temperatures in liquid nitrogen). In exploring the range of practices undertaken across various different heritage domains that share rationales in the maintenance of ecological, cultural, linguistic and biological diversity, it aims to explore the potential for innovative forms of knowledge exchange and the development of shared work practices between them.

Working across an expanded field of heritage that includes a more blended, complicated definition of natural/cultural and tangible/intangible heritage clearly has the potential to bring common interests in the documentation, cataloguing, maintenance and preservation of diversity across these various domains into sharp contrast. We might think here of the potential for indigenous categories of plant and animal species to provide alternative templates for recording, documenting and understanding the basis for biological diversity; the museum-like practices of collecting and documenting 'intangible' languages and their resonance with the practices of cataloguing and preserving in herbaria; and the shift in perception and practice that might come about from thinking of national parks as a form of outdoor museum or frozen zoo, or seed banks as a form of library or archive. These points of synergy and divergence are explored and emphasised in working comparatively across these various domains concerned with the conservation of different forms of diversity, and the worlding practices each enacts.

Profusion

A vast expansion of the production and affordability of material goods, and a democratisation of memory – seeing value in ordinary as well as in more singular personal histories and experiences – have contributed to a sense of there being a profusion and even excess of things that might be saved for the future (Macdonald and Morgan 2018a; Morgan and Macdonald 2020). In many societies, the number of things that people own has increased with each generation, with this even leading to the use of dedicated spaces outside the home – so-called 'self-storage' – for keeping what cannot be squeezed into it. One in ten US households make use of such facilities (Bell 2013). Professional 'decluttering' services have also expanded dramatically to help people sift the significant from the junk. This is accompanied by the growth of provision of specialist storage materials – allowing 'home curation' and 'auto-archiving' – and of online facilities for 'life chronicling', providing classificatory frameworks to help people select what is worth saving.

For museums – as institutions predicated on 'saving for posterity' – material abundance and the democratisation of memory create especially acute dilemmas, particularly for contemporary collecting. Storage is a major issue. Many museums have as much as 90 per cent of their collections in storage, and struggle with the high costs and inadequacies of this. Museums may also face backlogs of cataloguing the objects that they have collected. In the face of this, various museums and heritage organisations are reviewing collecting policies as a means of being more selective, while at the same time recognising what may be more diverse constituencies. Models such as the Australian Burra Charter are attracting attention for devising more selective value-based models for saving what will be the heritage of the future (Staniforth 2013), and there are also potential models from other studies of 'coping with overflow' (Czarniawska and Löfgren 2012). This includes considering possibilities of removing objects from museum collections in what is variously termed 'deaccession', 'disposal' and 'rationalisation' (see Chapters 10 and 11).

Accordingly, this theme looks at museums, and also at individuals in their personal lives and homes, to explore what is kept – either by active selection or other processes – in the face of a profusion of things, especially those produced by mass production. By bringing institutional (museums) and personal (homes) domains together, we aim to provide insight into how practices or approaches in each might suggest ways of doing otherwise for the other – particularly for coping with what is so often experienced as a problematic profusion of things. As we will see, this attempt to deal with profusion articulates with perceptions of future uncertainty, and experiences of addressing perceived entropic transformation, as well as with ambitions to recognise diversity in the creation of a future archive.

Uncertainty

Heritage is often said to be the human legacy preserved for the benefit of future generations. However, it typically remains unclear precisely when these future generations will live and how we can make the right decisions in the present with their best interests in mind. The main challenge lies in how to prepare for the future's inherent uncertainty. Heritage managers work with material that is testament to structural and enduring change. This perspective makes it possible for them to envision futures as different from our present as the Palaeolithic. Cultural and technological developments such as space flight and nuclear waste move our engagements with such futures from the conceptual to the strategic. Change and uncertainty provide a counterbalance to heritage tropes of stability and continuity. It is timely to explore whether we can envision change and uncertainty as desirable for heritage and conservation practice, thus turning a possible challenge into an opportunity.

Accordingly, this theme investigates how to perceive and deal with radical uncertainty about the distant future. To progress this aim, our research has considered how to preserve knowledge about sites for final disposal of nuclear waste (see Holtorf and Högberg 2014a; 2015a), the design of messages sent from Earth into outer space, long-term storage of information attached to ceramic data carriers, and selected practices of world heritage designation and management. This part of the book aims to explore these case studies in order to probe how conceptions of uncertain futures condition how we value and manage materials in the present (see also Holtorf and Högberg forthcoming a). Our ambition is to capitalise on the creative potential released by the common acknowledgement of an uncertain future across different kinds of organisations that are concerned with the management of future legacies, with the intention to conceive differently of heritage and how it is appropriately managed. What happens when we come to see nuclear waste as heritage? How can a space message transform perceptions of the human legacy? Can heritage and long-term memory help us to reduce the risks of future development on Earth? Does the perceived uncertainty of the long-term future even provide opportunities for heritage and conservation practice?

Transformation

As it becomes increasingly difficult to find resources for continued protection, and as accelerated environmental change threatens the integrity of many heritage assets, it has become clear that there is a need for experimentation with approaches that attempt to sustain the practice of cultural remembrance with materials that are allowed to change, or even disappear. Non-interventionist management approaches, while still relatively uncommon, are beginning to be explored through conceptualisations of curated decay (DeSilvey 2014; 2017) and heritage transience (DeSilvey 2012). These approaches locate heritage value in process, rather than permanence, and seek a collaborative, rather than an antagonistic, relationship with other-than-human agents of weathering, decay and colonisation. Accordingly, our work in the Transformation theme sought to explore how ecological entanglement and cultural remembrance is practised in relation to features and landscapes that are undergoing active processes of change and material transformation. The work in this theme sought to generate new ways of understanding our relationship to the past, and the future, as the distinction between natural and cultural heritage becomes unsustainable, and as tangible heritage features become integrated into other ecologies and systems.

We began our research on this theme with a comparative focus on management of built heritage and transitional landscapes. In built heritage contexts, we were interested in heritage management practices that accommodated and interpreted – rather than resisted – processes of ruination, decay, erosion and disintegration. In the domain of transitional landscapes, we sought to explore how heritage practice engaged with changing land uses, either through intentional programmes of rewilding and redevelopment, or through more indirect collaborations with processes such as coastal change and spontaneous re-naturalisation. Although we originally set out to compare these different domains, we subsequently shifted our focus to look at dynamics of change and transformation on different scales within and across three distinctive landscapes, nesting our interest in built heritage forms within the wider landscape contexts in which these forms are located. In the places we explored, the making of future heritage often involved maintaining continuity with the past through processes of change. These models of continuity and change clearly have the potential for application within other heritage domains, which have traditionally emphasised permanence and stasis in preference to the management of entropic change.

Cross-theme syntheses

One of the distinctive aspects of the research programme of which this book is an outcome was our attempt to facilitate creative contexts for inter- and intra-sectoral knowledge exchange among the various heritage partner organisations with which we worked. Accordingly, between each of the four thematic parts of the book are interwoven visual essays that document three significant cross-theme knowledge exchange workshops that we ran in Östhammar (Sweden), Kew (UK) and Suffolk (UK). These three events aimed to foster knowledge exchange across different segments of the heritage sector through a series of planned site visits, activities, presentations and discussions among specially selected groups of individuals from our partner organisations and others. The workshops aimed to explore and understand shared issues for the heritage sector, to engage our partner organisations in co-designing aspects of our research, and to integrate the ideas developed during these workshops into operational and policy perspectives. In addition, each project theme also held further knowledge-exchange events, as discussed in each thematic part of this book.

The final part of the book looks across the four themes to explore the theoretical and practical implications of the alternatives that they pose for each other, and for heritage more broadly. We conclude by reviewing how our comparative analysis of heritage practices as distinctive 'worlding' and future-making practices has contributed new perspectives on the operation of heritage in society, and its relationship to the construction of new realities.

Methods and approaches

It will by now be clear that we do not see conservation as simply happening within the boundaries of the historic site, the four walls of the conservation laboratory or museum, or within the fences that border the protected area or national park. A material-semiotic approach to conservation assemblages (see Harrison 2013a; 2016b; 2018) directs our attention to the ways in which heritage not only operates within such delineated spaces, but also to how it can act 'at a distance' – within bureaux or governmental offices, at international congresses, in the ethical guideline documentation of professional organisations, or within the shuffle of papers in court rooms. These operations of heritage may be just as important to understanding how heritage operates as ethnographic study located at the site of targeted preservation efforts.

'I can't tell you how many objects we manage, but I can tell you the number of records'. This is how the head of collections at a prominent national heritage management agency began a presentation on that agency's role in heritage conservation when describing it to an audience of professionals in London in 2016. In doing so, he raised an issue that became increasingly apparent to us as we undertook this research – which is that heritage is closely connected with, perhaps even defined by, certain data-driven, bureaucratic processes, and that metadata relating to objects in both *in-situ* and *ex-situ* collections are increasingly the focus of conservation efforts themselves. Historian of science Geoffrey Bowker writes of biodiversity as 'datadiversity' (2000; see also Devictor and Bensaude-Vincent

2016), not only to account for the ways in which worlds are only as diverse as the categorical systems built to measure that diversity, but also to highlight how data determines action back on the fields from which it is collected. The ways in which quite mundane bureaucratic practices make collections of many different kinds mobile and combinable (see Latour 1987; Bennett et al. 2017) – by way of lists, registers, records, databases – and how these 'tokens' (see Latour 2005) or data-objects become proxies for, and subject to, conservation practices themselves, constitutes an important area of focus for understanding how heritage 'works' and what heritage 'does' comparatively (Harrison 2016a).

In developing our methodological approach, we came to understand the transformation of such data-objects into the targets of conservation activity through reference to Latour's concept of 'immutable mobiles'. These are transportable textual or visual fragments, observations and representations of objects, places and phenomena that are collected from 'the field' and returned to 'centres of collection and calculation', where they are combined with other such objects and subjected to translation to produce forms of scientific knowledge that predicate action, including action back upon the fields from which they were collected (Latour 1987; 1999; see discussion in Bennett et al. 2017; Harrison 2018). An example of this is the ways in which, in *ex-situ* biodiversity conservation, the conservation of certain kinds of biological materials, in combination with different forms of data pertaining to those materials, comes to stand in for the conservation of the animal species from which those materials have been taken (Parry 2004; Van Dooren 2009; see further discussion in Part II, Diversity). Such biomaterials exemplify a process that could be understood to be common to *ex-situ* natural and cultural heritage conservation more generally (Breithoff and Harrison 2020a; 2020b). This work of translation, in which one thing comes to stand in for and represent another, can only be understood by working across multiple field sites and seeing each as part of a broader conservation process in relation to the others. Such a relational, distributed sensibility was central to the approach we adopted in the research discussed in the book.

Similarly, we observed throughout the course of our work how large international congresses, driven by a mobile group of 'experts' who circulate from field site to field site and promulgate the best practices that are developed at such meetings, have an important and lasting influence on the practices adopted at those sites themselves. Accounts of the politics of UNESCO World Heritage Committee meetings (for example, Brumann 2014; Meskell 2013; 2014; 2015b; 2018; Meskell et al. 2015; Winter 2014; 2015), and our reading of collaborative event ethnographies of International Union for

Conservation of Nature (IUCN) World Conservation Congresses and other major international biodiversity congresses and meetings (for example, Brosius and Campbell 2010; Fletcher 2014; Corson et al. 2014) inspired us not only to attend and participate in such meetings (alongside the more conventional 'local' sites of heritage practice that one might think of in relation to natural and cultural heritage conservation), but also to develop more multi-sited approaches to understanding heritage processes and practices. Our work is thus strongly influenced by multi-sited ethnography, and ethnographies 'in and of the world system', as Marcus (1995) has famously termed such approaches (or world system*s*, as we might wish to say, in recognising the multiplicity of such worlds). In working in and across a diverse range of sites associated with the domains of conservation practice with which we are concerned in this book, we aim to focus our attention on what anthropologist Anna Tsing (2005) refers to as 'zones of awkward engagement', spaces of friction in which the relationship between local actors and global processes are realised, producing conflict or consensus, but always acting back upon the worlds they themselves are engaged in generating. In doing so, we look to emphasise the relationships between people, 'things', institutions, corporations, governments and environments, as well as the ideological and epistemological structures that animate and give them meaning through specific forms of conservation practices.

Our focus on heritage practices as sociomaterial engagements directed toward assembling futures has also called for forms of methodological experimentation. Members of the research team come from a variety of different academic backgrounds (archaeology, cultural geography, history of science/science studies, intermedia, social anthropology), but our approach is broadly ethnographic, drawing on material, visual and sensory ethnographies (for example, Pink 2009; 2012; Meskell 2005; 2012a; Castañeda and Matthews 2008; Hamilakis and Anagnostopoulos 2009; Hamilakis 2011; González-Ruibal 2014), with a particular focus on sociomaterial worlds, emergent practices, and the 'happening of the social' (Lury and Wakeford 2012). In doing so, we build on a range of previous experimentation in more-or-less materially focused ethnographic methods across our research team (for example, Harrison 2002; 2004; 2017; DeSilvey 2012; Bond et al. 2013; Macdonald and Basu 2007; Pink and Morgan 2013; Pink et al. 2014). We do so against the background of the issues raised by the growing acknowledgement that we live in a geological era in which what we once took for granted as the 'human' and 'non-human' have also become folded together in complicated and imminently transformative ways (for example, Haraway 1991; Latour 2004; Dibley 2012). This is not necessarily the sort of work that might be most helpfully undertaken by a sole ethnographer-fieldworker (for discussion of this, see also Rabinow 2011 and González-Ruibal 2014), even though in some cases our work has been more conventionally anthropological in this sense. In other cases, our work has been undertaken collaboratively, and the data we report in this book have emerged from the nexus of our interactions with one another, with our professional collaborators (see further below) and with the sociomaterial worlds we study.

Like González-Ruibal (2014), we suggest that the rhythm of such ethnographic work might be more punctuated than conventional ethnography, and might involve more rapid and/or directed methods, in which participants are asked to re-enact particular quotidian processes for recording (using film, audio or other graphical methods) in ways that allow both informants and researchers to reflect directly on them (see Bartolini and DeSilvey 2020a). The work of Sarah Pink and colleagues on the use of short-term, multi-researcher ethnography within the field of health care provides another example of intensive, materially focused, 'applied' ethnographic research with significant implications for the kind of work we carried out (Pink and Morgan 2013; Pink et al. 2014). Importantly, we also tried to move beyond theoretical and conceptual perspectives that have been developed in other contexts, to explore the ways in which the various practices of heritage examined might themselves be generative of new and distinctive theoretical approaches to understanding the ways in which the future is cared for and curated across varied contexts. Visual research methods – especially the use of still and moving image as ways of documenting and interrogating the varied research materials and contexts within which we worked – played a key role in the research project (see also Sterling 2020). While the various visual essays presented within the book represent one snapshot of this, an online archive of our experimental ethnographic film work is also available (https://vimeo.com/heritagefutures).

In order to facilitate such co-created knowledge, we established a range of different contexts and collaborative forums within which to discuss heritage practices and processes across the different domains of practice in which we were working. In this way, our work has been strongly influenced by the forms of experimental, collaborative, 'para-ethnographic' practices that have characterised anthropological approaches to the contemporary (Holmes and Marcus 2005; 2008; Marcus 2013). In developing the research programme, we were particularly influenced by multi-sited para-ethnography (Rabinow et al. 2008), in which ethnographers come together with other expert knowledge producers in the development of shared, critical insights. To enable this, as mentioned above, we facilitated a series of inter- and intra-thematic 'thought experiments', collaborative knowledge-exchange events in which the authors and members of the various partner organisations with which we worked came together around field visits and collaborative workshops to explore shared questions relating to futures, world-making, and creative engagements with environmental change. These included a range of different kinds of activities – from collective visits to explore archival architectures at the site of the long-term nuclear waste repository that is currently being planned to be constructed in Forsmark, Sweden, by our partners SKB; to thought experiments relating to the different ordering and worlding practices across the various collections at Kew in London; to discussion of concepts of loss across natural and cultural heritage domains, with reference to climate-related coastal change on the Sussex coast. We participated as a group in a range of professional international and national scientific meetings, including the IUCN World Conservation Congress in 2016 held in Hawaii, USA; and the International Council on Monuments and Sites (ICOMOS) General Assembly and Scientific Symposium held in 2017 in Delhi, India, for which we developed and ran workshops aimed at creatively engaging and learning from natural and cultural heritage practitioners in relation to our project themes (see Figure 1.1 and Figure 1.2). We also facilitated

Figure 1.1 Delegates of the 19th ICOMOS General Assembly and Scientific Symposium in New Delhi playing 'The Thing from the Future' card game, which we adapted from that developed by the artists' collective Situation Lab for the event. Around 80 people participated in the game (photograph by Rodney Harrison).

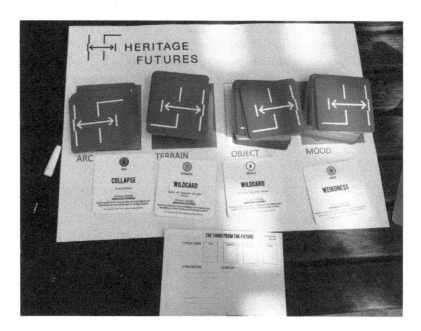

Figure 1.2   Detail of 'The Thing from the Future' card game (photograph by Rodney Harrison).

theme-specific workshops that identified the contributions that professional declutterers might make to rethinking issues of museum profusion, discussed shared problems of data, and explored transitional landscapes with creative practitioners and industry executives. Our work was further enriched by the opportunity to work with a number of creative practitioners, each of whom helped us to reflect not only on the practices of the organisations with which we worked, but also on our own academic practices and the worlds that each of these is also engaged in co-producing. In sum, this range of creative, visual, spatial and material ethnographies has allowed us to produce distinctive insights into our case studies, and has facilitated comparison across and between them.

***

This chapter has introduced the general conceptual framing of the book, its themes, methods and approaches, and structure. The next chapter explores in more detail some general questions of the relationship between heritage, heritage practices and the future, in order to provide background to the empirical material presented in each of the following four thematic parts. It also sets out in more detail the rationale for the project's empirical attention to various 'heritage-like' practices, in particular those concerning the management of waste, conceived here as another form of material and discursive legacy. As the chapter further explains, this inclusion was part of an attempt to create a groundbreaking and innovative programme of research that would expand and challenge the very ways in which heritage is currently conceived of, and undertaken globally in the future – to document contemporary practices so as to intervene directly in these various fields of heritage practice's futures.

Notes

1. In January 2020, the National Trust revised the order of words in their motto, from 'For ever, for everyone' to 'For everyone, for ever'. This was in part intended to reflect a rethinking of emphasis in its mission during its 125th anniversary year (Ingrid Samuel, personal communication; see https://www.nationaltrust.org.uk/blogs/directors-blog/hilary-mcgrady-celebrates-our-125th-anniversary). We maintain the original order here.
2. We use the plural 'heritages' here and elsewhere to emphasise the heterogeneity between the different fields of heritage practice that we explore empirically in the book. It is our contention that these different fields constitute different kinds of worlding practices, and hence work to assemble different futures. If these worlding practices are multiple, so are the future worlds they produce. Escobar (2018) and De la Cadena and Blaser's (2018) separate contributions to the development of the concept of the *pluriverse* – 'a world of many worlds' – helpfully captures the essence of our ideas regarding the ways in which heritage produces multiple overlapping worlds.
3. The working group Endangerment and Its Consequences: Documenting and Preserving Nature and Culture, led by Fernando Vidal and Nélia Dias, in which Rodney Harrison was a participating researcher, was part of the project Sciences of the Archive, based at and funded by the Max Planck Institute for the History of Science.

2
Heritage as future-making practices

Rodney Harrison

Introduction

This chapter develops themes introduced in the previous chapter relating to heritage, heritage practices and the future, and explores them in more depth. It focuses particularly on the development of heritage in the nineteenth and twentieth centuries, and its role in crafting particular kinds of imagined and desired futures. It then presents in more detail the general rationale for the book's comparative approaches, in particular its inclusion of waste management practices as part of a broader consideration of heritage management. These ideas form a general background to the thematic parts that follow.

A brief history of (heritage) 'futures'

The idea that heritage as a concept emerged, in Euro-American contexts at least, as a result of historical reconfigurations in cultural, social and practical relations with time, as part of the 'experience' of modernity, is now well established. (These ideas are précised in more detail in Harrison 2013a, 13ff.; but see counterarguments by Harvey 2001b.) Historians of heritage generally place the origins of the philosophies that are seen to underpin broadly 'Western' approaches to natural and cultural heritage conservation and management (in particular the rise of the national park movement and the development of a set of new symbolic relationships with cultural objects that were held to manifest national forms of heritage) in the context of late Enlightenment thought and the rise of nation states in the eighteenth and nineteenth centuries (for example, see Lowenthal 2015; Samuel 1994; Mandler 1997; Swenson 2014).

While the origins of museums, herbaria, zoos and other *ex-situ* collections lie much earlier, in the work of antiquarians and private collectors, heritage is widely held to be a distinctively *modern* notion. Kevin Walsh (1992; see also Jameson 1991; Brett 1996) suggests that it is the very way in which modernity contrasts itself in relation to its past that makes heritage such an important factor in determining how modern societies conceptualise themselves. As Osborne (1995, 13–14) notes, the 'time' of modernity is not straightforward, as it involves a complex doubling in which it defines itself simultaneously as both 'contemporary' and 'new'. In doing so, it constantly creates the present as a 'contemporary past' while it anticipates the future as embodied within its present. In other words, modernity creates for itself pasts and futures that are perceived to be both *immanent* (contained within) and *imminent* (impending) in the present (see further discussion in Harrison 2011). This simultaneity of the past and future in the present is part of the way in which the experience of modernity is emphasised as one of rapid progress and technological and social change (Berman 1983; Virilio 1986; Tomlinson 2007). Heritage in such contexts emerges as a set of material practices concerned with anticipating and resourcing more or less distant futures in the present. As I go on to discuss, these futures are often only vaguely defined. One of the ways in which heritage has typically attempted to preserve its objects of preservation for the future is through creating records, lists, catalogues – encyclopedic snapshots of its endangered subjects as microcosmic representations of the worlds from which they were drawn. As Elizabeth Edwards (2012, 7) suggests in her study of the amateur photographic survey movement in England, all such efforts to salvage through recording create 'an archival grid through which the past might be accessible in an imagined future'. Underpinning such efforts is a sense of moral obligation to that future, and in particular, to the 'future generations' who will inhabit it.

The concept of 'future generations' – which is itself closely related to a belief in the existence of certain collective and individual obligations to those future generations (as introduced in Chapter 1) – has a long and complicated history, which is intertwined with the philosophical justification for the conservation of nature and culture. John Ruskin's *Seven Lamps of Architecture*, published in 1849 and widely cited as one of the canonical texts of the late nineteenth- and twentieth-century architectural and historic conservation movement, frames the argument for honest or 'true' architecture (defined as a return to the authentic architecture of the Gothic) in terms of a series of moral obligations to future generations:

The idea of self-denial for the sake of posterity, of practising present economy for the sake of debtors yet unborn, of planting forests that our descendants may live under their shade, or of raising cities for future nations to inhabit, never, I suppose, efficiently takes place among publicly recognised motives of exertion. Yet these are not the less our duties; nor is our part fitly sustained upon the earth, unless the range of our intended and deliberate usefulness include *not only the companions, but the successors, of our pilgrimage*. God has lent us the earth for our life ... It belongs as much to *those who are to come after us*, and whose names are already written in the book of creation, as to us; and we have no right, by anything that we do or neglect, to involve them in unnecessary penalties, or deprive them of benefits which it was in our power to bequeath. And this the more, because it is one of the appointed conditions of the labor of men that, in proportion to the time between the seed-sowing and the harvest, is the fulness of the fruit; and that generally, there-fore, *the farther off we place our aim, and the less we desire to be our-selves the witnesses of what we have labored for, the more wide and rich will be the measure of our success*. Men cannot benefit those that are with them as they can benefit *those who come after them*; and of all the pulpits from which human voice is ever sent forth, there is none from which it reaches so far as from the grave.

(Ruskin 1849, 176, my emphasis)

Ruskin believed that such principles should apply even more strongly to the ways in which present generations should conduct themselves in rela-tion to historic monuments and buildings. Later in the essay, he writes:

... it is again no question of expediency or feeling whether we shall preserve the buildings of past times or not. *We have no right what-ever to touch them.* They are not ours. They belong partly to those who built them, and partly to all the generations of mankind who are to follow us.

(Ruskin 1849, 187, emphasis in original)

He continues:

What we have ourselves built, we are at liberty to throw down; but what other men gave their strength, and wealth, and life to accom-plish, their right over does not pass away with their death; still less is the right to the use of what they have left vested in us only. It belongs to all their successors.

(Ruskin 1849, 187)

Ruskin's work, and that of other Gothic Revivalists, strongly influenced William Morris and other founding members of the Society for the Protection of Ancient Buildings (SPAB), established in England in 1877, which applied his ideas to the 'problem' of what were perceived to be the unsympathetic restorations of ancient buildings during the Victorian era, arguing:

> … to put Protection in the place of Restoration, to stave off decay by daily care, to prop a perilous wall or mend a leaky roof by such means as are obviously meant for support or covering, and show no pretence of other art, and otherwise to resist all tampering with either the fabric or ornament of the building as it stands; if it has become inconvenient for its present use, to raise another building rather than alter or enlarge the old one; in fine to treat our ancient buildings as monuments of a bygone art, created by bygone manners, that modern art cannot meddle with without destroying.
>
> Thus, and thus only, shall we escape the reproach of our learning being turned into a snare to us; thus, and thus only can we protect our ancient buildings, and hand them down instructive and venerable to those that come after us.
>
> (SPAB 2017, n.p.)

A line of influence can be drawn from Ruskin's ideas through to the emergence of institutionalised and governmental forms of conservation practices during the late nineteenth century via the work of Ralph Waldo Emerson, whose transcendentalist writings about nature, along with those of his protégé Henry David Thoreau, became key philosophical texts of the fledgling national park movement in the United States, entrenching this notion of concern for future generations in national, and subsequently international, developments in nature conservation. Their writing significantly influenced John Muir (see discussions in Nash 1967 and Oelschlaeger 1991), who in San Francisco in 1892 founded the preservationist society known as the Sierra Club, which played a key role in the establishment of a number of the first US national parks, including Yosemite National Park. This was in turn based on the model of Yellowstone National Park, which had already by this time been gazetted by an Act of Congress on 1 March 1872, and which became the first 'wild' area reserved for recreational purposes under the management of the United States Federal Government. This is widely recognised as the first natural area specifically gazetted for conservation and recreational purposes.

In the UK, the Sierra Club's efforts were pre-empted by debates on the preservation of commons and other open spaces by groups such as the Commons Protection Society (founded in 1866) and the National Footpaths Preservation Society (founded in 1844), which were both influential in the founding of the National Trust for the Preservation of Historic Buildings and Natural Beauty in 1894, whose mission became the task of holding land and buildings in perpetuity for the benefit of the nation (The National Trust Act 1907). The role of nature conservation in resourcing the future was also explicitly referenced in the act that created the US National Parks Service, the National Park Service Organic Act 1916, noting that the role of the Parks Service was to:

> promote and regulate the use of the federal areas known as national parks, monuments, and reservations ... which purpose is to conserve the scenery and the natural and historic objects and the wild life therein and to provide for the enjoyment of the same in such manner and by such means as will leave them unimpaired *for the enjoyment of future generations.*
>
> (United States Congress 1916, my emphasis)

Of course, in establishing the philosophical justification for the preservation and conservation of nature and culture, such practices (and the belief systems that underpinned them) were also complicit in the production of distinctive notions of 'nature' and 'culture' in the process. These are issues that we address further in Part II, Diversity, and Part V, Transformation.

Another significant influence on the development of institutionalised heritage practices has been the ways in which certain state institutions emerged throughout the late nineteenth and twentieth centuries to mitigate increasingly severe inheritance and death taxes on the estates of the aristocracy and other economic elites. In the UK, the National Trust received many of its built assets and landholdings in the mid-twentieth century due to a number of factors, including the decline in the political power of the aristocracy, and loss of income from these estates themselves (Mandler 1997; Cowell 2008). Assuming ownership of these buildings and land, which would otherwise have been passed directly to the former owner's 'future generations', formed a template for understanding such activities as contributing to a collective *national* inheritance. The creation of a specific class of legally inalienable objects and places by way of national heritage legislation, and their passing from private to public ownership (or in this case, to a charitable trust), helped to emphasise this goal. Later legislation in many countries aimed to provide taxation relief for the private owners of scheduled buildings or which incentivised the adaptive reuse of historic building stock by offering tax credits on works to certified historic properties (see discussion in Murtagh 2006, 58–60, for example). The entanglement of heritage with concepts of inheritance has contributed significantly to its symbolic rhetoric, which normalises its activities by projecting the moral and political justification for its work on to a vaguely defined set of collective future beneficiaries.

The role of heritage conservation and preservation in resourcing the future was further reinforced in the suite of post-war initiatives that established a range of international conventions and protocols for the protection and maintenance of natural and cultural heritage, which were increasingly understood to represent universal and universally valued resources, the protection of which was undertaken for the common interest of both present and future generations. These conventions have each individually been treated in detail in historical perspective by a number of different scholars, and it is not our intention to explore them comprehensively here. The now well-known text of the 1972 World Heritage Convention exemplifies this in declaring:

> Each State Party to this Convention recognizes that the *duty of ensuring the identification, protection, conservation, presentation and transmission to future generations of the cultural and natural heritage* referred to in Articles 1 and 2 and situated on its territory, belongs primarily to that State. It will do all it can to this end, to the utmost of its own resources and, where appropriate, with any international assistance and co-operation, in particular, financial, artistic, scientific and technical, which it may be able to obtain.
>
> (UNESCO 1972, 3, my emphasis)

As it has developed over the course of the twentieth and early part of the twenty-first century in relation to the preservation of natural and cultural heritage, the concept of 'future generations' has also increasingly come to imply notions of *intergenerational responsibility*. One of the most widely cited examples of this is in the definition of sustainable development that was developed in the United Nations General Assembly's *Report of the World Commission on Environment and Development: Our Common Future* in 1987, more often known simply as the 'Brundtland Report' after the Commission's

Chair, former Norwegian Prime Minister Gro Harlem Brundtland (Brundtland Commission 1987). The report presents competing visions of possible futures. On the one hand, this future might be 'better' than the present:

> ... more prosperous, more just, and more secure. Our report, *Our Common Future,* is not a prediction of ever increasing environmental decay, poverty, and hardship in an ever more polluted world among ever decreasing resources. We see instead the possibility for a new era of economic growth, one that must be based on policies that sustain and expand the environmental resource base. And we believe such growth to be absolutely essential to relieve the great poverty that is deepening in much of the developing world.
>
> (Brundtland Commission 1987, 11)

Nonetheless, the report points to a series of interconnected crises, suggesting that the management of contemporary economic inequalities must be undertaken with a view towards the impacts of present behaviours on the future. In order to do so, *Our Common Future* suggests the need to develop understandings of sustainable forms of development in which economic development and attempts to increase contemporary global equality must be balanced with a view towards future environmental conservation:

> ... the Commission's hope for the future is conditional on decisive political action now to begin managing environmental resources to ensure both sustainable human progress and human survival. We are not forecasting a future; we are serving a notice – an urgent notice based on the latest and best scientific evidence – that the time has come to take the decisions needed to secure the resources to sustain this and coming generations. We do not offer a detailed blueprint for action, but instead a pathway by which the peoples of the world may enlarge their spheres of cooperation.
>
> (Brundtland Commission 1987, 11)

Iris Borowy (2014) shows how the definition of sustainable development adopted by the report avoids questions of political difference by its insistence on the *universal future benefits* of its recommendations:

> The Earth is one but the world is not. We all depend on one biosphere for sustaining our lives. Yet each community, each country, strives for survival and prosperity with little regard for its impact

on others. Some consume the Earth's resources at a rate that would leave little for future generations. Others, many more in number, consume far too little and live with the prospect of hunger, squalor, disease, and early death.

(Brundtland Commission 1987, 27)

The report's definition of sustainable development frames relations with future generations in an economic language of resource, capitals and debt by drawing comparisons between the contemporary conditions of poverty that exist in certain countries and the potential future global poverty that unsustainable contemporary development efforts have the potential to bring about (Nordblad forthcoming):

> The failures that we need to correct arise both from poverty and from the short-sighted way in which we have often pursued prosperity. Many parts of the world are caught in a vicious downwards spiral: Poor people are forced to overuse environmental resources to survive from day to day, and their impoverishment of their environment further impoverishes them, making their survival ever more difficult and uncertain. The prosperity attained in some parts of the world is often precarious, as it has been secured through farming, forestry, and industrial practices that bring profit and progress only over the short term.
>
> (Brundtland Commission 1987, 28)

Our Common Future is also explicit in denoting the future as vulnerable, threatened and at risk. The first chapter of the report is titled 'A Threatened Future', and it sets about delineating the symptoms and causes of this threat in subsequent sections on 'Poverty', 'Growth', 'Survival' and 'The Economic Crisis':

> We are now just beginning to realize that we must find an alternative to our ingrained behaviour of burdening future generations resulting from our misplaced belief that there is a choice between economy and the environment. That choice, in the long term, turns out to be an illusion with awesome consequences for humanity.
>
> (Brundtland Commission 1987, 36–7)

In doing so, *Our Common Future* exemplifies another contemporary heritage trope in appealing to a broader 'endangerment sensibility'. This concept, which was referred to briefly in Chapter 1 but which I wish to

expand on here, was coined and defined by Fernando Vidal and Nélia
Dias (2016a) in these terms:

> ... the notion stands at the heart of a network of concepts, values,
> and practices dealing with entities considered threatened by extinc-
> tion and destruction, and with techniques aimed at preserving
> them. An entity's endangered status crystallizes by way of its incor-
> poration into various documentary devices – archives, catalogues,
> databases, inventories and atlases. These devices materialize values
> that inspire an urge to perpetuate, but they do so through concrete
> objects and information they choose to archive, and the techniques
> they use to do so ... Endangerment, then, not only refers to states
> of the world that the sciences may identify and describe, but also
> names an individual and collective resource for apprehending the
> world at the levels of symbols and action.
>
> (Vidal and Dias 2016a, 1)

In designating this as a 'sensibility', Vidal and Dias show how, while not
universal, this way of conceptualising nature and culture is widespread
and pervasive, synthesising work on the history of the sciences and social
sciences that explores the role of the archive as an apparatus that not
only produces the world that it purports to document (for example,
Bowker and Star 2000) but also organises that world's time (for example, see Daston 2012) through its distinctive set of memory practices
(Bowker 2005a). The ways in which natural and cultural heritage has
been defined in relation to its own endangerment forms an important
basis for the arguments we pursue, but also raises the questions of the
politics of heritage in the sense in which endangerment contributes to the
moral weight of heritage practices, normalising and removing them from
critical scrutiny and hence sidelining the questions of power that have
formed a central focus for critical heritage studies (for example, Bennett
1995; Smith 2006; Macdonald 2009; Winter 2015; Meskell 2018).

The moral authority of conservation is also, as Vidal and Dias
(2016a) indicate, connected to emotional response. The concept of
'future generations' may also contain notions of generational differences
or model specific understandings of familial relations that address themselves directly to the emotional and affective qualities of the endangerment sensibility. One place in which these models of familial relations
are applied to broader social collectives is in the notion of the 'generation
gap'. Anthropologist Margaret Mead's (1970) study of the generation gap
in the book *Culture and Commitment: A Study of the Generation Gap* posits

certain fundamental differences in the ways in which different societies learn from one another to account for the emergence of what she suggested were new ways of learning and relating to the future that were developing at the time in which she was writing. Her thesis is that three different modes of social learning across generations can be distinguished based on global comparative anthropological analyses. In *postfigurative* cultures, social learning is achieved primarily through tradition, in which parents and elders are the primary source of social knowledge. In *co-figurative* cultures, social learning occurs primarily through peer-based learning, in which parents, elders and young people learn from their peers and one another. In *prefigurative* cultures, adults primarily learn from their children, suggesting that 'we are now entering a period, new in history, in which the young are taking on a new authority in their prefigurative apprehension of the still unknown future' (Mead 1970, 3). Of course, such theorising acts as both a reflection on and is simultaneously generative of certain sensibilities that relate to specific historical and cultural contexts. In the conclusion of the book, Mead seems to pre-empt the Brundtland Report's call to action on behalf of the future:

> We must place the future, like the unborn child in the womb of a woman, within a community of men, women, and children, among us, already here, already to be nourished and succoured and protected, already in need of things for which, if they are not prepared before it is born, will be too late. So, as the young say, The Future Is Now.
>
> (Mead 1970, 94)

In such an imaginary, the child often constitutes the emblematic figure of the future. But as Sarah May (forthcoming; see also May 2013) argues, this infantilisation of the future often underpins a patronising set of assumptions in which it is presumed that future generations will be less able to determine their own needs and values than present ones. Dirk Spennemann (2007a; 2007b) makes similar observations in charting the growing dominance of the concept of 'the future' in writings and slogans associated with local and regional historical societies in the United States, in suggesting that the appeal to the rhetoric of the future re-enforces assumptions regarding the capacities of contemporary heritage organisations to accurately predict future social values and tastes. As Edelmann (2004) notes, these future children are not really imagined to be 'real' children at all, but exist as a mechanism by which to delineate the limits of change on political discourse; such rhetorical devices re-enforce the norms of the present, rather than acknowledge the potential radical difference of the future. Högberg and colleagues' (2017) study of contemporary archaeologists and heritage professionals, based on interviews with 67 individuals working across at least eight countries (but primarily based in Sweden and the UK), suggests that many heritage managers today cannot easily express how they conceive of the future in the name of which they undertake their professional practice, or when that future will be, or how they believe their work will impact upon it. The future that these heritage professionals discuss in these interviews tends to manifest implicitly in their everyday work, but remains temporally close to, and generally mirrors, the present (see also Holtorf and Högberg 2014a; 2015b). These observations have been borne out in several different ways in the work of this project, as we go on to discuss.

The final aspect of the notion of future generations that I want to touch on in this chapter is its economic basis. This is particularly manifested in the notion of *intergenerational equity*. Contemporary debates relating to the global economic crisis have frequently blamed 'baby boomers' for current issues relating to global debt. The title of David Willetts' (2010) book, *The Pinch: How the Baby Boomers Took Their Children's Future and Why They Should Give It Back,* is typical of this trend, in which the past is viewed as having produced a future debt. But if the future is something to which contemporary societies are thought to owe a debt, how does one render it payable? In Wales in the UK, the Well-Being of Future Generations Act (National Assembly for Wales 2015) has provided for the appointment of a future generation commissioner whose duty is 'to act as a guardian for future generations' and 'to encourage public bodies to take greater account of the long-term impact of the things they do'. Aspects of what we might term the 'economisation', or rendering of natural and cultural heritage as distinctive forms of capitals, are pre-empted by the idea that these heritage 'assets' form kinds of natural and cultural 'resources', terms that have gained widespread prominence in heritage management throughout the second part of the twentieth century (for example, Lipe 1984). The bringing together of valuation of the environment and its weighing against the economy in the Brundtland Report discussed above also reflects this process by which heritage is seen as representing distinctive forms of capitals that can be measured and monetarised. Nonetheless, significant debates surround these attempts to render in monetary terms the values of nature and culture. Recent discussions of the concept of natural capital, itself an extension of the concept of cultural capitals, exemplify these developments (for example, see Helm 2015). Questions of the emergence of new forms of biocapital in relation to *ex-situ* biodiversity conservation practices are explored later in the book, in Part II, Diversity.

The question of the nature of heritage value has been a consistent theme in studies of cultural heritage since Alois Riegl's (1982) famous taxonomy of the range of contemporary and historic values that underpin what he termed the 'modern cult of monuments', first published in 1903. Over the past few decades, cultural heritage values have received increased attention in the work of academics, policymakers and practitioners alike (see the recent review of this literature in Fredheim and Khalaf 2016). And yet, it could be argued that much of this work has done little more than provide alternative typological systems for describing values that are already assumed to be inherent in heritage, rather than focusing on the processes by which these values are assembled or made (but see Heinich 2009; 2011). An additional problem is that most of these taxonomies of values work with what is essentially an economic model of value, which may obscure other forms of value. Important insights regarding the production of heritage values have emerged from ethnographic work that explores the ways in which certain kinds of practices of maintenance and care are involved in the production of different regimes of value (for example, Herzfeld 2004; Jones 2017). I will return to the concept of care (and its absence) shortly.

What are 'futures' and how are they 'made'?

If it is possible to suggest that the 'future' has long been implicated in debates regarding the conservation of natural and cultural heritage, what can be said of this notion of 'the future' itself, which also has a long history as a concept in both the popular and scientific imaginary (for example, Jameson 2007)? What are 'futures', and how might they be theorised and conceptualised? And in what ways do certain actions in the present open up, realise or produce different futures? These philosophical questions relate to issues of different conceptions of time (Gell 1992) and its politics (Osborne 1995).

The work of German sociologist Niklas Luhmann (1976) provides a helpful entry point to these questions. Dismissing the idea of time as universal, he suggests that social orders are also temporal orders; that is, different forms of society have distinct temporal dispositions by which they are structured and in which the relations between past and future will differ from one another. Furthermore, the forms by which observations of the future are integrated into different societies constitute an important way of distinguishing their operations from one another. In working through these ideas, he makes a distinction between 'present futures' and 'future presents'. Present futures are contemporary observations of possible futures; discourses and instruments work together to produce visualisations of potential outcomes that are made in the present. Future presents, on the other hand, refer to the relations that bind one actual operation or outcome to another as part of a sequence of actions and events in time. Drawing on German historian Reinhart Koselleck's (2004) distinction between the 'space of experience' and the 'horizon of expectation', and pre-empting the work of the American philosopher Marshall Berman (1983), Luhmann sees modern societies as distinguished by their orientation towards the 'new':

> Whereas the ancients started with generalizations of their everyday world by means of cosmological and theological assumptions and thought not of 'the' future but of coming events and the possibility of their privative negation, we experience our future as a generalized horizon of surplus possibilities that have to be reduced as we approach them. We can think of degrees of openness and call *futurization* increasing and *defuturization* decreasing the openness of a present future. Defuturization may lead to the limiting condition where the present future merges with the future presents and only one future is possible. Actually, the structure of our society prevents defuturization from going this far …
>
> (Luhmann 1976, 141)

Thus, for Luhmann:

> … modernity is linked to an intense futurization of the future … The present moment becomes the potential turning point between the future not yet determined and the past that is not any longer determining. The past and the future are not aligned automatically, but are articulated in the 'now'.
>
> (Opitz and Tellmann 2015, 111)

That is, societies are differentiated not only by their openness to different futures, but also by the ways in which pasts and futures are articulated in the present. He sees modern societies as characterised by the production of a present that is constituted through an ambiguous set of relations with pasts and futures in which they are simultaneously unbound from the present moment in a way that creates a heightened sense of uncertainty or 'risk' (see also Luhmann 1993).

The set of sociomaterial discourses that balance futurisation and defuturisation, or which seek to simultaneously hold possible futures open while also placing limits upon them, constitute the precise set of temporal practices that are exemplified by natural and cultural heritage conservation. Using Luhmann's language, conservation practices can be seen as apparatuses or 'technologies' that:

> … on the other hand, orient themselves to future presents. They transform them into a string of anticipated presents. They postulate and anticipate causal or stochastic links between future events in order to incorporate them into the present present. This implies two important reductions of complexity. The first transforms the character of events which are emerging recombinations of independent contingencies into a carrier function of the process of determination. The second brings into relief a sequential pattern, a chain of interconnected events; it sequentializes complexity by abstracting more or less from interfering processes.
>
> (Luhmann 1976, 143)

I have already discussed Vidal and Dias's (2016b) concept of the endangerment sensibility, but it has long been observed that 'heritage', both 'natural' and 'cultural', is generally defined within the context of some implicit or explicit threat to objects, species, landscapes or practices that are perceived to hold a form of collective value (for example, Holdgate 1999; Lowenthal 1985). These existential threats relate to the belief in more or less uncertain futures. One way in which modern societies manage the risk and uncertainty that arises from such implicit or explicit senses of threat is through placing increased trust in 'experts' and abstract 'expert systems' over local forms of knowledge (Giddens 1991, 29–32). Risk functions in Foucault's conception of modern societies as 'a governmental strategy of regulatory power by which populations and individuals are monitored and managed' (Lupton 1999, 87). Risk is calculated and defined by a range of 'experts' who produce statistics and data that make risk calculable and hence manageable. Harrison (2013a; 2016a), Rico (2015a; 2015b; 2016) and Meskell (2012b; 2014) have explored the links between the bureaucratisation and professionalisation of cultural heritage as 'modern' strategies for the care and management of heritage 'risk', making clear the connection between natural and cultural heritage conservation practices and the production of a broader endangerment sensibility that is characteristic of 'risk societies' (see Luhmann 1993; see also Beck 1992). The research collected in this book demonstrates that these practices can be studied not only historically, but also ethnographically, to illuminate the particular ways in which they enact and produce discrete (and often disparate) futures.

Anthropologist Paul Rabinow's reflections on Luhmann's work in his book *Marking Time* (2008) help to clarify this modern temporal order, which both gives rise to, and is sustained by, natural and cultural heritage practices:

> In our time, as never before, the continuity from past to future is broken. However, the one thing we do know is that much of what will be true in future presents will depend on current decisions. Decide now! [But] To complicate the picture, we do not have anyone who really *can* decide …
>
> (Rabinow 2008, 59, emphasis in original)

This produces a kind of pervasive ontological crisis; heritage is paralysed by the imperative to make decisions in the present that also hold open the possibilities of different futures in which those decisions may be rendered incorrect. It must act in the present in a way that maintains but also manages the openness of that future, that is, it exists in an ambiguous state in which it balances both practices of futurisation and defuturisation. Thus, as the late John Urry notes in his recent synthetic review of future studies in the social sciences, particular futures tend to be produced by the same anticipatory systems that have been built to plan for and predict them (Urry 2016, 9; see also Law and Urry 2004). This is not only because the power to realise certain futures is unequally distributed and prioritises those futures that benefit certain powerful actors and institutions, but also because specific planning and management systems can themselves enact and produce the precise futures they simultaneously resource and act to prevent.

To speak of 'futures' in the plural, as 'enacted' and 'made', seems to contradict the idea of the future as a 'reality' – a specific temporal and spatial zone of material and social experience. Here we confront a central problem not only of Luhmann's work, and the genre of future studies he is associated with, but also of the contemporary social sciences – how can we speak of something as simultaneously 'real' and also 'constructed'? And how can we talk about multiple real, coexistent constructed realities? The work of Michel Callon and Fabien Muniesa (for example, Callon 1998; 2005; Callon and Muniesa 2005; Muniesa 2014; Muniesa and

Callon 2007), which examines the ways in which the economy is simultaneously real and produced by the intervention of the same economists who claim to observe it (see also Hertz 2000), addresses this question directly. As Muniesa notes:

> … reality is indeed constructed, but it is so in the engineer's sense: the scientific fact stands objectively in the laboratory as the bridge stands firmly over the water, that is, insofar as it undergoes a laborious process of material assemblage. But that is not, alas, quite a common view. For constructivism to mean realism it has first to emancipate from the idea of 'social construction' that is often found in the social sciences and according to which reality would be located not in things but in what we think of them. And for realism to mean constructivism it has to avoid the temptation of considering reality as something that just stands there without taking the trouble to happen.
>
> (Muniesa 2014, 32)

Perhaps the most important finding to emerge from the history and sociology of the natural and social sciences over the past decades is that observation is always itself a form of intervention (for example, see Barad 2007; Daston 2012; Daston and Galison 2010; Latour 1987; 2013; Stengers 2000). My reference to the example of the economy here is not arbitrary – this is the very context in which 'futures' are 'traded', and in doing so, assembled and produced (see also Urry 2016, 8). And like the economy, as I have noted above, heritage is defined by its management practices – practices that are intended to control for uncertainty and to identify, define and secure the existence of their subjects into the future. These practices thus intervene in, and contribute directly to, the assembling of specific future worlds.

This brings us to the question of the capacities of different forms of heritage practices to generate specific kinds of futures – or what we might call their 'futurability'. Drawing on the work of Henri Bergson, Italian Marxist theorist Franco Berardi (2017, 3) uses this term to describe 'a layer of possibility which may or may not develop into actuality'. He suggests that futurability can be further broken down into a series of variables: *possibility*, *potency* and *power*. 'Possibility is content, potency is energy, and power is form' (Berardi 2017, 1). Possibility is always plural, while potency is the energy with which possible futures are actualised. Power is the selection and enforcement of specific futures, which simultaneously excludes others from being actualised. One aspect of the futurability of any set of practices can be found in their capacity to generate hope. In commenting on what they term the recent 'hope boom' in anthropology, Kleist and Jansen (2016) suggest that the current, accelerating interest in the topic reflects an increasing global sense of crisis, insecurity and uncertainty. Importantly, they note that hope arises from, and creates, specific dispositions towards the future – that specific formations of hope constitute discrete forms of temporal reasoning. Similarly, Appadurai (2013) has suggested that the politics of hope forms the foundation for an anthropology of the future. But as Ghassan Hage (2003) argues, hope also constitutes a form of governmental power in the sense in which hope is unevenly distributed, and the state's capacity to distribute hope articulates specific forms of biopolitics. Our work in this volume is situated within a broader set of anthropological interests in engaging seriously with the future – through studying scientific/institutional (for example, Paul Rabinow's work on biotechnology – see Rabinow 1996; 1999; Rabinow and Dan-Cohen 2005) or non-technical fields of practice (for example, religion and divinatory practices, see Zeitlyn 2012), which are explicitly concerned with future-making and, indeed, as an active form of speculative engagement with the future itself (for example, Salazar et al. 2017).

Heritage: Assembling, building and designing future worlds

In exploring the futurability of certain forms of natural and cultural conservation practices, and in bringing them into closer conversation with other ways of caring for, resourcing and realising specific futures, this book also addresses itself directly to, and attempts to advance, heritage studies as a field of research. I see it as making a sustained contribution to debates regarding the importance of material approaches to understanding 'official' and 'unofficial' heritage practices and their roles in building social worlds, and to the value of comparative perspectives in heritage studies. Such an approach should not be viewed as inconsistent with a consideration of the discourse of heritage and its knowledge/power effects; indeed, it would also draw on other important recent developments in the exploration of the sociomaterial effects of the politics of world heritage (for example, Brumann 2014; Meskell 2013; 2014; 2015b; 2018; Meskell et al. 2015; Winter 2014; 2015) and a consideration of the relationship between heritage, cosmopolitanism (Meskell

2009; Geismar 2015), and sacralisation and secularisation processes (for example, Byrne 2014; Rico 2014b) at a range of different scales (Harvey 2015; Baird 2017).

The book's arguments bring together a particular set of theoretical perspectives that have found increasing significance within recent critical heritage studies scholarship (see discussion in Harrison 2018). These include: a Deleuzian language of assemblage, as elaborated upon in the work of Manuel DeLanda (2006) and others, which helps to focus attention on the range of heterogeneous elements – objects, people, places, practices, pronouncements, bureaucratic apparatuses – that are brought together in 'heritage assemblages' (Bennett and Healy 2009; Macdonald 2009; Harrison 2013a; 2013b), such as museums and heritage sites, and the variable and dispersed manner in which they function; a materially focused reading of some of what have come to be known as the 'later' works of Michel Foucault, in particular *The Birth of Biopolitics* (2008) and *Security, Territory, Population* (2009), which elaborate on the concept of governmentality and the various apparatuses (*dispositifs*) by which it operates; an emphasis on more symmetrical approaches to understanding the distribution of different forms of agency across heterogeneous networks, including both human and other-than-human actors, which takes its cue from Latourian science studies (for example, Latour 1993; 1999; 2005) and actor–network theory more broadly; and the multinaturalism of ontological perspectivism, which is concerned with 'elucidating the multiplicity of forms of existence enacted through concrete practices' (Povinelli 2012). Here there is another connection with Bruno Latour's work on the politics of nature (for example, Latour 2004) and Latour's (2013) and Philippe Descola's (2013) enquiries into multiple modes of existence, as part of what has been characterised as a broader 'ontological turn' in anthropology and the social sciences more generally (for example, Holbraad et al. 2014; see reviews in Kohn 2015 and Holbraad and Pederson 2017).

The various chapters draw more or less explicitly on assemblage and actor–network approaches to show the value in seeing 'heritage' as a series of strategic sociotechnical and/or biopolitical assemblages composed of various people, institutions, apparatuses (*dispositifs*) and the relations between them (for example, Macdonald 2009; Harrison 2013a; 2013b; Bennett et al. 2017). Thinking of heritage in this way not only provides ways of interrogating how it operates at the level of both material and social relations, but also helps to focus attention on the particular constellations of power/knowledge effects that it facilitates, that is, the relationship between heritage and governmentality, where it advances more conventional concerns of discourse analysis in heritage studies (see also Smith 2006). Jane Bennett's (2010) discussion of assemblage theory shows how human and non-human agents cannot be separated from the ways in which they are arranged and the affordances of the various sociotechnical assemblages in which they are entangled. Thinking of heritage as an assemblage (*agencement*) means paying attention not only to individuals and corporations, and the discourses they promulgate or resist, but also to the specific arrangements of materials, equipment, texts and technologies, both 'ancient' and 'modern', by which heritage is produced in conversation with them. These specific arrangements of materials might include not only the 'historic' fabric of a cultural heritage site itself, along with the assortment of artefacts and 'scars' that represent its 'patina' (Dawdy 2016) of age and authenticity, but also the various technologies of tourism and display by which it is exhibited and made 'visitable' (Dicks 2004) as a heritage site. One might think of the governmental capacities of these various sociotechnical components, which together make up the heritage assemblage, in relation to the concept of an apparatus, as developed by Michel Foucault.

Paul Rabinow (2003, 49ff.) has shown how Foucault defined an apparatus as a device or technology that specifies (and hence helps to create) a subject so that it might control, distribute and/or manage it. Agamben (2009, 14) further defines an apparatus as 'anything that has in some way the capacity to capture, orient, determine, intercept, model, control, or secure the gestures, behaviours, opinions, or discourses of living beings' (and indeed, the system of relations between them). Examples might include the governmental capacities of the various modern and historic material interventions at historic cultural heritage sites – conservation methods and equipment, crowd-controlling devices, infrastructure associated with movement around a site, the various interpretive appliances that have been introduced alongside the affordances of the material that forms the heritage site itself, and the texts and discourses that give each of them their authority to control behaviour in specific ways. These devices and texts are arranged and assembled in precise and identifiable ways, the study of which allows their capacity to control and regulate behaviour, and the various networks of agency in which they are distributed, to be better understood.

So what is the 'world-making' work of heritage? Elsewhere, I (Harrison 2016b) have shown how heritage registers and lists of many different forms might be seen to act 'at a distance' to direct and constrain the management of both intangible and tangible forms of cultural heritage. One of the key outcomes of cultural heritage practices, for example, is the material and semiotic transformation of ruined and redundant objects, places and practices in a process by which they are given a 'second life' (Kirshenblatt-Gimblett 1998; 2006). Similarly, through the designation of protected areas, parts of the landscape are also transformed into 'wilderness' or 'nature'. But this transformation is not only discursive. The work of heritage transforms not only the conservation objects themselves (by way of conservation processes, for example, which may chemically or physically alter and transform the object into a piece of 'heritage'), but also the landscapes in which they are situated. One tends to think of heritage as something that is pre-existing and thus incorporated passively, or 'designed around' in rural and urban landscapes, but the decision to conserve and incorporate what had previously existed more simply as a 'ruin' or a 'wild' space into a landscape and to label it as 'heritage' is one that transforms the material world in particular ways. What I mean here is that a decision to build 'around', 'within', 'above' or 'below' is also a decision to build 'with' something – an archaeological site, part of a ruined building, a former factory, a nature reserve – and this is also a process of creating something new out of fragments (see also Shanks 2012). Preservation, in a very material sense, both resources and assembles future worlds. As Derrida (1996, 11) notes, there is 'no archive without outside' – the archive both reflects and, in doing so, actively organises and reorganises the world to which it refers.

Towards an ecology of heritage practices

If we are to see heritage practices of various kinds as enacting new realities through contingent practices of assembling and reassembling bodies, techniques, technologies, materials, values, temporalities and spaces in particular ways, what does it mean to speak of 'futures', 'realities' and 'worlds' in the plural?

> This is how I produced what I would call my first step towards an ecology of practice, the demand that no practice be defined as 'like any other', just as no living species is like any other. Approaching a practice then means approaching it as it diverges, that is, feeling its borders, experimenting with the questions which practitioners may accept as relevant, even if they are not their own questions, rather than posing insulting questions that would lead them to mobilise and transform the border into a defence against their outside.
>
> (Stengers 2005, 184)

Invoking Isabelle Stengers's notion of ecologies of practices, I draw attention to the relative autonomy of different domains of heritage practices, with each of these domains specifying particular objects of conservation and specific accompanying methods of management. Examples of such domains include the fields of biodiversity conservation, built heritage conservation and endangered language preservation, each of which identifies a specific risk (respectively, loss of biological diversity, loss of cultural patrimony, and loss of language and 'culture') and an endangered object ('biodiversity', 'built heritage' and 'language diversity'). Each of these domains applies its own specific techniques for identifying, collecting, conserving and managing the endangered object and the factors that are perceived to threaten it (see Harrison 2015; Harrison et al. 2016; see also Vidal and Dias 2016a). In thinking of how these domains exist contiguously and yet discretely from one another, I am influenced by German philosopher Peter Sloterdijk's (2016) characterisation of the contemporary condition as one in which humans increasingly occupy a 'foam' or complex ocean of fragmentary yet contiguous spheres. In so far as heritage is generally tasked with preserving its endangered object for the 'future', and each of these domains is concerned with establishing its respective conservation targets as both objects of knowledge and fields of intervention, these discrete yet adjacent heritage domains can be said to be actively engaged in the work of assembling and caring for future worlds. Although these domains of practice may sometimes come into relation with one another, and may be sustained by discourses that arise from others, they often operate in relative isolation. Central here is a plural notion of heritage ontologies – understood as the world-making, future-assembling capacities of heritage practices of different kinds, and the ways in which different heritage practices might be seen to enact different realities, and hence to assemble radically different futures (Harrison 2015; 2017).

In focusing on heritage practices, I make a distinction between *processes* and *practices*. Processes here represent descriptions of abstracted flows or movements, which in terms of actor–network theory might be understood as descriptions that help account for the ways in which specific sociomaterial networks are held together. Practices, on the other hand, refer to the actual things that human and non-human actors *do*. It is important to differentiate between generic or abstracted descriptions of the operations of networks as conservation processes, and specific ethnographic accounts of conservation practices, which, in sum, and through comparison, might be drawn upon to build up generalised accounts of such processes. The latter may be drawn on to understand the former, but they are distinct from one another.

Comparison and the conceptual affordances of heritage

One important argument we wish to pursue in the book relates to the value of comparative approaches to understanding what heritage conservation 'is' and 'does'. I use the terms 'comparison' and 'comparative approaches' to convey issues that are both methodological and conceptual, and I see comparison as valuable for a number of different reasons. I suggest that comparison can help to identify similarities and differences between conservation practices to generate understandings of model processes that can in turn help to account for how heritage functions and in what ways different kinds of heritage practices are articulated with, or are discrete from, one another. But perhaps more importantly, comparative approaches can also help to generate analytical concepts and provide a mechanism by which to reflect on our own conceptual frameworks. As such, these comparative approaches do not necessarily, or only, aim to find analogies or parallels among practices and institutions related with heritage, but can also encompass an enquiry into *how* conservation practices and institutions are dissimilar from one another and the reasons why they may differ. Articulating the differences between conservation practices, and exposing where they, and the values they generate, come into conflict with one another, constitutes a way of engaging with the politics and governmental capacities of heritage, which regularly makes appeals to universal values and 'best practices' in advocating for specific ways of conserving its endangered objects. Peter Van der Veer (2016) has recently argued that anthropology's comparative project remains vital for its ability to render and make translatable differences between cultures. I see these comparative approaches as key to addressing what I understand to be a principal aim of heritage studies, to critically engage its normalising and universalising tendencies, and to expose the social, political, material and cultural work it does.

I also see such comparative approaches as a way of working through the conceptual affordances of specific heritage practices and their objects of conservation to generate new ways of understanding the relationship between presents and futures. In using the term 'conceptual affordances', I draw on Martin Holbraad and Morten Axel Pederson's (2017, 199ff.) discussion of 'things as concepts', in which they argue the need for anthropological analyses to take account of the material properties of things and their potential to define certain forms of analytical thought. One of the conceptual affordances of the heritage practices we have engaged concerns the matter of conservation as 'care'. Here, one might think productively of the etymological roots of the word 'curate' in the

Latin word 'curare', to care. As María Puig de la Bellacasa (2017) argues, care as a concept is contested, political and sometimes hegemonic. It can constitute a responsibility or a burden. But it is also helpful to think with speculatively as a concept, in the sense in which it opens new horizons of possibility for ways of coexisting ethically in more-than-human worlds. What very explicitly connects the diverse range of practices we engage in this book – endangered language preservation, built and archaeological heritage management, deep-space messaging, nuclear waste disposal practices, rewilding, protected area management, museum work, informal practices of keeping and disposing within people's homes, biobanking, agrobiodiversity conversation, the preservation of natural and cultural heritage more generally – is that each one conceptualises itself more or less explicitly as a practice of caring for the future. These practices often involve meticulous and sustained acts of attentiveness to the needs of their endangered subjects; they are based in dialogical relationships in which those endangered subjects are not passive, but often active participants. As Annemarie Mol (2008) argues in her study of health care and patient choice, care should not be considered as a fixed category; in order to understand the 'rationale' or 'logic of care', one should study how care manifests in everyday practices. In exploring the diverse material ways in which futures are cared for and realised across a range of different cultural and geopolitical contexts, we aim to say something distinctive both about the nature of caring in more-than-human worlds, and about the capacities for those practices of care to realise specific futures, as well as the politics that determines the ways in which these practices can be deployed.

Legacies: Heritage and waste

I have already noted that one of the distinctive aspects of our analysis is to bring together heritage with other long-term material, discursive and political 'legacies' in the form of what is often negatively valued as 'waste'. Of course, this book is not the first to bring together the concepts of heritage management and waste management. Aspects of this comparison appear in the work of Mary Douglas (1991; originally published 1966), and in Michael Thompson's well-known book *Rubbish Theory* (1979), while, more recently, the geologist Marcos Buser (2016) has written on what he terms the 'heritage of toxic waste', to draw attention to the durability and persistence of chemotoxic and radioactive waste materials. A number of scholars (for example, Storm 2014; 2015; Schlanger et al.

2016; Joyce 2016; Maxwell 2016; Dawney et al. 2017; K. Brown 2019) have also explored nuclear power generation and waste disposal from a material culture studies or archaeological perspective in relation to issues of future material inheritances. Nonetheless, the rationale for this comparison is perhaps not immediately apparent, and deserves further consideration as part of the background to the inclusion of various of the case studies that the book explores.

I begin with the logics of bringing together questions of heritage and waste as interrelated spatial and discursive processes of managing forms of *redundancy*. As I have already noted, 'heritage' is a term that simultaneously identifies an object, place or practice as something that has value, and as something that is considered to be threatened or at risk. Waste, on the other hand, is a term that is clearly negatively valued – it designates a redundant object or useless by-product of some other operation. It is neither valuable nor at risk (although it might pose a risk to others). Yet both heritage and waste emerge from the same process of redundancy – these are both terms that denote superfluous objects that are no longer useful for the purpose for which they were originally produced. The museum and the rubbish dump might then be seen as two potential spatial end points for such redundant objects.

Or perhaps not so much end points, as points in a cycle of consumption and re-use, as categories of spatial and discursive placement. Kevin Hetherington (2004) argues that disposal is not just about questions of waste and rubbish, but is implicated more broadly in the ways in which people manage absence within social relations. Further, he explains that disposal is never final, as is implied by the notion of 'rubbish', but involves issues of managing social relations and their representation around themes of movement, transformation, incompleteness and return. He says that 'disposal is a continual practice of engaging with making and holding things in a state of absence' (Hetherington 2004, 37). While Hetherington's concern here is with practices of consumption more broadly, his focus on the work of maintaining absence draws out another similarity between heritage and waste, which is that both are defined by practices of maintenance and containment. Intangible heritage practices require performance to maintain and preserve, nature and biodiversity are actively managed by practices of ecosystem service repair and management, endangered languages are recorded and archived, become extinct and might possibly be rediscovered and live again. But the important point here is that heritage and waste occupy a series of 'other' spaces, outside of the realm of everyday life, set apart, sometimes hidden away in vaults, archives, banks, museums – repositories of different kinds.

To progress these concepts further, I briefly introduce two of these 'other places' to which we will return later in separate parts of the book. The first of these is the long-term nuclear waste and spent fuel repository site in Forsmark, Sweden, which is currently being constructed by SKB, the Swedish Nuclear Waste Management Company (see Figure 2.1). And the second is the Svalbard Global Seed Vault, currently the world's largest secure seed storage facility, located on the Norwegian island of Spitsbergen near Longyearbyen in the remote Arctic Svalbard archipelago, about 1,300 kilometres (810 miles) from the North Pole (see Figure 2.2).

I bring them together here not only to highlight the strikingly similar physical architectures of the two repositories, but also to think more broadly about the shared characteristics of such 'archives', which are built to contain and manage both heritage and waste. SKB's tagline, 'We take care of Swedish nuclear waste', invokes another connection between heritage and waste, in that both are designated as things that require human care. But if the robust security of biobanks and nuclear waste repositories tells us something of the similarities between heritage and waste in their managed depositions in these 'other places', what can one say about the absences and gaps in the landscape that are created by

Figure 2.1   Part of the network of tunnels at SKB's Final Repository for Short-Lived Radioactive Waste located at Forsmark in the municipality of Östhammar (photograph courtesy of SKB).

Figure 2.2 The 'Svalbard Tube' at the Svalbard Global Seed Vault (photograph by Rodney Harrison).

the gathering together of heritage and wastes and their storage in such a manner? And what happens when these affective materials leak from their repositories into the surrounding environment?

Drawing on the theme of cultural and historical debt in Derrida's *Spectres of Marx* (1994), Hetherington (2002; 2005; 2007) suggests that ghosts in the urban landscape represent the traces of unfinished or unmanaged disposal. One might think here of the ways in which heritage is always concerned with the maintenance of fragments. The almost fetishistic attempts to conserve the empty niche of the Great Buddha at Bamyan in Afghanistan following its destruction by the Taliban in 2001 exemplifies this pointedly (see Figure 2.3; see further discussion of absent heritages in Harrison 2013a). Similarly, the early twenty-first century is haunted by other ghosts of unmanaged disposals – the vast tracts of plastic wastes that converge within oceanic gyres (Figure 2.4 is a picture of part of the 'Pacific garbage patch', one of Timothy Morton's (2013a) hyperobjects), but perhaps even more problematic and more authentically haunting are the invisible anthropogenic waste products – carbon monoxide as an artefact of agriculture and industrial processes; chemotoxic wastes within waterways; the radionuclides within the Earth's

Figure 2.3 Matter out of place/ghosts of unmanaged disposals 1: the empty niche of the Great Buddha at Bamyan, Afghanistan, famously 'destroyed by the Taliban' in 2001 (photograph by Eric Sutphin CC BY 2.0).

Figure 2.4 Matter out of place/ghosts of unmanaged disposals 2: the Pacific Oceanic Gyre (photograph by Hagerty Ryan, courtesy US Fish and Wildlife Service CC0).

geology, which persist as atomic traces of nuclear energy production and warfare. These pollutants haunt as much because they constitute matter 'out of place' (Douglas 1991), and as such they help shine a light more intensely on the ways in which these repositories create new realities through their collecting and ordering practices.

One of the complex problems that the management of nuclear and other forms of hazardous waste presents is that the materials transform themselves over time. Marcos Buser (2016) points out that certain organic pollutants are transformed into what are termed 'metabolites' by bacterial or chemical decomposition, forming new materials that are often far more toxic than their parent materials. In the same vein, most of us are probably aware of the half-lives of nuclear materials and the ways in which they actively decay. On the other hand, decay contributes both positively and negatively to the aesthetic values of heritage (for example, DeSilvey 2017). The affective power of heritage sites, both positive and negative, also changes – sometimes less predictably, but it transforms nonetheless. Conservation and heritage work is framed as a process of slowing or managing such change and decay.

However, it is also clear that certain heritage sites become more or less toxic according to other contextual shifts in their social, material, political, economic or ecological environment. What might otherwise be valorised and protected as 'intangible heritage' might also form templates for identifying ethnic minorities and targeting them for expulsion, violence and genocides. Arjun Appadurai's *Fear of Small Numbers* (2006) considers the connection between globalisation and extreme culturally motivated ethnic violence in the genocides that occurred in the 1990s in eastern Europe, Rwanda and India, and subsequently in the 2000s in what has been termed the 'war on terror' – all of which arose under circumstances in which 'intangible' cultural differences among minorities became the focus for identifying specific groups for violence and genocide.

Another area where waste studies illuminates heritage is in thinking about waste and heritage as both contained within, and defined by, zones of exclusion, and I draw here on the work of historian of science Peter Galison (2015), who notes this resonance across waste and wilderness in his work. Both heritage and waste are articulated through practices of boundary maintenance and the selective exclusion of humans; nuclear waste management and wilderness management exemplify these similarities. Indeed, wilderness is defined precisely by the *absence* of human traces, and the boundaries managed to exclude such influences. International Union for the Conservation of Nature (IUCN)

Category Ib 'Wilderness Areas' are defined as 'Protected areas that are usually large unmodified or slightly modified areas, retaining their natural character and influence, without permanent or significant human habitation, which are protected and managed so as to preserve their natural condition.' They are 'large ... untouched areas where ecosystem processes, including evolution, can continue unhindered by human(s)' and should be managed in such a way as to limit any human visitation (IUCN 2020). But in many other, less extreme, ways, heritage is defined by its controlled access and restriction of human intervention – the ubiquitous glass case of the museum, the roped barrier that keeps visitors from private rooms in country houses, and the extreme isolation of the Svalbard Global Seed Vault, for example.

This physical and discursive distance also produces problems of communication that resonate across waste and heritage management. We have become used to the idea that the values of objects, places and practices managed as natural and cultural heritage are not necessarily legible to 'ordinary people', and that 'experts' must be engaged to 'interpret' the values of such places to the public. Their values are mediated by interpretive signage, by costumed guides, by maps and plans, through audio guides. Like heritage, nuclear waste management is dominated by questions of communicating the danger of buried nuclear waste to the life forms that will occupy and inherit this human heritage hundreds of thousands of years in the future. We explore these themes in detail in Part IV, Uncertainty.

Questions of overaccumulation haunt both heritage and waste too. The concrete forms that the various apparatuses that have been produced to identify and manage forms of heritage at risk – the registers that form a record of endangered species and ecosystems, the List of World Heritage in Danger, and so on – often do not include processes by which these objects may be removed from such registers. The overburdened museum storeroom or the domestic spaces of the cluttered attic become the emblematic symbols of these processes of overaccumulation of heritage. The overaccumulation of 'stuff', the durability of plastic wastes and their accumulation in alarming quantities in landfill, the problem of managing digital objects, e-wastes, noise and light pollution, and indeed the massive growth in human population itself, all speak to this same anxiety of enumerating growth in things as forms of overaccumulation. These are themes we explore explicitly in Part III, Profusion.

An obsession with memory practices also cuts across these fields. The work of nuclear semantics has at its core the study of intergenerational memory practices (Buser 2016). Andreas Huyssen (2003) points to the emergence of memory and its materialisation through memorials, museums and other cultural institutions as one of the key cultural and political phenomena of late twentieth-century modernity. Derrida's *Archive Fever* (1996) reveals the obsessive replication of such memory practices across many different practical fields. I take this term 'memory practices' from Geoffrey Bowker (2005a), who studies the proliferation of archival and other classificatory systems across various fields of natural science. Here, the archive stands in complicated relation with the future; it orders and makes new worlds in its structuring of reality. The potential for archives to order and produce realities underpins the work we present in Part II, Diversity, while the potential for such practices to change and, in turn, to transform realities, is addressed in Part V, Transformation.

But these acts of deposition, preservation and interpretation are as much practices of forgetting as they are of remembering, as archives are actively selected, selectively retained and impartially interpreted. These selective practices of remembering are also hierarchical practices of valuing. One is reminded of how the sites for the deposition of chemotoxic and radioactive wastes have also been selected in ways that reflect differentiation in the value of human lives between those who benefit from the consumption of the end products from which wastes are produced, and those who are forced to live among, and are most impacted upon by, the presence of those wastes in the environment.

****

This chapter has considered the relationship between heritage and the future, both as an imagined and aspiration goal on behalf of which both natural and cultural heritage is said to be preserved and managed, and as something that can be said to be actively built out of heritage conservation processes in the present. In Chapter 1, it was suggested that heritage practices can be broadly characterised with reference to a series of key processes – categorising, curating, conserving and communicating. The recognition of these generic processes invites an opening up of the empirical frame of heritage studies to other fields that also share such concerns. While waste is often characterised as the opposite of heritage, this chapter has suggested that it shares many of these concerns as a form of material and discursive legacy, the management of which is, like heritage, oriented towards the construction of particular kinds of actual and imagined futures. Accordingly, the book engages with a range of empirical case studies as representative of a range of different fields or domains of practice, some of which may be conventionally understood to be natural or cultural heritage fields, and some of which, such as waste management, might not. Nonetheless, all of these domains share common goals and frameworks (and often relate to one another in a variety of ways), which suggest the value of bringing such comparative perspectives to their study.

In the four thematic parts that follow, we explore the synthetic themes outlined in this chapter comparatively, drawing on empirical work undertaken over a four-year period by the book's authors and other affiliated members of our research team. We revisit them in more general terms in the final part, to reflect on the potential for such comparative work to generate new insights into natural and cultural heritage as future-making practices, and to reshape heritage and other forms of legacy-management practices in and for the future.

Part II
Diversity

What kinds of futures are realised by the preservation of biological, cultural and linguistic diversity – and what can each of these fields learn from one another?

3
Conserving diversity

Rodney Harrison, Esther Breithoff and Sefryn Penrose

The Library exists ab aeterno. *This truth, whose immediate corollary is the future eternity of the world, cannot be placed in doubt by any reasonable mind. Man, the imperfect librarian, may be the product of chance or of malevolent demiurgi; the universe, with its elegant endowment of shelves, of enigmatic volumes, of inexhaustible stairways for the traveller and latrines for the seated librarian, can only be the work of a god.*

Jorge Luis Borges, 'The Library of Babel' (2000 [1941])

Introduction

Let us begin with a riddle. What do red foxes, the Ainu language and tropical rainforest landscapes have in common?

All of these entities are classified (in one way or another) as endangered, and each is listed on a register that is in some way concerned with conserving plant or animal species, languages, landscapes or other forms of cultural or natural heritage. But it is worth pausing briefly to consider precisely what these lists and registers actually *conserve*. Because even though they list *individual* languages, cultures, animals, plants or landscapes, their conservation targets are rather articulated as different *collective* forms of 'diversity'. In heritage, it is customary to see the terms biodiversity, cultural diversity and linguistic diversity framed as *subjects* that are perceived to be at risk and that require specific forms of *action* to manage. But one might consider the discursive and socio-material steps that are involved in the gap that falls in the move between the focus on individual conservation targets – red foxes, the Ainu language, tropical rainforest landscapes – to the focus on meta-concepts that describe the conservation of different forms of collective diversity. These meta-concepts encode complicated relationships between parts and wholes. The diversity in biological or cultural diversity is so normative that it becomes impossible to imagine a scenario in which an ecosystem, landscape, national park, country, planet or other unit of analysis could ever be diverse *enough* – it represents a yearning for completeness and infinitude that, like that of other universal categorical systems (Bowker and Star 2000), constitutes what, in many cases, appears to be an impossible goal. Diversity is specified by way of a variety of indices, measurements and catalogues, designated at various degrees of risk (Turner 2007; Heise 2016), and is often represented metonymically: certain charismatic endangered objects, species, places, landscapes, languages or sets of practices come to stand in for the concept of biological or cultural diversity more generally. The conservation and management of individual components or conservation targets – individual languages, species, landscape units – and their respective collections, each contributes in part to the management of global biological and/or cultural diversity.

We began our work on diversity with a series of research questions. How is the concept of diversity understood, defined and mobilised across a range of different natural and cultural heritage conservation fields, and what kinds of social, material, political and ecological 'work' does this concept articulate in these different contexts? How are biological, cultural, genetic and linguistic diversity categorised and conserved, and what can one field learn from another? What are the range of practices undertaken across various different heritage domains that share an aim in the maintenance of ecological, cultural, linguistic and biological diversity, and what values are associated with these practices? And how might the boundaries between these different 'forms' of heritage be challenged, reconfigured or removed? These questions emerge from our broader consideration of the issues of future-making in heritage that are outlined in the introductory chapters of the book, and the general dominance of diversity as a concept that has driven a range of agendas – relating not only to 'what' is conserved, but *for, on behalf of* and *by whom* – across the heritage sector in recent times (see also Lee-Crossett 2018; 2019). They also emerge from observations of the growing dominance throughout the twentieth century of the concept of biological and cultural diversity, and its importance as a target for the conservation of nature and culture globally into the twenty-first century. Biological and cultural diversity have become such normative conservation targets that it is extremely uncommon to question their value or function. Our central provocation for both academics and practitioners is to challenge and problematise such notions by engaging these practices comparatively and critically, as individual and specific sociomaterial practices, to consider how and why they have come to dominate our understanding of the field of conservation, and the sociomaterial work that different fields accomplish by conserving such diversity.

As background to these questions, this chapter begins with a discussion of the emergence and function of various post-Second World War global organisations concerned with the preservation of cultural and natural heritage diversity, in particular the United Nations Educational and Scientific Organization (UNESCO) and its advisory bodies on natural and cultural world heritage (the International Union for the Conservation of Nature (IUCN), the International Council on Monuments and Sites (ICOMOS) and the International Centre for the Study of the Preservation and Restoration of Cultural Property (ICCROM)). This is not intended to function as a comprehensive history of natural and cultural diversity conservation, but instead to provide a contextual background to the case studies that form the focus of this part of the book. The chapter also provides a brief introduction to, and description of, the four different organisations with whom we engaged empirically to explore these questions through material and visual ethnographic research, and through involvement in our various thematic and cross-programme knowledge-exchange activities: the Nordic Genetic Resource Centre (NordGen) and Svalbard Global Seed Vault (SGSV), the Frozen Ark Project, the Endangered Languages Documentation Programme (ELDP) and the Herbarium at Kew. Each of these organisations is concerned with conserving forms of biological, cultural and/or biocultural diversity, and, as such, form relevant organisations working at regional, national and international scales across a number of countries with which to investigate these questions. Each organisation also, partially or predominantly, utilises *ex-situ* forms of conservation, drawing together collections from the field, and conserving them in a repository of some kind. While they have many things in common, they each approach their goal of conserving diversity in quite different ways, focusing on quite different conservation targets – seeds, the DNA of endangered animals, endangered languages and biodiversity, respectively. In addition to exploring these differences, we are also interested in the similarities between these diverse heritage domains, and what these similarities may have to tell us about how diversity conservation works more generally and the social, political, material and ecological 'work' that is performed by it. In doing so, the chapter also engages briefly with concepts of categorising and making worlds, and the concept of transactional realities, as key conceptual devices to which we will return in later chapters of this part of the book.

Subsequent chapters and visual essays focus on themes that facilitate these comparisons with finer granularity. Chapter 4 considers the relationship between field collecting and collections, suggesting that these constitute a kind of feedback loop in which the collections come to specify and define the fields from which their conservation targets are assembled. Chapter 5 compares different forms of *ex-situ* repository, drawing attention to their visual similarities and differences. Chapter 6 moves to the *ex-situ* collections themselves to show how they manipulate time and produce new forms of values. Chapter 7 looks at the role of parts and wholes in diversity conservation through a visual engagement with conservation proxies. Chapters 4 and 6 focus specifically on particular subgroups of empirical case studies and introduce each of the organisations we worked with, and how we worked with them, in more detail. Finally, Chapter 8 summarises the main findings of the work we undertook within the theme.

Diversity and endangerment

The introductory chapters of this book discussed the concept of the 'endangerment sensibility' (Vidal and Dias 2016b) as a component of the 'risk society' (Beck 1992; see Harrison 2013a; Rico 2015a; 2015b; 2016). This sensibility, which emerged during the twentieth century, connects together various registers and lists of threatened conservation targets; it manifested itself materially across a range of different forms of conservation activity in the later part of the twentieth century and continues to do so into the early part of the twenty-first. This concept of endangerment can be understood to be a motivating factor in connecting together a broad range of forms of natural and cultural heritage conservation practice, from cryogenic freezing to museum collecting, and from the conservation of biosphere reserves to the protection of world heritage sites. We have noted elsewhere that this endangerment sensibility is enacted by way of specific practices – listing, classifying, ordering, specifying, managing and preserving (see Harrison 2016b) – and that such practices can be studied not only historically but also ethnographically.

We introduce a further concept here, of 'transactional realities', which helps us to explain the relationship between conservation and (plural) world-making practices that underpin the research questions and empirical investigations that are a part of this theme. This derives from Michel Foucault's *The Birth of Biopolitics*, in which he notes:

Civil society is not a historical-natural given … [nor] a primary or immediate reality; it is something which forms part of a modern governmental technology … Civil society is, like madness and sexuality, what I call transactional realities. That is to say those transactional and transitional figures we call civil society, madness, and so on, which, although they have not always existed are nonetheless real, are born precisely from the interplay of relations of power and everything which constantly eludes them, at the interface, so to speak, of governors and governed.

(Foucault 2008, 297)

We suggest that the different forms of diversity that are articulated through the various lists and registers by which they are simultaneously quantified and designated as endangered – biodiversity, linguistic diversity, cultural diversity – operate as transactional realities through which the endangerment sensibility is articulated and produced. Our aim in this part of the book is to explore the practical and discursive means by which these transactional realities are produced, how they relate to one another, and what work they do in organising different realities, and hence in framing and producing different kinds of future worlds.

In his work on nineteenth- and twentieth-century anthropological field-collecting practices and their relationship with museum collecting, Tony Bennett (2013, 44–5; 2014; Bennett et al. 2017) has suggested that one of the important roles of such collecting practices is in producing 'working surfaces on the social', that is, in producing transactional realities that provide distinctive discursive and technical means by which human populations might be differentiated and by which specific forms of action on those differentiated populations might be mediated as a function of these relations. This is particularly the case in understanding the role of anthropological collecting in colonial contexts, understood broadly as two connected but distinct sets of relations – one spatial and one political – which help to illustrate the value of such an approach to archival and preservational practices more generally. The first concerns a regional distinction between the metropole and colony, and the role of anthropological museum collections in the production of similarly organised relations within metropolitan powers between the capital city and its various hinterlands. The second concerns the distinction between those mechanisms of governing that work through the forms of freedom they organise and those that operate coercively. These are most clearly apparent in the divisions that colonial governmentalities work through in designating sections of colonised populations (for example, indigenous peoples) as subject to directive forms of rule in which they are denied the attributes deemed necessary for liberal subjecthood: that is, the capacity to practise a responsibilised freedom. In the context of the *ex-situ* anthropological/cultural collections (and their associated field-collecting practices) with which Bennett and his co-authors are concerned, these transactional realities relate to the specific logics of particular colonial contexts and, as such, work towards the production of different governmental rationalities that are concerned with different ways of acting on sociomaterial worlds. These transactional realities and their associated governmental rationalities can be seen as plural worlding practices (see Barad 2007; de la Cadena and Blaser 2018; Omura et al. 2019; Breithoff 2020), and to exist as a function of specific configurations of *collecting, ordering* and *governing* practices (see Bennett et al. 2017).

There are two sets of relationships that emerge from this discussion that have relevance to our work with other forms of heritage beyond the ethnographic museum collections with which these arguments are primarily concerned (keeping in mind, as was noted in Chapter 1, that heritage is defined by its practices of categorising, curating, conserving and communicating). The first relates to how particular transactional realities produce specific governmental rationalities that are enacted through distinct collecting and ordering practices. If each transactional reality – or within the context of this discussion of diversity, each conservation target or goal – is produced through specific collecting, categorising, ordering and managing practices, this suggests that comparative approaches to these practices can help us to explore the different worlds that each form of heritage practice subsequently produces (see also Swanson et al. 2018). The second relates to the ways in which transactional realities are accompanied by particular forms of governmental rationalities, which constitute certain assumptions (and the actions that such assumptions predicate) that underpin the ways in which heritage is dealt with and managed. The elaboration of different categories of heritage and their appropriate means of management are each accompanied by their own associated notions of freedoms (for example, how they should be used and managed, and for whom), alongside the establishment of specific limits on those freedoms (limits on change to heritage fabric, authorised versus non-authorised conservation practices and so on). The important point to note is the way in which biological and cultural diversity conservation designates itself simultaneously as a subject of *enumeration* – it involves bureaucratic practices of identifying, counting and accounting for certain conservation targets in natural heritage management – and a field of *intervention* – it justifies and predicates certain actions on those conservation targets and/or the field(s) or context(s) in which those targets are contained (see also Bowker 2000). We will return to the concepts of transactional realities in Chapters 4 and 6. Before we do so, we look at the historical emergence of cultural and biological diversity as subjects and targets for conservation during the twentieth century, and the various transactional realities that came to be related to each.

Cultural diversity

The immediate aftermath of the Second World War saw the establishment of a series of international organisations concerned with the promotion and protection of forms of cultural and natural heritage. Here we discuss the emergence of these organisations, through which the notion of endangered diversity (both cultural and natural) has come to be articulated, defined and made actionable as a target for conservation and preservation by the various organisations that form the empirical focus of the rest of Part II, Diversity. Some aspects of this history are also relevant to case studies in other parts of the book.

UNESCO and its advisory bodies, including ICOMOS, ICCROM and IUCN, have been central to the development of what has been perceived to be a universally applicable set of criteria for the assessment, designation and conservation of 'world' heritage sites (Langfield et al. 2010, 5; Meskell 2018). Within this context, the concept of 'cultural diversity', as defined by the UNESCO Declaration of Principles of International Cultural Co-operation (1966) and the Universal Declaration on Cultural Diversity (2002), emerged as a specific conservation target and field of intervention. In the light of the atrocities committed under the name of racial science during the Second World War, the United Nations (UN) – created in 1945 with the aim of maintaining global peace and unity, and taking action on economic, social, humanitarian (and later also environmental) issues – sought to replace the concept of 'race' and its negative connotations with the concept of 'culture' (see Lentin 2005). This view was consolidated with the publication of *The Race Question* by UNESCO in 1950.

The UNESCO Universal Declaration on Cultural Diversity (2002) asserts that cultural heritage is the common heritage of humanity, enshrining difference as something that is both vulnerable to threats posed by modernity and globalisation, and also something intrinsic to social cohesion and global peace (UNESCO 2002). The subsequent 2003 UNESCO Convention for the Safeguarding of the Intangible Cultural Heritage and 2005 UNESCO Convention on the Protection and Promotion of the Diversity of Cultural Expressions each connect cultural diversity to human rights, thus making cultural diversity a unified project vital for the building of a sustainable future:

> Culture takes diverse forms across time and space. The diversity is embodied in the uniqueness and plurality of the identities of the groups and societies making up humankind. As a source of exchange, innovation and creativity, cultural diversity is as necessary for humankind as biodiversity is for nature. In this sense, it is the common heritage of humanity and should be recognized and affirmed for the benefit of present and future generations.
>
> (UNESCO 2002, Article 1)

The 2001 declaration goes on to promote cultural pluralism as 'conducive to cultural exchange and to the flourishing of creative capacities that sustain public life', and every person's right to cultural diversity, particularly in the context of minority groups and indigenous people (UNESCO 2002, Articles 2 and 4). As Harrison (2013a) has pointed out elsewhere, the idea of diversity as a universal human right has, however, the potential to distract from the ways in which cultural difference has often been (mis)used for political goals (see also Langfield et al. 2010) and for justifying different forms of liberal and illiberal practices of social governance on such differentiated populations (see further discussion in Bennett et al. 2017).

In 1952, Lévi-Strauss (1952) had already suggested that each culture contributed a unique and 'distinctive' part of a collective human diversity. As such, he argued that human progress, understood in its most fundamental terms as entering into the experience of modernity, was to be measured as the result of the interactions of different cultural groups, rather than being conceived of as the outcome of any cultural, biological or technological trait inherent to any of them. Progress was a function of intercultural knowledge, and thus, cultural diversity was integral to progress. But here, as Lentin (2005, 387) points out, lay a contradiction, because such intercultural dialogue would ultimately lead to the erosion of cultural distinctiveness, and hence of cultural diversity, rather than strengthening it. Bennett et al. (2017) show how this contradiction led to the development of special categories of endangered personhood – in particular the transnational concept of 'indigeneity' – which would require particular forms of conservation practices to maintain in the face of the inherent threats of intercultural dialogue and exchange.

Adding to the problematic notion of UNESCO's 'universal heritage' in relation to indigenous knowledges was the concept of 'intangible heritage'. Since the Rio Earth Summit in 1992 (UNESCO 1992), a broadening recognition of the importance of indigenous knowledges to an understanding of conservation had taken hold. Criticism – especially from 'Southern' states parties – focused around the observation that UNESCO's existing approach to world heritage valorised static, monumental forms of heritage, and offered no place for alternative understandings or conceptions of heritage. As part of the World Decade for Cultural Development (1988–97), the General Assembly established the World Commission on Culture and Development, which reported its findings in *Our Creative Diversity* in 1995. The report underscored cultural diversity as a global public good, while also highlighting the threat of homogenisation to traditional cultures (Graber 2006; Harrison 2013a).

Concurrently, an increasing understanding of the links between biological and cultural diversity emerged, fuelled by the perceived 'extinction crisis' (Maffi 2005; Krauss 1992). Gaining ground following the Rio Earth Summit of 1992, a new line of thinking established biological and cultural diversity as proxies for each other, with an observation that areas rich in one were usually rich in the other (Maffi 2005; Harmon 2002). Article 7 of UNESCO's Declaration on Cultural Diversity (2002) directly affirmed the analogy: 'cultural diversity is as necessary for humankind as biodiversity is for nature'. A loss of *bio*diversity would thus be perceived to mean a loss of *cultural* diversity, and vice versa, as species, cultures and languages were perceived to be inherently intertwined in what Maffi (2005, 602) has termed *biocultural diversity* or 'the diversity of life in all its manifestations – biological, cultural and linguistic, which are interrelated within a complex socio-ecological adaptive system' (see also Heyd 2010; Vidal and Dias 2016b).

Cultural diversity preservation via language documentation

Language diversity as a global conservation target emerged out of the development of these international protocols for the protection of cultural diversity. These protocols were being developed at the same time as the subfield of academic linguistics that deals with minority languages and a widespread observation of language loss. The rate of decline, if it continued unabated, was calculated as likely to reach a loss of between 50 per cent and 90 per cent of the 6,000-plus languages spoken globally by 2100 (Maffi 2005; Krauss 1992). (This figure has recently been adjusted downwards.) In 1987, the linguist Johannes Bechert, speaking at the Comité International Permanent des Linguistes (CIPL) conference, likened the predicted loss of Australian languages to 'the large-scale destruction of natural gene pools such as that in the tropical rain forests' (Himmelman 2008, 337). The conference resolved to prioritise the topic in the International Congress of Linguists, which met in Quebec in 1992, and undertook to commission a report on the state of the world's minority languages, which was published in 1991 as *Endangered Languages* (Robins and Uhlenbeck 1991). A 1992 publication (proceedings of the 1991 annual meeting of the Linguistic Society of America) edited by Ken Hale (Hale et al. 1992) further drew attention to the issue. Due to the attention and involvement in these activities of linguist Stephen Wurm, president of UNESCO's Conseil International de la Philosophie et des Sciences Humaines (CIPSH), the Endangered Languages Programme was formed in 1993, and an ad hoc committee constituted. A 'Red List' (see further discussion below) of endangered languages was drawn up, and published in 1996 as the first edition of the UNESCO *Atlas of the World's Languages in Danger of Disappearing* (Wurm 1996). In 2003, the UNESCO Ad Hoc Expert Group on Endangered Languages issued a document, *Language Vitality and Endangerment*, which laid out a set of criteria for measuring the level of endangerment of languages. It identified six factors on which to assess endangerment, scoring each from 5 (representing safety) to 0 (equivalent to extinction or near-extinction) (UNESCO Ad Hoc Expert Group on Endangered Languages 2003).

In 2001, UNESCO issued its Proclamation of Masterpieces of the Oral and Intangible Heritage of Humanity. A list of 'masterpieces' was duly drawn up, opening up the safeguarding approach to cultural acts beyond the 'tangibility' of built heritage. An earlier 'Recommendation on the Safeguarding of Traditional Culture and Folklore' (UNESCO 1989) had not received wide recognition, and was seen as a 'soft law' due to its lack of mandate or guidance on implementation (Aikawa-Faure 2009, 21). In part, the developing interest in these areas was driven by resistance to US cultural imperialism exercised by certain states parties – particularly France and Canada – to the imposition of US cultural exports. The complex UN negotiations over trade in television and cinematic output has played an important role throughout the emergence of cultural diversity as a conservation target for UNESCO, and the withdrawal from UNESCO of the USA in 1984, followed by the UK in 1985, effectively opened the door to more nuanced and informed approaches to cultural diversity (McDonald 2017, 167). The Universal Declaration on Cultural Diversity (UNESCO 2002), approved in Paris in 2001, is seen as a direct response to disputes of trade negotiations, with its primary aim being securing the sovereignty of states parties to exclude cultural output from trade liberalisation negotiations (Niedner-Kalthoff 2015; Pyykkönen 2012). It brought language into its auspices under the umbrella of human rights – as part of the right to expression of cultural diversity (Article 5: Cultural rights as an enabling environment for cultural diversity) – and embedded into Point 5 of its Action Plan, 'safeguarding the linguistic heritage of humanity' (UNESCO 2002).

UNESCO ratified the Convention for the Safeguarding of the Intangible Cultural Heritage in 2003. It built on the 2002 Declaration, again using a framework of human rights, but pushing a broader, more relativistic sense of culture. Article 2, which defined the possible forms that 'the intangible cultural heritage' might take, specifically included 'oral traditions and expressions, including language as a vehicle of the intangible cultural heritage' (UNESCO 2003). Although adopted in 2003, the Convention remains unratified by 17 of UNESCO's 195 member states, including the USA – which rejoined UNESCO in 2003 with the express intention of blocking the proposals – and the UK, although it claims to support the aims of the Convention (McDonald 2017, 169; Soukup 2006, 212).

After another long process of negotiation relating to the commercial and free trade implications, the Convention on the Protection and Promotion of the Diversity of Cultural Expressions was ratified in 2005. Article 6 of that convention proposes that states implement:

> … measures that, in an appropriate manner, provide opportunities for domestic cultural activities, goods and services among all those available within the national territory for the creation, production, dissemination, distribution and enjoyment of such domestic cultural activities, goods and services, including provisions relating to the language used for such activities, goods and services.
>
> (UNESCO 2005, 6)

Biological diversity

In the previous section, we outlined the ways in which the protection and promotion of *cultural* diversity came to be seen as the responsibility of a series of international non-governmental organisations concerned with the promotion of peace and sustainable futures. Parallel and often inter-related developments saw the establishment and increasing influence of a series of organisations concerned with the protection and management of *biological* diversity. The International Union for Conservation of Nature (IUCN, previously known as the IUPN – International Union for the Protection of Nature) was founded in 1948 at an international gathering of various government representatives and conservation organisations in Fontainebleau, France. The meeting, initiated by UNESCO and its first director-general, British biologist Julian Huxley, was established in response to an increasing universal concern with safeguarding the *natural* environment. As the only international organisation at the time focusing on biodiversity conservation in its broadest sense, the IUPN's main mission was to raise awareness of, and counteract, species extinction by establishing networks between the public and governing institutions from around the world (Holdgate 1999).

This, combined with the IUCN's efforts to guide conservation activities, led to the creation of the IUCN Red List of Threatened Species (henceforth, the Red List) in 1964. The Red List currently constitutes the most comprehensive, objective and scientifically grounded information source on the global conservation status of biodiversity. It is the result of 'assemblages of knowledge' such as the Red Data Books (Holdgate 1999, vi), which form global registers of biological species, their definitions and categories of threat: extinct, extinct in the wild, critically endangered, vulnerable, near threatened, least concern, data deficient, not evaluated. The Red Data Books' content is compiled and periodically reassessed and updated by an expert network made up by the IUCN Global Species Commission and the IUCN Survival Commission (SSC), as well as various other Red List partners, including universities and other research institutes, museums and non-governmental organisations (Fitter and Fitter 1987).

Over the years, the aim of the Red List has extended beyond the designation of threat status to include a substantial and hitherto unavailable accumulation and subsequent online publication of data on a large number of the world's species. Conservation efforts no longer follow 'priorities for extinction' (Collar 1996, 122) – favouring large charismatic animals already identified as at risk – but now target all kinds of species, as well as the ecosystems and habitats they inhabit (Rodrigues et al. 2006; Baillie et al. 2004). Despite the IUCN's best efforts, and it having been widely acknowledged as 'an increasingly powerful tool for conservation planning, management, monitoring and decision making' (Rodrigues et al. 2006, 71), the Red List remains an incomplete inventory, with gaps in knowledge and the threat statuses being based on less than 3 per cent of the world's almost two million known species, according to the *2004 IUCN Red List of Threatened Species: A Global Species Assessment* (Baillie et al. 2004).

Even though it has come to dominate the ways in which we understand, value and care for the 'natural' world, 'biodiversity' as a concept is relatively young, only emerging as a specifically identified target for conservation activity during the late 1970s and 1980s (Heyd 2010; Sepkoski 2016; Takacs 1996). The First National Forum on Biodiversity, held in Washington, DC, in September 1986, organised by conservation biologists E.O. Wilson and Walter Rosen (see Wilson 1988), is commonly held to mark the entry of the concept into international public discourse. But what does the term 'biodiversity' mean in this context? Since its introduction as a shorthand for 'biological diversity', the concept of 'biodiversity' has come to stand in for a range of different conservation targets, from individual species to landscapes and ecosystems, and the primary means by which the values of 'natural' heritage are articulated. Generally used to refer to and measure all categories of biological diversity and its abundance, including everything from 'alleles, to populations, to species, to communities, to eco-systems' (Sarkar 2002, 405; see also United Nations 1992), biodiversity has also acted as a more 'scientific' synonym for nature. Generally, biological diversity, the 'web of life' (CBD 2000), is considered to be something intrinsically good, the protection of which is paramount for the survival of humanity:

> Biological resources are the pillars upon which we build civilizations … The loss of biodiversity threatens our food supplies, opportunities for recreation and tourism, and sources of wood, medicines and energy. It also interferes with essential ecological functions.
> (CBD 2000, 3)

Still, the meaning of the term 'biodiversity' remains ambiguous, its definition continuously remoulded to fit the agenda and situation of the stakeholder(s) involved (Swingland 2001), but always framed in relation to broader narratives of extinction and loss. In the process, biodiversity has become a powerful concept employed across the natural and social sciences, as well as governmental and corporate agencies, to justify and frame interventions *in*, and actions *upon*, the 'natural' world (Bowker 2005a). In the field of ecology and conservation biology, the concept of biodiversity is conventionally approached as something that is of universal value and in need of protection (Perrings et al. 1992).

Classifying biological diversity as endangered involves a conscious decision to put it into a specific category that carries within itself connotations of loss, depletion and forgetting – negative or 'anti-values par excellence' (Vidal and Dias 2016a, 1) – that force one to see biodiversity as potentially inherently diminishing with time, and thus in need of saving (see Harrison 2017; see also Sepkoski 2016). To this way of thinking, biodiversity becomes something that is followed by the persistent 'shadow of extinction' (Van Dooren 2014, 8), and for which humans come to act as saviours of the victims of their own misdoings. Here, we draw on Van Dooren's (2014) definition of extinction as a slow unravelling of entangled lives that does not represent a single event but the unmaking of an interlinked ecological and social web of human and non-human species. (On the emerging field of extinction studies, see also Bird Rose 2011; Sodikoff 2012; Heise 2016; Bird Rose et al. 2017).

Sepkoski (2016) has drawn attention to the significant discursive shift that occurred with the introduction of the concept of biodiversity, from a focus on individual species or landscapes as conservation targets to the combined contribution of these parts to a whole. Importantly, he situates this move historically within a new understanding of the nature of species extinction, itself derived from the 'new catastrophism' of palaeontology and evolutionary biology. He notes that, in the nineteenth century, species extinction was commonly understood as a slow and normative process that contributed to the continuous renewal of a natural equilibrium: that as certain species went extinct, others, through processes of natural selection, would replenish 'nature's economy' (see discussion in Worster 1994) to maintain the balance of nature. Indeed, he notes that in this view, species extinction might even be viewed as progressive, weeding out 'unfit' species in favour of more adaptive ones (themes that reflect the work discussed in Part III, Profusion). The number of species in the world was thus understood to always be maintained in a stable state or, alternatively, might be understood to be steadily increasing with time. During the 1970s and 1980s, within the context of the development of systems and chaos theory, and of Cold War fears of possible nuclear planetary annihilation, Sepkoski notes that palaeontologists and evolutionary biologists began to question Darwinian models and the implication that extinction might be understood to be a function of the 'imperfection' of less-fit species. This coincided with the development of new theories of mass prehistoric extinctions related to catastrophic events, such as that of a meteorite impact event approximately 65 million years ago, thought to have brought the Cretaceous period to its conclusion.

The implication of these new theories was the perception that, while the 'natural' state of things was for species diversity to increase exponentially over time, the number of species had neither been stable nor had increased at a stable rate over the Earth's history, and that certain catastrophic mass extinction events had had a major impact on species diversity over time. Work on the nature of these mass extinction events suggested that the evolutionary lineages that survived such events tended to actually be more homogeneous in other regards: 'even if diversity – as measured by the sheer number of species alive – has increased, it has become a more homogenous kind of diversity, since those species are clustered within fewer and fewer higher taxa' (Sepkoski 2016, 77). Sepkoski points to the influence of these ideas on E.O. Wilson's work, in particular, in forming an accepted view of species extinction as an irreversible and potentially erratic and catastrophic process, where species diversity is endangered by the likelihood of such catastrophic processes, and likely decreases with time. Importantly, this view of biodiversity as a normative target for natural heritage conservation activity gained traction from its connection with other apparatuses (see Harrison 2013a; 2016b) that were developed to address the endangerment sensibility, in particular, as we have already noted, those concerned with the measurement of the endangerment of cultural and linguistic diversity (Maffi 2005). These notions of the inherent endangerment of biological, cultural and linguistic diversity are reflected in the aims of our case study organisations in various ways. We now introduce these four case study organisations briefly, before turning to look at them in more detail in subsequent chapters.

Introduction to the case studies

In the preceding section, we briefly outlined the historical emergence of biological and cultural diversity as transactional realities for conservation – concepts that mobilise particular forms of action, which make and remake parallel yet overlapping worlds around themselves, but that do not exist independently of the constellations of knowledge practices by which they are composed. Here, we introduce the four organisations with whom we worked directly as part of this theme. These share certain common practices of conservation via the formation of *ex-situ* collections of their respective conservation objects, motivated by the collection of data relating to these objects in their 'natural' environments. But they are also incredibly heterogeneous in the range of targets they address, and the means by which they do this. We aim to draw out this diversity of approaches in the chapters that follow this one.

NordGen/The Svalbard Global Seed Vault

The Svalbard Global Seed Vault (SGSV) is currently the world's largest secure seed storage facility. It was established in 2008 by the Royal Norwegian Ministry of Agriculture and Food; the Global Crop Diversity Trust (now known as the Crop Trust), an independent international organisation based in Germany (established as a partnership between the United Nations Food and Agriculture Organization (FAO) and the Consultative Group on International Agricultural Research); and the Nordic Genetic Resource Centre (NordGen). At a cost of US\$9 million to the Norwegian government, the construction of the SGSV began in 2005 as a result of the recommendations of the 2004 International Treaty on Plant Genetic Resources for Food and Agriculture, which created a global *ex-situ* system for the conservation of agricultural plant genetic resource diversity. Situated on the remote island of Spitsbergen in the Norwegian Svalbard archipelago, high in the Arctic north, it received its first deposits of seeds in 2008. In addition to their responsibilities for the day-to-day management of the SGSV, NordGen are engaged in a number of different initiatives concerned with the safeguarding and sustainable use of plants, farm animals and forests across the Nordic regions. NordGen itself was established in January 2008 as a cooperative initiative across the Nordic countries as a result of a merger between the Nordic Gene Bank, the Nordic Gene Bank Farm Animals and the Nordic Council for Forest Reproductive Material. NordGen is primarily financed by the Nordic Council of Ministers. Its main office and NordGen Plants are located in Alnarp, near Malmö, in southern Sweden. NordGen Farm Animals and NordGen Forest offices are located in Ås, near Oslo, in Norway.

The Frozen Ark project

The Frozen Ark project was originally established in 2004 at the University of Nottingham by the late geneticist Professor Bryan Clarke FRS and immunologist Dr Ann Clarke, as well as developmental biologist Dame Anne McLaren, in an effort to preserve the genetic resources of threatened wild species kept in zoos and aquaria around the world before they could go extinct (see Clarke 2009; Costa and Bruford 2018), assuming this extinction was a given. From the 1960s, Bryan dedicated much of his time to work on speciation in the *Partula* land snail, native to the volcanic islands of French Polynesia. It was around the same time that *Lissachatina fulica*, the giant African land snail was brought to the island of Tahiti for breeding purposes as a culinary delicacy – a decision with serious consequences. The snail spread to neighbouring islands and, in the absence of any natural predators, bred at such an alarming rate that the government decided to introduce the carnivorous Florida rosy wolfsnail (*Euglandina rosea*) to the island to control the quickly escalating agricultural pest. However, instead of eating its targeted prey, the new snail ravaged the *Partula* snail population, and within 15 years the latter had disappeared from most of the islands (Clarke et al. 1984). Realising the imminent threat of extinction to the species from human interference, Clarke and his team decided to collect live specimens of the remaining 12 *Partula* species, bring them back to the UK and freeze tissue samples in order to preserve their DNA and allow for further study; they also established an international captive breeding programme at the Zoological Society of London in the hope of reintroducing the snail to its natural habitat. The fate of the *Partula* was playing out before their very eyes, and the importance of collecting and preserving biological material from endangered animals eventually resulted in the creation of the Frozen Ark project (Costa and Bruford 2018). It operated for some years out of its institutional base at the University of Nottingham, which continues to provide laboratory and office space, but the project's research is now mainly carried out at Cardiff University.

The Herbarium at Kew

The Herbarium collection at Kew originates in the historic collections of the Hookers, father and son, and in the collecting expeditions of the nineteenth century. Joseph Hooker sent thousands of specimens back to his father at Kew from his expeditions – initially to the Antarctic (taking in the islands of the Southern Ocean), then to India and the Himalaya, and then to the USA (Goyder et al. 2012). Further specimens were sent by William Arnold Bromfield. The collection was bolstered by the donation of private collections, including those of the East India Company, and that of the botanist George Bentham. Influenced by the evolutionary theories of Darwin, but not based on evolutionary relationships, Bentham and Hooker's *Genera Plantarum* (1862–83) provided a clear, if not definitive, classification system that was used at Kew until recently, when the Angiosperm Phylogeny Grouping (APG) in its third iteration was adopted (Fay 2011). APG is based on DNA sequencing of plants, allowing an evolutionary family tree to be built (Chase et al. 1993; Wearn et al. 2013; APG IV 2016). The Herbarium at Kew currently holds six million specimens, and continues to accession around thirty thousand per year, describing around two thousand new species annually (Kew 2018).

Article 7 of the Convention on Biological Diversity (United Nations 1992) requires states parties to monitor and collect data on biodiversity. Following that, the Global Plant Strategy (most recently updated following COP10) sets out a set of objectives relating to plant conservation. Objective I states: 'Plant diversity is well understood, documented and recognized', and sets out targets that speak to the continued role of herbaria in documenting and recording the state and status of the world's plants. So-called 'Red List assessments' should improve the knowledge of plant conservation status through the documentation of a prescribed information set recorded during specimen accession (Willis et al. 2003, 1567). Since only 5 per cent of known plant species have been subject to Red List assessment, the possibilities of assessment in this long-established manner seem to provide an answer to the perceived need for increased understanding via documentation and *ex-situ* recording.

We also worked with the UK National Tree Seed Project (UKNTSP), part of a Kew-led project to collect the seeds of the UK's native flora and fauna and bank them – a process that requires a sample of viable seeds to be dried and frozen for potential future use, with priority given to maintaining the most threatened and/or potentially useful seeds (Kew 2018). Seeds are gathered from around the UK, and prepared and stored at the Millennium Seed Bank (MSB) in Sussex, UK. The MSB is a Kew-owned and run facility, purpose-built within the grounds of a National Trust property, Wakehurst Place, to house the seed collection at a site external to, yet directly related to, the Botanic Gardens at Kew. It is part of a global network of such banks aiming to store 25 per cent of bankable plant species by 2020. The UKNTSP is administered from the MSB and is a five-year project, begun in 2013, and funded by the People's Postcode Lottery, with the remit of collecting at least the top 50 species from a specially prepared target list.

The Endangered Languages Documentation Project

The Hans Rausing Endangered Languages Documentation Project (latterly, the Endangered Languages Project – ELDP) began at the School of Oriental and African Studies (SOAS), part of the University of London, in 2002, following the bestowal of a £20-million grant from the Lisbet Rausing Charitable Fund (now known as Arcadia). The grant enabled two activity strands: an academic programme that was to fund master's degree and PhD programmes at SOAS, and an archive of documented languages. The funding and programmes responded to the advent of documentation as a branch of linguistics, as opposed to description (see, for example, Himmelmann 1998). Applications are made to ELDP for projects to record an aspect of language (also understood as culture expressed within language) within an endangered language – identified as such through the criteria laid out in 2003 by the UNESCO Ad Hoc Expert Group. Through this mechanism, it funds documentary linguists to collect languages deemed to be in various degrees of danger – either from gradual sublimation by larger languages, or at risk of becoming moribund, to the extent of extinction. The ELDP relies on individual linguists to come forward with languages that they wish to study. Unlike some other diversity collecting institutions, there is thus no target list. Each linguist forms a corpus of work on the collected language, usually including a grammar and lexicon, and, increasingly, audio and video recordings. Further elements of the corpus might take the form of educational resources or academic articles. The whole is then stored (since 2014 as open access) on a publicly accessible database called the Endangered Language Archive. The ELDP also trains linguists in location-based field schools.

Methods

We worked with each of these four case study organisations in several different ways. First, we undertook empirical research over the course of four years, involving interviews with staff, volunteers and associates of the four organisations. We also participated in field-, collections- and desktop-based research projects through a series of multi-sited, embedded placements as a means through which to undertake short-term ethnographies (Pink and Morgan 2013) within each organisation.

The work we undertook within each organisation is described in more detail in the chapters that follow. Each of these four case study organisations was at the same time a project partner on the Heritage Futures research programme and, as such, representatives of the four organisations also participated in various collaborative knowledge-exchange events throughout the project, which aimed at understanding the work of each of the partner organisations comparatively and at co-designing research to address common issues for the sector. We organised one of these events in collaboration with the Alan Turing Institute, British Library and AHRC Heritage Priority Area on 'Heritage and Data' (see Harrison et al. 2017). Representatives of the four organisations also participated in the overall programme-wide knowledge-exchange events that form the subject of the three knowledge-exchange visual essays that are placed between the thematic parts of this book. In addition to the interviews and ethnographic observations, this part of the book also draws on these more experimental 'para-ethnographic' (Holmes and Marcus 2005; 2006; 2008; see Harrison et al. 2016) engagements with the organisations as part of the research programme. Finally, as we noted in the Preface and Acknowledgements and in Chapter 1 of this book, we participated in a number of international conferences, congresses and workshops at which various of these four case study organisations presented their work, or in which broader international research and policy initiatives that impacted on them were discussed. These included the IUCN World Conservation Congress in Hawaii in 2016, where we participated in the jointly organised IUCN/ICOMOS 'nature–culture journey' (itself co-organised by one of our advisory board members and the head of world heritage at IUCN), and an equivalent programme of events that took place at the ICOMOS General Assembly and Scientific Symposium in Delhi in 2017. We also brought together representatives of some of the organisations at project-sponsored workshops and festivals, including two Heritage Futures themed panels that we ran at NESTA's Future Fest in 2018. Engaging with the organisations in a number of different settings – on fieldwork, working in collections and laboratories, at international congresses and specially curated workshops – allowed us not only to collaborate with them in our research, but also to develop more nuanced and contextual understandings of how the organisations and their different conceptual framings of diversity functioned in different contexts.

Discussion and conclusion

As we suggested earlier in this chapter, the different forms of diversity that are articulated through the various lists and registers by which these forms of diversity are simultaneously quantified and designated as endangered – biological diversity, linguistic diversity, cultural diversity – operate as transactional realities that bind a range of different endangered objects together and help realise, justify and normalise a spectrum of different forms of conservation and management practices that are applied to them. These conservation practices range from the freezing of blood, skin and other biological materials from endangered animals in biobanks; to the documentation, collection and enumeration of plant and animal species in the 'wild' and their duplication in copies held in herbaria and zoos; to the recording and documentation of languages and cultural practices by linguists and anthropologists; and the conservation of agrobiodiversity as biocultural archives in the form of seeds.

The chapters and visual essays that follow each look across these case studies comparatively to explore the key themes that have emerged in relation to heritage diversity as a result of our research. The first of the two formal chapters (Chapter 4) focuses on the relationship between fieldwork and *ex-situ* collections. The second of the two formal chapters (Chapter 6) considers the different *ex-situ* biodiversity conservation practices documented across these case studies as distinctive temporal practices concerned with the production of specific futures and specific forms of biocapitals. These chapters are punctuated by two visual essays (Chapters 5 and 7), which provide visual means of comparing the practices and conservation objects across these four case studies. Throughout these chapters and visual essays, we touch on a number of other key themes that have emerged from the comparative elements of our research. These include the relationship between *in-situ* and *ex-situ* conservation practices, and the form of the repositories in which *ex-situ* collections are stored; the role of bureaucratic processes and data in conservation; and the role of funding arrangements in producing their own sense of endangerment within the very organisations that are tasked with managing it. In Chapter 8, we conclude this part of the book with some general observations drawn from the empirical case studies regarding the social, political, material and ecological work that is performed by diversity conservation practices across both natural and cultural heritage preservation.

4
Diverse fields: *Ex-situ* collecting practices

Sefryn Penrose, Rodney Harrison and Esther Breithoff

Introduction

This chapter compares the behaviours of parallel heritage fields engaged in the preservation of different forms of diversity in order to develop an understanding of the practice of field collecting and the assembling of *ex-situ* collections in the composition and maintenance of different heritage domains. We do this by comparing and developing a general understanding of common approaches to field collecting across the four organisations on which we focus in this part of the book. In order to draw out these common practices, we reflect here on the stages involved in the work of collecting the components that will become the *ex-situ* collection, work that is undertaken in the 'field' – a space that we argue is not independent of, but co-created by these collecting practices, and their respective *ex-situ* repositories and the ways in which they are organised. We have documented these practices through fieldwork and interviews with several organisations tasked with 'safeguarding' diversity within particular domains of heritage practice, as outlined in Chapter 3. These domains are constituted and occupied by various organisations and institutions engaged in the preservation of conservation *targets* (endangered objects). We aim to draw out the divergences, differences and similarities between the domains – and to address the collaborations between human and non-human actors and the different worlds these practices enact – in each of these cases.

The domains explored here are agrobiodiversity conservation, frozen zoos, endangered language documentation and tree biodiversity conservation. Organisations that work within these domains work to safeguard diversity. Within each domain, this diversity is represented by conservation objects (the target of that domain's conservation efforts): each object is a unit that represents, or is a sample of, a scattered whole. The associated conservation objects of the domains considered here are therefore the units that each organisation collects and conserves; specifically, crop seeds, animal species DNA, languages (represented by their grammatical and lexiconic components) and tree seeds. These objects represent storable components (see Breithoff and Harrison 2020a) that are constituted into organised, unitised, compartmentalised archives that operate as ostensibly future-proof proxies for the transactional realities they come to stand in for as part of their respective collection. Following their collection, these units become part of an *ex-situ* assemblage that is banked, or stored: they will no longer be located in their place of collection, and are instead transferred 'off site, or away from the natural location' (Park and Allaby 2013). We have already discussed how diversity involves complicated relations between parts and wholes. Each of these collections as a whole, as well as their individual components, somehow come to stand in for the form of diversity that each collection is concerned with conserving. This chapter is concerned with the process by which these components are specified and broken down in the field, before being reassembled as part of collections elsewhere. The mechanics of these collections will be covered in Chapter 6.

We introduce an important distinction here between sites of *in-situ* conservation – national parks, wildlife reserves, endangered languages preserved in place through educational programmes, or wild crop relatives growing alongside cultivated grain fields, for example – and the notion of 'the field', as a site of collecting from which *ex-situ* collections are constituted. In *Collecting, Ordering, Governing*, Bennett et al. (2017) propose the term 'anthropological assemblages' as a means of engaging with the ways in which, 'in their early twentieth century forms, anthropological museums operated at the intersections of different socio-material networks: those connecting them to the public spheres of the major metropolitan powers, those linking them to the institutions and practices of colonial administration, and those comprising the relations between museum, field, and university' (Bennett et al. 2017, 5). With regard to the last of these, Bennett (2013) has proposed the concept of 'fieldwork agencement' to refer to the immediate forces – transport systems, the mediating roles of missionaries or colonial administrators, the technologies of filming or recording, the use of tents as locations in close proximity to but distinct from 'the field' – which together organise the fieldwork situation. Key to Bennett's concept is a stress on the distribution of agency across the relations between human actors (anthropologists, indigenous 'subjects' and 'informants') and non-human actors, particularly in focusing on the role of the various technical instruments and devices (film and sound recording instruments, cameras, callipers, anthropometers and so on) that come to determine how data and other objects of collection are collected and processed (see further discussion in Bennett et al. 2017).

Paraphrasing but expanding on the concepts of anthropological assemblages and fieldwork agencements presented in Bennett et al. (2017; see also Bennett et al. 2014), Harrison (2018) posits the existence of 'heritage assemblages' that operate in relation to 'heritage recording agencements', which encompass:

1. the whole set of relations and processes, from origin and con- ception, which condition heritage experts' routes to, conceptions of, and modes of entry into 'the field' (in which the endangered object of heritage is situated, either *in situ* or *ex situ*), including the role of specific definitions and discourses of heritage within such processes in specifying both the forms of endangerment and the appropriate means of intervening in that condition;
2. the relations between heritage experts and the other agents – human and non-human – in the more immediate fieldwork con- texts in which data (and other objects of collection) are collected and subjected to initial organization and interpretation;
3. the routes through which these heritage experts and their assem- bled materials (collected conservation targets, site recordings, photographs, field notes, observations, plans and maps, etc.) return to 'base' (whether to a local field office, state government heritage agency, or office of an international NGO), the mecha- nisms through which the materials and data they have collected are subjected to institutionally specific processes of ordering and classification; and
4. the manner in which such materials and data are connected to the institutions and networks through which, whether in the public sphere, in relation to the tasks of bureaucratic administration, or those of social or environmental management, heritage is govern- mentally deployed, by either state or non-state actors, to intervene within and bring about changes in the conduct of specific (human and/or non-human) populations.

(Harrison 2018, 1376–7)

Drawing on micro-ethnographic fieldwork (Pink and Morgan 2013) – short amounts of embedded time spent with collectors in the four domains mentioned above – we use a comparative approach to describe how different organisations involved in these domains engage different forms of heritage recording agencements, and the transactional realities that such agencements produce. We identify common features and motivations across the domains that illuminate social and cultural operations – alongside other-than-human constitutive incidents – of such initiatives. By simultaneously attending to the structuring guidelines and protocols that determine *what* is collected and the more fluid, embodied and interactive (human–non-human; nature–culture; planned–unplanned; academic–practitioner; indoor–outdoor) *how* of collection as a practice, we aim to facilitate a more nuanced understanding of the creative ordering practices involved in the production of *ex-situ* worlds, and to develop a comparative approach to such collecting and ordering practices that may be of broader value to heritage studies more generally.

Collecting *situ*ations

In this chapter, we draw from empirical work with each of the four collecting organisations, undertaken by Sefryn Penrose and Esther Breithoff. As part of this comparative work, they undertook a series of interviews with staff, volunteers and associates of all four organisations, and also engaged in both field collecting and collections management and research through a series of multi-sited, embedded short-term ethnographies (Pink and Morgan 2013). The following vignettes act as windows into this work.

Seed

The fieldwork officer of the UK National Tree Seed Project (UKNTSP) is responsible for communicating with organisations with which his organisation is associated in partnership (such as the Forestry Commission and the National Trust). These organisations help in determining and directing which seeds will be collected from which trees, and where. He is also the finder of the trees and one of the collectors of seeds. Accompanied by volunteers from the Millennium Seed Bank (MSB) and elsewhere in Kew, he determines which seeds must be collected from which trees and in which zones. The UKNTSP uses the Forestry Commission's Seed Zones – areas of relatively similar climatic, geological and topographical conditions, to which seeds are native – and has plotted the distribution of tree species accordingly. Sefryn joins them collecting on the Gower Peninsula in Wales, Seed Zone 303. They are looking for broad-leaf lime, holly and yew.

As the Kew Land Rover crosses the border between the made road and the muddy track, they follow a representative of Welsh Natural Resources on the trail of some mature limes. Out here in the field, the strategy documents and species lists seem to belong to another, cleaner, place.

The guide stops on the wet, early-autumn track. He indicates the limes at the bottom of a gently inclined woodland. The project lead walks straight to them, pulls a branch down, and examines it closely. It has tiny brown hairs along the veins of the small leaves. But it has large burrs too. He takes a cutting and hands it to one of the volunteers. He identifies the tree as a hybrid – a cross between the large-leaf lime and the small-leaf lime. The give-away is the hairs and the burrs.

The cutting is taken back to the van. The volunteer lays it on a sheet of newspaper – Sefryn notices that the text on the paper is in the language Bahasa Indonesia, the paper an artefact from collecting trips much further afield – and the newspaper is laid on a blotting sheet. He marks the papers according to the numbers assigned to the trees by the project leader, and he ties a corresponding label to the cutting. He straps the plant press with difficulty, since one of the straps has a loose buckle. The other volunteer takes GPS coordinates of the trees, and the project leader hammers little silver tags into their trunks. The tags have 'UKNTSP' stamped into them.

As they walk, looking for more limes hidden more deeply in the woods, Sefryn asks the team what their academic backgrounds are. All three of the Gower team studied in associated disciplinary avenues to botany, but they now call themselves conservationists or conservation managers.

DNA

The Frozen Ark works to conserve tissue samples, cells and viable DNA from endangered species for research and conservation purposes. Although based in Nottingham, its interim director is a molecular ecologist based at Cardiff University. On Esther's visit to his lab, he introduces her to a senior conservationist from Sabah, Malaysia, studying for a PhD with him. The PhD researcher explains that protocols for transferring tissue and DNA across international boundaries have become highly regulated, and almost prohibitive. Although he cannot place a comprehensive set of samples from his collecting with the Frozen Ark, he is part of the network that supports the organisation's aim to establish a global database and expand a collaborative approach.

Esther interviews the PhD researcher in the lab. He has been collecting samples of proboscis monkeys in Sabah. He is plotting the phylogeography and the phylogenetics of the monkeys, monitoring their loss of habitat and population fragmentation. The sampling is based on an existing survey undertaken by fieldworkers, then a reconnaissance trip by boat, monitoring 'how big the group is; how high the trees are', taking GPS points along the way. Then he makes a return trip with the addition to the team of rangers and veterinarians. Back in their boat, they aim for collecting DNA from one monkey per night: 'We go at night. We're a little bit like commandos actually …' The monkeys are sedated, tranquilised by dart and tracked. The rangers use nets to catch the monkeys – still in the trees as the tranquilisers do their work – to avoid them being hurt by the fall. He prides himself that in sampling a hundred monkeys, none have been hurt so far. The process of sampling is time-consuming, he says, describing how the field centre is set up and the monkey is taken back to it. Once there, another team – of rangers and biologists – is ready to collect the samples, while the vet checks the monkey's vital statistics throughout. Blood samples are extracted by syringe; faecal samples are taken from the monkey's anal tract; saliva samples from its mouth. The monkey is marked with a biodegradable dye. When the samples have been taken, the monkey is returned to where it was found.

These are the sorts of samples collected by the Frozen Ark and other biobanks. As well as their research potential, they represent the preserved resource of endangered animals and the product of a continuing cataloguing and monitoring process undertaken by a team with multiple skill sets. The conservationist's organisation has 15 years' worth of proboscis monkey samples, tracking the health of the species as well as its 'metadata' – its geographical spread, evidence of its population, its diet and living habits.

Languages

The director of the Endangered Languages Documentation Project (ELDP) at the School of Oriental and African Studies (SOAS) puts Sefryn in touch with one of their former grant holders, who is working on a PhD under her supervision, preparing a thesis on noun phrases in the language that he studies.

The PhD researcher calls himself a language documentarian, not a linguist. During his previous postgraduate study in Tanzania, his professor gave him a copy of The Languages of Tanzania: A Bibliography *(Maho and Sands 2002), and told him to spend a weekend eliminating all the languages that had already been documented and had texts associated with them – grammars, dictionaries, ethnographies. Of the eight languages that remained after this exercise, the professor picked the one that was not Bantu* and sent the student on a 13-hour bus ride to document it. The language documentarian is a young man, but the time he has spent embedding himself in his study language is considerable. A couple of years after that first immersion, he received a grant from the ELDP to further his work. In between times, he worked in his deindustrialised home town for the Office of Public Engagement. Back in Tanzania with his ELDP grant, the links between cultures in his home town and his field site – both post-colonial transmogrified societies in the midst of deep change – became apparent. He formed an 'advisory group' consisting of his landlady and other local people that were interested in his project. His work on noun-phrases required significant spoken data. The language was becoming obsolete and was no longer learned by children. Many of the noun-phrases in which he was interested were pertinent to activities that were themselves passing – such as techniques of divination and crop preparation. The agricultural practices of the speakers had changed to adapt to monocultures of corn farming, and the practices and semantics of millet farming, and associated ceremonies of rainmaking and gourd use, had become more or less obsolete. He was just in time to interview a rainmaker before his death from tuberculosis. Rainmaking was a craft that had been persecuted by the colonial and post-colonial governments in the drive towards the displacement of the past for modernity.

Crops

NordGen's headquarters in southern Sweden stores crop seeds – a record of crop diversity in the Scandinavian countries – as well as their wild relatives. This is a genetic resource that can be regenerated to research or breed the properties of species no longer widely farmed.

The senior scientist in charge of the vegetable collection is a plant-breeder. For a long time, she ran her own commercial farm, and then she worked for a seed producer. Sefryn asks about her background as she drives her the short distance to an 'experiment' that she is conducting into the properties of species of carrot that are not 'described'. 'I'm not a botanist,' she says, explaining how she was invited to join NordGen due to her wealth of acquired knowledge of the genetic properties and behaviours of vegetables. Sefryn watches her working in the plot of wild relatives, laid out for a latitudinal study of their characteristics. She rummages dextrously among the spiderweb leaves to find the main umbel – the main 'flower' – for each variety. She takes their measurements down in a ledger and describes them – their attributes noted according to a universal protocol. Later, in one of the tunnels, where the cauliflowers grow, she tugs at an anomaly. It is about a foot taller than the rest of the crop. She laughs and pulls the outlier out of the *ground. 'The others would probably want to know what made it so, but I am a breeder. It shouldn't look like that.' It has mutated.*

NordGen is headquartered in the arable zone of southern Sweden. Even outside the NordGen plots, barley is swishing in the wind. Crouched in a 1.5-metre-square plot on a hot day, Sefryn cuts off the spears of old varieties of barley. It takes her a long time to do the first, to check with a stab of her thumbnail whether the barleycorns are ripe, a condition indicated by a sort of translucent white, like a grain of glutenous rice. The second patch is a different sort, and it takes her less than half the time. She begins to think that she has got her eye in – a phrase she is used to thinking in her cultural heritage work, dating materials by site, recognising historic patterns in maps. She keeps thinking of the Munsell Chart used in archaeology to distinguish soil types and how difficult it is to tell browny-red from reddy-brown. But she has not become more familiar with the techniques of barley harvest; it is just that the second plot is vastly different. It is brittle and delicate – it does not bend, it breaks. Her next patch is different again. It is tougher, although it looks more delicate. Thin black streaks, and a little black underlining – like a delicate use of kohl – makes it utterly distinctive. She is joined by a volunteer – they are running out of time, and she has finished her patch. Bent over all day in the field, she remarks on how fit all the harvesters must be and comments on Sefryn's unconditioned sore back. Another volunteer walks past. His phone, swinging from his waist, is playing heavy metal. 'Yoga,' her helper says. She commutes from a nearby city. The city seems a long way away from this field, with its hipsters, yoga and metal nights.

Building nature and culture *ex situ*

'We need to take steps to rebuild nature' (Lawton 2010, ix). So reads Professor Sir John Lawton's introduction to *Making Space for Nature: A Review of England's Wildlife Sites and Ecological Network*, putting in black and white not just the extent of the need to repair the 'damage' claimed to have been done in the past, but also proposing an explicit strategy to create: to *rebuild nature*. Lawton was chair of a UK government review into wildlife sites and their connectivity. The report presents its findings, particularly the debilitating effect on the environment of past practice, in a call for redemptive and pre-emptive action for the future. The conservation work that rebuilding nature (whether now *or* in the future) entails requires another layer of strategising. Groves et al. (2002, 502), in an article laying out the practicalities of conservation science, state: 'To represent the biodiversity of a region or ecoregion in conservation areas, we focus on conservation targets, the entities or features for which a conservation plan or project is attempting to ensure long-term persistence'. The entities are individualised into targets – strategies, objectives, selection criteria. Historically, collections were for the record: 'If maintained properly, specimens in every (natural history) collection can provide a permanent record of life on earth' (Mehrhoff 1997, 447). The record stands, for philosopher David Heyd (2010), as a response to collective shame at loss. But such collecting has become more purposeful, redemptive, conceptualised as providing the building blocks with which to *rebuild nature.* The Royal Botanic Gardens, Kew – the UK's foremost natural history research and archive collection – frames its UK National Tree Seed Project as a supporting mechanism, and the project's website states: 'The Millennium Seed Bank (MSB)'s UK activities seek to support this ambition [to rebuild nature] through the provision of suitable plant material and data to support conservation and research initiatives' (Kew n.d.). We discuss some of these concepts of restitution in relation to de-extinction programmes in Chapter 6.

The data-driven rebuilding of nature requires technological support, however. Here, the Kew strategy plugs into the database. Far from being a passive record, the database impels particular forms of action in (and on) the world (Braverman 2017, 134; Bowker 2000). In doing so, it is active in that world's production. The basic unit of collection is determined by the columnar fields of the database, which demand analysis and calculation. The database also encourages hierarchy: algorithms create importance. Ranking takes place – scientifically – chosen by algorithmic certainty. The development of the UK National Tree Seed Project target list is described in these terms: 'An initial target list for the project has been developed by ranking UK woody species according to key criteria such as conservation status, prevalence in the landscape, vulnerability to pests and diseases and native status' (Kallow 2014, 5). It is an example of how *ex-situ* collections have become a core component in the active selection of heritage materials for preservation. Storage repositories – held locally, regionally, nationally or internationally, by the relevant hierarchical state, sponsored or private apparatuses – have been part of heritage practice since its earliest days, but since the Second World War, such off-site collections have shifted in meaning (for the emergence and development of these global approaches, see, for example, Hale et al. 2013; Harrison 2013a; McDonald 2017; Pyykkönen 2012; Meskell 2018). Rather than being understood as passive stores of knowledge, or representations of an imperial or national agenda (see, for example, Bennett 1995; Hewison 1987), such repositories have taken on a quasi-practical role as spaces in which universal knowledges are stored with the understanding that their contents may hold solutions to problems presented in unknown futures (in which novel crop diseases have emerged, or species have become extinct, for example). *Ex-situ* collections have become part of a salvific heritage collecting agencement and, as such, they draw on appeals to a global responsibility to come together to protect – for the future – the component parts of the world's diversity. Article 9 of the United Nations Convention on Biological Diversity directly concerns *ex-situ* conservation, setting out the measures to which signatories must subscribe in undertaking the work of conservation (United Nations 1992, 7). The collections themselves comprise units (*components* in the wording of Article 9), neatly stored, often frozen, which represent the possibilities of *research, recovery, rehabilitation, resource* (to use the language of the Convention).

Collecting and defining the field

Latour (1993, 7) has written of the 'seamless fabric of … "nature-culture"' experienced by the field anthropologist, and the way in which ethnography enables the 'bringing together [of the] myths, ethnosciences, genealogies, political forms, religions, epics and rites of the people'. He advocates research that traces the networks that are simultaneously 'real, social and narrated' in the construction – or, in Latour's words, 'weaving' – of the world (Latour 1993, 9).

How does a comparative perspective on these field-collecting experiences inform a more productive understanding of the way that collectors, and collection protocols, shape *ex-situ* collections and, by extension, the latent worlds they might resource? Irus Braverman (2015, 3) states that 'lurking beneath the surface of the *in situ* and *ex situ* dichotomy are its older and seemingly less scientific cousins: wilderness versus captivity and nature versus culture'. However, she also makes space for the connection between the two. How otherwise can one get from one space to the other?

In the woods with the UKNTSP, Sefryn wonders about the identity of wilderness itself: Braverman borrows Thoreau's term *wildness* to problematise the dichotomy. Even deep in the woods, the impossibility of dividing nature from culture performs itself in front of us. In all these encounters, her perception is shaped by her own background in cultural heritage. It means that, although she struggles to distinguish lime species from each other, she can at least recognise that the trees to which they are first directed are part of an ornamental avenue – planted limes – and although they are mature, and well established in what the Ancient

Woodland Inventory of 2011 categorises as Restored Ancient Woodland (Natural Resources Wales 2011), even the name of the wood, 'Park Wood', alerts us to its existence as a cultural artefact – cultural ecofact, perhaps – too.

In *Friction: An Ethnography of Global Connection*, anthropologist Anna Tsing (2005, xi) reflects on her realisation that the 'forest landscape is *social*'. In her work on how the Indonesian rainforest is meshed within a capitalist system, she develops the concept of *friction* as a complicator: 'It was only by walking and working with [the local forest-dwellers] that I learned to see the forest differently' (Tsing 2005, xi). The distinction between these fields of collection and the metropolitan locales to which their varied objects of collection are returned is not straightforward. Sefryn notes that many of the woodland paths she walks with the Kew collectors are well trodden. The NordGen plots are on the edges of prime Swedish farmland. The language documentarian's informants speak at least one other language and drink from Coke bottles. These fields of collection reconstitute themselves as part of this process too – they have accommodated, and continue to accommodate, many kinds of stakeholders and changes.

Our informants' complex relationships with disciplinary expertise – or perhaps, more accurately, their self-acknowledged hybrid status as both professional and expert – recalls Dorinda Outram's (1997) distinction between 'indoor' and 'outdoor' science, and Kohler's (2006, 183) drawing out of the identities of the historic practitioners of 'outdoor science': 'their identity as scientists was complicated by the fact that they straddled the boundary between head and hand work, white and blue collar, craft and profession'. The collectors/fieldworkers claim a hybrid understanding of themselves – knowers of landscape and practitioners in the most practical sense. A background in forestry and a recreational interest in climbing mean that the UKNTSP project lead can access a remote lime on a steep riparian incline. The keeper of vegetables has a breeder's eye for characteristics, and a farmer's talent for growing. The language documentarian uses his skills from community facilitation not only to elicit the noun-phrase that constitutes the stuff of his PhD and his published papers, but also to deliver a sense of ownership to the communities with which he works, to help put in place a group that can, if it chooses to do so, continue the work that he started.

Field collecting as knowledge practices

In his discussion of the nineteenth- and early twentieth-century American natural history surveyors, Kohler compares the contemporaneous middle-class pursuits of outdoor recreation – 'hunting, foraging, camping'– with 'observing and collecting', noting the identical pleasures to be had from both (Kohler 2007, 444; see also Griffiths 1996). The fieldworkers and collectors that Sefryn and Esther worked alongside had their own expertise, embedded in the landscape, in tracking and tracing and finding. Kohler describes the feedback loop between practitioners and the repositories that they fed, and the circular process of categorising and collecting, as the collected was sent back, identified, categorised, and a request flung back for more. 'The places and conditions of collecting constitute an ideal medium for mixing expert and vernacular cultures', writes Kohler (2007, 444). Sefryn observed the UKNTSP project lead note trees that were not on his list, and take GPS coordinates for a curious apple tree and another unidentified fruit tree. This information will feed back into the project's database. It is partly the existing record, the record produced in the past that points towards what is now a past future, which brings the collector to their particular field, to engage in the 'continuation of collecting' (Ikin 2011; Kohler 2006). Knowing where you are walking is one thing, but knowing where to walk next is another. It is this practice in particular that has allowed the meaning of the collection to extend beyond the condition of the record. Where once the collection of the specimen was a means to an end – with the specimen understood as a 'manageable piece of the natural world' (Larsen 1996, 359) – it is now a means to a future. Records are 'part of the effort to preserve biodiversity' (Ikin 2011, 179), rather than insertions in the encyclopedia.

The admixture of learnt knowledge and embodied knowledge is explored in the work of a number of social scientists, with particular reference to the experience of being in the world – in the outdoors, in the elements, in the field. It is these acts of being in the world that directly inform the worlding acts of collection – the creation of the *ex-situ* resource. The felicities of the non-human – late springs, high winds, herbivores – determine, as they direct collectors to abandon the search for that seed, but also alert them to this. The experience is defined by the grounding: feet on the ground, eyes to the earth or its fruits, being alert to environmental subtleties, which may, through any number of felicities – high winds, late-fruitings, herbivores, access restrictions, malaria – determine that instead of this seed or that language, another is gathered for the *ex-situ* assemblage. Jane Rendell remarks on the act of walking, that it:

> ... provides a way of understanding sites in flux in a manner that questions the logic of measuring, surveying and drawing a location from a series of fixed and static viewpoints. When we walk we encounter sites in motion and in relation to one another, suggesting that things seem different depending on whether we are 'coming to' or going from'.
>
> (Rendell 2006, 188)

As Tim Ingold (2010c, S136) writes, 'far from being subsidiary to the constitution of knowledge, this ground, and the ways we walk it' lies at the core of knowing. In their work on fieldwork as a manifestation of expertise, geographers Peltola and Tuomisaari (2015, 2) expand on Ingold's (2010c) observations to suggest that 'expertise is not about accumulating information but rather a capacity: sensitivity to cues in the environment and an ability to respond to those cues'. In a sense, this is the same sort of knowing that characterised the older practices of field collecting, and its transmutation into *ex-situ* 'field laboratory' work (see, for example, Kohler 2006; Bennett et al. 2017).

Academic expertise and the practical vernacular touch each other in more obvious ways too. 'Local knowledge of the landscape, other natural features including local climate, and an understanding of modifications to the local environment are always valuable', reads Section 11.1.4 of the chapter on 'Botanical Collecting' in the *Oxford Handbook of Linguistic Fieldwork* (Conn 2012). The history of collecting is peopled by local teams, knowers of landscape beyond collecting disciplines and beyond recreation. This history is cumulative and recursive. Rocha et al. (2017), in their work on agrobiodiversity, document a chronology of state-sponsored expeditions to collect what is now called germplasm from agricultural crops, beginning in 2500 BC. 'Plant expeditions' and 'collecting missions' – exploration and belief – continue to be terms employed in the collection of plant genetic resources. Again, the knowledge of terrain, and behaviours, is a necessity. Accessing local skills – forest rangers in Sabah and Gower, rainmakers in Tanzania: people with knowledge of the spatial–temporal state contiguous with the now – is a necessity in the building of a future resource.

In practice, as with the trees and the monkeys, the intuitive sense of looking and knowing slots into the framework dictated by the target list in a far more complex and connected way than the collection of species samples as a practice might suggest. The need for the conservation targets, the details of their acquisition, and their broader corpus of metadata map on to each other when they are finally assembled *ex situ*, and when the contextual embodiment of the act of collection disappears. In his study of soil analysis in the Amazon, Latour (1999, 42) responds to this element in the creation of data: 'One should never speak of "data" – what is given – but rather of *sublata* – that is, of "achievements"'. Notwithstanding the problematic restructuring that the ontological work of Latour's shifts in Latin terminology performs, this reconceptualising of data as something to be worked for – achieved – captures the acts of harvest, of gleaning, of generation, of comprehension, that both biological and cultural heritage collectors do.

Performing practice

Each spear of barley is dropped into a paper bag. It is a performative gesture. Sefryn periodically checks the bag for insects. Written on it are her initials, the number from the barcoded label in her plot, and the date. The inside of the bag is another inner frontier – the edge of the field; the liminal space between nature and culture. She has already categorised by what she has selected and what she has left to be mown and mulched later on – selection skills she learned quickly following explanation, then observation, then trial and error. The manager of the barley plots has already categorised the barley that he has chosen to regenerate here.

The language documentarian's masses of recordings, hours of videos, and photographs of things discussed will feed into the laboratory offering of the grammar and the article on the noun-phrase that he plans for the language, and edited examples of speech and gesture. In archaeology, this is the on-site work that means that the archaeological fieldworker does not go home with all the stones in the ground (Hodder 1999). This is the constitutive work of cyclical selecting too.

But for now, the collected objects and recordings are unprocessed knowledges – the fruits of collecting – and they represent the doing and the act of fieldwork, rather than the forms of knowledge they will be used to produce when returned to base and processed, alongside other data objects collected during other field expeditions in other places. These are not the data for the database, but the spoils of the expedition. For now, they are individual things, but still absorbed in context, from places that the fieldworkers and Sefryn have been and seen. They are not (yet) abstract collections of metadata in unprocessed or processed bundles. They are categories that have been created, spatial and locational, in the cultural domain of the field.

The end of the expedition is marked almost ritualistically, performatively – a beating of the bounds – by the cleaning of their boots. Water is poured into a plastic tub, and they use it and scrubbing brushes to remove the accrued mud from their boots. They pat them dry with paper towels and then spray the boots with a disinfectant. It is a performance suited to the aims of the trip, to collect the endemic native trees from their ancient woodlands. You do not need to have your eye in to see the effect of ash dieback as it spreads, and the haunting of Dutch elm disease is ever present. The plastic ziplock bags with the labels, the herbarium press, the GPS consoles are all loaded into the boot of the car, and the team head back to the Millennium Seed Bank with the fruits of their labours. In the evening, they find a pub in a village halfway back to their accommodation. It is on a tree-less Elm Street.

Discussion and conclusion

In this chapter, we have explored the practices of four organisations and their associated collectors through a framework that links certain heritage recording agencements and their material networks with the transactional realities that each produces. Each organisation represented within this study maintains or coordinates *ex-situ* collections of certain conservation objects in order to preserve diversity for the future. The four organisations can be seen to work in parallel, undertaking stages of work that more or less map on to each other's modes of practice. Broadly, they identify, collect, prepare, conserve, store and share information on the conservation objects of their *ex-situ* collections. These practices correlate with the general set of four – categorising, curating, conserving and communicating – which we noted in the first chapter of the book as characterising all heritage practices more generally.

By combining empirical study with concepts drawn from Barad's (2007) agential realism and actor–network theory, drawing closely on a discussion of biological and cultural diversity as transactional realities, we suggest that these collectors are 'worlders' themselves, both in the field and as *ex-situ* traders between the present and the future perfect (or that-which-will-have-been). By doing so, we have tried to show that the collectors are hybrids: repositories of knowledge of both field and conserved object, and privy to the secrets held by both (Latour 1993, 30). To become an *ex-situ* 'proxy' (see Chapter 7), the conservation object – the seed, language, or DNA sample – must be collected. In order to be collected, the future present is calculated, with a strategy set to enact it, and the article in need of being sent to the future is identified. A hierarchy of frameworks is deployed to structure the practices of collecting. The significance of these practices is that they illuminate the specific ways in which futures are enacted and performed, and have agency and urgency in the present, dictating and constructing the way that heritage organisations respond to (and produce) the anticipation of loss in their daily work practices. We will now move from the field to the *ex-situ* repository to explore in more detail how the various collections themselves speculate upon the scarcity and endangerment that they are created to preserve against, and in doing so, how they build multiple parallel future worlds.

5
Repositories

Sefryn Penrose, Rodney Harrison and Esther Breithoff

Art critic Hal Foster (2004, 5) has written that contemporary artists working with museum collections and archives bring to the fore the 'found yet constructed, factual yet fictive, public yet private' nature of all archival framing. That is, all practices of collecting entail selection, storytelling practices of interpretation and the transformation of space. The evocation of the work of the biodiversity repository often falls into the biblical storytelling bracket: these are the arks wherein the future of the Earth is contained, wherein the wealth of species that is lost (or to be lost) is preserved for future use (or 'recovery' or 'rehabilitation', as Article 9 of the international Convention on Biological Diversity on 'Ex-situ Conservation' decrees (United Nations 1992)). The evocation of the ark does useful work, epitomised perhaps by the Svalbard Global Seed Vault, on top of the world, in the natural frozen wastes of the Arctic Circle, yet containing proxies for the world's crop resources.

But, writing of 'institutional spaces' in his introduction to a photo essay of that name, documentary photographer Peter Metelerkamp (2013, 523) articulates how 'structures and spaces speak equally of culture when they are most quotidian, "ordinary", and unselfconscious'. The structures and spaces of Article 9 are the structures and spaces of banking the world's biodiversity, the genetic resource. In this photo essay (see Figures 5.1 to 5.15 at the end of this chapter), we shift the framing from the contained and the container, and what they stand for, to the contain*ing*: to what Thom Van Dooren (2017, 5) calls 'technologies of stasis, united by a common effort to hold species in limbo', in which biobanks are seen as forms of modern frozen archives (see also Radin 2017; Radin and Kowal 2017) dominated by generations of freezers, from domestic white goods repurposed, to catering-class chrome, to specialist liquid nitrogen tanks. Degrees of coldness are indicated and assured by the ubiquitous seven-section LCD number display. Freezers are numbered, or named. They are alarmed. Frost is a hazard of time, use and space. Of the oldest freezers still used at Alnarp, where NordGen is headquartered, the seed technician says, 'they work perfectly so long as no one touches them'. It is a joke, of course, but these are 20-year-old domestic consumables.

Collecting institutions are as bound into the disciplinary cultures of collecting as they are into the cultures of conservation. Each repository displays the hallmarks of its institutors and investors. At the Herbarium at Kew, the years of specimen collecting are documented by the variety of deposit notation, the story recorded as much about collector as daisy or landscape. An entire freezer at NordGen is devoted to the collection of a retired botanist with a private interest in barley. The Kew-authorised specimen cards, however, each stamped *Herb. Hort. Kew*, tie the erroneous, the donated, the old, into the technology of contemporary banking practice, of *fit*, and the old barley specimens have the viability checked, and are absorbed into the system via the standard aluminium specimen envelopes. The dimensions of archive boxes are given to depositors at Svalbard, but it remains the job of each depositing nation to find the box to fit. Deposit boxes are bespoke wood from North Korea, clear plastic from Peru, black plastic archive boxes by far the most ubiquitous, but they all fit their allocated space on the metal rack shelving. As time passes, though, these technologies might change, and the holders for the vials of molecular DNA marginally alter across deposits – yellow to red, now with more holes, now bespoke, now with barcodes – and it makes the fit a little less tight. These technologies of dormancy keep the future-worlds of diversity on ice – suspended in the institutional contexts of vial, envelope, file, box, freezer, shelf – away from life – light, moisture, heat, change. As in banks, the blandness of bureaucracy of containing belies the speculative effect it represents. The technologies of dormancy employ the mundane method of 'ticking-over' through the tried and tested, anticipatory futures fixed firmly in the *now*.

Figure 5.1 Boxes of seed samples stored inside one of the three identical vaults in the Svalbard Global Seed Vault (photograph by Rodney Harrison).

Figure 5.2 Live exhibit of ancient grains held by NordGen at the Botaniska Trädgården (Botanical Gardens), Lund, Sweden (photograph by Sefryn Penrose).

Figure 5.3 The Frozen Ark, Nottingham (photograph by Esther Breithoff).

Figure 5.4 The family Compositae in the Herbarium at the Royal Botanic Gardens, Kew (photograph by Sefryn Penrose).

Figure 5.5 Freezer held at *c.*−20°C, Frozen Ark/Molecular Ecology and Evolution Research Laboratory, Cardiff University (photograph by Esther Breithoff).

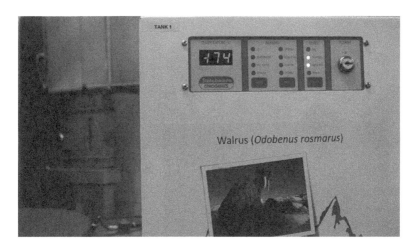

Figure 5.6 Liquid nitrogen tank, Molecular Collections Facility, Natural History Museum (photograph by Sefryn Penrose).

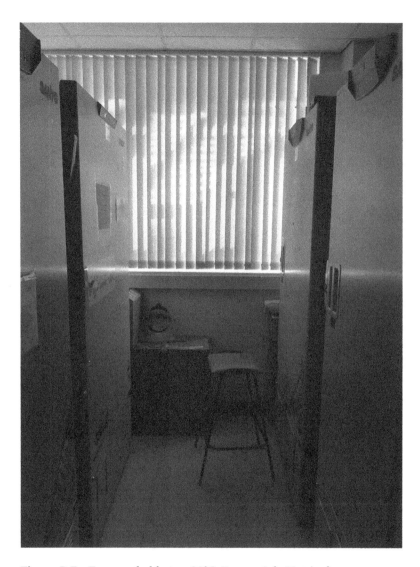

Figure 5.7 Freezers held at *c*.–80°C, Frozen Ark, Nottingham (photograph by Esther Breithoff).

Figure 5.8 DNA specimen vials, Frozen Ark, Nottingham (photograph by Esther Breithoff).

Figure 5.9 Molecular DNA freezers held at *c*.–80°C, Frozen Ark, Nottingham (photograph by Esther Breithoff).

Figure 5.10   Molecular DNA specimen boxes, Frozen Ark, Nottingham (photograph by Esther Breithoff).

Figure 5.11   The entrance to the Svalbard Global Seed Vault, showing the artwork *Perpetual Repercussion* built into its ceiling (photograph by Rodney Harrison).

Figure 5.12 Frozen Ark, Nottingham (photograph by Esther Breithoff).

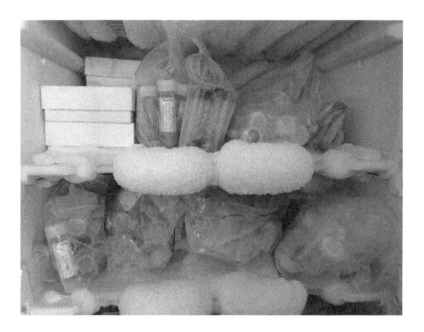

Figure 5.13 Inside one of the freezers at the Frozen Ark/Molecular Ecology and Evolution Research Laboratory, Cardiff University (photograph by Esther Breithoff).

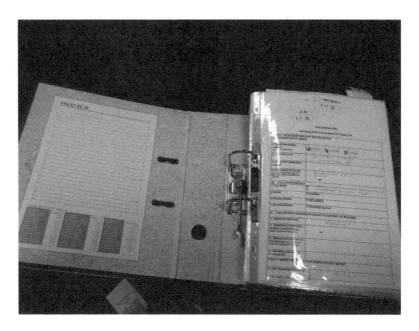

Figure 5.14 Squirrel monkey DNA voucher specimen, Frozen Ark
(photograph by Esther Breithoff).

Figure 5.15 Entrance to one of the three identical refrigerated storage
recesses inside the Svalbard Global Seed Vault (photograph by Rodney
Harrison).

6
Banking time: Trading in futures

Esther Breithoff and Rodney Harrison

Introduction

In this chapter,[1] we shift from *ex-situ* field collecting to the worlding practices enacted by the repositories in which collected tokens are organised, ordered and stored. In doing so, we focus specifically on the future-making practices inherent in the work of global agrobiodiversity conservation and non-human animal endangered DNA cryopreservation, drawing on our research with the Nordic Genetic Resource Centre (NordGen), the Svalbard Global Seed Vault (SGSV) and the Frozen Ark project. In the chapter, we observe a contemporary shift in the meaning of the practice of collecting, archiving and safeguarding such plant and animal biomaterials. From an initial 'heroic' narrative that cast such biobanks in a static, dormant role – isolated arks to carry endangered DNA into an uncertain future (Doyle 1997; Watson and Holt 2001; Bowkett 2009; Chrulew 2017) – we detect a recent shift to a more active function that acknowledges their potential for reanimation of genetic material in future biosocial and biopolitical programmes, including the well-publicised 'restoration' of the International Center for Agricultural Research in the Dry Areas (ICARDA) seed bank in Syria, and in so-called 'de-extinction' initiatives. We suggest that the role of such institutions has transformed from repository to speculative reinvestment: the 'arks' that stored and safeguarded genetic samples for survival within an endangerment narrative (see Turner 2007) have altered to become 'investment banks' where genetic materials can be actively reworked and revived to build new futures (see also Bowker 2005b; Heatherington 2012; Chrulew 2017).

Where the new forms of biocapital generated with such repositories seem to reflect reformulations of late capitalist values (for example,

Doyle 1997; Shukin 2009; Thacker 2010), in this chapter we consider the ways in which a critical perspective on the operations of these enterprises might help us to bring new insights to bear on the latent possibilities contained within these reservoirs of cold-stored and frozen seeds and DNA. We suggest that unravelling the details of the temporal orientations of conservation practices and their underpinning sociotechnical and biopolitical processes helps us to understand the ways in which conservation practices of different kinds are not normative, but vary across time and space, actively shaping different kinds of future worlds. In doing so, we draw on approaches to the study of archives and collections that emphasise the ways in which their collecting and ordering practices not only reflect, but actively intervene within and shape, the worlds they order (see further discussion in Bennett et al. 2017). Our examination of global agrobiodiversity conservation and endangered DNA cryopreservation programmes reveals the complexity of temporal aspects of biodiversity conservation, as well as the complicated ways in which conservation practices both 'archive' diversity and generate and accumulate latent forms of biocapital (Helmreich 2008; Sunder Rajan 2006) in their aim to secure genetic resources for the future.

The predicted loss of two-thirds of the world's vertebrate population by 2020 (WWF 2016), and a similarly bleak outlook for invertebrate species, has intensified biodiversity conservation efforts globally. These take the form of both *in-situ* conservation programmes (for example, through the designation of protected areas) and *ex-situ* captive breeding programmes (for example, in zoos and aquaria). More recently, these *ex-situ* conservation efforts have accelerated as a result of the DNA 'revolution', through the development of organised archives of non-human animal and plant biomaterials that aim to document and preserve genetic information on the biology, ecology and evolutionary history of threatened plants, mammals, birds and reptiles in the form of viable cells and DNA preparations, before it is irretrievably lost (Corley-Smith and Brandhorst 1999; Watson and Holt 2001; Friese 2013; Costa and Bruford 2018). Genetic resource banking – the freezing of plant and animal genetic material for *ex-situ* storage, and its use in research within a present-day and potential future context – has emerged as a response to what has been understood to be a contemporary extinction crisis, and in many cases, cryobanks have come to be seen as the only and last resort for recording and storing biological material from endangered species for potential future retrieval.

The practice of freezing and storing biological material (including blood, germplasm, embryos, tissues and somatic cells of non-human animals) in genetic resource banks for the advancement of human medicine and the development of agro-industries is not a new development in scientific research (see further discussion in Radin 2015; 2017; Radin and Kowal 2017). Nonetheless, it is only recently that *ex-situ* cold and cryogenic practices have become a leading and driving force in biodiversity research within the context of endangered species conservation (see Gemeinholzer et al. 2011; Wildt et al. 1997; see also Howard et al. 2016 and Wisely et al. 2015 on the ferret biobank) – with biobank facilities such as the Smithsonian, the San Diego Frozen Zoo® and the genetic repository at the Natural History Museum in London collecting blood, tissues, cell cultures, eggs, spermatozoa and embryos specifically for conservation purposes, and the global expansion of regional and national seed banks for agrobiodiversity conservation. According to its website, the Zoological Society of San Diego (ZSSD) Center for Reproduction of Endangered Species (CRES) now stores 'the largest and most diverse collection of its kind in the world', with over '10,000 living cell cultures, oocytes, sperm, and embryos representing nearly 1,000 taxa, including one extinct species, the po'ouli' (San Diego Zoo Institute for Conservation Research 2020, n.p.). Since its foundation in 1975, the San Diego Frozen Zoo® has become an irreplaceable and continuously expanding source of biological information for significant scientific advancements in fields such as conservation, medicine, assisted reproduction, evolutionary biology, physiology and wildlife medicine (Chemnick et al. 2009).

In a paper on the Frozen Zoo® concept published in 1984, Benirschke advocates:

> Biologists at zoological gardens have a unique opportunity – if not an *obligation* – to preserve materials for scientific study. At a time when biomedical capabilities are expanding rapidly, we find ourselves in the position that biological resources are dwindling rapidly. Many forms of life are at the point where extinction is imminent, yet the animal or plant has not become understood in any of its major biological ways.
>
> (Benirschke 1984, 325, our emphasis)

Benirschke's words convey an urgency not only to save dwindling genetic material for scientific study in the present, but to safeguard it for an undetermined future in which humans will be in a better position to extract from it as yet unrecovered information. (They also provide the key to understanding the role of such facilities in contributing to the growth of new forms of biocapital, as we will discuss later.) Here, cryobanks become the harbourers of 'time-travelling resource[s]' (Radin 2017, xii), which are both enactors of, and produce templates for, 'futures in the making' (Adam and Groves 2007, 17; Turner 2007). Genetic resources of endangered animals, for example, have enabled developments in reproductive technologies to maintain genetic diversity that have already produced promising 'real-life' results in a number of conservation programmes (for example, Howard et al. 1992; Wildt et al. 1997). As such, frozen zoos and other non-human biobanks are driving ongoing research into cloning, de-extinction and reintroduction of endangered and once-extinct species (see further discussion in O'Connor 2015; Shapiro 2015; Pilcher 2016). Cryobanks thus facilitate human intervention in the categorisation and manipulation of biological diversity in standardised data management systems, turning the 'wild' into 'managed natures' (Buller 2013, 183), and thus opening up seemingly endless possibilities for what Donna Haraway (2011) calls, the 'reinvention of nature'. These developments are likely to have significant impacts on what we might now, in the light of the recognition of the Anthropocene epoch, term the 'Human Planet' (Lewis and Maslin 2018).

The Svalbard Global Seed Vault

As has already been noted, the Svalbard Global Seed Vault (SGSV) is currently the world's largest secure seed storage facility. It was established in 2008 by the Royal Norwegian Ministry of Agriculture and Food; the Global Crop Diversity Trust (now known as the Crop Trust), an independent international organisation based in Germany (established as a partnership between the United Nations Food and Agriculture Organization (FAO) and the Consultative Group on International Agricultural Research (CGIAR)); and the Nordic Genetic Resource Centre (NordGen). At a cost of US$9 million to the Norwegian government, the construction of the SGSV began in 2005 as a result of the recommendations of the 2004 International Treaty on Plant Genetic Resources for Food and Agriculture, which created a global *ex-situ* system for the conservation of agricultural plant genetic resource diversity. Situated on the island of Spitsbergen in the Svalbard archipelago, it received its first deposits of seeds in 2008.

NordGen is responsible for the day-to-day operations of the facility, and maintains a publicly accessible database documenting its samples. The SGSV holds in its frozen repository approximately 1.06 million accessions and 681 million seeds, provided by 87 depositor institutions, sourced from almost every country in the world (Svalbard Global Seed Vault 2010). Each accession represents a sample taken of a specific living crop population from a specific geographic location at a specific point in time, and is usually made up of approximately five hundred individual seeds. Depositing institutions first dry the seed accessions to limit their moisture content to 5–6 per cent, and then seal them inside an individual airtight aluminium bag. These bags are packed into standard-sized crates and stacked on shelving racks within one of the three separate, identical storage vaults, each measuring approximately 9.5 × 27 metres, which are refrigerated to maintain a constant temperature of −18°C. These vaults have been excavated approximately 120 metres into the side of a sandstone mountain at a height of 130 metres above sea level; entry to the vaults is via a 100-metre entrance tunnel. Equal parts bunker and frozen 'ark', the dramatic facade includes a commissioned artwork, *Perpetual Repercussion* by Dyveke Sanne, which 'renders the building visible from far off both day and night, using highly reflective stainless steel triangles of various sizes' (Norwegian Ministry of Agriculture and Food 2015). The cold climate and permafrost ensure that, even if power were to be lost, the storage vaults would remain frozen for a significant period of time, even taking into account the possible effects of climate and sea level changes. 'Designed for [a] virtually infinite lifetime', it is perceived to be 'robustly secured against external hazards and climate change effects' (Norwegian Ministry of Agriculture and Food 2015).

Rodney Harrison and Sefryn Penrose visited the SGSV in October 2015, spending several days in Spitsbergen, during which time they interviewed NordGen staff involved in the work of the seed vault. They were able to observe the arrival and accessioning of seed samples and to discuss the processes by which samples are X-rayed and deposited in the vault. NordGen staff also participated in a number of our cross-theme knowledge-exchange events, and other talks and activities, giving us an opportunity to return to discuss many of the issues that this visit first raised.

The SGSV is not a conventional seed bank, but was conceived of as part of a global system to facilitate the secure storage of a duplicate 'backup' of seed accessions held in national and regional repositories:

> Worldwide, more than 1,700 genebanks hold collections of food crops for safekeeping, yet many of these are vulnerable, exposed not only to natural catastrophes and war, but also to avoidable disasters, such as lack of funding or poor management. Something as mundane as a poorly functioning freezer can ruin an entire collection. And the loss of a crop variety is as irreversible as the extinction of a dinosaur, animal or any form of life.
>
> (Crop Trust n.d. a, n.p.)

These backup sets of seeds are stored free of charge and are held as part of an international agreement in which the seeds remain the property of the depositing institution, and are available for withdrawal only by that institution, at any time. It is thus not an active gene bank, but a literal 'vault' containing a secure stock of duplicate accessions, which can be used if seed stocks from the depositing institution become depleted or lost. The need for such a facility seemed clearly demonstrated when, in September 2015, scientists from ICARDA who had lost access to their gene bank facility in Aleppo, Syria, requested the return of seeds deposited in the SGSV, to reconstruct their collection in a new facility in Lebanon. This first withdrawal of seed samples from the SGSV as a result of the ongoing conflict in Syria was reported widely in the media, and seemed to indicate that the SGSV was already fulfilling a purpose that had previously been assumed would arise in a more distant future (most often framed within the temporal horizon of medium- to long-term global climate change; see Fowler 2008), thus justifying the significant investment in this global 'insurance policy'. The manager of the new ICARDA gene bank facility in Terbol, Bekaa, was reported to have said of the withdrawal of seed samples, 'It [SGSV] was not expected to be opened for 150 or 200 years ... It would only open in the case of major crises but then we soon discovered that, with this crisis at a country level, we needed to open it' (Alabaster 2015, n.p.).

Banking diversity, making futures, securing hope

In articulating the need for such a repository, the mission of the SGSV is framed within what we might see as a fairly conventional articulation of the endangerment sensibility and its accompanying entropic view of the relationship between diversity and time. The Crop Trust, as the charitable organisation responsible for funding the ongoing operations of the SGSV and the preparation and shipment of seed from developing countries, perhaps articulates this most clearly in its explanation of the purpose of the SGSV: 'The purpose of the Svalbard Global Seed Vault is to provide insurance against both incremental and catastrophic loss of crop biodiversity held in traditional seed banks around the world. The Seed Vault offers "fail-safe" protection for one of the most important natural resources on earth' (Crop Trust n.d. b, n.p.). It continues:

Crop diversity is the resource to which plant breeders must turn to develop varieties that can withstand pests, diseases, and remain productive in the face of changing climates. It will therefore underpin the world food supply … the Seed Vault will ensure that unique diversity held in genebanks in developing countries is not lost forever if an accident occurs.

(Crop Trust n.d. b, n.p.)

In these statements, we see all of the conventional articulations of what we have elsewhere referred to as an 'entropic' view of diversity (see Harrison 2017; Breithoff and Harrison 2020a; 2020b; but see DeSilvey 2017 for an alternative reading of this term in relation to heritage, loss and change), including the potential loss of diversity through catastrophic incidents and the need to build resilience in the face of such changes.

However, the situation becomes somewhat more complicated when we consider the operation of the SGSV in relation to the global system of agrobiodiversity conservation and, in particular, the relationship of the materials stored in the SGSV to the specific conservation targets of agrobiodiversity conservation practices. As Sara Peres (2016) shows, seed banks were originally developed as part of a strategy to ensure the maintenance of crop genetic diversity in the face of widespread adoption of a small number of high-yielding crop varieties during the agricultural industrialisation and modernisation of the twentieth century. The freezing of seeds would enable the maintenance of agrobiodiversity without the need for ongoing cultivation of old crop varieties, resulting in an 'archive' of the evolutionary histories of crop varieties that might be of use to future generations of agricultural scientists and farmers.

The notion of 'genetic erosion' fundamentally underpins this global system. First coined at the 1967 FAO/International Biological Program Technical Conference on the Exploration, Utilization and Conservation of Plant Genetic Resources (Pistorius 1997, 2), the concept gained strength from its resonance with the, by then, well-known concept of soil erosion, suggesting that the full range of both wild and domesticated genetic diversity, threatened with 'erosion' by agricultural modernisation programmes, was fundamental to future food security (see Fenzi and Bonneuil 2016, 74–6). 'Landraces', localised genetic variants of crop species resulting from both cultural and natural selection processes, were seen to represent a bank of genetic diversity that held potential for future crop improvement to both mediate the effects of future climate change and develop resilience to future diseases (for example, see further discussion in Hummer 2015).

Peres (2016), drawing on the work of Parry (2004) and Van Dooren (2009), goes on to show that the present system of gene banks is the outcome of debates in the 1960s and 1970s surrounding the most appropriate methods of agrobiodiversity conservation – *in-situ* or *ex-situ* – in which the frozen seeds held in seed banks across the world came to act as 'proxies' for crops. These debates were closely related to, and indeed stimulated, the development of broader technologies of *ex-situ* cryogenic, as well as other cold and frozen preservation practices, across a large number of different fields of conservation (see Radin 2016; 2017; chapters in Radin and Kowal 2017). Elaborating on the temporal aspect of seeds as proxies, Peres argues that frozen seeds could become records or 'archives' of a crop's evolutionary history because they were preserved statically and latently, and as such they might be 'recalled' in the future (see also Bowker 2005a):

> Seed banks can therefore be imagined as repositories that enabled the 'recall' of genetic diversity, both by committing it to memory and by allowing it to be recovered from cold storage for use. By evoking both these meanings, the concept of recall conveys how the conservation of old landraces is entangled with concerns regarding their future use. Seed banks thus function as archives that make records of the past of crops accessible in the future.
>
> (Peres 2016, 102)

It is worth thinking through in more detail the concepts of the archive, and of the relationship between the seed, its genetic material, and the biosocial record of a crop's evolutionary history. Peres (2016) posits that seeds are individual records of a crop's evolutionary history; from this framing, we extrapolate that the seed functions as the 'document' within the accession 'folder', which is a component of the gene bank as 'archive'. However, we want to suggest a more complicated, nested relationship in which we might consider each seed to also function as a form of biosocial archive in its own right. Each seed holds within its genetic material records of localised crop experimentation and natural and cultural selection, which, although partial and iterative, describe histories of agricultural activity that may extend back in time to the earliest prehistoric experimentation with domestication of crop species. These seeds could thus be characterised, as Van Dooren (2007, 83) does, as archives of 'inter-generational, inter-species, human/plant kinship relations'. In relation to the ICARDA accession withdrawal, the gene bank manager was also quoted as saying, 'When you trace back the history of these seeds, [you think of] the tradition and the heritage that they captured ... They were maintained by local farmers from generation to generation, from father to son and then all the way to ICARDA's gene bank and from there to the Global Seed Vault in Svalbard' (Alabaster 2015, n.p.). While each individual seed may only record the outcomes of particular processes of natural and cultural selection, in the sense that these are 'inscribed' in the genetic material of the seed itself, holding these seeds at low temperatures would potentially halt the genetic erosion that might occur *in situ* through a combination of natural and cultural processes. Thus, the cumulative (meta)archive of the SGSV conserves not only genetic agro-biodiversity, but also individual archives (seeds) that contain a series of specific biological-historical accounts (genes) of multispecies biosocial relations.

If the nature of the SGSV is complicated by this articulation of a more intricate, nested relationship of document to folder to archive, it is even further complicated by its relationship with time, and with the forms of diversity it holds in its repository. In freezing crop seeds as archives that map global genetic diversity from different points in time, each of which contains echoes or fragments of the diversity of past multispecies biosocial processes, the SGSV intervenes in the normative, entropic decay of diversity, 'banking' a record of past and present genetic diversity in frozen, arrested time. As in Radin's (2013) account of frozen blood and tissue samples, the values of these collections are banked as *latent values*, which are only to be realised at some future moment in time. In conjunction with ongoing processes of *in-situ* agrobiodiversity maintenance, themselves subject to continuing processes of natural and cultural selection that alter contemporary global agrobiodiversity, the vault's collection reverses the entropic process of diversity decay by increasing global crop genetic diversity. It does this because *in-situ* conservation (working through time) goes on producing other, new forms of agrobiodiversity, while *ex-situ* conservation (working through frozen time) maintains older diversity into the future, thus increasing global diversity overall.

The Crop Trust suggests:

> The Vault is the ultimate insurance policy for the world's food supply, offering options for future generations to overcome the challenges of climate change and population growth. It will secure, for centuries, millions of seeds representing every important crop variety available in the world today. It is the final back up.
>
> (Crop Trust n.d. a, n.p.)

But the notion of a 'backup' here, which implies that duplicate accessions remain (biologically and socially) functionally equivalent, belies the complicated biosociotechnical and discursive shifts that occur within the repository, which, along with the possibility of further genetic changes within cold storage (for example, Soleri and Smith 1999), mean that which is deposited is fundamentally transformed by the process, creating something significantly different in *ex-situ* conservation when compared with that which is conserved *in situ*. In this sense, the operations of the SGSV seem to hold much in common with other archives, where the materials contained are reconfigured and acquire new forms of significance through their archival deposition (for example, Stoler 2009). They also have in common the idea of the archive as a place in which different forms of relations are ordered and shaped, and which in turn shape and order the worlds to which these archives refer (for example, Joyce 1999; Bowker 2005a; Bennett et al. 2017). As such, the SGSV as meta-archive also constitutes its own biosocial record of specific, historically embedded, neo-liberal practices of multispecies relationships – that is, the attempts to mediate modernised agriculture through *ex-situ* conservation that emerged in the latter part of the twentieth century.

This, in turn, contributes to the accumulation of forms of biocapital by the SGSV that are different to those values that accrue within the national and regional gene banks providing their 'duplicate' samples to the SGSV. These biocultural values draw not only on the added prestige derived from belonging to the 'global' seed vault – as part of the 'final' backup – and from the specific stories (for example, the Syrian withdrawal) associated with objects contained within it, but also, through processes of genetic shift, to the addition of novel forms of biodiversity to the frozen, latent life contained within its archive. If the metaphor of a 'backup' is only partially accurate, then, its designation as a '*bank*' in this process of the creation and accumulation of new forms of biocapital seems far more apposite (see also Bowker 2000; 2005b).

It is perhaps no coincidence that the conservation target of such activity is the seed. It acts here both as physical container for genetic material and as poignant symbol of latent potential and hope in securing uncertain futures. By intervening directly in 'natural' processes of entropic diversity decay and providing 'fail-safe' protection for 'one of the most important natural resources on earth' (Crop Trust n.d. b, n.p.), the SGSV offers 'options' to future generations in responding to climate and population change:

The power of seed can be explosive. Not just because it can force its way through rock-hard soil to reach the sunlight, but also because it is at the centre of many political processes. The rights relating to the genetic material of plants, animals and micro-organisms have been a key issue of contention between industrial and developing countries.

(Statsbygg 2008, 8)

Ghassan Hage (2003) discusses the state's capacity to distribute hope as a form of governmental power. Similarly, in offering a sense of hope and security against uncertain global futures, agrobiodiversity banking is also a practice that is caught up in processes of the generation and differential distribution of forms of power. The biopolitical concerns articulated in these processes contribute to the management of risk and uncertainty by establishing certain frameworks for intervening in, and shaping, the future through the maintenance of a 'bank' of genetic materials that might form the basis for future crop experimentation, and thus future forms of life. While the global system (of which the SGSV is a part) is one in which there are significant regulatory frameworks for the sharing of plant genetic resources for food and agriculture, it is nonetheless one in which the authority to determine access to those resources is vested in national governments. Here, this global system's objective to conserve a universal, biosocial archive for humanity is disrupted by issues of national sovereignty in ways that echo those of other international conservation instruments, such as the UNESCO World Heritage List (for example, see Harrison 2013a; Meskell 2014). This is a notion we will now explore in more detail in relation to another biobanking initiative, the Frozen Ark.

The Frozen Ark

The UK registered charity the Frozen Ark is a frozen zoo which aims to conserve cells and DNA of endangered non-human animals. The goal is for the Frozen Ark to become both a physical and an open-access virtual biobank that stores, manages and safeguards biological material from the world's threatened species, and connects researchers on a global level. Founding partners include the London Natural History Museum and the Zoological Society of London, as well as the University of Nottingham, which provides laboratory and office space and serves as the seat of the Frozen Ark, while research is now mainly being carried out at Cardiff University. At the time of writing, its consortium of zoos, aquaria and other conservation bodies amount to 27 national and international partners from all over the world (Costa and Bruford 2018). The apocalyptic message conveyed by the project's logo, a 'stylised ark on stormy seas' (Chrulew 2017), is both clear and urgent: in the face of anthropogenic ecological loss, the collecting, storing and managing of biological material from endangered species might be the only chance for humanity and the species with which we cohabit the planet. Yet, unlike Noah's Ark, which, according to the Genesis flood narrative, carried a male and a female of all the world's animals to save them from extinction by drowning, the Frozen Ark is a 'cryogenic' or 'technoscientific ark' (Parry 2004) that adheres to its website's motto of 'saving cells and DNA of endangered species' – materials that act as *ex-situ* proxies of the living species they were taken from (see Chapter 7).

The work presented here draws primarily on a six-week intensive placement undertaken in 2017, during which Esther Breithoff worked with Frozen Ark team members and conservation biologists based in the Molecular Ecology and Evolution research laboratory at Cardiff University, and a number of additional interviews and laboratory visits to Frozen Ark team members based at the University of Nottingham, and with affiliated researchers at London Zoo and the Natural History Museum. During the Cardiff placement, Esther shadowed staff and students in the laboratory, interviewed them about their work, and completed desktop research tasks in support of the production of a report on the ethics of non-human biobanking. Further, Frozen Ark staff participated in various collaborative knowledge-exchange events throughout the project, which aimed at understanding the work of each of the partner organisations and co-designing research to address common issues for the sector. This section also draws on these more experimental 'para-ethnographic' (Holmes and Marcus 2005; 2006; 2008; see Harrison et al. 2016) engagements with the organisation as part of the research programme over a longer, four-year period.

The University of Nottingham currently provides two *c.*–80°C freezers storing just over seven hundred blood and tissue samples obtained from endangered non-human animals from UK-based zoos and aquaria. The charity's collection consists of samples from a number of different animals, including the scimitar-horned oryx (extinct in the wild), the Colombian spider monkey, pileated gibbon, siamang gibbon, lar gibbon, snow leopard and Malayan tapir (all endangered). When our researchers visited the Nottingham laboratory, we were shown how information on all the samples stored there is organised in physical file folders, and includes, among other details, an internal identification number, a universal zoo number, the species, type and location of sample, what it is preserved in, sample quality and, where applicable, a Whatman FTA card.[2] The Frozen Ark's interim director, professor of biodiversity and conservation geneticist Mike Bruford, based at the University of Cardiff, indicated that the ultimate objective is to form a confederated model that functions as both a physical and virtual infrastructure, storing and managing the genetic material from endangered species, sampled in the wild and in zoos and aquaria, from all over the world. At the time of writing, CryoArks is in the process of being established, a Cardiff-based and BBSRC-funded (UK Biotechnology and Biosciences Research Council) initiative resulting from a collaboration between the Frozen Ark and some of its partner institutions, as well as the UK node of the European Association of Zoos and Aquaria (EAZA) biobank. Due to limitations imposed by the Nagoya Protocol, which is published by the Secretariat of the Convention on Biological Diversity and ensures 'the fair and equitable sharing of the benefits arising from the utilization of genetic resources, thereby contributing to the conservation of biological diversity and the sustainable use of its components' (CBD 2011, Article 1), CryoArks will be mainly focused on the UK and Ireland, whereas the Frozen Ark has a global remit. To this end, it has already started cataloguing samples of extinct, endangered and threatened[3] species held by consortium members, and is aiming to increase the number of, and coordination between, consortium members. Unlike other biobanks around the world (such as the San Diego Frozen Zoo®, or the Smithsonian Biobank), which intend to form a single point on Earth where genetic material from all over the world is being stored inside a central biobank, the Frozen Ark aims to be a Nagoya-compliant backup storage facility for institutions that, for various reasons, cannot store their own samples, or would like to have duplicates of existing collections and to hold centralised records relating to a distributed network of physical biobanks that store biosamples of endangered non-human animals (much like the SGSV does for seeds).

Based on interviews with the charity's staff undertaken during Esther's lab placement in Cardiff, and subsequently with staff based in Nottingham, it is apparent that the Frozen Ark's concern for preservation of genetic material for future generations initially outweighed active conservation efforts. With species going extinct all over the world, and the dramatic anticipated loss of genetic information, the Frozen Ark eventually decided to change from acting purely as a repository to become an active collection. This decision seems to have been influenced partially by the emergence of new experimental genetic work, but also reflected a change in philosophy about the Ark's role. 'The focus was always for the future', reflects Jude Smith, who has been the charity's administrator from the beginning, 'but as we've got on, it has become really obvious that the future is here now, you know, it's now.'

This new approach, described as more 'pragmatic' by professor Bruford, recognises the need to boost the profile of the charity in order to deliver on its promises for the future: the collection, safeguarding and managing of biological and genetic material from endangered species for both anticipated and unanticipated future uses. The vision is for the Frozen Ark to become an active and ethical facility for genomic resource management that helps to identify and prioritise which animal species are at risk of extinction, and are thus in need of sampling, and to develop the most effective techniques of collecting, storing and managing biological material. In its educational role, the Frozen Ark supports institutions both in the UK and abroad with setting up their own biobank facilities and/or successfully managing already existing repositories. According to the charity, its main goals are:

> i) coordinating global efforts in animal biobanking; (ii) sharing expertise; (iii) offering help to organisations and governments that wish to set up biobanks in their own countries; (iv) providing the physical and informatics infrastructure that will allow conservationists and researchers to search for, locate and use this material wherever possible without having to resample from wild populations.
>
> (Costa and Bruford 2018, n.p.)

In the current absence of coordination and lack of shared protocols and databases between different biobanks nationally and internationally, the Frozen Ark plans on setting up a virtual stand-alone open-access database connecting existing biobanks on a global level. This would facilitate increased access to research material for researchers and conservationists internationally. The Frozen Ark sees its role in safeguarding and managing genetic diversity as part of a joint effort between *ex-situ* and *in-situ* conservation practices. Cryostoring biomaterial of endangered species in freezers and liquid nitrogen tanks – although space effective – does, however, come with a high carbon footprint, which one could suggest ultimately increases the threat of extinction to the animals it was designed to protect. The Frozen Ark website emphasises that establishing and maintaining a global biobank at present is also a costly undertaking that has suffered from a lack of funding since its inception:

Time is running out for many species. Conservation efforts will undoubtedly save some but we must preserve the genetic record of all endangered species for our future. Time is also running out for the Frozen Ark, which has been running with volunteers on a shoestring budget for several years. Help us save Nature's genetic heritage so that future generations can enjoy the natural world as we have all done.

(Frozen Ark 2020, n.p.)

Like the endangered species whose biological material it aims to secure in the race against irretrievable loss of biodiversity, the Frozen Ark itself also senses a risk of its own endangerment in articulating these difficulties of establishing long-term funding to secure its future operations. These issues of uncertainty relating to the securing of ongoing financial resources for the organisation's research and collections were a regular topic of discussion – in the laboratory, in conferences, and in more formal interview contexts. They form another of the various ways in which the urgency of the work of the organisation, and biodiversity conservation more generally, are expressed.

Playing God in the Anthropocene: Biodiversity, cryopreservation and future-making

In 1993, the Steven Spielberg film *Jurassic Park* seemed to offer an improbable view of an alternative future in which long-extinct species could be regenerated from ancient DNA. We have shown that initiatives to collect and store the raw materials for such a process in the form of frozen blood, tissue and other human and non-human animal organic materials have a much longer genealogy. However, recent developments in genetic rescue programmes that aim to revive extinct and threatened animal species suggest such genomic engineering is scientifically possible. Several projects that sound equally implausible – including 'genetic rescue' projects currently being undertaken by Revive and Restore (reviverestore.org) to recreate extinct passenger pigeons and woolly mammoths – are likely to realise results within the next decade (for example, see Jørgensen 2013; Shapiro 2015). Sherkow and Greely (2013) explain that the three approaches that appear most likely to yield results are back-breeding, in which selective breeding is used to produce the phenotypes of extinct species; cloning using cryopreserved tissue; and genetic engineering using whole genome sequencing and the editing of DNA in cells from genetically similar extant animals. In many ways, these projects constitute a realisation of the latent futures that are resourced by frozen zoos and cryopreservation technologies. The move within the Frozen Ark away from perceiving its role primarily as a passive collecting institution for the future, to one of active experimental conservation in the present, exemplifies the ways in which such collections resource the development of new realities in which the possibilities of reviving extinct species through hybridisation with extant ones is increasingly becoming fulfilled. But in their enabling of certain forms of what Vidal and Dias (2016a, 1) helpfully term 'restitution fantasies', they also re-enforce dominant (although not uncomplicated – see Dibley 2012; 2015) forms of anthropocentrism, which remain barely hidden within the Anthropocene chronotope (see Pratt 2017), in the fulfilment of humanity's ultimate mastery over nature: the ability to resurrect the species that we have ourselves rendered extinct. The quest for such a reality is embodied in the Frozen Ark's own creation narrative, in which the founders' attempts to save the *Partula* land snail through more conventional methods of captive breeding are unsuccessful, and force them to turn to cryopreservation for future hybridisation and de-extinction programmes as the last hope for this totemic species.

From ark to bank: Biodiversity and biocapital

It is in the transformation of these latent possibilities into new economic (as well as ecological) realities that we are able to determine shifts in the nature of biobanking facilities and the forms of value they both generate and are caught up within (Shukin 2009). A significant literature in science studies, which develops and expands upon Foucault's 'late' work on biopower/biopolitics, has traced the development of what Cooper (2008) terms the 'bioeconomy' since the 1970s in the specific relations of biotechnology, neo-liberal politics and economic policy (for example, see Doyle 1997; Thacker 2005; Rose 2007; Waldby and Mitchell 2006; Shukin 2009; Franklin 2013; Cooper and Waldby 2014). Central to the bioeconomy has been the emergence and evolution of a range of new forms of 'biocapital'. We draw on Helmreich's (2008; see also Sunder Rajan 2006) definition of biocapital as the surplus values generated by the commodification and circulation of forms of biological life within economic systems. Helmreich points out, however, that biocapital is understood and deployed in a number of different ways by scholars across science studies, and itself may manifest in a range of different forms, as parts of different sociomaterial assemblages. It is the ways in which bio-capital emerges flexibly and replicates itself across these different socio-material assemblages that concerns us here. Given the significance of the study of concepts of value to critical heritage studies, we might ask: how have cryobanks such as the Frozen Ark contributed to the development of new forms of value? And in what ways are those new values accumulated and distributed within the bioeconomy?

In his influential paper, which originally developed the concept of the Frozen Zoo in 1984, Benirschke observes the relationship between the growth of cryopreservational technologies and the dwindling biolog-ical resources these are produced to conserve. As biodiversity (bearing in mind that this concept is itself plastic and subject to shifts in meaning) diminishes, the value of these banked biomaterials increases both indi-vidually and collectively. As we have argued in relation to the work of seed biobanks, these processes are forms of *speculative biocapital accu-mulation*, banking on, yet simultaneously imaginatively resourcing, the development of the biotechnologies that will realise these future values. Thus, extinction, biobanking, biocapital and biodiversity come to be linked in a complicated network of values within the emerging bioeco-nomy. In its speculation on, and investment in, the anticipation of loss, the work of the Frozen Ark (and the field of biodiversity cryopreserva-tion more generally) can also be understood to represent a response to neo-liberal economics in the ways in which it constitutes an optimisation of the use of space and resources. Cryobanking 'represents a technically viable method for helping to conserve species biodiversity, without hav-ing to maintain large captive populations of each organism' (Hosey et al. 2009, 319, as quoted by Chrulew 2017), nor, indeed, the designated landscapes in which these organisms might conventionally be preserved (as national parks, for example). As Chrulew (2017, 297) goes on to surmise from these comments in his own discussion of the Frozen Ark, 'the forms of preservation and exchange made possible by the frozen zoo transform the relationships between humans, animals, and technologies, reorganising space and time beyond familiar constraints in the interests of optimal efficiency and diversity'.

The ability of biodiversity conservation to designate conservation proxies that are immutable, combinable mobiles (in the Latourian (1987; 1999) sense) is thus central to the ways in which biobanks function within a bioeconomy to accumulate biocapital. As Harrison (2017) has observed of the seeds in *ex-situ* seed banks, while these are conceptualised as cop-ies of biomaterials held in other collections (or, as we qualify here, not so much copies as fragments of the original sample that remain authentic at the level of the DNA – indeed, as Chrulew (2017) notes, doubles of doubles held in captivity that are themselves doubles of wild animals), they are not, in fact, duplicates, as their presence within these particular biosocial archives allows them to accumulate new forms of value and, indeed, possible new genetic characteristics that do not directly replicate those from which they were originally copied. This is again reflected in the change of perception of the function of the Frozen Ark, from repository – where frozen biomaterials would be collected untouched for the future, to speculative reinvestment – where such biomaterials would be part of active and ongoing genetic experimentation with saving threatened species and potentially reversing extinction, in particular through the generation of hybrids that combine genetic materials from both living and extinct species. Finally, cryobanking reconfigures relationships between life and death. Talking in the context of frozen genetic material from humans, Lemke observes that:

> ... 'human material' transcends the living person. The person who dies today is not really dead. He or she lives on, at least potentially. Or more precisely, parts of a human being – his or her cells or organs, blood, bone marrow, and so on – can continue to exist in the bodies of other people, whose quality of life they improve or who are spared death through their incorporation. The organic materials of life are not subordinate to the same biological rhythms as the body is. These materials can be stored as information in biobanks or cultivated in stem cell lines. Death can be part of a productive circuit and used to improve and extend life. The death of one person may guarantee the life and survival of another. Death has also become flexible and compartmentalised.
>
> (Lemke 2012, 95)

Similarly, biotechnologies employed by the Frozen Ark allow for the breaking down of species into a range of components at the biomolecular level, which allow for almost endless recombination (Doyle 1997; Chrulew 2017), further complicating the question of the relevant units by which biodiversity might be measured, and the relative values of such units and their proxies. The importance of the late capitalist context of these developments cannot be overstated. This extension of life and expansion of what constitutes biological reproduction is a function of what Cooper refers to as the bioeconomy's transformation of biological life into surplus value (Cooper 2008; see also Shukin 2009; Thacker 2010). As in the case of Svalbard Global Seed Vault, the operations of the

Frozen Ark can be understood to accumulate and generate surplus value through reversing what are perceived to be 'natural' as well as humanly produced entropic processes of biodiversity decay (Sepkoski 2016); but importantly, the new forms of value that it produces are not simply inherent to its proxies themselves, but also derive from the latent (see Radin 2017) potential for new and experimental forms of life that they may be used to produce. In this sense, the Frozen Ark contributes to what Radin (2015) terms a form of 'planned hindsight' – it realises its own technofutures through its collecting policies in the present. Its latent generation of future value in the form of biocapital requires direct speculation upon the extinction and biodiversity loss that it is created to secure the present against. The Frozen Ark counter-intuitively depends upon the future biodiversity loss that it works against, but simultaneously anticipates, in its present operations.

Conclusion

Our aim in this chapter has been to critically explore the field of *ex-situ* biodiversity cryopreservation and its place in the late capitalist global economy by exploring how biobanks speculate upon, and help to realise, new futures as a response to an anticipated global loss of biodiversity. These might be understood to constitute specific materialisations of forms of more or less 'hopeful' futures (see Kleist and Jansen 2016 and further discussion in Chapter 2). In the work of the SGSV, we see specific forms of hope and security generated through practices of banking genetic diversity, in response to conditions of future global uncertainties regarding climate and population. We have used our work with the SGSV and the Frozen Ark as a starting point to begin to think about the reorganisation of biodiversity values that the rise of such facilities reflects, and the largely unexplored relationship between biodiversity conservation and the bioeconomy more generally. We want to be clear that this is not intended as a criticism of the work of the organisations, the individuals who work for the organisations, or of biodiversity conservation more generally, but is 'critical' in a broader sense of trying to begin to understand how biodiversity conservation is caught up in, and simultaneously generative of, new systemic networks of power relations within the context of late capitalism. If biodiversity conservation is viewed through the lens of a critical exploration of the forms of value it generates and their interactions with one another, *ex-situ* biobanks are no longer dormant genetic 'arks', but rather 'investment banks' that accumulate and produce value through speculation upon the forms of extinction that they themselves seek to build resilience against through their reconfiguration of post-genomic life. Biobanks are not simply passive collecting institutions, but through redefining both what constitutes 'nature' and the ways in which nature might be conserved, their operations are generative of new values, new forms of life and new sociomaterial worlds.

We have also sought to introduce some new critical concepts to the comparative study of biological diversity preservation practices, oriented towards the understanding of such practices as forms of future-making in which each set of practices is understood to produce its own distinctive future worlds. We see these concepts as potentially also helpful in rethinking *cultural* diversity preservation practices. One might argue that the newly emergent bioeconomy discussed here constitutes the logical product of a recognition of our current epoch – the Anthropocene – as one in which humans have become the primary force of global geological and climatological change (for example, Lewis and Maslin 2018). These biotechnologies and their resultant post-extinction imaginaries are the ghosts that haunt the landscapes touched by the violence and conflicts of modernity, and the monsters that emerge out of the resulting hybrid human/non-human social relations, which Tsing et al. (2017) and their contributors see as defining the post-Anthropocene planetary poetics. Of course, the notion implied within the idea of the Anthropocene is precisely that we live in what Marris (2013) terms a 'post-wild world'. In presenting the distinctive future-making practices of this particular field of *ex-situ* biodiversity cryopreservation, we also aim to demonstrate the value of understanding and engaging critically and comparatively with cultural diversity preservation practices, and the distinctive futures they enact and resource.

Notes

1. This chapter draws on material previously published as Esther Breithoff and Rodney Harrison (2020a), 'From Ark to Bank: Extinction, Proxies and Biocapitals in Ex-Situ Biodiversity Conservation Practices', *International Journal of Heritage Studies* 26 (1): 37–55; Esther Breithoff and Rodney Harrison (2020b), 'Making Futures in End Times: Nature Conservation in the Anthropocene', in Rodney Harrison and Colin Sterling (eds) *Deterritorialising the Future: Heritage in, of and after the Anthropocene* (Open Humanities Press); and Rodney Harrison (2017), 'Freezing Seeds and Making Futures: Endangerment, Hope, Security, and Time in Agrobiodiversity Conservation Practices', *Culture, Agriculture, Food and Environment* 39 (2): 80–9.
2. A commercially available paper card containing chemicals that stabilise nucleic acids on contact for long-term storage of DNA at room temperature. These cards are often used for collecting and storing DNA in the field by pushing or blotting specimen fluids such as blood, saliva or plant materials against the card for later extraction in the laboratory.
3. These terms have specific technical definitions that relate to the categories established by the International Union for Conservation of Nature (IUCN) Red List of Threatened Species.

Proxies

Esther Breithoff

We have already noted that the concept of biological and cultural diversity in heritage is an ambiguous and plastic one, encoding complicated relationships between parts and wholes (see Chapter). It is realised by way of indices, measurements, and catalogues of endangered objects, practices, places and species, designated at various degrees of risk (Turner ; Vidal and Dias b; Heise), and is often represented *metonymically,* as certain charismatic objects and species come to stand in for the concept of biological and cultural diversity more generally. Familiar examples are the individual starving polar bear as a symbol of the environmental impacts of anthropogenic climate change, or the last speaker of an endangered language as the sole custodian of an endangered culture or way of life.

One aspect of how *biodiversity* as a concept is realised is by way of proxies that represent units – individual animals, species, protected areas, ecosystems – on which certain forms of conservation processes might be enacted (for example, see Heise). The term 'conservation proxy' has a specific meaning in conservation biology, and describes how certain units of analysis (species, landscapes, soils and so on) act as indicators of the relative 'health' or diversity of a particular system or larger unit of analysis – a national park, an ecosystem, a waterway and so on (these meanings are discussed further in Part V, Transformation). These surrogates or flagship species become a shorthand measurement to guide the distribution of resource or to measure the intensity of action that is required on a particular system (for example, Caro).

But there is another, equally important way of understanding the concept of proxies in relation to *ex-situ* biological as well as cultural diversity conservation practices. This is in the way in which certain kinds of biological and cultural materials, in combination with different forms of data pertaining to those materials, come to stand in for biological or cultural diversity, and/or the individual species or cultures from which those materials have been taken (Parry ; Van Dooren ; Bennett et al.). The transformation of such objects into the targets of conservation activity themselves can be understood in relation to Latour's concept of 'immutable mobiles' in the history of the development of modern sciences. These are transportable textual or visual fragments, observations and representations of objects, places and phenomena that are collected from 'the field' and returned to 'centres of collection and calculation', where they are combined with other such objects and subjected to translation to produce forms of scientific knowledge that predicate action, including action back upon the fields from which they were collected (Latour ;). In the case of the Frozen Ark, the Svalbard Global Seed Vault (SGSV) and Kew, biological materials (including cells, DNA samples, and seeds, plants and flower specimens) act as *ex-situ* proxies of biodiversity in 'nature', and as such, these materials, their containers and the data pertaining to them increasingly become themselves the focus of conservation activity. Similarly, at the Endangered Languages Documentation Programme (ELDP), the digital records of languages become proxies for endangered languages and cultures. (See Figures . to . at the end of this chapter.)

But the application of these concepts to such repositories also suggests certain ways in which Latour's model might be modified to accommodate the more complicated sets of relations that have arisen in the late modern cultural and biological economies in which such collections have come to proliferate. One example of this is the seemingly problematic use of the term 'centre of calculation' to describe *ex-situ* biodiversity conservation repositories such as seed banks and frozen zoos. Whereas Kew could be argued to draw together collections from across the world into a central place that builds a world around these collections, and thus represents a conventional 'centre of calculation', the Frozen Ark and the SGSV are composed of consortia of zoos, aquaria and other conservation bodies. Like cultural collections (for example, see the discussion of the relations of French metropolitan and colonial museums in Bennett et al.), centres of calculation may be distributed and operate across multiple centres as part of a confederated model. Importantly, these are held together by virtual networks, in this case databases containing information relating to samples of biomaterials from plants and non-human animals, which manage and constrain the ways in which data are collected and that render them able to be combined and manipulated in specific ways. These more complicated sets of relations are similarly realised through the relations of the Frozen Ark and the SGSV with other institutions, where they act as a 'backup' or copy of copies held in other biobanks. Even though these are 'copies', they are also perceived as authentic or 'immutable' at the level of the DNA sample (see further discussion in Harrison and Breithoff and Harrison a). The conservation of such biomaterials is a form of 'latent' or 'deferred' conservation in the sense in which these cells and data are frozen for future scientific research, which may aid conservation efforts in some, as yet undefined, manner. In this way, such biomaterials, as proxies for biological diversity held in *ex-situ* collections, exemplify a process that could be understood to be common to *ex-situ* natural and cultural heritage conservation more generally. The futures that are realised and populated by such proxies do not so much conserve realities *as they exist in the present*, but rather invent *new forms of future natures* in which conservation is perhaps better understood to function as a form of 'invention' (see further discussion in Part V, Transformation).

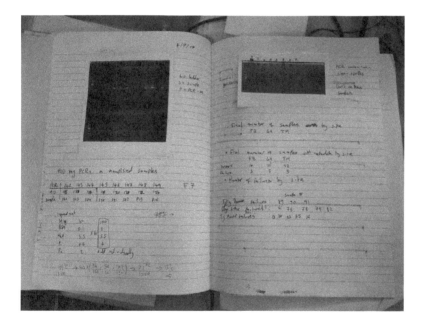

Figure .   Lab book entry showing PCR data (amplifications of a known section of DNA often used to identify the presence or absence of a genetic trait) and agarose gel images (the fluorescent rectangles visible in the images identify the presence or absence of a genetic trait), which act as proxies for the flycatcher bird. Frozen Ark/Molecular Ecology and Evolution Research Laboratory, Cardiff University (photograph by Esther Breithoff).

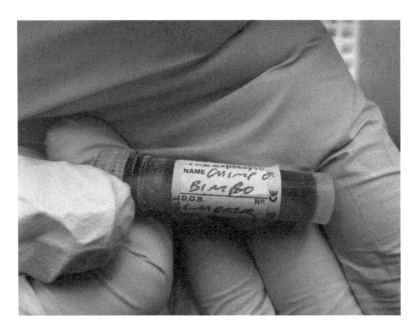

Figure .   Frozen blood sample of a chimpanzee, stored in one of Frozen Ark's c.–°C freezers at the University of Nottingham, as a further example of a biomaterial proxy of the animal from which it was extracted. Frozen Ark, University of Nottingham (photograph by Esther Breithoff).

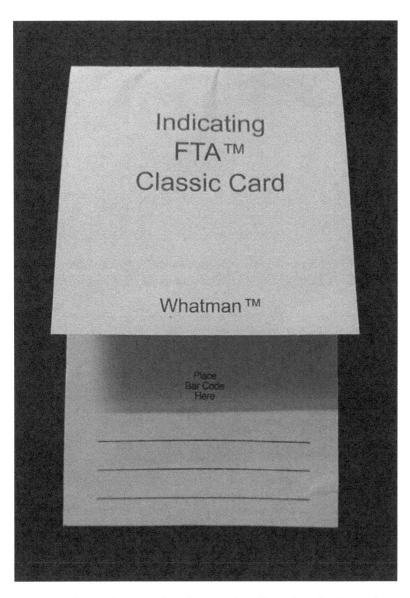

Figure . The FTA is a paper-based system that allows the collection and storage of DNA (mostly from blood and buccal swabs) by dabbing a bit of the fluid into one of the pink circles inside the card. It allows a quick and safe storage of DNA without the need of liquid nitrogen and freezers, making them a practical alternative when sampling in the field. Unfortunately, the cards are expensive and only allow four samples per card. Such technologies make the collection, transportation and subsequent storage of DNA/ biomaterials as conservation proxies possible. Frozen Ark/Natural History Museum, London (photograph by Esther Breithoff).

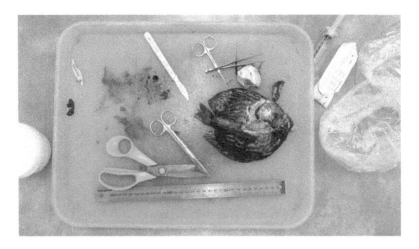

Figure . Dissection of fish to remove samples for cold and chemical storage, Zoological Society of London (photograph by Sefryn Penrose).

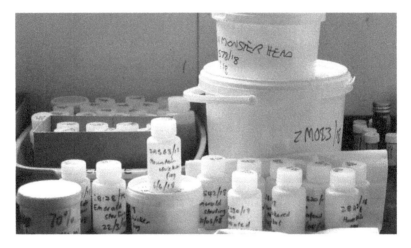

Figure . Samples of animal parts stored in ethanol, Zoological Society of London (photograph by Sefryn Penrose).

Figure . Pressed and dried plant specimens at the Herbarium at Kew (photograph by Rodney Harrison).

Figure . Boxes of seed specimens stored at the Svalbard Global Seed Vault (photograph by Rodney Harrison).

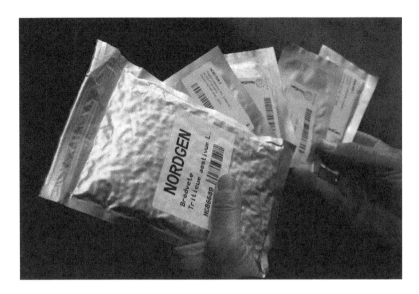

Figure . Accessions of seeds, stored in aluminium pouches, Svalbard Global Seed Vault (photograph by Riccardo Gangale, courtesy of Landbruks-og matdepartementet CC BY-ND .).

Figure . Agricultural seed specimens, Svalbard Global Seed Vault (photograph by Riccardo Gangale, courtesy of Landbruks-og matdepartementet CC BY-ND .).

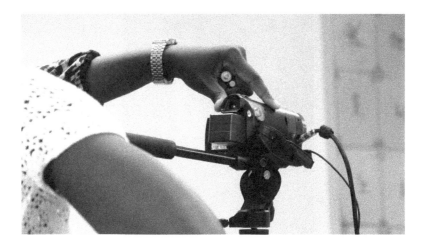

Figure .   Digital audio and video recording at an ELDP training workshop on the practices of language documentation at the Netherlands Institute in Morocco, Rabat (photograph by Sefryn Penrose).

Figure .   Entering information into the ELDP endangered language database at a training workshop in Rabat, Morocco (photograph by Sefryn Penrose).

Figure . Laptop holding central sample database at the Molecular Ecology and Evolution Laboratory, Cardiff University (photograph by Esther Breithoff).

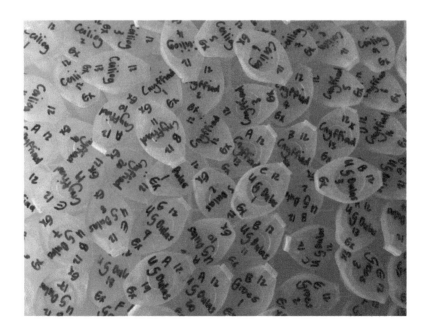

Figure . Cryopreserved DNA sample tubes stored in the Molecular Ecology and Evolution Laboratory, Cardiff University (photograph by Esther Breithoff).

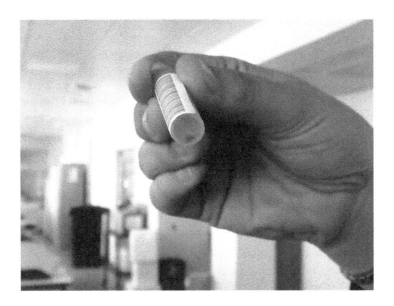

Figure . Barcoded cryopreserved DNA sample tube, Molecular Ecology and Evolution Laboratory, Cardiff University (photograph by Esther Breithoff).

Figure . Samples of domestic ferret fur in envelopes at the Molecular Ecology and Evolution Laboratory in Cardiff (photograph by Esther Breithoff).

8
Towards the total archive

Rodney Harrison and Esther Breithoff

'This is supposed to last for eternity', exclaimed Åsmund Asdal at the
Nordic Genetic Resource Centre in an interview with *The Guardian* in
May 2017 (Carrington 2017, n.p.). Rising temperatures and melting permafrost, which were widely reported in the media as being the results
of climate change, had led to the ingress of water and damage to the
entrance of the Svalbard Global Seed Vault (SGSV) less than 10 years
after it was first constructed. Although no water came in to the areas of
seed storage themselves, and the main functional parts of the Seed Vault
were not flooded, the episode had major impacts on the media's vision
of, and trust in, the future-proofing qualities of the world's largest crop
seed 'backup' facility. Uncertainty has replaced eternity, as the future one
secures against is always changing. Nonetheless, in an effort to make it
withstand changes in climate and the test of time, the Norwegian Ministry for Agriculture and Food together with Statsbygg[1] have since invested
in a major technical upgrade of the seed bank – a costly initiative about
which Asdal comments:

> We don't believe that the Seed Vault should be used as an exam-
> ple of problems caused by climate change, because we do not have
> any scientific evidence proving that this is the case. The upgrade is
> being done to secure the Seed Vault for the future, where climate
> change is one of the factors. It is fixing some initial weaknesses at
> the construction, and it is increasing the security against unfriendly
> actions, through installing new doors, barriers and surveillance sys-
> tems. This is also the reason for implementing stricter visitor poli-
> cies. So our focus is that the Seed Vault provides security for future
> food production in agricultural regions in a changing climate.
>
> (Asdal 2019)

Nonetheless, the instigation of these new works – which involve the complete replacement of the 'Svalbard Tube' access tunnel with a new, watertight concrete tunnel, the addition of a new service building, the excavation of two additional large storage vaults and works to re-establish the permafrost in the soils surrounding the vault – shows how the future is a moving target, and how changing understandings of the future will have an ongoing impact on how diversity is managed and conserved in an unfolding present.

Our aim in this part of the book has been to consider the role of 'diversity' as a concept in mobilising conservation activities across a range of different heritage domains, and to compare and contrast the different forms that these actions take. We have done so with specific reference to four organisations – the Endangered Languages Documentation Programme (ELDP), NordGen/SGSV, Kew and the Frozen Ark – each of which is concerned with the conservation of different forms of heritage diversity, and each of which approaches this goal by focusing on quite different conservation targets – endangered languages, crop seeds, both living and preserved plant specimens, and DNA samples of endangered animals respectively. Nonetheless, we have observed similar processes and ideas at work in each of these organisations, which could be said to undertake their work in broadly similar ways. They each collect materials from the field, which constitute partial components towards the conservation and management of the form of diversity with which they are concerned. These materials, along with observations relating to them and the contexts from which they are collected (in the form of data, photographs, field notes and so on) are assembled together and returned to a repository – a 'centre of collection and calculation', in Latourian terms – where forms of knowledge and decisions about how to manage those fields from which the objects were collected, as well as the objects themselves, are produced. In doing so, we argue that these repositories act like investment banks in the sense in which they produce new forms of value by speculating on the forms of endangerment that they are built to secure against. They also, as in Latour's discussions of biologists in the Amazon in *Pandora's Hope* (1999), produce forms of governmental knowledge that 'act back' on those fields by specifying the way in which they should be understood and managed. These generic relations between fields of collecting, *ex-situ* collections and *in-situ* forms of heritage management show strong similarities across all of the heritage domains with which we have worked. They work together to initiate and maintain significant 'looping effects' (see Hacking 1995; see further discussion in relation to collections in Bennett et al. 2017), wherein each of the varied forms of conservation we studied helps to justify and reinforce the discursive and material work of the other. We suggested that 'biodiversity', 'linguistic diversity' and 'cultural diversity' operate as transactional realities through which the endangerment sensibility is articulated and produced. This concept has been helpful in demonstrating the practical and discursive means by which 'diversity' is produced as a normative conservation target; how the various ways of understanding that diversity have come to relate to one another, both historically and in the present; and how they organise (different) realities and hence work – separately and collectively – to produce different kinds of future worlds.

We have also shown how each of the organisations and their respective heritage domains specify proxies that come to stand in for the conservation targets that the objects they collect constitute a sample of – as well as standing in for other, broader categories of conservation meta-objects, each of which contributes to the conservation of diversity overall. Indeed, the ability to increasingly break each of these conservation targets down into smaller and smaller components – not just a bird, which represents a part of an ecosystem, but microscopic samples of cryopreserved bird DNA, for example – shows how diversity conservation seems to exhibit a general movement towards the ever-increasing specification and collection of smaller and smaller parts of wholes. It is possible to argue, as Chrulew (2017) does of the Frozen Ark, that this constitutes a sort of neo-liberal optimisation of the use of space and resources. But it also seems to contribute to similar kinds of issues to those we discuss in Part III, Profusion – which Harrison (2013b) argues elsewhere relate to a general tendency historically over the late twentieth and early twenty-first centuries for heritage to expand exponentially to increase its fields of governance over an ever-increasing range of objects, places and practices.

Part of our work has involved questioning the boundaries between natural and cultural heritage, which still, despite much critique, seem to represent significant differences in the conservation and management of different forms of heritage – differences of definition that are partially produced by the different kinds of practices to which individual objects are subjected. In the visual essay 'Collections as techniques of worlding' (Chapter 16), we address this question directly, looking at the ways in which the same objects can be treated and valued very differently depending on the collection in which they end up at Kew (for example, herbarium, economic botany collection, seed bank, gardens and/or other living collections).

We have also seen how what constitutes diversity is very much defined by the categories that are devised to quantify it – or more accurately, to quantify its *loss* – and that different paradigms produce different ways of understanding diversity. These categories have been argued to be 'world-making' as they provide specific kinds of templates for organising reality, and both mobilise and facilitate specific forms of action on the world. Diversity conservation and management practices, particularly those of *ex-situ* collections, can also be understood to be future-making practices because these collections speculatively resource the development of new technologies to realise their latent potential. Recent advances in the use of cryopreserved DNA in de-extinction and cross-breeding programmes represent a good example of this. But we might also suggest that the heterogeneity of such diversity conservation practices themselves leads to a profusion of futures, not all of which work in concert with one another. We will consider the more general questions of the sustainability of conservation practices that these observations raise in the concluding part of the book.

One of the objectives of our comparative work across these differ-ent fields was to consider shared responses to common problems across them. One of the common issues that emerged for our group of partners related to the maintenance and preservation of data. Data – often meta-data related to other conservation objects in a collection – have increas-ingly come to be seen as proxies, or objects in need of conservation, in their own right. These issues emerged particularly strongly in the work-shop we co-organised with the British Library, the Alan Turing Institute and the Arts and Humanities Research Council Heritage Priority Area in June 2017 on this topic (see Harrison et al. 2017). While it is acknowl-edged that the future use of 'big' data, and the way in which it develops in relation to heritage practice, is likely to have transformative effects on how heritage conservation organisations collect, curate and care for both natural and cultural heritage, the question of how we should pre-serve such data and hold it (and related code and algorithms) to account is becoming increasingly important. Alongside the rise of algometric decision-making and public policy development, data science outputs themselves must become a matter of public record that need to be pre-served to ensure future accountability for the decisions and priorities that these data have been used to justify.

A further shared challenge we identified in all four case studies relates to the impact of bureaucratic protocols and the mismatch between national and international instruments, in the sense that they simultane-ously facilitate and constrain conservation efforts. For example, on the one hand, the Svalbard Global Seed Vault and Frozen Ark both largely owe their existence to developments that arose as a result of the signing of the 1992 multilateral Convention on Biological Diversity (United Nations 1992). On the other hand, the 2010 supplementary agreement to the Convention, the Nagoya Protocol on Access to Genetic Resources and the Fair and Equitable Sharing of Benefits Arising from their Utilization to the Convention on Biological Diversity (CBD 2011), implements strict guidelines on the collection and cross-border distribution and sharing of benefits from genetic resources in order to protect developing countries from potential exploitation. This has raised concerns for the Frozen Ark over the added red tape and the restrictions on research and conservation efforts that such added bureaucratic processes and legislations will inevitably create. Diversity conservation could thus be said to be both a product of, and simultaneously constrained by, such bureaucratic instruments and procedures.

Another common issue to emerge from our work is the significance of funding. Rather than the level of endangerment, it is often funding that determines conservation priorities, and the urgency and forms of action that are taken in relation to different kinds of endangered objects, places, practices and species. In many ways, this is also an artefact of the neo-liberalisation of conservation (a point developed in relation to bio-banks in Chapter 6), but it gives many of the agencies that are tasked with the conservation of natural and cultural diversity an additional impetus and urgency in relation to their work. Time may be 'running out' for the objects, species, places and practices such agencies seek to preserve, but it is also sometimes 'running out' for those agencies themselves. Insofar as such practices actively build future worlds, it may not be so much the meek, but the charismatic and cute that will inherit the Earth, because it is far easier to raise public and private funds for them. Such observations have an important role to play in rethinking both natural and cultural heritage preservational practices and their roles in remaking more or less diverse planetary futures.

We noted in the introduction to this part of the book that the fields of diversity conservation are strongly normative ones, in which the inherent value of diversity is rarely questioned. What we discovered in our comparative analysis is that what that diversity *means* and the different kinds of *actions it mobilises* are in fact highly variable. It is clear that the units by which diversity is monitored – be it landscapes, plant or animal species, languages, cultures – are only ever as diverse as the categories that are devised to enumerate that diversity. These categories are, in turn, often produced to measure absences or endangerment of diversity. Not only does this inflect the conservation of heritage diversity with its own kind of pathos or yearning for completion, in which the collection can only ever be an incomplete and diminishing sample – which we have referred to as an 'entropic' view of the relationship between diversity and time – but it also produces what Jacques Derrida (1996) might characterise as its own kind of 'archive fever', in which these different repositories and conservation activities multiply and reproduce. So, for example, during the time we worked on this book, a new global seed vault, which largely replicates the function of the Svalbard Global Seed Vault, opened in India. Located 17,300 feet above sea level in the snow-covered Himalayas, Chang La Vault, India's own 'doomsday' vault stores five thousand duplicate seed accessions, and is at the time of writing (after the SGSV) the second-largest cold-storage seed bank in the world (Pal 2018). Similarly, in 2018, China opened its new National Gene Bank in Shenzhen, which aims to be the world's largest gene bank, with a 'library' of ten million samples of animal, plant, microorganism and human body cells, that partially replicates the work of the Frozen Ark.[2] This replication and duplication of collections raises questions of the sustainability of heritage practices (see also Harrison 2013b), a subject to which we will return in the overall conclusion to the book.

We also suggest that different ways of understanding diversity produce quite different templates for collecting, ordering and governing heritage, and hence produce quite different future worlds as part of the heritage 'pluriverse'. We have shown how certain kinds of conservation activities normalise the selection and isolation of certain kinds of conservation targets, and specify particular management regimes that should be applied to them. In doing so, each practice is selective – certain objects, plants, DNA samples or languages are selected for documentation, preservation, conservation and management over others, and in this process are selectively transmitted into future worlds (while others are not). The claims of heritage to resource the future are not simply clichés – these activities provide material and discursive raw materials for future speculative world-making. An example of this is the emergence of scientific de-extinction practices as a result of the discovery and development of DNA cryopreservation and the implementation of DNA biobanks globally.

This raises the question of what heritage might look like in the *absence* of biodiversity or cultural diversity as conservation targets. This question is quite difficult to answer, because the idea of heritage itself is so completely tied up with the question of diversity and endangerment that it is difficult to disentangle them from one another. However, we are aware that alternative ways of conceptualising obligations to the future are present in a range of different contexts. For example, Deborah Bird Rose (2003) worked with Australian Indigenous New South Wales National Parks and Wildlife Service staff to develop alternative ways of thinking about national park biodiversity conservation and management based in kinship relationships, in which organising principles associated with notions of familial relations with the world based on ideas of respect, loyalty and care might underpin radically different models of conservation practice. Importantly, these models are equally concerned with more familiar notions of sustainability (see the discussion in relation to the Brundtland Report in Chapters 1 and 2).[3] These to some extent mirror Donna Haraway's (2015, 161) suggested rallying cry for the Chthulucene:[4] 'Make Kin Not Babies!', which she proposes in her discussion of the need to find new, more sympathetic relationships with the world in the light of the recognition of the widespread impacts of anthropogenic ecological and climatological change on both ourselves and the multiple other species with which we share worlds. As such, she proposes less genealogical ways of understanding kinship and more contextual ones, based on the need for cooperation to help reconstitute 'refuges' and to help rebuild damaged, collaboratively constituted worlds. Such models force us to rethink the normative modes of diversity conservation and the values and relationships that are produced and reproduced by them.

We hope we have also shown why, and in what ways, these different 'templates' (by which we mean different 'transactional realities', or different ways of defining and making diversity quantifiable) for understanding diversity and its relationship to heritage 'matter'. We use the term 'matter' here in two ways – both in the sense in which they 'count' and also in the sense in which they are material worlding practices, 'matter*ings*', which help compose and hold together different kinds of material and social worlds. It is only through a critical and comparative engagement with such practices, their associated transactional realities and governmental rationalities – and the collecting, ordering and governing practices that arise from those governmental rationalities – that we can begin to understand how such practices 'matter' in both senses of the word.

Our work has also raised important issues that relate to, and cut across, the book's three other themes. Diversity is often collected to manage *uncertain* futures. In the examples of the biobanks discussed in this part that articulation of managing biological diversity to secure against future uncertainty is explicit. But we have also seen how the futures that different forms of diversity are being managed *for* also change, as in the case of the SGSV mentioned above. This brings us to our next point, which is that diversity can be seen to have its own form of ontological *profusion* problem. We see this in the duplication and replication of conservation targets across different repositories, and the formation of multiple proxies and multiple methods of conservation (for example, *ex situ* versus *in situ*) for the same conservation targets. Diversity collecting also often seems to work against the recognition of transformation/change in the ways in which change is articulated as threatening or non-normative (as in much heritage), but diversity collecting does in fact often accommodate or even encourage change, resourcing speculation and the production of new futures, and in this sense connects with the work on *transformation* in Part V. We will return to discuss these cross-cutting points in the concluding part of the book. It is to the questions of profusion that are raised by heritage to which we will next turn.

Notes

1. Statsbygg, the Norwegian Directorate of Public Construction and Property, is a government agency that manages property owned and operated by the government of Norway.
2. Current Frozen Ark director Mike Bruford was involved in advising on the establishment of the Chinese National Gene Bank.
3. Rodney Harrison worked for the New South Wales National Parks and Wildlife Service, and was involved in the research group that commissioned this study.
4. Haraway (2015, 160) uses this term in complement to the terms 'Anthropocene', 'Capitalocene' and 'Plantationocene', as a 'name for the dynamic ongoing sym-chthonic forces and powers of which people are a part … These real and possible timespaces are not named after SF writer H.P. Lovecraft's misogynist racial-nightmare monster Cthulhu (note spelling difference), but rather after the diverse Earth-wide tentacular powers and forces and collected things with names like Naga, Gaia, Tangaroa (burst from water-full Papa), Terra, Haniyasu-hime, Spider Woman, Pachamama, Oya, Gorgo, Raven, A'akuluujjusi, and many many more. "My" Chthulucene, even burdened with its problematic Greek-ish tendrils, entangles myriad temporalities and spatialities and myriad intra-active entities-in-assemblages – including the more-than-human, other-than-human, inhuman, and human-as-humus.'

Cross-theme knowledge-exchange event 1

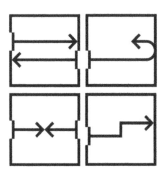

9
The hundred-thousand-year question

First cross-theme knowledge-exchange workshop, 8–11 March 2016, Forsmark and Stockholm, Sweden

Sefryn Penrose, Rodney Harrison, Cornelius Holtorf and Sarah May

When we decide to conserve something for the future, we need to think about where we will store it. How will our storage facilities do the work of conservation? How long will they be there? What kind of futures are made by doing this? How will these facilities be known, interpreted and used in the future?

Our first project-wide knowledge-exchange workshop took place 8–11 March 2016 in Forsmark (Östhammar Municipality) and Stockholm, Sweden (see Figures 9.1 to 9.12 at the end of this chapter). Organised by Sarah May, Rodney Harrison and Cornelius Holtorf, in collaboration with Sofie Tunbrant from the Swedish Nuclear Fuel and Waste Management Company (SKB) – the company charged with the disposal of nuclear waste in Sweden – the project group and invited project partners and guests engaged in a series of site-based tours, workshops and talks. Our group of around 25 academics and practitioners visited the site of Sweden's repository for short-term radioactive waste, which is also the proposed site of the final repository for high-level radioactive waste that is to last at least one hundred thousand years (see further discussion in Part IV, Uncertainty). Such repositories, like museums and seed banks, are examples of *ex-situ* conservation. Together, we aimed to explore the different kinds of sites, practices, architectures, concepts and technologies involved in conservation for the future.

We asked our participants to think about the differences and similarities between their respective fields of conservation, and their practices and processes. We asked how the range of different architectural and technological forms across the various domains in which they work might influence these practices, and the values and meanings attributed to the objects contained within them. We also asked each participant to bring an object that they might want conserved for a hundred thousand years – the period that SKB must envisage for the safe management of nuclear waste – as a focal point for various workshop activities over the course of the week.

SKB brought us to the site in which tunnels underground will become vaults for the safe storage of the carefully prepared and sealed copper canisters of spent fuel, a hundred thousand years into the future. With this very real task in mind, overlooking the site of the vaults, the team used the objects that they had brought in a *thought experiment*: envisaging what we really mean when we talk about preserving things into the future. Do we think enough about who the people of the future that we claim to work for *are*? And what will those future people actually *want* of the heritage we preserve for them?

With these objects in front of us, these questions became stark in their relevance to the work of the Heritage Futures team and our project partners. Some had chosen objects that represented their work: Mark Nesbitt from the Royal Botanic Gardens at Kew in London brought fair trade dark chocolate, representing both the heritage of the Earth's botanical resource, and also the cultural memory of its use and recent work to promote its 'fair trade'. Åsmund Asdal of NordGen, and responsible for the Svalbard Global Seed Vault, brought barley, sealed in the aluminium envelopes that keep the seeds dry and safe in the frozen vault at Svalbard. Others chose items more personal to them: Heritage Future's Sarah May brought her son's milk teeth; Boris Wastiau, who directs the Musée d'ethnographie de Genève (MEG), brought a copy of his first monograph, illustrative of his career, the pattern of work in his discipline and, in its essence, a contribution to knowledge – a sly nod, he admitted, to the vanity of heritage. Others sought to select something illustrative of the era in which they had lived: co-investigator Sharon Macdonald brought a selfie stick, purchased especially for the event, and indicative of technologies and materials of our era and also of its societal practices. There was a playful aspect to some of the objects – participants wanted to play tricks on the future: Sharon liked the idea of the future's potential problems in interpreting her object. But several participants wanted to be helpful: their objects were intended to be more than curiosities to the people of the future. Rebecca Green of the Frozen Ark brought a camping fork – a symbol of how we have lived, and a potential tool. SKB's Sofie Tunbrant brought a draft document designed to be distributed to the archives of the world, indicating the nature, history and location of Sweden's nuclear waste: a practical gift detailing one sort of storage of a challenging heritage. Åsmund's barley could be propagated by the people of the future and used to make beer. At least one of the participants, Anders Högberg, wanted to express from the outset his wariness of the desire to push into the future the things of now. He brought that thought wrapped in a box as his object.

The objects were photographed both digitally and with a Polaroid camera – a resurrected artefact itself – and in being so, the objects were already entering a realm of heritagisation: representative of a curatorial event that itself would become of the past. The peculiar process and 'look' of the Polaroid photographs gave all the objects a kind of intimacy that only some of them had arrived with: a layer of affect representative of their very recent past – their selection from shelves, shops, bedrooms, jewellery boxes; their journeys; and their arrivals at Forsmark.

The workshop was augmented by keynote talks by Martin Kunze on the Memory of Mankind project – another kind of repository of heritage – and by Jon Lomberg of the One Earth: New Horizons Message project. Both projects imagine – even materialise – the projection of the world's knowledge resource into an uncertain future. Over the course of the workshop, participants increasingly saw their work as making futures, rather than conserving pasts, and we recognised that these futures were not all the same as each other's.

At the end, Mark Nesbitt invited participants to consume the chocolate he had brought. It was an apt ending to our first knowledge exchange, the first engagement of our partners with each other, and with the big questions of the future with which the research programme aimed to wrestle.

The objects themselves can be viewed in the short film available at https://vimeo.com/187859927. A film, *Gifts to the Future (Episode 1)*, covering the entire workshop is available at https://vimeo.com/178724619.

Figure 9.1   Swedish winter landscape, with the nuclear facilities of Forsmark in the background (photograph by Rodney Harrison).

Figure 9.2   On site at Forsmark, Inger Nordholm of SKB explains where the company intends to deposit Sweden's nuclear waste for millennia to come (photograph by Antony Lyons).

Figure 9.3 The planned repository for spent nuclear fuel at Forsmark (image by Lasse Modin, courtesy SKB).

Figure 9.4 Exhibition of the results of a thought experiment: all participants were asked to bring an object that they might want conserved for a hundred thousand years (photograph by Cornelius Holtorf).

Figure 9.5 Three gifts for the future, selected by Jon Lomberg (photograph by Cornelius Holtorf).

Figure 9.6 Åsmund Asdal's barley seeds, to be conserved for the future (photograph by Cornelius Holtorf).

Figure 9.7   Joint seminar in Stockholm: how can we learn from each other to inform long-term conservation practice across different sectors? (photograph by Cornelius Holtorf).

Figure 9.8   Artist Jon Lomberg of the One Earth: New Horizons Message project looking into his own space artwork (photograph by Sarah May).

Figure 9.9 Martin Kunze of the Memory of Mankind project sends greetings to the future (photograph by Cornelius Holtorf).

Figure 9.10 A member of the next generation of humans: co-investigator Caitlin DeSilvey's son, born on 8 March 2016 (photograph by Russ Johnston).

Figure 9.11 SKB's Sofie Tunbrant presents a message to the future (1) (photograph by Antony Lyons).

Figure 9.12 SKB's Sofie Tunbrant presents a message to the future (2) (photograph by Antony Lyons).

Part III
Profusion

In the face of a profusion of things – mass produced for mass consumption – what gets kept for the future?

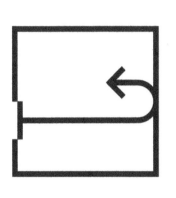

10
Too many things to keep for the future?

Sharon Macdonald, Jennie Morgan and Harald Fredheim

In some ways, profusion could be said to be an inexorable condition of heritage: there is more that could be conserved than possibly can be, at least according to current technological and space-time conditions. Moreover, as a mode of according value, heritage is selective – it operates by much not making the cut. Valuable past – heritage – swims in a sea of, and is effectively buoyed up by, all that sinks into oblivion (see also Chapters 1 and 2 in this book). In some contexts, however, there is a particularly heightened sense of there being a profusion of objects, places and practices – even 'a growing sense of too muchness', as Elizabeth Chin (2016, 7) puts it – that might be saved. What are the consequences of such profusion for heritage futures? How and in what ways do some things – and some of their accompaniments – rather than others come to be kept?

To make active selections about what should be conserved, a panoply of heritage institutions and practices has developed in most countries of the world. For example, UNESCO World Heritage listing – in which there is typically a profusion of applicants, relatively few of which are successful – is discussed in Part IV, Uncertainty. By contrast, however, the heritage institutions researched in Part II, Diversity – namely the Svalbard Global Seed Vault, Royal Botanic Gardens Kew, the Frozen Ark and the Endangered Languages Documentation Project – operate against a presumed backdrop of diversity loss, and thus seek to preserve as much of the perceived dwindling profusion as possible.

In this part of the book, our concern is primarily with the keeping of material culture that takes the form of things or objects[1] – sometimes, as we show further below, variously labelled as 'stuff', 'treasure' or 'heritage'. We focus on museums – institutions that are culturally tasked with selecting which objects (and whatever else is presumed to go with them) are to be saved for posterity, and also on homes, where we look at domestic practices that shape what is kept for the future.[2] Although such domestic practices might initially seem to be less obviously about heritage-making, they are a key domain for determining what will be inherited by future generations. Moreover, this inheritance is not necessarily restricted to within families, but is also a source on which other kinds of heritage-making may draw. This is the case for the museum collections of contemporary (that is, of the present or recent past) 'everyday life' – usually called 'social history' collections in our primary geographical research location of the UK – that are the focus of our study, whose collections often contain objects that previously lived in people's homes (and were subsequently gifted to the museum or otherwise acquired by it). As such, then, we are looking here at two interlinked heritage domains – museum collections of contemporary everyday life, and homes – both of which, we contend, face a profusion predicament, namely, many more things that could potentially be conserved for the future than can be. We ask how, in the face of this predicament, do some come to be kept – to 'remain' or 'make it' into the future – while others are not?

The profusion predicament

In choosing the term 'profusion' rather than negatively loaded terms such as 'overload' or 'excess', or positively connoted ones such as 'abundance' and 'plenty', our aim was to keep the question of evaluation open – to be able to see whether and in which specific contexts having a lot of things from which to select between might be regarded as an advantage rather than necessarily as a problem. Nevertheless, the research was also framed in relation to a widespread contemporary popular discourse of concern about various forms of 'overload' and 'excess'. As Orvar Löfgren and Barbara Czarniawska (2012), who use the term 'overflow', describe:[3]

> 'It is simply too much!' has become a common complaint in contemporary Western societies, where many people often feel they are living in a situation of overflow because they have to deal with a steadily growing amount of commodities, technologies, and time constraints. Too much information, too many market choices, too many responsibilities, and too many social relations, is the common complaint.
> (Löfgren and Czarniawska 2012, 1–2)

In relation to the focus of our research, recent years have seen such concerns repeatedly raised in relation to objects in domestic contexts, especially in media coverage of cases of hoarding (Frost and Steketee 2011;

Herring 2014). Reality television series such as *Hoarders* in the US (first broadcast in 2009) and *The Hoarder Next Door* in the UK (first broadcast in 2012) are just one indication of a recent widespread popular interest in people with what is presented as a pathological attachment to stuff. Fuelling that interest seems to be a fear that many of us could find ourselves on the road to such a pathology, as James Wallman argues in his popular book, with the telling title, *Stuffocation* (2015, 99): we are collectively suffering, he claims, from 'a clutter crisis' and 'the dark side of materialism'. That many people are seeking a way out from this seems to be substantiated by the expansion of advice and services to help people to 'declutter' (see Belk et al. 2007; Wallman 2015; Newell 2014; Kilroy-Marac 2016), to find ways to 'cope with overload', or to adopt lifestyle strategies such as minimalism (Klug 2018). The books and television shows of Japanese tidying guru, Marie Kondo, have created a worldwide enthralment with her KonMari Method (a term based on her name), meaning to radically reduce the number of one's possessions by getting rid of those that do not 'spark joy'.[4]

While, as far as we are aware, museums have not adopted KonMari, or 'kondo-ing' as it is sometimes called, they have seen a growing discourse about insufficient storage space and a search for solutions to a perceived problem of expanding collections – solutions that include increased interest in and practice of 'disposal', that is, removing objects from collections. A survey of almost 1,500 museums in over a hundred different countries reported two in three saying that they lacked space, one in two complaining of overcrowded storage units, and two in five noting large backlogs of objects to be accessioned (ICCROM and UNESCO 2011). That one possible solution to this overcrowding might be getting rid of some objects seems to indicate, as Mirjam Brusius and Kavita Singh (2018, 13) note, that 'an important taboo that has long been part of the museum world seems to be dissolving'. When, in the course of our research, we brought a professional domestic 'declutterer' together with various museum staff and others to discuss issues of profusion, this struck a nerve and generated much interest, not only among those present (see Chapter 11).[5]

We should emphasise that, in holding this event, and in our research overall, our aim was not to help museums – or people in their own homes – to declutter, although for those seeking to do so, our research has something to say, for which see the final chapter of this part of the book (Chapter 15). Rather, our remit was to explore whether and in what circumstances profusion was an issue for museum staff and for people (who were not diagnosed as hoarders) in their home lives. We wanted to know how they chose what to keep, and also how, even in the absence of acts of choosing, some things survive into the future and others do not. What practices and evaluations were involved? What features of objects – such as their size, weight or durability – might also influence whether they would remain rather than be removed or leave? And what might happen – in theory at least – if some practices or ways of thinking were transferred from museums to homes and vice versa?

Although our research began with the idea that we currently face a particular profusion predicament, it could be argued that there is inevitably an abundance of objects – and even of kinds of objects (depending on quite how 'kind' is defined) – that might be collected by museums or kept in homes. There have always been more things that *could* be collected and kept than are actually preserved for the future. In the face of many things, there is still a question of what and how many will be *pulled into* homes or museums. Likewise, whether there is even seen to be a profusion of objects that might be kept is not simply an empirical matter, dependent on actual numbers of things. Rather, it is also perceptual – that is, whether a certain number of objects will be perceived as many, or a profusion, or not, is also in the eye of the (culturally and historically located) beholder. Moreover, it is not necessarily inevitable that even when there is a perception of there being an abundance of things, that this is regarded as a problematic 'too muchness'. That abundance may be relished, as seems to have been the case, for example, for nineteenth-century ethnological collectors (Penny 2002), and as could be said to be the case, perceptions of loss notwithstanding, for some of the domains discussed in Part II, Diversity. Furthermore, in some contexts it may seem quite obvious what to keep, there being a confidence about what should be selected from the profusion of possibilities. Likewise, what counts as 'too much stuff' for one person or institution can be very different for another (Miller 2008; Stevenson 2018).

Despite these caveats, however, we contend both on the basis of the widespread discussion of domestic hoarding, stuffocation, decluttering and so forth on the one hand, and museum anxieties about collecting strategies, storage space and disposal on the other – as well as on the basis of our empirical research – that it does make sense to talk about a contemporary profusion predicament in relation to certain kinds of things. Moreover, while the profusion predicament is undoubtedly perceptual – and a struggle with 'too much stuff' is something that those we studied discuss – it also has particular historical and cultural roots.

More and more things

Especially charged with causing stuffocation and other profusion problems are manufactured goods. While it is certainly not the case that these are the only things accused of causing problems for museums and homes, they are at the forefront of blame and of a wider, moralised discourse about 'too muchness', as Chin (2016) explains in her partly Marxist-inspired analysis. The background to this is the development of industrialised capitalism, which laid not just the foundations for being able to manufacture more and more things relatively quickly and easily, but also established an economic and social system that was based in the constant production of more things.

Technological advances, especially in relation to electronics, also fuelled the production of new things – further intensified by changes in production techniques, such as shorter production runs, which have increasingly allowed for more differentiated products aimed at more specific market segments, and for ever more rapid cycles of fashion, fuelling what is sometimes referred to as hyper-consumption or turbo-consumption (Campbell 2015; Schor 2008). Already, innovations from the 1970s, such as floppy discs and video recorders, have become archaeological curiosities, and one survey estimates that the range of different Android devices – numbering in the tens of thousands – increased six-fold between 2012 and 2015 (Mirani 2015). Fast fashion stores, such as H&M and Zara, have not only expanded massively worldwide, they bring new ranges to their stores every few weeks (Joung 2014).

Producing more things makes no sense, however, without people ready to buy them. In other words, we also need to understand why people might pull more and more things into their homes – at least temporarily. There is a considerable literature on techniques such as advertising that developed to encourage and sustain consumer demand (for example, Tungate 2007; Turow and McAllister 2009), as well as on developments such as fashion (for example, Wilson 2003; English 2013) and 'planned obsolescence' of manufactured goods, in order to help ensure that people would continue to buy afresh rather than just keep what they already have (for example, Tischleder and Wasserman 2015; Strasser 1999; 2015).

Nevertheless, the desire for new things should not just be taken as a given, the psychological phenomenon of 'new possession rush' notwithstanding (Campbell 2015). Rather, this itself needs to be seen within a wider positive cultural evaluation of the new and the novel, even while interest in and desire for the old and the antique are not necessarily displaced, and indeed may even be intensified as our own research below also shows. The increased purchasing of more things is enabled in part by a rise in overall incomes and a relative decrease in the costs of many products (Campbell 2015). More fundamentally, however, it also requires a desire to buy new things even before the earlier ones have become obsolete or worn out. Central here, as various sociologists have argued, are changing ideas about selves – with these now generally being less ascribed but instead more changeable, flexible, liquid or even multiple (for example, Campbell 1987; Giddens 1991; Bauman 2000; Bell and Hollows 2016; Hazir 2015). Objects are bound up with how people are seeking to define themselves, including imagining what they could potentially become in the future (Campbell 1987). This fuels consumption, as new products allow for fantasies of self-realisation; in effect, visions of new, future selves. At the same time, however, this does not necessarily mean that old things are just discarded, for objects are invested with many meanings, including as carriers of memories, emotions and relationships.[6] All of this, then, contributes both to the production of more and more things and also to the likelihood of individual people possessing more things over the course of their lifetimes than did people in pre-industrial times. Indeed, research shows that people living in industrialised Western countries today typically have vastly more objects in their homes than did earlier generations (Arnold et al. 2012).

As far as museums are concerned, the increase of manufactured and consumer goods relates most directly to those museums that collect such objects, which, as we have already noted, generally go under the label of 'social history' collections in the UK. Such collections are the focus of our research described in the following chapter. For museums more generally, however, the fact that they are expected never to get rid of anything once it has become part of their collections (even if, in practice, they do – see, for example, Lubar 2017), means that they are inevitably accumulative – they 'pile up' more and more (see Harrison 2013a, 2013b). Here it is worth noting that the great wave of public museums in the nineteenth and twentieth centuries coincides with capitalist production being in full swing – and thus with an expansion of commodities and consumerism (Pearce 1999; Lubar et al. 2017). On the one hand, museums seemed to help to legitimate a 'mania for collecting [in which] domestic collections flourished and remodelled interior spaces into esthetic and historic museums of themselves' (Maleuvre 1999, 4). On the other hand, however, perhaps they 'could act as a kind of moral antidote' to consumerism and its treating of things as ephemeral 'by illustrating careful and meaningful selection' (Macdonald 2006a, 86). In any case, over time, without processes of removing items from collections, these could only grow bigger, and in the face of worlds of things that themselves constantly expand – as do manufactured items – this could only lead to profusion.

In the case of social history collecting, however, it is not only the number of new things that causes the challenge – as became very evident in our research. Compounding the sense of a profusion predicament is the movement of which the development of social history itself was a part, namely, the democratising attempt to collect from a wider range of the population. While the early social history movement called for attending to the lives of the working class and of women, this has been expanded to many other forms of social diversity, such as of racial and ethnic heritage or of sexuality, often expressed as 'communities' (Macdonald and Morgan 2018a). This recognition of the worth of collecting more histories from more and diverse communities has, then, also led towards museums seeing more and more things as not just possible candidates but even as desired items for collecting, as we discuss further below.

Alternative responses to profusion

Faced with more and more things, the following options – alone or in concert – are logically possible: (1) acquire and keep as many as possible, inevitably in more crowded conditions – that is, allow more and more to enter into the home or museum; (2) avoid acquiring more or only do so very selectively at low numbers; (3) expand or improve methods of storage (so as to be able to acquire and keep more); (4) get rid of some things that have already been acquired. As we will see in the chapters that follow, all four of these can be seen – to different degrees and with fascinating twists – in both the museum and the domestic domains.

As noted at the beginning of this chapter, selecting certain things as worth keeping for the future, and putting effort of care into conserving them, is to accord them value (Heinich 2009; 2011); and this has its correlate in that those not selected – or that are deselected through getting rid of them somehow – are not valued or are devalued. And because objects are often associated with people, non-selection or divestment of some kinds of things is easily regarded as a devaluing of particular people, memories and histories. This makes selecting what to keep for the future and, even more emphatically, deciding what no longer to care for, or to actively get rid of, so fraught. As Petra Beck (2016, 127) puts it: 'dealing with things always means dealing with relations'.

A significant literature across a number of disciplines has been devoted to theorising relationships between keeping and disposal, especially the ways in which value is constituted in relation to that deemed waste or rubbish (see especially Hetherington 2004; Gregson 2011; Lucas 2002; Thompson 1979; see further discussion in Chapter 2). In a context of escalating production and consumption – and ensuing profusion of things – questions of waste and sustainability become all the more pressing. The options are not, however, simply limited to the either/or choice of keeping or disposing. As we will see in Part IV, Uncertainty, for example, even that which has been 'disposed of' may well endure for a long time. And as we see in both Part II, Diversity, and Part V, Transformation, there is a wide range of forms of keeping and divesting, constituting, in effect, a spectrum or repertoire of possibilities.

Below, we briefly highlight something of this repertoire, as illustrated in existing literature relating to domestic and museum contexts. This can be seen as both background and supplementary to the empirical research that we present in the following chapters.

Repertoires and relativities of domestic keeping and disposal

In her work on domestic practices, Nicky Gregson (2011) chooses to use the term 'ridding' in order to illuminate the range of forms that disposal of objects might take. As she and others emphasise (for example, Crewe 2011; Appelgren and Bohlin 2015a; 2015b; Bohlin 2019), how and to where something is got rid of, including how irretrievably, can be highly meaningful and carefully differentiated. This is nicely illustrated, for example, in a recent paper by Melanie Lovatt (2015), in which she discusses the struggles – the 'push and pull' – and often nuanced decision-making over which 'trajectories' items from a deceased relative take – what is given to whom, what goes to the charity shop and what is thrown away.

Just as 'ridding' may cover a wide range of different practices, so too may 'keeping'. Visibility and display – and often subtle and shifting differentiations of value – are at issue too, as is shown, for example, by Drazin and Frohlich's (2007) study of which photographs are framed and which are left unframed and stuck with magnets on to the fridge in English homes. Drawing on museum practices, whether objects are arranged into a collection, and how they are cared for and displayed, can also be an indication not just of how they are valued but also of specific personal histories, memories and relations (Belk et al. 1991; Pearce 1998; 1999; Elsner and Cardinal 1994; Martin 1999; Shamash 2014). So too can the designation of some objects as heirlooms (for example, Joyce 2000; Cieraad 2010), souvenirs (for example, Stewart 1993; Hitchcock and Teague 2000) or other special carriers of memory. It is perhaps no surprise that there has been increased use of the term 'curation' in contexts including the domestic in recent years (for example, Balzer 2015; Bhaskar 2016) – offering as it does a mode of careful selection and arrangement of things in contrast to supposed 'overload' – and we deploy this below, too, in part in order to highlight the links between domestic and museum practices. A further instance of curation, in its original sense of care, is the tending to objects at home, including their repair, maintenance and preservation (for example, Gregson et al. 2009; see also http://repairacts.net), which can be seen as at least partly analogous to conservation and restoration within museums.

Attention to storage practices encourages understanding the home, as Cwerner and Metcalfe (2003, 229) put it, 'not simply as a place for living' but as 'a set of spaces, channels, and flows, as objects and people find their way into, through, and sometimes out of' it. Moreover, storage constitutes an interesting and often liminal value space for domestic objects, as both Sasha Newell (2014) and Sophie Woodward (2015) argue in their respective discussions of 'closets, attics, basements, garages, and storage units' (Newell 2014, 209). The possibilities for further liminal keeping have been expanded in recent years by the development of commercial self-storage facilities. In the US, which saw the first such facilities in the 1960s, one in ten households now uses them, in a total storage area equivalent to three times the size of Manhattan Island (Eldrige 2017; see also Bell 2013). In Europe, where the development is more recent and not so intense, there has been a sizeable increase in self-storage, with the UK accounting for nearly half of the use of self-storage (FEDESSA 2018; SSAUK 2019). In ethnographically exploring practices of using commercial self-storage facilities, Petra Beck (2016) productively plays with the term 'self-storage' to trace the kinds of selves that are created through what is located and done there, arguing that storage and discarding should be regarded as creative processes alongside acquisition. Others too point to the sometimes complex considerations, as well as the emotions, involved in selecting the fate of certain things, be it giving them to friends or relatives, or to charity shops, sending them for recycling or reuse (see also, for example, Appelgren and Bohlin 2015a; 2015b; Bohlin 2019), putting them into the bin, or even – as we will see below – taking them to museums.

Repertoires and relativities of museum keeping and disposal

In museums too there is a spectrum of forms of keeping. As in homes, there is the issue of whether things are kept in view or out of sight. For museums in the UK, the issue of objects not on open display has come to be increasingly politicised since the 1980s, when neo-liberal audit culture approaches cast things not on public display as wasteful (Macdonald and Morgan 2018a), although this has taken on a different political inflection in relation to repatriation debates (see Brusius and Singh 2018; and see also Tythacott and Arvanitis 2014). So-called 'visible storage' – in which large numbers of objects are displayed openly to the public more or less as they would be in storage – making objects accessible via digitisation, and various forms of 'revisiting' stored collections, have been some of the major responses to this (for example, Griesser-Stermscheg 2013; Brusius and Singh 2018; Reeves 2018; Thiemeyer 2018; Macdonald 2020). Alongside these attempts to open up the collections, however, are others, such as the increased tendency to separate stores from exhibition spaces, and often to locate the former at considerable distances from the museums (often in warehouses on industrial estates) and from people likely to visit (if this is even allowed). The physical organisation of objects within museum storage is reflective not only of various classifications, but also influences the accessibility of objects – such as which are on high shelves or at the back of drawers – and their 'findability', as well as influencing how many objects can be stored within a given space. The Musée d'ethnographie de Genève (MEG), for example, has reorganised much of its collections by size and conservation requirements, rather than by the more usual typology of geographical area, in order to maximise the number of objects that it can store.[7] Visibility and access are also shaped by infrastructures of information, as provided by the structuring of databases, categories and metadata, content and degree of detail of what is recorded (Geismar 2018). Furthermore, there are relativities of keeping constituted by the specific ways in which objects are cared for and preserved, which contribute to how likely certain objects are to make it into the future and for how long.

Ridding of objects from museum collections is a subject that is often said to be 'controversial' (NMDC 2003, 3; Simmons 2015), with the term 'disposal' having been called a 'dirty word' (Goldstein 1997; Vecco and Piazzai 2015), 'never to be uttered aloud' (Greene 2006, 7). Nevertheless, at the same time as wider discourses of problematic domestic profusion have come on to the agenda, so too has disposal from museums (see Chapter 11, and Macdonald and Morgan 2018a; Morgan and Macdonald 2020). As in domestic contexts, removing things from collections may take a range of forms. As set out in the ethical guidelines of the Museums Association (2015), the first recourse should be to try to 'transfer' an item to another museum – thus allowing for its reuse and, in effect, as with gifting domestic items to relatives, keeping it in the family. 'Deaccession' refers to the formal process of an object no longer being part of a collection – an action that does not necessarily physically remove it from the museum space. Equally, it is possible for an object to remain legally part of a museum's collection while being physically moved elsewhere, such as for long-term loan, as is sometimes also done as a form of repatriation. And while 'disposal' is a generic term for both legal and physical removal from the collections, the term 'rationalisation' is increasingly used, surely at least partly in order to sound less terminal. Alongside these, there have also been a range of other, sometimes creative, approaches, such as forms of reusing (Morgan and Macdonald 2020).

Staying and leaving

Pervasive in the literature briefly reviewed above is language that presumes human agency and intentionality – even if authors sometimes recognise the agency of things. Terms presupposing human agency include 'acquiring', 'keeping', 'holding on to' and 'conserving' on the one hand, and 'disposal', 'ridding', 'letting go' and 'divestment' on the other. In some contexts, these certainly are appropriate, as, for example, when museums are undertaking 'deaccession' of objects in their collections or people are 'decluttering' their bedrooms. We therefore use such terms when such intentionality appears to be involved. But as our research below shows, sometimes things just 'stick around' – that is, they are not so much actively 'kept' as merely 'staying put' – or they 'disappear', perhaps lost, or somehow 'leave' (albeit more often a home than a museum), without this being part of a conscious human act of 'removal'. For this reason, we also supplement the existing vocabularies, where appropriate, with terms that refer to objects as variously 'staying' or 'remaining', 'leaving' or 'departing'.

So, not only what is selected and kept, but also what somehow 'sticks around' or 'remains' into the future, as well as what does not manage to 'make it' or 'stay', in the face of the multitude of things, is the focus of the profusion research. How we conducted the research is described below.

The profusion study

As noted above, we primarily conducted our research in and on the UK. Issues of full museum storage – and discussion of ways of addressing this – have been voiced especially strongly in the UK, and within Europe the UK is at the forefront of utilising self-storage facilities and offering professional decluttering services (see, for example, Wijsmuller 2017; Stevens 2018). The Association of Professional Declutterers and Organisers, UK, was founded in 2004 (www.apdo.co.uk/our-organisation). Our reading and consultation of documentary sources, such as museum policy documents and statistics on self-storage, however, was wide-ranging and not restricted to the UK, and we also undertook some direct investigation of cases elsewhere, including in Germany, China, New Zealand and Switzerland.[8] Our research beyond the UK suggests that concern with profusion, and looking for ways of dealing with it, is widespread, although there can be significant differences between countries with respect, for example, to the legal frameworks for removing objects from museum collections or infrastructures for recycling. Analysis of this is beyond the scope of this particular research, however, and the following chapters focus on the empirical research conducted in the UK. Each chapter also explains the research methods adopted for each domain in more detail.

In outline, however, for both the museum and the domestic dimensions of the research, we undertook wide literature and general research, including attending events of relevant organisations, and coupled this with more targeted ethnographic research. The latter, conducted primarily by Jennie Morgan, involved more in-depth discussion, and witnessing of infrastructures as well as practices. One feature of our ethnographic approach was to allow, as far as possible, respondents to raise their own issues and concerns rather than to remain constrained to questions framed by us. For this reason, we did not separate off a specific study of 'the digital', but were concerned instead to see where this topic arose in relation to our more general interest in what people keep for the future and how they keep it.

Most of the museums that we researched ethnographically were independent or local authority museums with social history collections. Part of our rationale here was that compared with larger or national museums, smaller or more local ones tend to be less studied and reported upon. We were also already aware that many such museums face storage constraints – although we did not yet know to what extent, or quite what the implications might be in practice. The research included interviewing museum staff and those in museum organisations, as well as some longer fieldwork and filming. Subsequent to this, and conducted primarily by

Harald Fredheim, further contextualisation was also undertaken through a survey, its analysis and a structured knowledge-exchange event conducted with museum staff.[9] The aim of this mix of approaches was to be able both to hear the spoken rationales for what was being selected for the future and to see something of the infrastructures and practices involved.

With respect to domestic practices, the approach was also mixed and selective. As it was necessarily small scale, it was shaped not by trying to cover particular demographics but, rather, focused on instances of personal keeping or ridding, especially at 'critical life moments' – such as moving home or dealing with the belongings of a deceased family member. At such moments, decisions about whether to keep certain items or not come to the fore, allowing for investigation of the possibilities contemplated as well as those actually taken.

What follows in this part of the book

By looking at two interrelated, cultural domains – museums and homes – that face particularly acute dilemmas over the profusion of possibilities regarding what to keep for the future, we seek to show the practices, assumptions and struggles involved in each. Two substantial chapters discuss what we call curating museum profusion (Chapter 11) and curating domestic profusion (Chapter 13) in turn. As has been noted by various commentators recently, in popular culture, the language of 'curating' has increasingly been extended beyond the sphere of museums and galleries (Balzer 2015; Bhaskar 2016). In an analysis that complements our own, Michael Bhaskar (2016) writes of this as a response to 'a world of excess'.

In these chapters, then, we first outline the methods deployed in each domain in more detail, before discussing how profusion is experienced in each. This is followed by attention to the strategies for dealing with profusion, which brings processes and practices of acquisition, keeping and disposal – as well as ways in which things might also otherwise remain or depart – into view. In both cases, we give particular attention to storage – as infrastructures of keeping and containing – and to the digital – so often imagined as a way of potentially 'solving' the dilemmas of material profusion.

The two visual essays (Chapter 12 and Chapter 14) focus respectively on each domain, probing particular aspects of the research in more depth, highlighting some of the specific methodologies and collaborative approaches that we employed. Chapter 12 does so in relation to the survey of museums and an interrelated knowledge-exchange event, and explores especially the question of how museum staff experience profusion, thus building on the previous chapter. Chapter 14 looks at an arts–research collaboration that invited individuals to share reflections on their relationships to objects, and ideas about selecting and keeping them for the future, so complementing the material presented in Chapter 13, 'Curating domestic profusion'. In the final chapter of this part of the book (Chapter 15), we seek to look across the two domains and reflect on how approaches to profusion within each might potentially be deployed in the other, and even, perhaps, elsewhere. Are we doomed in our struggle with the profusion of things, or are there sources of hope?

Notes

1. There is a considerable but far from consensual literature on the use of these terms (and other linked ones, such as 'artefacts', 'possessions', 'stuff'), with various differentiations being made (see, for example, Pels et al. 2002; Morgan 2011; Brown 2015; Macdonald 2020). Here, we do not seek to impose stringent definitions, and we are attentive to how they are used in the domains that we research. Having said that, we use the term 'objects' not only in the sense that it is formally used in museums, that is, to refer to items that are part of museum collections, but also more broadly to indicate specific items – from the broader mass of things or material culture – that are singled out, one way or another, as possibly worth selection for keeping. Such items are not necessarily 'material' in a narrow sense – for example, digital images might be collected in museums and homes. Nevertheless, our primary focus is on the material, although we offer some reflections on the digital too (including its material implications, such as its need for certain hardware that may also become redundant).
2. We use the terms 'domestic' and 'homes' – and sometimes 'personal' – to describe our research focus, which was mainly through attention to particular individuals and with reference to certain specific 'critical life moments', as we describe further in Chapter 13. As we did not much focus on whole households and their members and interrelationships, we chose not to use 'households' as we had done in the original research proposal.
3. Löfgren and Czarniawska claim that 'overflow' is evaluatively open, although they also write of it as something that 'must be "managed"' (2012, 1) and see 'excess, surplus, overspill' as 'synonyms'. They also make a good case for 'overflow' as a term with productive hydraulic metaphors and linkages. See also the visual essay by Antony Lyons (Chapter 26). For information about the Managing Overflow project, see also: https://gri.gu.se/english/research/mof+eng.
4. Her first book to be published in English was *The Life-Changing Magic of Tidying Up* (Kondo 2014). This has since been translated into many other languages and has sold more than ten million copies (www.mariekondobooks.com). See also: https://konmari.com/pages/about. In 2019, a television series called *Tidying Up With Marie Kondo* was launched on Netflix streaming service.
5. See: https://heritage-futures.org/curating-domestic-profusion-workshop/.
6. There is an immense scholarship on this, some of which we mention in the chapters that follow. Among the key works: for museums, see the work of Pearce (for example, 1992; 1994; 1999) and Dudley (2010); for domestic settings, see, for example, Csikszentmihalyi and Rochberg-Halton (1981) and Miller (2001; 2008).
7. We thank the museum's director, Boris Wastiau, for organising a visit of the stores.
8. We have reported briefly on these elsewhere: https://heritage-futures.org/travelling-future-taking-profusion-theme-new-zealand/; https://heritage-futures.org/interview-lili-fang/. The following includes reference to cross-theme considerations: https://heritage-futures.org/berlin-thought-experiment-heritage-futures-visits-carmah/.
9. Harald Fredheim joined the project in May 2018. Jennie Morgan took up a full-time lectureship at the University of Stirling in June 2018, continuing work on the project but at a necessarily scaled down extent.

11
Curating museum profusion

Harald Fredheim, Sharon Macdonald and Jennie Morgan

Figure 11.1 Pots and pans on a museum shelf (photograph by Jennie Morgan, courtesy of CultureNL Museums).

Imagine a museum storeroom lined with shelves and racks (such as in Figure 11.1). These are filled with boxes and objects, labelled by number and name. On one shelf sit a dozen or so radios, mainly from the 1950s, hefty things with dials and wood veneer. On another is a collection of similar looking copper and cast-iron pots and pans from the nineteenth century. A tall shelving unit is packed with ceramics – teacups, bowls, jugs, plates – and other, unidentifiable, things. A bedframe leans against one of the few bare areas of wall; a butter churn stands on the floor at the end of an aisle. In a corner, two tables and a desk with a computer are piled high with paperwork, ring binders, and yet more objects. A woman apologises when we enter: 'I'm so sorry about the state of this room. We're just in the process of trying to clear the mega-backlog. Not that I can claim this is new – to be honest, it's always like this!' She gestures us to sit down and tells us about what she describes as 'my big headache':

> It's just so hard to know where to begin – and where to end. There's so much that we *could* collect and that we *could* display, so many stories that we *could* tell. Already, we have so much. Actually, we even have so much that we haven't fully catalogued or researched yet – our backlog is pretty scary, well, as you can see – those things on the tables over there waiting to be catalogued are just part of it. And don't even ask about digitisation. We are hardly alone in this. So many museums are in this position. Our storage is already filled to bursting point, so it is really hard to justify collecting more. But at the same time, we have a duty to future generations to actually try and show the way things are today. Are there ways of putting on the brakes and saying enough is enough? You want to know what we collect and why – and it's a good question. But to be quite honest, I think that sometimes it's more a matter of having to decide what not to collect – not that that makes it any easier.[1]

At face value, museums can be seen as agencies for managing profusion. They are designed to hold, organise and present an abundance of things; glass cases and labels project a sense of cleanliness and order. This is what the public expects of museums, and what museums expect of themselves. As our research revealed, however, in the face of a profusion of things, museum staff may struggle to maintain such order – especially behind the scenes in storerooms. One of our survey respondents expressed, for example, that she is 'ashamed of the state of the collections at the moment so would prefer the public are not aware of the state of things'. While other museum staff who deal with collections – who today are often referred to as working in 'collections management' – may not share this feeling of shame, or may not do so to the same extent, our research showed clearly that a sense of struggle to select the 'right' things to keep for the future, and to care for the objects that already have been selected, is widespread.

In this chapter, we turn to our empirical research on museums to explore how staff working with museum collections experience the profusion of things that could be collected, how they address the manifestations of profusion they experience, and, more generally, how they go about making selections of which objects to save for the future.[2] As explained in Chapter 10, we identify these practices of selection as valorising – that is, they not only reflect value judgements but also, through selection, retention, care and disposal, create value (see Heinich 2009; 2011; Harrison 2013b). Below, we outline in more detail the methods used in our museum research, and discuss how the different methods have informed each other, before sharing some of our findings about how museums in the UK that collect everyday objects from the recent past or contemporary present perceive and address the profusion predicament. In doing so, we explore the professional practices of museum staff, providing their own views on how they decide what is significant enough to warrant keeping for the future. We also foreground the futures that staff see themselves working for, and reflect on the futures that current practices are creating.

Methods

The main empirical work done by the Profusion theme in the museums domain consisted of interviews with, and observations of, museum practice, a UK-wide survey and two knowledge-exchange events. The more qualitative research of interviewing and observing museum professionals was conducted first, providing a series of questions to be explored more quantitatively through a survey. These results were discussed with sector representatives, to provide further contextualising qualitative research material. We worked closely with the Arts Council England (Yorkshire) and the York Museums Trust, who provided an invaluable sounding board, helping us to formulate questions and approaches, as well as to network us with specific museums and organisations, and to participate in our theme-specific (as well as in one project-wide) knowledge-exchange events. The New School House Gallery, York (see Figure 11.2), acted as host for our first event – in which we invited Dr Zemirah Moffat, an anthropologist and professional home 'declutterer', to collaborate with us on leading a workshop for museum directors, collections staff and academics researching in related areas.[3]

The 'domestic declutterer meets museum staff' event was an element in a raft of research approaches designed to help us grasp how museum staff experience profusion, and their roles and possibilities in relation to it. Others included going to conferences and workshops of museum organisations, where we networked with key policymakers (such as the

Association of Independent Museums, the UK Museums Association, and the Collections Trust), especially when issues of contemporary collecting or disposal were on the agenda; reviewing literature produced by the sector; and visiting specific museums. The latter entailed meeting with various museum staff, sometimes more than once, and usually visiting storage spaces, in which case photography was generally used alongside observation and semi-structured interviews. One focus for this qualitative work was an in-depth case study with York Museums Trust, which facilitated visits to several of their museums including, repeatedly over a period of six weeks, the York Castle Museum (a local museum of items of everyday life of the recent past). We supplemented this case with a range of short visits to another eight museums with social history collections or departments, including those that had undergone considerable reorganisation and refinement of their collecting approaches. Our fieldwork provided opportunities to observe museum staff carrying out a review of collections, developing what they called 'rationalisation procedures' (to help refine what should be kept and what disposed of), and making decisions about disposal. This resulted in 21 recorded interviews, each lasting between one and three hours.

Figure 11.2 The New School House Gallery, York, host of our first Profusion theme knowledge-exchange event in 2016 (photograph by Jennie Morgan).

To help contextualise and further expand upon this qualitative work, we also undertook a survey on contemporary collecting and disposal.[4] This was designed with many open-ended questions in order to be used predominantly qualitatively. Distributed widely to museums in the UK through email lists, via social media and directly to museums whose websites suggested they might collect everyday objects from the present or recent past, it received 93 responses from individual museum staff. Although this provided some quantifiable results, the numbers are not large and there may be various biases in who responded, so we resist using exact values in their interpretation, as shown on the reproduced data discussion cards in our visual essay on sharing experiences and responses to museum profusion (Chapter 12). In a further knowledge-exchange event, at the National Railway Museum, York, results of the survey were made available for discussion by participants, who included survey respondents from a wide variety of museums, as well as represent-atives from a selection of other organisations. By discussing the results in this way, we were able to feed back reflections by participants into the research process, and thus to further enhance our understanding.

Below, we first address how profusion is experienced by museum staff in our research, before turning to their strategies for dealing with it. By highlighting the relativities and repertoires of keeping and disposal, and the reasons why objects otherwise remain in or leave collections, we hope to add nuance to debates about how many objects museums are collecting and disposing. Ultimately – by thinking in relation to the domestic domain, as well as other Heritage Futures domains – we seek to contribute to thinking further about how heritage-making in relation to profusion might be approached differently in the future.

Experiences of profusion in museums

> We also wanted to unearth the hidden treasures within our store, which had been obscured from us, possibly for decades, due to the sheer volume of material which had been collected.
>
> (Russell n.d., n.p.)

This statement, about the rationale behind a major review and ration-alisation project in the social history collection at the Museum of Lon-don, aptly illustrates how museum staff often describe profusion in their museums. Our research has identified three main sources of profusion in museums that together constitute the sense of 'too-muchness' we call the profusion predicament. These are: (1) the sense of there being many things that have not yet been collected, but might be worth keeping for the future; (2) an abundance of accessioned objects already in store; and (3) backlogs of acquired objects that are yet to be formally accessioned. We discuss each of these in turn below but first note how concerns about profusion arose post-1980 in UK museums.

The Museum Accreditation Scheme, which was launched in 1988 partly in response to the growing numbers of independent museums at the time, addresses potential profusion by requiring bespoke collections development policies that outline what museums do and do not collect, as well as regulating and documenting disposal procedures (see MLA 2004). A year later, a report called *The Cost of Collecting*, commissioned by the Office of Arts and Libraries (1989), claimed that 80 per cent of UK collections were in storage – a figure that was widely discussed as indicative of problematic over-collecting.[5] This became still more explicit when the National Museums Directors' Conference issued a report in 2003 with the title *Too Much Stuff? Disposal from Museums* (NMDC 2003). Other guidelines, such as the Museums Association's 'Code of Ethics' (2015), likewise include emphasis on careful selection and management of collections. (For 'effective' collections, see also Cross and Wilkinson 2007; Museums Association 2012.)

Although there has been a clear move towards more open discussion of deaccession and disposal, as we have charted more extensively elsewhere (Morgan and Macdonald 2020), quantitative studies (and also our own survey) do not demonstrate that this has resulted in a marked shift in collections development practice (Museums Association 2012). Nevertheless, we may be at a turning point. The Museums Association's 2018 *Museums Taskforce Report and Recommendations* argues that the defining challenge for collections development in museums is 'that many museums have full stores, [with] collections acquired inconsistently and gaps in collections knowledge'. Therefore, it is 'necessary to break the cycle of having too much material that is not being used or delivering public benefit, not enough information about what museums have, and insufficient capacity to manage collections and make confident and informed decisions' (Museums Association 2018, 5). The subsequent recommendations stress the need for museums to 'review the impact of collections development policy and practice over the last decade' and take 'a collective responsibility to resolve the gap between theory and practice' (Museums Association 2018, 6). So let us, then, turn to practice to explore how museums are experiencing and responding to profusion through the everyday performance of creating value and futures by selecting and caring for objects in collections.

All the things that might be worth keeping for the future

Choosing what to keep for the future is a daunting prospect, especially when doing so for society rather than for oneself. As one curator told us, 'the important thing as a curator is to try to be objective … and I think that is obviously where it's very different from what you might do in your normal house'. Despite this particular curator's aspiration to 'objectivity', many of the curators with whom we spoke expressed less confidence in there being an objective position – and many spoke instead in terms of 'stories', thus suggesting more subjective modes of selection, as we discuss further below. That 'contemporary collecting' was perceived to be an especially challenging form of collecting was also evident from responses to our survey. As a curator at a local authority museum put it, 'what is material culture in the twenty teens? I get that the Museum of London or the V&A might be able to make a reasonable stab at this but local museums? Might we end up with the twenty-first century equivalent of multiple Victorian mangles? Is that OK?'

There is also a growing awareness of the ephemeral nature and rapid pace with which things can come and go, which forces the issue of collecting despite uncertainties around which objects to keep for the future. As one curator who showed us the industrial history collection with which he works put it:

> One thing is that, in a way, we're too late now if we want to collect some objects. Some gaps in our collections will never be filled because there's simply nothing left, and perhaps decisions were made in the past about what should be kept and what shouldn't, which we might look back on now and say 'well, maybe we would have done it differently'. There's lots of things that have been preserved en masse – railway locomotives, traction engines … whereas there are other objects that we don't collect.

These connections drawn between concerns about selecting the 'right' objects to keep for the future and critical assessments of past collecting practices that contribute to current profusion predicaments are good examples of the future projecting we observed curators to be engaged in as they navigate profusion. Concerns about how past collecting has caused both 'gaps' and 'duplicates' in current collections shape how museum staff think about collecting for the future.

The local authority museum curator quoted above also explained that selecting what to keep was being made more difficult by mass production, not only because there are more things from which to choose, but because mass-produced objects seem to her to not be sufficiently meaningful for telling more local stories. Neither, however, does she regard very individualised or personal objects as sufficient to do this:

> Are objects instruments of reflecting social history and were they ever adequate to this role? In mass production era are they meaningful enough? In an LA [a local authority museum] your job is more or less about reflecting the history of your borough and its residents. But if nothing is especially borough-typical (everywhere has a Tesco for example) what do I seek? We did a project about loss and lost objects a couple of years ago and most of our youth group identified either a piece of jewellery someone had given them or their mobile and mobile charger as the things they cared about. I've no shade to throw on either of those but if my job is to tell the story of my borough then the very personal or the extremely ubiquitous somehow don't quite cover it for me.

The profusion of mass-produced items, and the accelerated appearance and disappearance of new things, is undoubtedly a challenge for many collections staff. How many models of mobile phones to collect was an example that was given several times. More recently, the sense that museums should also be collecting digital objects – whether computer games and software, images, videos, documents or social media – has added further to the profusion of things that could be collected, although one curator stressed that despite rhetoric that may suggest the relative 'newness' of digital collecting, this is something that museums have 'been dealing with for years'. Our research provided many and diverse examples that curatorial ambitions for such collecting could occur – especially that focused on social media associated with contemporary events (for example, 'Brexit' (the exit of the UK from the European Union), the Scottish Independence referendum, the Arab Spring, the Black Lives Matter and Me Too movements). As one curator responsible for digital collecting in her institution put it, 'contemporary collecting and digital is one, because digital is the medium to document contemporary stuff that's happening'. Continuing, she reasoned that, 'all these things are happening digitally now', which thus requires – in her view – museum collecting to respond in order to 'document' these social and political movements, as well as the everyday experience of them. Equally important, however, was curators' wish – and sense of duty – to collect in such a way as to represent greater social diversity. Collecting to address what were regarded as imbalances in previous collecting was frequently articulated as an ambition, or an area of practice being developed, although we found less evidence (in our fieldwork and survey) of such ambitions being fully integrated into collecting policies or practice in a way that curators themselves perceived to be entirely satisfactory. More typically – and paralleling the rise of 'cultural diversity' as a conservation target discussed in Part II, Diversity – it was expressed in terms of a need to collect objects from 'different communities' or as 'diversifying the collections' to be able to tell many different 'stories' in the future.

Accessioned objects already in stores

These ambitions of further developing collections and filling identified subject 'gaps', which were sometimes formalised as 'priority areas' in collections development policies shared with us, are complicated by the absence of gaps on most shelves in museum stores. These subject or conceptual 'gaps' or 'deficits' may also relate to changes in the kind of information being recorded about objects. It is now widely acknowledged, and is supported through our findings, that museums today want to present objects with more information about the individual lives and events with which they were entangled, or what is often referred to as 'telling stories'. Some collections staff tell us that this shift towards richer contextual information has been particularly influential in making existing objects in the collections less usable than they were previously. While the objects could illustrate a particular type or category they are now perceived as not having sufficiently relevant or significant stories to tell.

In the acquisition meetings that we observed, participants typically considered, discussed, and sometimes vigorously debated, the kinds of 'stories' that objects might tell. Objects regarded to hold potential to tell not only a story, but different kinds of stories, appeared to be especially appealing. Conversely, those items without a story, or with only one, were less likely to be collected, unless another feature added significance (such as being particularly rare; of use for researchers; holding social, historical or cultural value; filling a collections gap; or being needed for an exhibition). This strategy of seeking to acquire fewer material things overall, but ones that can tell more, and more diverse, narratives, is a prevalent response to managing profusion in museums. Coupled with the quest for more 'diversity' introduced above, this results in a situation in which – when evaluating both existing collections and what might yet be acquired – there is a sense of what one curator described as 'a great volume of material', but that it is at the same time potentially insufficient for the uses museum staff now intend for it. As one social history curator put it:

I think it's our instinct as curators to try to collect. Particularly in social history, there are so many different stories to try to tell and I think politically the focus on inclusion and trying to represent all communities, all people, all stories, is a real driver and we're very conscious of where the gaps are.

Despite widespread 'respect' for the decisions and actions of their predecessors – a point made repeatedly by our interlocutors – many museum staff working with collections referenced what they regarded to be poor collections decisions made in the past. Many professionals whom we visited and interviewed, and virtually all of our survey respondents, said that they have objects in their collections that they would not collect if building the collection from scratch. A curator in one of the museums we visited put it this way:

> We have really suffered from over-collecting of past curators in terms of people who have particular interests or even contacts, where it has meant that things have come into the collection that, perhaps, there's too much of one thing in terms of it being over-represented to the detriment of other areas that may have been neglected.

Another, rather bluntly, said: 'You think about the things that people have collected and you think "would I have collected those?" God, no, that doesn't tell the story in a way I want it to.'

Museum staff responding to our survey identified improving documentation and collections care as their primary responsibility to future curators and publics, and they were eager to pass on the collection 'in a better state' than it was in when they had received it. A collections manager at an independent former local authority museum in Yorkshire described how this commitment shapes her current practice:

> The disposal procedure is so time consuming and you're usually dealing with a 'the sins of our fathers' scenario where ill-informed and indiscriminate collecting in the past has led to masses of unsuitable material clogging up stores. So, my approach to collecting is to consider whether I will be creating similar problems for my successors, which encourages me to be much stricter when making acquisition decisions.

This collections manager explains how past collecting decisions not only weigh on current collections staff in the form of reminders of the fraught nature of selecting the 'right' objects to keep for the future,[6] but also how the very real physical manifestations of these decisions also present real challenges in fitting new acquisitions into already 'full' storerooms. A full museum store, as described in our opening vignette, is the most readily recognisable manifestation of profusion in museums, and one that adds to collection staff's experience of profusion as a predicament in several ways.

There is the pragmatic and very real challenge of not being able to fit more into what is already squeezed, with curators sometimes describing this to be 'a massive issue' or their organisation being 'at a critical level' in terms of needing storage. This not only reduces collecting (as the surveys we cited above illustrate) but may also shape what is collected. For example, we learnt from sitting in on meetings where decisions are made about possible acquisitions, that the size, storage implications (such as if items require specialist or conservation-grade enclosures) and present or anticipated future conservation needs are often all considered. Perhaps most challenging of all is that these needs are not always known for objects already in store, especially those that are yet to be catalogued and make up part of what is often referred to as 'backlogs'.

Backlogs of acquired objects yet to be formally accessioned

Documentation is a major concern for a large proportion of the collections staff with whom we have interacted, and collections reviews often highlight errors and absences in documentation systems, with forgotten objects sometimes being 'discovered' in storerooms. Many museums complain about having poorly provenanced items that may have no contextual documentation whatsoever. Some museums have not fully migrated their documentation from systems used in the past, especially if transferring from paper to digital records. Objects sometimes disappear in the cracks between systems, through records being lost or by not having been properly documented when brought into the collection. As a result, several curators we engaged with have described situations in which further collecting has been put on hold until they are able to 'get a handle' on their existing collections. Our survey also more specifically revealed that this is especially common in museums with large accessioning backlogs. This refers to objects that have been acquired – that is, been brought into the collection – but that have not yet been added to formal accession records. Many curators understandably feel it is irresponsible to add to a collection when they do not know what they already have and do not know when they will find the time to process objects that have already been selected:

I think looking back we're still dealing with the mass of acquisitions that came in, in the '70s and '80s. Accreditation has been a huge driver in helping us manage that in a consistent way and in a professional way and making sure that when something is collected it doesn't just arrive in the museum and then sit in a cupboard of doom – we have a number of cupboards of doom – for ten years and then people like us now come along and have to try to deal with that when we're lucky if there's an entry form, never mind any sort of cataloguing information. So, I don't think it's a bad thing that has stopped. There's a much more rigorous approach to the collecting we do now, so that the documentation is in place and we're not leaving black holes for our successors, but that all adds to the barriers, I suppose, to collecting in a wider way.

Many of the respondents to our survey explained that they could not give accurate figures about how many objects they collect and dispose of on average each year because the numbers fluctuate greatly and because the numbers of objects accessioned and deaccessioned do not accurately reflect how many objects are acquired and disposed of. This is because backlogs of objects that have not yet been formally accessioned in museum registers can be the main source of objects added to accession registers or removed from collections. One collections development officer responding to the survey explained that 'in 2017, 1,409 new records were created, but many of these would have been for objects that were acquired many years ago, but for which appropriate documentation had not yet been created'. These backlogs are recognised as a significant problem in the sector, and museums are required to have a plan for how they will be overcome as part of the accreditation standard. Their size is measured periodically in surveys administered by the regional Museum Development Network, and in 2018 the Collections Trust launched a programme of support to specifically help museums 'banish the backlog' (S. Brown 2019).

Strategies for addressing museum profusion

In the face of the profusion predicament, museum organisations, museums and curators – individually or in concert – have developed strategies for dealing with it. Some of these are relatively instrumental and formalised – namely policies and procedures for collections development, significance assessment and rationalisation (see Figure 11.3), whereas others are more by default or informal, such as not, or rarely, collecting due to lack of space.

Figure 11.3 Infrastructures for managing profusion include policies and procedures for collections development, documentation and significance assessment (photograph by Jennie Morgan, courtesy of York Museums Trust).

Making selections: Collections policies and assessments

Museums use collections development policies to outline what they do and do not collect. These operate primarily to limit what is collected and provide curators with institutional support to let some things go. Required for museum accreditation, they are also widely felt by our survey respondents to help them make better collecting and disposal decisions, most importantly by countering what they describe as 'individual bias' and the accepting of 'unsuitable donations'. One specific form of excess that these documents are considered to safeguard against is curatorial enthusiasm (or 'passion', as it was sometimes described) for collecting from narrowly focused areas in their subject. At one museum we visited, a registrar showed us one such example catalogued in the electronic database: a 'collection of 176 fruit wrappers' purchased from a local market.

Collections development policies outline what museums want to collect in quite broad terms. As in various other areas of cultural and natural heritage management, more specific tools have also been developed, especially what are called 'significance assessments' – in which individual objects' 'significance' is judged according to a range of criteria through formal processes (see Macdonald and Morgan 2018b). Unlike collections development policies, processes for formal significance assessments are not a requirement for accreditation and our results suggest that their use varies greatly across the sector. While some museums have shown us their formal templates, others report that they consider similar criteria, but through less formal processes, including curatorial judgement gained from accumulated experience of working with collections. Nevertheless, our survey results suggest that museums' processes for assessing significance, whether formal or informal, are overwhelmingly felt to help make better decisions. Common to these approaches is understanding the 'significance' of an object as the sum of its cultural values and its usefulness as a museum object.

Both collections development policies and significance assessments are positioned by museum staff to be more objective and collective mechanisms by which museums make strategic decisions about potential acquisitions. Several of our survey respondents mentioned that formal policies are helpful in relation to the sometimes diplomatically awkward matter of rebuffing an offered 'gift' – 'without putting donors off should they find other items of interest in the future', as one curator at an independent museum in Scotland put it.

Moreover, several survey respondents flagged that putting a collections development policy online helps keep unwanted donations from ever making it to the museum. While this might be the perception of museum staff, our homes study did not indicate that people who approach museums with donations are necessarily reading these policies, and (as we discuss in Chapter 13) typically approach museums motivated by other goals than helping them to acquire objects in identified priority areas.

Any such guidelines need to be put into practice – which might also bring them up against further material or unanticipated considerations. One curator we visited to talk to about social history collecting explained how she went about the process in ideal cases. First, she considers a new acquisition's 'relevance' to specific areas of the museum's collecting policy, or how it will 'enhance the collection' (including if it would address any perceived gaps or weaknesses). She then described a 'secondary' level of considerations, including 'the history of the object, its background and context' (or what is usually talked about as being 'provenance'), and also the proposed acquisition's 'use', including its 'display' and 'research' potential (or 'what we could do with it', as she put it). 'It can't just be something that you're just sticking in a box and never having display potential,' she summarised, adding that a new acquisition would be more likely to be collected if it had the capacity to 'open up different strands of potential interpretation' so that it could be 'used in very different ways' – that is, as we discussed above, tell multiple kinds of stories. In many ways, what is involved here is providing formal and informal procedures that help to remove the disquieting sense that one might be getting it wrong, including by limiting the extent to which decisions are felt to be 'subjective'. It is also about using documentation of processes to try to show future curators that 'we tried', as it was sometimes put to us.

Yet in practice, there can still be other considerations that come to bear. As we noted above, some curators described a tendency to be more lenient about accepting objects that do not take up much space. Moreover, as one curator from Scotland noted in response to our survey, '[policies] are guidelines and can still clearly be bent if you wish to acquire something, or conversely can be enforced to the letter if you don't. There is still flexibility in them, which is useful.' What is particularly interesting here is that he identifies the room that policies leave for subjective curatorial judgement as *useful*. While some curators find the seemingly objective nature of policies reassuring, others value the space they provide for individual judgements within this structure.

Infrastructures for containing it all: Collections review and storage solutions

During many of our visits to museums, we met collections staff either undertaking – or who had recently completed – collection audits (see Figure 11.4). One typical outcome of such audits is the reorganisation of the storeroom to maximise available space, and museum staff showed us, often with a sense of pride, newly installed dedicated 'storage solutions', such as archive boxes, modular shelves, enclosed units and sliding racks. Here, collections review, leading to storeroom reorganisation, is intended to address profusion in museums by literally attempting to better contain it all by improving storage systems. While on tours of museum storerooms, we learnt about different modes of storing collections, which revealed a wide spectrum from 'open' to 'deep' storage. The latter suggests that one profusion strategy might be a partial removal of objects by containing them in the farthest recesses of facilities, usually off-site from the museum exhibitions and offices of museum staff. Although we did not learn of any actual examples, staff also considered future possibilities for more 'joined-up' approaches to storage across the sector – for example, by housing the collections of several different museums from one region in a centralised facility. While collection audits, also called

Figure 11.4 A social history curator works in the storeroom at our partner organisation, York Museums Trust, on a collections audit. This process is sometimes used by museums to reorganise collections in storage (photograph by Jennie Morgan, courtesy York Museums Trust).

'reviews', are becoming increasingly common, there is no central or linked database for collections across the UK. We have repeatedly been told that it would help museums to act on their audits – either by adding or removing objects from their collections – if they had a better sense not only of what they, but also of what other museums, already have.

These kinds of themes were illustrated when we attended a professional training event in Manchester on the topic of collection reviews. Here, it was stressed that a collection review can lead to many different outcomes, which may or may not include disposal. This corresponds well with our broader results, which highlight that most reviews lead to a very small number of disposals, but instead focus on enhancing staff understanding of collections or lead to a reorganisation of storage. As a result, the term 'rationalisation' is increasingly used rather than 'disposal'. In one of the rationalisation projects we learnt about through our museum visits, this was explained by one curator as follows:

> This isn't a disposal project, it's actually the collections that are left behind. It's as much about them as what we're disposing. It's what we're keeping, we're doing it for those objects, really, as much as anything and so that is, for us as a museum, a very important outcome. That what we're left with is a refined collection. We want to be able to use it. It has research academic potential that we can start to release because we can manage it better.

As this quotation shows, while space is an important factor, rationalising collections is also about the capacity to care for and use objects effectively, not merely about having enough space on the shelves.

The digital

We remained open in our study to tracing if and how digital technologies were deployed in relation to profusion predicaments in museums. We found no instances in which objects were being digitised rather than physically kept by the museums in our study, and when we discussed this possibility with them, they usually responded negatively. 'Heavens no!' declared one, 'that wouldn't be right, would it? We are supposed to keep the real things.' Indeed, rather than solving any sense of a profusion predicament, digital objects and technologies generally seemed to exacerbate it.

They did so, first, by adding another set of 'objects' that might potentially be acquired. With regard to collecting social media using automated software, one curator surmised that 'you could easily binge collect'. Another curator saw such collecting as well-nigh impossible, as 'the digital can be so broad and it changes too fast'. Problems of collecting the digital were also seen as arising from the fact that the 'technology' and 'infrastructure' required to translate 'captured' digital content (such as tweets inputted into an Excel spreadsheet) from a mass of content into usable museum resources are not yet sufficiently developed. In addition, curators spoke about the difficulties of navigating copyright, or of the future preservation challenges of software and hardware required for using digital objects. One curator, who collected video games from the 1990s onwards, reasoned:

... all these hardware and software are now completely obsolete. Even if it was a video game from the '90s that was created on Windows, it was Windows 95. Windows 95 is totally incompatible to whatever Windows we have now ... So you either had to find a Windows 95 computer to extract the file and then simulate it to a Windows 2010, which has to be refreshed and integrated as Windows progresses.

Although there was a widespread sense that the digital could not replace collections of physical objects, the use of electronic and online databases is seen by many curators as helping to keep information that they believe should be collected about collection items.

Mostly, however, we encountered a sense that creating digital records, and digitising objects and information about them, were adding to, rather than ameliorating, the 'backlogs' discussed above. So, not only was the digital not regarded as a satisfactory solution for limited physical storage space, it was also pointed out to us that digital storage is not resource or cost free. 'The two big conceptions of digital is that digital is free or cheap', one curator told us, noting that 'people don't understand how big files are, or [that] you have to have different files, like your raw file or digital preservation file, and then your access files. That's a lot of storage'. For these and other reasons, then, the digital is considered – in its own ways – to be complex, desirable and offering some potential future avenues for addressing profusion, but also simultaneously adding to it.

Curating loss: Rationalisation, transfer and disposal

Permanently removing objects from a collection is increasingly recognised as an important element of responsible collections development, and the Museums Association's 'Disposal Toolkit' (2014) outlines how museums can go about doing this without breaching their 'Code of Ethics' (2015), which is enforced by accreditation. Despite efforts to facilitate permanently removing objects from collections, disposal is still widely considered a last resort. A curator at a local authority museum explained that she has 'a number of things earmarked for disposal and would follow the disposal criteria of the sector of course, but I am still currently hanging on to things as I don't quite feel ready'. This sense of not feeling ready, or the emotional difficulty of going through with disposal, is something we have come across repeatedly – also retrospectively, as in the case of a house steward at a National Trust property in South East England, who explained that she has 'had to accept the loss of items from the collections for good reasons, even though I found the process painful'. Such comments indicate that the emotional cost of letting go might even potentially be experienced as too great for museum staff to actually do it. We certainly learnt of objects that, although the formal decision had been taken to release them from collections, remained in museum storerooms, often awaiting a 'suitable' new location to be found. Curatorial concern with 'suitability' for future trajectories of objects perhaps reveals the kinds of affective and moral judgements underpinning the act of letting go.

The procedures that need to be followed – the forms to be filled in and the identification of possible new homes – can also, paradoxically, require such a degree of work as to render attempting to dispose of items more effort than museum staff feel able to undertake. This is why a documentation and collections officer in South West England retains hundreds of identical milk bottles. She explained that 'we don't need them all and being local they are of no interest to anyone else, which makes it simpler for us to leave them taking up space in the store than to attempt disposal'. While we had agreement to spend time observing a social history curator doing a collections rationalisation, with one intended outcome being identifying possible items for disposal, our visits were curtailed because the curator had to put this work 'on hold' as it could not be fitted in with other commitments. These anecdotes suggest that many collections staff may already intuitively know what was recently demonstrated by a study focusing on archaeological collections – namely, that rationalisation projects are generally not a cost-effective means of providing storage space (Baxter et al. 2018). Nevertheless, most of our survey respondents did not feel it should be made easier to dispose of objects from social history collections.

A major concern for collections staff is how potential news of disposals will be received by members of the public, and a number of curators with whom we have engaged have called for more care around the language used for what is increasingly referred to as collections 'review' or 'rationalisation' projects. This finding is supported by an earlier public consultation on disposal by the Museums Association (2007, 11), which found that 'the word "disposal" conjures negative connotations, including suspicion, shock and scepticism'. One of our survey respondents argued:

> We need to get away from using the word 'disposal'. To the public, it implies putting an object in the skip. 'Deaccessioning' is ghastly museum jargon. We are now using the word 'transfer' as our first preference, and then 'removal' for those cases where, after advertising, the item has not been placed in the public domain and is going elsewhere, or is being recycled.

'Transfer' is already widely used to distinguish objects that move between institutions that provide public access from more controversial sale, recycling or destruction, and our interactions with museum staff suggest that such 'transfers' are felt to be far less emotionally charged than outright 'disposal'.

In practice, the vast majority of decisions that lead to permanent removal of objects from collections are relatively uncontroversial, as they take the form of transfers to other institutions or the destruction of objects that have deteriorated beyond repair or consist of dangerous materials. Less than a third of our survey respondents have disposed of objects for reasons other than poor condition in the last five years, and several of those who have done so explained that this was for safety reasons or because they have duplicates. However, as demonstrated in this chapter, this does not mean that museums do not keep objects that, if they were faced with collecting them now, they would no longer collect: for a variety of reasons, such objects remain.

Increasingly, as part of the greater openness to discussing the removal of objects from collections, creative forms of 'de-growing' collections are being contemplated, and even being put into practice (Morgan and Macdonald 2020). One example involves donating tools to charities that refurbish them and put them back into use. A recent Museum of London collections review and rationalisation project focusing on its social and working history collections disposed of just over five thousand duplicate and surplus objects (Stephens 2015; Mendoza 2017, 45–6). Many of these objects were transferred to accredited museums, yet a key aim was to seek more innovative routes and recipients for disposal. The museum gave over one hundred duplicate objects to the 'Workaid' charity, which redistributes items (such as tools, sewing machines and books) to communities for the learning of new skills. The museum also gave duplicated traditional tools used in manufacturing (such as carpentry, shoemaking and metalworking) to universities for teaching students about historic crafts, and for use in training this new generation of craftspeople (Russell n.d.). Several respondents to our survey expressed an interest in working with artists to similarly transform disposal projects in generative and socially meaningful processes (see Das (2015) for a similar example of a UCL-based project). This clearly resonates with the approaches described in Part V, Transformation, which seek to 'transform loss', and we see great potential for work along these lines in the museum sector in the future.

***

In this chapter, we have explored how profusion is experienced by the museum staff working with social history collections in the UK, and have outlined some of their strategies for dealing with it. We have explored some of the relativities and repertoires of keeping and disposal that we have observed, and we have discussed reasons why objects variously remain in or leave collections. We turn now to our visual essay on one of the knowledge-exchange events that informed our findings, before moving in the following chapters to explore how profusion is experienced and approached in homes.

Notes

1. This is a semi-fictionalised description based on a composite from our research. It also features in Macdonald and Morgan (2018a).
2. Some of the results discussed in this chapter have been published previously in Fredheim, Macdonald and Morgan (2018), Macdonald and Morgan (2018a), Macdonald and Morgan (2018b) and Morgan and Macdonald (2020).
3. For further information about this event see: 'Meaningful Objects: Stories and Videos from the Domestic Profusion Workshop (https://heritage-futures.org/curating-domestic-profusion-workshop/).
4. For more extensive results from the survey, as well as further information about its design and questions, see Fredheim, Macdonald and Morgan (2018).
5. For further discussion see Macdonald and Morgan (2018a) and Morgan and Macdonald (2020).
6. Rodney Harrison discusses this as the 'affective weight' of objects that forms part of the 'curatorial responsibility' or burden in *Reassembling the Collection* (2013c).

12
Let's talk!

Harald Fredheim

Throughout our research on profusion, we have had the privilege of learning alongside colleagues working in museums. We also organised two events that attempted to give the museum staff we engaged with opportunities to share experiences and approaches directly with each other. Our second event, Museums for Profusion, was designed to follow on from our Contemporary Collecting and Disposal survey that was distributed in July 2018. The survey built on results from our ethnographic museum study and asked probing questions to understand the scale at which objects are entering and leaving social history collections in the UK, what museum staff think about the sustainability of their collecting practices, how they view the changing roles and responsibilities of curators and publics, what their experiences of creative approaches to contemporary collecting and disposal are, and more. Museums for Profusion invited survey participants and other museum colleagues to engage with our preliminary analysis of the survey results, share experiences of profusion, and think about how contemporary collecting and disposal might be approached differently in the future.

The event was held at the National Railway Museum in York, during September 2018. As in the ethnographic research on museum profusion, the focus was on allowing our museum colleagues to speak to and address their own experiences and questions around profusion in museums. In contrast to the survey, which necessarily consisted of a set of questions, the event was designed to facilitate networking and discussion around participants' own interests in our emerging results. When registering for the event, participants were asked to provide 'a question you would like to ask' and 'a question you would like to answer'. These questions were printed on personalised networking cards and provided to participants when they arrived on the day of the event (see Figure 12.1a and Figure 12.1b). The cards provided an optional networking aid before the formal programme began and during breaks. Some participants used the cards actively, to exchange contact information or discuss their questions printed on the back, while others chose not to, and left their cards behind at the end of the day. This was one of the ways in which we sought to facilitate meaningful encounters for our participants, while trusting them to know how to get the most out of the day for themselves.

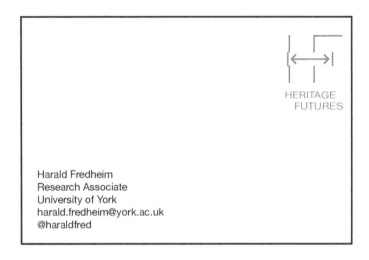

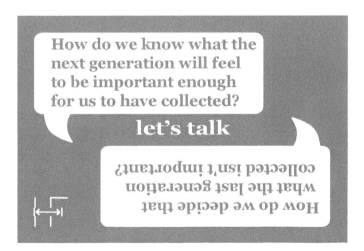

Figure 12.1a/b   The networking cards contained contact information provided by participants on the front, and questions participants wanted to ask and be asked on the back. The examples displayed above are taken from two different cards (Megan von Ackermann).

In order to deliver an event driven by participants' interests in our research on profusion in museums, and that foregrounded peer learning and participants' agency, Dr Megan von Ackermann was commissioned to co-design data discussion cards that illustrated the preliminary analysis of our survey results at a glance. Megan is a graphic designer and archaeologist who has developed a specialisation in data visualisation. Together, Megan and I divided a selection of the survey results into eight thematic data discussion cards, which provided the structure for unmoderated discussions at our Museums for Profusion event. Each participant was presented with a set of the eight data discussion cards, printed on A5 cardstock, and asked to explore them with colleagues from other museums seated around their table (see Figure 12.2). Participants were invited to speak freely, and to note down on blank cards provided any questions or comments they wanted to feed back into our research.

After inviting survey respondents to attend the event, we extended the invitation to members of Museum as Muck and Museum Detox, which are networks for UK museum professionals identifying as working class, and Black and Minority Ethnic, respectively. In this way, the museum staff who had responded to our survey were given an opportunity to engage with our preliminary analysis of their responses and have a say in how these were presented in our report, while also giving

Figure 12.2 Knowledge-exchange participants discuss the data discussion cards with colleagues from other museums (photograph by Ben Jancso/Baluga Photography).

museum staff from under-represented demographics an opportunity to weigh in on profusion and the future of social history collecting. Most importantly, networking cards, ample breaks and unmoderated discussions allowed all our participants to spend time with each other and to reflect on their own practice (see Figure 12.3). Many of the reflections they chose to share with us formally are reproduced on blue and purple 'cards' in our report, *Profusion in Museums* (Fredheim, Macdonald and Morgan 2018).

On the pages that follow, I have reproduced the data discussion cards designed for the Museums for Profusion event (see Figures 12.4 to 12.11). Each of the cards represents a discrete theme or topic, with the exception of the first card, which provides an overview of the museums represented in the survey responses. The cards can be approached in any order, but here the order in which they are presented is: growth, policies, acquisitions, disposals, futures, transparency and participation. As at our knowledge-exchange event, I prefer to let them speak for themselves, and invite you to glance over them and use the ones that grab your attention to consider the futures that profusion is shaping for museums.

Figure 12.3 Knowledge-exchange participants reflect on insights from the data discussion cards and feed back their reflections on blue and purple Heritage Futures postcards (photograph by Ben Jancso/Baluga Photography).

Distribution of social history collection sizes

| 1000 | 1,000-5,000 | 5,000-20,000 | 20,000-100,000 | 100,000+ |

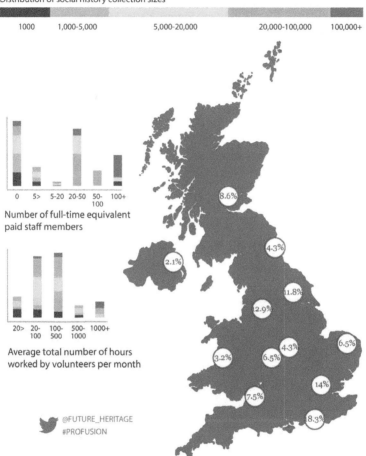

Number of full-time equivalent paid staff members

0   5>   5-20   20-50   50-100   100+

Average total number of hours worked by volunteers per month

20>   20-100   100-500   500-1000   1000+

@FUTURE_HERITAGE
#PROFUSION

8.6%
4.3%
2.1%
11.8%
2.9%
6.5%
4.3%
3.2%
6.5%
14%
7.5%
8.3%

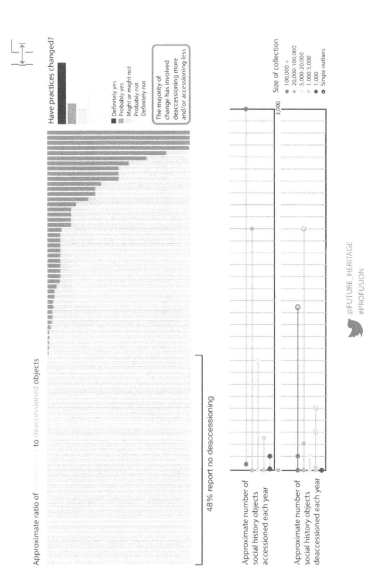

Have practices changed?

- Definitely yes
- Probably yes
- Might or might not
- Probably not
- Definitely not

The majority of change has involved deaccessioning more and/or accessioning less

Approximate ratio of accessioned to deaccessioned objects

48% report no deaccessioning

Approximate number of social history objects accessioned each year

Approximate number of social history objects deaccessioned each year

3,000

0

Size of collection
- 100,000 +
- 20,000-100,000
- 5,000-20,000
- 1,000-5,000
- 1,000
- Single outliers

@FUTURE HERITAGE
#PROFUSION

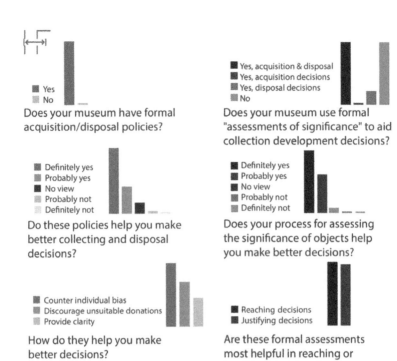

Yes
No

Does your museum have formal acquisition/disposal policies?

Yes, acquisition & disposal
Yes, acquisition decisions
Yes, disposal decisions
No

Does your museum use formal "assessments of significance" to aid collection development decisions?

Definitely yes
Probably yes
No view
Probably not
Definitely not

Do these policies help you make better collecting and disposal decisions?

Definitely yes
Probably yes
No view
Probably not
Definitely not

Does your process for assessing the significance of objects help you make better decisions?

Counter individual bias
Discourage unsuitable donations
Provide clarity

How do they help you make better decisions?

Reaching decisions
Justifying decisions

Are these formal assessments most helpful in reaching or justifying decisions?

"[Policies] are guidelines and can still clearly be bent if you wish to acquire something, or conversely can be enforced to the letter if you don't. There is still flexibility in them which is useful."

Definitely yes
Probably yes
No view
Probably not
Definitely not

Do you wish your museum had formal guidance documents for significance assessments?

"focus" "clear"
"standardised"
"informed"
"objective"
"rigorous"
"consistency"

@FUTURE_HERITAGE
#PROFUSION

How do you think these would help you?

Yes
Not anymore
No

Do you accept object donations to your social history collection from the public?

Do we really understand the scale of profusion?

"We let it be known what we would like to collect."

Does your museum purchase social history objects for your collection?

Yes
Not anymore
No

"Our collecting is manageable in its passive form. We are unable to be more active in our collecting as we do not have the time to do so or the space to put the collections that we could acquire."

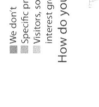

We don't
Specific projects
Visitors, social media, interest groups

How do you solicit donations?

"We don't have to, donors come to us."

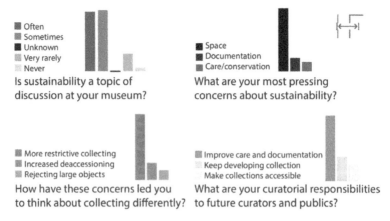

Often
Sometimes
Unknown
Very rarely
Never

Is sustainability a topic of
discussion at your museum?

Space
Documentation
Care/conservation

What are your most pressing
concerns about sustainability?

More restrictive collecting
Increased deaccessioning
Rejecting large objects

How have these concerns led you
to think about collecting differently?

Improve care and documentation
Keep developing collection
Make collections accessible

What are your curatorial responsibilities
to future curators and publics?

Are we thinking
about the future,
or a continuation
of the present?

Definitely yes
Probably yes
No view
Probably not
Definitely not

Museums keep objects for the future. Do you think the
time-frames social history objects are kept for should be
approached differently to those of objects in other types
of collections, such as art, natural history or archaeology?

Which futures for social history collecting are our
"profusion-coping-mechanisms" creating?

What will social history collecting look like
in your museum in 50 or 100 years time?

@FUTURE_HERITAGE
#PROFUSION

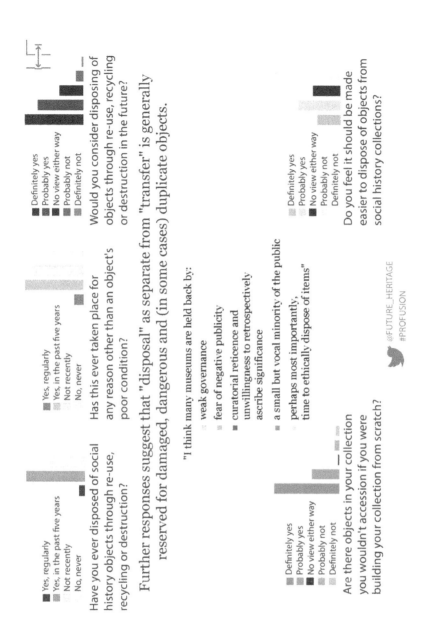

Definitely yes
Probably yes
No view either way
Probably not
Definitely not

Would you consider disposing of objects through re-use, recycling or destruction in the future?

Further responses suggest that "disposal" as separate from "transfer" is generally reserved for damaged, dangerous and (in some cases) duplicate objects.

Yes, regularly
Yes, in the past five years
Not recently
No, never

Has this ever taken place for any reason other than an object's poor condition?

Yes, regularly
Yes, in the past five years
Not recently
No, never

Have you ever disposed of social history objects through re-use, recycling or destruction?

"I think many museums are held back by:

- weak governance

- fear of negative publicity

- curatorial reticence and unwillingness to retrospectively ascribe significance

- a small but vocal minority of the public

perhaps most importantly, time to ethically dispose of items"

Definitely yes
Probably yes
No view either way
Probably not
Definitely not

Are there objects in your collection you wouldn't accession if you were building your collection from scratch?

Definitely yes
Probably yes
No view either way
Probably not
Definitely not

Do you feel it should be made easier to dispose of objects from social history collections?

@FUTURE_HERITAGE
#PROFUSION

"The governing body will ensure that both acquisition
and disposal are carried out openly and with transparency"
- ACE, Collections Development Policy Template

- Documentation / meeting minutes
- Policies publicised
- Follow industry guidelines

How does your museum ensure that
acquisition and disposal are carried out
openly and transparently?

"Minutes of the meeting
are recorded and
would be accessible
if anyone did an FOI request."

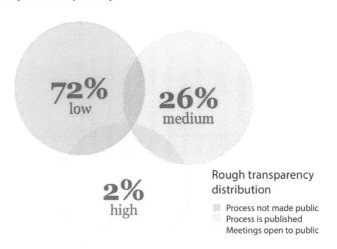

72% low

26% medium

2% high

Rough transparency
distribution

- Process not made public
- Process is published
- Meetings open to public

"Final approval is made by elected councillors
at sessions that the public can attend, details then
published online. All approved objects are
advertised in Museums Journal."

@FUTURE_HERITAGE
#PROFUSION

1% yes   no

Are your museum's collections development meetings open to the public?

- Definitely yes
- Probably yes
- No view
- Probably not
- Definitely not

Do you think they should be?

"It might help decisions to be more consistent
but it may slow the process down.
I am ashamed of the state of the collections
at the moment so would prefer the public
are not aware of the state of things"

Have you ever invited members of the public to inform your acquisition or disposal decisions?

Was it helpful?

Do you hope your museum invites the public to participate in future acquisition decisions?

Do you hope your museum invites public participation in future disposal decisions?

Why?

- Foster and reflect public ownership
- Valuable public expertise
- Value openness and transparency
- Public lack expertise and objectivity
- Difficult in practice
- Lack of time and resources

Are you happy with who is involved in making decisions about the acquisition
and disposal of social history objects at your museum?

 @FUTURE_HERITAGE
#PROFUSION

13
Curating domestic profusion

Jennie Morgan and Sharon Macdonald

Fieldwork visits to talk with people in their homes about 'profusion' were often characterised by a common experience. This was learning about what one person called 'my cupboard of doom'. 'Packed to bursting point', as she put it, with various household items – clothes, sports equipment, luggage, computers, Christmas decorations, gardening tools and children's toys – she thought that such cupboards 'are probably common to lots of other homes'. Her perception was confirmed by our research. It was not uncommon for people to refer to, or sometimes to even show us, a specific storage cupboard (or loft, basement, chest of drawers or purpose-designed 'storage solution') perceived to be full to the brim. Indicating their ubiquity, these were usually spoken about in a matter-of-fact way, and often accompanied with expressions hinting at a perceived unruliness, or even burden of the things contained within – 'I really *do* need to sort it all out'; 'I can't even show you because there is no space to get in'. Although a common feature of domestic life, such spaces are typically unremarked upon and kept out of sight of visitors.

In this chapter, we explore whether profusion is a predicament for individuals in domestic contexts, and, if so, how it manifests and is experienced, and with what it is connected. Figure 13.1 illustrates a proliferation of everyday domestic items, where 'too much stuff' – or what might also be called the material culture of contemporary everyday life[1] – is perceived to be on the brink of overflowing the capacity to reasonably contain it. Here we look into how people in their own homes deal with the potential mass of things that they might and often do acquire. We examine what this profusion means for actual experiences and practices within homes, especially as those homes in the UK are smaller than those in many European countries (SSAUK 2018, 15). As with museums,

Figure 13.1 An example of a 'cupboard of doom' (photograph by Jennie Morgan).

judging and selecting what is or is not worth keeping for the future is effectively a constitution of value. Here too, this is not just – and indeed is only infrequently – about monetary worth but is about organising relations between people and things, and also about social and familial relationships, one's own sense of self and specific kinds of ideas about the future. By highlighting a repertoire of relativities of keeping and discarding – which our research showed to be especially acute at critical life moments, such as moving house – we explore how curating profusion is not simply reducible to dealing with large quantities of things. Rather, it is entangled with managing the sociomaterial relationships that characterise present and future domestic lives.

Below, we present results in two main sections that mirror those of the previous chapter. The first focuses on how people in their own homes experience profusion. The second builds on this to look at the strategies that they deploy for coping with this. We trace how value, emotion and the physical qualities of objects work together to sometimes create unsatisfactory and emotionally exhausting situations experienced as what we call the 'profusion predicament'. Before doing so, however, we briefly sketch how the research was conducted.

Methods

As with the museum research, our domestic study included doing semi-structured interviews and using participant-led elicitation techniques (for example, inviting participants to 'show' as well as to 'tell' us about what they are keeping for the future)[2] – in this case, with people in their own and other people's homes, as well as with professionals. It also included observational visits, some of which involved taking photographs and making short research films (see Figure 13.2).[3]

Figure 13.2   Filming during a household visit (photograph by Shelley Castle).

Here, too, specifically orchestrated encounters were also part of the method, with the Declutterer event mentioned in the previous chapters providing information on domestic practices as well as on those of museums. In addition, we used an extended creative collaboration with Shelley Castle of Encounters Arts, which led to a public arts-research event, as described in Chapter 14.[4]

We visited 16 homes (sometimes more than once) and also undertook further interviews about personal strategies for dealing with profusion, with 29 people in total being included in the study. In addition, three professional 'declutterers' and the founder of Storii (an online app for digitally organising 'life moments') were interviewed, and we visited and spoke with staff at a self-storage facility. Furthermore, as we constantly found ourselves thinking about our own practices, we also came to acknowledge this as an integral, 'auto-ethnographic' part of our research.[5]

Our study did not aim to account for variations associated with economic, age, class or ethnic differences between domestic settings – although it did include a mix of men and women, different ages (our youngest participant being 19 and the oldest in their 70s) and professions. Rather, it sought to highlight *some* of the potential different ways of assembling domestic future heritages in relation to the struggle of being faced with a potential overload, not only of things, but also of information and choice. Within this, there was some emphasis on exploring the movement of things (and, to an extent, ideas and practices) between homes and museums by including in the research people who had offered items to museums. Our museum partners (introduced in Chapters 10 and 11) helped us to recruit such participants.

Experiences of profusion

Most people visited in domestic settings described the storing of everyday household items as challenging; many talked about ambitions to 'streamline', 'minimalise' or 'better organise' both material and digital things. Some talked about matters such as the environmental effects of plastics in the ocean, or the impact on personal well-being of 'digital overload'. Alongside recognising the dilemmas of a profusion of things, some also identified reasons for it and their own ambivalence in relation to it, especially with regard to what has been called (and as we introduced earlier) the 'pursuit' of 'newness' (Campbell 2015). For example, one participant explained:

I've got loads of stuff, and I suppose that's why I'm ambivalent because I actually don't really want any more stuff. But I think it's part of twentieth- or twenty-first-century life that there is this kind of feeling that buying just one more thing on Amazon or buying just one more – having just a slightly different car or a slightly different motorbike is actually going to sort of push you over the edge towards happiness. And there is that, certainly when you get stressed or tired or anxious, there's almost this kind of knee-jerk reaction to sort of try to buy something. I've got ambivalent feelings towards that sort of thing.

It is clear here that acquiring more things is also an emotive matter. So, too, is trying to manage the things one owns. The description of a woman needing to control her 'cupboard of doom' above (Figure 13.1) – and the very language of 'doom', with its evocations of an impending negative future – is but one such example, as we discuss further in Chapter 15.

Popular media descriptions of a struggle with profusion – including television programmes such as the UK-based *The Hoarder Next Door* (first broadcast in 2012) and books (and the accompanying television series) such as Marie Kondo's (2014) *The Life-Changing Magic of Tidying Up* – were sometimes mentioned by research participants. These tend to present the accumulation of things as not only a practical issue but also as a mental burden[6] – an idea expressed by others too. At our Declutterer event, Dr Zemirah Moffat (an anthropologist and professional home 'declutterer') told us how 'clutter comes from the Middle English word "clotter", or blood clot' and that 'clutter clearing releases you and your belongings back into the flow of life, so they are no longer stuck and neither are you'. Adding to the emotional dimension of profusion is that questions of how to deal with it tend to become most intense at critical life moments, such as moving house or sorting out an inheritance of material things. These are times that might be affectively fraught in any case, but dealing with accumulated stuff – and deciding what to keep and what to discard – becomes especially entangled in the forging of social relationships and crafting of desired lives in the present and future.

It was clear from individuals who were sorting out the contents of the homes of deceased relatives – undertaking a 'house clearance' to identify which items would be retained and which would be discarded – that the sorting required time and energy, with people often describing undertaking regular and ongoing moments of activity spread over an evening, a week or a weekend each month. It was not uncommon for our participants to have worked on a house clearance for a year or more.

Specific kinds of things were considered especially troublesome. Often this was due to the material, physical qualities of the things themselves. For example, several people showed us what was sometimes called 'brown furniture' or large-scale pieces of wooden furniture – wardrobes, chests of drawers, vanity cabinets – dating from the 1950s and 1960s. Usually too big to fit into contemporary homes, and viewed as unfashionable, such furniture was difficult to sell or even give away. Nevertheless, those clearing the homes of relatives were reluctant to discard the furniture because of the perceived quality of the carpentry and wood: 'it's too good to take to the tip', 'it seems a shame to chuck it out because they don't make them like this nowadays', said one person. Dealing with such tricky items was sometimes described to be an 'exhausting' or 'emotionally tiring' experience.

In response, some individuals spoke of wanting to avoid 'passing on' to the next generation accumulated things, which might come to be seen as a burden. This mirrored the experience of museum curators grappling with the burden of past collecting decisions discussed in Chapter 11. As one woman put it when recounting her experience of clearing her parents' house:

> We were trying to think of, well, if something happened to myself and my husband [and] the kids had to clear the house out, we wouldn't want them to have to go through the same process as what I was going through, and having to spend lots and lots of time going through.

A desire to develop strategies to avoid passing on what might later turn out to be a burden was expressed by other people we met. For example, one married couple who were beginning to declutter their own house, with the view of possibly 'downsizing', joked that they might ask their two adult children to identify items they would like to inherit by putting stickers on them (one colour per sibling) so that they 'could then get rid of everything else!' While this was expressed with humour, it reflected how many of those people we met seek to tackle domestic profusion in the present, rather than leaving this for future generations to deal with.

It was not uncommon for people to describe how sorting in critical life moments such as 'house clearing' or 'downsizing' had prompted them to reassess what they were keeping in their own homes, and to begin to consider much more carefully what they would acquire, hold on to and bequeath to others. In doing so, they might even subject things that they had previously considered to be self-evident to keep (including a diverse mix of objects such as family photographs, jewellery, personal documents, furniture, ornaments, clothing and religious objects) to questioning and even reassessment ('will they *really* want this?'). In effect, in critical life moments, people become aware that they are agents of future heritage-making.

Strategies for addressing domestic profusion

In domestic settings, individuals tackle what they see as excess things by making selections about what and what not to keep through processes they variously called 'sorting', 'organising' or 'sifting through'. In our auto-ethnography, we observed how we are constantly engaged in such practices in our homes, even if we do not think, or talk with others, about these much. For example, Jennie Morgan has what she calls a 'one in, one out policy', whereby for anything newly acquired something else is selected to be discarded. In a strategy that is also adopted by others, here we see a clear attempt to balance what stays and what leaves. Other strategies adopted by those we met are discussed below.

Figure 13.3   A collection of model trains (photograph by Jennie Morgan).

Making selections: Determining value through systematic approaches

The model trains in Figure 13.3 belong to a man who self-identified as a 'born collector'. His collections – of model trains, but also road signage, bicycles, books and glassware – filled many parts of his home, workplace and other storage locations that we visited. While at first glance this appeared to be a very broad accumulation of things, he described himself as having 'a systematised, controlled, collecting type mentality'. Jennie's field notes record:

> The collector describes to me three principles: 'genre', 'definitive' and 'connoisseurial' collecting. *Genre* collecting, he tells me, is the ambition to broadly acquire certain kinds of things – 'everything with a road sign on it'. He explains that this is 'the most uncontrollable' type of collecting because it holds potential to proliferate until 'it can get completely out of hand'. The second and third principles seem intended to set stricter limits. He describes *definitive* collecting as the attempt to acquire 'one of everything' within a defined series or category of things – for example, 'every model of Hornby train ever produced'. *Connoisseurial* is more controlled still, by 'picking and choosing' – or selecting a single outstanding example – 'the best' or 'one good one'. Yet even within these broad approaches, the collector describes how it is necessary to undertake further 'filtering' by using a range of additional criteria (e.g. 'use', 'historical interest', 'rarity', 'taste' and 'condition'). Otherwise, he tells me, the risk is becoming utterly overwhelmed 'by crates of stuff'.

Here, having a clear rationale defines 'a collection' and distinguishes it from being an unruly or 'uncontrolled' mass, or 'crates of stuff'.[7] This 'mentality' sets limits by providing criteria to link items into a related group, giving them meaning as a whole, and from which the collector can then choose to include some things, and to exclude others; or to 'draw the line' by having 'a control factor', as he put it. From Jennie's field notes:

> On the one hand, it might be said that this self-identified 'serious collector' is a special case when compared to other people in our domestic study, who did not see themselves as collectors.[8] Yet, there are more similarities than one might initially imagine. While others we met were not as practised expressing the motivations, judgements and assumptions that shape their selections, it was evident that their choices were not done in an entirely ad hoc manner. They similarly used systematic approaches, or what we can consider modes of determining value.

This was illustrated by the case of a woman clearing the house lived in by her two parents, who had died within the past year. Showing items she was sorting through, such as clothing, books, kitchen equipment, ornaments and personal documents, she described her approach. This included working systematically 'room by room'; making decisions about similar categories of objects, or 'grouping like with like' (as one declutterer characterised this common strategy); and working first with objects considered self-evident to keep, or what she called 'the easy things' with obvious financial value, use or strong affective response, such as sentiment or nostalgia. She also thought carefully about her motivations for keeping, explaining how:

> It was balancing 'OK, my mother was very keen on this' but what is its future? Can I afford to keep it, do I have the room to keep it or is it in a suitable condition to keep? For example, there was an ornament my mother did love but it would never have been displayed anywhere in my house, but the hand was broken as well, so that couldn't go to the charity shop. I think I put it in recycling or landfill, I can't remember, but regardless, I was torn between that because I know my mother had loved it, but it was broken and I had no use for it, and then I didn't want our house full of clutter for our children to have to throw away when we're dead. So, it had to go.

Even in this short extract from a much lengthier conversation, a range of different 'pull' and 'push' factors (Lovatt 2015, 24) are flagged through the participant's description of struggling to decide or feeling 'torn'. Some things exert a 'pull' to be kept 'for memories', or a perceived responsibility to care for these on behalf of others ('something that my mother would have wanted to keep'). Yet these same things may also exert a 'push' to be discarded because they are broken, have no identifiable 'use', are not considered aesthetically pleasing ('it would never have been displayed anywhere in my house'), or are simply too big to transfer.

These kinds of struggles were typical of our conversations with other individuals, and illustrate the broad range of values and emotions informing what is selected to keep for the future in domestic settings. These include 'functional use', 'monetary value', 'beauty', 'rarity', 'age', 'memories/sentiment', 'biographic marker' (being associated with a key life event or experience) and 'obligation', as we discuss further in Chapter 15. This is not intended to be an exhaustive list, but rather begins to reveal what is at stake and what people see as relevant to address when making selections. Unlike the museum professionals we discussed in Chapter 11, who increasingly use 'significance assessment' frameworks, people in their own and other people's homes did not appear to attempt to rank these values and emotions, yet in practice, matters such as the size or storage requirements of an object often sealed its fate. Perhaps not surprisingly, as the examples above illustrate, these factors sometimes conflicted, simultaneously pushing and pulling, thus imbuing selection with a sense of uncertainty.

It was common for participants to explain to us how in making selections they wanted to 'respect' not only the reasons why something had been acquired in the first place, but also the further decision to hold on to it over time. In homes, value appears to be added to objects the longer they are kept and as they are pushed through critical life moments. Value is produced in the process of attending to things and deciding how to handle them. One possible result is that it is more difficult to let these things go – indicated when people expressed discomfort with making a decision to get rid of something perceived to have been held on to over time. This was illustrated during one of our visits, when a householder pointed out a collection of umbrellas (see Figure 13.4), explaining how she had accumulated these because she 'just loves umbrellas' and having 'different colours' to 'suit your mood'. Considering a potential near-future 'downsize' of where she was living, she explained that she 'wasn't too concerned' what would happen to the umbrellas from any associated sorting (thus indicating her willingness to consider letting them go), apart from two specific umbrellas: one that had belonged to her grandfather, and another, a cotton parasol, that had belonged to her grandmother (and for which she had an accompanying photograph showing her grandmother in her early 20s with the parasol). Both umbrellas were damaged, with ripped fabrics and no longer functioning mechanisms, but she explained how she would like to keep these 'old' things that had previously been acquired by their original owners, and then kept and later given to her by other family members:

> It's just, you know how you get handed down things, and I just wouldn't throw it out … I mean, I wouldn't really have kept that [umbrella] because it's all torn and ripped and what good is it. Whereas the parasol, although it's stained, it is still usable, not that you're going to use it.

Continuing, she mused, 'anything old, I mean I couldn't bear to throw it out, you know, belonging to other people'.

Figure 13.4 Umbrellas (photograph by Jennie Morgan).

This example, as well as others we encountered, indicated that even when a value judgement has been made (such as an item being broken with no identifiable future use), the emotional cost of actually letting go may be experienced as too great to actually do it. We saw this too in our museum study through the objects that, although the decision had been taken to remove them from collections, remained in storerooms. This was further emphasised when participants described how – due to specific material, sensory, aesthetic or other qualities – objects appeared to come to stand in not only for the past decisions and value judgements of others, but also for memories and characteristics of the person themselves. A cheap novelty egg timer, in the shape of a chicken, was one of the few items a son kept from clearing his father's home because it 'reminded' him of his 'sense of humour'. Other people similarly spoke about items they felt compelled to keep because – as we were told on various occasions – to do otherwise 'would be like getting rid of them' ('them' being the person to which an item had originally belonged, or from whom an item had been gifted).

Not only did these emotional ties shape what was kept, but they also influenced the kinds of futures that people tried to shape for objects that were let go. Over almost two years, one woman in her 20s clearing the house of her deceased 'Gran', recounted to us (via intermittent email, photographs, telephone and Skype interviews) the great effort she went to in order to discard items in a manner of which grandmother, whom she described as not wanting 'any waste', would have 'approved'.[9] Yet this had led to an unsatisfactory situation with regard to a large 1950s sofa, which she was struggling to sell because the only way would be 'for much less than it could be worth', which she felt 'would be disrespectful' to her grandmother's 'frugality'. When we first encountered her, after unsuccessful attempts at selling the sofa, she had offered the item for donation to a local museum. She explained:

> For someone who is house-proud, and who saved up for this stuff, that's what she would have wanted to do. She wanted people to come and see her house, so why don't we give it to somewhere where they can see it, because that's exactly what she liked!

There is, of course, much more that could be said here, beyond the scope of our discussion. The bigger point to be made is that addressing profusion through making selections is not only to deal with its material manifestation, but various other sensory, emotional, symbolic and relational proliferations that can be carried with things. By making selections, especially about the things that are kept, the sense that specific items hold value may even be increased (as suggested by the difficulty of parting with items known to once have been 'loved', even if they no longer hold any perceived use, value and/or meaningful connection to current recipients). Value emerges not simply through the decision to acquire something in the first place, but is produced through the ongoing decisions and practices of retaining.

Infrastructures for containing it all: Household storage and caring for things

Another way that profusion is addressed in domestic settings is through attempts at containment, especially through ongoing practices of storing and caring for things. We have already in this book seen other architectures of containment for managing heritage, especially in Part II, Diversity, but also in our discussion of museum collections review and storage solutions in Chapter 11. Here, then, we delve further into these infrastructures by looking at where things go in homes when they are kept, what forms of storage and practices of care are used and what people hope will happen to these things.

In most of the homes that we visited, things selected as worth keeping for posterity did appear to warrant special practices of care and maintenance. Items were routinely stored apart from everyday use, in lofts, basements, garden sheds, cupboards and/or under the bed (see Figure 13.5), as well as in purpose-designed containers, including albums, display cabinets or shelves, and boxes.

Figure 13.5 A storage loft: the domestic equivalent of the museum storeroom, or deep storage? (photograph by Jennie Morgan).

Some of these practices shared similarities with how museums care for their collections. First, by removing items from everyday circulation by storing these in set-apart places, with the loft or the basement being the household equivalent, perhaps, of the museum storeroom – or even a form of 'deep storage', given that items in these areas were often inaccessible. Second, through practices of care that perceived items to be at risk of not being there in the future – by being lost, destroyed or simply disintegrating over time – without some form of active intervention by their owners.

This was illustrated during one visit, when a woman showed us a set of dolls' houses that she was keeping for her grandchildren for when they are older. She holds on to these despite her grandchildren showing little current interest in them, thus framing the future of these things as uncertain. The children are not permitted to play with these 'unsupervised' in case they accidentally break them, and she explained that she had glued some of the furniture inside to try to mitigate it from being lost. She had also taught her grandchildren how to clean the houses carefully using a selection of bristle brushes and tweezers to dust (see Figure 13.6).

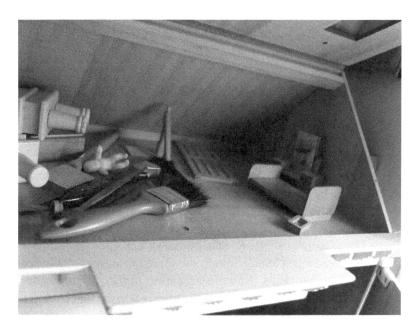

Figure 13.6   Tools for caring for a dolls' house (photograph by Jennie Morgan).

This was a practice she also used for her own large collection of dolls:

> They were in a cabinet originally, like when I got married before the kids came along, my little niece, believe it or not, she's the only one that really likes dolls. And she used to come over and I'd give her

the brush, and she would slide the cabinet and she would take them all out very carefully. I wouldn't let any of the rest of them do it, but I knew [she] was like myself, she liked dolls. So, she would clean them and put them back, and then obviously with [having] the kids they sort of got neglected a wee bit when you have babies. Then, when I cleaned them it was a quick [makes blowing noise] back in the cabinet sort of thing. When we moved to the second house, I had got another cabinet made because I did away with the original one. It was a long one. It didn't take as many dolls but had glass shelves so you can imagine they needed dusting regularly because it wasn't airtight. Then when we came here, I kept it for a while, but this living room is too small and that was when they all got boxed away. I had the porcelain ones going up the stairs, I had them sitting there, and maybe one sitting there [points to area in living room], because by that time my boys were older and weren't going to wreck them. But then when the grandkids came along, the dolls got put away as well because I didn't want them busted.

Another way she was attempting to care for this collection, in light of a potential 'downsize', was that she had offered it for donation to a museum in a city in a different part of the country from where she lived. This was a city she had enjoyed visiting many times on holiday and to where she was contemplating relocating.

Many other participants shared her idea that things kept for posterity require special practices of storage and care. Typically, this involved trying not only to maintain the physical integrity of objects, but also to deliberately add value in ways that might ensure their future chances of survival by being retained rather than discarded. Above, we have already seen how people might identify specific future recipients (informally, but also through leaving things to named benefactors in wills). More creative strategies were also used. For example, one woman we met told us how she had lodged a handwritten letter inside a clock she had inherited from her great-aunt, to describe what she called the clock's 'story'. She told us how she asked her father to write this letter – 'the story of its history' – because:

If you lose the story, then it's just a thing. I suppose it's just a thing anyway, but it's got an extra value. So, just a clock that looks like that, it might be attractive, it might be an antique, it might be worth financial money, but ... with a story it's got an emotional value, a historical value, rather than just a financial value. It's the emotional and historical value that I care about.

The woman's letter-writing strategy attempts to add *specific kinds* of values that signify the clock's importance to her, and to communicate these values to future generations, thus increasing the likelihood of the clock being retained when she eventually passes it on to her children. Given her emphasis on 'stories' – a theme that also emerged in our museum study (see Chapter 11 and also Macdonald and Morgan 2018a) – it is not inconsequential that she works as a museum professional. Yet trying to retain information to add value to objects was witnessed across the homes we visited. Other participants similarly kept notes with objects, original receipts, photographs of previous owners using or wearing items, the names of individuals or locations by writing these on to photographs, and additional information compiled from doing research into the family history of inherited objects or documents. While we observed a range of special practices of care and storage, the ability of items – especially those reasoned to have durable material qualities – to persist without any such active intervention was also flagged (as *The Human Bower* visual essay in Chapter 14 likewise illustrates). The persistence of objects over time, without active intervention, was sometimes considered to enhance their value, as indicated when people described attachments to things that they had unexpectedly found after forgetting about and not particularly missing their disappearance.

The Digital

Finally, it is important when looking at strategies for addressing profusion in homes to briefly note that we did not find digital recording or storage to be considered a solution. Our visits suggested that digital technologies are not widely used to address the profusion predicament, and more typically are regarded to create their own struggles. For example, people often described having many digitally created photographs, but not yet having developed effective systems for storing, organising, retrieving, and ultimately being able to view and use these. One woman told us she had thousands of digital photographs stored across a laptop, mobile phones, a camera and 'cloud'-based storage. She was frustrated that these were 'very disorganised', and yet told us that 'to go back and put them in any sort of order' by introducing a system, such as 'tagging' the photographs with 'categories' pertaining to the subject of the image ('holiday' or 'engagement', for example), would 'be a really time-consuming job'. Without systems to order and organise, digital objects can also be considered a burden. However, although holding potential to overwhelm, this woman also indicated how the digital is experientially different from material profusion. She reasoned that for these digital photographs – in contrast to the boxes of photographic prints stored in her home – 'you don't really see it as taking up an awful lot of space. You sort of say, "Oh, it's fine. There's thousands there. It'll be fine!"' Some factors that were flagged above as acting as a strong 'push' from the home, such as limited space, are perceived to disappear with the digital and in doing so propel further towards accumulation. Moreover, anxiety about technology failure in the future was also expressed. Some people described trying to mitigate this risk – for example, by backing up files on different storage devices, or printing paper images and/or albums from digital files.

Curating loss

We have discussed how our fieldwork revealed the different ways that people in domestic settings develop strategies for addressing profusion. Beyond their own strategies, participants were also aware of the professional and semi-professional services for tackling profusion, such as 'declutterers' and 'self-storage'. Talking to professional 'declutterers' (or 'organisers', as some call themselves) indicated that such services offer practical support through systematic approaches to releasing things from homes, as well as helping with the physical 'heavy lifting' work involved (as one put it). We learnt of a range of 'tips', such as the 'one in, one out' strategy introduced earlier. With wardrobe decluttering, one professional organiser's approach was to ask clients to put the clothes hangers facing one way, and then to turn them around once an item is worn to assess, after a set period, what has been 'actually used'. But beyond these kinds of practical strategies, professionals also understand their work to offer emotional bolstering for what – as this chapter has already illustrated – is a process experienced, in many cases, with deep uncertainty or even difficulty. One professional organiser described how this translates into her approach for working with clients in their homes:

> When I'm with somebody, I start and just stand beside them, because ultimately it's them who will decide what goes out. It's not me who decides. They decide. So, I initially stand beside them and they're taking a small section of the room and we're looking at it and I'm sitting there. They're saying, 'Oh, I'll keep that' and I'll say to them, 'What do you think? Do you think you can let go of that, or would you like to think about that for a minute? We could put it in the "thinking box"', or 'I'm definitely going to keep it' or 'we

could recycle or give [it] to charity?' So they've got options here. They've got four options. They are then making the decision about where they're going to put it … But the idea for me standing beside is not to put too much stuff into that thinking box, because all we're doing is moving from there to there. So, as the time goes on, she is becoming more relaxed. She is going, 'Oh this is great.' There's an uplifting in the person. 'This is great. I've wanted it out of my house for ages. It's going out.' So, as she starts to relax, she starts to get faster as well, so I then move slightly further away from her. I'm still alongside her, but I'm now doing a section and she's doing a section, and for the main stuff I'm just putting it out but anything I come across, I'm saying, 'What you think about this?' 'Oh yeah, I want to keep that.' So, we're working alongside and as the hours go on I'm actually getting further away from her, and she's doing it faster and she's making big decisions, and in the meantime she has told me the whole story of what has happened. And by the end, it's a strange thing, but by the end of it, every single person that I've worked with, by the end of it, they're giving you a hug when you leave. They're like, 'I just feel so much better.' That's what I mean about – instead of just going in and just chucking everybody's stuff, it's about coaching them through, deciding what they're going to give away, or throw away, or recycle, or keep.

This lengthy quotation illustrates how practical and emotional support are entangled in how the professional organiser understands, as well as approaches, curating loss from homes – here, by physically standing next to a client for 'emotional support' and offering a range of options for discard, including a liminal 'thinking box'. She also spoke about offering clients options for the objects that remain – including, for things such as photographs, if these will be put 'out on display' or rather stored, in specific containers, in areas such as the loft.

While none of the householders in our study were using services such as these, most were actively involved in some form of 'decluttering' as a mode of getting rid of things. Although people appeared to think that keeping a selection of certain kinds of things for the future is a good thing to do, equally apparent was a perceived need to streamline, purge or let go.[10] This usually involved relocating objects to friends and family, and charity shops, and selling to others via online forums for second-hand goods. Beyond the specific details of each, our visits illustrated a broadly shared concern among people in homes with 'losing well'.[11] What we mean by this, here, is the desire to craft acceptable futures for objects leaving homes. The quotation above, and our visits, show the great effort and care that goes into attempting to shape certain kinds of futures, not simply for things that remain, but also for those which leave homes. This was certainly further illustrated through the preferences that people indicated for using certain routes (or 'options') for discard; those that provide opportunity for the 'use' or 'functional' value of objects to be revived, or otherwise maintained, appeared especially popular – such as giving items (for whatever reason they were being released) to friends, family or colleagues. Many people emphasised their concern to avoid adding to growing landfills by not releasing items in ways that would categorise them as 'waste' or 'rubbish' through 'binning' or 'taking them to the tip'. One professional 'organiser' we spoke to pushed this further by musing that while, in her view, 'the media makes it out that we're a throwaway society', and that the built-in obsolescence of consumer goods (which we mentioned in Chapter 10) means that some things inevitably disappear because they are not constructed for longevity, her professional experience leads her to believe that people tend not to simply throw things away. Instead, as she put it, there is 'that kind of responsibility built into us that we shouldn't be throwing this away'. Certainly, for most people we visited, losing things by binning was considered to be an option only to be taken if all others – such as 'giving' or 'recycling' items into new contexts of use – had been exhausted.

It is perhaps not surprising, then, that giving things to charity was frequently used, not least because people described this to require less time, mental effort and emotional burden than (as we have seen above with one woman and her grandmother's furniture) trying to sell items, or find other people to give them to. Yet, many people we spoke to also recounted their frustration that charity shops did not accept certain categories of things for legal reasons or due to space constraints. One professional organiser recounted difficulty finding a new home for a large quantity of paperback books, partly due to storage issues in charity shops, but also because of a perceived lack of desire from any potential future recipients, given digital technologies competing with analogue. She told us how:

> Nobody wants them. I can't find anybody who will take these books. I've been all over the country. I cannot find anybody who will come and pick up books because they're going to be on a Kindle and they're going to be stored in that way in the future.

In an interesting parallel with museums, our research noted that some charity shops make available on their websites lists of what they are unable to accept – or what might be considered a type of (de)collecting policy – including things with a perceived health or safety risk, such as used bedding, electrical items, or furniture lacking evidence of meeting contemporary fire-safety standards.[12]

Such examples reveal how a strong impetus to 'lose well' by maintaining or reviving the potential value (economic, but also use value) of items shapes how items leave homes. Donating to museums was talked about in ways that indicated it satisfies perceived commitments to objects by museums having appropriate storage facilities and conservation skills to care for things in ways not always possible in the home. As we have already shown above, donating items to museums appeared to fulfil felt obligations and relationships to other people, including the deceased. Typically, people who had approached museums to donate objects had seen similar categories and periods of items on display – 1960s hair curling tongs, a Hoover or television set – and reasoned curators would want more examples. There was also a view that objects could have 'historical significance' (as several put it) beyond importance to families or individuals, and by relocating objects to museums where, it was imagined, they could be 'seen', 'enjoyed' and 'appreciated' by a wider audience, this value would be better realised. While not explicitly discussed with people in our study, it is entirely conceivable that this also fulfils a desire of families and individuals to be seen and appreciated, creating their own legacies of significance through the gifting of things to heritage institutions. Gifting to museums can be understood to be motivated by a desire to satisfy people's emotional commitments, especially by using them as repositories for the kinds of troublesome objects (discussed above) that they do not wish to, or cannot, retain but that they struggle to let go due to perceived responsibilities and emotional ties. In some scenarios, gifting to museums may even avoid having to make difficult selections in the present, and thus deferring agency to another site of future heritage-making. This was certainly how some museum curators saw it, perhaps sighing over the 'unsolicited donations' that had arrived at their desks.

***

This chapter has shown how selecting items for future posterity involves relativities of keeping and discarding. This spectrum is shaped both by practical considerations, such as space or the ongoing use of an item, and also by emotional attachments and moral judgements, including ideas about what might be an acceptable future trajectory for things. Here, we have also seen how museums feature as one ideal new home for the things people care about but do not want to keep, or can no longer keep, themselves. Before looking at further actual and potential exchanges between museums and homes, we continue with a focus on personal selection of objects for the future, through discussion of *The Human Bower*, an interactive public artwork created in collaboration with one of our creative fellows.

Notes

1. This category in itself partly fuels the profusion predicament through what has been called its 'mutability' or ability 'to be all things to many people' (Hackett 2017).
2. Our approach draws on previous research experience using interventional techniques, including those described in Pink and Morgan (2013).
3. For examples of short films made from the domestic study, see *On Collecting* (https://heritage-futures.org/on-collecting) and *My Dad the Collector* (https://heritage-futures.org/torbays-hidden-treasures/).
4. See www.encounters-arts.org.uk for further details. Also https://heritage-futures.org/torbays-hidden-treasures/ and https://heritage-futures.org/the-human-bower/.
5. This 'auto-ethnography' included being open to creatively addressing the issue – for example, through 'play' by participating in the Minimalism Game (www.theminimalists.com/game/). We thank Ricarda Maria Schmidt for introducing this to us. Elsewhere, Jennie has characterised 'auto-ethnography' as being defined by 'self-observation', or 'a process and product of drawing on personal experiences, emotions, thoughts, and feelings to better understand those of others' (Morgan and Pink 2018, 402). We were also inspired by scholars researching in related areas drawing on self-reflexive analysis (for example, Bell and Bell 2012; Chin 2016), perhaps indicating the widespread ubiquity of profusion in contemporary Western life.
6. This is taken even further in the recent pathologisation of certain kinds of people–object relations, and the associated language of 'clutter' or 'hoarding', as discussed by Herring (2014).
7. This understanding resonates with Sharon Macdonald's (2006a) discussion of collecting. Similar points are made by anthropologist Katie Kilroy-Marac (2018), who explores 'rules' for organising, ordering, arranging and distinguishing personal 'hoards' from 'collections'.
8. Although, as cultural-geographer Nicky Gregson (2011, 106) has argued, most homes could be regarded to have some kind of 'collection' 'through their use of storage systems to display, as well as hold and order, consumer items'.
9. Of relevance here is Gregson et al.'s (2007a) analysis of the complex negotiation of 'love relations' involved in divestment.
10. A phenomenon explored by others in the domestic setting, most notably through the work of cultural geographer Nicky Gregson (see Gregson et al. 2007b; Gregson 2011), but also studies of divestment through recirculation (for example, Appelgren and Bohlin, 2015a).
11. The language of 'losing well' was introduced by Ingrid Samuel of the National Trust during the knowledge-exchange event described in Chapter 23, and is discussed further in Part V, Transformation, and Part VI, Future heritages. See also Caitlin DeSilvey's (2017) work on 'curating decay'.
12. See, for example, www.bhf.org.uk/shop/donating-goods/book-furniture-collection-near-me/items-we-can-not-sell.

14
The Human Bower

Jennie Morgan

This visual essay focuses on creative practice as a route for addressing questions of future keeping. Susan Hogan and Sarah Pink (2010), who explore the synergies between feminist art therapy and anthropology, argue that making and reflecting upon art can bring forth 'interior states', including 'imaginative worlds', that might not be expressed by talk alone. Through the images and text that follow, I aim to illustrate the methodological value of creative collaboration for examining processes of selective keeping and future-making. I document a participatory arts–research collaboration with Encounters Arts associate Shelley Castle, which led to the interactive public artworks *The Story in the Object* and *The Human Bower*.[1] The process of designing and facilitating these events generated rich insights into what people decide is worth keeping for posterity, and how these decisions and actions play a role in creating the future. As one participant in *The Human Bower* put it, 'it has opened my mind to the process of making these choices' to realise that 'the seed of the future is here'.

In July 2017, Shelley and I visited a range of people in their homes across the Torbay area (including Torquay, see Figure 14.1 and Figure 14.2 – all figures are at the end of this chapter). Torbay is a region on the south coast of the UK characterised by a curious configuration of profusion and scarcity. On the one hand, it is known as 'the English Riviera', due to a mild climate and lasting popularity as a holiday resort. Yet others have noted Torbay's towns and villages to be a 'casualty of the recession', or economic downturn, in the UK from 2008 (Savill 2009). The ever-changing fortunes of 'a century of playtime' are reflected in the flaked paint of an abandoned shopfront, one of the many that I noticed while visiting the region's towns (see Figure 14.3 and 14.4). These were in stark contrast to the bustling restaurants and souvenir shops servicing the waterfront tourist trade. During visits to people in their homes, we asked people to show and tell us about things they are keeping for future posterity (see Figure 14.5). Toys, a garden ornament, a hiking guidebook, an antique clock, circus programmes and a Palaeolithic hand-axe were some of the diverse objects discussed, to which Shelley responded by making *in-situ* 'object portraits' (see Figures 14.9 to 14.11). Shelley described making these portraits 'to connect with the object (and therefore the owner) in a deeper way while the owner talked about them'. This fieldwork was a type of collecting in itself – a drawing together of narratives, photographs, sketches, experiences and people – which Shelley then assembled (including domestic objects loaned by the people visited) into the temporary *Story in the Object* installation at the Torre Abbey Museum. What cut across the things collected, as Shelley has reflected, 'was that the objects resonated a highly personal charge' for their owners, which 'seemed to be passed on during the telling of their story'.[2] Keepers' selections appeared invested with layers of emotion, sentiment, nostalgia, relationships and personalities, which acted as a powerful pull (or 'charge'), making not keeping these treasured things inconceivable.

Having delved into the personal significance that elicits attachments, and adds value to things, the next phase in the collaboration attempted to shift from individual to more collective approaches. Inspired by the Australasian male bowerbird, who builds a structure assembled from twigs and attempts to entice a mate by decorating it with objects (often discarded detritus from human life-worlds), Shelley and I co-designed *The Human Bower* event, which was held over a weekend in May 2018 in the gardens of Torre Abbey Museum. Starting with a 'guided conversation', participants were asked to contemplate what they would like the future to look like, and then what they thought could be held on to so as to make that happen. People then selected words distilling the essence of each conversation to write on to willow branches (harvested by Shelley from a local grower undertaking annual coppicing), which they bound with brightly coloured threads, before adding to the Bower. For those who wanted to do so, these words were also written on to stones and placed in front of the Bower to mimic the bird's practice of 'displaying' its treasured things.

The event enabled people to consider their active role in imagining, designing and creating futures. Those who took part reported feeling 'more hopeful' after making the Bower, and feeling better able to express their ideas about the future, and to appreciate their role in building futures. As one person put it: 'I feel more optimistic about the future and, through thinking about [it from a] "human scale", more able to envisage it'. Others commented on the need for actions of 'un-making' to create desired futures, or letting go of what is considered redundant, outmoded or (at worst) obstructing desired futures. As another person put it:

> Assuming that what we surround ourselves with (objects, people, thoughts) will inform our attitudes and hopes for the future, can we ritualistically say goodbye to things/connections and particularly 'monuments' that give power or prestige to values that we want to leave behind? … I like the idea that some communities ritually burn or purge their collections/histories to have a spring clean or fresh start – not just get rid of stuff but to actively burn the ground etc. for new growth. I like that our idea of 'preserving our heritage' might become flexible to the idea that 'history' must physically erode, change and die – and that doing this allows all things to change and grow physically but also perceptually (e.g. narrative transformation).

These activities created a specific temporal pace – a slowness – in striking contrast to the speeding up we discussed in the introduction to this part of the book as fuelling contemporary profusion. Shelley's wider practice often asks people to participate in some form of 'making' to help people 'shift into a different mode' that enables them 'not to feel too watched', but to bring forth their hopes, ambitions, thoughts and opinions through what she calls 'a sideways glance'. Allowing time and space to think, talk, share and make, *The Human Bower* event similarly revealed (to return to Hogan and Pink's (2010) arguments) 'imaginative worlds' that may otherwise go little commented upon. The specific qualities of futures were articulated, as some people taking part described orienting themselves towards futures being much the same as today, while others predicted a radical and (typically) dystopian break. Participants commented, for example, on the anticipated natural and cultural effects of climate change. Caring for the natural world and each other, as entities perceived to require active intervention to ensure they will be there in the future, was a key theme to emerge over the weekend.

Strikingly, stuff, or the material culture of everyday life, was noticeably absent from the Bower in contrast to the earlier fieldwork leading to *The Story in the Object*. A common theme, from participants' written responses to what they thought should be let go of to make desired futures happen, was what one person called an 'addiction' to consumer culture, characterised as the accumulation of more and more material things. Another person wrote that they would like the future to be 'less materialistic' by letting go of 'too much choice of material things' and by 'only buying objects that are useful or beautiful'. They concluded that 'recycling and upcycling is the only way forward'. Similarly, someone else expressed that building *The Human Bower* 'reminded' them 'how, with time to think and room to make and talk, people and stories are what matters to me, and that material objects are the "vehicles" for those connections'.

These comments provided insight into people's experiences of the profusion predicament. They indicated a desire to be surrounded with fewer material things, but also to choose much *more carefully* those objects, that might help them to build more meaningful relationships – or 'connections' – with other people, the urban or natural environments in which they live, and wider social groups such as 'communities' or 'neighbourhoods' that provide a sense of belonging and identity. They reveal that it is the 'story' – or what may be characterised to be the meanings, significance and values – carried with and communicated through objects, that is the 'glue' that builds such connections. This theme has emerged elsewhere in this part of the book, including in the museum study in Chapter 11, where curators were concerned to put relationships between objects and people at the heart of collecting (see also Morgan and Macdonald 2020). The images that follow further illustrate these ideas, as well as the process of this arts–research collaboration, and the objects, stories and experiences generated (see Figures 14.1 to 14.18).

Notes

1. The latter also formed part of the Heritage Futures exhibition at Manchester Museum.
2. See https://heritage-futures.org/torbays-hidden-treasures.

Figure 14.1 Torquay (England), the place of the collaboration, 2017 (photograph by Jennie Morgan).

Figure 14.2 Torquay (England), the place of the collaboration, 2017 (photograph by Jennie Morgan).

Figure 14.3 Shopfront. Torbay, on the south coast of England, is characterised by a curious configuration of profusion and scarcity, 2017 (photograph by Jennie Morgan).

Figure 14.4 Shopfront. Torbay, on the south coast of England, is characterised by a curious configuration of profusion and scarcity, 2017 (photograph by Jennie Morgan).

Things kept for posterity

Ring: a gift from her mother-in-law (the previous owner)
Wooden box: for keeping 'treasures'
Notebook: for writing and keeping 'thoughts'
Portrait of a dead dog: ashes also
Photograph of children: printed from a digital image made by a friend
Stone that looks like a raptor: found when beach-combing
Mantle clock, antique barometer: 'treasured things' 'for the children'
1980s toy panda bear: 'lost' in childhood, replica 'found' on eBay in adulthood
Theatre tickets, circus programmes: reminder of 'adventures' pre-children
Hand axe: 400,000 years old, or 'a forever thing'
Coin collection: displayed in a case with printed labels
Guidebook for coastal footpath: she might put it in her coffin when she dies to mark a significant life achievement?
'Angel' garden ornament: possibly pass on to 'spiritual' grandchild
Nothing: as does not especially want to keep anything for the future|

Figure 14.5   A list of things people showed the author and the artist during their visits to people in their homes, as wanting to keep for the future.

Figure 14.6 The keeper of this stone found it 'fossil hunting'. It is small and robust, so he has not done anything special to care for it, but 'carelessly' kept it in a coat pocket. He would be sad if it were lost because it intriguingly looks like a raptor, 2017 (photograph by Jennie Morgan).

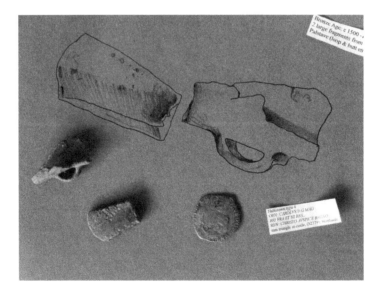

Figure 14.7 A collection of archaeological fragments kept by one man. He described these to be 'forever things', which he hopes will outlast humans. He has written labels describing what these things are, 2017 (photograph by Jennie Morgan).

Figure 14.8 The owner of this mantle clock described how she has put a handwritten note inside explaining its significance. When she gives it to her children in the future, she hopes it will help them to understand why she wants it to be kept, 2017 (photograph by Jennie Morgan).

Figure 14.9 Shelley Castle, Encounters Arts, sketches 'imposter bear', a soft toy the adult owner bought online to replicate a bear she had loved and lost as a child. Sadly, it did not look or feel the same as the original. She hoped to get rid of it, but her children have become attached, so she now feels unable to do so, 2017 (photograph by Jennie Morgan).

Figure 14.10 *Imposter Bear*, ink drawing by Shelley Castle, 2017 (© S. Castle).

Figure 14.11 Shelley Castle makes an 'object portrait' of a doll loaned for *The Story in the Object* installation. The doll was made by the lender's mother, rediscovered some 35 years after it was last seen, and has a pair of her mother's silk stockings coming out of the bottom of the legs, 2017 (© S. Castle).

Figure 14.12 *The Human Bower,* 19–20 May 2018, Torre Abbey Gardens, 2018 (photograph by Jennie Morgan).

Figure 14.13 Co-designing *The Human Bower* event to bring anthropological and creative practice together for investigating future keeping, 2018 (photograph by Jennie Morgan).

Figure 14.14 *The Human Bower,* 19–20 May 2018, Torre Abbey Gardens, 2018 (photograph by Jennie Morgan).

Figure 14.15 Binding willow branches for *The Human Bower*, 2018 (photograph by Jennie Morgan).

Figure 14.16 Careful selections: placing willow branches and futures into *The Human Bower*, 2018 (photograph by Jennie Morgan).

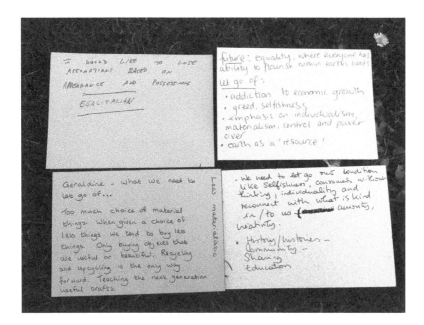

Figure 14.17 Imagining, designing and creating futures: participants in *The Human Bower* reflected on what should be kept and let go of to make desired futures, 2018 (photograph by Jennie Morgan).

Figure 14.18 Releasing what is not needed to make desired futures: posting reflections into 'Geraldine', an ex-street performer's barrow, *The Human Bower* event, 2018 (photograph by Jennie Morgan).

15
Doomed?

Sharon Macdonald, Jennie Morgan and Harald Fredheim

As we saw at the end of Chapter 13, sending items from a home to a museum is a way of removing them from one's immediate surroundings, but it is certainly not about stopping them from being kept for the future. On the contrary, it is a way of trying to ensure that they endure for longer than things usually do in domestic time frames, for 'the future' in domestic temporalities is usually only envisaged, if at all, as at most a generation or two. Museums, by contrast, promise a longer, generally unspecified, future – 'for posterity'; a future, moreover, in which objects will be valued as official *heritage*.

In this final chapter of the part of the book detailing our work on profusion, we bring together our two domains to reflect on the implications of our research for heritage futures. Looking across and between museums and homes, we highlight some of their commonalities and differences, especially with regard to how they negotiate the question that we posed at the start of Part III: *In the face of a profusion of things – especially those mass produced for mass consumption – what gets kept for the future?*

As has been clear from the preceding discussion, there are no definitive blueprints for determining what is kept – and, as such, no single answer to the question. Rather, in both museums and homes, sometimes relatively systematically and sometimes more provisionally, people try to figure out how to deal with what in both domains is widely regarded as a profusion – and often a 'too-muchness' – of things that have already been kept, as well as ones that might potentially be acquired. Amid our various interlocutors' attempts, however, certain motives and other influences have emerged as especially salient for shaping what is kept, and what is not, as we discuss further below. In each domain, we have also identified a range of strategies for 'coping with profusion', and thus for potentially avoiding being doomed to feeling overwhelmed by too much stuff.

In the final part of this chapter, then, we speculate on how some of these might be deployed in the other domain, and on the implications of this for heritage futures more generally. First, however, we further introduce the cross-domain insights from our research by turning to our discovery of 'cupboards of doom' in both museums and homes, and to what this suggests about keeping for the future.

Cupboards of doom

The cupboard of doom is a kind of purgatory for things whose fate is as yet undecided. What goes into a cupboard of doom might just turn out to be worth keeping, perhaps to be useful in some way, but such is the degree of uncertainty about this that not only are its contents hidden from view, they are not usually even accorded any kind of organisation. Instead, things are piled up, 'packed to bursting point', and are described as having been 'shoved' or even 'hurled' in there.[1] In the museum, the things in cupboards of doom are not 'accessioned' – that is, they are not formally part of the museum's collections. Perhaps they will, one day, become so. But as they probably lack accompanying documentation, they are more likely to be doomed to not being kept for the long term – if, that is, anybody ever gets around to 'sorting them out'.

The cupboard of doom is a further example of the relativities of keeping that we discussed in the introduction to this part of the book (Chapter 10). Like attics, basements and self-storage units – where the cupboard of doom might even be located – it is a space of 'absent presence', to use Kevin Hetherington's (2004) term (though not quite as he does). But in its naming and degree of intense disorder, it is an even more vivid expression of the profusion predicament. Sometimes talked about with embarrassment or even shame – manifest in a reluctance to show it, perhaps – the cupboard of doom speaks even more eloquently than those other spaces of the sense that things can be 'a burden' or 'get out of hand'. Although some of what goes into the cupboard of doom might one day find a new space and life in the museum or home, the word 'doom' implies considerable pessimism over the likely future of things accumulated in this way. Unlike Sasha Newell's (2014, 187) findings, the objects in cupboards of doom seem to be less often 'endowed with personhood, making them inalienable from the individual self and especially the collective identity of the family'. Instead, the 'doomed' things seem – as the very word 'doom' implies – to be further on the spectrum towards alienability, moving on and away, perhaps to more terminal disposal.

Nevertheless, the fact that things still lurk in such cupboards speaks to a reluctance to chuck them out. Such reluctance might potentially be understood psychologically, in terms of more general negative emotions around 'letting go' and 'loss'. While our research showed reluctance to dispose of things – and feelings of being troubled by doing so – in various other instances, it was certainly not a universal experience. Indeed, it runs counter to the positive feelings that decluttering is often said to generate. Rather, reluctance to dispose was linked either to specific things – and perhaps the human relations entangled with them, which could take the form of senses of obligation to keep things, or of affective attachment – or, as seemed most significant for the cupboards of doom, could centre on concern over possibly throwing out something that one might, in the future, wish one had not.

In addition, however, reluctance to 'tackle' cupboards of doom related to not wanting to have to deal with the stuff – to make decisions about it – at all. A cupboard of doom always needs sorting out; it is always there as a kind of reprimand for having not done so. It is not surprising in this light that the curator in the museum chapter (Chapter 11) spoke of her relief at having devised a careful acquisition process that would, she hoped, mean that the museum would no longer create cupboards of doom. She hoped thus to be able to foreclose the postponing of decision-making to the future that such cupboards allow or even encourage.

Getting rid of cupboards of doom, then, could be seen as one strategy – others of which we will see below – for dealing with profusion. But we should not forget that the cupboards themselves are also such a strategy. They are a deferral tactic that also allows for acquiring-without-fully-acquiring, for keeping-while-not-fully-keeping – even for nearly-but-not-really-disposing. As such, they illustrate well that keeping and disposing are not simply either/or binary options but are part of a spectrum that is characterised by degrees of visibility, organisation and care that are variously accorded to things.

Cupboards of doom also illustrate that storage infrastructures are variable in their capacity to contain profusion. Alongside the orderly modes of storage – especially, though not only, evident in museum shelving and drawers – are also, frequently, if not universally, less organised modes of keeping. These are especially important for things that either do not easily fit into existing classifications or physical spaces, or that, while kept, are especially close to not being.

These cupboards can also be used to make a further general point from our research, which is that what counts as profusion is not just about absolute numbers of things, but often hinges more on whether they are contained and containable by available storage. Recall the collector in Chapter 13, on domestic profusion. Despite a clear profusion of things in his home, he operated what he saw as a careful system to avoid being deluged with 'crates of stuff', and the many things he owned were carefully ordered by his own – very museological – system. What spells a sense of 'too-muchness' is more things arriving than can be properly organised and stored, the building up of backlogs and stuffed drawers – and cupboards of doom, especially when their doors no longer can be closed.

Let us turn, then, to provide a brief schematic account of the various factors we have seen in the previous chapters that influence what is kept or what somehow or other ends up staying around, and what, for one reason or another, leaves the museum or home.

Why some things stay and others leave

Although the primary focus of our research was on what is kept for the future, we found ourselves also looking at what is not kept – at practices such as domestic decluttering and museum disposal. This was not only an artefact of our research methodology, but also reflected what can be seen as a finding, namely, that what is kept is not necessarily what is actively selected but can simply be what remains, what is not disposed of. This is especially the case in homes, where we also sometimes found that some interlocutors seemed to have given little prior thought to what they would keep for the future. While there were others who certainly did so, as we have described, for many, domestic keeping for the future was not a specific organised – we might even say museological – activity, but something more provisionally pieced together from decisions about specific objects or just from what was not discarded. Nevertheless, all such keeping – and its closely entangled counterpart of disposing – was shaped by various values and other factors. Below, building on the previous chapters, we list those that we identified – in effect, through grounded theorising – in our research. For any particular thing, the relativity of its staying or leaving – including the particular routes on which it might go (for example: in the case of homes, to a member of one's family; in the case of museums, to another museum) – is generally shaped by a mixture of these values and factors, sometimes characterised by struggle or push-and-pull. As our research also showed, many of these values and factors are imbued with emotion, with individuals in both domains sometimes talking in terms of feelings, which might also make rationalising decisions seem awkward or inappropriate.

1. **Memory-value** – that an object is regarded as a carrier of significant personal or collective memory, and that it can potentially work as such in the future, was undoubtedly a key value in both domains, especially for more active forms of selection for the future. In some cases we witnessed, the search for the right kinds of objects to perform this future heritage work was very marked. Some kinds of memories also loomed large, and could be regarded as subcategories of memory-value. This included the following. **Place-value** – objects selected to carry memory connected to specific locations – was significant in both homes and museums. **Event-value** – to remember specific moments – could also be seen in both, working in terms of specific life events for personal remembering (for example, a birth) or events in collective histories for museums, although the latter could sometimes play a part in personal collecting too. **Memory of individuals** – that is, the recollection of specific people – was also characteristic of both domains. While these forms of value were shared, museum selections were more likely to be characterised by notions of 'representativeness', though these were not entirely absent in homes.

2. **Obligation** – senses of obligation to keep, and sometimes also to acquire, things were evident in both domains. This could even be to the extent that people said that there were things that they would prefer to get rid of but that they felt themselves obliged to keep. For museums, this sometimes lay in what was seen as a fundamental duty to keep what had been given to them for preserving for perpetuity. More specifically, however, there were cases of gifts (in museums, usually called donations), which in both domains established relational links to people, which meant that getting rid of something could feel like a disrespect for that relationship – the equivalent of failed reciprocity in Maussian exchange analysis (Mauss 1990). In addition to this **gift-value** was also sometimes a sense of obligation to objects on account of the fact that they had already been around a long time – thus, what we might call **time-value**, or, more specifically, respect for **staying power.** Things that had been kept a long time – either in museums or homes – were seen to somehow have *earned* a right to remain.

3. **Materialities** – the physical qualities of objects also shaped staying power. Some were seen as too large, fragile or awkward to move. Furthermore, the small and relatively invisible could also have staying power, hidden in storage or even in cupboards of doom, thus evading routine clearing up, decluttering or disposal. Such materialities could, equally, shape whether something was acquired or not in the first place – would

there be sufficient space for it or, particularly for museums, might its conservation demands be too much to cope with?

4. **Use-value** – in homes, especially, many objects are acquired for their functionality and they often remain because they are regarded as useful. In museums, objects are normally taken out of their everyday use but nevertheless museums may acquire objects in order to use them in exhibitions. Increasingly, it seems, many museums acquire objects in relation to specific exhibitions rather than to complete collections, and in some cases they seek forms of temporary or provisional acquisition, such as through loans or (particularly for museums of contemporary everyday life) objects that are displayed in exhibitions but that are not formally accessioned for long-term futures in the museum.

5. **Rarity and age-value** – in both domains, the fact that an object is rare or old (which is not necessarily equivalent to having staying power within a location) could be a reason for acquiring and keeping certain things, or for seeking good future homes for them. These were not, however, prominent values in our research settings. For museums whose focus is not on the contemporary everyday, these values are likely to be more significant.

6. **Aesthetic value** – the beauty of certain things was also not a prominent value in the domains that we studied. It was occasionally mentioned in both domains, although the objects judged lovely were not necessarily so by canonical criteria. As has been argued elsewhere in relation to aesthetic judgements, it seems likely that in some or even many cases when objects were judged beautiful their place in more specific regimes of value, notably their memory-value, were at play (Bourdieu 1984).

7. **Financial value** – although monetary or financial value is sometimes considered to be especially significant in capitalist societies, the monetary worth of things was only rarely mentioned in either museums or homes, and was not usually given as a reason in itself for acquiring or keeping something (indeed, cost was more likely to be a reason *not* to acquire something). Partly due no doubt to the fact that our focus was on everyday and, especially, mass-produced things, when monetary value was mentioned, it was usually in relation to something having now gathered financial worth, perhaps due to its rarity.

It is worth here comparing these with the values identified by Nathalie Heinich (2011) in her research on heritage: (1) authenticity; (2) ancientness;

(3) rarity; (4) beauty; and (5) signification. We too identified rarity and beauty as relevant values, and while 'ancientness' was not pertinent in our case, some kind of age-value nevertheless was. What she calls 'signification' has strong overlap with our 'memory-value'. 'Authenticity' she considers to be 'an absolute value … the very core of heritage' (Heinich 2011, 123). That there was virtually no discussion of authenticity in our research sites might, then, be seen as surprising. One explanation might be that it was so taken for granted as to never need to be mentioned. In some ways that was the case: the origins of these mostly fairly new objects were not in question, and it is usually only when authenticity is doubted that it is explicitly invoked. In addition, however, the criteria for selection and keeping that we witnessed seem to suggest senses of authenticity that might be broader than the scientifically asserted 'bond between … the object and its origin' (Heinich 2011, 123) that is so central in Heinich's research on French national heritage administrators (see also Heinich 2009). Rather, what we have here called memory-value might be seen as providing the authentic links in relation to the kind of heritage on which we focus. Our research thus also contributes to findings of others concerning the variable forms of authenticity evoked in relation to different kinds of heritage and heritage-making (Wang 1999; Jones 2010).

Where our research also departs from that of Heinich – despite her emphasis on looking at the actual criteria used in the practice of selecting what should be accorded the status of national heritage – is that we also give recognition to the more practical, material, contingent and personally inflected influences on what is kept. Although these loom especially large in homes, they are also, as we have seen (perhaps primed by our attention to homes), present in museums.

All of these various factors – values, obligation and duty – can contribute to a profusion of things in both museums and homes. In particular, they can support a situation in which more things are pulled in and kept than are pushed or otherwise drift out. By thinking further about these factors, however, we can perhaps also see ways of coping with what can sometimes become problematic profusion.

Coping with profusion

In our research in both homes and museums, we witnessed the implementation of strategies to either limit acquisition or to encourage objects to leave the premises – or both. The speed of entry and leaving was, however, significantly different in homes and museums: the former typically acquire many more things and also discard them more readily and rapidly. Museums, by contrast, are institutions of more considered and limited arrivals and – even more so – departures. The ways in which they each manage their different temporalities of object-flow, however, may also potentially offer some possibilities for each other of dealing with what both often experienced as problematic profusion of things.

Beginning with acquisition, the museums' slower modes of acquisition potentially might be adopted, at least in part, in domestic settings. Particularly in light of considerations of sustainability, thinking more explicitly about objects being around for a long time can help to act as a brake on the fast consumption patterns discussed in the introduction to this part of the book. This is a point made by decluttering advice too, with Zemirah Moffat, at our 'declutterer meets museum staff' event, reminding participants of William Morris's maxim to 'have nothing in your houses that you do not know to be useful, or believe to be beautiful'. That this directly indexes values that emerged as significant in our research shows too that more explicit reflection on the 'value-work' that each object is intended to do could contribute to more considered – and therefore limited – acquisition. Museums might further refine their own practice in this regard too, as is already under way in the form of establishing typologies of values and processes of what is usually called significance assessment, which are intended to create criteria to help decide what should be selected and preserved for the future (see Fredheim and Khalaf 2016; Macdonald and Morgan 2018b). What such processes can also do is to ensure that objects are selected with sufficient documentation to make them usable in the future – the lack of such information having clearly showed itself to be problematic for many museums in our study. Tacking back to homes again, such documentation practices might also be employed for selected things to be kept for the future in homes – the equivalent perhaps of the annotated photograph album rather than the mass of unlabelled and unsorted pictures.

This brings us to the question of the digital – with its greater saving of physical space – possibly replacing material acquisition or keeping. Although we have personal experience of only keeping digital documents and of purchasing fewer physical books, and there are cases of people adopting such strategies in quite radical forms (see, for example, Portrait 1, in Miller 2008), we saw no concerted moves in this direction in our research. Indeed, what we witnessed was more to the contrary, namely that the digital became an added burden, especially for museums, which are sometimes concerned about whether they should also collect digital objects, and with digitisation of collections becoming another task to accomplish (perhaps with inadequate resources).

Given that the sense of obligation in relation to gifts emerged as especially significant in our research ('Donations – everybody's nightmare!' exclaimed one curator), strategies to allow for not feeling bad about not accepting or keeping them seem worth addressing, if ending up with too many things is to be avoided. Such strategies are already emerging in popular literature, such as James Wallman's *Stuffocation* (2015), with its advice to individuals to request as gifts contributions towards experiences (such as a meal out) rather than durable objects. Museums in our study revealed a range of approaches, from carefully worded letters to explain why they could not accept certain donations, to installing a prominent display of objects that they had already rejected. Staff concern about hurting people's feelings was also reflected in the fact that they sometimes suggested other institutions that might be willing to accept the donation – as part of the looking for alternative future trajectories, rather than outright binning, that was more widely characteristic of the treatment of many objects, especially gifts. At one of our knowledge-exchange events, there was also talk of asking those making donations to make a further financial donation to contribute to the costs of future storage and conservation. This was judged to be a good idea, but, perhaps because it infringed upon the ethics of the gift, was also judged hard to implement and 'may be a bit cheeky'.

Although many things depart from homes, as we saw in the introduction to this part of the book (Chapter 10) and in our curating domestic profusion chapter (Chapter 13), there is still often an experience of more and more things building up, with certain kinds of things being especially likely to be retained or, at least, not pushed out. These were especially those things connected with memory-value or holding certain obligations, in other words, carrying certain relationships – although other factors discussed above, such as physical qualities, could also be involved. Advice from declutterers to ritualise processes of discarding, perhaps even seeing it as a kind of 'death' that needs a period of 'bereavement' – as was suggested by a participant in our 'declutter meets museum staff' event – or Marie Kondo's advice to thank objects before saying goodbye to them, were seen as potentially helpful in such circumstances. Also crucial was what would happen to objects later, with certain routes, such as to charity shops where they could have a new life with somebody else, for example, often being preferred over the rubbish bin.

For museums, as discussed above, removing objects that have been accessioned is a subject that has come to be openly addressed relatively recently, and is characterised by legal as well as moral and cultural considerations. In relation to senses of problematic profusion, however, it was something that many of the museums that we studied were interested to at least contemplate and, as described above, we followed some cases of how they went about doing so. What was especially clear in these cases was that there was felt to be a strong need to 'do it properly', to ensure that there would not be discarding of things whose loss might be regretted in the future. This has led to the expansion of rationalisation processes for doing this. Insofar as these processes entail considering each object against certain specified criteria, they are not dissimilar from domestic decluttering processes. They typically differ, however, in that the museum processes themselves usually entail careful documentation of what is being deaccessioned and where it goes. Potentially, that might be adopted in homes too but, in this case, it would probably simply make the task of discarding all the more onerous. As with homes, however, consideration of where objects will go is very important in how acceptable their departure is seen to be by those involved. That they first be offered to another museum is expected by professional codes of ethics (Museums Association 2014; 2015). Even beyond this, a hope for 'good homes' is generally preferred and, in relation to this, forms of new life for objects, such as the Museum of London sending deaccessioned hand tools for reuse, are emerging as part of the increasing emphasis on museum disposal. Other approaches and strategies also emerged across our two domains. These included, for example, the idea of museums having periodic systematic reviews of what they hold – the equivalent of a spring clean perhaps;[2] or for both domains to think of objects not as necessarily enduring for ever, but as having a certain 'shelf-life' or natural lifespan (Morgan and Macdonald 2020; see also Harrison 2013b suggesting periodic review of heritage listings).

***

The latter idea also took shape partly in relation to thinking about and with the other themes in Heritage Futures. Diversity, Transformation and Uncertainty all, in various ways, challenge modes of imagining or performing heritage as something static, unchanging and performed once and for all. Instead, they show in various ways and to varying extents, as appropriate to the different domains with which they deal, possibilities of working with change and even, as one of the participants in our final knowledge-exchange workshop expressed it, of 'losing well' (see footnote 11 of Chapter 13, as well as further discussion in Chapter 23 and Part V, Transformation). In contexts in which the profusion of things seems increasingly unsustainable, and even threatening of doom, acquiring and keeping well seem to be equally crucial. In Part IV, Uncertainty (following the visual essay documenting the second of our three cross-programme knowledge-exchange events on collections as techniques of worlding), we turn to consider the contexts of the management of different forms of toxic heritage over very long-term futures in which such considerations become particularly acute.

Notes

1. Quotations here and in the following description are from previous chapters and from the post 'The Cupboard of Doom' on Tania Kindersley's (2011) blog.
2. See the blog about the Profusion research, 'Holding on to the past: Why decluttering is such a dilemma' (University of York 2016).

Cross-theme knowledge-exchange event 2

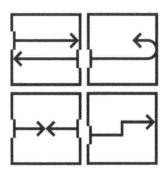

16
Collections as techniques of worlding

Second cross-theme knowledge-exchange workshop, 28 February–
2 March 2017, Royal Botanic Gardens, Kew, UK
Rodney Harrison and Sefryn Penrose

We have already noted in Part I of this book that observation is always itself a form of intervention (for example, see Barad 2007; Daston and Lunbeck 2011; Latour 1987; 2013; Stengers 2000) – that realities are built, designed and held together by observational and ordering practices. In heritage, the classificatory systems employed to order and account for different conservation targets are also systems for specifying and accounting for forms of risk – factors that are seen to endanger those objects, places, practices, languages, people, plants and animals that different organisations collect, curate and care for (or, perhaps, do not – as discussed in Part V, Transformation). These classificatory systems produce different transactional realities (see the discussion in Part II, Diversity), which relate to a broader 'endangerment sensibility' (see Vidal and Dias 2016a) and order and hold together worlds in different ways.

The second Heritage Futures cross-theme knowledge-exchange event took place from 28 February to 2 March 2017 and was co-organised by Sefryn Penrose and Rodney Harrison, along with members of the Kew Science team at the Royal Botanic Gardens at Kew (see further details below and Figures 16.1 to 16.12 at the end of this chapter). We invited individuals from a range of different heritage organisations who are involved in the work of collecting, conserving, curating and caring for heritage in its many forms to come together to explore how their practices and procedures contribute to defining and shaping material and discursive legacies that build different futures. In particular, we asked participants to focus on how the different classificatory systems that underpin different kinds of collections contribute to the construction of different kinds of coexistent worlds and to consider how these different worlds might have different and sometimes conflicting conservation priorities.

Kew, with its various very different collections – including the Herbarium (see Figure 16.1 and Figure 16.2), Economic Botany Collection, Library and range of 'live' collections – was the ideal location in which to explore these questions. We saw clearly how the same objects might be classified and treated quite differently in these different contexts, and be used in quite different ways in setting conservation priorities, and in documenting and understanding diversity and its loss in different contexts. Through close observation of the practices of one specific organisation, we hoped to stimulate each participant to reflect on their own practices afresh as part of this 'para-ethnographic' co-investigation into the collections as 'worlding practices' (see Barad 2007).

Participants were asked to consider a series of questions during the various workshop activities, site visits, tours and talks to give focus to these workshop themes. These were as follows:

- What are your own/organisation's/field's classificatory/collection/curation practices?
- What is the background/foundation of these practices (for example, disciplinary, practical/pragmatic, historical)?
- How do the classificatory systems that underpin your objects of conservation relate to the collecting and ordering practices you employ? To what extent do the practices relate to specific ways of categorising risks?
- What are the stated aims of your organisation/organisational practices?
- What restrictions do you face in fulfilling them?
- What is the place of the future in your practices and in your understanding of your work?
- When is the future that you are conceiving of (if you are …)?
- Do you consider this future in relation to other futures/the future of others?

The workshop began with introductions to Kew and its collections led by our hosts Mark Nesbitt (curator, Economic Botany Collection), Caroline Cornish (principal researcher, Mobile Museum Project, Royal Holloway) (see Figure 16.3), Nina Davies (assistant curator, Africa and Madagascar) and Clare Drinkell (assistant curator, Asia), and a tour of the Herbarium and Economic Botany Collection led by David Goyder (research leader, Africa and Madagascar). We then received an introduction to classification from Gemma Bramley (research leader in the Asia Team), after which participants, using the biscuits they were asked to bring with them, were invited to create their own categorisation systems – based on a range of factors such as shape, colour, size, filling and coating – to show how each creates its own world of values around itself (see Figure 16.8).

Tours of the Herbarium, Economic Botany Collection and Tropical Nursery helped us to understand the different forms of collecting that are undertaken by the organisation, and how these reflect different values and conservation priorities (see Figures 16.4 to 16.6, Figure 16.9 and Figure 16.10). We also considered the ways in which classification is represented by data and metadata records, reflecting philosopher of science Geoffrey Bowker's (2000) observations of biodiversity as 'datadiversity'. Eve Lucas (research leader, Integrated Monography), described how the new system of phylogeny (the study of the evolutionary history and relationships among individuals or groups of organisms) has recently caused a major reconsideration of existing taxonomic systems for organising the plant world. Where taxonomies have previously made reference to similarities and degrees of difference in plant morphology and composition, new approaches to phylogeny, built on new developments in understanding of DNA, have provided new and quite different templates for ordering and classifying plants. At Kew, the Angiosperm (flowering plants) Phylogeny Group's fourth iteration of its phylogenetic taxonomy (APG IV), published in 2016 and partly developed by Kew practitioners, has been introduced and has led to a major reorganisation of Kew's collections and how they are understood. We drew on this specific case study to think more generally about how shifts between old and new categorisations change practices (and, in turn, the worlds that such practices produce).

Kew curators Nina Davies and Clare Drinkell then led a beginners' workshop in plant pressing – the practice of creating specimens for the Herbarium – handing out cuttings for the participants to attempt to press themselves (see Figure 16.12). Begonias, ferns, cacti, papyri were flattened on to Kew's specimen papers, and accompanying sheets filled out, describing the characters of the plants. These practical insights into the heritage practices of our partner organisations have helped us and other project participants to understand in a more intimate way how specific heritage practices are performed and enacted, and the implications of such practices in the work of conservation globally.

In the evening, our speaker Mandana Seyfeddinipur, director of the Endangered Languages Documentation Programme (ELDP) at the School of Oriental and African Studies (SOAS), helped us to consider in more detail how the questions we had been considering in relation to botanical specimens might also apply to other forms of cultural collections.

We came together on the final day of the workshop to consider in more general terms the themes of the workshop. If heritage involves the conservation of different kinds of endangered objects in the present for the future, what is the precise relationship between the ways we order those conservation objects and the future worlds these practices produce? And how can an understanding of the relationships between collecting, ordering and worlding practices help us to make better decisions in the present about the legacies we bestow upon the future? We left Kew with a clearer sense of the ways in which different classificatory systems build different kinds of worlds, and where these might resonate or come into conflict with one another.

Figure 16.1   Inside the Herbarium at Kew (photograph by Rodney Harrison).

Figure 16.2 Cabinets inside the Herbarium at Kew (photograph by Rodney Harrison).

Figure 16.3 An introduction to the history of Kew with Caroline Cornish (photograph by Rodney Harrison).

Figure 16.4   Workshop participants enjoy a tour of the Herbarium at Kew with David Goyder (photograph by Rodney Harrison).

Figure 16.5   Workshop participants in the Economic Botany Collection, Kew (photograph by Rodney Harrison).

Figure 16.6   Inside one of the cabinets in one of the older wings of the Herbarium at Kew. Folders with a red line denote type specimens (photograph by Rodney Harrison).

Figure 16.7 Workshop participants undertook a number of creative tasks inspired by Kew's collections (photograph by Rodney Harrison).

Figure 16.8 Biscuits organised on a sliding scale of beauty during one of the workshop activities (photograph by Sefryn Penrose).

Figure 16.9   Tour of the tropical nursery, Royal Botanic Gardens Kew (photograph by Rodney Harrison).

Figure 16.10   Inside the tropical nursery, Royal Botanic Gardens Kew (photograph by Rodney Harrison).

Figure 16.11 'Listening' to bees in *The Hive*, an immersive artwork designed by UK-based artist Wolfgang Buttress, originally created for the UK Pavilion at the 2015 Milan Expo (photograph by Rodney Harrison).

Figure 16.12 IUCN director of world heritage, Tim Badman; artist Pernilla Frid; and Heritage Futures co-investigator Caitlin DeSilvey, learning to press plants during the workshop (photograph by Sefryn Penrose).

Part IV
Uncertainty

How does the perceived uncertainty of the long-term future provide opportunities for heritage and conservation practice?

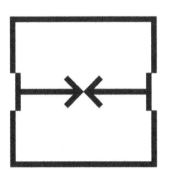

17
Uncertain futures

Sarah May and Cornelius Holtorf

You can be sure that if a model says the world will end in 50 years, the model itself will be gone in 25.

Steve Fuller (2013, n.p.)

The demand for certainty is one which is natural to man [sic], but is nevertheless an intellectual vice ... To endure uncertainty is difficult, but so are most of the other virtues.

Bertrand Russell (1950, 27)

Planning for an uncertain future: Practices in four domains for the long term

Uncertainty is a basic element of anticipating futures – we can always be surprised, even as one month becomes the next. Sociologists have taken many different approaches to the way that we manage this uncertainty in everyday life, especially as it relates to the idea of risk (Beck 1992; Zinn 2008; Miller 2009). Uncertainty has also become a major topic of discussion in both natural and cultural heritage conservation (see Henderson 2018; Chilvers 2008). Futures studies and forecasting work on the general assumption that the further we imagine into the future, the greater the uncertainty of what will actually happen becomes. It is reasonable to presume that the basic conditions of life will stay stable for the next few years; many people hope for stability through a lifetime. But no one would expect that communities a thousand, ten thousand or one hundred thousand years hence would live like humans do today, and share their priorities, understandings and ways of communicating. Changes – in climate, demography, technology, social structure, health, even biology – are to be expected over long time frames. Usually, people manage this uncertainty by simply not thinking about it. But there are a number of domains of practice where uncertainty is managed professionally. We explore some of these in this part of the book.

In heritage management, uncertainty about the future is often figured as an inevitable challenge for all planning – something to factor in, to prepare for. As discussed in Part I, this is in keeping with thinking associated with risk cultures (Douglas and Wildavsky 1982; Beck 1992; Lupton 1999; Samimian-Darash and Rabinow 2015), where anticipation and predictability are considered to be desirable and uncertainty is minimised. To this way of thinking, appropriate management procedures (and practices) will reduce uncertainty and allow for the future to be predicted and controlled as much as possible. This confidence in the capacity of management to control uncertainty falls away when one considers the deep time frames that we work with in this part of the book. When we are thinking one hundred thousand years (or more) ahead of us, uncertainty regarding the details of that future is unavoidable.

In this part of the book, we discuss our work with four different domains of practice, each of which share ambitions to manage deep time frames that reach into the distant future and the need to manage uncertainty. These domains of practice deal with nuclear waste, a space message, a long-term storage site and world heritage respectively.

The **Swedish Nuclear Fuel and Waste Management Company (SKB)** (www.skb.com) is responsible for the management of Swedish radioactive waste, which mostly derives from nuclear power plants. In 2011, SKB applied to the relevant authorities to build and operate a repository for spent nuclear fuel some 500 metres below the ground at Forsmark in the municipality of Östhammar, north of Stockholm. The challenge is to deposit and store this material safely for one hundred thousand years. In this context, SKB has been taking part in ongoing discussions of records, knowledge and memory in nuclear waste management (Schröder 2019). Anders Högberg and Cornelius Holtorf have collaborated with SKB since 2011, investigating the implications of considering nuclear waste as a particular kind of cultural heritage that we leave behind for future generations (Högberg et al. 2017; Holtorf and Högberg forthcoming c; see further discussion in Chapter 19). Archaeologists have expertise that is relevant to deal with the task of communicating across very long time periods. In this case, the challenge is to inform hominids (or, indeed, other sentient biological organisms) living thousands of years from now about the nature and significance of this particular legacy from the nuclear age, so as to prevent inadvertent intrusion. In March 2016, the Heritage Futures project visited the site at Forsmark during its first knowledge-exchange workshop, organised in collaboration with SKB (see Chapter 9).

The **One Earth: New Horizons Message** is a space message proposed for transmission to NASA's *New Horizons* spacecraft, which was launched in 2006 and is now travelling at high speed beyond the boundaries of the solar system. Initiated and directed by artist Jon Lomberg, the idea of the project is to create a digital successor to the legendary 1977 *Voyager* Golden Records, for which Lomberg was the design director. The new message will take the form of a globally crowdsourced collection of text, pictures, sounds, software and other content stored in the computer memory of the *New Horizons* spacecraft. The message is intended to be a decipherable greeting to any extraterrestrials who find the spacecraft in the far future, as well as a self-portrait of humanity on Earth. The process of creating this particular legacy for the universe in eternity is also a message to humans on Earth about the heritage we share on this planet (see further discussion in Chapter 20). At the time of writing, the project has failed to gain NASA's formal support and has not been implemented.

The **Memory of Mankind (MOM)** (www.memory-of-mankind.com) project involves long-term storage of stoneware ceramic tiles containing a printed, analogue record of our time. Created and managed by the ceramicist Martin Kunze, it is proposed that a large collection of these data carriers containing huge amounts of information will be stored for up to one million years in the salt mines of Hallstatt in the Salzkammergut area in Austria. Under these conditions, it is thought that this 'time capsule' will be protected from oblivion caused by the possible consequences of ecological, economic or other processes leading to the loss of data, especially of digital data, which is particularly fragile. The MOM preserves a wide range of information about our age; it amounts to a particular form of cultural heritage preserved as a legacy for the long-term future (see further discussion in Chapter 21).

World Heritage Sites are selected by UNESCO on the basis and by the mechanisms of the 1972 Convention Concerning the Protection of the World Cultural and Natural Heritage (World Heritage Convention; UNESCO 1972) (https://whc.unesco.org/). This Convention has been signed by nearly 200 states parties, and at the time of writing there are more than 1,100 sites inscribed on the World Heritage List. It recognises in its Preliminaries that 'the cultural heritage and the natural heritage are increasingly threatened with destruction', and considers that 'deterioration or disappearance of any item of the cultural or natural heritage constitutes a harmful impoverishment of the heritage of all the nations of the world' (UNESCO 1972, 1). According to Article 4 of the Convention, each state party recognises therefore 'the duty of ensuring the identification,

Figure 17.1 The village of Glenridding and Ullswater lake in the Lake District in the UK (photograph by David Iliff CC BY-SA 3.0).

protection, conservation, presentation and transmission to future generations of the cultural and natural heritage' (UNESCO 1972, 3) inscribed on the list. We focused in particular on the Lake District in Cumbria, United Kingdom (see Figure 17.1), which was inscribed as a cultural landscape on the World Heritage List in 2017. Its value has been officially described in these terms:

> The combined work of nature and human activity has produced a harmonious landscape in which the mountains are mirrored in the lakes. Grand houses, gardens and parks have been purposely created to enhance the landscape's beauty. This landscape was greatly appreciated from the 18th century onwards by the Picturesque and later Romantic movements, which celebrated it in paintings, drawings and words. It also inspired an awareness of the importance of beautiful landscapes and triggered early efforts to preserve them.
>
> (UNESCO 2017, n.p.)

We found during our fieldwork that the Lake District relates to the theme of uncertainty and connects to our other domains of heritage and conservation practice in several ways. The region's inscription on UNESCO's list of World Heritage Sites allowed us to consider practices associated with world heritage inscription, its immediate aftermath, and World Heritage Site management and 'transmission to future generations' more generally. We also looked at how the practices involved in managing uncertainty affected nuclear waste management and related landscape practice on the coastal fringes on the western side of the district. Sometimes called 'The Western Lakes' and sometimes called 'Britain's Energy Coast', this area has a series of small towns that service some high-profile industries. The biggest employer in the region is Sellafield Nuclear Site, the first nuclear power station in the world and one of the most complex problems for decommissioning and management of nuclear waste. The location of the site, and the expertise of those who work there, make the siting of a final repository for nuclear waste seem attractive to planners. But local resistance has required a rethink, and only low-level waste is to be managed there in the long term. The Lake District is also home to one of the UK's Dark Sky Discovery Sites, in Ennerdale. These sites are managed to reduce artificial light, allowing for astronomical observation and appreciation of the night skies. The Science and Technology Facilities Council conduct regular dark sky sessions at the Lower Gillerthwaite Field Centre, which encourage amateur astronomers and members of the public to explore deep space. These outreach sessions helped us consider the role of space and space messaging in contemporary culture. In this sense, the Lake District became a central case study, as there we were effectively able to pin down many ideas, concepts and practices related to the notion of uncertainty of the future.

The specific domains considered here are distinctive for the very long time frames within which those futures are conceived of; they engage with 'deep time' (for example, Benford 1999; Ginn et al. 2018). In practical terms, these domains consider the future as 'eternity', and assume some kind of persistence, perpetuity and timelessness in their activities, where their own realms do not fundamentally change but essentially stay the same. A final nuclear repository and a long-term information storage site are not envisioned to be opened and reorganised at some point. Likewise, World Heritage Sites on Earth and messages in outer space, once created, are assumed to be preserved and valued for all time. But any such timeless stability is far from certain, even absurd.

We have a range of words in common parlance to deal with these long time frames: 'forever', 'eternity', 'perpetuity'. Each of these words has a slightly different nuance and is commonly used in different but overlapping fields (see also Part V, Transformation). 'Perpetuity' is most commonly used in legal discussions to distinguish between fixed arrangements (such as a 100-year lease) and those which have no end date. 'Eternity' is more often used in philosophical and religious discussions, and references a notion of persistence and permanence in the face of change. In Aristotelian thinking, time is defined as the 'moving likeness of eternity', which does not move but is unchanging (Roark 2011, 24). This notion of eternity as outside the uncertainties of time is also reflected in Christian thought. In a recent treatise on Britain's future, Bishop John Setamu (2015, 25) argues that it is the present that is uncertain; the eternal future is set by God's plan. 'Forever' is perhaps the most commonly used and the least well defined, so that its inclusion in heritage strategy is both immediately comprehensible and beyond critical assessment (see further discussion in Chapters 1 and 2 of this volume).

But while the practice of World Heritage management may not fix its futures beyond these philosophical framings, nuclear waste management, deep-space messaging and, to a certain extent, long-term information storage, work in more concrete and specific definitions, sometimes referred to as 'clock time' (and this approach is also clear in the Long Now Foundation's, 10,000-year Clock of the Long Now project). The time frame it takes to send a message to deep space can be calculated through the speed of spacecraft and the distances involved. The long-term storage of information is planned for in relation to known rates of decay for different media and of the geological changes of the surrounding rock. Most famously, and perhaps most crucially, the half-life of radioactive material determines the length of time it needs to be managed to avoid harm to humans and other animals.

Nonetheless, while these deep times may be a matter of physics and geology rather than philosophy, they are still open to political discussion. The binding regulations of the United States Nuclear Regulatory Commission require the disposal of high-level radioactive waste in a geological repository at Yucca Mountain, with safe performance for ten thousand years after disposal (UN NRC 2009, § 63.113). In Germany, on the other hand, national legislation of the Repository Site Selection Act (Standortauswahlgesetz) stipulates that similar material needs to be deposited in a geological repository that has best chances to provide safe storage for one million years (Federal Ministry of Justice and Consumer Protection 2017, § 1 (2)). These differences in part reflect the character of the underlying political discussions that are framed by the futures under discussion in given societal contexts. While to those outside of the waste management sphere these time frames may seem indistinguishable, and indeed incomprehensible, to the engineers with legal responsibility for them, they are all too real.

One way to reconcile timeless futures and eternity with the clock time of nuclear waste may be to consider kairological time (from the Greek *kairos*), described by Gault (1995, 155) as: 'a time of opportunities and events. It is the time of right times, the right times for things to happen ... If we feel a hunger and consequently announce "It is time for lunch"'. While nuclear waste management refers to 'clock time' futures, the political

Figure 17.2 Erich Berger and Mari Keto's installation *Inheritance* consists of a box to be passed on as an heirloom and heritage to future generations, but it is also a repetitive ritual and intangible inheritance. Part of the exhibition Perpetual Uncertainty, curated by Ele Carpenter and held at Malmö Art Museum in Malmö, Sweden, 24 April–26 August 2018 (photograph by Daniel Lindskog).

concern is for the right time, the time when the radiological nature of the material can be managed without containment. This is referenced in an artwork by Erich Berger and Mari Keto called *Inheritance*, a piece of jewellery made from uranium, packaged with a measurement system to determine how radioactive it is (see Figure 17.2). Each generation is invited to measure the radioactivity and decide whether to store or wear the jewellery. By the same token, the information storage sites and the space message imply the arrival of the moment of discovery and revelation by future genera tions and extraterrestrial intelligence respectively. Time that is responsive to the moment of opportunity may help us bridge the different methods of understanding the long time frames in our comparative domains (see also the discussion on time in Chapter 24).

Comparative approaches and methods

The domains of practice described in this part of the book sit at strange interstices between local and global practices. The World Heritage

Convention was developed at the same time as other international conventions intended to define what Brumann and Berliner (2016, 8) have referred to as 'superordinate level of concern … on the high seas, outer space and Antarctic', and is linked to UNESCO's purpose of fostering world peace and human rights globally. Although World Heritage Sites themselves have very firmly defined local borders and constitute prime examples of national heritage, many practices associated with their inscription and management are inherently global, constantly referring to global documents, bodies, politics (Brumann and Berliner 2016). Similarly, although nuclear waste is managed in very well-defined and controlled locations, national and international regulation and politics dominate the practices of that management. Space messaging locates the Earth within the galaxy, but associated practices tend to be national yet with transnational and global aspirations. The long-term information storage at the MOM is intended to be secure for the future of 'civilisation', as conceived globally, but it draws to a great extent on central European content and on the specific local affordances of the Hallstatt salt mines (including their World Heritage status). For this reason, although our empirical research has drawn heavily on place-based investigation on our case study of the Lake District, it has also drawn on multiple other investigations, and on non-localised sources evoking global dimensions.

During fieldwork, both on geographical locations connected to each of our examples and at the computer from which we accessed relevant documents on the internet, we took an iterative approach to engagement between the different elements of these heritage assemblages (see Harrison 2013a; 2018), looking for conjunctions and disjunctions between them. We met nuclear waste experts in Paris and Stockholm, Jon Lomberg of the One Earth: New Horizons Message project in Hawaii, world heritage experts in Delhi and Nara, and Martin Kunze of the Memory of Mankind facility in Hallstatt. We worked with the different strands of texts and documentation that accrue around our examples, alert to the distinctions of purpose and audience between (for example) strategic documents, strategy papers, minutes, instructions, letters, publicity documents and academic texts. We considered how these resonated with the personal understandings of deep time held by different people involved with the case studies, using semi-structured interviews, ethnographic approaches and lessons gained during our knowledge-exchange workshops.

We took a similar approach to the material culture and landscape of our central case study in the Lake District, including some formal recording and some less-structured engagement to see how the different aspects reflect and create the complex understandings of deep time that may support or undermine the formally expressed views we describe from the other aspects. A key part of this engagement was developing 'film-as-method' interactions in order to frame them for analysis rather than solely to produce outputs. The process of filming places the researcher in a different relation to the material than note taking, still photography and audio interviewing. It particularly highlights aspects of movement and change in the landscape. Similarly, the process of film editing draws attention to the connections and disconnections between field sites and participants (see Chapter 1 and Bartolini and DeSilvey (2020a) for more detailed accounts of how film-as-method was used in the Heritage Futures research programme). We cycled between these different elements, returning to each with insights from the others.

Since the purpose of our work has been comparative, our focus has been on the connection – or indeed lack of connection – between domains (observations that were also made in each of the other thematic parts of the book, and to which we return in the concluding part). We have not attempted to describe or analyse practice in any one domain; rather, we have explored the nodes and modes of connection, the framings from one domain that illuminate practice in another. At times this has felt unmanageable. What we write is not primarily about the Lake District, or nuclear waste management, or World Heritage Site management, or space messaging or long-term storage. It is about how practice in those domains engages with the long-term futures that are uncertain, but nonetheless frame their purpose.

In addition to fieldwork in places where futures are managed, we have also engaged with the practices of management at international meetings, notably the Organisation for Economic Co-operation and Development (OECD) Nuclear Energy Agency's Record, Knowledge and Memory Project meeting in Paris in 2015, the International Union for the Conservation of Nature (IUCN) World Congress in Hawaii in 2017 and the International Council of Monuments and Sites (ICOMOS) World Congress in Delhi in 2018 (see further discussion in Chapter 1). Our observations of and engagements with these meetings form an important part of our empirical work. We also on several occasions (in Paris 2015, in Forsmark and Stockholm in 2016 (see Chapter 9), in London at Kew in 2017 (see Chapter 16) and in the Lake District in 2017) brought representatives from various of our four domains together to stimulate direct 'knowledge exchange', involving mutual listening, learning and inspiration.

From risk to opportunity: An intellectual framework

The concepts of certainty and safety are semantically closely connected. In German and Swedish, common terms for uncertainty (*Unsicherheit* and *osäkerhet* respectively) refer to a lack not only of predictability but also of reliability and safety. Uncertainty can thus be read as a judgement, especially in relation to nuclear waste, as if it were the role of these domains to achieve safety by obliterating uncertainty.

Even in English, uncertainty is often seen as a problem because it involves risk. The future is contingent and uncertain in the sense that what exactly is going to happen in the future cannot be known in the present. The more distant the future we consider, the more open it becomes. This profound uncertainty invites futurologists, clairvoyants and prophets to provide certainty about the future. In between total ignorance and certain knowledge lies the future that, in modern societies, is planned for in everyday life and managed by political, social and cultural institutions. The intention is to optimise outcomes in the future, despite its uncertainty. Often this means to anticipate threats and risks and take suitable precautions (for example, in relation to the possible impact of climate change). But it can also mean to contribute actively to a history of long-term change and transformation (for example, the future of Europe). In modern societies, heritage is accordingly either preserved against anticipated threats and risks (for example, scheduled sites – see also Part V, Transformation) or maintained as living heritage in continuous transformation (for example, living languages – see also Part II, Diversity, on languages as heritage).

According to Barbara Adam and Chris Groves (2007), there are alternatives to the way modern societies manage the uncertainty of open futures. Some societies attempt to make the future more certain (for example, by making it more legible and patterned) through an emphasis on natural cycles, cultural traditions and social obligations. An ethically motivated view of the future emphasises instead a mindset of care for future generations (like parents caring for their children) and a call for forgiveness about the unknown consequences of our actions.

Such thoughts informed our thinking throughout the duration of the project. We have gone through a number of distinctive stages in our own thinking, as our understanding evolved through fieldwork, joint presentations, joint writing and many discussions. Asking how the uncertainty of the deep future is conceived of and managed in different fields of conservation practice, we initially contrasted continuous with discontinuous futures perceived in heritage. Very simplified, in the perception of the future as continuous, we are on our way into the future, continuing with what we are doing. A continuous future assumes a development, with changes that are gradual but seamless. For example, during our research in the Lake District, we visited the World of Beatrix Potter museum at Bowness. Here, visitors were invited to preserve the favourite radishes of Peter Rabbit for future generations by continuously planting them in their gardens (and not by embalming them!), accepting the variable impact of local conditions and also of slow mutations. By the same token, as explored in Chapter 18, local shepherds are trying to continue their way of life under ever-changing circumstances. In this logic, we can be *proactionary*, accepting risks in order to seize emerging opportunities for continuous development, while trusting in human ingenuity and judgement (Fuller 2013). A challenge is how conditions can be created that facilitate appropriate change (see also Part V, Transformation), and in particular how such change can be controlled so that it keeps occurring in a sustainable way and does not prevent further changes to occur later on. In this way of thinking, the original state of cultural heritage is not necessarily superior to subsequent transformations and resurrections.

On the other hand, according to the perception of the future as discontinuous, it is the future that is approaching us, prompting us to anticipate and react to what will be in store for us, often perceived as a threat. Such futures conceptualise uncertainty in terms of risk and perceive a loss of continuity as a threat we need to address. According to this logic, we must be *precautionary*, anticipating risks in order to control them and thus be able to maintain what we have thankfully inherited from the past (Fuller 2013). Here, uncertainty is associated with a future collapse of some kind, creating a gap of continuity, a discontinuity. This perception of the future is common in many heritage practices (Benford 1999). For example, in Great Britain, red squirrels are endangered, at risk of becoming extinct, and must be saved untainted in a fight against their rivals, the non-native grey squirrels. Across our four domains, there was a fairly similar understanding that the future holds threats of loss that need to be minimised in the best possible ways. Uncertainty was perceived as something that ultimately is a problem, a liability, something that threatens what we hold dear or in other ways is important to us, and what we would like to keep and maintain. That applied to the intention of the World Heritage programme to preserve 'the heritage of all the nations of the world' (UNESCO 1972, 1) against various threats of destruction as much as to the responsibility of SKB to prevent any stored radioactive waste from ever spreading into the natural environment and negatively affecting many creatures' health and well-being (see also Chapter 19, on toxic heritage). The One Earth Message and MOM are conceived in terms of maintaining accessibility and intelligibility of important information across very large temporal distances and under all conceivable eventualities.

The archaeologist Guy Middleton has been studying why archaeological narratives of collapse are so popular. He argues that the anticipation of collapse, signalled by preparing to communicate across that gap, can provide an opportunity too. Somewhat counter-intuitively, it can increase our sense of power and control, acting almost in metaphysical dimensions when our judgement is required, with consequences for the future:

> Turning that to the possibility of near-future collapse, by imagining ourselves standing on the precipice of some epochal change, we make ourselves feel more important – we are living at a key time and we have the power to affect global civilisation, either positively or negatively.
>
> (Middleton 2017, n.p.)

It is no coincidence that several of the domains we studied are often perceived in precisely such terms. With the prospect of future collapse, how we act today is portrayed as decisive and as affecting global civilisation in profound ways: Will the world heritage be preserved? Can nuclear waste and records of our time be securely stored for the benefit of future generations? Will the human messages sent to outer space ever be received by their intended audiences? Our four domains catch the human imagination because they allow people to engage with challenges that ultimately may have a bearing on the fate of humanity. They make us reflect on responsibilities that are larger than each of us, they give us a sense of focus and purpose, and they create meaning where there was doubt.

At this point in our thinking, the risk of a discontinuous future had become considerably less threatening in our appreciation of uncertainty across various domains of heritage. We were therefore very open to the proposal for heritage studies to embrace uncertainty, presented in *The Future of Heritage as Climates Change*, edited by David Harvey and Jim Perry (2015b). In their perspective, the uncertainty of heritage futures can be seen as a space of creativity to be explored in order to realise the potential of managing heritage in the present. They do not see uncertainty as a negative thing, to be overcome or denied. Indeed, the changes that people cannot predict may be thrilling, beneficial and stimulating, or also terrifying, destructive and oppressive. But whenever we speak of forever, we can be certain that changes will come.

Uncertainty regarding the future is a precondition for human freedom and responsibility, both in relation to what we think and what we do. If the future were controlled by the present, then we would lose the freedom of thought and action that we value. In this sense, uncertainty makes us free indeed (O'Malley 2015). Here we see why it makes sense to ask, as we came to do, to what extent we might turn an apparent challenge into an opportunity by envisioning uncertainty as desirable for heritage and conservation practice. This is the perspective we are developing in some detail in the following chapters in this part of the book.

In what follows, we present something of an intellectual patchwork, composed of specific observations made during our empirical studies and the various thought experiments they inspired. Chapter 18 contains an ethnographic account of a shepherd and her practice in the Lake District, during the time that the World Heritage Site nomination was being evaluated by UNESCO. In Chapter 19 we discuss the concept of toxicity in relation to nuclear waste and heritage. This is followed in Chapter 20 by a discussion of two space initiatives on the micro-messaging website Twitter. In the visual essay presented in Chapter 21, we explore long-term information storage at the Memory of Mankind in Hallstatt. In our concluding chapter, we review our work on the theme as a whole, and take stock of some lessons learned about collaborative practice and how to manage uncertain futures.

18
A shepherd's futures: Shepherds and World Heritage in the Lake District

Sarah May

The Lake District is a large and heterogeneous region in the north-west of England, which has been managed as a unit since 1951, when it was created as one of the UK's first National Parks. It comprises 13 separate valleys, the hills (also known as fells) between them, and the many lakes and rivers in the valley bottoms. Inscribed in 2017 as a World Heritage Site, it is now managed by a partnership of 25 organisations, who came together for the nomination process and have jointly agreed a management plan. Each of these groups has a different relationship with the site. Some own land, some are run by members, some are government funded and have statutory responsibilities. Some of them, such as the Environment Agency, Historic England and the National Trust, have national remits, while some are local governments, charities and businesses. Some of these represent groups of individuals who have had traditional responsibility for land management, such as the Herdwick Sheep Breeders' Association.

We originally chose the Lake District as a case study for our work on the theme of uncertainty in heritage practices because it was a candidate for World Heritage Site nomination. We wanted to see what future-making practices were involved in the process of World Heritage inscription and how those practices would produce new futures and perpetuate existing ones. The Lake District has been nominated as a World Heritage Site before. In 1987, the International Union for Conservation of Nature (IUCN) determined that there were 'more outstanding examples of glaciation and wildlife'. In 1990, when the International Council on Monuments and Sites (ICOMOS) evaluated it, they 'questioned the importance of Wordsworth in world terms' (Gfeller 2013, 491). Gfeller (2013, 491) has argued that this was one of the things that led to the new World Heritage Site category 'Cultural Landscape'. Harrison has discussed the development of this category in more depth, including its relationship to intangible heritage, a relationship that runs through much of this chapter (Harrison 2013a, 114–39).

The cultural landscape that the Lakes has been inscribed for has been established through fell shepherding. The management of the fells as commonage for sheep has determined many other aspects of landscape development, from ownership to drainage. This, in turn, has inspired artists and writers to celebrate a 'shepherds' republic' that responds to that landscape. Early heritage campaigner, Beatrix Potter, specified that native Herdwick sheep should be kept on the substantial tracts of land that she left to the National Trust. The World Heritage nomination recognises the importance of this landscape: 'The interaction between agro-pastoral farming and the natural features of the English Lake District has produced a landscape of great harmonious beauty which in the 18th century attracted the interest of the Picturesque Movement' (LDNPP 2016, 271).

There are some who worry that the wrong values have been valorised in this designation. George Monbiot, a major proponent of rewilding (see also Part V, Transformation), has coined the epithet 'sheepwrecked' to characterise the ecological status of this landscape (Monbiot 2013). He presents the UNESCO decision as an ill-informed error. But his most substantial piece on the matter indicates that he does not understand the designation or management practices involved (Monbiot 2017). He represents designation as an attempt to set the present in stone, something that cannot be undone, and foresees no change. He overlooks the management plans, periodic reports and even the removal of the designation that all form part of how World Heritage Sites are managed. Yet he could hardly be blamed for this, given that heritage is almost always presented as a slowing or halting of change, or a return to the past, when, in fact, as we argue in this book, heritage is often more about imagining and assembling different kinds of *futures*.

There is much critical work on the operation of the World Heritage Convention and its practices (for example, Brumann and Berliner 2016; Meskell 2014; 2018), but my interest here is in the future-making aspects of heritage practices. Studying a World Heritage Site, particularly one that has been a candidate for so long, presents special challenges. Perhaps counter-intuitively, by producing a sense that everything is known and accounted for, the vast volume of documentation can impede understanding. I hoped to find a way through this forest of discourse by working closely with individuals to understand their practices. In this, I follow Brumann and Berliner (2016, 2), who draw a distinction between ethnography and impact studies – claiming that their work foregrounds the local social situation, rather than a conservation agenda.

Just as World Heritage Sites provide a fertile ground for what Tsing (2005) terms 'friction' between global and local practices, so too do they provide an excellent ground for similar relations between the contemporary and the eternal. As Brumann and Berliner (2016, 14) note, 'within, around and alongside … transnational pockets, local life continues, often with limited direct contact to the emissaries of the wider world but deeply affected by their presence and decisions taken elsewhere'. Present concerns also continue in similar relation to the perpetuity that the outstanding universal value is being managed for. The moment of inscription calls a desire for transformation and yet, 'In European countries by contrast, World Heritage often adds only rather thin layers to long-established national conservation frameworks and decades- or even centuries-old local adaptations to a heritage regime' (Brumann and Berliner 2016, 14). The desire for continuity comes into conflict with that desire for transformation.

My fieldwork in the Lake District was undertaken with the people who are managing and living in this landscape, building and juggling these diverse futures. Mostly they work for the present, or the immediate future. But their practices are underpinned by these bigger futures.

The practice of World Heritage Site management is always as much about managing people as it is about managing sites, landscapes and buildings. Even single building inscriptions have many stakeholders, and cultural landscapes have many thousands. In the Lake District, these relationships are held within the Lake District National Park Partnership. In the course of the research for this project, I spent time with managers from the National Trust, businesspeople running businesses drawing on the World Heritage 'brand', artists and community organisers. But my most long-lasting and entrenched relationship was with a shepherd.

Shepherds, and farming more generally, were key to the World Heritage Site bid. Indeed, the Herdwick Sheep Breeders' Association, represented by the National Farmers' Union (NFU), is a key partner in the consortium that brought the bid for World Heritage status to UNESCO. Importantly, the successful bid followed an economic feasibility study carried out by James Rebanks (2009), who has since found fame as 'the Herdwick Shepherd'. His books about his life and his farm have been on international bestseller lists (Rebanks 2015; 2019), and he has a following of fifty thousand for his Twitter account, which shares images and details of farming life, including live tweets of lambing (@herdyshepherd1). Although the economic report is not mentioned in the nomination document, it was crucial to creating the partnership that put forward the bid. This indicates the centrality of fell shepherding to the heritage of the Lake District. The Cultural Landscape designation on the World Heritage List always requires the presence of a mixture of tangible and intangible heritage features and values. Fell shepherding creates the landscape of the Lake District, and shepherds must participate in that practice in order to perpetuate it.

In autumn 2015 and in spring and summer 2017, I spent time with a shepherd named Andrea Meanwell. I made contact with her through Twitter because she expressed interest in both heritage and the future, and was interested in the research I was carrying out as part of this project. Andrea has published two books (Meanwell 2016; 2017), writes for *Cumbria* magazine and has her own substantial following on Twitter (@ruslandvalley), so she is used to reflecting on and discussing her practice and its importance. In this chapter, I describe how my time with Andrea, observing her practice and listening to her talk about it, helped me explore questions of participation and endangerment. While farmers often have other enterprises, the way that she and James Rebanks have other careers and engage with public debate is unusual, and this makes Andrea a particularly helpful interlocutor in helping me to reflect on these questions.

Heritage practices

In any circumstance, farming is a conglomerate of practices, which individual farmers negotiate according to their particular circumstances and skills. In the Lake District, these are complicated by the heritage status of this life and the ways in which it constructs the cultural landscape managed as World Heritage. In addition to being a component of the World Heritage bid, shepherding is a livelihood for hundreds of families in the Lake District. Many of these families have been farming for many generations. Most of these farmers are keenly aware of the heritage value placed on their practice, and a handful incorporate this awareness into their practice.

Before I begin, I want to lay out my understanding of what practices are and how they relate to future-making. As discussed in Chapters 1 and 2, the Heritage Futures research programme aimed to study *practice* as opposed to *discourse* – here I am interested in what people do and how they assemble living and non-living networks to do these things. I am interested in the comparison between practices acknowledged to be heritage practice and those that are generally not viewed that way.

I follow Schatzki (2010) in his understanding of practices as materially constituted relationships. Like Hand et al. (2005, 6.8), I 'focus on the relation between the material, the conventional and the temporal, as configured through practice. What are the terms and conditions of inter-dependence and how obdurate are the conventions and habits that arise as a result?'

As noted in the introductory chapters, one of the key features of practices is that they unfold in places. Different places privilege differ-ent groups of practices, so in a gallery, artistic practices have a stronger claim than others (Leach 2007, 180). Similarly, heritage practices are foregrounded in a World Heritage Site, so the process of inscription we followed in the Lake District is a process of understanding an ever-increasing range of practices as they become enfolded with, and some-times recognised as, heritage practices.

As practices are inherently spatialised, they are also temporal, which makes them interesting for studying processes of future-making. As Adam and Groves (2011, 18) have argued in relation to economic insti-tutions, it is the practices, such as cost–benefit analysis and future dis-counting, not the discourse 'through which these institutions construct futures which effectively institutionalize irresponsibility, exploiting the future in the narrow interests of the present'. Do all heritage practices construct these futures in the interests of the present? I would argue that they do not. The practices described in this chapter intend to bring the future into the present, to care for it in similar ways.

Groves has also explored how practices relate to attachment in uncer-tain futures. Discussing how a driver engages with 'An imagined future in which the material infrastructure on which Ronald's preferred style of driving depends is degraded [, it] is one in which he finds it hard to picture a place for the competences, ideals, and forms of friendship that he iden-tifies as central to his identity' (Groves et al. 2016, 321). Any individual's set of practices intertwine and resist categorisation. When I joined Andrea as she went out to check on sheep in lamb, we talked about a vast range of things: land ownership; changes in her business strategy (and the variable cost profile of sheep by breed and gender); I watched her tag newborn lambs and talked about how a new gatepost had changed the drainage in a field; we talked about relationships between neighbours and agencies and governments. In the following section, I lay out a selection of themes that emerged from my observations of her practice. Moving between field observations and reflections based on discussions in the wider literature, I draw out relationships between humans, animals, materials and places to sketch how these practices constitute heritage and create futures.

A shepherd's future-making practices

When I met her, Andrea had been farming for six years. She had a small mixed flock of sheep, which she kept on a patchwork of land, both near her house in Rusland Valley and separately on land associated with Blawith Fell. In addition to her 50 sheep, she had some cattle and some fell ponies. Although her aim was to develop a strong flock of Rough Fell sheep, she had other sheep as well – some, such as the Ronaldsay sheep, because she was participating in research about rare breeds and some, such as the Ouessant, because they were more profitable. Although her family had a history of farming, she had pursued a successful teaching career before returning to farming in search of a more meaningful life.

From the complexity of her practice, I have selected the following themes through which to explore the concerns outlined above: caring, breeding, land management, bureaucracy and public engagement.

Caring

A large proportion of Andrea's time is spent caring for animals (see Figure 18.1). She visits her animals every day to feed them and count them, and to look out for and treat fly strike, lameness and other common ailments. These practices are closely entwined with breeding, discussed below, because spending time with the animals helps her decide which she will breed, what her future flock will look like. They also create and maintain individual affective relationships.

On my first visit, it is autumn. Andrea explains that she is feeding the sheep in order to keep them tame; they do not need extra feeding yet, but if she feeds them regularly, they will come to her when she needs to give them medicine or any other thing where she needs to get them to be manageable. Two of the sheep do not come when she calls and shakes the bucket, so she goes to find them and make sure that they are all right. She crosses a gap in the wall around this field. The sheep are all right. She explains that she bought them from an auction the other week. They have not fully settled in yet and are not used to the routine. She is not worried as long as they are all right – they walk off into a further field. We notice that one of the sheep is limping. She wrestles it until she can see the foot it is favouring, and clears out some shingle that it has between its toes from the hardstanding of the hay barn – 'It's OK, it's not smelly, so it's not bad.'

Figure 18.1 Caring is a complex practice that begins when a lamb is born. But the practices of breeding and bureaucracy begin at the same time. The lamb is assessed for its value to the flock and tagged with the marker that stays with it through life (photograph by Sarah May).

Baraister reminds us of the importance of care:

> To care is never simply a matter of labour or simply a matter of a wish to repair the world. To care is to deal, in an ongoing and durational way with affective states that may include the racialized, gendered and imperially imbued ambivalence that seeps into the ways we maintain the lives of others. Care is an arduous temporal practice.
>
> (Baraister 2014, 29)

In Andrea's case, her reputation for caring has led her to adopt lambs that other shepherds dismiss. This has made it more difficult for her to develop the flock she wants. Her care in the present is in conflict with her desire for the future flock.

Andrea reflects on what it is to be a female farmer. Most of her cousins married farmers. If she had done that, she would never have been able to have her own flock. The decisions about the flock would have been her husband's; she 'would have made the soup'. She can only think of one other shepherdess in the Lake District – she tweets as @barefootshepherdess. Her flock was originally a joint enterprise with her husband, but she took it on when the marriage broke down, so Andrea is pretty distinctive in terms of running her own flock this way. She says there are some women in the ring at auctions showing and selling their sheep, but mostly these are young women, 15–16 years old and not yet married. This is linked to her role as nurse for orphan sheep. She says that being a shepherdess is more challenging than her former career as a teacher – a more interesting challenge, with more going on, changing more often.

One of the lambs is small, has not grown; she calls him Roughy. He was left in the hedge by his mother at birth; the ewe nursed the other twin, but did not bother with him. Andrea does not think he will survive the winter, although she is not completely certain. It transpires that she is regularly given orphan lambs to bottle feed because she is 'soft' and does not like to see them die. As a result, she has quite a mix of sheep, in addition to the Rough Fell sheep that are her focus and ambition. This work is usually carried out by the wife of the farm, but she takes lambs from farmers who have no wives. Her son says to her, 'If you don't take them, they'll smash them against a wall'. She's not sure if that is true, but she would rather take them than see them left. It is a lot of work, through the night, but she has always enjoyed it since she was a small girl on her uncle's farm. Caring for animals, looking after their well-being in the broadest sense, is a major motivation for her.

This caring practice builds Andrea's sense of place. She works in these fields every day. The attachment is not simply to the land but to the relationships with the animals, the care that she enacts while working. It also depends upon and enacts knowledge and skill that she inherited from her family and that she passes to her children. Each generation enacts it differently. The continuous future she seeks to build depends upon these rhythms of care. The longer-term futures of the other themes are stitched into life by care.

Breeding

Since the future that Andrea is working towards is a strong flock of Rough Fell sheep, breeding is a core practice for her. Choosing which ewes to breed, how to arrange a tup to service them, buying in new sheep and judging the quality of the flock as it matures are all connected through an understanding of what a Rough Fell sheep should be. This is codified in flock books published annually by the Rough Fell Sheep Breeders' Association. The characteristics of the breed have changed over the last century, the greatest difference being a substantial reduction in the size of the fleece. Since wool is now so cheap, it costs more to shear a sheep than can be got from its fleece, so a long fleece has little value. But the judgement of living sheep against that code is a skill and a practice that takes time to develop.

Andrea showed this skill when I visited her during servicing. We went through into the second field away from the road, where older ewes were being kept with a tup who had been put with them in the last few days. Three of the ewes have been serviced and showed raddle, the red waxy substance applied to the underside of the tup so that it will mark a ewe that has been serviced. We discussed her ambition: her plan as a farmer is to breed a strong flock of Rough Fell sheep. By a strong flock, she means a substantial group who mostly show the characteristics of the breed clearly. She reckons she has two now that are 6/10, and the rest are less than that. She will improve her flock by breeding, and especially by careful attention to the tup. The judgement begins at lambing. As soon as a lamb is born, its potential value to the flock is assessed.

Before I met Andrea, I followed the practice of James Rebanks, a shepherd, a heritage consultant and an author, as discussed above. His public draw is the detail and immediacy of the shepherding life, exemplified in his live tweeting of lambing. Of course, lambs represent spring for some people, so in addition to the 'live' temporality, there's a strong focus on seasonality. Highlighting seasonality is part of creating 'time-lessness' – cyclical time stands in opposition to 'the arrow of time', so each spring is *spring*. It is clear that Rebanks also feels the future very closely in these lambs. He sees them as his economic future, and also looks to develop relationships with them.

But breeding is not only about creating a flock that displays unified characteristics. Andrea's uncle was instrumental in setting up a 'cascade' breeding system that underpins UK meat production. Hill sheep are bred with Leicester sheep to produce a variety called 'mule sheep'. These sheep have the 'milkyness' of a Leicester, so they can have at least two lambs at a time, combined with the hardiness of the hill sheep, which means they need less medication and survive environmental fluctuation better. The mule sheep are bred with a meaty sheep (Texel) and it is the resulting lambs that are sold for meat throughout the UK. Rough Fell and Swaledale are both suitable for this cross, but Herdwicks are not. So, the breeding of hill sheep is required for the maintenance of a national flock. She has two mule sheep (which have more spirally fleece), but she does not breed them herself. Some people near the coast, who have good grass and warmer conditions breed them, but mostly they are bred elsewhere with sheep from here. Since the mule sheep are cross-bred with the meaty sheep and the lambs are eaten, they need a supply of newly bred mule sheep every year.

The 'cascade' means that the practices that are valued as heritage in the Lake District are also integrated outside of the designated World Heritage Site. The breeding that happens here is central to the health of the national flock. This sense of the value of heritage is apparent in heritage-based placemaking as well – certain places hold a stock of value from which other places can replenish their identity.

The second time I visited Andrea, her focus had shifted to greater financial viability, and our conversation demonstrated how near to impossible that is, and how closely related this is to breeding (see Figure 18.2). A well-bred ewe can be sold to another farmer; a male lamb that will not be raised as a tup can only be sold for meat. The gradation in value from a breeding ewe at £90 to a male lamb for meat at £23 is pretty steep, and the male lambs barely make the cost of their feed back. A ewe that does not conform to breed is, like the males, sold for meat. But that judgement is individual. Andrea tells me a story of a lamb that was born with a beautiful face, but when fully born exposed the disappointment of a black tail, which sealed its fate as not breeding stock. There are also fashions: sometimes a white face is prized, sometimes a spotty face. These characteristics may not be linked to real strengths: the bones are more important than the markings. The only sheep she keeps that consistently make money are the miniature Ouessant sheep, which she sells to heritage sites and smallholders, largely because they are decorative. They can sell for £300, and there is no question about good breeding. The people who buy them do not consult flock books.

There are differences of opinion between Andrea and her son about what makes a 'good' Rough Fell sheep. Although she passes her knowledge on, her son makes his own judgement. Her uncle is respected for his experience and knowledge, so if something happened to him and her cousin took over, his reputation would pass with it, but in Andrea's case she has to build her own reputation.

The practice of breeding relies on selection and perpetuation, which are key elements of heritage practice. There are clear crossovers here with themes explored in this book in Part II, Diversity, and Part III, Profusion. This breeding is where value is created and it also drives the financial

Figure 18.2 Andrea sees the future of her flock in increasing quality and consistency, but she knits hats with the wool of the alpaca she has, and sells them as part of the suite of public-facing practices that keep her farm viable in the present (photograph by Sarah May).

sustainability. Nonetheless, the categories are not fixed. There are changes in preference over the century, between generations. Judgement is both an individual preference and a skill that is valued at shows and auctions.

Land management

Land management is perhaps the practice with the most direct connection to tangible aspects of landscape – this is the creation of the landscape that is valued in the 'Outstanding Universal Value' criterion used by UNESCO to consider World Heritage status. Andrea's land management begins with purchasing land, and moves on to being part of a group of common rights to graze a fell, to boundary maintenance, and a practice of grazing known as 'conservation grazing', in which the animals are key actors in the perpetuation of particular forms of biodiversity.

When I visited Andrea, she kept her sheep on three separate plots of land that she owns, having bought them separately when she has had money at the same time that the land became available. She says that this is the way it is for people in the area unless they have inherited a farm, in which case their land is much more likely to all be in one block (see Figure 18.3).

She explained that even small blocks of land are increasingly difficult to come by, since so many people want to 'own a little bit of the Lake District'. People buy land to use for camping (for their own use), or even buy it sight unseen to avoid inheritance tax. A plot of two acres, which she might use for keeping a tup isolated, recently sold in her valley for £64,000. Land used to be around £2,000 an acre, then went up to £10,000, but £64,000 suggests that the value has become free

Figure 18.3 Andrea's land is dispersed, and her land-management practice relies on her Land Rover Defender. When Land Rover ceased production, the value shot up, and this vehicle was stolen in a rash of thefts across the Lake District. Like land value, heritage and rarity, the uncertainty of increased value impacts her practice (photograph by Sarah May).

floating – not actually the use value of land, but a speculative invest-ment. As we drove, she pointed to a small plot she had hoped to buy but not succeeded, which has been bought by people who camp on it. I asked, how many days a year can you get campers, and she explained that it was for their own camping, not to charge others. But she said that they camp about five days a year, and they do not seem to have much fun as it is often raining.

Most land is sold by auction. She managed to buy both her house, with its land, and the first plot she brought me to by direct reference to the future. As soon as the auction signs went up, she came, with her children, to the seller and said: 'Don't sell this by auction. Please sell it to us, we have a stake in this place, we want to live here and make our future here.' In the case of her house, they had to buy it within seven days in order to circumvent the plans for auction that were already with the lawyers.

We came to her land, which is off a lane behind a gate, and she explained that this land, at Blawith, has commonage rights attached that mean she could graze 64 sheep on the fell, but it is a Site of Special Scientific Interest (SSSI),[1] and Natural England says it has enough sheep – any more would be unfavourable, so she cannot put them on. She could assert her rights, but this would annoy her neighbours, and she is buying land piecemeal from one of them. Her fellow commoners say she should just put the sheep on without saying anything, but it would annoy them if she came into conflict with Natural England. She tells me that another friend is selling up because they are putting cattle on commons that have been vacated by sheep – they have put more than their rights, and their neighbours are furious.

As we drove, Andrea also pointed out a plot of land that is not being farmed and is being overrun by bracken and other scrub: 'There, that's what rewilding looks like, isn't it awful?' Rewilding is a strong concern for her, and also an irritation. She is very irritated both by the propos-als to reintroduce lynx and by the people on Twitter who tell her to stop resisting it, who do not understand that this is her land – that the fell is her land just as much as the field. They tell her not to worry because there would be compensation for sheep that are killed, 'but how would they like it if I put a tiger in their back garden?' 'People sitting in Manchester reading the summer paper, and they say, "I come to the Lakes sometimes, I'm not a city person at heart"'. She says that compensation for a sheep misunderstands what sheep are. It is not just money, it is an individual: 'I can't just go and buy any sheep, it might not like my land, it might not suit the other sheep, it might jump out' (see Figure 18.4).

Figure 18.4 Each sheep is an individual. Andrea's resistance to rewilding includes outrage at the thought of 'compensation' for predation, as if sheep simply represent money (photograph by Sarah May).

Rewilding is a broader topic of concern in the management of the World Heritage Site, as discussed above. The landscape geographer Kenneth Olwig (2016) has argued that rewilding continues enclosure politics, while fell shepherding continues the vestiges of pre-enclosure land use, and therefore increases biodiversity. Some of the more general issues related to rewilding practices are examined in Part V, Transformation. Here it is worth noting that Andrea sees her land-management practice as being diametrically opposed to rewilding.

Her land at Blawith has four fields, some of which have quite a lot of rushes. However, the walls between the fields were quite broken down, so it was hard for her to manage the land for improvement. She applied for a Countryside Stewardship grant to repair the walls, with the help of her son, who has a flair for stone walling. After she repaired the walls, she brought fell ponies to graze. These ponies can eat rushes, unlike sheep, so they clear the rushes from the fields, and the sheep move through them in a different cycle. The relationship between wetland, stone walls, government grants, skilful children and hardy ponies exemplifies the materiality and temporality of her practice. The land seems fixed, but it is always changing, and management intervenes in that change – to stop succession, to control the flow.

Bureaucracy

As Bennett and others have argued in their book, *Collecting, Ordering, Governing: Anthropology, Museums, and Liberal Government*, practices of bureaucracy have both defined heritage historically and given it much political power (Bennett et al. 2017; see also Harrison 2013a; 2016b). As the process by which different regimes of governance are negotiated, bureaucracy plays a similarly central role in the practice of fell shepherding in the Lake District. As farming is also a business, Andrea's practice includes navigating the bureaucracies of applying for grants (as discussed above), tendering for tenancies, supermarket deals, and even direct sales of meat. The materiality of bureaucracy is shifting, from what Mathur (2016) refers to as its 'paper-y tangibility' to digital networks. Hybrid systems that mimic paper forms but disseminate them through digital systems can make bureaucracies even more complex.

Andrea has been told that four thousand grants on a particular scheme were to be given throughout the UK, and that they expected thirty-two thousand applications. Actually, there were only two thousand applications, because the application process was so onerous. But because the four thousand grants are spread out by allocation across the country, she is not guaranteed a grant despite the fact that they are undersubscribed. She says that the form took her and her father a week to complete, even though they both have degrees and are used to filling out such forms.

Andrea's negotiation of bureaucracy also relates to the constraints on her land use that come from the multiple heritage designations. She says that one of the reasons that 'offcomers' feel that they have a right to argue for rewilding is because it is a National Park. People therefore feel that it is in some sense a place that belongs to everyone. (These issues of ownership of heritage – 'for ever, for everyone', in the words of the motto of the National Trust – are discussed in more detail in Part I of this book). When I first visited her, Andrea was not sure what she thought of the World Heritage Site bid. She spoke with James Rebanks to ask him what the benefits would be, but she still felt confused about the change and any benefits that may ensue. In discussions with the National Trust regarding a prospective tenancy, she raised how the bid would benefit her, but the representative could not give her anything concrete. The potential political benefits of the cultural landscape designation, especially in dealing with issues such as rewilding and rocketing land prices, may be the most important aspects of the change in status for her. Since the Outstanding

Universal Value on which the bid is based is linked explicitly to fell farming, then things that undermine fell farming could be discouraged. But, of course, that is not a direct benefit to her. Also, World Heritage Site management has little legal force, so the new governance may make little difference.

The change of governance associated with 'Brexit' (at the time of writing, the proposed exit of the UK from the European Union) may have much greater impact, both on Andrea's practice and on the landscape of the Lake District. Of the seven people who attended her commoners' council, six said that they would go out of business immediately if the Single Farm Payment were cut. Bureaucratic regimes can change quickly and can have knock-on effects on all other forms of practice. In this landscape, these kinds of changes are more likely to cause discontinuity than other changing futures, such as climate change.

Public engagement

I was initially surprised to find that public engagement was an important part of Andrea's practice. While public engagement is common in heritage practice (and 'communication' is one of the four processes that we identified as common to all heritage practices – see further discussion in Chapter 1), I had expected shepherding to be less concerned with communication. As discussed above, Andrea may be a particularly communicative shepherd, but the precarious nature of upland farming means that, like heritage, it needs public support.

Some of her practice is advocacy, explaining the importance of fell shepherding to the public. This is very similar to heritage practice in other domains. She runs tours of her farm, engages on social media and writes books; she even has an online gift shop selling hand-knitted products, some of which use wool from her animals. She also advises the Cumbria Wildlife Trust and runs short courses on conservation grazing. All of these practices seek to inform and enthuse. They rely on the other practices for their value, but take a very different type of skill and resource.

She also runs two holiday homes for tourists, another practice that involves maintenance and bureaucracy in equal measure. One of the main draws of World Heritage Site status is an increase in tourism, but for many people in the Lake District the current levels of tourism are unwelcome. The economic model put forward by James Rebanks promotes a change in the nature of tourism to promote more middle-class tourism. Does the shepherding landscape persist because the tourist future wants it? What does it mean to be timeless in a changing world?

Writing

It is worth considering Andrea's writing practice in more detail because writing and writers are another aspect of the Outstanding Universal Value of the Lake District. Andrea's books are largely narrative non-fiction, with some aspects of memoir and poetry. Her writing draws heavily on her own experience to create a sense of place and tradition. It is also advocacy – it builds support for the policies that support upland farming that I discuss above in relation to bureaucracy.

The arguments about rewilding and land ownership are being played out very clearly through writing. People making their case not to each other, but to various readerships, only some of which have direct power in the Lake District. I am also thinking about who writes, and how. There are links to the way that Wordsworth wrote about the Lake District, and all the other 'authors'. But are James Rebanks and Andrea Meanwell of that tradition, or claiming another? Is he an author or a shepherd? It is not just books and journal articles. Blogging, and even Twitter and Facebook, create futures too. There is a profusion of writing: newspaper articles, reports, meeting minutes, letters. It may be that in terms of time spent, more time is spent on writing than on any other practice of future-making in the Lake District. How is it done? On paper? On screen? During the evening? During the day? Apologised for? I think about my own writing practice – why I do it, and how I hope it will influence the future. For some (like Meanwell and Rebanks), it provides an income stream that will let them continue to do other things they want – but it is more than that, because it creates the imagined Lake District that should/will endure.

Most of these practices are aimed steadily at the present, but they have been very influential in future-making in the Lake District since the nineteenth century. Writing has many different temporalities in practice as well as in the effect. How does tweeting relate to writing books or policy documents? Does writing seek to create or influence far futures as well as close ones, or only some writing? Is there a sense of permanence in 'putting it down on paper', or is it part of the care that creates the 'thing' that moves forward on its own?

Uncertainty and a present unfolding

Andrea says that farming is a never-ending project, not like building a house. The constant interaction of all these different practices moves towards the building of a 'good flock', but the definition of 'good flock' shifts even as she moves towards it. Looking at these practices in relation to uncertainty, continuity and discontinuity are just issues of scale. Discontinuities are continuously produced. They are bridged in many different ways, some of which produce more change than others. A Rough Fell sheep now is very different from a Rough Fell sheep a century ago but it is still called a Rough Fell, so the sense of an identity has been held. But if you wanted the genetic 'stock' of the earlier sheep for something, you are out of luck. Similarly, the Lake District has been inscribed as a World Heritage Site; there is a clear boundary around it. This can maintain its identity, but it might look and work very differently in even a hundred years.

Practices are intertwined. Feeding sheep, breeding sheep, managing land for sheep, buying land for sheep, managing finance to buy land, engaging in public debate – a shepherd juggles all practices, and futures emerge. James Rebanks left Twitter in summer 2018, at the same time that he resigned from a government panel on National Parks (*The Telegraph* 2018). He had received substantial personal attacks from people who see farming in the uplands as unsustainable. The demands of being a public shepherd are high. Shepherds now occupy a mix of roles in the public imagination – from Wordsworth's image of a republic of free men, to harbingers of the Anthropocene. The significance of sheep and shepherds to the Lake District as a World Heritage Site seems more relevant than ever, encapsulating and provoking wider arguments about our global relationship with landscape. But these cultural tropes skate over the practices that are actually involved in the intangible heritage and landscape creation of keeping sheep. In June 2019, Andrea was appointed farming officer for the Lake District National Park Partnership. She brings her care and insight to a new set of practices, more closely associated with professional heritage management. She has passed day-to-day farm work to her son, placing the next step in her future-making practice. In the next chapter, we consider a different form of uncertainty in relation to heritage futures through a discussion of 'toxic' heritage.

Note

1. An SSSI is a nature conservation designation in the United Kingdom that provides certain kinds of protections for the land and natural resources contained within it. These are administered by Natural England, a non-departmental organisation that is sponsored by the Department for Environment, Food and Rural Affairs.

19
Toxic heritage: Uncertain and unsafe

Gustav Wollentz, Sarah May, Cornelius Holtorf and Anders Högberg

Introduction

As we saw in the previous chapter, the uncertainty of the future is both a risk and an opportunity for contemporary 'living' cultural heritage, such as shepherding in the English Lake District. But this uncertainty of the future is perhaps particularly pertinent when the legacies concerned are toxic to humans and other biological organisms. This is the case for radioactive waste that is to be safely managed in the long term by companies such as the Swedish Nuclear Fuel and Waste Management Company (SKB) and Radioactive Waste Management (RWM) in the UK. One preferred location for the UK geological repository for long-term storage of radioactive waste is Ennerdale in the Lake District, not far from Sellafield, the former power plant and former reprocessing site where high-level waste has been stored until now (Carrington 2018). This physical proximity to what is, at the time of writing, the UK's newest World Heritage Site, the English Lake District, has led us to consider the conceptual proximity of heritage management and nuclear waste management. While Buser (2016) has considered the idea that toxic waste may itself be heritage (and see further discussion in Chapter 2), we go further here, exploring whether there are instances when heritage itself may be seen to be toxic. The term 'toxic heritage' is deliberately provocative in this argument, both drawing attention to the comparative practices in the two domains of World Heritage Site management and nuclear waste management, and extending established understandings of difficult heritage (for example, Macdonald 2009).

We argue that the two management regimes have more in common than one may think (see also Holtorf and Högberg 2013; 2014a; 2015a; 2015b; 2016; Högberg and Holtorf 2016). Both heritage management and nuclear waste management share concerns with sustainable preservation, secure storage of material items, long-term memory keeping and knowledge transfer to future generations. Both management regimes are also characterised by a felt responsibility towards the future, which is manifested in a perceived duty not to leave a legacy harming or threatening future generations' quality of life, whether in the form of hazardous waste containing radioactive material that will survive for too long or in the form of valuable heritage that will not survive long enough.

Using nuclear waste and its management as a point of departure, we here develop the concept of toxic heritage and argue for its conceptual value to heritage studies, complementing rather than replacing existing concepts such as 'difficult' (Macdonald 2009), 'negative' (Meskell 2002), 'dark' (Kobiałka 2018; Seitsonen 2018) and 'dissonant' (Tunbridge and Ashworth 1996; Kisić 2016) heritage. The field of heritage is to a large extent about how we manage human and natural legacies, and finding suitable ways of management is particularly important when the heritage is toxic, in the sense that it endangers important values. Both nuclear waste and cultural heritage are managed and contained through specific regulations (as a result of a sense of responsibility/duty), and through values of 'exceptionalism' they are set apart from other forms of waste or from unofficial heritage due to a perceived sense of risk (see Harrison 2013a; Rico 2014a; 2015a). Indeed, it can be argued that it is a perceived sense of risk that drives both nuclear waste management and cultural heritage management, and that it is this risk that leads to a need of 'containment' through regulations (see May 2009 for a discussion of how framing things as endangered domesticates them). But can the disturbing or unwanted past be safely contained, and would such a containment even be desirable? We suggest that the notion of 'toxic heritage' helps to unpack and critically investigate these issues.

We will begin by introducing nuclear waste management and its challenges in relationship to heritage management, before we introduce the concept of toxic heritage in detail. We will go on to discuss circumstances under which heritage may become toxic, why it may become toxic, and the challenges of determining and managing toxic heritage. These challenges will be discussed in relation to issues of 'uncertainty' and 'unsafety'. Thereafter, we will contextualise our argument by looking briefly at toxic heritage in a very different context: former Yugoslavia, where the heritage of recent conflict has the capacity to undermine contemporary social safety. Finally, we conclude by tying the threads together, and discuss the benefits of an integrated approach in order to understand and manage both forms of toxic heritage.

Nuclear waste and cultural heritage management

Worldwide, there are at the time of writing more than 250,000 tonnes of high-level nuclear waste, with an additional 12,000 tonnes being added every year (IAEA 2018). The current favoured method for discarding this waste is disposal in mined tunnels drilled into stable geological formations several hundred metres below the surface. The process of selecting appropriate locations for such final repositories of high-level radioactive waste is now well under way in several countries (Swedish National Council for Nuclear Waste 2019). The goal is to isolate nuclear waste from the human environment, near enough permanently. It takes a hundred thousand years or more before highly radioactive nuclear waste is no longer deemed dangerous for human beings. Present and future generations of sentient biological organisms are therefore faced with the task of safeguarding this hazardous waste for very long time periods. After the waste has been finally disposed of underground, we need, among other things, to transmit information over thousands of generations concerning the location, character and content of these large underground repositories (Schröder 2019). This is at the same time both an impossible and a necessary task. Any physical marker at the location is unlikely to persist over such long time periods, given the expected impact of major climatic changes including, for example, a new ice age during which massive layers of ice will abrade the surface of the land (Ahlbom et al. 1991). Archives containing written records will be kept all over the world, but we cannot guarantee that they will survive sufficiently long. Moreover, we know neither which written languages will be understood nor whether pictograms or symbols will be interpreted in the way we meant them (Wikander 2015a; 2015b). In fact, we cannot even be sure that the hominids or other sentient biological organisms receiving our messages will belong to the species Homo sapiens, which is not older than c. 300,000 years and may not exist in the same form a few hundred thousand years ahead. No one can honestly claim to be able to transmit information reliably many thousands of years into the future.

Stonehenge is an exceptional form of cultural heritage: it may not be older, but it attracted more interest over the centuries than related prehistoric monuments. By analogy, nuclear waste can be said to be the 'Stonehenge' of toxic waste: it is not necessarily more long-lasting or more dangerous to living beings than other forms of toxic waste, but it attracts a particularly large amount of attention in society, from media to politicians to grass-roots activists. Indeed, criticism has been raised about the lack of informed future perspectives with regard to other forms of toxic waste, such as that of tar sands (Westman 2013) or coal mines (Okrent 1999, 887–90).

Nuclear waste management aims to create a sense of safety due to a perceived risk to present and future generations. The prime strategy for this is containing nuclear waste in deep geological repositories, with the help of a strict protocol of regulations and requirements. If this protocol is not met, there could be repercussions affecting humans, wildlife and the environment at large. It has proven to be of utmost importance to build a sense of public trust in the capability of the responsible institutions to manage the repositories and contain the nuclear waste without any additional threats to present and future generations. If a sense of safety and trust is not produced among the local population, they will most likely oppose the presence of the repository, as occurred at the planned Yucca Mountain Nuclear Waste Repository in Nevada, USA that has now been abandoned (Kunreuther et al. 1990; Macfarlane and Ewing 2006; Endres 2009; see also Sjöberg and Drottz-Sjöberg 2001; Andrén 2012 for a parallel discussion in Sweden).

Similarly, heritage management often operates under a perceived sense of risk and in the framework of endangerment (Vidal and Dias 2016a; see discussion in Chapters 1 and 2 of this book). Certain forms of tangible/intangible heritage are framed as in need of protection because they are threatened by contemporary circumstances, for instance the 'spatial cleansing' occurring as a result of modernity (Herzfeld 2006; González-Ruibal 2008; Connerton 2009), war (Sørensen and Viejo-Rose 2015; Walasek 2016; Pollock 2016) or climate change and the natural disasters that follow (Jones 1986; Solli et al. 2011; Hambrecht and Rockman 2017). As discussed in Chapter 2, this concept of a heritage at risk, or endangerment sensibility, underpins and justifies the conservation and protection of all heritage. However, alternative perspectives highlighting how 'change' is both inevitable and a potential positive value in heritage have also been put forward, and they call for a more nuanced understanding of heritage conservation and risk (DeSilvey 2017; Holtorf 2018a; papers in DeSilvey and Harrison 2020).

Indeed, both nuclear waste management and heritage management are often preoccupied by a need to create safe spaces, not only in terms of preserving and maintaining tangible and intangible heritage or keeping toxic waste away from humans, but also in terms of *not* creating a sense of unsafety. This can be exemplified by looking at Trinidad Rico's research about the nomination process of UNESCO World Heritage Sites. She found (Rico 2008, 349) that 'The process of nomination to the List actively discourages contestation, through the decontextualization of specific sites, as they are required to fit a predefined language embodied in a set of criteria, and to define geographical boundaries that may isolate them from their spatial, and to some degree cultural, contexts.' More generally, cultural heritage is commonly associated with values such as 'beauty' and 'perfection', and notions of being 'sacred' and 'admirable' (see, for example, Macdonald 2006b, 19), which stand in sharp contrast to contestation and unsafety. This becomes especially poignant in the case of difficult heritage, of which nuclear waste is one example, since such heritage tends to, and should, be 'permanently unsettling' (Macdonald 2009), in order for it to pose uncomfortable but important questions that in turn will make it emotionally and socially relevant (Wollentz 2017a).

One excellent example of employing radioactivity, and questions surrounding nuclear waste, in such a way is the exhibition *Perpetual Uncertainty*, curated by Ele Carpenter and most recently showcased in 2018 at the Malmö Art Museum in Sweden (see Figures 19.1 to 19.4 and Figure 17.2). This exhibition, comprising 27 works in total, uses the perpetually changing characteristics of radioactivity to reflect upon memory, time and knowledge. In contrast to how heritage and nuclear waste is commonly managed, the aim of this exhibition is to produce a sense of uncertainty rather than certainty, through emphasising instability rather than stability. Before we develop the argument further, it is necessary to position and define the concept of toxic heritage in relationship to other terms within the field.

Toxic heritage

The subfield of 'difficult' (Macdonald 2009), 'dissonant' (Tunbridge and Ashworth 1996; Kisić 2016), 'negative' (Meskell 2002), 'undesirable' (Macdonald 2006b) or 'dark' (Kobiałka 2018; Seitsonen 2018) heritage has emerged within the last 20 years (Samuels 2015), owing significant impetus to the seminal work of geographers John E. Tunbridge and Gregory J. Ashworth in *Dissonant Heritage: The Management of the Past as a Resource in Conflict* (1996). While the concept has gained more attention and significance in academia within recent decades, it has perhaps been recognised within heritage management for considerably longer than it has featured in scholarly discussions. In a thoughtful article on the topic, the anthropologist Joshua Samuels (2015) argues that the various terms are more or less used by scholars to designate the same phenomenon, which is the meditation on managing a problematic or disturbing past. Nevertheless, they hold different connotations. Negative heritage, for instance, is simultaneously a value statement and refers to heritage that 'becomes the repository of negative memory in the collective imaginary' (Meskell 2002, 558); for example, the site of a terrorist attack. Within recent years, difficult heritage has become the most common term to use (see Macdonald 2009) and, as emphasised by Samuels (2015), the relative neutrality of the word 'difficult' is a benefit. In defining dissonant heritage, we draw on the work of Tunbridge and Ashworth (1996), which was later developed by Laurajane Smith (2006), in seeing all heritage as inherently dissonant, because 'all heritage is uncomfortable to someone, not only because any meaning or message about a heritage place may "disinherit" someone else, but because heritage has a particular power to legitimize – or not – someone's sense of place and thus their social and cultural experiences and memories' (Smith 2006, 81). Dissonance does not necessarily lead to conflict, but if the dissonance is not addressed, or if it is silenced (see Trouillot 1995), the risk of open conflict increases considerably (see, for example, the discussion of the post-Franco 'Pact of Silence' in Spain in Viejo-Rose 2011, 150–95; also, in relation to the Heritage Futures research programme, see Raxworthy 2018).

While it is important to keep in mind that all heritage is, and should to some extent be, difficult to present due to heritage being inherently dissonant, it is necessary for analytical purposes to define 'difficult heritage' as a specific form of particularly unsettling heritage, due to its connection to violence, war or otherwise traumatic memories (see Logan and Reeves 2009; Drozdzewski et al. 2016). Heritage becomes especially difficult to reconcile when 'one's own people or country are the perpetrators' (Macdonald 2016, 270). With all these terms already in use, where does toxic heritage fit in? We use the term 'toxic heritage' to describe instances in which forms of difficult heritage come to endanger certain core values in society (such as equal rights and opportunities, peaceful coexistence, freedom of speech, health and well-being), most often because of a lack of responsible management. We are open to the fact that what exactly constitutes these core values may differ from context to context, especially regarding so-called non-Western societies. The heritage professional needs to listen, accept and be open-minded to different ways of understanding heritage and relations to the past and to the world (for example, Orange 2015; Kiddey 2017), but *also* have a critical and engaged voice that does not fall prey to 'reactionary populism' (Gonzaléz-Ruibal et al. 2018; see also Brophy 2018).

Figure 19.1 Malmö Art Museum welcoming visitors to Perpetual Uncertainty: Art and Radioactivity. The exhibition brought together 29 international artists investigating the relations between nuclear power, radioactivity, deep time and cultural heritage.[1]

Figure 19.2 Ken and Julia Yonetani, *Crystal Palace: The Great Exhibition of the Works of Industry of all Nuclear Nations* (2013). The work consists of 31 chandelier frames refitted with uranium glass and UV lights, representing each of the states using nuclear technology in the contemporary world.

Figure 19.3   Robert Williams and Bryan McGovern Wilson, *Cumbrian Alchemy* (2014). This installation investigates speculative relationships between the nuclear industry, radioactivity, landscape, archaeology, folklore and popular culture in the British region of Cumbria, which includes the Lake District.

Figure 19.4   Andrew Weir, *Pazugoo* (2017). These 3D-printed figures and cast prototypes are inspired by ancient renderings of Pazuzu, the Babylonian–Assyrian demon of dust, plagues and misfortune. They are intended to mark underground perimeters of deep geological repositories for nuclear waste.

As stated above, heritage risks becoming toxic especially when its dissonance is being silenced or disregarded. Therefore, we argue that the inherent dissonance, and potential difficulty, in heritage may be seen as a resource for triggering different sets of engagements and responses (see also Kisić 2016, 31; De Nardi 2017), rather than as a problem in need of being resolved through containment (Wollentz 2017a). We are here distinguishing between three different but highly interrelated forms of toxic heritage:

1. *When heritage is forgotten so that important stories may not be transmitted further:* A pertinent example would be the history of colonialism, specifically the silencing of the causes motivating, and the human rights violations resulting from, colonialism (see McAtackney and Palmer 2016).
2. *When a heritage is remembered in order to promote a specific and exclusive version of the past:* A pertinent example would be a postwar silencing of the suffering experienced from each side of a war instead of a focus on shared suffering, as occurred in the aftermath of the breakup of Yugoslavia (see, for example, Duijzings 2007).
3. *When heritage is designed so that it supports dangerous politics:* The seminal edited volume, *The Invention of Tradition*, by Eric Hobsbawm and Terence Ranger (1983), provides several examples of how political institutions in Europe during the nineteenth century invented traditions in order to *claim* an ancient and self-given origin of the novel construction of the nation. These invented traditions still legitimise present-day understandings of the nation that can be dangerous.

These three forms (forgotten, selective and invented) are often interconnected, and incidents of toxic heritage can seldom neatly be placed into one of these categories; instead, it can include elements of all three. Furthermore, a heritage based on a selective process of remembering and forgetting is, to a large extent, unavoidable and not, in itself, a cause for concern (Forty and Küchler 1999; Connerton 2008; 2011, 51–82; Harrison 2013a, 166–203; Wollentz 2019). The entanglement of forgetting, selection and invention are highlighted in Penrose's (2017, 171) discussion of neo-liberal ruins: 'Memory mourns the past. What remains, decays'. To avoid the pitfalls of such heritage, it is crucial to ask *how*, *where* and *why* certain memories are promoted at the expense of others, and which and – even more importantly – *whose* silences are produced in the process. Further, Sara Perry (2019) has recently argued that it is precisely the emotionally connected arguments that create value in heritage. We will now outline challenges in managing and understanding toxic heritage with a focus on uncertainty and unsafety.

Uncertainty

Nuclear waste is inherently 'hazardous' to biological organisms, including humans, through its radioactivity. The same cannot necessarily be said of the physical properties of heritage. However, we cannot be certain that nuclear waste will always be perceived as predominantly hazardous waste posing a threat to humanity, and that its physical properties, notably the radioactivity, will always be its most significant or most interesting characteristic. New technologies, such as transmutation, may allow using nuclear waste to generate further energy or for other purposes, so that this waste becomes a precious resource. Additionally, radioactive material has proven to be a creative resource in the visual arts, for instance within the *Perpetual Uncertainty* exhibition, mentioned above. Artist James Acord (1944–2011) became the first and thus far only private individual in the USA licensed to own and hold radioactive materials. Although radioactive substances can be very dangerous, for example when they enter the food chain or are used in dirty bombs, the locations of their storage or disposal do not have to be seen forever as areas of deadly threats, but may, given time, be transformed into altogether different things. This is not to deny or ignore real dangers posed by radioactive material to future generations but more to look at these dangers in the present from a different perspective on their possible future context. Who would have thought, back in the late 1980s, that the area around the destroyed reactors at Chernobyl, although in places still radioactive, would become something of a nature reserve, which has now happened after a process of auto-rewilding (Kruse and Galison 2011; see further discussion of rewilding in Part V, Transformation)?

What we find significant to pinpoint is that, despite attempts of containment through regulations, in order to create and maintain a sense of safety due to a perceived risk, there is still a large degree of unpredictability and uncertainty concerning nuclear waste. The material is by its very nature unstable, as radioactivity is caused by unstable atomic nuclei emitting energy. Moreover, we cannot predict or determine for certain whether it will be interpreted and treated as *waste* in the future. Further, radioactive waste is constantly changing as its level of radiation gradually decreases. These processes of ongoing transformations occur over immense timescales (one hundred thousand years or more). They are evocatively captured in the artwork *Inheritance* by Erich Berger and Mari Keto, which was exhibited as part of the exhibition Perpetual Uncertainty (see Figure 17.2). The installation exhibits radioactive jewellery meant to be inherited over generations. A casket includes the material and instructions for measuring the radioactive levels of the jewellery as it is passed to the next generation, in order to control if it is ready to be used. If determined to be not ready for use, the jewellery is safely stored again, awaiting coming generations to test its hazardousness.

Similar to radioactive waste, we argue that difficult heritage is 'perpetually uncertain'. Sites that are connected to death, suffering and violations of human rights, such as Auschwitz, can be used to foster dialogue about the past and personal reflection concerning the values of human lives. For instance, that is the aim of the International Coalition of Sites of Conscience (Ševčenko 2010; 2011), which is a network of historic sites aimed at using difficult heritage to promote human rights issues. If managed in an inclusive manner, without silencing dissonance, such sites may not be toxic heritage in the sense that they do not endanger certain core values in society, as defined above.

However, toxic heritage does not necessarily have clearly demarcated beginnings or endings in time. This can be illustrated through the notion of 'imperial debris', as introduced by Ann Laura Stoler (2008; 2013) and further examined by Laura McAtackney and Russell Palmer (2016), referring to how imperial processes and colonial institutions can persist and saturate people's lives over considerable time periods. In fact, 'imperial debris' often underlies and structures post-colonial settings, and carries on through material remains such as overgrown ruins of colonial institutions and in concrete neighbourhoods of low-income high-rises. Approaching such sites from the perspective of nuclear waste bodes the question: do empires have a half-life?[2]

Certain forms of heritage, such as that of colonialism, may have a pervasive and subjacent character that makes them especially toxic. There is no general way, no one-size-fits-all model, of how to transform any of the three forms of toxic heritage, as defined above, into something more positive or constructive. Neither are there any guarantees that a site that has transformed from toxic heritage will remain that way. Indeed, that is the very nature of perpetual uncertainty: heritage is changing. Instead of seeing change as a cause for concern, it may be better to approach it as an incentive to take account of uncertainty rather than sidestepping it (see also Part V, Transformation). By taking account of uncertainty, heritage management will be better able to respond to the changing characteristics of heritage.

Unsafety

It is not always necessary, or beneficial, to make toxic heritage safe. In fact, it is pertinent to question if 'safe' heritage is what is needed (see also Macdonald 2009; Harrison 2013a). Both heritage and nuclear waste management have commonly sought single stable solutions to their responsibilities: they have often been keen to establish long-term preservation that effectively place their respective object of attention in a timeless state of permanent existence and unchanging value. An illustrative example is when UNESCO, supported by the World Bank and other international and national actors, reconstructed the famous bridge Stari Most (see Figure 19.5) in Mostar, after it had been destroyed by the HVO (Croatian Defence Council) in November 1993. The aim was to transform the reconstructed bridge, which was reopened in 2004, into a monument with universal values that would symbolise the healing of a divided city (UNESCO 2005, 35). However, criticism has been levelled against UNESCO in the goal of finding a single stable solution (that is, a reconstructed Stari Most) for a long-term and complex phenomenon such as a post-war reconciliation process (Grodach 2002; Makaš 2007; Walasek 2016; Forde

Figure 19.5   The reconstructed Stari Most bridge in Mostar, Bosnia and Herzegovina (photograph by Gustav Wollentz).

2016). The point is that heritage can achieve more if a single stable solution is avoided and 'change' is accounted for rather than downplayed. By so doing, heritage can be involved in difficult but necessary processes that do not necessarily end at a certain point. Responsibilities towards present and future generations do not stop with the reconstruction of a building. Instead, they are ongoing and continuously evolving. As evocatively expressed by Lisa Baraitser (2015, 29), professor in psychosocial studies, when elaborating on the relationship between care and time: 'Care is an arduous temporal practice that entails the maintenance of relations with ourselves and others through histories of oppression that return in the present again and again.'

Indeed, responsibility to present and future generations is crucial both within heritage management and nuclear waste management. In nuclear waste management, this sense of responsibility is not solely concerned with keeping radioactive waste away from human beings at all costs, but also to *allow* future generations to make their own informed decisions and potentially create new meanings and values surrounding nuclear waste, which may be fundamentally different from our present understandings. Only through approaching nuclear waste management as an ongoing and continuous process involving several actors in society, institutional and non-institutional, will there be a possibility of keeping the memory of the geological repositories alive for thousands of years (see Pescatore 2018). Similarly, as we argue throughout this book, in cultural heritage management, a sense of responsibility to future generations is not only about conserving heritage at all costs in the face of a perceived risk, but also about facilitating future generations to make their own meanings and values in relation to heritage. Just as in nuclear waste, these meanings and values may be very different to our current ones (see also Högberg et al. 2017). Therefore, a high degree of flexibility is required, in which responsibility is seen as an ongoing process without beginning and end. Such a flexibility demands a responsiveness to change.

Rather than focusing on control, containment and regulations, on creating a safe heritage through stable solutions, there may be a benefit in focusing on the issue of responsibility to the present as well as to the future. Sometimes a responsible heritage management may be to protect and contain heritage due to a perceived risk (natural disaster, war, spatial cleansing and so on). On other occasions, a responsible heritage management may be the opposite: to allow for heritage to be uncontained and, subsequently, to produce a sense of unsafety.

Toxic heritage in former Yugoslavia

In this section, we would like to root our argument in a particular case study through examining toxic heritage in former Yugoslavia. The reason why we focus on this particular region in the context of toxic heritage is because its heritage became politicised, conflicted and targeted for destruction during the wars that led to the dissolution of the Socialist Federal Republic of Yugoslavia, and the legacies of the wars are still informing attitudes and responsibilities towards the heritage. However, before such an undertaking, we find it useful to discuss the article 'The Jurassic Park of Historical Culture' by Antonis Liakos and Mitsos Bilalis (2017), which draws upon popular culture to provide a framework for understanding the nature and role of historical culture. Liakos and Bilalis argue that the past has a way of unexpectedly and uncontrollably intruding upon and influencing the present, similar to the dinosaurs brought back to life in *Jurassic Park* (1993; see also Chapter 6). As the authors write: 'No one is safe from the past; no one knows when, under what conditions and which species of dinosaurs will start to awaken and start to revive past wars' (Liakos and Bilalis 2017, 210). They distinguish between a 'closed' and an 'open' past, with the former having no real consequences for the present, while the latter is demanding justice or vengeance. Comparable to how the dinosaurs in the first *Jurassic Park* film are controlled and managed through fences and regulations and placed in a theme park as a tourist attraction, the past is managed, controlled and made safe through museums, monuments, and popular films and books. Nevertheless, the past is unpredictable and potentially toxic: 'the presence of the past may prove deadly; dead memories are thirsty for blood, and there are many killer dinosaurs in the park. Nationalism is one of the bigger ones' (Liakos and Bilalis 2017, 209). And, of course, those of you who have seen the films know how fleeting the sense of safety proved to be, no matter how securely the dinosaurs were contained.

This can be exemplified by looking at the rise of nationalism during the breakup of Yugoslavia in the 1990s. During the wars, politicians and military leaders were regularly drawing upon the past to legitimise further violence. Most famously, the medieval 1389 Battle of Kosovo, between the Ottomans and a coalition of Christian forces, was frequently employed by the infamous convicted war criminal Ratko Mladić to legitimise the genocides occurring in Bosnia and Herzegovina against the Bosnian Muslim population (Duijzings 2000, 201–2; 2007, 142–3). Repeatedly, the myth of the battle has been misused by Serbian politicians, academics, public figures and religious leaders to claim an 'eternal' right to the land of Kosovo, opposed to the Kosovo Albanians (Duijzings 2000, 176–202; Bieber 2002; Djokić 2009; Čolović 2011). This rhetoric of entitlement was most famously expressed during the 600th anniversary of the battle in 1989, when Slobodan Milošević gave a speech at the Gazimestan monument (see Figure 19.6), where the battle is supposed to have taken place. At every so-called Vidovdan, a celebration held annually for the anniversary of the battle on 28 June, Serbians gather at the monument, singing nationalistic songs and wearing nationalistic clothes. These practices have less to do with history and more to do with the reconstruction of the past in the present and using it to make claims on the future (Hobsbawm and Ranger 1983; Connerton 1989). Therefore, the Gazimestan monument, in its present-day role and purpose, is an example of toxic heritage as defined above, including both selective and invented elements (Wollentz 2019).

Within popular, and occasionally academic, representations of the Balkans, the region is often characterised as 'haunted' or 'burdened' by a toxic past of 'ancient ethnic hatreds', to the point that people are sometimes simply portrayed as passive victims who are powerless in the face

Figure 19.6 The Gazimestan monument, Kosovo (photograph by Gustav Wollentz).

of a violent past that in turn motivates further violence (see, for example, Kaplan 2005). Such a representation may seem to superficially align with the argument by Liakos and Bilalis (2017) in regard to the uncontrollable and intrusive nature of the past. However, it is a problematic and, indeed, harmful representation, which has a long history of Eurocentric and colonial roots (Todorova 1997; Ramet 2006; Kolstø 2005). Such a representation diverts attention from the crucial issue of responsibility and downplays human agency. It highlights the necessity to focus on how the past is being instrumentalised by actors, who are often directed towards the future *rather* than the past. This is not to diminish the significance of a historical understanding of the causes motivating the outbreak of ethnic tension and violence, but a call for the necessity to position representations and experiences of the past within the current political and social framework, in which a selected past may receive a specific purpose and role.

The socialist heritage in former Yugoslavia provides a case in point. The heritage of socialism tends to pose an uncomfortable dilemma, both for the political elites, who are often driven by a nationalistic agenda, and for international organisations, which often regard liberal values as the norm (Kisić 2016, 173–87, 266–9). After the war, which led to the dissolution of Yugoslavia, the ideology of socialism building upon the identity of workers was replaced by a neo-liberal and post-industrial society, in which the identity of workers was not valued. This process silenced the workers' identity within the public space. In many cities, such as in Mostar, in Bosnia and Herzegovina, socialist monuments were either neglected – for example, the Partisan Memorial Cemetery (Partizansko groblje) (Barišić et al. 2017; Murtić and Barišić 2019) – or replaced with new 'exclusively ethnic' monuments (Wollentz 2017b; Wollentz et al. 2019). Therefore, the industrial heritage of socialism evokes 'potential for negotiation of identities that would offer an alternative to divisions along ethnic and religious lines that currently dominate the post-Yugoslav spaces' (Petrović 2013, 96).

In an insightful study on the post-war heritage of Sarajevo, Piro Rexhepi (2018, 13) argues that projects supported by the European Union tend to produce 'Ottoman or Socialist histories as temporary misalignments from the European linear path [which] forecloses any possible alternative futurities'. Rexhepi's study suggests that the European Union has ideas of what constitutes a 'safe' and 'unsafe' heritage in Sarajevo, and enforces this through financial support to 'safe' heritage (Austro-Hungarian)[3] and a neglect of heritage that is deemed 'unsafe' (most notably socialist). Safety is thus induced through regulations, containment and management (or the lack of it), but this safety is not innocent. For instance, the colonial aspects of the Austro-Hungarian heritage are neglected in favour of recognising it as 'European', in opposition to 'Ottoman' (Muslim) or 'socialist' (communist), notwithstanding that the European Union itself has a long history of colonialism. Here we can note how the criteria for determining safe/unsafe heritage are based on a highly selective process of remembering and forgetting. However, a growing body of research is recognising how a silencing of the socialist heritage in former Yugoslavia is not accepted freely by people. Instead, it leads to reactions in the form of protests (Kurtović and Hromadžić 2017), youth activism (Carabelli 2018; Wollentz et al. 2019) or simply a silent resistance.

This underlines that the toxicity of heritage is not inherent, but a product of how it is managed. Therefore, it is crucial to understand the dynamics at work, and ask on what criteria a certain site of heritage is regarded as toxic, and whether such a categorisation is aligned with the experiences/memories/perspectives of the population living close to or at the site. Indeed, what is considered toxic heritage by certain groups may be considered valuable heritage by others, while the very process of categorising toxic heritage may hide historical injustices. The past will be managed, contained and regulated and, following the analogy introduced by Liakos and Bilalis (2017), a Jurassic Park will be created out of it: a zone of safety. Nevertheless, it is not possible to control the past, because people have their own experiences, memories and interpretations, and may refuse any top-down representations of the past – that is, they may try to rescue the dinosaurs that are held in prison. This is one of the main reasons why we argue that heritage is perpetually uncertain. Sometimes, the sense of safety created by maintaining heritage is an illusion that hides deep injustices and forces silences. As the heritage of socialism in former Yugoslavia informed us, recognising a silenced past may be a source for personal and collective resistance, empowerment and emancipation. Through unravelling the past as a domain of competing claims and identities, which in turn are building upon conflicting interpretations, memories and narratives, we will become better adept at responding to change by acknowledging the unpredictability and uncertainty of heritage.

Conclusions

Toxic heritage is defined as a specific form of difficult heritage, when the heritage in question threatens core values, such as equal rights and opportunities, peaceful coexistence, freedom of speech, health and well-being. We distinguish between three different but highly inter-related instances of toxic heritage: forgotten, selective and invented forms. Throughout this chapter, we have argued that heritage man-agement and nuclear waste management share important concerns and challenges, and we have focused particularly on a shared aim of containment due to a sense of risk, a similar uncertain and unstable character and a shared sense of responsibility to future generations. We hope to have shown the benefits of an integrated approach to difficult heritage.

Our conclusions are fourfold. First, the toxicity of heritage is not related to its content (for instance, due to a connection to death or violence) but to its management and to the narratives for which it is used. This is analogous to toxic waste, which – managed safely – might also be a resource. Second, both toxic waste and toxic herit-age are perpetually uncertain, that is, they are changeable. Heritage managers have little control over these changes because they are often driven by wider processes. However, if we take account of the muta-ble nature of the material, we can make clear how it is managed so that people dealing with the changes have the information to make useful decisions about it. Third, it is far from obvious that creating a 'safe' past will necessarily reduce the toxicity of heritage. Occasionally, we need to allow for heritage to be uncontained and potentially pro-duce a sense of unsafety. Furthermore, the very process of creating a 'safe' past may hide historical injustices and force silences, and may therefore result in a toxic heritage. Thus, it is necessary to question on what criteria a certain past is regarded as safe/unsafe. Finally, instead of aiming to find single stable solutions in dealing with toxic waste/ heritage, we suggest that responsibilities to present and future gener-ations need to be seen as ongoing and continuously evolving, without beginning or end. In so doing, and in line with other discussions in this book, heritage management will become better at preparing for, and responding to, change over time. This underlines the argument we have made throughout this part of the book, that uncertainty can be an opportunity. This is as true for the management of toxic and dangerous materials as it is for the topic of the next chapter, the messages sent to spacecraft that could represent humanity to extraterrestrial futures. In both cases, uncertainty inspires us to engage with values, and an open, engaged stance produces better results.

Notes

1. Figures 19.1 to 19.4 all photographed by Daniel Lindskog, from the exhibition Perpetual Uncertainty, produced by Bildmuseet, Umeå University, curated by Ele Carpenter, and shown at Malmö Art Museum in Malmö, Sweden, 24 April–26 August 2018.
2. Half-life is defined as the time it takes for a quantity to reduce to half its initial value. It is often used to designate the gradual disintegration of the atoms of radioactive material, that is, radioactive decay.
3. Between 1878 and 1918, Bosnia and Herzegovina was de facto ruled by Austria-Hungary, as part of the Austro-Hungarian Empire, after more than four hundred years of Ottoman rule (1463/1482 to 1878). Nevertheless, it was not formally annexed by Austria-Hungary until 1908.

20

Micro-messaging/space messaging: A comparative exploration of #GoodbyePhilae and #MessageToVoyager

Sarah May

Introduction

Heritage has always been an integral part of space exploration. When Neil Armstrong landed on the moon he claimed to be doing so 'for all mankind', but he planted an American flag in the ground. Heritage creates space as a cultural field. Alice Gorman points out that space heritage, like heritage on Earth, includes the unintentional remains of our activities as well as the statement pieces that we would like to be remembered by. So, both Armstrong's footprint and the flag that was left are heritage (Gorman 2015; 2016). But space exploration also engages heritage practice by creating space as an exhibition, even an archive of material that represents 'the best of humanity' (Wolfram 2018). When the *Voyager* spacecrafts were launched on their journey out of the solar system, our collaborator Jon Lomberg was part of a team which aimed to include a message from Earth for any beings that might find it. This message selected sounds, music, art and other imagery to represent humanity and the Earth to a future, extraterrestrial audience (Paglen 2013).

Lomberg has continued the work of space art and space communication, and most recently established the One Earth Message (OEM) project, which planned a crowdsourced message to upload to the *New Horizons* spacecraft as it exited the solar system, having passed Pluto, and headed out into the galaxy. The selection of components for that message, the processes of negotiation and the technological practices involved in leaving it on a spacecraft to be found by unknown beings after the death of humanity, show the ways people reflect and construct themselves in the mirror of 'forever'. This selection and curation, and the concern with the ways in which these components will be received in the distant future, have clear parallels in other kinds of heritage practice described in this volume.

Jon Lomberg, the leader of the OEM project, has significant experience with such initiatives. As mentioned, he worked with Carl Sagan on 'Sounds of Earth', a record pressed in gold and encased in instructions for use that was loaded on to the two *Voyager* spacecraft before they were launched to explore the outer solar system. That project was completed quickly, and a handful of people made all the decisions about what to include and how to communicate with beings that may share nothing more with us than the capacity to send technology into space (Sagan et al. 1978; Paglen 2013). A follow-on project that sent a CD on the *Viking* lander to Mars had a similarly small project team, but a much closer audience: the CD is a message to future humans as they land on Mars, to remind them of the dreams and stories that propelled them there (Lomberg 2018). But both of these projects struggled with representing cultural and natural diversity, as they were put together quickly by small groups of individuals from broadly similar socio-economic, cultural and political backgrounds and from a single country (Vakoch 1998; Goldsmith 1990).

OEM sought to broaden participation in deep-space communication and in so doing bring the people of the world together to present themselves to the universe. But while anyone who heard about the project could contribute, the data space available would be restricted. Because the message was not a feature of the *New Horizons* mission from the beginning, it would be uploaded through transmission to the spacecraft after it had passed Pluto – the larger the message, the more difficult the transmission (Lomberg 2018). Further, the project team were keen to frame it as a message that could conceivably be understood, rather than a set of sounds, texts and images. So, the project team planned to select and compose a message from crowdsourced contributions.

OEM worked through many different channels, but in the end decided it would not be possible to add a message to *New Horizons*. Reflecting on the fact that a new message would not be uploaded, Lomberg explored how the cultural materials that were sent with *New Horizons* (some coins, a flag and the ashes of the discoverer of Pluto, Clyde Tombaugh) are not suitable as representatives of humanity. He pointed out that they are all American, rather than global, and that no thought had been given to the possibility of interspecies communication (Lomberg 2018).

The decision to send these items makes little sense in terms of communicating with a future non-human species, but it sends a clear, if parochial, message to the people of contemporary Earth. The coins come from the states that produced the spacecraft, the flag represents the USA and the ashes are those of the individual genius associated with one of the main scientific targets of the mission. The message for earthlings is: 'Space exploration is a matter of territory, a matter of pride, a matter of individual genius.' This matches well with the Cold War origins and neo-liberal development of space exploration (Ehrenfreund et al. 2010; Geppert 2012; Gorman 2009). A message such as this asserts that current social structures will persist, and that humanity can be represented through the aspirations of one nation or indeed one person.

As space exploration has moved from its Cold War origins to a neo-liberal capitalist model, including venture capitalists, the creation and transmission of messages has similarly become individualised (Gorman 2018). Rather than an official team composing a message to be included at launch, there have been many opportunities for individuals to create heritage to be conserved and communicated in space. In this chapter, I examine two messaging events and their profile on the micro-messaging platform, Twitter. I will explore how these campaigns constructed heritage and compare it with the earlier coordinated heritage practice represented by the selection of materials to be sent as part of the original *Voyager* message.

Twitter is a social media platform that broadcasts short messages from anyone with an account. Despite being castigated for its rapid, aggressive mode of discourse, it has become an important social and political sphere over the last 10 years. Heritage scholars have considered how Twitter constructs communities (including through exclusion) and how this form of communication creates new forms of heritage practice (Richardson 2014; Richardson and Lindgren 2017; Bonacchi et al. 2014; Bonacchi et al. 2018). It has become similarly important to the discipline of science communication (Waters and Williams 2011; Côté and Darling 2018). Since communication, both with the contemporary inhabitants of Earth and future inhabitants of deep space, has long been an integral part of space programmes, it is no surprise that space agencies have used Twitter as part of their strategies.

Philae: Messages and memorials

In 2016, the European Space Agency (ESA) completed a mission to explore and land on the comet 67P. The *Rosetta* spacecraft that conducted the mission was named after the Rosetta Stone – a tablet carved in 1976 BC that played a key role in twentieth-century decipherment of hieroglyphs. In homage to this, it carried a small disk, etched in 1,000 languages (ESA 2002). But when the spacecraft landed it also brought with it a set of messages crowdsourced through social media.

Two weeks before the ESA uploaded these messages to *Rosetta*, communications between *Rosetta* and *Philae*, its lander on the comet, were switched off. These messages are from anyone on Earth who wanted to say goodbye to the lander using the Twitter hashtag #GoodbyePhilae. It is hoped that the data storage, and thus the messages, will survive the crash landing. Although the #GoodbyePhilae messages look to the future, they are framed by the ESA as a goodbye, a memorial to a robot.

The Rosetta mission had a major outreach component that used social media extensively. Both *Rosetta* and the *Philae* lander have been anthropomorphised. They are the stars of a cartoon series popularising their explorations for children, and each has a Twitter account. When *Philae* separated from *Rosetta*, it was given a 'younger brother' persona, and photographs sent from the lander are referred to as postcards.

Philae also took on a role of underdog due to a problematic landing in which the robot bounced a number of times and came to rest in the shadow of a boulder. This caused problems with communication and operations throughout the rest of the mission. When the lander went quiet because its solar generator could not start up its systems, many of the followers of the Twitter account reported that they were in tears. When the comet moved closer to the sun again, the lander 'woke up' slightly sooner than expected. There was some communication back with *Rosetta*, and then no more.

The *Philae* Twitter account sent out one last message (see Figure 20.1). As goodbye messages, the responses to this are essentially a memorial, a requirement for the future to remember something that is important to us. Although focused in relation to a person or event, memorials are always about the people creating them as well. They are about immortality in the face of mortality. As Binyon's famous First World War memorial poem 'For the Fallen' has it, 'They shall grow not old, as we that are left grow old' (Binyon 1914). This memorial to *Philae* has some

Philae Lander ✓
@Philae2014

I'm far from Earth&Sun!I'd love to take memories of
YOU with me. Please send me a postcard from home!
#GoodbyePhilae dlr.de/blogs/en/deskt...

3:03 PM · Jul 26, 2016 · TweetDeck

Figure 20.1   The tweet calling for messages with the hashtag
#GoodbyePhilae (@Philae2014/Twitter).

John Mason
@johnmason1971

Replying to @Philae2014 and @ESA_Rosetta

Just don't do a V'ger and return in a few hundred years
to destroy your creator!

1:39 PM · Jul 27, 2016 · Twitter for Android

Figure 20.2   Some tweets expressed a fear that *Philae* would enact
science-fiction futures (@johnmason1971/Twitter).

awareness that the future may not be like the present. It calls upon an
unknowable future to think of us, but also calls on us to imagine a future
that might care to do so. The messages represent a relatively unmediated
view of what people on social media take from the mission, how they feel
about it and how they want to be remembered in relation to it. In that,
the #GoodbyePhilae upload creates a memorial future related to, but distinct from, other space messages.

Reflecting on the content of the messages, there is some discussion
of what the future might be; consideration of aliens finding the lander
and the messages; contemplation of the lander travelling through space
with the comet and seeing things but not communicating them with us;
and anxiety (slightly ironic but also sincere) around the *Voyager* narrative (related to the film *Star Trek: The Motion Picture* (1979), in which the
fictitious *Voyager 6* spacecraft returns to Earth hundreds of years hence to
communicate its accumulated knowledge, but attacks humanity because
it does not recognise us as 'the creator' – see Figure 20.2).

Philae asked for postcards, and a lot of the messages conform to
classic postcard imagery – mostly landscapes, a lot of flowers, almost no
animals (see Figure 20.3 and Figure 20.4). There is also a focus on 'my
place', so gardens, views from windows and the beauty of the individual
point of view.

Jan R. Zelinski
@DrPioneer18

@Philae2014 #GoodbyePhilae ...Goodbye Philae...with Greetings from Egypt...

2:06 PM · Jul 27, 2016 · Twitter Web Client

Figure 20.3 A 'postcard' from Egypt for *Philae* (@DrPioneer18/ Twitter).

But not all the photographs are classic postcards. In keeping with the *zeit-geist*, there are many selfies, a mix of groups and singles, often holding signs, which are usually messages addressed to *Philae*. These, in common with tweets without photographs, usually thank *Philae*, or praise him for his efforts and say it is time to rest. Quite a few say 'thank you for your service', which is a common phrase for thanking military veterans

If you haven't yet, say #GoodbyePhilae to @Philae2014 lander with a picture! See them at flickr.com/DLR_de

1:42 PM · Jul 30, 2016 · TweetDeck

Figure 20.4   A seaside 'postcard' for *Philae* (@DLR_en/Twitter).

in the US. All of these seem to suggest that the anthropomorphism allows people to identify with the robot as a friend and by extension allows them to feel the extension of humanity into space.

But with that attachment comes sadness at the death of the robot. A lot of the tweets suggest genuine sadness and a real sense of mortality. While some tweets point to the anthropomorphism and the manipulative nature of the public engagement, the sense that the robot is dying calls to the concept of eternity (see Figure 20.5).

The messages also contain a fair amount of references to popular culture, including films – mostly but not all science fiction, especially the death scenes of robots. There are also messages expressing hopes for future loves. There is a smattering of Shakespeare, as well as Dylan Thomas: 'Do not go gentle into that good night'. People also shared a wide range of music, but mostly it was sentimental music from the 1970s, such as 'Dust in the Wind' by Kansas – not necessarily the music that best represents humanity; simply the music that the loss of the lander calls to mind to the individual. There is almost no mention of politics – except a tiny handful of jokes and one image of a dead child in Aleppo. The messages in this memorial have perhaps more in common with the flowers and teddy bears left on the roadside at the sites of car crashes, or those

Figure 20.5 The 'death' of the lander prompted emotional responses (@NickyWoolf/@KingdomOfTheEgo/Twitter).

left to commemorate celebrities (Graves-Brown and Orange 2017), than with the wreaths left at war memorials (despite the military connotations of 'service'). This suggests that the future of space exploration is shifting from the imaginaries of military conquest so prevalent in the 1960s to one in which even the robots are individuals exploring and finding the freedom of space.

The personal nature of the memorial suggests that it is our own individual lives that should be remembered by the future, rather than an abstract or aggregate 'humanity' or even 'nation'. Even where cultural references are included (such as music), it is personal taste and memory, rather than pieces from a 'canon' or highlighting particular cultures, as might be the case in relation to the selection of places made for the World Heritage Site list, for example (see further discussion in Chapter 18). This is in contrast to the disk that was sent with the spacecraft when it was launched (http://rosettaproject.org/disk/concept/), which has the more traditional future-making task of saving human culture from oblivion.

It is also a very emotional message. Whether laughing or crying, this memorial humanises the robots of space futures by imbuing them with emotion. Future-making is neither wholly rational nor wholly strategic, but crystalises hopes and fears. A mosaic image of the lander composed of images from the messages expresses the way the lander is (and space futures are) humanised through the initiative (see Figure 20.6).

Figure 20.6 A mosaic image created from all the messages sent under #GoodbyePhilae encapsulates the group value of the messages (DLR German Aerospace Centre CC BY SA 2.0).

Message to *Voyager*

In 2017, to mark the 40th anniversary of the *Voyager* launches, NASA ran a social media competition to select a single 60-character message to be beamed to the spacecraft. The winner – 'We offer friendship across the stars. You are not alone.' – was submitted by Oliver Jenkins, and was 'sent to the stars' by William Shatner, the actor who played Captain James T. Kirk in *Star Trek* (NASA 2017). This different kind of institutional engagement, and different set of rules for selection, created a different kind of engagement with the message and, by extension, with its future audience. As with the ESA initiative described above, NASA collected social media messages across a number of platforms over two weeks using the hashtag #MessageToVoyager. From the thousands of messages, a team at NASA selected 10 finalists, which were then subject to public vote. Although no messages submitted after 15 August were considered, the hashtag continued to be used in much the same way before and after the deadline for submissions. This suggests that being part of the discussion on social media was more important to contributors than actually sending their message to *Voyager*.

Although the NASA team recorded more than thirty thousand messages across all platforms using the hashtag (NASA 2017), reading through these messages reveals that a much smaller number were actual messages and that there were even fewer messages that were not jokes. The 10 finalists are much more formal in tone than the majority of messages. Some are quotations from poets and two are quotations from Carl Sagan. Even when crowdsourcing, the lure of authority is strong. The finalists are mixed in their intended audience. Some are messages to *Voyager* itself (like the *Philae* messages); some, including the winner, are for beings that might find *Voyager* (mirroring the original *Voyager* Golden Records).

Oliver Jenkins, who submitted the winning message, is a British autistic man, and he felt that the selection of his message was a great honour. He featured on the cover of the November 2017 issue of *Your Autism* magazine, with the headline 'Reach for the stars and you just might get there'. A year later, he tweeted that it was probably the greatest achievement of his life. Other finalists were similarly proud, and their achievement was seen to reflect well on their countries of origin. Both the Mexican and Belgian embassies supported and promoted their entrants' messages. This was a message framed as speaking for all of the Earth.

Thirty thousand initially sounds like a large response, but in comparison with other hashtags it is relatively small. In April 2019, thirty-five thousand people responded overnight to a single tweet by Donald Trump regarding the television programme *Game of Thrones*. While social media usage has increased over the two years between these events, thirty thousand responses is not, in fact, a global message.

A large proportion of those responses were promotions of the initiative, encouraging people to submit a message, vote and 'tune in' to watch the message being sent, and celebrating that the message had been sent. Hundreds of tweets were expressions of dismay and cries for help because of the 'mess we've made of the world'. Well over a hundred of the tweets were complaints about Donald Trump. Even after the winning message was beamed to *Voyager*, many tweets suggested that it was over optimistic: 'Nice message but unreal. We cannot even be friendly with each other on earth? How could we with Alien lives', tweeted @CaptAI in 2017.

Social media is always intertextual. In addition to the quotations from serious entries, many were quotations from popular culture, including, not surprisingly, references to the plot of *Star Trek: The Motion Picture* discussed under the *Philae* messages above. The hashtag also became entangled with another hashtag – #gishwhes – a hashtag related to the 'greatest international scavenger hunt'. Hundreds of tweets with this hashtag asked *Voyager* to pick up things such as milk, or chastised it for taking too long at the shops.

There was less engagement with this initiative than with the *Philae* initiative discussed above. The competition and the sense of speaking for humanity gave it greater prestige, but fewer people actually contributed messages. There is a greater sense that the message 'represents humanity', but it does not humanise *Voyager* in the same way that the final messages humanised *Philae*.

The designation of something as heritage here on Earth is firmly controlled by procedures, and often by legislation. But perhaps space heritage is more akin to the erection of statues on Earth – something in which heritage professionals rarely have a say. Both terrestrial and space heritage are taken as representations of all humanity, but rarely do most people have a say in how either is constructed.

Another piece of space heritage, left on the Moon after the first landing, expresses this clearly:

HERE MEN FROM THE PLANET EARTH
FIRST SET FOOT UPON THE MOON
JULY 1969, A.D.
WE CAME IN PEACE FOR ALL MANKIND
NEIL A. ARMSTRONG MICHAEL COLLINS EDWIN E. ALDRIN, JR.
ASTRONAUT ASTRONAUT ASTRONAUT
RICHARD NIXON
PRESIDENT, UNITED STATES OF AMERICA

Discussion

A catalogue of all artefacts and messages that have been sent beyond the atmosphere describes hundreds of initiatives, some public and formal, some almost ad hoc attempts to assess these materials to determine the best way to represent ourselves (Quast 2018). But is the real purpose to represent ourselves to aliens, to a distant future, or to explore how we see ourselves? Stephen Wolfram has considered the problem from the point of view of computer science and concludes: 'We should think of the beacons we send as monuments. Perhaps they will be useful for some kind of "afterlife." But for now they serve as a useful rallying point for thinking about what we're proud of in the achievements of our civilization – and what we want to capture and celebrate in the best way we can' (Wolfram 2018, n.p.).

But the cultural aspects of space programmes are rarely thought through in such detail. Discussing a decision to programme the Mars rover *Curiosity* to play 'Happy Birthday' by vibrating its sampling systems at different frequencies, Florence Tan, Sample Analysis at Mars (SAM) electrical lead engineer, NASA Goddard Space Center, said, 'Music brings us all together, so this is fun' (NASA Goddard 2013). However, in 2017 the practice was discontinued: '"In a nutshell, there is no scientific gain from the rover playing music or singing 'Happy Birthday' on Mars," Tan said. In the battle between song and science, science always wins' (Koren 2017, n.p.). Although cultural heritage is a consistent feature of space programmes, it is essentially seen as a 'fun' extra, easily handled as a hobby by engineers, and personalised by astronauts – a sideshow.

Nonetheless, the message initiatives examined here show some important features of how people assemble the futures embodied in space travel. The most striking feature is personalisation, even narcissism. This is at the root of many of the negative reactions described above. But there is always narcissism in heritage – the desire to codify social and cultural value and ensure that it persists beyond our lifetime. That narcissism is only acceptable if it is shared. Wanting people to remember me forever is arrogant, wanting people to remember 'our culture' is acceptable, honourable even. The difference between them is in the practices of selection (as discussed in Chapter 2). This formal process of selection is also being considered in space, as the proposal for a 'planetary park system for Mars' shows (Cockell and Horneck 2004). The desire for perpetuity, not to be forgotten, is an individual desire. But there is also a longing for connection. As Oliver Jenkins's message says: 'We offer friendship across the stars. You are not alone.'

21
The one-million-year time capsule

Antony Lyons and Cornelius Holtorf

The Memory of Mankind (MOM) storage project aims to preserve, in perpetuity, stories and snapshots about our era. It is an ambitious time capsule, with a global content. Protected deep in an active salt mine, the information imprinted into ceramic tablets has the potential to survive for more than a million years. For more than 10 years, ceramicist Martin Kunze has been developing – and since 2012, also physically creating and managing – this repository in the Hallstatt salt mines in the mountains of Austria (www.memory-of-mankind.com). Anyone desiring a dose of immortality can arrange to have information (text and graphics) printed onto the extremely durable ceramic data carriers.

Kunze says:

> Isn't it an exciting era we live in? Within a generation we witness our world's fundamental change. So many stories to be told, some with pride, some with regret, some are touching, and – to be honest – some of them at least embarrassing. MOM tells our story, complete, not whitewashed. If we don't write it down now, it will probably be lost forever.

> (MOM 2018)

Behind the MOM project is a logic of rescuing the memory of global society in our age. But MOM is at the same time more than a response to a threat. It also translates a scenario of loss of information into an opportunity to reflect and create something that is valuable in the present, because it addresses uncertainty yet promises (much like a deep-space message; see Chapter 20) to endure over the very long term.

The photographs in this visual essay (see Figures 21.1 to 21.10) form a pictorial record of a visit in 2018 by Antony Lyons to the site of the MOM facility in Hallstatt, Austria (except where noted otherwise).

Figure 21.1 Martin Kunze in front of the MOM storage boxes containing numerous ceramic tablets (photograph by Daniel Lindskog).

Martin Kunze has a particular view of the future, which MOM aims to address: 'In a few decades, every trace of our digital photos, emails and blogs will have faded and in a few centuries, nobody will any longer know who we were or how we lived and what we lived for' (MOM 2013). Because magnetically encoded digital data is vulnerable to degradation and to major disruptive events such as an electromagnetic pulse (for example, from an atomic weapon or a powerful solar coronal blast), MOM has been seeking alternative storage solutions to prevent data loss and enable access, in the distant future, to historical records of our time (see Figure 21.1). In this sense, the intention of MOM is related to the ethics and politics of conservation:

> The MOM project aims to preserve today's stories in order to pass on our present to give the future a past. A gift both to our grand-children and to a civilization far beyond the digital age. So we leave more than nuclear waste, global warming and countless energy drink cans …
>
> (MOM 2018, n.p.)

Figure 21.2 A printed ceramic MOM tablet, with information about the Heritage Futures project (photograph by Antony Lyons).

The Memory of Mankind project aims to preserve a record, or a snapshot, of our time, protected from possible oblivion caused by the consequences of ecological, economic or other processes leading to the loss of electronic and indeed other data. Based on this logic, the strategy is to establish an analogue storage site, using durable materials. In this initial phase, the content is preserved on stoneware ceramic tiles (or 'tablets') (see Figure 21.2), but research and development is already under way to create more compact, and even longer-lasting, 'ceramic microfilm' and a ceramic optical data disk.

Kunze managed to win support for MOM from several established heritage institutions, including the Natural History Museum in London and the Art History Museum in Vienna, the University of Vienna and the Mozarteum in Salzburg. They have immortalised images and descriptions of parts of their collections on a series of tablets. He has also been discussing with the nuclear waste sector the possibility of storing on such tablets information about nuclear waste repositories in order to regain access in the event of failure of other information preservation strategies.

Figure 21.3 The town and lake of Hallstatt (photograph by Antony Lyons).

Nestled on the shore of the Hallstätter See, Hallstatt is a well-known archaeological site in contemporary Austria (see Figure 21.3). Centred around the salt workings in the high valley several hundred metres above the lake level, remains of human habitation date back to the Neolithic, but are especially prominent from the Late Bronze Age (c.1500 BC) through to the Iron Age up until the so-called Hallstatt Period (c.350 BC). Salt was a very important commodity in this time, as it was one of the main means of preserving meat and other foodstuffs.

In a poetic echo of the MOM process and ambitions, the salt in the mine cavities has preserved a unique assemblage of prehistoric artefacts for our time. Many of these artefacts are tools and personal belongings associated with prehistoric mining practices, providing more or less direct insights into past ways of life.

Figure 21.4   World Heritage view (photograph by Antony Lyons).

The cultural landscape of Hallstatt-Dachstein/Salzkammergut was inscribed as a UNESCO World Heritage Site in 1997 (see Figure 21.4). The official description of the site expresses the recognised significance:

> Human activity in the magnificent natural landscape of the Salzkammergut began in prehistoric times, with the salt deposits being exploited as early as the 2nd millennium BC. This resource formed the basis of the area's prosperity up to the middle of the 20th century, a prosperity that is reflected in the fine architecture of the town of Hallstatt.
>
> (UNESCO 1997, n.p.)

In the assessment of the area, it was appreciated that it 'retains all the elements linked to evidence of salt mining and processing, associated timber production, transhumance and dairy farming, and still retains the harmony that attracted the 19th century artists and writers'. It is also acknowledged that this cultural landscape 'has not, and does not, suffer from the adverse effects of modern development' (UNESCO 1997, n.p.). In this passage, it remains somewhat unclear, in larger temporal perspective, what is meant by 'modern' and 'adverse'.

Figure 21.5 One side of a MOM token measuring 6.5 cm in diameter, for locating the storage facility. On the reverse of the token, the relative position of the site in relation to the lake is shown, with the connection to the salt mine. The entrance is therefore indicated to within 10 metres. Everyone who deposits a ceramic tablet will receive one such token (photograph by Antony Lyons).

Looking to the distant future, the predicted survival chances of the Memory of Mankind is based on the geological action of the salt seams, which over time will continue to deform to completely envelop the ceramic containers. The plan is for locatability to be optimised by the distribution of (eventually) tens of thousands of small ceramic plaques, or tokens, that describe the exact location of the storage vault (see Figure 21.5). These tokens will be distributed around the world. A future society will only be able to access the preserved information if it is capable of understanding the geographical information on the token and can excavate down to the site of the ancient mine (see Figure 21.6).

Paradoxically, if found and accessed in the near future (as many time capsules are), the opening of the Memory of Mankind will jeopardise the permanence of the information it holds, since it will not necessarily be possible to close the storage again securely and effectively after exposure. Given that the holdings cannot easily be returned to their original slumber, one of the challenges of the project is how future generations will be able to judge whether the time has come to open, access and make use of the MOM.

Figure 21.6 Access to the mine is by a mining train. At the end of the tunnel, 400 metres inside the mountain, is the site of MOM (photograph by Antony Lyons).

Public national archives are subject to state-controlled requirements. MOM is not bound to these aims. This time capsule however contains documents, which seem not worthwhile being preserved on the first sight, but representing a reflection of ourselves, of our time and therefore being of cultural-historic value on the long term.

(Dr Claudia Theune, professor of historical
archaeology, University of Vienna, Austria)

The Memory of Mankind Project is an expression of human creativity and the desire to leave something of ourselves for distant generations to discover and from which they may learn… . Just thinking about this project provides a time perspective that puts the events of our own time into proper historical context.

(Jon Lomberg, project manager, One Earth:
New Horizons Message)

Figure 21.7   Part of the process of making the tablets: applying the ceramic print layer before kiln-firing (photograph by Antony Lyons).

The MOM content-creation process is a very open one, accepting online proposals from anywhere in the world. This bottom-up creation of the MOM content is innovative. Heritage choices, guidance and decision-making have largely been within the purview of professional experts. Simple text contributions are free, and by making a (geographically variable) payment, other content may be contributed – from individuals and institutions. Additionally, content from everyday printed material (daily editorials of major global newspapers, magazines and so on) is being automatically compiled. An important feature of the MOM process is that a duplicate ceramic tablet is delivered back to the provider of the content. This therefore forms another distributed durable record and – for the holder of the duplicate – creates an imaginative link to the primary MOM storage site.

There are many levels of storytelling at play: there are the stories collected in the making of the tablets (see Figure 21.7); the stories expressed in the content itself; the story of the assembly and future of the storage site; and the diverse stories of the journeys of the duplicate tablets and MOM tokens, as they are distributed around the world. The journeys – through space and time – of both the original and the duplicate are both highly unpredictable (see Figure 21.8).

Figure 21.8 The ceramic tablets are stored in heavy, thick-walled ceramic boxes; they will be moved deeper into the mine tunnels before eventual sealing (photograph by Antony Lyons).

> There are so many questions at the philosophical level of the project that I think are just so interesting – even the definition of what is important, what is relevant, what is actually interesting? How do you define those things? How do you define past and future, and how will we communicate in the future? … It's not about storing every single piece of information that we have, but giving a perspective, and giving a snapshot of what we are as a society today.
>
> Catherine Plaut, MOM project coordinator (MOM 2017)

Figure 21.9   Ceramic microfilm – the next generation of the MOM storage facility (photograph by Martin Kunze).

The next phase for MOM preservation is to use 1-millimetre-thick ceramic sheets, encased in wafer-thin layers of glass. A high-energy laser is used to write into these, and one 20-centimetre piece of this microfilm can store five million characters (see Figure 21.9). Initial plans are for one thousand of the world's most important books or texts to be preserved in this way. They will be chosen by combining published lists using an algorithm developed by the University of Vienna.

What exactly is the legacy created in the Hallstatt mine: will the MOM eventually be remembered for the content of its data carriers or for elaborate twenty-first-century efforts to preserve a legacy for the deep future? Will our descendants nostalgically remember remembering?

Figure 21.10 'Glück Auf' (photograph by Antony Lyons).

'Glück auf' (see Figure 21.10) is a traditional miners' greeting in German. It means: 'Good luck!'

22
Uncertainty, collaboration and emerging issues

Cornelius Holtorf and Sarah May

'How is the uncertainty of the deep future conceived of and managed in different fields of conservation practice?' When we designed our original research question, we assumed we would find not only a variety of possible responses to the widespread understanding that it is hard to know much about the future – and even harder, the longer you think ahead – but also a variety of answers reflecting the different legacy-related practices we were studying. However, we learned quickly that this was not the case. A perception of the future in terms of risks, managed to anticipate threats and prevent loss, generally prevailed wherever we looked. Our research interest therefore moved in a new direction as we began to explore to what extent one might turn an apparent challenge into an opportunity by envisioning uncertainty as *desirable* for conservation practice – and indeed for heritage management. The specific examples that we got to know better during the course of our research illustrated that uncertainty does indeed hold opportunities, and may even be preferable to a future we could be certain about, even in terms of conservation.

In short, uncertainty is desirable because it opens the door for change. As much as every transformation provides obstacles, it also offers opportunities (see also Part V, Transformation). We cannot hold back the flow of time and history. Nothing is ever given; nothing can be conserved indefinitely. The limits of planning have been summed up by Steve Fuller (2013, n.p.): 'You can be sure that if a model says the world will end in 50 years, the model itself will be gone in 25.' Further, if we would like things to be different to how they are now – good news! They will be. If we shift our view of the future to flow, then we recentre ourselves. We can and we should push the flow as we want it to be (see also Chapter 26).

Obviously, future heritage users will have their own priorities and interpretations. Heritage, after all, is a social and interpretive practice. As Chapman (2018, n.p.) argues, regarding historical scholarship, 'historians of the future have the same rights to cognitive self-determination as historians in the present: it is not our place to seek to define and constrain future possibilities'. Moreover, just as our children make their own lives, partly in opposition to what they receive from us, future generations will make their own futures. UNESCO may see heritage as a gift from the past to the future (Von Droste zu Hülshoff, 2006; see further discussion in Chapters 1 and 2 of this book), but an unwanted gift can be a burden. How can we know whether future generations will want these gifts? (May, forthcoming).

Uncertainty, in our framing, allows for freedom and creativity, for broad participation and engagement, and for exploiting favourable circumstances. But uncertainty also demands responsibility and invites affection, love and care for living beings. Indeed, for all the uncertainty there is, maybe all that matters in the end is a mindset of love, and care – much in the way that parents feel for the next generation of humans (Adam and Groves 2007; 2011). The complexity of this care, and the ways that it takes account of the more-than-human, is a key question in contemporary ethics (for example, Puig de la Bellacasa 2017) and, indeed, is a core concern across all four of the themes in this book. This is most obvious within our research in the exploration of shepherding as heritage practice. It is care in the present that creates a desirable future. It is also apparent in our assessment of space messaging on Twitter. When asked to send a message to the future, people are overwhelmingly gentle, personal. The anthropomorphism of robotic spacecraft elicits care and affection.

But how do we show genuine affection, love and care when it comes to designing nuclear waste repositories? Perhaps the Dutch intermediate repository for nuclear waste, which we visited in autumn 2017 outside Vlissingen, can suggest a way to draw ethics of care from one domain to the next. Recognising that it will be a century before there is sufficient waste or resource to build a final geological repository, the Netherlands has built a temporary repository for the next century. It is designed to keep the material safe, but also to keep the question of its long-term future in the minds of the Dutch people. In cooperation with artists, the buildings are painted in bright colours, with the chemical formula of the waste in large letters. The building for spent fuel will be repainted a different colour every 10 years to remind people that the material inside is changing. The design keeps the attention of the present, not by frightening us, but by making it intriguing and welcoming engagement (Codée and Verhoef 2015). If we begin with care in the present, we can care for the future.

However, heritage practice also does constrain future possibilities, by choosing what pasts to push into the future and, indeed, in other choices with political, social and economic ramifications. While historians of the future may have cognitive self-determination, we still have some influence on the material and social worlds in which they operate. This concern for the welfare of future generations is one of the reasons why it matters what we do today, not least regarding the cultural heritage and other legacies we are going to leave behind (Holtorf and Högberg forthcoming b). We are not responsible for making future people happy, but, while acknowledging the specific conditions of uncertainty both as a threat and as an opportunity, we can attempt to make decisions from which they might really benefit. This involves a commitment to be explicit about what futures individuals and organisations are planning for, how they are addressing the ways in which the future will differ from the present, and how exactly they think their work in the present will benefit people in the future. A logical next step would be to move from a comparative analysis of different ways of future-making in contemporary heritage and conservation practices, as we have presented in this book, to planning for specific possible uses and benefits of heritage in future communities.

Lessons from collaborations across four domains

An important insight from our research is that collaboration with non-academic partners inevitably has different aims than the academic pursuit of knowledge and debate, conducted in forums such as academic conferences or publications. Martin Kunze of the Memory of Mankind project (MOM) was always keen to learn how to improve on his own long-term storage project in the Austrian Alps. Both Gustavo Araoz of the International Council on Monuments and Sites (ICOMOS) and Giovanni Boccardi of UNESCO (who was meeting us in a non-institutional capacity) had their own far-reaching ideas for the future development of heritage theory and heritage management in the context of various policies, and they very much appreciated the inspiration and critical feedback we offered them. All three had strong intellectual interests, connected with their own practices. Although that made conversations easy, it was also clear that they were interested primarily to advance their own specific activities and not so much in our larger academic project trying to synthesise and theorise, eventually resulting in academic publications such as the present book.

Our collaborators from Swedish Nuclear Fuel and Waste Management Company (SKB) were mostly interested in demonstrating to wider audiences that the challenges of long-term, safe storage of nuclear waste are connected to other domains in society, and not unique to them; they wanted to connect their own questions about the future with those of others in society and therefore welcomed the opportunity to come into contact with other contemporary future projects, not least to establish their own endeavours as a case study in the academic field of heritage studies. Similarly, Jon Lomberg of the One Earth Message project expressed that, for him, our project was an opportunity to cast as wide a net as possible in attracting interest and support in his own future-related project. He also appreciated that our invitation had enabled him to fly from Hawaii, where he lives, to Europe for a publicity and marketing tour to attract support for his space message project. Both partners formulated aims and expectations of our collaboration that were far from our own, but of course they made perfect sense from their perspectives.

Initially such responses made us question the purpose of collaboration in an academic project. But we realised quickly that what we had gained was in fact insight into how to make our work relevant to partners in society at large and, thus, even from an academic perspective, how to make our work more significant than it might otherwise have been. There is strong demand for academic expertise beyond academia, but that demand does not necessarily match how we may prefer to see and portray ourselves as academic researchers. If we seek to make a direct impact on society with academic research, which of course we should, the first step is to learn to listen and to be willing to collaborate on equal terms with partners pursuing their own agendas. We learned that it takes time and commitment to generate understanding for each other's work, engender mutual respect and build trust between partners in different sectors and professions. Although they do not need be uncritical, such collaborations require a willingness to advance unfamiliar agendas and to try new formats. That does not necessarily sit well with the short time frames and expected levels of output recognised by academic funding bodies and recruitment panels. But this only shows where academia still has a lot to learn itself. Our work has most certainly benefited our collaborative partners in the way they had hoped. This will continue to do so while we remain in contact with each other: as with academic partnerships, such collaborations continue in various ways even after a project has formally ended.

At the same time, there are also academically important lessons for our research topic, which we learned from the collaboration and which we think are relevant to our partners too. In particular, our comparative approach has allowed us to recognise and appreciate some of the important contributions that each of our domains has to offer the others, which was one of the main aims of the research programme as a whole (see discussion in Part I, Heritage futures). These are as follows:

- The nuclear waste sector shows how future planning can be done systematically and professionally. The cultural heritage sector in particular can draw inspiration from that work to overcome its own professional naivety regarding the future (Högberg et al. 2017).
- The cultural heritage sector, including World Heritage Site management, has come a long way in appreciating and managing the politics and ethics of heritage and the need to involve multiple stakeholders in its work; other realms, such as nuclear waste, space messages and even the MOM project, can learn that social contestation is part of the normal state of affairs of all legacy management and heritage processes, not a kind of negative interference. The resulting tensions, and the way they are overcome together with other stakeholders, eventually make the significance of heritage in society stronger, not weaker (Harrison 2013a).
- The deep-space message excels in prompting us all to consider heritage in terms of our collective legacy on Earth, transcending the boundaries that are dividing humanity. This challenges UNESCO and ICOMOS in particular on how to select and conserve a human legacy on Earth that may create genuine human unity, rather than local and national distinction and division.
- The long-term information storage at MOM facilitates broad participation in society and mobilises not only citizens and families but also a range of different organisations in society in long-term legacy work. The underlying commitment to inclusivity and the implied willingness to embrace a profusion of information creates benefits in societal resonance that should be very attractive even to a space message from humanity, the undertaking of building a final repository for nuclear waste, and not least the sustainable management of cultural heritage.

One of the key findings of our research is that managing uncertain human futures with the help of different manifestations of cultural heritage can benefit from the four specific strengths just described: systematic planning, appreciating relevant politics and ethics, transcendence of boundaries dividing humanity, and broad participation in society.

The various domains we have worked with illustrate the specific benefits that each strength offers. If nothing else, this suggests to the professional cultural heritage sector that solely expert-driven conservation and legal protection anticipating specific threats is not good enough, even if relevant stakeholders are invited to participate in this work. In order to be prepared for an uncertain future, the cultural heritage sector will benefit from more systematic planning, transcending existing boundaries and facilitating broad participation across a range of different sectors in society.

Issues emerging for the future

The assumption that the future is mostly significant to present-day heritage management insofar as it holds risks and threats to preservation is ultimately problematic. Saving or rescuing heritage is not necessarily by default the most appropriate strategy for sustainable development and a better future for humanity. However, the sincere commitment of many professional colleagues and our collaborative partners to save or rescue heritage demands respect. For them, if we put enough effort into it, we *can* ensure that past legacies are preserved, or that future populations will not be harmed by nuclear waste, or that non-humans will understand our space messages, or that the tiles deposited in MOM will be discoverable in thousands of years.

On the other hand, many social benefits of heritage are not threatened by destruction, and they may be renewable (Holtorf 2015). There may even be significant gains from destruction, as the planetarium in Montreal reminded us (which we visited in connection with attending a major conference in the city): after the dinosaurs died out, partly due to a meteorite impact, mass extinction proved to be a source of renewal as new life forms emerged, in that case paving the way for the emergence of humans on Earth (see also the discussion of biodiversity and evolutionary models in Chapter 6). Similarly, as we argued in Chapter 19, on 'Toxic heritage', there may be heritages and materials it would be good to get rid of. Not all change is a threat, and destruction can be an opportunity as well as a risk. An alternative strategy, replacing tropes of risk and threats, may therefore be based on notions of change, growth and transformation (Holtorf 2015; DeSilvey 2017; papers in DeSilvey and Harrison 2020).

The persistence of a preservation-focused future orientation may relate to our desire for personal persistence, or, to see it from the other side, our fear of death. Terror Management Theory (or TMT) posits that awareness of our own mortality is implicated in identification with groups and ideals that we believe will survive beyond our lifetimes (Reicher 2014; Sani et al. 2009). The greater our anxiety about impending death, the stronger our affiliation with, and defence of, the values, beliefs and heritages of groups we identify with, 'because groups that extend beyond one's mere personal existence, both backward and forward in time, and that are perceived as long-lasting and quasi-eternal entities, are potent symbols of transcendence' (Sani et al. 2009, 244).

While the future will never become the present, always slipping forward into the yet-to-be, we still have responsibilities to those who come after us. They are not simply abstract vessels of our current anxieties. Part of the discussion of nuclear waste management has involved formal ethical consideration of our responsibilities to future generations. In 1995, the International Atomic Energy Agency (IAEA) issued the Principles of Radioactive Waste Management as a part of its safety series. According to Principle 5, the waste shall be managed 'in such a way that will not impose undue burdens on future generations' (Bråkenhielm 2015, 397). In Sweden, this ethical consideration has been described as the *principle of (intergenerational) autonomy*, 'in which every generation should have the autonomy to manage and use spent nuclear fuel in whichever way they see fit' (Bråkenhielm 2015, 399). What if we were to apply this principle to heritage? For instance, many of the commemorative regimes associated with the centenary of the First World War require that future generations do the emotional labour of remembering our war dead. The principle of intergenerational autonomy would require us to manage that heritage in such a way that future generations had no responsibility for it and could do whatever they see fit.

In this situation, our research focus eventually came to move beyond the notion of uncertainty, and started to address a widely felt need to promote sustainability and foster resilience for future generations (Holtorf 2018). Sustainability requires resilience, and ultimately depends on the ability to embrace change and absorb disturbance. Sustainability is thus not necessarily based on preservation, but rather on the ability to adapt to loss and transformation. This insight may provide the biggest challenge for the cultural heritage sector in the broadest sense, relating as it does to all four of the themes explored in this book. What does it mean for the legacies we leave behind to be able to absorb loss and transformation? To make it specific, how are World Heritage Sites and nuclear waste repositories to reckon with loss and transformation? Or how can a space message or a deep storage facility absorb disturbance and still be meaningful? The toolbox of heritage professionals will need to contain more items than conservation and preservation in order to be equipped to provide solutions for such issues. In the next part of the book (following the visual essay documenting the third of our three cross-programme knowledge-exchange events, on Transforming Loss), we turn to consider certain cases in the management of heritage in which change is acknowledged, actively managed for and even embraced.

According to the Long Now Foundation (Brand 2008), the most important aspect of future thinking is not to anticipate in detail what will happen and plan now for all eventualities. Instead we need to integrate future thinking into everyday decision-making, being aware of the future we assume in the decisions we make and the practices in which we engage, while realising that there are alternatives. In that sense, it may be more important to keep asking about the future than to have good answers. This is related to the idea of futures literacy, where students are asked to interrogate specific anticipated futures for their underpinning assumptions. This allows humans to act in the present to work towards desired futures, rather than simply bracing against seemingly inevitable futures (see also Sandford and Cassar forthcoming).

Our research has examined practices in heritage and related domains. It has given us a clearer understanding of the assumed futures inherent in these practices, but more importantly raised further questions about alternative futures that could be assembled through development of these practices. These are issues which are foregrounded in the following part of the book, which focuses on the theme of transformation.

Cross-theme knowledge-exchange event 3

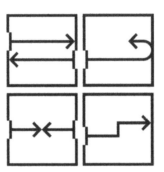

23
Transforming loss

Third cross-theme knowledge-exchange workshop, October 2018, Woodbridge/Orford, Suffolk, UK

Nadia Bartolini and Caitlin DeSilvey

How can those responsible for caring for landscapes and historic features respond to change and loss positively and proactively? Natural and cultural heritage features are continually affected by transformative processes, some of them inevitable (such as weathering and climate change) and others intentional (such as strategies applied to manage profusion or enhance biodiversity). Our third and final knowledge-exchange workshop, which took place in early October 2018 in Suffolk, UK, aimed to explore heritage management practices and philosophies that seek to accommodate transience and transformation (see Figures 23.1 to 23.8).

Heritage Futures programme partners the National Trust and the Coastal and Intertidal Zone Archaeological Network (CITiZAN) collaborated with members of the Profusion and Diversity themes (Nadia Bartolini, Caitlin DeSilvey, Sefryn Penrose and Rodney Harrison) in creating a workshop to explore how loss could be seen as *both* a pressing challenge and an untapped opportunity for the emergence of alternative values, relationships and material configurations.

The four-day workshop in Suffolk brought together 30 heritage researchers and conservation practitioners in a series of activities and conversations designed to work across different parts of the heritage sector and integrate operational and policy perspectives.

Workshop discussions were grounded in field excursions on the second day of the workshop to Orford Ness – a shingle spit off the Suffolk coast, partly owned by the National Trust and discussed at length in Part V, Transformation – and Orford Castle – an English Heritage site that is also home to the community-run Orford Museum.

Figure 23.1 Workshop participants on the ferry to Orford Ness (photograph by Cornelius Holtorf).

Orford Ness is a place characterised by ongoing change in both its historic built environment and its natural landscape. On the day of our visit, the workshop group took a short boat journey over the River Ore to access the spit (see Figure 23.1). National Trust and CITiZAN experts guided the group around the isolated and exposed landscape (see Figure 23.2), sharing their knowledge about the site's dynamic coastal environment

Figure 23.2a Participants exploring the AWRE site (photograph by Caitlin DeSilvey).

Figure 23.2b   View of Stony Ditch, the control room, power house, Black Beacon and the lighthouse (photograph by Antony Lyons).

and exploring the relict structures and features associated with the twentieth-century occupation of the spit by the Ministry of Defence for classified research and weapons testing. Since the early 1990s, the National Trust has managed elements of the site's built environment through a policy of 'continued ruination'. Discussions in the field touched on the aesthetics of loss and decay; the accommodation of natural forces, such as erosion and ruination, and the resulting loss of control; and the balance between efforts to avert loss and efforts to restore and conserve (in relation to both natural and cultural features).

During a conversation inside a former Atomic Weapons Research Establishment (AWRE) laboratory building, one National Trust staff member reflected on the tension between different approaches in the organisation's decision-making about the future management of the buildings (see Figure 23.3):

> You know people want to see it because it's got historical signifi-
> cance, it's got nature taking over, it's got the aesthetics of things
> falling apart, which is, you know, pleasing to some degree ... it's
> the peeling paint and the sounds in the roof, clanking about, and

Figure 23.3 Workshop participants inside one of the AWRE laboratory buildings observing decay (photograph by Antony Lyons).

the birds in the ducting. There's something quite spooky and emotionally powerful about all that, and also [something] about the political element of it. I came to this site and I thought, yeah, great, you know nature taking over, the Cold War, that's all gone now, we should be allowing it to – you know – scab over if you like. But when you're here, and you talk to the people about the significance to them, how emotionally connected they are, because of the significance of the work they were doing, you start thinking, yeah, maybe we should hang onto it and present what they're feeling about it. Because they see it as a cautionary tale, because they see it as something significant to protect the nation, and you could see things like that happening again, so should we be remembering that and remembering why that was so important?

Orford Castle, on the mainland just over the river from Orford Ness, is an English Heritage property that is also home to the Orford Museum, a small local collection whose curator and volunteers, constrained by space and resources, continually grapple with difficult questions about deaccessioning and potential loss (see Figure 23.4). The museum curator provided

Figure 23.4 Workshop participants visiting Orford Castle and Orford Museum (photograph by Tanya Venture).

participants with an assessment of the perception of loss through different registers. For instance, she observed how loss can result from the ways in which museums choose to accession and deaccession objects, but frequent staff turnover at local museums can also lead to the loss of institutional memory and a particular ethos of care. These observations resonate particularly with the work detailed in Part III, Profusion.

The field excursions provided the workshop participants with a grounded appreciation of the challenges faced by professionals and practitioners dealing with the prospect of loss in relation to the buildings, landscapes and objects that they manage. On the third day of the workshop, keynote presentations and workshop sessions focused on the potential for framing loss through alternative values and emerging relationships, and on the opportunity to develop new modes of engagement and interpretation. Three sessions brought together views from different practitioners, working in different heritage-related fields.

In the first session, National Trust staff shared their thinking behind the development of conservation management plans at two sites where change is inevitable and imminent, Orford Ness and Mullion Harbour. The Orford Ness plan was used as a prompt to discuss challenges and opportunities associated with the coordinated management of natural

Figure 23.5 Workshop session on 'making heritage' (photograph by Tanya Venture).

and cultural heritage landscapes. The following open discussion explored whether a philosophy of loss and transformation can provide the basis for more collaborative and holistic approaches.

The subsequent session examined rewilding as a heritage-making process that seeks to enhance and produce biodiversity, although it is often perceived to have the opposite effect on cultural diversity, overlooking or erasing traditions and practices embedded in the landscape (see Figure 23.5). The workshop speakers, however, challenged this interpretation and offered examples of how rewilding can foster the emergence of new connections and values, through the production of future ecologies, economies and cultures that link to the past in unexpected ways.

The final session focused on the problem of profusion in museum and other contexts. Speakers suggested approaches that might be used to frame disposal and deaccessioning as creative and productive processes. Discussion drew out different ideas about possible solutions to over-accumulation and considered whether 'letting go' may present new opportunities for organisations and people to engage with museum collections.

On the final day of the workshop, a senior representative from the National Trust (and member of the Heritage Futures advisory board) offered her reflections on the workshop.[1] She focused her comments

Figure 23.6 A community of plants that has established in one of the AWRE structures since the National Trust's acquisition in the 1990s (photograph by Caitlin DeSilvey).

around what she identified as 'two kinds of letting go'. One kind is intentional and controlled, and involves making decisions about how to cope with anticipated change proactively, through drafting of management plans and other tools for 'letting go well'. She observed that this kind of planning is not very good at coping with ambiguity, and that planning processes may need to change to allow for more iterative and flexible approaches. The second kind of letting go she described as the process of 'letting go of control', which 'is the opposite of making an intentional choice'. She talked about the challenge of giving over control to natural processes, and to communities, and suggested that new strategies are needed to help both practitioners and publics cope with the resulting uncertainty, 'becoming comfortable when we don't know what the outcome is'.

The open discussion that followed focused on thinking about what a framework for managing loss and change, directed to stakeholders in the heritage and conservation sectors, might look like. Workshop participants were also asked to think about possible guidelines for communication and engagement with diverse publics around themes of loss, change and transformation. Five breakout groups considered these topics from the perspective of different stakeholder groups – stewards, public bodies, communicators, consultancies and communities. Each group produced a set of recommendations and reflections. Five key points, distilled from the group conversation, address possible directions for the future of sites and features in transition, such as Orford Ness.

The first point relates to *temporality*. As a site in the process of transformation, it is important to facilitate short-, medium- and long-term planning, with regular intervals of review, reporting and re-evaluation, to allow for long-term flexibility and to enable integration of feedback from various stakeholders and adjustment of targets as necessary. Change is always occurring, but some change processes are slower than others (for example, enabling fauna and flora to adapt to emerging conditions, or letting a building gradually decay). Integrating management across the natural and built environment would open up options for interpreting different scales and speeds of change, and managing for 'process rather than product' (see Figure 23.6).

The second point considers the use of *storytelling* as a means to connect people with objects and the landscape. Acknowledging non-human as well as human stories can enhance the connection to place and encourage appreciation of ongoing change. The interpretation of a coastal site, for example,

Figure 23.7 Chinese water deer at Orford Ness (photograph by Dave Crawshaw, courtesy of the National Trust).

should be balanced with information about how climate change and erosion has historically shaped and reshaped the environment. Interpretation could also focus on how a disused site has, through time, provided new habitat for native and non-native flora and fauna – like the Chinese water deer that escaped from a mainland collection of exotic animals several decades ago and have since established on Orford Ness (see Figure 23.7). With this holistic vision in mind, visitors could then be asked: what stories will we be able to tell about this place in fifty, or five hundred, years?

The third point that emerged from the workshop is that, when managing a complex and dynamic site, managers need to take into account a *broader conception of heritage* that incorporates both natural and cultural heritage. In a survey conducted with CITiZAN staff and volunteers in July 2016, a total of 82 per cent viewed 'the whole' of Orford Ness as being 'heritage' (see Figure 23.8). Recognising both the cultural and natural elements of sites as heritage does not mean preserving everything, however. It is important to highlight that most volunteers surveyed were accepting of the loss of material remains, but felt that a record should be preserved. In keeping with this volume's broader themes, 'heritage' is seen as something *made in the present for the future*, and inclusive of a range of materials and processes.

Figure 23.8 Workshop participants on Orford Ness, walking towards the lighthouse (photograph by Tanya Venture).

The fourth point engages with the concept of *innovation* as a way of exploring the possibilities that emerge as structures decay and landscapes transform. Many of the public bodies responsible for cultural and natural heritage conservation and policy have a renewed interest in public engagement, 'putting people at the heart of the environment' and 'support[ing] the co-creation of ideas' (Natural England 2016, 4, 7). An expanded concept of public engagement may lead to the development of innovative interpretation strategies that tell the story of ongoing process and involve people in monitoring change over time, or that use new technologies to allow people to see the landscape in different ways.

The last point recognises that good listening is an essential part of *communication* and that consultation needs to allow for meaningful incorporation of feedback to give people a voice in adaptation planning at sites in transition. Communication should not be just about broadcasting a message or a decision: it is a two-way process that needs to be supported and sustained, through challenges such as staff changes and budgetary constraints. New mechanisms may be needed to engage people in understanding conservation philosophies and decisions, and to give them confidence to share their thoughts about long-term plans for the future of sites. Scheduling regular meetings with interested stakeholders to take stock of how things are progressing would be beneficial to keep communication lines open, and to allow people and sites to adapt to changes over time.

These general observations related to the topic of this particular workshop, but they also provided a helpful conclusion to our series of cross-theme collaborative knowledge exchanges. As such, they are broadly relevant not only to the kinds of transformational heritage landscapes in which this workshop was situated, but equally to natural and cultural collections and to living traditions or various forms of 'intangible' heritage.

Notes

1. These comments can be read in full in context at https://heritage-futures.org/reflections-transforming-loss.

Part V
Transformation

What are the future-making processes and practices involved in heritage landscapes that are undergoing significant change and transformation?

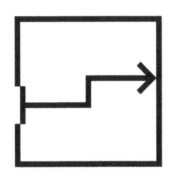

24
Living with transformation

Caitlin DeSilvey, Nadia Bartolini and Antony Lyons

Heritage transitions

In contemporary public discourse, cultural and natural heritage is often framed through reference to a relatively narrow range of desired attributes: stability and integrity (built heritage); indigeneity and diversity (natural heritage); and tradition and continuity (intangible heritage). The broad-brush assumption that value is secured through some form of protection masks a more complex situation on the ground, however, where practitioners are often keenly aware of the need to manage change, rather than arrest it. In an influential 1994 paper, Alan Holland and Kate Rawles wrote, 'conservation is about *negotiating the transition from past to future in such a way as to secure the transfer of maximum significance*' (Holland and Rawles 1994, 46, emphasis in the original), and many conservation practitioners and heritage professionals understand their role in this vein, working with a background assumption that some change is inevitable and appreciating that perpetuating meaning is often more important than preserving fabric (Douglas-Jones et al. 2016). This pragmatic position sits in tension with much wider policy, however, where there remains a prevailing commitment to protect 'heritage assets' from damage, decay and destruction – and any other forces, cultural or natural, that may lead to 'substantial harm or total loss' (in the terms of the UK *National Planning Policy Framework* (MHCLG 2019, 56)). The most common response to a perceived threat is to take measures to guard against further change, with 'loss aversion' as the primary goal (Holtorf 2015).

It may be, however, that the time has come to surface some of the hidden sympathies that heritage practice harbours for a more adaptive and expansive conception of conservation. The awareness of living in a world undergoing significant transformation, with certain planetary processes accelerated by global climate change (against background trends of human population growth, habitat destruction and species loss), defines our contemporary moment. At the same time, the resources available for preservation-as-usual are drying up in the face of economic austerity and uncertainty. In recent years, the recognition of widespread ecological and social change has been attended by the emergence of new theoretical approaches, understanding heritage as a socially embedded, future-oriented process through which the past is brought into the present to shape new practices and environments. These approaches frame heritage significance as an emergent, relational property – not an inherent quality linked to the preservation of specific material states (DeSilvey 2017; Harrison 2013a; 2015; Harrison et al. 2016; Pétursdóttir and Olsen 2014a; 2014b). Change and transformation has been reframed as an integral element of heritage, with the potential to generate new connections between the past and the future and between human and more-than-human agents.

Recent work has also shown how understanding long-term past trajectories of change can generate more expansive and creative possibilities for responding to anticipated future change (DeSilvey et al. 2011; Fincher et al. 2015), and explored how traces of the past can be brought into focus through attention to processes of erosion and emergence, involuntary remembrance and layered time (Geissler et al. 2016). Heritage can act as a focal point for resistance to change, but it can also create opportunities for communities to come to terms with change and act as a resource for the emergence of alternative practices that use the past to foster resilience and reciprocity (Harvey and Perry 2015a). Increasingly, heritage practice is also departing from 'top-down' decision-making and agenda-setting, to encourage more mobile and inclusive forms of engagement, and appreciate heritage significance as a dynamic, social process (Jones 2017).

Working at this interface, our research sought to understand how the practice of future-making is sustained (or enhanced) in relation to heritage materials and landscapes that are undergoing active processes of change and transformation. We chose to work with the concept of transformation because it allows for the inclusion of multiple processes and potentialities, incorporating changes in composition and structure, but also in character and condition. Throughout the research, we sought to track how transformations that are interpreted as 'harm' or 'loss' on one register can also provide opportunities for the emergence of other relational configurations and trajectories. Our research set out to consider the current and future dilemmas associated with the management of change by working within two domains of practice: the management of built heritage and the management of transitional landscapes. Our focus in built heritage contexts was initially on instances where there was some accommodation or apreciation of ruination and material transformation. Within the second domain, we aimed to explore landscapes defined by dynamic processes of rewilding, re-naturalisation and coastal change. We identified three case study sites where both sets of domains were present, but as we began our fieldwork, we came to appreciate the ways in which these initial comparative fields of practice were folded into each other, with processes of managing change playing out at different scales and through different contexts. A particularly geographical orientation informed our interest in the complexity of place and landscape as it is produced at the intersection of practice, process and representation, and we made the early decision to direct our focus on the relationship between the structural and the landscape scale within our sites, and across sites.

The landscapes we chose to work in are all undergoing transformation at a scale and a velocity more pronounced than the background condition of change characteristic of comparable landscapes. In each of the sites, a transition in land use is implicated in (but not fully responsible for) transformative processes. In mid-Cornwall, UK, pockets of post-industry coexist alongside active extraction of china clay (kaolin) deposits. In Portugal's Côa Valley, the shift to a post-agricultural ecology and economy is being facilitated through a pilot 'rewilding' initiative. On Orford Ness, Suffolk, UK, post-military management has been guided by a unique accommodation of dynamic structural and coastal change. In these places, the making of future heritage is not about conserving objects or artefacts as stable entities but about maintaining continuity with the past *through* processes of change and innovation (Poulios 2010).

By working across domains and with local collaborators, we gained insights into how managers and stewards accommodate and negotiate ambiguity, instability and emergent process, and in doing so are forced to acknowledge the entanglement of conventional categories of 'natural' and 'cultural' heritage management (although it should be noted that the label 'heritage' was not always central to the concerns of the people we encountered). We also came to appreciate how, by cultivating an openness to novel forms and multiple, overlapping temporalities, such sites unsettle conceptions of heritage time premised on a return to past states and baseline conditions. These two thematic findings – around managing entanglement and surfacing alternative temporalities – are central to the research that we discuss in the other chapters in this part of the book, and they will be returned to in the conclusion. Before introducing this content in more detail, we provide a brief introduction to each of our case study sites and collaborating organisations.

Sites and synergies

In mid-Cornwall's china clay country, north of the town of St Austell, more than two centuries of industrial extraction, on an increasingly large scale, have produced a patchwork, punctured landscape mosaic. Imerys, a multinational company based in France, continues to extract deposits of kaolin (decomposed granite), mostly in massive open pits, using heavy machinery and involving a substantial processing infrastructure (pipes, roads, plants, tunnels, tracks, tanks). Other areas are now 'post-operational' and so held in limbo, awaiting redevelopment or reuse, but in the meantime (often over decades) undergoing re-naturalisation, either intentionally (with replanting of heathland and forest) or passively (with rogue plantations of rhododendron and other 'invasive' species). Around the edges and in isolated pockets, elements of the industry are conserved in facilities managed by the Wheal Martyn Trust and the associated China Clay History Society. Many more features are left to decay in semi-wild dereliction. Industrial ruins and waste tips are scattered throughout the landscape. No one really knows what to do with these remainders, although some of them have accrued value as local landmarks and are celebrated as icons of industrial heritage. 'Preservation' of such features is problematic, however, and regional heritage bodies, who recognise the continual change brought about by evolving industrial process *as* the heritage of this landscape, have struggled to find a clear way forward (Kirkham 2014). One of our thematic knowledge-exchange events, facilitated by the organisation Future Terrains, was informed by their experience in developing culturally sensitive responses to post-industrial transition in similar landscapes globally. As we will go on to show, the clay country provided a remarkable laboratory for exploring the relationship between ongoing transformative process and heritage-making (see Figure 24.1).

Figure 24.1   Aerial view from the year 2000 of Wheal Martyn Clay Works (centre), which shows the post-operational Lansalson Pit and the working Wheal Martyn china clay pit, operated by Imerys Minerals Ltd (photograph courtesy of Wheal Martyn Trust).

In the Côa Valley, in north-east Portugal, a UNESCO World Heritage designated prehistoric rock art site shares a landscape with a rewilding initiative, led by a local organisation, Associação Transumância e Natureza (ATN), and supported by Rewilding Europe. In the Côa, as in much of rural southern Europe, a decades-long trend of land abandonment has transformed the landscape: small villages have gradually become depopulated, and olive groves and arable fields have gone to scrub. ATN was established in 2000 to restore habitat for raptors and other species in the abandoned agricultural lands. In 2012, they joined Rewilding Europe through an initiative that sought to release semi-wild horses and cattle (and, eventually, ibex and other large herbivore species)

Figure 24.2　Horse release in August 2016 in Cidadelhe, Portugal (photograph by Caitlin DeSilvey).

to the landscape (see Figure 24.2). We worked with ATN to understand their plans to transform the landscape into an ecologically rich mosaic that resembles (but does not replicate) what it was in the past, twenty thousand years ago, when representations of horses and other animals were carved into the stone along the river gorge. But this transformation is uneven: the introduced animals still need care and management; traditional practices of animal husbandry intersect with rewilding agendas; ruined houses are restored to accommodate eco-tourists. The 'new natural heritage' (Jepson and Schepers 2016, 2) produced by rewilding opens up new engagements with the deep past, while other local initiatives, such as the Memory Archive project hosted by ACÔA (Friends of the Côa Museum and Archaeological Park), work intergenerationally to record place-memories of the recent past before they are lost.

Orford Ness is a 15-kilometre-long shingle spit off the east coast of England. Here, the intentional management of change and ruination in (selected) built structures left behind by the Ministry of Defence is set against a backdrop of continual coastal erosion and longshore drift. Coastal erosion uncovers archaeology as well as erasing it, and the National Trust (partial owner of the Ness) works closely with the Coastal

Figure 24.3 One of the former AWRE research laboratories at Orford Ness, with the Orfordness Lighthouse in the background (photograph by Antony Lyons).

and Intertidal Zone Archaeological Network (CITiZAN) to record features as they are exposed and then lost. We undertook ethnographic research and worked on knowledge-exchange activities with both organisations to explore the dynamic and fluid nature of this place and to understand how this quality is celebrated by local managers, visitors and creative practitioners – change is the constant that links the past and the future here. But there are also nodes of attempted durability/fixity that work against this – a local effort to protect the lighthouse from inevitable erosion, for example, and the maintenance of selected structures in a state of arrested decay (or in active use for offices, accommodation and interpretation). Some of the Ministry of Defence structures were listed decades ago, but the iconic Atomic Weapons Research Establishment (AWRE) facility was only designated as a Scheduled Monument in 2014 (see Figure 24.3). Historic England holds that the designation does not trigger a presumption of protection, but they admit they have no control over how other people interpret the significance of such designations. In our research at Orford Ness, we sought to understand these tensions between process and preservation as they played out in relation to specific features and their futures (see also Chapter 23).

Methods, approaches and collaborative process

The research that forms the empirical focus of this part of the book was undertaken by two cultural geographers, Caitlin DeSilvey (CD) and Nadia Bartolini (NB), and one creative practitioner, Antony Lyons (AL). We adopted a variety of methods and approaches over the course of the research, including both parallel and concurrent enquiries. The authors each had independent involvements with the sites, interlocutors and research materials. The Côa Valley research is informed by ethnographic fieldwork undertaken in October/November 2015 (AL, NB and CD), August 2016 (CD), October 2016 (AL and NB), April 2017 (AL), October 2017 (NB) and June 2018 (AL). Semi-structured, informal and group interviews took place with land managers, local residents, business owners, archaeologists and conservationists. Participant observation was conducted in a variety of different sites and at local events, and we also analysed promotional and strategic planning material produced by local and international organisations. In addition, Antony adopted a 'shadowing' strategy with selected field operatives. At Orford Ness, the authors partnered with the National Trust and CITiZAN to explore the heritage practices involved in managing and recording Orford Ness's dynamic landscape. The investigation at Orford Ness consisted in Nadia's ongoing observation of archaeological training and recording sessions that CITiZAN organised for community volunteers, her participation in various related meetings, and a series of interviews with National Trust and Historic England staff. On site, Nadia worked in partnership with CITiZAN to film ongoing activity associated with the recording of Orford Ness's 'at risk' coastal structures and features (see Figure 24.4). Nadia and Antony also undertook joint fieldwork, and Antony participated in an intensive residential sound-recording workshop with Chris Watson, a leader in this field. In 2019, at the end of the project, Antony conducted an artist-residency at Orford Ness resulting in a site-specific creative installation. Data gathering in the clay country research involved a range of methods: accessing digital archives of planning and policy documents; interviewing key stakeholders; visual ethnography; field excursions; and knowledge-exchange events (see Figure 24.5). Antony's clay country artist-residency involved research fieldwork, exhibition and a participatory project with a local school. Broadly, his work comprised contextual practice-based research (Sullivan 2009) conducted in tandem with the academic team. The radically mixed methods adopted in our research generated a rich body of material, only some of which is presented in this book. Other outputs included papers in peer-reviewed journals, films, blog posts, exhibitions and conference presentations.

Figure 24.4 Nadia Bartolini filming CITiZAN staff and volunteers at Orford Ness in January 2017 (photograph by Lara Band, courtesy of CITiZAN).

Figure 24.5 Antony Lyons leading discussion at the Sky Tip, north of St Austell, Cornwall, during a May 2018 knowledge-exchange workshop (photograph by Caitlin DeSilvey).

At all three of these sites, our research was made possible by the generosity of our collaborators and the organisations they work for, who opened up their practices – and the philosophical underpinning of these practices – to scrutiny, and engaged enthusiastically in conversation about what they do and why they do it. It should be noted, in relation to these collaborations, that the topics we were considering at these three sites are inherently political and social, in that they involve decisions about what aspects of place to privilege and protect, and which elements to relinquish or reconfigure. In the sites we studied, we also identified occasional tensions between top-down institutional agendas and the perspectives of local practitioners and community members. The programmes of land-use change affecting our case study sites involve various forms of consultation and engagement with stakeholders, and multi-stranded efforts by the managers or stewards to reach out and enable participation. But progress and implementation in these sites is inevitably slippery, messy and tangled, and power dynamics (including land ownership) can be an impediment to consensus building. The material in the following chapters reflects on some of these dynamics, but it represents the perspectives gleaned by us as researchers, not necessarily that of our collaborators. Where there are potential differences in opinion and interpretation, we have tried to be sensitive to this.

Although our research approach was grounded in collaboration and co-creation, we were always aware of inevitable 'insider and outsider' dynamics, and the difference between being embedded locally (as a resident or practitioner) and being a 'visiting researcher'. Where possible, we chose methods that allowed for sustained and meaningful engagement with both places and their people – shadowing practices in the field, co-creating knowledge-exchange events, drafting shared guidance, producing films and installations, designing creative collaborations and engaging in extended dialogue. It should also be mentioned, in the spirit of the broader research project on which this book is based, that our research practice involved collaboration with non-human others, as well as human ones (see further discussion in Part I of this book). Much of the narrative and practice around (heritage) landscape transformation centres on the role that non-human species – primarily plants and animals – play in shaping and sharing places. In the following chapters, we have sought to develop new ways of telling these stories and also of acknowledging the agentic influences of elemental forces and processes (water, fire, ice, weather and climate). Following contemporary ecologically infused writings (such as Haraway 2003; 2006; Tsing et al. 2017; Morton 2011; 2013a), we have focused in our writing on specific entangled relationships (more on this below). In the case studies we present, there is evidence of an emerging interest in working with (as opposed to resisting) these agencies, even in operational land-management situations. This manifests as acceptance of flooding and coastal change, accepting the inevitability of fire and embracing processes of ruination and invasion. The need to find accommodations and ways of co-working with these forces is beginning to register in the agendas of progressive and imaginative practitioners, and we aim to document some of that work here.

Managing entanglement

As mentioned previously, one theme that emerged across all three of our study sites was a recognition that attention to process and transformation blurs and complicates categories of natural/cultural heritage management. In institutional frameworks, cultural and natural heritage management have – to a large degree – been kept separate, with distinct areas of expertise and oversight. At the international level of UNESCO's World Heritage Framework, the International Council on Monuments and Sites (ICOMOS) is responsible for cultural sites and the International Union for the Conservation of Nature (IUCN) for natural sites, and similar arrangements hold at a national level (Historic England and Natural England in the UK, for example). There has recently been a recognition of the need for more collaborative management approaches across natural and cultural heritage, but integration has been difficult to achieve (Larwood et al. 2017; also see further discussion in Part II, Diversity). In wider academic discourse, there has been an increasing focus on entangled eco-cultural worlds, and a call for approaches that can attend to the imbrication of natural and cultural heritage (Harrison 2013a; 2015; DeSilvey 2017). Some of this work draws on theoretical resources offered by assemblage thinking, as a means to trouble the nature/culture binary and to articulate the complex relationships between agents (biological and other), institutions, policies and practices in assembling 'nature-cultures' (Haraway 2003). In our own research, we sought to attend to the way assemblages are distributed, involving the careful selection of certain elements, while purposefully discarding others (this theme is explored in more depth later in this section). But we found that it is one thing to call for the dissolution of binary categories and quite another to realise this in practice, in specific places, where managers are bound by policies and plans that may reinforce this division.

One concept that we have found useful for thinking out of, and across, the bounds delineated by frameworks of natural and cultural heritage is that of the 'ruderal'. We explore this concept in more detail in the chapters that follow and in the conclusion to this part of the book, but a brief definition is needed by way of introduction. The word 'ruderal', with its roots in the Latin word for 'rubble', refers to opportunistic plant species that take root in disturbed or interrupted environments (see Figure 24.6). Interestingly, one definition of the ruderal suggests that this disturbance is introduced by human agents, while the other suggests a more indirect 'interruption', without specifying the agent of disturbance. In both inflections, disruption creates the conditions of possibility for the emergence of new (plant) communities, often perceived as 'weeds' or 'invasives'. On a global scale, the concept of the ruderal resonates with theories of 'inhuman nature' (Clark 2011) and the continual disturbance generated by forces outside human control – disease, fire, severe storms, geological upheavals. Others have used the concept of the ruderal as an analytic framework for rethinking cultural migration, human/non-human relations and unintended ecologies (Stoetzer 2018), and also for thinking about the cultural relevance of the ecological concept of the 'back loop', which asserts that systems do not remain in a steady state, but experience continual phases of collapse and unravelling, followed by creative phases of 'release and reconfiguration' (Wakefield 2018).

Figure 24.6 Classic ruderal species, including rosebay willowherb, growing on the shingle at Orford Ness (photograph by Antony Lyons).

In Chapter 25, we explore how the management of the transitional landscapes and features involves spatialisation strategies that intensify the complexities of the nature–culture dynamic. In the sites we studied, the management of change and transformation, while accommodating certain expressions of dynamic process (such as ruination and landscape rewilding), also involved the reinforcement of boundaries and establishment of distinct territories. On the one hand, there is an implicit acknowledgement of entangled naturecultures, but this acknowledgement is often attended by a desire to manage the resulting ambiguity, and to contain the effects of the unpredictable and indeterminate forces that are being invited in. The chapter uses concepts of 'fixing' and 'lines of flight' to explore these tensions as they were encountered in the three sites. Related themes also run through Chapter 26, in relation to ideas about fluidity, braiding and 'ongoingness'. Rather than focusing on the management of entanglement as such, the chapter highlights creative expressions of uncontrolled fluidity of processes and the emergence of novel, hybrid eco-cultural paradigms and possibilities. In Chapter 28, we develop the concept of 'ruderal heritage' in more detail and explore its potential contribution to innovation in heritage practice and scholarship.

Temporality and flow

The concept of perpetuity, indexed in statements such as the National Trust's 'for ever, for everyone', and discussed in detail in Chapters 1 and 2, implies a responsibility to ensure the continuation of a heritage asset (be it an object or a cultural landscape) indefinitely into the future.[1] It is premised on a conception of time as linear and sequential, broken into 'periods of significance', with a clear demarcation between 'the past' (history) and 'the future' (forever). The assumption is that intentional material preservation provides a 'window' or 'portal' into a world that is safely located somewhere 'behind' us spatially – in David Lowenthal's (2015) terms, 'the past is a foreign country' that we can visit, but not dwell in. Within this framing of time and materiality, there is an imperative to 'save' heritage that is deemed to be 'at risk' of irreversible transformation, prey to all of the antonyms of 'perpetuity': ephemerality, impermanence, temporariness, transience.

A few decades of scholarship have convincingly argued, however, that what and how we choose to preserve often tells us much more about our values in the present than about the past and the people who inhabited it (such as Harrison 2013a; Harvey 2001b; Smith 2006; Holtorf 2012). Recent work has also focused attention on the way the material remains of the past are always co-present, open to reactivation either through intentional or through involuntary encounters, and, as such, 'heritage' is only one way – and a relatively limited one at that – of experiencing a connection with 'the past' in the present (Macdonald 2013). Some of this work has highlighted how such a 'presentist' perspective unsettles the chronological, historicist 'time regime' (Hartog 2016). Laurent Olivier muses on the implications of this re-evaluation of historical time:

> ... if historical time ... no longer ... links, little by little, events which strictly follow on from each other – in a word, if time is now released – it can then create a correlation between events which are very distant from each other. If the past remains embedded in the present, it can therefore reawake[n] and reactivate in the present processes which were thought to be over for good, because they belonged to a past which was over and done with.
>
> (Olivier 2004, 209)

Olivier writes of composite, heterogeneous time, characterised by the persistence of elements of the material past in present physical environments. Such persistence is witnessed in examples such as the rock art in the Côa Valley (see Figure 24.7) and it has a particular role in defining

Figure 24.7 Bovines painted on a granite cliff face in Cidadelhe, Portugal, approximately ten thousand years ago (photograph taken by Mário Reis in 2015 and enhanced using DStretch, courtesy of Côa Museum/Côa Park Foundation Archives).

the character of layered and entangled places. These ideas are explored in depth by geographers in relation to specific urban environments and cultural landscapes (Pred 2004; Crang and Travlou 2001; Bartolini 2013; Bastian 2014; Massey 2006). Extending this focus on temporality, Bruce Braun has recently argued that the Anthropocene calls for an understanding of time that acknowledges both how the 'past haunts the present' (Braun 2015, 240) and how time flows 'toward us, from the future to the present' (Braun 2015, 239).

These more open, contingent conceptions of time have a particular salience in relation to landscapes characterised by transformation and dynamic change, such as those we studied. We did come across some examples of attempts at conventional preservation, in efforts to restore a landscape to an eco-historic baseline or a structure to an original condition (where the will and the resources allowed). Much more common, however, was a sense of time (and place) permeated by residual traces and temporal juxtapositions. Some of these traces indexed futures that never came to pass, while others provided openings to plausible future trajectories. The concept of relational time (Harvey 1996; Fitzpatrick 2004) perhaps provides a more useful lens for understanding the complex and multiple temporalities at play in these landscapes, and the way they emerged in specific moments of encounter. This is a theme taken up by Timothy Morton, who has argued for a reconsideration of the relationship between aesthetics and temporality: 'space and time are emergent properties of objects', he writes (Morton 2013b, 35). Morton suggests that we live in a world that 'times' actively around us, as different configurations of objects and agents come together and apart (Morton 2011).

In the following chapters, we apply the ideas of Morton and others to unravel the complex temporalities at play in the landscapes we studied. In Chapter 26, Antony imaginatively explores cycles within deep time, and resonances between the three case study sites, utilising a hybrid 'geopoetic' style, anchored by the analogy of 'fluvial-journeying', exploring 'channels', 'floodplains' and 'oxbow lakes'. Themes of temporality and complexity also emerge in Chapter 25, where Nadia addresses strategies for managing ambiguity about past/present/future time. In Chapter 28, we return to the discussion of temporality, framed by three different temporal modalities: open time, wild time and drift time.

In addition to the substantive chapters described above, this thematic part also includes a collaborative visual essay (Chapter 27), in which the members of the research team have compiled their reflections on a series of images, in a conversational format. In the concluding chapter (Chapter 28), as noted above, we return to our two thematic foci – on managing entanglement and surfacing alternative temporalities – and explore the relevance of these ideas for both our case study sites and wider heritage practice.

Note

1. The concept of protection 'in perpetuity' was embedded in the founding of the organisation (Sutton et al. 2017, 11), and the Act of 1907, which formalised the organisation's structure and purpose, states an intention of 'permanent preservation'. As noted in Chapter 1, in January 2020, the National Trust revised the order of words in their motto, from 'For ever, for everyone' to 'For everyone, forever'.

25

Fixing naturecultures: Spatial and temporal strategies for managing heritage transformation and entanglement

Nadia Bartolini

Introduction

One of the aims of the research we carried out was to better understand how a focus on process, rather than permanence, works to blur the distinction between natural and cultural heritage. As fieldwork progressed during the three-year period, we realised that the management of change and transformation, while accommodating certain expressions of dynamic process (such as ruination and landscape rewilding), also involved the reinforcement of boundaries and establishment of distinct territories at the three sites. These efforts often appeared designed to manage the ambiguity associated with the accommodation of change and to contain the effects of unpredictable and indeterminate forces. In this chapter, I explore how managing conservation and preservation initiatives in transitional landscapes involves spatialisation strategies that intensify the complexities of the nature–culture dynamic.

The complexities in question are associated with the relationality of nature and culture, as well as the interconnectivity of beings (see Harrison et al. 2004). This particular understanding of the entanglement of nature and culture finds resonance with Donna Haraway's concept of 'nature-cultures', which appreciates the combination and the co-production of human and non-human relationality (Haraway 2004; 2008; in relation to heritage, see Harrison 2013a; 2015). When describing Haraway's concept, John Law (2004, 4) indicates that, 'Natures, then, are partially connected to humans: they are partly being made together.' The concept of 'naturecultures' also resonates with the preoccupations of geographers when considering interactions in place. As Doreen Massey (2005, 67) notes, 'The specificities of space are a product of interrelations – connections and disconnections – and their (combinatory) effects.'

The entanglements and assemblages that occur in any given location, and the consequences of such relationality, may be outward-facing (through networks that branch out) or inward-facing. In *Space after Deleuze* (2017), Arun Saldanha investigates the spatialisation of Gilles Deleuze's thinking, particularly following his collaboration with Felix Guattari. In the book, Saldanha homes in on how space shapes thinking, not simply as a theoretical imaginary, but as part of the very fabric of being: 'Space *is* difference, multiplicity, change, and movement, not some separate formal realm that would frame them' (Saldanha 2017, 3, emphasis in the original). One of the key spatial terms used by Deleuze and Guattari is the notion of 'territory' as a conceptual frame to articulate flows (an element that will be further discussed in Chapter 26), encounters and concatenations: 'Territorialization requires a dynamic coming-together of heterogeneous components set loose from elsewhere. Something is *de* territorialized only to be *re* territorialized within a new configuration' (Saldanha 2017, 113, emphasis in the original).

The ways territories are understood – how they are made and reconfigured, as well as how they are perceived – draws in elements that *create* places. This is more than place-making: it is about how things are activated, purposely separated and also how things become and are born out of 'lines of flight' (Deleuze and Guattari 1987, 3). While Deleuze and Guattari associate lines of flight with 'the potentiality for politics at the heart of capitalism' (Saldanha 2017, 35), we can also understand heritage through the notion of lines of flight. Such a perspective allows us to look beyond elements that are simply settled and collected: lines of flight evoke the *potentialities* that can emerge, even though their paths may be uncertain. Taken together, the entanglement of naturecultures, and the lines of flight, occur in place. And in relation to the empirical focus of this part of the book, it is places that are transforming – transitioning from one land use to another – because it is through the gradual transformation of sites that we can notice the practices that are put in place to manage an environment that is in the process of becoming, that is not yet 'fixed' or consolidated in form.

In this chapter, I will investigate our three fieldwork sites through the concept of naturecultures and their spatial configurations. I wish to consider how naturecultures are assembled, and also how spaces that organise connections are developed through conservation management decisions, heritage-making practices and cultural signifiers. This will be explored through the concept of temporal and spatial 'fixes', a concept first introduced by David Harvey in 1981, and subsequently revisited in 2001, when Harvey clarifies the variegated English meanings of the word 'fix':

> One meaning, as 'the pole was fixed in the hole', refers to something being pinned down and secured in a particular locus. The idea is that something is secured in space: it cannot be moved or modified. Another, as in 'fix a problem', is to resolve a difficulty, take care of a problem. Again, the sense is that things are made secure, but by returning things to normal functioning again (as in 'he fixed the car's engine so that it ran smoothly'). This second meaning has a metaphorical derivative, as in 'the drug addict needs a fix', in which it is the burning desire to relieve a chronic or pervasive problem that is the focus of the meaning. Once the 'fix' is found or achieved then the problem is resolved and the desire evaporates. But, as in the case of the drug addict, it is implied that the resolution is temporary rather than permanent, since the craving soon returns.
>
> (Harvey 2001a, 24)

What Harvey (2001a, 24) specifies is that, in his initial study on capitalism's geographical expansion, he was referring to the second definition of the 'fix' in terms of how 'capitalism, we might say, is addicted to geographical expansion much as it is addicted to technological change and endless expansion through economic growth'. Nonetheless, Harvey notes that this expansion does not preclude a fixity in space. Indeed, he plays on the various meanings of fixity to engage with the mobility of capital, and how 'capitalism has to fix space … in order to overcome space' (Harvey 2001a, 25).

These concepts related to the fixing of space, and the temporality associated with solving particular dilemmas, resonate with what we encountered in the field sites we investigated in our research on heritage transformations. Fixity is also a useful concept to explore the entanglement of naturecultures and the '*re* territorialisation' of new configurations in the study of heritage-making practices through change. This chapter will explore each of these field sites through three spatial themes: marking territories in the rewilding landscapes in the Côa Valley in Portugal; carving paths in the clay country landscape around St Austell, Cornwall, UK; and defining edges at Orford Ness, Suffolk, UK. Through these spatial themes, I will draw out how heritage-making practices temporally 'fix' places in order to cope with the challenges that transitional landscapes pose to conventional heritage management, with their expressions of the 'unfixed' and continual 'becoming'.

Marking territories

> Blimunda walked thousands of leagues, nearly always barefoot. The soles of her feet became hard and scarred like the bark of a tree. Those feet walked the length and breadth of Portugal, on several occasions they even crossed the Spanish border, because Blimunda failed to notice any line on the ground dividing this territory here from that territory there, she simply heard a foreign language being spoken and turned back.
>
> (Saramago 1998, 342)

In his book *Baltasar and Blimunda*, set in eighteenth-century Portugal, writer José Saramago weaves a tale where the boundaries of fiction and reality are blurred, and where the search for love intersects with the search for freedom. Blimunda spends years travelling throughout Portugal to find her beloved Baltasar. The theme of the traveller is a recurring one for Saramago; his non-fiction book, *Journey to Portugal* (2013), accompanied us on our first fieldtrip to Portugal, as we landed in the coastal city of Porto and drove across the country to reach the Côa Valley near the Spanish border. Like the traveller in *Journey to Portugal*, as we travelled east and north, we witnessed the changing landscapes, the gradual depopulation of human inhabitants and the transition into rougher and wilder territory.

However, our journey did not end once we arrived in the Côa Valley. Rather, we continued to travel, going from one rural village to another, from one rewilding reserve to the next. Along the way, we encountered different horse breeds, geologies, cultures and dialects – all different, yet familiar; all distinctive, yet linked. Like Blimunda, we sometimes failed to notice the lines that divided territories. After several fieldwork trips, however, we started to distinguish these divisions, and if we failed to do so ourselves, others would point out the signs where the lines were drawn (see Chapter 27 for a discussion of signs).

Rewilding is widely understood to be an approach in which human intervention in landscape processes is significantly reduced, so that nature can 'look after itself' (Navarro and Pereira 2012, 904). However, our fieldwork in Portugal has shown that rewilding – at least in its early stages – also involves defining areas and practices that serve a specific purpose in rewilding the landscape. From our observations, rewilding is also a process through which territories are created and marked, facilitating a series of temporary fixes. These attempts to manage an uncertain future landscape, and to engage in experimental conservation practices, sometimes involve (paradoxically) reasserting nature–culture boundaries. Associação Transumância e Natureza (ATN) holds various properties across the Côa and Douro Rivers in a mix of freehold and rental arrangements. The main rewilding area, Faia Brava, is the most cohesive territory of the reserve, totalling 1,000 hectares. Since 2012, ATN has been involved in the reintroduction of 'semi-wild livestock' such as horses, so that their grazing can 'restore the natural mechanisms that maintain the landscape mosaic' (ATN 2015, 10; see also DeSilvey and Bartolini 2019).

There are three horse breeds native to Portugal: Garrano, Sorraia and Lusitano. During fieldwork, ATN provided access to visit the different breeds in the different territories where they had been introduced. The short- and medium-term strategy for the reintroduced Garrano horses is to keep them in the core Faia Brava reserve, separate from other horse breeds (interview 11 October 2017). Garrano horses are sturdy and familiar with rugged terrains. Outnumbered compared with the other breeds, most of the 80 Garrano horses in Faia Brava have been purchased through annual livestock fairs and private networks (see Figure 25.1a). The 'fixing' or containment of the Garranos enables the horses to roam a much larger fenced terrain, compared with ATN's other properties, to develop relationships within their own breed and to find themselves in an environment where they can 'adapt the wilderness back' (interview 8 October 2016; Grange et al. 2009). ATN's other horse breeds are also 'fixed' to other territories. ATN monitors five Sorraia horses in Middle Côa, a place that has a very different environment to Faia Brava, and that is considered much more amenable to the Sorraia breed: it has a flatter, lusher landscape that is easily accessible to the river (see Figure 25.1b). While there is no verifiable evidence that the Sorraia horse is specifically 'ancient', there seems to be consensus that it is nonetheless considered 'a primitive horse and is believed to be the primary ancestor of the Iberian horses' (Luís et al. 2007, 25). ATN is, however, less concerned with establishing pure 'ancient' breeds (interviews 9 October, 11–12 October 2017); rather, they seek to associate horses with a Côa Valley landscape to which they can most easily adapt. Here, the 'fixing' seems like a matchmaking between horse breed characteristics and a suitable environment.

Figure 25.1a Garrano horses being released in Faia Brava in August 2016 (photograph by Caitlin DeSilvey).

Figure 25.1b Sorraias at Middle Côa in 2018 (photograph by Nadia Bartolini).

Quinta do Sol, a 70-hectare property contiguous to the Faia Brava reserve is another location that is part of the rewilding initiative; in this area, Sorraia horses mingle with mustangs. According to ATN, this is a provisional arrangement – a temporary home for the horses. Once they begin to breed and appear to be healthy, the plan is to move them to Middle Côa. In effect, Quinta do Sol acts as a temporary fix where breeding and observation of the offspring takes place until such time as they are ready to be delivered to their more permanent home. But this is not the only time that horses are moved around properties; they are also moved to provide other landscape management services.

One of ATN's founders highlights that in this area 'the cornerstone of rewilding is reintroducing grazers'. The importance of the reintroduction of horses at Faia Brava is summed up by both conservation managers and local residents: one of their main jobs is 'to clean' and, therefore, to reduce fire risk in the scrubby vegetation that has established in the area in the absence of agricultural use. As Chapter 28 highlights, there is a long-standing tradition in this farmed landscape of carrying out controlled burning. Yet, in some instances, fire can burn out of control, as was the case in October 2017, when the increasing death toll due to wildfires precipitated the resignation of Portugal's interior minister (Agence France-Presse 2017). Another ATN founder and current guest-house owner told us when interviewed in 2017 that the 2003 fire that destroyed over 215,000 hectares of land was a turning point for the conservation organisation: ATN decided to start monitoring fires, and assist in replenishing the depleted landscape. This involved hiring interns to monitor and to help with tree planting, but also, importantly, the reintroduction of Garrano horses to start grazing. During informal interviews, local residents also recognised the value of the horses, seeing them as 'doing a job by cleaning' the landscape, and the hostel owners in the village of Cidadelhe have noticed a decrease in wildfires in the area, which they attribute to the presence of the horses. Because the rewilding properties are not necessarily connected to one another, ATN uses trailers to move horses from one part of their reserves to another. The movement of horses is a temporary fix that solves two problems for non-humans and for humans: it ensures that the horses are fed and that grazing is done on as much of the rewilding area as possible to reduce the risk, and spread, of fire.

A number of other properties are used to temporarily house the horses. For instance, a 7-hectare plot of land located north of Almeida was described as 'a kind of hospital'. During the dry conditions of 2017, multiple interviewees recalled that some 20 Garrano horses suffering from heat exhaustion or lack of water were brought here for three to six months so that they could recuperate before being moved back to Faia Brava (see Figure 25.1a). ATN has negotiated to manage another small plot of land near Figueira de Castelo Rodrigo, where it has moved a young Lusitano horse donated to the organisation: its development will be monitored in case one day it can be cross-bred.

It can be argued that ATN's involvement in locating and relocating the horses demonstrates the high level of intervention in this rewilding initiative, as well as a means to manage nature conservation and cultural heritage referents in the area. During an interview, one of ATN's founders pointed out that one needs to see rewilding in this landscape as a process where present practices are small steps to reaching future goals. The small steps in question consist in both species management and in spatialised practices where horses are 'contained' for specific purposes. Spatialising the horses solves certain present problems for ATN, but may also involve unmarking and 'unfixing' these territories in the future in order to achieve a particular (human) desired nature.

Steve Hinchliffe (2007, 44) highlights that: 'Matters are sociable rather than natural or social. And being sociable they can change.' The sociability between the reintroduced horses, as well as their relationship with more-than-humans and their adaptation into the Côa landscape, speaks to how new forms of sociality become heritage. This appreciation of the social as bounding – rather than dividing – humans and non-humans goes alongside the recent call to develop approaches that consider human and non-human perspectives and their relationality (Buller 2015). By keeping species separate, and by engaging in wildlife management through breeding and 'hospitalising', ATN fixes and reterritorialises in its own way: species are being conserved and managed, and caring is occurring in the present for the future. In this sense, heritage-making is not only a product of sociality, but also about the desire embedded in creating new natural heritage for the future.

Carving paths

I saw that no-one watched me,
And the hard white flakes began to fall
Between sleepers, into ruts of the path:

And beyond the siding the main line turned away,
Like my heart, towards open clay.

                    (extract from 'Exit', in *Clay Cuts*, Jack Clemo 1991, 44)

Born during the First World War to a clay-kiln worker, Reginald John ('Jack') Clemo was a renowned Cornish poet and lifetime resident of the clay country whose writings were inspired by the everyday lives of the working-class community and the landscape that was being carved out before him. As he outlines in *Clay Cuts*: 'The realism and symbolism of these poems could only be achieved by a poet who was born, as I was, in a workman's cottage with many bristling clay-pyramids visible from its windows' (Clemo 1991, 8). China clay extraction took hold in mid-Cornwall in the mid-eighteenth century, when Plymouth chemist William Cookworthy discovered that the white feldspar of granite decomposed to create kaolinite, which could be used in the making of white porcelain (Thurlow 2005). Geologists engaged in a form of geotourism in the St Austell area in Cornwall, initially to visit the industrial tin extraction landscapes. As tin extraction shifted to china clay extraction, other non-scientific travellers followed suit, especially after the arrival of railway travel in the mid-nineteenth century. The depiction of the area in popular culture touched on both its romantic and its deeply industrial associations (Bristow 2016; Trower 2009).

    The china clay process involves extraction (also called 'winning the clay') through the use of high-pressure washing techniques and processing (refining and drying) activities that involve the production of a vast amount of waste material, which was traditionally deposited in the landscape in conical clay tips. Engagement in these activities defined the identity of workers in and around St Austell for generations. In the 1930s, Clemo went deaf and by 1955, he was blind. His poems therefore are resoundingly located in time and space, witnessing a time when the landscape still featured the white pyramid forms that were emblematic of the mid-Cornwall china clay landscape (see Figure 25.2). Since then, much has changed: in the 1950s and 1960s, the china clay industry production methods were modernised; the French company Imerys took over the conglomerate English China Clays (ECC) in 1999; china clay production shifted to other areas around the world, notably Brazil; and many extraction sites were eventually classified as non-operational.

    Today, the clay landscape could be described as a liminal space, something not quite 'fixed', a place that remains open to interpretation. This might be because it could be seen as vacillating between the place it was in the past (and the remnants and relics that index the heritage of china

Figure 25.2 Sign for the St Dennis, Cornwall primary school depicting china clay tips known locally as 'Flatty' and 'Pointy' (photograph by Nadia Bartolini).

clay extraction) and what it is in the process of becoming (as the industry continues to transform the landscape, with increasingly automated processes). In the meantime, however, this ill-defined landscape has meaning for present-day populations, who cherish the area's mixed and messy natural and cultural heritage, and see value in both the re-naturalised post-operational landscapes and the evidence of ongoing extraction (see, for instance, ClayFutures 2009). As china clay production changed, so has people's experience of the landscape: from identifying with the iconic 'Cornish Alps' during the peak of the china clay industry to new generations who will only know the rolling hills of re-vegetated waste tips.

For locals and visitors alike, one way to experience the china clay landscape is through the numerous paths and trails that permeate the St Austell area. Since taking over from ECC 20 years ago, Imerys Minerals Limited, which owns over 5,500 hectares in mid-Cornwall, has created over 40 kilometres of permissive footpaths and trails (Imerys, n.d.). Imerys have been partnering with government agencies and developers in restoring non-operational lands to different uses for local communities. These formal and informal paths are part of the heritage-making practices in the landscape and provide another means to understand how naturecultures are assembled; not as delineated and bounded areas, but rather as pathways that gently carve through the landscape and reveal a combination of physical features (such as geologies and vegetation types) and cultural heritage (memories and post-industrial remnants). Locals participate in maintaining the paths and they have become part and parcel of the well-being of the community. As one local council representative mentioned to us during an interview in 2016:

> Cornwall has a community of active people, and I am very confident in saying this, like nowhere else in Britain are people engaged at a community level in their historic environment like they are in Cornwall... just everywhere you go in Cornwall you will find community groups actively using their heritage, conserving it and going out in [various places in Cornwall] clearing sites and clearing the vegetation off just for the love of it. And having a huge impact on the experience of the visitors who come, and by extension, they are contributing to the economy by going out and clearing off the monuments and keeping the paths clear and practical conservation works ...

The council representative mentions clearing twice in this extract, linking heritage and conservation with tidying up – an attention to detail to encourage public access to the paths. Yet it also suggests that heritage is not unruly but, rather, clean and uncluttered. The level of care attributed is akin to that which is done around a home: tidying up the garden, sweeping the leaves and branches from the front steps, leaving the path to the front door clear of debris. However, with some groups of volunteers, such as the Tregargus Trust, clearing paths requires an assessment of naturecultures, and a recognition that the clearing of paths around, in this case, re-vegetated industrial ruins, involved acts of destruction as well as conservation: 'You have to draw a line somewhere between what is gonna destroy the valley and what we destroy – what we shouldn't be doing' (WildWorks 2014, 00:25:05). The management of the paths, and the related decision-making practices that ensue, is more complex than the notion of 'tidying up'. It involves a consideration of the naturecultures from varied perspectives that defines how the temporal and spatial fixing will be deployed in the present. One of the clay country paths, known as 'Eden Project to Wheal Martyn', is described as 'cross[ing] woodland, heathland and pass[ing] by working mines and clay pits' (Clay Trails n.d., n.p.). This path highlights what is arguably the most impressive display of iconic features, particularly in terms of landscape changes resulting from industrial activity.

The three distinct landscape features resulting from china clay extraction and processing are clay pits, clay tips and mica lagoons. At the post-operational Carclaze site, just north of St Austell, all three can be seen. In

May 2018, we brought a group of participants in a knowledge-exchange event to this site, where Peter Herring from Historic England described the writings and early lithographs of geotourists as a form of the 'industrial sublime' (see also Bristow 2016). At Baal Pit, we were able to witness remnants of the industry: the mica lagoon, the chimney of the engine house at Pentruff and 'the gravel pumps on an incline … used in the 1980s to pump the clay and sand out of the pit' (Tonkin 2007; Bristow 2007, 4; see Figure 25.3). When observing the scenery at Baal Pit, most of the participants were, like us, impressed by the view – and its mix of physical attributes and unorthodox aesthetic beauty. This is in itself paradoxical, considering the violence which the traditional process of washing and breaking the clay involved: using direct water jets called 'monitors' pressured up to 300 psi (Thurlow 2005). With such pressured force, it is no wonder that the term 'landscape scars' (Storm 2014) comes to mind when considering the force put upon the natural environment to extract the desired product for consumption.

Yet, the 'wounded', lunar-like landscape also enabled other opportunities to emerge: 'As you round the corner of the path you'll be able to see into Baal Pit, a disused china clay pit, whose surreal landscape has featured in Dr Who' (Clay Trails n.d., n.p.). In February 1971, filming for six episodes of the British science fiction television series *Doctor Who*, titled 'Colony in Space', took place in Baal Pit, which doubled as the planet Uxarieus in the year 2472. The storyline involves human colonists, who

Figure 25.3   Baal Pit (photograph by Nadia Bartolini).

are struggling to live on the planet, and invaders from the Interplanetary Mining Corporation, who arrive to plunder the planet of the mineral duralinium. The screenshots from the episodes (Figures 25.4a and 25.4b) allow a comparison between the condition of the pit during filming in 1971 and the state of the pit in 2018.

Figure 25.4a Screenshot from BBC1's *Doctor Who*, 'Colony in Space', Episode One.

Figure 25.4b Screenshot from BBC1's *Doctor Who*, 'Colony in Space', Episode Two.

A different natureculture entanglement is evident here. As the world's longest-running science fiction television series (Nicol 2018), there is no denying the iconic status of Doctor Who, a Time Lord, in the mindset of UK popular culture. *Doctor Who* has a reach that goes beyond class, gender and regional divisions. It is also intergenerational, as extended families sit in front of the television to watch the yearly rendition of the *Doctor Who* Christmas special. As Nicol (2018) highlights, the popularity of *Doctor Who* merits attention because it draws on aspects of British national identity and politics. Concurrently, this touches on how heritage narratives are woven in popular culture (see Holtorf 2010). What this case in Cornwall adds is the association of *Doctor Who* with a real landscape in Cornwall, a landscape that is not only described as 'surreal', but also represented as futuristic. By including a mention of the filming of *Doctor Who*, the Clay Trails path narrative reinforces the juxtaposition of times in a place that simultaneously represents past, present and future. The natureculture entanglement here blurs the boundaries between fact and fiction, as popular culture is bound up in the 'lines of flight' of Baal Pit.

However, *Doctor Who* was filmed at Baal Pit in 1971, so almost half a century separates these two landscapes. In the last couple of decades, Imerys has been partnering with government agencies and developers in restoring non-operational lands to different uses. In 2008, a proposal was put forward to create 'eco-communities' on a number of non-operational sites in the clay country. In 2017, the UK government granted support for the company Eco-Bos to develop the site at West Carclaze, with the promise of a garden village creating 1,500 new homes and associated services, amid a heritage park that features the iconic Sky Tip (see Figure 25.5).

During the planning approval process, local residents had opportunities to voice their concerns, and some people pointed to the potential harm the development (and the creation of new multi-purpose paths and facilities) could have on the existing network of paths:

> Maslow's Hierarchy of Needs tells us we all need to have a home we feel safe in and this new public footpath (but which also would be used for motorcyclists [and] horse riders too) … [would] creat[e] a noise nuisance where none exists on this land at present … [and] would result in all of us feeling unsafe.
>
> (Cornwall Council website, comments from 27 March 2015)

Figure 25.5 The Sky Tip, with the Cornish flag planted at the summit (photograph by Nadia Bartolini).

> I object to the above planning application for several reasons:...
> People use the existing countryside, admire it, walk along it on paths.
> It is a peaceful sanctuary absolutely necessary in today's society.
> (Cornwall Council website, comments from 26 May 2015)

Here, both objections highlight how paths conjure up feelings of safety and tranquillity. This resonates with some of the themes discussed in Part IV, Uncertainty, particularly through the ways that toxic forms of heritage are made safe. One could suggest that the paths that are carved into the china clay landscape are a means to cope with change. By using the paths to experience nature, even if this nature has been produced through intensive industrial activity, local populations can make a claim to the kind of nature they desire, and their preference for accessing it (see Tilley and Cameron-Daum 2017). The paths speak of the past, present and future; they relate to an industrial time when humans 'wounded' the Earth to extract the resources that gave them jobs and pride. And along the way, the paths recognise how this industry also enabled a time-travelling representation associated with heritage narratives from contemporary British popular culture. The tension between a positive past (associated with employment and a sense of regional identity) and a negative one (damaging nature) is partly reconciled with the paths: the paths do not forget, yet, they have nonetheless become, as one of the comments above mentions, a 'sanctuary'. In the present conjuncture, as a landscape that is still in the process of '*multiple* becomings' (Massey 2005, 173, emphasis in the original), paths enable a temporal 'fixing' of the dilemma between what was, what is and what will become. Here, naturecultures are understood through the paths: moving across and circulating through the china clay country.

Defining edges

> Certainly we have plenty of [coast]: the shoreline of the UK mainland alone is more than five times as long as that of France, and once you add Ireland and all the islands of both countries, you have a lot more edge than middle.
>
> (Kingshill and Westwood 2012, xi)

There has been much written about the post-military site of Orford Ness. It is a place where Cold War secrets abound and, as time goes by, these secrets are gradually resurfacing into the public domain. The military's attraction to Orford Ness emerged in 1913: War Office correspondence from the time highlights the 'island' nature of the site, which afforded 'privacy' to classified military operations (Heazell 2010, 24). From the outset, Orford Ness's unique geography was valued by the War Office 'to enable certain experimental work' to take place (Heazell 2010, 23). Indeed, still today, one National Trust employee interviewed in 2016 refers to its past in ways that highlight its 'edginess': 'a lot of what went on here was cutting edge sort of experimental, the first of something that happened'.

Although it is occasionally accessed from a land bridge near Aldeburgh, visitors to the shingle spit usually take the ferry across the River Ore to reach Orford Ness, which has the not unwelcome effect of restricting visitor numbers. Known as 'the island' by locals (Wainwright 2009), one could posit that for the War Office, it was viewed as an island because its location was 'on the edge': not quite an island, but separate from the mainland. Today, Orford Ness is owned by the National Trust, and here again, for a conservation organisation, it is seen as a property 'on the edge': not quite a typical National Trust property. When the Trust acquired the site in 1993, decision-makers vacillated between tidying it up and returning it to 'wilderness' (Wainwright 2009, 136). This 'edge-land in flux' resonates with the poetic text drafted by Antony Lyons in his discussion of 'sensitive chaos' (see Chapter 26).

Orford Ness remains an ill-defined and perplexing place. While it may be made of edges, it is still difficult to determine where those edges are. One of the boundaries that is in flux is the edge of the shingle spit itself, a rare geological formation notable for the fact that the shingle supports a vegetative community of rare plants. As Angus Wainwright (2009, 134–5) mentions: 'This shingle structure is very dynamic, building up in some areas and eroding in others and the beach can change shape overnight.' Its malleable edge therefore renders the site less 'fixed'.

Since purchasing Orford Ness in 1993, the National Trust has balanced their management of the site's combined cultural and natural heritage. Staff and volunteers work hard to maintain the site and its landscape to benefit both wildlife and visitors. In light of the varied areas that require care and preservation, different management approaches are used to 'preserve the character of the landscape and protect the wildlife' (National Trust n.d. a). If landscapes have distinctive characters, so do humans and organisations. One National Trust employee who was present when the organisation purchased Orford Ness, and who was interviewed in 2016, explains the mindset at the time: 'The National Trust are a very tidy organisation. They are used to looking after gardens and country houses and things. The instinctive approach of the National Trust [at Orford Ness] was to tidy everything up.' He goes on to highlight the 'natural instincts' humans have when managing the site:

> I also remember the first volunteers that arrived looking around for things to do. They started edging around all the roads where the vegetation was growing in to make them look neat. That's an instinctive approach. When you have a different philosophy, it does need to be written down to guide people.

The act of tidying up can be understood as a means through which cultural and natural heritage management manifests itself (see Harrison 2004). The tidying up outlined in the quotation above is not unlike the perception of clearing the paths in Cornwall – a form of domestication to tame the spread of the flora. Yet here, the tidying also refers to the National Trust itself, and the ideal of the organisation's 'for ever, for everyone' motto mentioned in Chapter 24, which assumes that management is meant to fix features in perpetuity. At Orford Ness, the tidying of the paths is described as 'edging', a term that suggests defining the edge between the concrete paths (which existed prior to the National Trust's purchase of the property) and the vegetation. Defining the edges and clearing up the paths are what the National Trust employee mentions to be 'instinctive'. However, an examination of the history of management at the site reveals that this 'edging' is not applied evenly to all areas on the site, and that the maintenance of 'edges' involves philosophical as well as practical considerations.

In the early years of the National Trust's ownership, the organisation developed a management plan that sought to describe the significance of the aesthetic, symbolic and historical characteristics of Orford Ness, and to identify distinct 'character areas' (Wainwright 2009). It was only after this broad analysis of the site's qualities that a general philosophy of non-intervention was adopted for a designated part of the site (DeSilvey 2017; Wainwright 2009). This philosophy was initially targeted at the already decaying Atomic Weapons Research Establishment (AWRE). It was then 'applied with varying degrees' in other character areas, including the old airfield, the grazing marshes and the open shingle (Wainwright 2009, 140).

As Wainwright (2009) mentions, a side effect of implementing this philosophy was to restrict unattended access to the public for much of the area. Furthermore, as the site still includes unexploded ordnance, visitors are asked not to stray from the waymarked concrete paths and trails. This spatial fixing of where visitors can go, and when they can view the site on accompanied tours, enables the National Trust to control the impact of visitors. The threat of stepping on a bomb if one strays off the path has the effect of creating an invisible fence between the paths and the open shingle, mitigating impact on the fragile shingle vegetation. Restricting visitor access also has the effect of benefiting the preservation of natural and cultural heritage in the long term, and of enhancing 'the feeling of solitude [which] is so important' to experience the unique atmosphere of Orford Ness (Wainwright 2009, 141).

The philosophy of non-intervention has enabled the National Trust to fix one of their dilemmas at the time – how to cope with the inherited legacy of the decaying concrete AWRE structures – but it has generated other challenges. An interviewee recounted how during the 1990s, with the end of the Cold War, a large number of former defence sites were being sold, some of which had clear historical significance while others were more recent. The AWRE structures were potentially too contemporary to be considered to have historical value, residing on the edge of being 'significant'. In designating some areas of the site, including the AWRE facility, for non-intervention, and others for intensive restoration, the National Trust effectively established a network of boundaries and edges at the site. In the years following this decision, the National Trust has worked with the unpredictability of nature and, concurrently, the varying degrees of uncertainty generated by the experiment with the philosophy of non-intervention. In the former grazing marshes on the inland side of the spit, intensive intervention has occurred through conservation management work to enhance habitats, following a four-year Future for Wildlife project funded by the European Union's LIFE + Nature programme (National Trust and RSPB 2014). Between 2010 and 2014, a total of 2.5 kilometres of new ditches were dug to develop new habitat and move water around the site (National Trust and RSPB 2014, 3). To revitalise the coastal marshes that had been levelled for the use of military aircraft in 1913, and subsequently for agricultural purposes, three hectares of new saline coastal lagoons were created, with a further three hectares restored with a new system of pools, water controls, pumps and sluices in order to keep sustainable food supplies for breeding and migratory birds (National Trust and RSPB 2014, 4–5). This 'fixing' of nature is both spatial and temporal, and could be seen as a means to correct what had taken place in the past.

The National Trust finds itself at a crossroads, 25 years after acquisition of the site, as it reassesses how to move forward and develop a joint conservation management plan that encompasses both natural and cultural heritage. During those 25 years, however, the production of new forms of heritage has been occurring at the interstices – or at the edges – of official management frameworks and practices: the AWRE structures have gained more value as their historic significance has been recognised, most recently through granting of Scheduled Monument status in 2014; birds and other living beings have adopted the AWRE structures for nesting (see Figure 25.6); and new records of threatened features on the coast have been uploaded by the Coastal and Intertidal Zone Archaeological Network (CITiZAN) (see Bartolini and DeSilvey 2020a). These are just some examples that highlight how the entanglement of naturecultures at Orford Ness involves negotiation of fuzzy boundaries where fauna and flora share the same spaces as cultural heritage.

In the midst of conversations about how to manage the future of Orford Ness, the philosophy of non-intervention has enhanced relevance in relation to the impending threat of climate change, and the need to explore new ways of 'living with change' (DeSilvey 2017; Heathcote et al. 2017, 97; DeSilvey and Harrison 2020; see further discussion in Chapter 23). Part of the responsibility of heritage organisations is 'to understand what future changes we might expect' (Heathcote et al. 2017, 89). In the

Figure 25.6 Bird's nest in decayed AWRE building (photograph by Nadia Bartolini).

current conjuncture, what is anticipated is accelerated climate change and the intensification of forces that are beyond human control (as mentioned in Chapter 24). On the coast at Orford Ness, these forces are particularly acute, where disturbance gradually shapes the landscape, and ruderal processes take hold. The philosophy of non-intervention suggests new possibilities for appreciating heritage in the midst of mutability, and for caring without conserving in aspic (DeSilvey 2017). As non-human agency – in the form of sea level rise and intensified storm activity – alters our coastal landscapes, humans will gradually need to react to change, and develop heritage values amid transformation.

Conclusion

In this chapter, I have focused on how Donna Haraway's (2004; 2008) non-dualistic notion of 'naturecultures' can be understood and applied through reference to the spatial and temporal fixes that occur in transitional landscapes across three different sites, in Portugal and in the UK. I drew on David Harvey's conceptual framework of 'the fix' to reflect on the ways that boundaries are created and maintained through specific management decisions (see Harvey 2001a). The connections between the three field-work sites in the UK and Portugal were explored by using spatial themes: marking territories, carving paths and defining edges. While each site was spatially categorised, it is not impossible to imagine shifting one spatial metaphor to another site. Indeed, as each of these fieldwork sites are transitional, and therefore unfixed, so too are the processes that are taking place at each site. Application of these spatial metaphors to analysis across the sites can introduce new ways of navigating complex heritage landscapes and suggest new future directions for heritage research and practice.

For instance, in the Côa Valley, I discussed how rewilding practices in the present work to mark territories that separate reintroduced horses in order to 'fix' certain problems. But if we consider how paths are carved into the Côa Valley, we obtain different perspectives on future possibilities for this landscape. The Grande Rota is an ancestral walking trail that links historical villages, and it passes through the Faia Brava rewilding reserve on its 200-kilometre journey from the Côa River spring (at Fóios, Sabugal) to the river mouth (at Vila Nova de Foz Côa) (see Bartolini and DeSilvey 2020b). The intersections between paths of the past and new paths created by the reintroduced horses in the present might suggest alternative future heritages for humans and non-humans. Alternatively, in Cornwall, I considered how the paths carved through the china clay landscape allow people to encounter and appreciate both the re-naturalised landscape and the industry's cultural legacies. However, the new garden village development at West Carclaze, which will introduce new homes and feature a heritage park with the Sky Tip as its centrepiece, is a formalised process of marking and fixing territories through residential zones, parks and leisure, and 'wild' areas – not unlike the 'edging' that takes place in the landscape at Orford Ness.

In this chapter, I specifically examined the attempts to temporally and spatially fix places as a means to cope with change and transformation. This resonates with the arguments made in Part II, Diversity, about the ways that biobanks 'slow' or 'freeze' time and the ways in which spatial containment works to preserve collected matter. However, in our research for this part, processes of fixing and containing were always partial and incomplete, and heritage management was continually challenged by the intersection of multiple processes and potentialities. By attempting to manage or control one area, other opposing forces (inadvertent or not) may intervene to produce tensions, and hence complicate desired future trajectories. Perhaps heritage management could benefit from embracing the concept of naturecultures, accepting the ways in which humans and non-humans collaborate and compete to generate 'lines of flight', and exploring the range of alternative future possibilities arising from them.

26

Sensitive chaos: Geopoetic flows and wildings in the edgelands

Antony Lyons

> *riverrun, past Eve and Adam's, from swerve of shore to bend of bay,*
> *brings us by a commodius vicus of recirculation back to Howth Castle*
> *and Environs.*
>
> *A way a lone a last a loved along the*
> > James Joyce, *first and last sentences from* Finnegans Wake *(1939)*

Introduction

The geographical settings for this essay are the three edgelands-in-flux described in Chapter 24. Through a creative lens, my core focus is on dynamics of flow and release in the context of transformation in natural/cultural heritage. In these sites, fluidity and change unfold across a spectrum of spatial scales and processes – including coastal reshaping, landform erosion, structural disintegration, and penetrative action of moulds and fungi, among other things. Flows also operate within processes of species evolution and the dynamics of invasiveness, mobility and disappearance. The myriad of lenses for observing the cultural constructs of landscape and place can include: landscape character, landscape art and aesthetics, historical enquiry, conservation planning and political ecology. Over recent decades, hybrid, process-based approaches of 'deep mapping' and 'geopoetics' have been brought to bear in landscape situations, as methods for conducting creative research and assembling knowledge (Magrane 2015; Springett 2015). Their adoption as part of contextual art-practice-based research (Sullivan 2009) can involve interweaving strands of the past in the speculative co-creation of futures and novel eco-social paradigms. As a creative practitioner, engaged in practice-as-research, I draw on these approaches for expression and sharing, via the production and co-production of assemblage works, embracing videosonics, intermedia installation, photography and writings. These activities emerge from extended immersive fieldwork and attunement, augmented by contextual artistic research and archival explorations of selected geographical areas, in dialogue with collaborators, interlocutors, scientists/ecologists and other workers. Co-creative productions distilled from these slow, deep encounters with ecologies of place can suggest and reveal some of the complex braidings and tensions inherent in nature–culture relationships and transformations. A feature of my approach is the crafting of situated deep-time and Anthropocenic readings of landscape transformation processes.[1] Thus, both the geological and geographical are introduced as essential ingredients in assembling imaginative 'geopoetic' laboratories of place-dynamics (Lyons 2019).

In this chapter, I employ a triptych of film-poems (produced for the Heritage Futures project) as contemplative mirrors to initiate reflection on some observed flows (or currents) within the three Transformation theme case study sites. From a geopoetic perspective, filmic methods expose contrasting light and shadow, in both technical and psychological senses. Juxtaposing the real and imaginary, the intuitive and the factual, I undertake a metaphorical watery journey, which is, simultaneously, a narrative record of an exploratory research journey – condensing, flowing, soaking-in, leaking-out. Specifically, in relation to the geopoetic, my approach resonates with the writings of the poet-philosophers Don McKay (2011), Kenneth White (2003) and Robert Frodeman (2003), and others, such as ethnologist Mairi McFadyen:

> As a cultural project, a geopoetic creative ethnology can inspire a radical process and re-engagement with a broader and deeper understanding of culture in this place, not by looking back and re-performing fixed heritage, but by generating new meanings.
>
> (McFadyen 2018, 13)

In the Côa Valley (north-east Portugal), we find prehistoric animal rock engravings sitting alongside, and infusing, active efforts aimed at species protection and 'rewilding'. At Orford Ness (Suffolk coast, UK), the geological deep-time pasts and futures of this ever-morphing shingle spit form a kind of meta-narrative frame within which more ephemeral narratives play out – including visitor strategies, conservation (or not?) of Cold War concrete laboratories and defiant efforts to defend a lighthouse from the encroaching, eroding sea. In this setting, there is also rewilding, although most of this is passive, occurring through natural succession and limitations on human action. Finally, in the Cornish 'claylands' (UK), there is an ebb and flow of vegetation and 'overburden'. For over 150 years, human industry has scraped away the living biological layers of plant and soil. Now, with the contraction of the mining industry, through both abandonment and planned 'restoration', there is the slow return of richly diverse ecological ground cover. This echo of the return of vegetation to post-ice-age landscapes, but here – and now – in Cornwall, there is an extra, novel boosting from introduced 'exotic' species.

Using film-as-method observations and water-derived metaphors and allegory, I address the braided themes of:

- heritage landscape change and adaptation as braided meshworks of flows
- multi-species entanglements and 'wildings' as hybrid (heritage) futures with novel, mutating ecologies, within a nature–culture continuum
- multi-temporalities and imaginative modes of place research, including deep-time and geopoetic perspectives.

The following section presents brief descriptions of three long-take 'videosonic poems' that were created during the fieldwork (see Figure 26.1).[2] They are contemplations of water (in the form of mist or fog) and of heritage-in-flux. In their absorption with 'time', there are resonances with Morton's (2017, 69) discussion of '"nowness", a shifting haunted region like evaporating mist, a region that can't be tied to a specific time-scale'. In the remainder of the essay, I go on to explore entangled aspects of the local heritage contexts, through the braiding of themes that resonate with the river journey as a metaphorical carrier.

Three videosonic poems: Spectral reflections in the mist

The first of the videosonic poems, *Sky Tip Circumstance*,[3] features a hill of waste material. The edited footage is a time-compressed version of a single continuous take, recorded – handheld – for over 30 minutes, from the shelter of my mobile studio/campervan. The circumstance was happenstance, serendipitous. The occasion presented itself after many visits, over the course of a year, to the environs of the 'Sky Tip' mound outside St Austell in Cornwall – the centre of a long-established industry of kaolin mining. Over time, this waste heap gradually inserted itself on my radar, partly due to its imposing visual presence, its distinctive pyramidal outline being clearly visible on the horizon when viewed from high ground over 20 miles away. Beyond the role it plays in helping to define the visual character of the local landscape, there are also strong personal and community attachments. For some, it is a marker of a lifetime of work 'winning the clay'; for others, a symbol of a proud Cornish identity to be emphasised by flying the flag bearing the white cross of Saint Piran at the summit; and for many young people of St Austell, it is a place of freedom, an in-between zone, a wilding space of escape.

Staying with the rubble (see Haraway 2016), the explorations at the Sky Tip carry echoes of time spent at another huge – and once white – artificial mound of rubble in southern England, namely the Neolithic Silbury Hill, near Avebury in Wiltshire, separated from the Sky Tip by hundreds of miles and in age by thousands of years. Silbury's form is more rounded now but its dimensions are very similar and – as at the Sky Tip – the 'positive' volume of the mound is partnered by the 'negative' void of an adjacent pit. At Silbury Hill, this void space is a sculpted depression – water-filled in wintertime – which has been speculated by some to form a vast pregnant female form (Dames 1992). In legend, King Sil is said to be buried deep in the mound, seated on a golden horse.[4] Numerous archaeological digs have shown no evidence of any burial, nor of treasure. In Cornwall, the flooded pit next to the Sky Tip might similarly be positioned as a site of speculation and fantasy. Aerial photography (see Figure 26.2a) reveals a cross-shaped earthwork emerging from the water, echoing, for me, the semi-submerged land-art earthwork *Spiral Jetty* by Robert Smithson, located in the Great Salt Lake in Utah, USA (see Figure 26.2b). In speculative mode, could the inspiration for the water-framed earthwork here at the Sky Tip be a reference to the symbolic cross frequently seen fluttering at the summit (see Figure 25.5)?

The second of the videosonic poems, *NebulousNess*,[5] similarly records mist rolling across another in-between 'limbo landscape'.[6] This was filmed, again for 30 minutes, at Orford Ness, and features a now defunct (but much contested) lighthouse, slowly appearing out of the sea mist, only to fade back into the white-out oblivion – a metaphorical ending that resonates with the impending fate of the physical lighthouse structure. The coast here is shifting, receding, and the Orfordness Lighthouse will almost certainly be removed – or completely transformed – by the action of coastal erosion or controlled demolition within the next year.

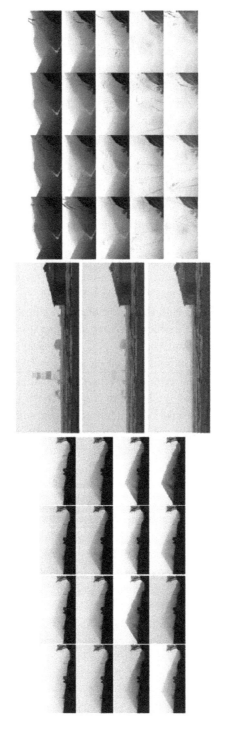

Figure 26.1 Video triptych by Antony Lyons (*Sky Tip Circumstance, NebulousNess, Côa Valley*), selected stills.

Figure 26.2a   Cornwall clay-mining pit with Sky Tip (lower right).
Google Earth historical imagery, 31 December 2005 (© Getmapping plc).

Figure 26.2b   Robert Smithson's sculpture, *Spiral Jetty* (photograph by
Jacob Rak CC BY-SA 4.0).

It's part of my life; it's part of my heritage … we're fighting tide, weather, you know, erosion, but we'll keep her here as long as we can keep her here. That's the main goal.

(Mark Thacker, lighthouse volunteer, BBC News 2018)

Coupled with a sonic mix recorded on 'the island', this vignette reflects on the slow shifting and drifting of the terrain, the materials and the anchors of identity or belonging. Particular historic structures or buildings become a blur and, instead, attention is drawn to phenomena of flow, emergence and change in this dynamic, liminal place. For me, this sense is enhanced by the knowledge that just offshore lies the extensive sunken land mass of Doggerland – the once human-inhabited, now drowned, world, which has lain submerged for nearly ten thousand years.

During fieldwork in the Côa Valley in eastern Portugal, storm conditions provided a fortuitous opportunity to similarly observe and record a 'limbo landscape' state, which is presented in the third film-poem, *Côa Valley*.[7] Not imminently threatened with destruction or oblivion, this rugged valley was, however, facing inundation by the planned Foz Côa Dam project in the early 1990s, and is now the site of a major experimental rewilding initiative. Once again using moving-image as an observation and reflection method, my aim of capturing the shifting nebulous valley conditions for a similarly 'long-take' was cut short by the mounting vigour of an intense storm – a visceral reminder of the powerful elemental watery forces that will continue to transform this landscape over the course of deep time.

While this triptych of recordings dwells primarily on elemental, and weather-related, forces of change and disappearance (and reappearance), there are nevertheless some fleeting presences of living ecologies. Trees and grasses bend and dance in the wind. Animals flit in and out of the frame. This multi-species theme of landscape transformation will be a thread in the fluid tapestry presented here.

Water and flow: A looping choreography

Working in the research context of the Transformation theme, I position water-flow as a metaphorical device for assembling interpretive responses to these morphing, eroding places that – for me – form an atmospheric and effective nexus. Neimanis (2014, 5) writes, from a hydro-feminist perspective, that, 'as a lively and unruly substance, water strains against the bounds of its geophysical containments – levees break, skies open, pipes burst – and this wilfulness pertains equally to water's capture by discourse'. Water also seems to be an appropriate (if elusive) metaphorical carrier due to its tangible centrality to the geographical situations of these three study sites (present in the form of river, sea and pit-pools), and its inherent qualities of mediation and in-between-ness (Illich 1986). Its relevance is also evident through the working of its agency at a range of scales, and finally through its manifold tangible and intangible interactions with 'heritage' (be it 'cultural', 'natural' or 'naturecultural').

Using this river-journey metaphor echoes Latour's use (in discussing artworks and the 'auras' of facsimiles) of 'a river's catchment, complete with its estuaries, its many tributaries, its dramatic rapids, its many meandering turns and, of course, also, its several hidden sources' (Latour and Lowe 2011, 4). Revisiting a theme of water and geopoetics, previously introduced in 'Sunless Waters of Forgetfulness' (Lyons 2019), I have approached these landscapes through the lens, and aesthetic perception, of what Schwenk (1996) terms 'Sensitive Chaos'.[8] Furthermore, my observations on multi-species entanglements involve 'staying with the trouble' (Haraway 2016), and resonate strongly with the animistic, more-than-human perspectives of Abram (1997). My exploratory journey also intersects with the diverse contexts of (practical) ecological rewilding and the philosophical 'dark ecology' of Morton (2016).

In creatively viewing landscape change over time, Ingold's (2010a; 2010b; 2015) ideas of woven, emergent 'meshworks' and 'lineology' have relevance. For Ingold (2013, 25), 'Artisans or practitioners who follow the flow are, in effect, itinerants, wayfarers, whose task is to enter the grain of the world's becoming and bend it to an evolving purpose.' For the creative fieldworker, or geopoetic practitioner, this journey necessarily embraces both embodied site-specific research and imaginative, intuitive dream-logic excursions, involving juxtaposition, challenge and constructive critique: 'Like Beuys' social sculpture, as creative fieldworkers, "we make the field, but the field also makes us", creating "new mental cartography"' (McFadyen, 2018, 11, quoting Kenneth White).

In my fieldwork-based explorations and imaginative assemblages, there is a concatenation of seeking, gathering, editing (film and sound) and public sharing; each stage is imbued with its own rhythms, pattern-awareness and expression. In poetry – as in landscape change – there are slow, long rhythms, with different frequencies of change in every setting – everywhere filled with ambiguities, hidden presences, softer reflections:

Everything washes away
Disappears in the mist (of time)
Vorticity, spirality, circularity

Water and vegetation act in concert
– both powered by the sun – shaping and
re-shaping this land.
Water is ephemerality, transience, spectral
Time-frames: in geological time, the continents 'drift'
The coastal edges 'pulse', tides.
Human insignificance. Not in relation to an all-powerful god,
but in the face of universal, planetary processes.
Anthropocene?

(text from the Limbo Landscape Lab exhibition, 2018,
Antony Lyons)

Riverrun

The flow here is through a terrain of the imagination, although it intersects with some situated practices and principles of heritage landscape
management and protection. Like the concept of 'landscape', heritage
is a human intervention or construct, a cultural formulation by groups
or individuals, or one fabricated in relation to other species. When we
move beyond heritage as a commodity, or even an industry, we begin to
enter the fuzzy and friable territory of an all-pervasive culture and 'really
deep ecology' (Morton 2009), and of being part of the 'nature–culture
continuum' (Massumi 2002). In this chapter, I regard heritage not as
legacy or stasis, but essentially as being in 'flow' (as a boat/vessel/ark is
in the flow). The legacy of change; the legacy *is* the change; 'rust never
sleeps'. Weaving geopoetics and geomorphology, each stage of this poetic
water cycle is a nexus point of consilience and connotations. Addressing
heritage (time-based natureculture), the narrative journey is broadly linear, yet the channels converge, bifurcate and intertwine.

In the cloud: Atmospherics and aesthetics of mist

These kinds of natural phenomena, like fog, like mist, which render
the environment and one's ability to see it almost impossible, have
always interested me greatly.

(Sebald 2010, 82)

The aforementioned three anchoring moving-image works are mist-
laden sequences. Mist has connotations of mysteriousness (and thus the

sacred, spiritual, spectral); of disappearance, transience, dispersion. The mood, or atmospherics, may also be one of fear and miasma. Mist is neutral, stoic and sparse; but miasma is more brooding and threatening, darker. It suggests a kind of descent – a 'dark ecology' (Morton 2016), or the elegiac declensionism of the Dark Mountain Project (www. dark-mountain.net). Through this glass darkly, I dwell on the woven meshes of relationships between topics such as (re)wilding, sanctuary and evolving growth. Increasingly, the dynamics of material metamorphosis and biological cycling and regeneration are seen as an ongoing continuum. The ex-military site of Orford Ness represents 'the first time the National Trust consciously placed as much emphasis on atmosphere and association, and it's also the first time they said let's just let the buildings fall down … let them crumble over time …' (Woodward 2002, 223). The 'continued ruination' of some of the structures at Orford Ness was explored in depth by DeSilvey (2017) as a potential model for a more porous and process-based heritage practice.

My triptych of films exhibits a post-human ambience – elemental and dark, embracing feral-ness and ongoingness. In the Cornish piece (*Sky Tip Circumstance*), the composition within the frame includes a lone leafless tree, buffeted by the wind – a scene reminiscent of the perennial (instructed)[9] scenography of the theatrical staging of Samuel Beckett's *Waiting for Godot*. Cloud, mist and fog bring us humans into more intimate connection with visceral moistness. Enveloped in the mist, there can appear to be a suspension of flow, and time also, awaiting the vectors of rains and streams, the portents of future floods. These nebulous meteorological states are preludes to the flows and torrents that follow on – washing and sculpting the landforms as well as human and animal structures. All that is solid melts into water.

Rainfall: Eroding, dissolving, transforming

In the third film-poem of the tryptych (*Côa Valley*), as cloud slowly envelops the Côa River valley, the accompanying torrents of rainwater are palpable. Through watching – and listening – the viewer is encountering some of the flows that have contributed to the formation of this valley. The recording location is a promontory on the route of the 'Biologists' Track', a trail once used by shepherds bringing their herds to these steep valley sides. Abandoned for decades, more recently biologists and wildlife tourists have begun to use the trail for monitoring and birdwatching. It crosses an area that was purchased by Associação Transumância e Natureza (ATN) in 2012, as part of an extension of the private Faia

Brava Nature Reserve (the nucleus of a now much larger intentional rewilding zone). Here we are at the confluence of participating erosional stormwater flows, river channels, old pastoral-shepherding pathways and new interventionist 're-naturing'. In the mesh of activity, there is a blurring between the cultural and natural realms. In *The Spell of the Sensuous*, anthropologist–magician David Abram (1997, 32) speculates that 'despite all the mechanical artifacts that now surround us, the world in which we find ourselves before we set out to calculate and measure is not an inert or mechanical object, but a living field, an open and dynamic landscape subject to its own moods and metamorphoses'.

In an echo of this, the situation in Cornwall – at the eroding Sky Tip – braids together landscape character, waste management, stormwaters, urbanisation, trespassing, invasive species and much more. In this dynamic mining area, 'emotional reference points may be forced to change several times, leading to disconnection, disorientation, a sense of loss and hopelessness' (Whitbread-Abrutat 2018, n.p.). Evidence from aerial and satellite photography reveals the progressive development of storm-related deep gullies in the sides of this mountain of micaceous sand – sharp furrows like the *sastrugi*[10] of the polar regions or those of the Loess Plateau of China (see Figure 26.3). Wrinkles in the physical landscape … and in time.

The 'heritage question' here is also very tangled. A high proportion of the local terrain is fenced off and festooned with a plethora of 'Not a play area' signage (see Figure 26.4). However, there exists a widespread informal culture of gaining access – of assuming (or reasserting) rights of access, and dissolving or eroding the land-use boundaries. These *are*, in actuality, play areas. And it was all once farmland, not very long ago.

On the mound of the Sky Tip, for this subculture of access/trespass and transgressiveness, the erosional features add to the land's attraction as an adventurous play zone. In contrast, to develop a new 'garden village' around the base of the mound, the mining company (and partners in the housing scheme), need to portray the hill as having a manageable stability risk, and to emphasise that the feature will remain out of bounds. Perpetually?[11] An environmental impact assessment for an earlier version of the development plans stated that management 'through inspection, monitoring and maintenance by the responsible party, together with any mitigation identified through future stability assessments, will reduce the potential impact from global and/or local slope stability. Access to the Great Treverbyn Tip[12] will be restricted' (Savills 2014, 45).

On Orford Ness, despite the heavy – and dramatic – visual presence of some of the monumental concrete structures (and the congruent heaviness of their histories and resonances), the overall human imprint is

Figure 26.3 Letterpress printing plate for the Limbo Landscape Lab exhibition poster, highlighting the furrows in the Sky Tip mound (photograph by Antony Lyons).

Figure 26.4 'Stay out'/'Not a play area' signs, Cornwall (photographs by Antony Lyons).

relatively light-touch and will, in time, crumble and dissolve away. Under the impact of weathering, the immense concrete structures are slowly transforming, as evidenced by the formation of calcium carbonate stalactites and stalagmites (Figure 26.5). The concrete Cold War monuments are, in effect, dissolving and flowing; slowly metamorphosing; a form of

Figure 26.5 Stalactites on Orford Ness (photograph by Antony Lyons).

'leakage': 'Or in a word, things leak, forever discharging through the surfaces that form temporarily around them' (Ingold 2010b, 4).

> FUNGAL FUTURES
> Fungus and bracken heal the wounds
> Re-covery …
> Fungus and bacteria re-create the soil
> The soil scraped away (to where?)
> Scraped away to win the clay
> There is no play in the clay
> 'THIS IS NOT A PLAY AREA'
> This is a clay area
> Fungus is a bogeyman
> Fungie is our friend
> 'Plants make up about 80% of all
> biomass on Earth. Bacteria comes in second
> at 13% and fungus is third at just 2%'
>   (text from the Limbo Landscape Lab exhibition, 2018,
>   Antony Lyons)

Marshlands: Enmeshments, entanglements

Referring to Deleuze and Guattari's 'rhizome' networks, Ingold (2010b, 12) writes: 'Personally, I prefer the image of the fungal mycelium … what is crucial is that we start from the fluid character of the life process, wherein boundaries are sustained only thanks to the flow of materials across them.' In the bog and the mire, we encounter the slow fertility (and carbon-capture) of multi-species life forms. Haraway (2016, 11) posits a new paradigm of 'kinship' for 'multi-critter humans … manifold forms and manifold names … in all the airs, waters and places of the earth', and suggests that 'we require each other in unexpected collaborations and combinations, in hot compost piles', 'recuperating Terra's pluriverse … not "post-human" but "com-post"'. In *Walden*, Thoreau (1960, 119) asked, 'Am I not partly leaves and vegetable mould myself?'

In more-than-human socio-naturecultural relations, there is no point-source nor 'main channel', but instead a multitude of mycelial entanglements and rhizomic relationships. Where does a river start/end and 'not river' begin? This part of the present river journey is also concerned with mosses, joining the other colonisers of scraped-bare denuded rock surfaces of the clay-mining areas, together, in the dampness, re-making life-supporting soil. 'When I speak of the entanglement of things I mean this literally and precisely: not a network of connections but a meshwork of interwoven lines of growth and movement' (Ingold 2010b, 3). Some of the significant more-than-human others we encounter in this entangled mesh include fungi and lichens, preparing the ground for the plant succession (and success?) to follow. In Cornwall, these complex land-transforming interactions and relationships – including with the human realm – were brought into focus in the study site, where I uncovered a discarded, glass-framed 'uncontrolled mosaic'[13] of mining-zone aerial photographs and incorporated this object into a site-specific installation – the Limbo Landscape Lab. Over time, behind the glass frame, moulds had invaded the photographic-paper surface, gradually obliterating the features and detail of the mining landscape, resulting in a new intricately textured co-created surface (see Figure 26.6).

Tsing (2015, 282) dwells on the 'overgrown verges of our blasted landscapes – the edges of capitalist discipline, scalability, and abandoned resource plantations. We can still catch the scent of the latent commons – and the elusive autumn aroma'. She explores fungal ecologies and forest histories to speculate on modes of cohabitation within multispecies landscapes. An alternative view is presented by Crist. For her, the recent explosion in attentiveness to the meshing of the social and the natural conceals the 'assimilation of the natural *by* the social' (Crist 2016, 28, emphasis in the original).

Figure 26.6 Photographed detail from mould-affected 'uncontrolled mosaic' of aerial photographs, Cornwall. Part of Limbo Landscape Lab installation (photograph by Antony Lyons).

> Co-creating with the non-human (anon.)
> A landscape of magma, granite, soil, vegetation (anon.)
> Farms, woodland, lanes, churches (anon.)
> A network of tin-mines (anon.)
> The clay pits and tips (anon.)
> The pilot and photographer that took the aerial photographs (anon.)
> The assembler of the images (anon.)
> The printer and framer (anon.)
> The creeping moulds (anon.)
> The observer – you (anon.)
>
> (text from the Limbo Landscape Lab exhibition, 2018, Antony Lyons)

Dams: Power, control, fixity and protest

> Nothing is weaker than water,
> But when it attacks something hard
> Or resistant, then nothing withstands it,
> And nothing will alter its way.
>
> Tao Teh Ching (via Bruce Lee)

In considering this nexus, or pattern, of water flows, there are the important heritage-related topics of power, control and decision-making – Whose heritage? Who decides? Which voices get heard? Which do not? What stories are not remembered? (See, for example, Harrison 2013a; 2015.) In this section, dams – real and metaphorical – signify hierarchical control: 'authority' versus 'grass roots'. In these landscapes, in different ways, there are ongoing tensions between the positions of top-down institutional 'experts' and the local or community outlook. Some of this has already been outlined in Chapter 24. The apparent progress in 'community participation' in these sites is inevitably slippery, messy and tangled. And little is done to address an 'elephant in the room', which is the disparity of positions of power and land ownership in such dialogues. In *Ways of Seeing*, John Berger (1972, 87) suggests that the way we view landscapes is 'ultimately determined by [new] attitudes to property and exchange'. There are issues too around the human desire to hold on, 'fix' or stabilise, as explored in Chapter 25. Fixity is a continuation (of status quo), and, in one sense, this continuation can be regarded as 'sustainability'. At play also, along with the materiality – and transformation – of things, places, landscapes, there are the meanings we impart, both tangible and intangible.

A recent report (Rivers without Boundaries 2019, 6, 78) found that 'despite the drastic decrease in hydropower development in recent years, the number of conflicts between water infrastructure and World Heritage values has been steadily increasing', and 'a recurring characteristic of hydroelectric dam projects has been the absence of processes for free, prior and informed consultation and consent among indigenous peoples and other traditional communities'. In 2001 and 2003, I spent time in the valley of the Guadiana River in southern Portugal, before and after it was flooded by the huge – and controversial – Alqueva Dam[14] project. My main focus was the impact on the unique ecology of the *montado* cork-oak forest habitat, which includes the critically endangered Iberian lynx. In 2011, as artist-in-residence at the Grand Canyon (USA), I again found myself in a close encounter with a dammed (or damned?) landscape – that of the Colorado River, whose waters no longer reach the once fertile delta region in Mexico, evocatively described by Aldo Leopold nearly a century ago. In the video-essay *No Concept*,[15] based on these two riverine encounters, I contemplated the changes, displacements and sense of loss in the 'post dam-nation era',[16] and the entanglements of landscape terrains with human and non-human ecologies. This has a bearing on one of our study sites. The valley of the Côa River was facing inundation by the planned Foz Côa Dam project in the early 1990s. EDP, the Portuguese electricity-generating company began work on a 100-metre-high dam across a gorge close to the

Figure 26.7 Foz Côa Dam protest, 1995 (photograph by Teresa Silva).

mouth of the river. After four years, the project was abandoned, due to the protest campaign to save and protect the very significant Palaeolithic rock-art engravings found in the gorge (see Figure 26.7). The 1995 rallying cry (derived from a song by the hip-hop group Black Company) was 'The engravings don't know how to swim!' ('As gravuras não sabem nadar!'). The Portuguese president, Mário Soares, admitted that the rock engravings of the region 'really do not know how to swim', marking the turning of the tide against the plan to submerge this important cultural heritage site – subsequently classified as a UNESCO World Heritage Site.

White waters: Turbulence, oppositions and conflict resolutions

> 'Now I am become death, the destroyer of worlds' as Oppenheimer quoted Krishna in the Bhagavad Gita, is a phrase that has real resonance in the dereliction of Orford Ness, as Sebald discovered, and more so when one discovers the use of the ruins Sebald reflected on.
> Duncan Kent, 2018 (National Trust officer, formerly based at Orford Ness)

Within the white-water rapids of rivers, we find the turbulent flows of oppositional forces. Rock meets water; flows are disrupted, broken up and reconstituted. In these study sites, I have become interested in some contested or antagonistic practices and aspirations, involving both tangible and intangible heritage.

War, conflict and opposition are foregrounded at Orford Ness. Here, the social and cultural milieux confront the geological. 'Blue Danube' meets 'Red Beard'.[17] The history of the place is deeply entwined in the making and testing of weapons of war. There is a lot of attention (professional and public) paid to the preservation and study of military–industrial heritage. However, there is also a fascination with a unique landscape aesthetic that some describe as 'post-apocalyptic', and a place where some visitors feel a therapeutic quality of escape into a (temporary) refuge of 'otherworldliness'. In this landscape of flint (shingle) and steel (debris), there is little escape from resonances and reminders of destructive impulses and warfare (including the shadow of nuclear war). The site is littered with bomb craters, rusting mangled metal, razor wire, melted glass and signs warning of 'unexploded ordnance'. The visitor exhibition features an empty atomic bomb casing. The vegetation itself echoes this violent history, with the common occurrence of rosebay willowherb (also known as 'bomb-weed' or 'fire-weed'), a typical first coloniser of bomb sites (see also Chapter 24). Characterised by this particular sense of drama and atmosphere, Orford Ness plays a role as a 'dark tourism' destination, often eliciting comparisons to another famous 'restricted area' – 'the Zone' in Andrei Tarkovsky's influential 1979 film, *Stalker*. On Orford Ness, oppositions come to the fore in relation to public access, heritage management and coastal 'defence' strategies. For an interval of nearly 20 years, the ex-military 'zone' was unguarded, and there was unfettered access by local walkers, scrap-metal salvagers, fishermen, 'vandals' and so on (Heazell 2010). Acquisition by the National Trust in 1993 brought an end to this free-for-all. Antagonistic relationships have especially come into focus in relation to the aforementioned lighthouse (DeSilvey 2017). There remains, today, a lack of consensus on the way forward in dealing with the messy entanglement of physical flows, human attachments, heritage considerations and future visions. The action of water will be the ultimate arbiter.

Intangible heritage can often have socio-therapeutic value, in the sense of transformative mediation and conflict resolution. In the visits to the Portugal study site, I heard of a local tradition of 'duelling songs'. The Portuguese vernacular 'song-duel' style (*cantigas ao desafio*) is something that I first encountered as part of creative research in the north of the country in 2013. This tradition of improvised singing intrigued me then and I was fascinated to hear of the possible survival of a variant in the Côa villages, for example in Cidadelhe, one of the villages adjacent to the Faia Brava protected (rewilding) area. After the first field visit, I was keen to encounter and experience a 'song-duel', so during follow-up fieldwork,[18]

I asked one of our local research assistants to explore the staging of such a happening or performance. However, it seems that this was never a strong tradition in this locality and it has now waned completely. The few remaining musicians-singers no longer engage in the antagonistic song-duel, but they did share an improvised *fado* tradition with us. The playful (and mocking) song-duel tradition could be viewed as 'liminoid' activity. According to Turner (1982, 54–5), such forms of ludic or play rituals can be used 'to "cool" those "hot" from the warpath' and 'are often parts of social critiques or even revolutionary manifestos … exposing the injustices, inefficiencies, and immoralities of the mainstream economic and political structures and organizations'.

Not many miles from Orford Ness (in the rural fenlands of Cambridgeshire and in urban Peterborough), Bakewell et al. (2019) describe the staging of a theatrical, comedic storytelling form of collective conflict resolution, dealing with antagonisms around water management and urban–rural tensions. Stories (or 'cases') were presented by a variety of local community and organisational representatives. The inspiration for this, and the key structural components, were derived from study of an active tradition in Sardinia called *La Rasgioni* (The Reasons), where, through the scenography of a ritualised 'court', the aim was 'to develop "polyphonic narratives"' and 'bring together different types of knowledge, facilitate social learning … to preserve community cohesion and to reinforce local relationships by co-designing the resolution to a conflict' (Marino 2014, 71). In the emphasis on 'subversion, comedy and satire' and 'challenging current social (often hierarchical) dynamics', this appears to share some commonality with the duelling songs as a means of publicly airing private grievances, resolving conflict and enabling 'unheard voices to be listened to' (Bakewell et al. 2019, 81).

> Refuge/Refugia/Refugee
> Migrant, alien species
> Invasiveness, protection
> The claylands are a mosaic of refugia
> There are Monkey-Puzzle forests transplanted from Chile.
> There are Rhododendron forests from Iberia
> Fuchsia from the Caribbean
> Montbretia from the grasslands of southern Africa
> And Madagascar
> What is the colour of the future?
>   (text from the Limbo Landscape Lab exhibition, 2018,
>   Antony Lyons)

Channels and ox-bows: Flooding, spilling over, invading, sanctuary

For Heraclitus the 'same rivers' are made up of flows of 'different and different waters' which 'scatter and … gather … come together and flow away … approach and depart'.[19] The mainstream overflows and merges with the fertile edges. In flood conditions, there is heightened risk of destruction, but it coexists with benefits to soil fertility and nourishment (the River Nile being the example par excellence). Floods are crucial components of natural flow regimes and they are vital for maintaining a diversity of habitats. Here, imaginatively, non-human natures come centre frame, enabling expansion on the theme of 'invasiveness' and adventitious nature, touched on earlier. Like a river channel, the movement and flow of species is an ongoing struggle between simultaneous constant change and the resistivity to change; also, that between growth and collapse. Today, many landscapes of transformation, or transition, are to a large extent self-transforming, untended or 'released'. Into the vacuum and limbo-ness, there come flows of 'invasive', 'alien', 'non-native' species. Within such overflowings and migrations, climate change is part of the story-weave. For instance, the recent appearance of a processionary pine moth on Orford Ness (the first ever sighting in the UK) may herald an 'invasion' of this problematic and potentially dangerous species, currently widespread in southern Europe. Climate change is a likely contributory cause of its northern spread. Vegetation and soil regeneration are fundamental to ecosystem recovery and ecological healing in degraded and destroyed landscapes. In many cases, emergent conditions of novel/ hybrid ecosystems are likely to be more in evidence in ruderal (see Chapter 24) post-mining, post-agricultural and post-military settings. Invasiveness is a thorny issue and there are often divergent views. Despite recent leaps in understanding, the subtle currents of the vegetative world still elude us and human judgements of 'beneficial' and 'aggressively invasive' may be found lacking. Haraway (2016, 101) writes: 'One way to live and die well as mortal critters in the Chthulucene is to join forces to reconstitute refuges, to make possible partial and robust biological-cultural-political-technological recuperation and re-composition.'

Oxbow lakes (see Figure 26.8): on the face of it, these zones are 'out of the loop' (see also the reference to 'back loop' in Chapter 24), bypassed, maybe an anachronism. But on the flip side, they are refuges and sanctuaries. The former mining clay-pit pools in Cornwall also function as an (uncontrolled) mosaic of refuges and sanctuaries. As in the geopolitical and social human spheres, the difference between 'invasion' and 'sanctuary' is one of subjective viewpoint or perspective.

Figure 26.8 Mississippi River Meander Belt (detail of Sheet 4). From *Geological Investigation of the Alluvial Valley of the Lower Mississippi River* (Fisk 1944, Plate 22, Sheet 4).

While being guided around the shingle expanse of the Orford Ness site, I was informed of the intention to use chemical spraying to clear away the encroaching red valerian (*Centranthus ruber*), primarily because it is an invasive alien garden-escape plant and can displace the protected shingle ecology.[20] In my Orford Ness film-poem piece *NebulousNess*, a Chinese water deer appears in the frame (as do rabbits, hares and various birds). These deer, and some other 'exotic' species (such as the Reeves's muntjac), are escapees that have made their way here – some by swimming – and found refuge. And, in an echo of human refugees from war-torn lands, pheasants – which are extensively hunted on 'mainland' Britain – have also found their way on to the Ness, and have formed a breeding colony in this safe haven. As one of numerous China-related reverberations on Orford Ness, the Mandarin duck (*Aix galericulata*) is an interesting case. Brought to England from China in 1745, it is now regarded as an introduced non-native species. However, this is not the whole story. The species was already present in pre-glacial British fauna, evidence of which is found in the Pleistocene strata of nearby Norfolk (Harrison 1979, 277). Thompson (2014) examines such examples and challenges simplistic binary notions of 'native' and 'alien' as applied in a natural heritage context.

Delta and shore: Recursive space and time

The texture of the delta exhibits a complexity of bifurcations and confluences (see Figure 26.9): splitting, rejoining, braiding, recursiveness. Human (and more-than-human) evolution is increasingly found to have similar non-linear recombinant patterns. Places and organisms are both stable and shifting, or chaotic, depending on the scale of observation or the time frame (see Figure 26.10). Coastal zones are especially heterotopian.[21] The coastal shingle spit of Orford Ness exhibits a heritage of battling: against the sea ('holding the line' to protect the lighthouse, the marsh-grazing lands and the military complexes), and battles also to keep open the estuary shipping channel. Woodward (2002, 224) describes 'the wind whipping the grey sea on to the shore, flinging the shingle at the concrete walls, and oxidising the rusty coils of wire, jagged metal and snapped railway lines'. Orford Ness is a place with a constantly changing landform anatomy – shifting, drifting, migrating via longshore drift, undergoing a churn of simultaneous loss and creation. It is a place where 'processes' are laid bare; the slowly accumulating shingle waveforms are an echo of those dissipating on to the shore. As a coastal site,

Figure 26.9 The International Space Station Program. Madagascar delta. Astronaut photograph ISS008-E-19233 (detail). Photographed 25 March 2004 (courtesy of Earth Observations Laboratory, Johnson Space Center).

with sea and weather forces acting as the major agents of change, the sinuous fluidity of the form of the shingle spit is observable even within our human lifespans. In a single generation, major reshapings and disturbances occur. Accepting these changes involves more than simply 'letting go'. Instead, it is about seeking new ways to find coherence, and to slipstream, with change itself. Plant life, water flows, weather patterns, climate changes, and so on, all have unpredictable and unmanageable ways and impulses of their own.

The shingle mass will endlessly continue in its pattern of long-shore drift. The extensive 'reclaimed' marshlands will be transformed by rising sea level. Meanwhile, the plant communities that cling to the inhospitable surface of the slowly shifting ridges and waves of shingle are likely to outlive any human influence. Over geological time, the pulsating dance of transgressing seas and ice-age melting episodes will once more inundate this land mass – destined to share the fate of the drowned world of Doggerland, with its mammoth, elephant and horse bones, now lying offshore under the North Sea. Living with transformation on this morphing coast necessitates living with very

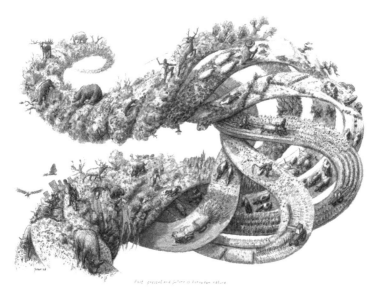

Figure 26.10 Past, present and future of European nature (courtesy of Jeroen Helmar/Ark Nature).

fluid hopes and visions for the longer future. Zooming out and zooming in reveals the fractal, recursive qualities of the waveforms of Orford Ness – reveals the Sensitive Chaos.

Ongoingness, returning: 'a commodius vicus of recirculation'

> Consequences overwhelm their causes, and this overflow has to be respected everywhere, in every domain.
>
> (Latour 2010, 484)

(Re)wilding and ecological restoration activities can be seen as forms of circling, or spiralling, back. They are seeking 'same, same, but different', hybridised, reimagined, with no real possibility of re-creation or replication of what went before. *Ongoingness* and *morphogenesis* can describe processes of shaping, over different scales of time and space. There is no loss, no decay, nor detritus, nor remnant, nor ruin; everything is *in* process and *is* a process.

I have touched on ways in which creative (geo)poetic perspectives may help to illuminate heritage landscape situations and play a part in future-speculations. In the Heritage Futures workshop described in Chapter 9, it was suggested that – for communicating perceptions of risk over hugely long timescales (in the particular case of radioactive waste storage/disposal), the best we can do is to pass on our advice to the next generation, and for this to be repeated across future generations, like a childhood game of 'whisper down the line'. In this whispering milieu, there is room for play. This *is* a play area. In the foregrounding of a fluid sense of 'play', rather than structured critique, there is some resonance with the 'entangled pluriverse' and 'compositionist' ideas of Latour (2010). These are not 'the days of miracle and wonder',[22] but we are experiencing 'the age of wonder at the disorders of nature' (Latour 2010, 481). No longer is it 'the time of avant-gardes or that of the Great Frontier, the time of manifestos' (Latour 2010, 472). In Latour's view, these have long passed. His 'compositionism' (posited as an alternative to 'critique' and even as a successor to 'nature') carries the 'smell of "compost" itself due to the active "de-composition" of many invisible agents' (Latour 2010, 473, 474). His compositionists believe that 'there are enough ruins and that everything has to be reassembled piece by piece' (Latour 2010, 475). Out of these reflections on 'heritage', 'landscape' and 'ongoingness', I have extracted currents and flows that carry ideas of expanded connection and co-creation with more-than-human realms, welcoming the complexities of relationships with multi-species and material meshes – water, vegetation, animals. These are, of course, accompanied by some hard-to-classify – and always wilded – 'in-betweeners': viruses, lichens, slime-moulds, prions. Of the ex-military zone of Orford Ness, Woodward (2002, 224) writes that 'Half-buried by shingle, the labs seem half-man, half-Nature'. Hybridity emerges from the confluence of entanglement and temporality, and it is expressed in the form of novel concepts of nature and culture. Ruins are a form of morphing hybrid – in between the aggregate material (stone, sand, clay and so on) and the maintained, functional structure. The latter is ceaselessly becoming ruined and on a trajectory to returning to the 'same, same, but different' basic materials. A process of endless becoming.

Recent critical heritage perspectives have begun to reassess relationships between cultural and natural ecologies, and to provoke questioning of power dynamics, privilege and decision-making, critiquing protection/conservation practices (for example, Harrison 2013a; 2015; DeSilvey 2017). Hybridity is an essential quality of the watery zones of floodplains, deltas and salt marsh. Cross-pollinations, recombinant ecologies, graftings and fusings are also about the 'evolution' of novel ecosystems – those that are the result of deliberate or inadvertent human action. Such 'emerging ecosystems' are characterised by new species combinations and the potential for changes in ecosystem functioning. What might this offer for future visioning and 'future-making'? Perhaps increased embracing of elements of dark ecologies, contamination and the 'feral' – that is, fluxes and hybrids between domestication and control; wild and untamed; healing and restoration. Ingold (2010b, 3) writes that 'a focus on life-processes requires us to attend not to materiality as such but to the fluxes and flows of materials. We are obliged, as Deleuze and Guattari say, to follow these flows, tracing the paths of form-generation, wherever they may lead'. This echoes an exploration of pathways (past, present and future) in the previous chapter, in relation to these three heritage landscapes; or, as Heraclitus noted, *panta rhei* ('everything flows').

At the (non-)conclusion, I return – or recirculate – to the triptych of film-poems introduced at the start of this chapter. What I wish to highlight is a tension between presence and absence, 'a shadow play of presence and absence intertwined' (Morton 2017, 69). This tension does not exist solely within the landscapes and objects depicted, but manifests also through the ways in which the 'long-take' method allows the audience experience to be simultaneously present and distant. Alison Butler (2017, 187) describes how – in discussing this aspect of the work of American film-maker James Benning – 'impressions of immediacy and estrangement, proximity and distance, are combined in a work simultaneously "framed" as an art object and a view of the real world'. The idea of 'heritage' serves to frame the world for us, but this creates a separation – one that may be bridged through creative, intuitive journeys; journeys that loop around in a world of ongoingness. There is a logic, but it is the logic of the delta and whirlpool.

Notes

1. In May 2019, the Subcommission on Quaternary Stratigraphy Anthropocene Working Group formally proposed (to the International Commission on Stratigraphy) the establishment of the Anthropocene epoch in the geological timescale. It defined this new 'chronostratigraphic' epoch as 'the period of Earth's history during which humans have a decisive influence on the state, dynamics, and future of the Earth System'.
2. The terms 'long-take' and 'capture' are used in this chapter, despite implicit extractive connotations. This point finds some echoes in the chapter's reflections.
3. *Sky Tip Circumstance* (8 min., time-compressed), https://vimeo.com/267828721 (a co-creation with composer–guitarist Adrian Utley; originally screened in 2018 as part of the site-specific installation work, *Limbo Landscape Lab*).
4. This relates to a common folklore archetype of the 'King Under the Mountain' – a king, or hero, who slumbers, but will one day reappear to save his people.
5. *NebulousNess* (10 min., time-compressed), https://vimeo.com/243714198 (originally screened in 2019 as part of the site-specific installation work, *Sensitive Chaos*).
6. 'Limbo Landscape Lab' is the title of a creative project connected to Heritage Futures: https://heritage-futures.org/limbo-landscape-lab-wheal-martyn/.
7. *Côa Valley* (6 min. 30 sec., time-compressed), https://vimeo.com/378012906 (planned as part of a site-specific installation work).

8. The German Romantic writer Novalis called water 'Das Sensible Chaos' (The Sensitive Chaos), and Theodor Schwenk wrote a book of the same name. It was also the title of a site-specific intermedia installation by Antony Lyons at Orford Ness in 2019.
9. The instruction given by Samuel Beckett regarding the set of *Waiting for Godot* was: 'A country road. A tree. Evening.'
10. *Sastrugi* are sharp irregular ridges formed on a snow surface by wind erosion and deposition. They are found in polar regions and open sites such as frozen lakes in cold temperate settings, and were recorded by both Scott and Shackleton in Antarctica.
11. See also the discussion of 'fixity' – in relation to this site – in Chapter 25.
12. The official name of what is commonly known as the 'Sky Tip'.
13. Uncontrolled mosaic: a mosaic composed of uncorrected photographs, the details of which have been matched from print to print, without ground control or other orientation – accurate measurement and direction cannot be accomplished.
14. This project was primarily for water supply and waterside leisure/tourism development. The latter has not materialised in any significant way.
15. https://vimeo.com/51288400
16. A term from *Running Dry: A Journey from Source to Sea Down the Dying Colorado River*, by Jonathan Waterman (2010, 9).
17. Two of the code names of projects that were part of the secret UK nuclear weapons programme tested on Orford Ness (https://historicengland.org.uk/listing/the-list/list-entry/1416933). *Blue Danube Redux* is the title of a video-work component of The Sensitive Chaos installation by Antony Lyons (2019).
18. Conducted with Nadia Bartolini.
19. Heraclitus River Fragment B12.
20. UK and European designations for the site require it to be managed, to protect the unique habitat.
21. After Foucault, heterotopias are defined as sites that somehow mirror and at the same time distort, unsettle or invert other spaces (www.heterotopiastudies.com).
22. Songwriters: Forere Motlhohcloa/Paul Simon, 'The Boy in the Bubble', lyrics © Universal Music Publishing Group.

27
Signifying transformation

Caitlin DeSilvey, Nadia Bartolini and Antony Lyons

In all of the landscapes we explored for this project, we arrived as out-siders, trying to read unfamiliar places and spaces to understand their textures and trajectories. Although all three of us brought different per-spectives and methodologies to bear on the research, we shared an initial instinct to look for 'signs' in the landscape that would help to orient us towards the underlying practices and relationships that made each place unlike any other. This visual essay touches on the practices of significa-tion we observed in the landscapes we studied and their relation to past futures and future pasts. We try to share our initial impressions and our observations about who the signs were created by and intended for. The images and text also, however, index the kind of conversation and col-laboration that characterised our shared work on heritage transforma-tion. We did not always see eye to eye, but part of our research process involved trying to understand and articulate our different perspectives. This chapter shares the kind of musing and shared sense-making that usually gets smoothed out in the presentation of academic research. In the end, this commitment to ongoing conversation produced, we think, a richer and more nuanced body of knowledge than we might otherwise have generated.

Caitlin DeSilvey (CD): In *Journey to Portugal*, José Saramago (2013, 190) describes a visit to Cidadelhe, where he noticed a carving lodged in a lintel: 'A bird settled on the head of a winged angel, between animals that could be lions, dogs or wingless griffins.' When we looked at this carving on our first visit in 2015, the Associação Transumância e Natureza (ATN) rewilding coordinator saw lions and bears – symbols of the past (and future?) wild. I saw dogs, animal companions. It's not possible to know what the person who created the carving intended to signify, but what we see in the present says something about our particular sensibilities and desired futures.

Nadia Bartolini (NB): I had not noticed the lintel until it was pointed out to me. When I came upon that area, I was drawn by the open doorway, the darkness within. Part of me felt like I was trespassing, but the space was completely accessible. I was an outsider who wanted to find out what was inside, what secrets I could uncover.

Antony Lyons (AL): For me, this signifies a journey. Not the locally linked story of one of Saramago's other books, *The Elephant's Journey* (2010), but the flow and movement of objects and symbolism. It was speculated by Bárbara, our archaeologist interlocuter and collaborator, that this carved piece, and others to be found in the village, may have been trans-located from the nearby ruined castle – or 'citadel' – that gives the village its name. At one time, this location was a significant border outpost, and a place of authority and domination. We are here in the once-contested borderlands … but the focus of geopolitics moves on: people move on; animals move on.

NB: When I took this photo, I had spent the day filming Coastal and Inter-tidal Zone Archaeological Network (CITiZAN) archaeologists and trained volunteers, who were measuring and recording features on Orford Ness, in this case, the former coastguard cottage. I decided to step back from the action and noticed a spot where things had started to gather around a National Trust sign: a coat, bags, a water bottle and thermos mug, and an assemblage of materials found during the recording: Danger – Electricity.

CD: I like the way the faded 'No access' sign indexes a moment of anxiety about risk and potential liability. In this photograph, the 'unsafe structure' is surrounded by community archaeologists recording its dimensions, and its demise, albeit with permission. There are other transgressions in the photo as well – the ad hoc pile of artefacts at the base of the sign signi-fies the impulse to collect, to take objects out of context and to rearrange the archaeological deposits at the site, creating unofficial *ex-situ* collec-tions driven by curiosity.

AL: The assemblage is interesting. I'm thinking of preservation, and reflecting on the work of Memory of Mankind (MOM), and their engage-ment in deep-time preservation. Very little in this scene will survive intact (or even partially so) across the span of a single human genera-tion. Everything is on a journey; and some journeys are temporally short. Coastal wave action and other dismantling/recycling processes will migrate and morph these things into different forms and places. Possi-bly the 'Danger – Electricity' message may remain legible over a much longer time frame. As in the MOM archive in the Austrian salt mine, it is a ceramic 'message to the future'.

AL: What will survive? 'Nature' appears in many guises in this image (including twice as text), but the moss and lichen growth represent inexorable, slow processes and life forces that have no need for, and pay no heed to, human machinations. The logos here will become defunct as a multinational corporation gets 'taken over', or a governmental quango gets reorganised and rebranded (English Nature was replaced by a new body, Natural England, in 2006). 'Goonvean', however, is a place name that was borrowed by a company; these names often have cultural persistence even through disruptive times.

CD: For me, this rewilded sign says something interesting about the future natural heritage that failed to materialise as anticipated. The sign is a legacy of a 1990s English Nature restoration initiative, which set about 'putting back the wild heart of Cornwall' by replanting post-operational clay workings with certain heathland species. The motto under the Imerys logo is 'Back to nature'; most of the company's signs now carry the motto 'Transform to perform'. In this image, the agency of moss and moisture has overwritten a projection of happy heathland with an untamed alternative.

NB: Imerys, English Nature and Goonvean. Companies, projects and organisations. All working on/with landscapes, reworking them, shaping them. Amidst mining activities, restructuring hierarchies and project management timetabling, vegetation creeps on, oblivious to human concerns and categorisations.

AL: Paleolithic rock-art engraving. Ibex. Some speculate that these engravings may have been intended as signs. One local archaeologist–guide that I met surmised that the engravings could once have marked habitual river-watering locations for various animals hunted by humans. A kind of 'advert', or something akin to the hobo 'code' of scratchings and graffiti symbols left on buildings and fences by itinerant workers in the early twentieth-century US as guidance to avoid trouble, or to direct fellow travellers to generous homes and available food. Like all prehistoric rock art, answers to questions of intended meaning will forever remain as speculation.

CD: The ibex, with its distinctive backswept horns, looking through thousands of years along the same river valley. The impossibility of knowing what these animal figures signified intrigues me. Archaeologists leave their options open – this carving could have had some spiritual significance, or it could have been purely practical, like a Palaeolithic road sign: 'look here for these creatures'. Or maybe it marked the bounds of a hunting territory? Or indicated a ceremonial gathering space? The carving wears these speculations lightly, not particularly bothered by 'meaning'.

NB: When I was given a tour of some of the engravings by Bárbara, the archaeologist, I was always surprised to find figures in the markings. I only saw lines everywhere. Lines that I thought were 'natural' striations in the rocks themselves. But as the lines were traced by Bárbara, I would start to see the figures that I was meant to see. And then, like in a Rorschach test, I could only see the figure. Part of me just wanted to go back to not noticing the human imprint: I wanted to see an indiscriminate series of lines, jumbled together, so that I wouldn't be able to distinguish the human from the non-human, but only see the rock again.

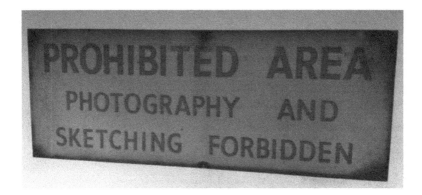

CD: These signs at Orford Ness clearly aren't meant to be heeded, yet they have been left casting out their redundant messages and they function to make people feel (in a rather limited way) like they are being risky and deviant just by being on the Ness. They work through a temporal disjuncture – that was then, this is now. It reminds me of the standard Orford Ness guide's comment: 'A visit to Orford Ness should be safe, but not necessarily comfortable.' The edge of danger is part of the allure of this place, carefully cultivated and just a little bit contrived.

AL: Based on perusal of online records, blogs etc., this 'Prohibited area' sign is one of the most photographed objects on Orford Ness. I'm guessing that there is an attraction to the sense (or echo) of transgressiveness. I find it interesting that, unlike other signs still scattered around the ex-military area, this particular one has been moved and mounted inside the small interpretation building. It is now a protected object – perhaps an acknowledgement that it encapsulates that edginess that is today one of the USPs (unique selling points) of this location.

NB: These remnant signs are some of my favourite things at Orford Ness. In my collection of photos at the site, about 30 per cent are of these signs. I think the reason I like them is that they are part of the 'affectual infrastructure' of Orford Ness: the signs already tell you something about the site and one cannot escape the signs when experiencing the landscape. They signal a different time: in the digital age it is hard to imagine a time when 'sketching' was potentially a prohibited activity. They also signal a different place: a dangerous, secretive environment bounded by military defences.

CD: Which way for the clay? This photo shows the tip of the Sky Tip and the trail signage in 2014, before we began our research. I think what drew me to this image at the time was the rather obvious framing of different 'directions' that the clay country might take – towards the industrial heritage repackaging represented by the Wheal Martyn Museum (now the Wheal Martyn Clay Works) or the redemptive restoration oasis that is the Eden Project. As the project ends, the distinction between these destinations seems less clear. The 'garden village' development emerging around the Sky Tip contains elements of both possible futures, and others.

NB: Caitlin highlights the different destinations that clay pasts and futures can take. The museum reinterpretation and restored clay pit theme park are located in opposite directions, with the ubiquitous, inscrutable Sky Tip set squarely in the middle. The image posits an interesting geographical disposition, as if time is severed in/from space, a notion that Henri Bergson (2007 [1888]) sought to explore when conceptualising the term 'multiplicities' – not as juxtapositions, but as sequences in duration. The clay landscape demonstrates how multiplicities of pasts and futures balance on the hinge of the present.

AL: I have spent many hours walking the land around this hill of mining waste – the Sky Tip, or more formally known as the Great Treverbyn Tip. The tip, and the land around, is a restricted area, fenced off and festooned with 'Keep Out' signage. The intention of the authorities is that everyone will stick to the designated paths and trails. But the Sky Tip has a magnetic attraction: it invites people towards it and, frequently, on to its slopes. For me, this photo conjures up the coexistence of many 'cultures' that can occupy a space, a place. Like the largely uncontrolled vegetation seen in the image, the future of human–land–place relationship here is uncontrollable, unknowable.

NB: The Côa Museum and Archaeological Park is located in the town of Vila Nova de Foz Côa. As we were walking along the streets of the town, we saw a number of depictions of the animal engravings: mosaic designs, and this painted figure on the side of a residential apartment block and above public toilet facilities. While one can visit the original engravings *in situ*, representations of these animal images can be found everywhere in the area. They are so common that they become an unnoticed part of everyday life, juxtaposed amidst sleeping dogs, decorative plants and drying laundry.

AL: A representation of a Palaeolithic engraving from the nearby Côa River gorge, very similar to the earlier photograph of the ibex. But underneath is something functional, practical, quotidian – the public toilets. Of course, the rock carving outlines have become a brand – on merchandise, billboards, tourist leaflets etc. The rock-art 'attraction' is bringing a welcome economic boost, after decades of decline and depopulation. The balance between turning the zone into a 'theme park' and maintaining a sensitive stewardship is tricky and much contested. Another resonant balancing act is seen in some of the towns and villages – between interventions of modernist architecture (as in the photo) and the traditional vernacular style.

CD: For me the punctum in this image is the pillowcase or cot sheet billowing out from the balcony. The swell of the fabric is echoed in the swell of the hind end of the carved ibex in an interesting way. But mostly it seems to index the very simple fact of inhabitation – the living alongside animal others and representations of animal others that has characterised life in this landscape for millennia. These images are now represented to market the town, but are also, as Nadia says, utterly ordinary.

AL: A juxtaposition of arrows. For me, these signify flows – of people along the very restricted and defined pathways of the Orford Ness site; and the water flow of the Côa River in Portugal. The old granite bridge connects two villages, and this bridging point was important before the advent of widespread car ownership, which now facilitates the – much longer – journey by road. The confinement to the marked paths on Orford Ness is a cause of disconnection. The visitor is not allowed to interact with the essential materials of the place – shingle, rusty metal remains, ruderal vegetation, Cold War concrete artefacts. One set of arrows is about enabling free-flowing hydrodynamics; the other about control, confinement.

NB: Arrows signal the path to take. At Orford Ness, Harald demonstrates the strangeness of some of the wayward signs, when options suddenly present us with a choice of path. The arrows on the bridge in the Côa Valley in Portugal seem to point to the water. Are these stone arrows meant for humans? Did they have meaning for its architect? Perhaps their materialities signal meaning. It would be easier to redo the arrows on the Ness: change their direction, delete one arrow, add a new one. The bridge arrows seem more fixed, solid, requiring significant tools to dislodge.

CD: I remember standing on the bridge and wondering about the arrows, and the mason who carved these elements of the bridge to set together like giant Lego bricks. The sharp end of the arrow points upstream, and presumably was engineered so that the flowing water would split smoothly and run around the piers to flow downstream. But it seems an unusually thoughtful modification for such a simple structure and would have involved some additional effort to carve the point instead of a flat face. Is this a traditional regional bridge design or an innovation by a creative stoneworker? The Orford Ness arrows, on the other hand, appear to be created with spray-paint and a stencil, so some skill involved, but perhaps more in the maintenance than the initial making.

NB: When we first visited the China Clay History Society (CCHS), this framed photograph of a St Austell welcome sign was located on the floor, leaning against a wall in the map room. We drew it to the attention of the CCHS members, all of whom had worked in the china clay mining industry. It seems that this is a photograph of an actual road sign on which edited words were added to the original photograph. The edited sign was created as a 'protest' to literally re-inscribe the area's mining history and heritage, and it was included in the exhibition Metalliferous Mining in the St Austell Area that ran in March 2010 at Wheal Martyn Clay Works. Since we took this photo in 2015, this mounted copy of the edited sign image has been moved to an unknown location. If one day it is found, it will be left to someone in the future to reconstruct and interpret its story.

AL: The adaptation ('defacement'?) of this roadside sign – or the photo of the road sign – is in a style very different to the more usually encountered graffiti scrawl. The 'mining' overlay is very carefully applied. Precision work. This echoes the engineering and technical pride that exudes from the ex-miners, in person, and from their assemblage of archive records. For them, this industry has been a multigenerational feat of ingenuity, inventiveness and intense focus. Not the mere shopkeeping nor 'wheeling and dealing' of the marketplace. Also, although this is an 'entrance' sign to a town, it also has a flavour of those 'heritage place' road signs, which – for most travellers – merely emphasise what they are missing, as they race past.

CD: It is the 'overwriting' that makes this sign meaningful. The sign captures one way of framing a place, and the replacement of one word signifies a world of meaning about marginalisation, resistance, community pride and identity. There is also a Russian-doll nesting going on here, with each layer of representation suggesting a viewer with a slightly different orientation and intention – the person who took the photograph of the sign while it was *in situ* at the edge of St Austell; the person who edited the photograph of it as a prompt for critique; Nadia's photo of us looking at the sign; and finally, the reproduction of these images here, in an academic book.

CD: It was so hot in the Côa in August that we could only go out in the very early morning and in the evening after the sun went down. We stopped in the lengthening shadows to look at the landscape as it gradually shed the day's heat. I photographed Russ with little Leif strapped to him, looking at the umber glow of the stripped cork trunk. On a previous visit in 2015, we had come across the cork trees on the path from Algodres to Sabóia – as we left the village and entered the Faia Brava reserve the tiny, scrabbled fields and olive groves gradually gave way to scrubbier and wilder growth, but the cork trees persisted, still part of a land-based livelihood.

AL: The mark on the cork oak tree is purely functional, a marker of the year (2016?) in which the bark was stripped off. This knowledge needs to be passed on, remembered – but only for 9 to 12 years, as that is the usual harvesting cycle for the bark. These trees are fairly isolated examples in the Côa area. Further south, especially in Alentejo, they form a crucial part of the economics of the *montado* agro-sylvo-pastoral system, where they are interspersed with the holm oaks that provide food (acorns) for the gastronomically celebrated free-roaming Iberian black pigs.

NB: It's interesting reading Caitlin's description of the image she took, as I wasn't present during her visit. I saw other numbered trees in other similar-looking areas in the Côa. The markings are striking and, to me, they distinguished the trees individually: I would notice them more. In a way, they remind me of the schist and granite rocks in the valley that are 'marked' by carvings or red ochre paint; the rocks standing out from other unmarked rocks. It is difficult not to see human imprints on the landscape, the ways humans cannot help but engage with the land.

AL: The first image is one of a few different variations on a theme that can be seen throughout Cornwall's clay-mining area. I find it a curious warning and it indicates the existence of differing perspectives and expectations. A large proportion of the local land is fenced off and 'out of bounds'. However, there is a common culture of gaining access – of assuming rights of access. These *are*, in actuality, play areas. And it was all once farmland, not very long ago. The second warning sign is from Orford Ness: keep off; keep away. And like the previous image, once again an open palm. In a 'deep time' reflection, these remind me of the prehistoric handprints (often stencils) in blood-red ochre or charcoal that are found throughout the world, some dated to over 30,000 years ago. Today, we are familiar with the meaning of the diagonal-line warning (Don't!). We can but speculate on the meaning of the ancient handprints. Messages to the future? Markings associated with initiation, ritual or shamanism?

CD: You touch on an interesting ambiguity about these signs – in order for the warning to make sense, the area behind the sign has to be already perceived as a potential 'play area' of some sort – unbounded and unrestricted. As I understand it, English China Clays had a general policy of allowing public access, perhaps not officially but effectively turning a blind eye to all of the informal community uses of the post-operational lands. When Imerys took over, this began to change, partly because they took their liability seriously, not necessarily out of a desire to assert their ownership. Speaking to people who grew up in the area, they used these spaces all the time, for biking and playing and messing around. This is harder now. I love the resonance with the ochre hand (?) at Las Cabreias in the Côa, where Pedro brought us on our first visit.

NB: Antony points to a common (Westernised) culture of gaining access and of distinguishing where access is privatised. At our knowledge-exchange event in Cornwall, there was mention of the commons and how to bring land back to 'the people'. But if Imerys owns 98 per cent of the clay landscape (freehold surface and mineral rights), then what is the extent of the commons? At Orford Ness, access is challenged by having to cross the River Ore to get to it. In the Faia Brava reserve, where the red ochre painting is located, there are porous gates. Speculating on the red ochre painting, perhaps the paint has faded or bled out and we're missing part of the picture. Is it a human hand, or could it represent other more-than-human parts of the landscape, perhaps a tree trunk with roots reaching down?

28
Processing change

Caitlin DeSilvey, Nadia Bartolini and Antony Lyons

Concluding and carrying on

In this final chapter we return to the two core themes introduced in the first chapter (Chapter 24) in this part of the book – managing entanglement and apprehending landscape time – to draw out some of the resonances between our three empirical cases. In doing so, we explore the binding potential of key concepts, including 'ruderality' and alternative temporal modalities. We also acknowledge how our complementary perspectives allowed us to critically engage with the practices and processes at play at each site, and reflect on the implications of 'heritage in transformation' for heritage practice and scholarship going forward. Where appropriate, we open out connections to other parts in the book, tracing points of contact and coherence, as well as difference and divergence. In the spirit of cross-fertilisation, we offer a few initial insights here. In relation to the themes explored in Part II, Diversity, for example, we can see – despite a shared focus on animal diversity – a contrast between the contained conservation of specific species and materials and the embrace of emergent alignments of diverse species, places and processes. The focus of Part III, on profusion as a problem of perception (as much as a practical reality), maps onto the way in which transformation emerges in this section as a background state common to all landscapes, which is only perceived as an object of concern in certain contexts. In relation to Part IV, Uncertainty, reflections on the inherent unsustainability of long-term, deep-time preservation have particular salience in relation to the unstable and uncertain cultural ecologies that we have explored in this section.

Managing entanglements, tensions and transformations

One thing we became aware of early on in our research was the need for new conceptual language to better frame our understanding of what was happening at the sites we were studying. The available terms for describing and defining heritage places and spaces often did not seem able to adequately capture the complexity we encountered in the field. We also, as we carried out the research, became very conscious of the way in which our different methodological approaches revealed different avenues for reflection and knowledge production.

Chapter 25 homed in on David Harvey's idea of the spatial 'fix' to capture how places are territorialised and re-territorialised, made and unmade (see Harvey 2001a). We explored how such processes unsettle the common conception of heritage as a stable, fixed entity that persists in time. Rather, through a reworking of Deleuze and Guattari's (1987) 'lines of flight', we came to appreciate the ways that bottom-up initiatives create opportunities that provide a means to cope with changing land-scapes and changing identities – in effect, attempting a reconciliation with uncertain futures. Chapter 26 focused on connections between the study sites and – utilising a riverine metaphor – tuned in to tensions, relation-ships and processes that are always 'in flow'. With the anchor of a family of short-film pieces produced for the Heritage Futures project, Antony explored nature–culture braidings within the conceptual framework of a watershed, or catchment, nexus. He emphasised the enhanced dynamism of these landscapes and, in a nuanced way, challenged the tendencies of heritage management to contain, control and 'fix'. The concept of 'fixing' is seen to work in multiple ways, some of them in tension with each other.

One concept that we brought into the discussion in Chapter 24, and that we explore further here, is the concept of the 'ruderal'; this term has been in the background in the subsequent chapters, particularly in relation to the exploration of disturbance and ecosystem dynamics. The relevance of this concept in our work suggests that there is scope for what might be called 'ruderal heritage' research, which would be focused on ongoing instances of both destruction and renewal, destabilisation and resilience – receptive to the opportunities that emerge from disturbance and the asso-ciated 'arts of living on a damaged planet' (Tsing et al. 2017; also Haraway 2016). We have already explored how a focus on heritage process, rather than heritage preservation, involves a continual folding and fraying of imposed categories of natural and cultural heritage management. In the discussion below, we push this further, to consider how a ruderal heritage framing would allow us to further open up the possibilities of collaboration with the non-human and with forces beyond our control.

Ruderal thinking at the margins

Our three study sites are all characterised by significant historic 'disturbance', as a result of mining (Cornwall claylands), agriculture (Côa Valley) and military testing (Orford Ness). They are each also undergoing
transformation, as they shift away from these modes of use and occupation. In the clay country, past disturbance by industrial excavation has
created pockets of enhanced biodiversity, most noticeable where zones
have been allowed to revegetate on their own (see Figures 28.1a and
28.1b). As explored in Chapter 26, these zones abound with ubiquitous
post-disturbance 'ruderal' species – buddleia, bramble and bracken, for
example – but are also inhabited by escaped exotics, such as rhododendron. These 'pioneer' species are rapidly taking over the post-operational
lands, and their presence is the source of a mixed response – part appreciation, part exasperation. Rhododendron is 'the bane of our lives', mentioned one heritage site manager. But in the community consultation
carried out in 2008 in relation to development proposals, people often
described the unruly vegetation on the post-operational lands as part of
the character of the landscape, and something worthy of protection. One
resident of the area near West Carclaze commented, 'Keep this old clay
area green and scrubby and wild and open to the public' (ClayFutures
2009, 85).

The rhododendron and the buddleia are unlikely to merit protection
any time soon, but the clay country is also home to several rare species
designated and protected for their natural heritage value. In one case, the
act of 'protection' is far from straightforward, however. One ruderal bryo-
phyte (moss) species, the Western rustwort (*Marsupella profunda*) needs
disturbed and exposed substrates to survive; it is a pioneer that colonises
unshaded or lightly shaded clay and granitic rocks. In the 1990s, the moss
was identified in several sites in and around both dormant and active
pits, and some of these sites were subsequently protected with Site of
Special Scientific Interest (SSSI) and Special Area of Conservation (SAC)
designations. Because the necessary disturbance was absent, however,
the moss became shaded by encroaching gorse and bramble. The plants
are now largely extinct in the designated areas and the species has been
categorized as 'Vulnerable' on the International Union for Conservation
of Nature (IUCN) Red List (Hodgetts 2011). Natural England has identified 'refuge' sites for species translocation and entered into a collaboration with Imerys to help replicate the heavy industrial activity that will
maintain the unique ecological conditions required to maintain viable
populations (Callaghan 2014). In this paradoxical instance of ruderal
heritage in action, the conservation of natural heritage is only possible

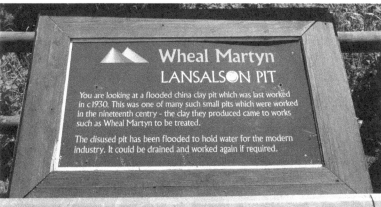

Figure 28.1a/b Lansalson Pit, its banks overgrown with ruderal species such as buddleia, rhododendron, bramble and bracken, and below it, the Lansalson Pit interpretation: 'it could be drained and worked again if required', at Wheal Martyn Clay Works (photographs by Nadia Bartolini).

through the 'periodic large-scale disturbance' brought about by extractive intervention (Callaghan 2014, 7).

In the Côa Valley, management of ruderal species – and analogue ruderal thinking – is central to both the rewilding effort and wider communities of interest. The local shepherds and farmers have a well-established tradition of seasonal burning, which they use as a management tool to encourage the growth and regeneration of forage. One business owner from a village adjacent to the reserve, interviewed in 2016, made the observation that fires are part of the 'memory and identity' of the area. As farming practices have been gradually withdrawn from the landscape, however, pioneer species such as broom have begun to grow in greater densities and – partly due to the high flammability of broom – fires have become more intense and destructive (occasionally threatening the remnant cork and olive trees, which can withstand moderate wildfires but may be killed by high-intensity blazes). On our first visit to the area in 2015, staff from Associação Transumância e Natureza (ATN) told us about the local perception of the unworked landscape as 'unclean' and dirty, and their concern about fire-setting by a shepherd in one of the villages. A few years prior to this, they had taken the shepherd to court for violating the new restrictions on fires in the Faia Brava Reserve (Leuvenink 2013, 20). As part of the rewilding of the area, ATN aims to disrupt the cycle of burning and the continual reversion to first-stage succession to allow woody tree species to become established and to eventually recreate a semi-forested landscape mosaic. The grazing and browsing of the horses and cattle is intended to keep the ruderal species in check and make the landscape less vulnerable to damaging fires, as other species gradually move in and the system gains resilience. Following years of conflict and disruption, local residents are now becoming more accepting of ATN's strategy, in part because some of these strategies have involved local residents witnessing the benefits of reduced fires (and in some cases participating in the management practices) (DeSilvey and Bartolini 2019). In this landscape, fire is both an expression of intangible cultural heritage and a contested ecological agent, managed by conflicting interests. But the conflict and disturbance has catalysed a tentative transition into a future state in which the entanglement of natural and cultural heritage becomes the basis for a new shared understanding of landscape dynamics.

On Orford Ness, we have been working with partners to understand how heritage is made (and unmade) in this unique environment. The Ness harbours many ruderal species, as the previous military disturbance and constantly shifting shingle provide the unstable substrates needed for their survival. Some of these species are considered to be invasive 'weeds', while others, such as the yellow-horned poppy (*Glaucium flavum*), are deemed to be 'native' and thus worthy of conservation – although the challenges here are not dissimilar to those posed by the management of the clay-country moss. Caitlin photographed a yellow-horned poppy on the beach crest south of the lighthouse in March 2012, and then six years later she came upon a poppy uprooted by a recent storm in more or less the same location, its roots exposed and the plant toppling down the beach crest. The toppled poppy could be seen as evidence of the destruction caused by accelerated, anthropogenic climate change, including sea level rise and increasing storm intensity. But this species is adapted to disturbance. It makes its home in the mobile shingle and also among the military ruins – around the edges of concrete bases, inside roofless structures and in crumbling foundations scattered with tossed shingle. For the poppy, like the moss species introduced above, disturbance is essential for its survival.

We can find a loose cultural analogue to the poppy in a derelict wooden police tower, which used to stand a few hundred yards south of the lighthouse. The tower was built in 1956 as an observation post for the Atomic Weapons Research Establishment (AWRE) security police, located inside a defensive perimeter fence. In a 2009 National Trust survey, the tower was still secure, but by 2012 its foundation was very close to the beach crest (see Figure 28.2). By the time of the first Coastal and Intertidal Zone Archaeological Network (CITiZAN) survey in 2015, it was gone; in a survey the following year, volunteers recorded a series of photographs of the foundation slab reduced to broken blocks of rubble (CITiZAN n.d.) (see Figure 28.3). We returned to the site with CITiZAN in March 2018, and all that was left was a fragment of concrete jutting

Figure 28.2   The remains of the police watchtower, visible in the distance on the beach crest (top left-hand corner) in 2012 (photograph by Caitlin DeSilvey).

Figure 28.3 CITiZAN-trained volunteers recording the remains of what was thought to be the base of the watchtower at Orford Ness in 2016 (photograph by Nadia Bartolini).

out of the steep beach face and a few other fragments scattered down the beach. The mood of the survey team was not mournful, but curious, forensic: the loss of the feature, in a sense, justified the labour spent surveying, measuring, documenting and recording (see also Bartolini and DeSilvey 2020a). It also became clear that only three years after the collapse of the tower, people no longer agreed on exactly where it had stood. One of the National Trust employees claimed that the feature recorded by CITiZAN was not the police tower base, but another eroding concrete foundation. We discussed the tower over breakfast in the Orford Ness bunkhouse, looking at old maps and photographs, comparing and considering. One of the CITIZAN staff shared a 1951 image she had found of a similar tower located north of the lighthouse, and posited that the tower in question was not built in 1956 but was relocated from the other site. Uncertainty, in this instance, created openings for dialogue and deliberation; history frayed and had to be woven back together. A lively dialogue about the past in place was generated out of disruption and erosion of evidence, in a collaborative process arguably more productive and generative than a passive encounter with the static tower as a piece of 'heritage'. Here, we found a heritage practice that was not trying to hold back change, but was working with it, and finding opportunities for engagement and (re)connection.

As well as a background condition of disturbance, we observed in our study sites a dynamic between intentional ecological restoration and emergent 'recovery'. Rewilding – or re-naturing – is being practised in varying degrees at all of the three locations, either through spontaneous re-naturalisation or deliberate reintroduction. For the managers and local people that we have been in contact with, there is a recognition that changes in practice will produce unpredictable 'new natures'. New natureculture environments are, of course, always in the process of emerging and becoming (Massey 2005). However, in the places we studied, we became aware of different, and sometimes conflicting, temporalities at play around these processes: some practices sought to accelerate ecological change while others sought to slow it down. One shepherd in the Côa Valley commented: 'Nature just takes over … I don't really understand why [ATN] are spending money to buy lands; I think that rewilding will just happen naturally' (quoted from DeSilvey and Bartolini 2019, 105). Here, the shepherd alludes to a process of 'natural' unmanaged rewilding, which plays out on a slower timescale than the one set by rewilding managers, who are intervening to produce the conditions necessary for the recovery of certain ecosystem functions and processes. We turn to the conceptualisation of time, and its speeds and scales, in the next section.

The surfaces and undercurrents of alternative temporalities

In Chapter 26, Antony used the metaphor of an oxbow lake to explore concepts of refuge, sanctuary and legacy. The formation of an oxbow lake also opens up an opportunity to think about the temporalities of the flows that exist in the process of its becoming. As faster-flowing water erodes the riverbank on the outside bend (concave banks), slower-flowing water deposits silt and sediment on the inside bend (convex banks). Over time, this process has the effect of modifying and closing the curves of the river channel, until eventually the water breaks through into a new channel. Having thus been cut off from the main water flow, the oxbow part of the river becomes a stand-alone lake. This oxbow lake can be a haven for new wildlife; however, it often dries up as water evaporates. The processes that exist in the oxbow lake formation include notions of 'slow' flow, 'fast' flow and time as an extended durational framework through which a variety of evolving actions physically change the environment – which in turn provides a sanctuary in which new natural habits may emerge. This simple 'natural' metaphor highlights the paradoxes of 'protection' and also the juxtapositions of 'fixity' and 'flow'. We develop these ideas further in relation to temporality by testing out three alternative temporal modalities – open time, wild time and drift time.

At the northern entrance to Blackpool Pit, a redundant china clay working pit, a broken sign hangs from the gate: 'This gate ... be closed ... time', it announces (the fragment reading 'must ... at all ... s' hangs askew) (see Figure 28.4). In actuality, of all of the sites we studied, it was in the clay landscape that we found time to be most radically 'open'. It is a place where multiple times exist in close proximity and where startling continuity gives way to radical discontinuity across the width of a hedge boundary (as in Figure 24.1).

Wheal Martyn Clay Works exists as an island of 'heritage time', where the past is presented for consumption and celebration – in this sense, perhaps, its temporality is one of 'closed time', in which the past is ostensibly no longer open to revision and reimagination. It is the only industrial site in the clay country designated as a Scheduled Monument, and also the only china-clay site acknowledged in the marketing for the UNESCO Cornish Mining World Heritage Site. The rest of the patchwork

Figure 28.4 Sign at Blackpool Pit, Cornwall, 2014 (photograph by Caitlin DeSilvey).

industrial landscape, with its inholdings of active industry, is still too unsettled to be labelled as heritage. The museum island is set in a sea of temporal flux: museum visitors are invited to walk to the edge of an active open pit to view the ongoing transformation of the landscape; across the valley lie fields bounded by ancient hedges (see Figure 24.1). Many other sites in the clay country lie in an extended post-operational limbo, where their fate remains open and unsecured – partly because of the industrial landowner's reluctance to designate areas for heritage or recreation because it would foreclose on the opportunity for them to bring them back into active production (thus 'sterilising' remaining kaolin deposits). One former Imerys employee recalled a case in which a flooded pit was offered to the community for use as a boating lake; a few years later, when the company needed to use the pit to store slurry, people were upset about the withdrawal of the recreational use. Now the company is careful to allow alternative use of post-operational lands only if they are certain that they will not need to reopen a site in the future.

The landscape poses a conundrum for local archaeologists and heritage managers. It is broadly acknowledged that the china clay industry 'eats its own heritage' through the destruction caused by ongoing extractive process, but an archaeological report from 2014 points out that post-extraction processes of restoration and reclamation, re-profiling and re-vegetating, can also lead to 'loss of historic landforms and the blurring or masking of historic landscape character' (Kirkham 2014, 149). 'There is a potential risk that authentic features of the modern and historic industry, with the particular historic, evidential, communal and aesthetic values attached to them, will be progressively erased' (Kirkham 2014, 149) – but the risk of this erasure is one that many local people are willing to accept if it means that the industry will continue to provide employment and maintain the viability of their communities.

The archaeological report goes on to articulate a further risk: 'The risk posed is that the physical evidence on which an appropriately detailed and comprehensive archaeological and historic record of an important modern industry should be based could vanish or be significantly damaged before it receives the attention which future archaeologists, historians and societies might require' (Kirkham 2014, 149). Who are these 'future archaeologists, historians and societies', and can we assume that values in the future will be the same as those in the present? What does 'preservation' mean in such a temporally scrambled landscape, where the possibility of upheaval is ever-present, and where elements of the past are continually overwritten and re-inscribed? There is an implicit recognition of this puzzle in the official report: 'The very large scale on which modern clay working is carried on poses evident problems for meaningful future "preservation" of a significant proportion of its key components' (Kirkham 2014, 149). The question of 'closed time' versus 'open time' remains unresolved.

The Côa Valley presents a slightly different kind of temporal riddle, with the deep past (indexed in the rock-art tradition, which begins in the Upper Palaeolithic twenty thousand years ago) set in relation to the deep future (and the long-term landscape transformation envisioned by the rewilding initiative). The rock art, with its 'universal value' ostensibly protected in perpetuity by its UNESCO World Heritage Site designation, provides imaginative fodder for radical transformation, which may or may not impact on the context in which the carvings are set. In this place, past traces are reactivated to support the creation of desired futures. While the conservationists responsible for managing the Faia Brava reserve take care to explain that the Palaeolithic carvings do not provide a literal reference for their reintroduction plans, they value the carvings as a 'portrait of what people saw and valued' in the ancient landscape, and also a record of the way that humans and animals have coexisted in the Côa for thousands of years. Their interest is not in the rock art in isolation, but in, as one manager commented, the 'landscape behind the engravings'. For them, the rewilding initiative is not about reaching some arbitrary baseline of pre-historic wildness, but about the process of enabling nature to 'become wild' again, in the context of the present. It is also about enabling local and visiting populations to rekindle a connection with non-human animals and open landscapes, as an alternative to perceiving land as an individually owned asset that must be worked to be economically and socially productive.

In the Côa, the temporal framework provided by linear, chronological time fails to explain patterns of recurrence and reinvention expressed in the relation between the rock art and the rewilding initiative. Here, we can begin to see how the 'process-oriented ethos' that defines ecological approaches to rewilding (Jepson and Schepers 2016) could be adopted to enliven our understanding of how the world 'times'. Wild time, which can be seen as a manifestation of 'open time', might encourage recognition of the way time flows and eddies, speeds up and slows down, iterates and irritates, pleats and plaits (Serres and Latour 1995) – processes that resonate with the braided water channels described in Chapter 26. In such an alternative framework (or 'returning'), it is possible to imagine that the ancient rock-carving tradition – which persisted unevenly into the twentieth century, with engravings of animals, trains and other features

Figure 28.5 Twentieth-century engraving of a train with a visible date (1944), located in the vicinity of a watermill in the Côa Valley, in the Rêgo da Vide site near the town of Vila Nova de Foz Côa (photograph taken by Fernando Barbosa in 1995, courtesy of Côa Museum/Côa Park Foundation Archives).

created by workers in the mills along the river – could be reactivated (see Figure 28.5). One archaeologist with a deep attachment to the region commented in 2016 during an informal interview that she would love to 'restart the artistic cycle of the Côa', allowing people to express themselves through art, in order to 'continue to give life to this [tradition], and not just freeze it in time'. Such an intervention, which would be considered sacrilege to some, could be seen instead as an expression of connection and continuity (see also Luís and García Díez 2008).

If the dominant clay country temporality is about 'open time' and the Côa is about 'wild time', then Orford Ness is perhaps about 'drift time', characterised by a fluid mixing of deep geological timelines with relatively short human ones (and their associated dark histories). The Ness is a structure resulting from the combination of wave action and processes of longshore drift, but the concept of drift also has a wider resonance. Þóra Pétursdóttir (2020) argues that a metaphor of 'drift' can open up alternative ways of knowing and reasoning with heritage matter(s). In relation to temporality, drift time suggests cycles of deposition and erosion, accretion and absence. From any elevated position on the Ness, it is possible to detect distinctive patterns of shingle ridges and swales, mostly set in an alignment roughly parallel to the current shoreline. The landforms function as a rough geological clock, showing the incremental development of the spit over the last five thousand years. Each ridge represents a past shoreline or major storm event.

The 'clock' is not entirely reliable, however: according to the guidebook, 'unlike the growth rings of a tree, shingle ridges do not necessarily show a progressive sequence of time. In many places an older series of ridges has been destroyed and replaced by a new series. So the age of the formation of Orford Ness still confounds experts' (National Trust n.d. b, n.p.). The cuspate pattern of the Ness has also been formed by continual processes of longshore drift, with prevailing currents gradually eroding the nub – or 'nose'/ness – at the spit's midpoint (near the lighthouse) and accreting new shingle to the south. Successive generations of lighthouses have fallen as this process reshapes the spit. The lost lighthouses can be read as points on the drift-time clock, with the current structure now reaching its eleventh hour (DeSilvey 2017, 157). Set against this backdrop of geological time, the fate of the military ruins of the twentieth century take on a different aspect. The labs and test cells of the AWRE facility have now been left on their own for many decades, first from outright abandonment by the Ministry of Defence, and then through the National Trust's policy of 'continued ruination', as discussed in the preceding chapters. Their gradual colonisation by opportunistic plants and animals (and their inexorable decay by other forces) can be interpreted as a vivid expression of ecological time (Walker and Wardle 2014) as it unfolds in relation to human time.

As evidenced in the discussion in Chapter 26 about the 'ongoingness' of Orford Ness, drift time is complicated. This complexity is something that the National Trust has attempted to grapple with through the most recent iteration of the Spirit of Place statement of the site, which also indexes processes of deposition and erosion in relation to the history of the site:

> It is a landscape and seascape that slips away to the endless line of the horizon. Lost in the vast scale you can feel liberated but at the same time oppressed and challenged … A place of secrets, physically inaccessible and once deliberately concealed: a former Official Secret now decaying physically, metaphorically and morally, imperceptibly revealing its myths, stories and meaning. Where once experimentation, creation and destruction combined to perfect the physics of warfare, wildlife now thrives …
>
> (National Trust 2015)

The excerpt recognises time as a composite, relational phenomenon, set within a dynamic and ever-shifting present. The National Trust seems to have accepted that caring for a place 'in perpetuity' may sometimes involve taking a step back and seeing places as they are caught up in ecological and geological processes that operate on much longer time frames than our limited human perspective usually allows for.

Inevitable change

The ideas explored in this part of the book open out possibilities for a critical heritage practice oriented to latency and release, and instability and emergence, rather than preservation and perpetuation. Memory and materiality are unhitched from the presumption of stability and stasis to instead work through change and disturbance, and attend to instances of both destruction and renewal, disturbance and resilience. Across the fuzzy nature/culture divide there is evidence of a loosening of the control implied by ideas of 'preservation' and protection, allowing for the emergence of a sensibility attuned to flow and perpetual transformation.

The process-based, transformative heritage frameworks we have been exploring are linked to a parallel shift in ecology and conservation, where there has been a recent re-evaluation of core ecological concepts and practices (Marris 2013; Thomas 2017; Jackson and Hobbs 2009). Assumptions about ecological succession towards stable climax states are being replaced with new paradigms that explore the significance of ongoing disturbance and dynamic change in the formation of non-equilibrium and novel ecosystems, as explored in the discussion in Chapter 26 about invasive species and emergent ecologies. The implications for the practice of ecological restoration have been profound, as summarised by Stephen Jackson and Richard Hobbs:

> ... perhaps the most natural feature of the world in which we find ourselves is continual flux ... If natural states are elusive, if the environment is always changing and ecosystems are always coming and going, and if multiple realisations are normal, then the premises underlying ecological restoration to a historic standard come into question.
>
> (Jackson and Hobbs 2009, 567–8)

In a recent interview, ecologist Chris Thomas discusses the pervasive tendency for ecologists to interpret ecological change (usually the arrival of new species, or the shifting habitats of established ones) as 'further evidence that the world is deviating from some imagined, idealised state, set at an undefined time in the past'. But, he claims, 'We need to avoid interpreting change as loss when change is inevitable' (Nesbit 2018, 40–3). There are gains as well as losses in change, he argues, and we need to be more open to the potentially productive aspects of change. In light of the landscapes discussed in this part of the book, it seems that rather than talking about loss and 'letting go', we should focus instead on embracing metamorphosis and 'letting be' – or even relinquishing and releasing. Such an approach may be particularly appropriate in relation to the entangled heritage naturecultures we explore in this section, but it also resonates in other contexts, such as museum practice, where some form of deaccessioning and 'letting go' may be crucial to the attempted maintenance of order.

As with any paradigm shift, the embrace of a 'heritage in transformation' will be uneven and contested. This was evidenced in some of the complexities and contradictions described in Chapter 25 and Chapter 26, as well as in the visual essay in Chapter 27, which highlights the discrepancies between what we are led to see on the surface and the deeper meanings underlying the processes and practices at play (see Figure 28.6). Through a focus on place-based, practice-led research we have come to understand how heritage practitioners and conservation professionals are already embracing transformation and change in the work that they do, although such approaches are often in tension with background expectations and policy frameworks. Given robust platforms for conversation (such as the knowledge exchanges trialled in the Heritage Futures research programme and documented in Chapters 9, 16 and 23), we see potential for meaningful and productive 'co-influencing' and a resulting shift in viewpoints around these themes. What seems to be certain is that, in the future, skills related to heritage adaptation and cultivated reciprocity with non-human others and forces will be as important as traditional skills related to heritage conservation and preservation.

Figure 28.6　One of the banners at the entrance to the Eden Project, Cornwall in 2016, showing 'before and after' images of the former clay pit (photograph by Nadia Bartolini).

Part VI
Future heritages

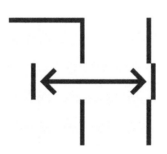

29
Discussion and conclusions

Rodney Harrison, Caitlin DeSilvey, Cornelius Holtorf, Sharon Macdonald, Nadia Bartolini, Esther Breithoff, Harald Fredheim, Antony Lyons, Sarah May, Jennie Morgan and Sefryn Penrose

Introduction

This book has aimed to explore how heritage practices, broadly defined, might be understood to contribute to the making of future worlds. Drawing on a range of ethnographic and creative visual methods, the four main empirical parts of the book have each focused on a specific theme or challenge for heritage – Diversity, Profusion, Uncertainty and Transformation. Within each theme, investigation of a series of case studies has allowed us to explore how these challenges motivate particular approaches to conservation and preservation in a range of different contexts. This chapter aims to bring together the findings of each of these thematic parts to explore how the four themes relate to one another, and to draw some general conclusions from comparisons across them. In doing so, we also aim to explore a wider set of considerations: how the different contexts in which our research was situated have shaped our observations of different practices, concepts and approaches; the ways in which local institutional factors and actors influenced these practices through various forms of engagement, expression, resistance and/or contestation; and the implications of the geographical, political, social and ecological contexts in which the research was undertaken, and how these influenced the findings of the study. In developing a comparative investigation of heritage practices across a range of different domains, we have been particularly keen to consider a breadth of different kinds of actors operating at a range of different scales – from individuals to households to multinational institutions; both official and non-official actors; and governmental, intergovernmental and non-governmental organisations. Accordingly, we discuss the implications of these factors for the findings of the study as well. The chapter also reflects more broadly on the approaches and methods employed in our research, in particular its collaborative 'para-ethnographic' approach to working with project partners, and the limits of these approaches. It then considers what the comparative perspectives employed here reveal about the 'futurability' (or future-making capacities) of the different forms of heritage and heritage-like practices discussed. The chapter concludes with reflections on the main findings to emerge from this work, which (perhaps counter-intuitively) relate to the long-term *unsustainability* of conservation and preservation practices. Here we also highlight how the work points towards ways of doing and researching heritage *otherwise*.

Comparisons across the four themes

Diversity and absence

The first empirical section of the book explored how 'diversity' emerged historically as a normative conservation target across a range of different forms of natural and cultural heritage preservational practices throughout the course of the twentieth century, and explored a range of different ways in which diversity is 'created', understood and preserved in practice today. These ranged from the recording and archiving of endangered languages in the Endangered Languages Documentation Programme (ELDP); the cryopreservation of endangered animal DNA at Frozen Ark; the cold storage of crop seeds at the Svalbard Global Seed Vault (SGSV); and the collection of a 'total archive' of plant specimens within the Herbarium at Kew. Each of these was considered within the context of the more general framework of natural and cultural heritage conservation that is provided by the operations of the various international conventions and organisations, including the International Union for the Conservation of Nature (IUCN), the International Council on Monuments and Sites (ICOMOS) and the United Nations Educational, Scientific and Cultural Organization (UNESCO). While mindful of the fact that such practices are also common to *in-situ* forms of conservation, it focused particularly on *ex-situ* diversity collecting practices and the relationship between collecting such endangered objects in the field and the various institutional and intellectual processes that were applied to these objects as they were collected and returned to a repository (zoo, museum, bank, archive, catalogue, collection) of some kind. Drawing on a broadly Latourian conceptual framework, it showed how new forms of knowledge about the places from which these objects were collected were generated by their coming together in such a way at particular 'centres of collection and calculation', where endangered objects are brought together and identified, ordered and arranged in specific ways that allow them to function as 'proxies' for the endangered objects they come to stand in for in such repositories.

However, it is clear that issues of 'Diversity' related more generally to many of the other empirical examples we studied. Building more diverse collections, representations and workforces is a general and often stated aim across the cultural and natural heritage sectors (for example, see Lee-Crossett 2019). In museums concerned with collecting from contemporary everyday life, as discussed in Part III, Profusion, attempting to include 'more diversity' has been one push towards increasing the size of collections. Rewilding practices, as discussed in Part V, Transformation, are concerned with accessing past genetic diversity to back-breed and reintroduce what we might term 'new' wild species into anthropogenic landscapes. De-extinction technologies are also increasingly being directed towards the prevention of species extinction by their application to increase fertility and 'restore' wild populations of critically endangered species (for example, see Jones 2014). In Part V, Transformation, we noted not only various practices and policies relating to the conservation and management of IUCN Red List 'endangered' species at their case study sites (for example, clay country mosses and rare plants at Orford Ness), but also the ways in which such sites hosted new or novel ecologies relating to their previous and ongoing uses, including the presence of Chinese water deer and the ways in which habitats were being managed for migratory birds at Orford Ness.

Simultaneously, the Transformation case studies also spoke to issues relating to the *absence* of diversity and its effects. In both the Côa and Orford case studies, social and cultural diversity were seen to have diminished through processes of depopulation and intentional isolation, respectively, which presented challenges for collective governance and decision-making. Both case studies also raised questions of saving or 'banking' current diversity for the future. The idea of providing protected refuge or sanctuary as a prelude to hoped-for future expansion of biodiversity was common across both study sites. The practical application of these ideas at both sites is focused on functional landscape repair and the (re)generation of habitat complexity.

Waste and value

The ways in which Profusion and Diversity operate as transactional realities in relation to heritage practices (see Chapter 5) means they also operationalise judgements of value and mobilise certain actions as a result of these judgements. In relation to those cases studied in Part III, Profusion, these values underpin and account for those things that are kept and those that are discarded in a range of institutional and non-institutional contexts. At the most basic level, as discussed in Chapter 2 and running through the case studies in Part IV, Uncertainty, these practices of valuation also underpin the distinction between 'heritage' and 'waste'. In the Transformation theme case studies, these judgements can be seen in operation in relation to the concept of 'invasive species'. These species are targeted for eradication in the name of conservation. They are seen as competing with, and hence incommensurate with, the conservation of other, more vulnerable, endangered, and hence more valuable, species. These underpinning value judgements motivate intensive human interventions of active and selective conservation and de-extinction on the one hand, and 'weeding out' of what, drawing on the work of Mary Douglas (1991), we might term species 'out of place' on the other hand. Such practices are undertaken to either aid or work against what may be perceived to be slower, more 'natural' processes of species regeneration and rewilding, or, in relation to the Diversity case studies, increasingly accelerating anthropogenic processes of species extinction. The issues raised by the delineation of heritage's alters – weeds, waste, clutter, rubbish and so on – go beyond mere questions of semantics to determine how the objects, places and practices thus defined are treated and managed.

Issues of diversity clearly also motivated the practices explored in Part IV, Uncertainty. The apparently more 'open' and democratic approach of the One Earth: New Horizons Message project to crowd-source a message to send into space was explicitly set against previous approaches, including that of the selection of materials to be presented on the *Voyager* Golden Records. The evocation of collective and universal humanity that these projects imagine invites critical questioning relating to the politics of representation and recognition, questions that have long formed a focus for critical investigation of cultural heritage and museums. But such projects – with their focus on the planetary scale – also remind us of one of the key findings of Part II, Diversity, that diversity is scalar and relates as much to the categories that are invented to quantify and record diversity *loss*, as it does to any form of independent measurement. A similar, passive (and hence ostensibly more democratic) approach is also taken in the Memory of Mankind (MOM) project, which in theory accepts content of any kind from anyone who wishes to provide it. This apparent inclusivity might be seen to be positive in terms of participation, an issue that needs to be considered alongside general provisos relating to access to the means by which materials might be selected and sent to the archive, and the interest in participation, which is necessarily limited to certain individuals and groups. It should be beneficial in terms of addressing questions of diversity of representation. But it nonetheless raises questions of the potential for a profusion of materials to amass within the archive. While there may be abundant space for data in the storage facility and on the ceramic tiles used, it raises questions about who will manage the huge amounts of data it may ultimately contain and to what purpose? Does the fact that we do not know what is going to be considered significant about our own time, or what the future needs, justify the means to try and preserve as much of the present as possible?

Stories and surplus

It also became apparent that, while helpful as an organisational device for this study, the four themes we investigated had different analytical statuses, and as such they each did different kinds of 'work' in relation to the heritage practices we observed. Diversity is explicitly mobilised as a concept to drive and target conservation activities across a range of different domains of conservation practice, as a normative and 'positive' aim of conservation work, while Profusion is generally not. Profusion was deliberately chosen by the researchers working on that theme as a more value-neutral term than some of the possible alternatives, such as 'excess'. As such, it afforded attention not only to 'negative' phenomena, such as 'clutter', but also to more 'positive' links, especially social history museum curators' attempts to create more 'inclusive' collections and exhibitions as part of a wider 'democratisation of the past' (see also Macdonald and Morgan 2018a). This also connects with the less directed, apparently more open approaches of the Memory of Mankind and One Earth: New Horizons Message projects, but also, by way of its resonance with general concepts of 'crowdsourcing' and 'citizen-recording', with the work of the Coastal and Intertidal Zone Archaeological Network (CITiZAN) at Orford Ness and, indeed, with the significant size of the volunteering sector within natural and cultural heritage conservation and management work more generally.

Links between Diversity and Profusion were also evident in the research. For example, it is clear that attempts to divers-*ify*, or to incorporate diversity in various forms (ranging from kinds of things to, more recently, addressing issues of social diversity) is one of the factors that is perceived to be leading to further profusion in museums, in the sense in which widening a collection requires one to acquire more stuff that has previously sat outside of formal collections policies. In particular, the move by museums to collect items representing the 'contemporary everyday' (and thus 'diversify' beyond a conventional museological focus on high culture) was perceived by the curators worked with to have a major impact on the profusion predicaments they were experiencing/navigating. In many ways, what is involved here is a similar attempt to capture diversity and to conserve it for the future as the biodiversity repositories discussed in Part II, Diversity. The argument does not, however, work in quite the same way for domestic settings. Except in the cases of more museological collecting being undertaken in homes, preserving (and enumerating) a diversity of items for the future was not at the forefront of domestic keeping and discarding strategies. At the same time, however, as Part III, Profusion, points out, the diversification and the increasingly subtle variations of material goods, as part of post-Fordist production and consumption cycles, itself encourages the buying of more and more items, which then accumulate in homes, as well as posing a challenge for museums about what to collect from the diverse range of items available.

The framing of diversity conservation objects as kinds of proxies also resonates with how contemporary everyday objects are used in museum collections. While social history collection has included wholesale rescue in the past, generally objects today are collected to *represent* or stand in for certain things, people, identities, ideas or practices – increasingly referred to as 'stories'. The research presented in Part III, Profusion, shows that the shift to 'stories' as the focus of collection has altered understandings of significance, to the extent that some objects are now less valuable because they do not lend themselves to telling stories – that is, they are not efficacious as proxies. The idea of proxies also relates to how diversity and representation is presently approached in social history collections in the UK and elsewhere. Some museums are concerned that their collections no longer are representative of their communities and, as part of their efforts to 'represent', they seek to build collections that better reflect changing demographics. The late capitalist and neo-liberal logics of needing to collect 'smaller and smaller parts of wholes' in diversity conservation (Chapter 6) also resonates with how collections reviews, museum rationalisation projects and household decluttering 'top tips' emphasise freeing up space by keeping only the 'best examples' or by insisting that objects 'carry their weight' – and ideally can serve multiple functions or be used to tell a range of different stories (thus representing the 'most efficient' proxies). While this focus on efficiency could be framed as an expression of neo-liberalism, it can also be a pragmatic response to recognising the scale of profusion (all the things that could/should be collected), and that in order to be able to use what collections have effectively, it must be done at a manageable scale. Elsewhere, in relation to the work of museums, Macdonald and Morgan (2018a) have referred to this as a form of 'pragmatic utopianism' – of holding on to collection ambitions while being realistic about achieving them.

While diversity is an important concept in museums, it remains poorly defined and thus difficult to measure either qualitatively or quantitatively on anything like a 'Red List' in these contexts. This does not mean that ideas about what diversity means do not shape ambitions for managing, using and building collections in museums, but that it is less common to work to specific diversity criteria or targets. This relates to the point about stories above. Some collections might be said by curators to be more diverse because they cover different social classes and genders – even though they may not have diverse collections with regard to race, or other categories. There is no clearly agreed measure for quantifying 'diversity' within these forms of collections, so the aim of achieving more diverse collections is difficult to quantify.

Resources and motivations

One significant issue that emerged across many of the domains of heritage practice we studied is the ways in which funding and resources, rather than conservation priorities, often drive the conservation and preservation agenda. In Part III, Profusion, a lack of resources was found to constrain collecting and restrict more 'active' or 'curatorially led' approaches, resulting in a reliance on self-selecting donors. Funding also indirectly impacts decisions about objects – for example, many museums will not accept 'large' objects because they take up more space, or objects with complex conservation needs. In Part II, Diversity, it was noted that funding constraints often mean that particular kinds of 'charismatic' species receive more conservation attention than other, less appealing, often 'less human' ones. In Part V, Transformation, funding constraints are seen to create certain limits on the nature of the conservation activities that are undertaken in each of the three landscapes. Funding also puts certain constrains on the long-term memory projects discussed in the Uncertainty section, both in terms of the amount of information that might be stored and the means by which it might be maintained into the distant future. In the Côa Valley, ambitious rewilding visions are partly motivated by the desire to create employment through eco-tourism and a means for younger people to remain in an isolated rural area, which, like other parts of the country, has experienced significant rural depopulation. At Orford Ness, the innovative cultural heritage management strategies of 'curated decay' (DeSilvey 2017) are to some extent motivated by an awareness of the potentially enormous costs of maintaining the massive concrete buildings.

Holding on and letting go

Questions of the relations between heritage and waste resonated throughout the different themes of the study in several ways too. Most explicitly, of course, in relation to the management of toxic forms of waste discussed in Part IV, Uncertainty, but also in relation to questions of relative value that arise in discussions regarding what to keep and what to discard, as discussed in Part III, Profusion, and when it might be desirable to 'let go' of control and allow for change and decay, in Part IV, Transformation. Similarly, in Part II, Diversity, it was shown how a Darwinian framework had characterised certain (non-adaptive) forms of genetic and biological traits as waste, to be bred out of the gene pool through 'natural' selection. It was only over the course of the twentieth century that the current understanding of diversity as inherently valuable (Sepkoski 2016) emerged as a transactional reality to determine current approaches to the maintenance and regeneration of both biological and cultural diversity as a matter of such extreme urgency.

These questions of what to 'save' and what to 'let go' are also often framed in terms of more or less implicitly 'moral' judgements. So, for example, repatriation or 'return' of cultural objects by museums to stakeholders and descendent communities might be deemed to be a morally acceptable form of deaccessioning, while discarding or selling objects on an open market would be seen to be morally incorrect. In diversity conservation, biodiversity and cultural diversity are framed as the 'right thing' to conserve, but there is significant variation in the ways in which different organisations attempt to do so, and these different approaches can have significant impacts. To take an extreme case, there is a long history of national parks being created in landscapes occupied by indigenous people, who come to be forcibly removed in the name of 'conservation' (for example, Zerner 1999; Stevens 2014). As we write, in India almost two million people face eviction from what many claim are traditional ancestral lands under a Supreme Court ruling to evict communities living in protected forest areas (Withnall 2019). Indeed, much of heritage conservation, both natural and cultural, is framed in normative, moral terms. This is evident in the 1972 World Heritage Convention, which evokes in its Preamble 'the magnitude and gravity of the new dangers threatening' cultural and natural heritage, and argues that, since the 'deterioration or disappearance of any item of the cultural or natural heritage constitutes a harmful impoverishment of the heritage of all the nations of the world', there is a strong need 'for all the peoples of the world, of safeguarding this unique and irreplaceable property ... as part of the world heritage of mankind as a whole' (UNESCO 1972, 1). We have seen it as our role in the book to critically probe such normative tendencies in heritage. Similarly, what is perceived as morally right in the present can be applied to objects, places and practices from the past, but perhaps not to the future – this makes discarding or 'letting go' of heritage difficult because instinctively it may feel that there is no future moral compass to evaluate such decisions against, unless it is related to a contemporary framework.

The sacred and the profane

The language of salvation and sacrifice also reminds us of the ways in which heritage, even if an intentionally secularising discourse, also has something of the sacred about it. Conservation and preservation requires certain leaps of faith – trust in the future to maintain the conservation decisions that are made in the present, and belief that one can 'know' the needs of the future (issues discussed at length in Part IV, Uncertainty). It also invokes forms of purity; the categorical systems that are used to measure forms of biological, linguistic and cultural diversity are troubled by hybrid forms and alternative taxonomies, as the Diversity and Trans- formation parts of the book showed. In many ways, the language of heri- tage is one that allows people to describe an experience of the sublime that might otherwise be described as religious.

Pushing this observation a bit further, we might note that if heritage is defined by those objects, places and practices it is charged with 'saving', we rarely pause to consider its opposite effects: the ways in which it also involves forms of sacrifice. The explicitly apocalyptic Judeo-Christian religious connotation of the Frozen Ark discussed in Part II, Diversity, for example, also reminds us of those animals that were not selected and were sacrificed to the Genesis story flood. These sacrifices might take one of several different forms. It is clear that in certain circumstances, saving one endangered object, place, species, ecosystem, language or practice might also facilitate the sacrifice of others, through the ways in which limited resources become channelled into one conservation activity over another. 'Saving' one part of the landscape, in the form of a national park or gazetted area, for example, might also facilitate specific forms of polluting or environmentally damaging 'non-conservation' activities outside of its borders, because people are perhaps less worried about the degradation of certain parts of the landscape if they think that others are 'taken care of'. This raises questions of the management of borders, which were prevalent throughout the case studies in Part V, Transformation, for example. And, as in the extreme example from India discussed above, conservation and preservation can often create conflicts over resources, and competing sets of rights and interests in them, meaning that an apparently 'positive' decision to conserve will always impact negatively in some way on those who compete for these resources. This observation invites a radical rethinking of heritage and its material-discursive effects. We cannot understand the designation of protected buildings or landscapes without looking beyond the gazetted structure or reserved area to consider the potentially 'negative' actions that such conservation activity may permit. In natural heritage conservation practices, it is common to talk about certain forms of sacrificial landscapes that are used for recreational activities. Their potential for biodiversity conservation is 'sacrificed' for raising awareness of conservation issues and for recreational use. Objects that are deaccessioned from museum collections might also be understood as sacrificial items. And in another related example, the clay country waste tips discussed in Part V, Transformation, are currently not listed, partially because there are simply too many of them; there is here a counter-intuitive sense of waiting until more disappear before they can be recognised as valuable, at risk and hence worth protecting.

Perhaps more fundamentally, each of the themes asked, in different ways, *why we conserve at all* in each of the domains studied. Part III, Profusion, noted a number of reasons why individuals, households and museums keep things and, in particular, those reasons that can lead to profusion, including 'values', 'obligation' and 'duty'. These motivations for keeping were common to all of the domains explored in this book, more or less explicitly. Part IV, Uncertainty, particularly emphasised the ways in which an often unspecified sense of obligation to the future frames much of the work that takes place across nuclear waste management and other long-term memory projects. Within Part V, Transformation, the work in Cornwall emphasised a sense of 'overspilling', or 'too much-ness'. This included responses to rampant vegetative growth and invasive species 'taking over'. This has obvious links with the observation of the Profusion theme, and the perception – in both domestic and institutional settings – that over-abundance of 'stuff' is exerting constant pressure to declutter, to dispose of or to simplify. The imperative to find increasingly economical ways of conserving conservation proxies in the form of tiny samples of DNA in biobanks also speaks to this pressure to minimise, optimise and pare back, which ran across case studies in all of the four themes.

On the inevitability of change for heritage in the Anthropocene

The half decade or so that passed between our conceptualisation of this project and working on this monograph of its findings has witnessed a complete transformation of public understandings of anthropogenic environmental change. The work of climate activists (in particular Greta Thunberg and the wave of climate crisis strikes she inspired) and extinction awareness campaigners (such as those working under the banner of Extinction Rebellion) has raised international public consciousness of the inevitability of change, and it is now widely acknowledged and understood that humans have modified the climate and environment to such a significant extent that it is no longer possible to assume that the geology, ecology and climate of the planet will remain in a stable state, even over the scale of individual human lifetimes. Over the course of our research, as the world and these environmental issues 'heated up', in many instances the work of the case study organisations documented in this book gained an increasing sense of urgency, and public discourse regarding climate change and extinction seemed to accelerate. This general emergence of intense public discussion of climate change, the Anthropocene and the sixth mass extinction forms an important back-drop to the work we present here.

As such, all of the themes engaged more or less with the concept of Uncertainty, in the sense in which heritage itself is driven by the idea of resourcing uncertain futures, but they did so in a way that became increasingly explicitly articulated as our research unfolded. The work documented as part of the Diversity and Profusion themes acts on similar precautionary principles to that in the Uncertainty section – the underpinning assumption being that, because we do not know what the future will hold, we should cover our bases and keep as much as we can. So, for example, the conservation of crop seeds in the SGSV is understood to operate as a kind of 'insurance policy' against global climate change, disease or crop extinction. Similarly, keeping things because they might 'come in useful' one day was characteristic of both museums and households in the Profusion case studies. The various organisations discussed in Part V, Transformation, with its focus on changing landscapes, all more or less explicitly worked within a general framework of resourcing the future in anticipation of some form of ecological, social and climatological change.

The *ex-situ* collecting observed in both Part II and Part III is generally positioned in response to change – with the implicit assumption that change (or the loss of biodiversity, cultural diversity, traditions, languages and ways of life) is necessarily 'bad' and something to be resisted. Simultaneously, however, there is often an acceptance that change is inevitable, and that change may make those things that are collected in response to threat/risk valuable in new (and unexpected) ways in the future. Such a framing was apparent in the media reporting of the Syria seedbank, which formed the focus for the first active 'withdrawal' of seeds from the Svalbard Global Seed Vault (Chapter 6). Similarly, as discussed in Part III, Profusion, collecting everyday objects could be seen as a form of resource speculation for the production of new futures. In homes, this has been demonstrated as householders have recounted finding objects that – while not specifically kept by others or themselves – have taken on particular meaning or value, in sometimes unexpected or surprising ways. Keeping hold of objects in homes also has complex relationships with change: sometimes specific objects are held on to so as to try to engineer new futures, while in others they are retained for continuity between the present and the past.

These observations of the extent to which an accelerated public consciousness of climate change and extinctions are impacting significantly on the heritage sector are not unique, but resonate with the work of others (for example, Harvey and Perry 2015b). If heritage could be defined precisely through its relationship with endangerment (see Vidal and Dias 2016b; see also Harrison 2013a; Rico 2015a; 2016), as a form of 'loss aversion' (Holtorf 2015), as we discussed in the introductory chapters to this book, these observations are likely to have a profound effect on the sector and the varied practices by which natural and cultural 'legacies' are managed in and for the future. Grounded as it is in sustained analysis of cultural responses to perceived loss and endangerment, heritage studies is perhaps uniquely positioned to provide critical perspectives on the current global crisis and the anticipation of widespread attrition and extinction across a range of cultural, social, geographical and ecological contexts.

In the face of accelerated climate and environmental change, promises of conservation and perpetuation are looking increasingly unsustainable. If climate change predictions are accurate, then some form of heritage loss, particularly in coastal contexts, appears to be inevitable and heritage values may need to adapt to reflect this new reality (Harvey and Perry 2015a; Koslov 2016; DeSilvey 2012). 'Loss and change are part of life, and part of the currency that gives our heritage value,' argue Hannah Fluck and Meredith Wiggins (2017, 167): 'It is not so much loss that is problematic, but how individuals, communities and societies choose to deal with loss.' In many cases, cultural heritage represents and provides evidence of a history of continuous change, loss and transformation. Awareness of this history, promoted by heritage, could become an important source of cultural resilience (Holtorf 2018).

The actual process of 'dealing with loss' in heritage practice and policy is still in its early stages and often more about recognition of the problem than formulating response. The US National Park Service, in its 2016 *Cultural Resources Climate Change Strategy*, made the bold statement that, 'We will ensure that our management options recognize the potential for loss … Managers should consider choices such as documenting some resources and letting them fall into ruin' (Rockman et al. 2016, 34). In the UK, Historic England has committed to 'develop an approach for dealing with inevitable change, including loss' (Fluck 2016). As yet, however, responses have tended to focus on refining systems for assessing significance and setting priorities for conservation, and making difficult choices about where to direct limited resources. Strategies for the intentional management of loss – of integrity, form and fabric – are still underdeveloped (although see Harvey and Perry 2015b; Hambrecht and Rockman 2017; DeSilvey 2017). Only two World Heritage Sites (out of more than 1,100) have ever been delisted, both under very special circumstances when their core values were threatened (see discussion in Harrison 2013b). The World Heritage Convention has no regular mechanism for reconsidering inscribed places as judgements and values change over time. While it is now widely recognised that key concepts of heritage interpretation, such as authenticity, are culturally specific and variable in space, it has not yet been fully understood that they are also variable over time (Holtorf and Kono 2015).

These questions are also fundamentally political ones. Whose stories are collected, remembered and celebrated, and whose are forgotten? How are the limited funds for nature conservation distributed among the world's endangered species? Who decides what gets lost and what to save? While these discussions have dominated the consideration of the politics of representation in cultural heritage for decades, they are equally applicable to issues of natural heritage conservation (for example, see Orlove and Brush 1996; Zerner 1999; Tsing 2005; Benson 2010; Bird Rose et al. 2017). Increasingly, heritage scholars are adopting integrated approaches to examine the politics of loss in both cultural and natural heritage contexts. A recent study of the effects of sea level rise on Kiribati, a low-lying island nation in the Pacific Ocean, for example, engages with questions about the extent to which an indigenous, largely oral culture can be 'preserved' outside its 'natural' and dynamic setting (Woodham et al. 2018). In this context, the conventional question of whose heritage is to be preserved is reversed to engage instead with the question of 'whose heritage will be lost?'

Doing heritage otherwise: Accepting and embracing uncertainty, loss and change

One of the aims of the book was to investigate and explore a range of different approaches to natural and cultural heritage preservation and conservation, and to draw on these to consider how heritage might be done *otherwise*. Observations of the inevitability of change from inside and outside of the sector suggest that such approaches are urgently needed. Each of the four themes allowed critical reflection not only on how the uncertainty of the future in the light of predicted loss and change were resisted through certain forms of heritage practice, but also on how loss and change might nonetheless be seen as a source of creative dynamism for heritage and other material and discursive legacy management practices.

The findings of Part III, Profusion, suggest that a shift from *product* to *process* might be helpful in museums and homes – in coordination with explicit future-thinking and planning over longer time frames. Thinking more holistically at the scale of whole collections and what it is hoped they achieve socially, or how collections are to be used in meaningful ways, rather than in terms of individual objects, seems to move some of the profusion 'problems' documented in that theme of this research forward in meaningful ways. In homes, such approaches were observed in people decluttering by making decisions about specific things or categories of things. This is also seen in the professional and semi-professional work of declutterers, both in our study and beyond (such as the KonMari Method).

Nonetheless, the rationalisation/decluttering projects examined in our research are still mostly about prioritisation to cope with profusion – with saving everything as the (impossible) goal and loss/transformation as the least desirable option. There is a movement towards making loss less undesirable and this is especially accepted in homes (for example, with the wider cultural emphasis in developed countries on associating well-being with having *less*). But what our study reveals is that a lot of work is still required to actually 'let go' in homes and museums – not only practical work, but also in terms of emotional labour – to unbind the ties and investments made in things. More could be done to explore the role of ritual in this context – but foregrounding loss as potentially positive (not as something that could be made less bad) often seems at odds with current conservation policy goals. Here perhaps, museums and other formal heritage institutions could learn from households, where more regular moments of letting go seem to occur at key stages in the life biography. There may be productive scope in thinking of both *ex-situ* and *in-situ* collections of natural and cultural objects through more biographical frames in this way. In the Diversity theme, the researchers found fewer engagements with the positive aspects of 'loss', but we did observe ways in which certain kinds of *ex-situ* collections create the conditions for transforming and realising both new approaches to conservation *and* new forms of diversity – and in doing so, resourcing new futures. The active role of humans in transitional landscapes as a form of future-making also formed an important part of the underpinning philosophy of many of the initiatives explored in the Transformation theme.

During the third and final cross-theme knowledge-exchange event, held at Orford Ness in Suffolk (see Chapter 23), we talked a lot about 'loss' of heritage and the idea of 'letting go well'. Advisory board member Ingrid Samuel reflected on this idea of engaging change productively by making a distinction between two kinds of 'letting go' in heritage. The first, she suggested, related to letting go of certain cultural or natural heritage resources and meant having the confidence to make decisions about what *not* to actively conserve. This requires respect and understanding, and the support of the sector to accept change as inevitable. The second, she suggested, was more generally about practitioners and heritage managers themselves letting go of control and embracing uncertainty.[1] This requires not only a positive attitude towards change, but tools and techniques for dealing socially, politically and materially with ambiguity. She suggested that one important part of this was language, that the term 'change' might be a lot more helpful in such contexts than the term 'loss'. Her suggestions resonate closely with the findings of our Uncertainty and Transformation themes, of the need to see transformation and uncertainty as an opportunity, rather than as an obstacle, as well as with Profusion, with possibilities for museums to use deaccessioning to address their fundamental values and longer-term aims.

This idea of embracing uncertainty and transformation across the natural and cultural heritage sector seems full of potential. Throughout the project, we found that, while many natural and cultural heritage professionals and organisations work in service of the future in one way or another, they do not often think in concrete ways about what this means. For example, in the Profusion theme, we saw how collections staff see their work as inherently future-focused, but generally do not specify the future to particular timespans and tend to regard it as both open-ended and inherently uncertain. In the second cross-programme knowledge-exchange event, at Kew, we saw how a new way of organising the collections did inject some more specific future-thinking into the work of the organisation (see Chapter 16). There is a lot of scope for further work here around explicit future-thinking and embracing uncertainty, and what that might look like. Here, some of the practice in homes could provide inspiration for more concrete future-thinking. In homes, people tend to think of the future through social and familial relationships, and sometimes articulate these futures vis-à-vis actions of inheritance-making, by making decisions in the present shaped through a desire to acquire, keep and pass things on to specific individuals whom they anticipate will value these things, often within one or two generations (see further discussion in Part III, Profusion). Similarly, the long-standing discussion about the preservation of records, knowledge and memory in the nuclear waste management industry has much to offer the heritage sector here, as discussed in Part IV, Uncertainty.

Our work points to both the inevitability and the creative potential of loss and change. Such observations seem inescapable for heritage in light of the current recognition of the Anthropocene, or the 'climate change era' (Solli et al. 2011; Harrison 2015; Harvey and Perry 2015b; Lorimer 2015; Olsen and Pétursdóttir 2016; Harrison and Sterling 2020). However, we should be careful not to overestimate or romanticise the emancipatory potential of such processes. In *Rubble*, Gastón Gordillo (2014) reminds us of the inequalities of power that underpin processes of ruination in many global contexts. Navaro-Yashin (2012) and Dawdy

(2016) articulate how those objects, places and practices that are transformed through processes of destruction and loss are also deeply politically contested. Nonetheless, it is clear that the more sophisticated ways of understanding, anticipating and engaging forms of uncertainty, change, transformation and loss outlined here point not only to challenging new ways of 'doing' and practising natural and cultural heritage preservation, conservation and management, which derive from embedded, collaborative, co-created, comparative research, but also map out important new lines of enquiry for heritage studies in the future.

Collaborative approaches

One of the most challenging aspects of the project, both for us as academic researchers and for the collaborators from inside and outside of the sector with whom we worked, was the ambitious collaborative agenda we had set for the project. These collaborations took several different forms and varied in intensity and scale. Engagement with particular project partners to co-design knowledge-exchange workshops, both within and across the various themes – some of which are illustrated in the visual essays that make up Chapters 9, 16 and 23 – was necessarily thorough, and involved co-creating a programme of activities that would not only give participants from other fields of practice an insight into their work but would also challenge the group to think critically and collectively about some of the most pressing issues for the sector, including the long-term future, extinction and diversity, and environmental (and climate) change. The depth of the engagement with each organisation also varied. In most cases we engaged deeply with key individuals from within each organisation, who often took on the role of 'critical friend' in commenting on, and helping us to frame, our research and its outcomes in a way that would be legible and useful for the sector. This was particularly the case for our advisory board, composed of senior people from across the fields of natural and cultural heritage conservation and waste management.

In other cases, particularly where we were able to arrange embedded periods of ethnographic fieldwork, working with and alongside collaborators, we engaged directly with a broader cross-section of the organisation and its associated field of practice. In yet other cases, we were able to access a large audience from across a particular domain through attending and participating in large international professional meetings and congresses, where we were not only able to disseminate the results of our work, but also enlist new collaborators and gain further insights into the ways in which each of the domains we studied functioned. We learned that it takes time and commitment to generate understanding for each other's work, engender mutual respect and build trust between partners in different sectors and professions. Such investment does pay off in the end, but it is not always the kind of labour that is easily justifiable either in academic terms or in the priorities of workloads for individuals within each of the partner organisations. Although our agendas were not always familiar to our collaborators, we nonetheless experienced a great willingness to collaborate and engage in critical thinking about the aims of the sector. Our research would not have been possible without the generosity of our various partner organisations, many of whom we engaged on difficult and even controversial topics.

Indeed, the inherently political nature of many of our interests – in the sense in which they go very much to the heart of which objects, places and practices to privilege and protect, and which elements to sacrifice, let go or rework – often meant that we needed to tread carefully as researchers. Many of the organisations that we worked with had little experience of being the subject of ethnographic interest themselves. Simultaneously, in some cases the professional contexts in which we worked, especially biobanking and other technical fields, were unfamiliar to us as researchers, and this meant that there was necessarily a steep learning curve to understand the dynamics of each field. The relationships of trust took time to build and meant we needed to accept occasional misunderstandings and allow time to learn on both sides of the academic/professional divide. But to characterise this as a clear distinction between practitioner and researcher presents a false distinction. Many of the authors of this book have worked within the same (or similar) professional or policy contexts to the ones we were studying and, as such, the boundaries between these different roles were not always clearly drawn. In many ways, this gave us unique access and insights into the issues faced by our collaborators and the sector as a whole. In some cases, we were also turning a lens on ourselves as researchers and our own practices throughout the project. This was particularly facilitated by our work with various creative practitioners, who reflected as much on us and our practice as researchers, as on the practices of the various sectoral collaborators with which we worked. This was also the case with the creative and documentary film-making undertaken by various members of the project team, which allowed us to reflect in many different ways on our own work and to find new ways of 'seeing', documenting and engaging with the practices we were researching (see further discussion in Bartolini and DeSilvey 2020a).

Collaborating with such a large and diverse group of non-academic partner organisations raised a number of challenges. One familiar experience throughout the project emerged from the ways in which particular key terms – heritage, conservation and preservation, for example – carried quite different meanings in the different contexts in which we were working. This sometimes generated misunderstanding, or a sense of using the same words to speak a different language. We found we could not assume a common understanding of even the most central concepts or terminologies. Although this was sometimes frustrating, we also found it helpful in terms of our own assumptions to challenge and define key terms that we had often used without giving them much thought. In our collaborative knowledge-exchange events, thinking through the dominant meanings of different concepts within the various different fields across which we were working often produced new and surprising insights, which facilitated broader discussions. In some cases, we also experienced challenges in our collaborations due to shifts in priority and agendas, and turnover of staff with whom we had been liaising closely within organisations. Sometimes this meant that plans had to be altered, or organisations had more or less capacity to be involved than had originally been planned. It was not always easy for us to understand precisely what was happening because these organisations were, understandably, dealing with issues of their own (including funding challenges) – issues that were not always evident to us as researchers from the outside. This meant we had to adopt a fairly agile and flexible attitude to planning events, particularly those that took place later in the project, a significant time after the participation of these different organisations had originally been solicited.

Nonetheless, despite these challenges, these engagements were undoubtedly productive for several reasons. Working closely with our partner organisations not only gave us privileged access to document the 'behind the scenes' heritage practices we wished to explore, but also helped us to frame our research and research questions in ways that would be legible to heritage practitioners and would have an impact on the sector. Our sector collaborators facilitated deeper knowledge about the various fields we studied, but also frequently raised important issues to think about and fruitful ideas to explore in the project, some of which led to important intellectual and practical detours that had a significant influence on the shape of the research programme and this resultant monograph. In addition, these partnerships provided practical advice and assistance with access to relevant collections, institutions and contacts within and across the various domains we researched. Engaging with our partner organisations in several different settings – on field-work, working in collections and heritage sites, at international con-gresses and specially curated knowledge-exchange workshops – meant not only that they could play a part in co-designing our research; it also allowed us to develop more nuanced and contextual understandings of how the organisations functioned in different contexts. The complex, messy, conceptually slippery practices we were able to document as a result of this belie the neat, smooth processes documented in policy and management documents, and show how complicated and contextual the range of approaches to conserving, preserving and managing the lega-cies of the past in the present really is. Participation in international pro-fessional conferences enabled us to get at least some glimpse into issues and approaches in various countries beyond those dozen or so countries in which we were directly working.

Heritage as future-making practices

Throughout the book, we have documented the practices of a range of individuals, groups, governmental, non-governmental and intergovern-mental organisations, each of which has aimed to resource the future in some way. We have argued that this future is not a generic outcome of heritage or conservation practices, but arises from the *specific* material and discursive practices that work with *particular* materials, gathering together *specific* human and non-human agents in a *precise* time and at a *particular* place. Quite different futures emerge from the varied practices we have documented – futures that may diverge significantly from, or even oppose, futures planned or created through the work of others.

What actions might flow from this recognition that certain heritage domains build their own distinctive worlds and their own particular futures? We argue that it is only in taking a comparative approach to understanding specific fields of heritage practices that we might reflect on, and explore, the possibilities inherent in reaching across these dif-ferent fields of practice to work towards the assembling of common or shared futures. By reframing heritage as future-making practices – and rethinking the relationships between these various modes of future-making or worlding practices – we suggest that these various practices of assembling and caring for the future might be creatively redeployed to generate innovation, foster resilience, encourage sustainability and facil-itate the building of 'common worlds' (Latour 2014) between and across them. As Arjun Appadurai (2013, 3) has recently noted, 'the future is ours to design, if we are attuned to the right risks, the right speculations, and the right understanding of the material world we both inherit and shape'. It is only in developing a shared and comprehensive understanding of the ways in which current speculations regarding what (and how) to conserve in the present actively shape our material, ecological and social futures that we will be able actively and consciously to do so. We have found that it is as much in the actions of *not* saving – of neglecting, discarding, losing, overlooking – that heritage futures are shaped, as in the implications of specific conservation and preservation practices themselves.

In the empirical research we conducted across the various case studies, we uncovered a range of different kinds of futures and temporalities that were implied, imagined and produced as a result of the conservation and preservation practices we studied. In the work of many natural and cultural heritage management organisations, there was often a taken-for-granted idea about 'the future' and 'posterity' as something that they work for, without a clear sense of when that future would precisely come. This sometimes took the form of 'forever' or a 'distant' future, but often not a specific temporal horizon. However, there were some exceptions to this. In homes, futures were at least sometimes framed more specifically within one or two generations. The nuclear waste management industry works to long and very specific temporal horizons, ten thousand, one hundred thousand or even one million years. Likewise, the Memory of Mankind project aspires to preserve its collections for up to one million years. In the first cross-theme knowledge-exchange event (Chapter 9) and in our Profusion work we found that putting specific time lengths into discussion with collections managers could significantly alter the ways in which individuals and organisations thought about their collections, what should be in them, who they were being kept for and what would be the appropriate means by which they should be conserved. These findings have profound significance for the heritage sector.

Conclusions: On the unsustainability of conservation practices

The ubiquitous narrative of a need to save or rescue heritage generates much attention in contemporary society and is prevalent throughout the heritage sector. But at the same time, in the course of our research, we found that there is little attempt to map the ways in which different kinds of conservation and preservation practices relate to one another, and where they may compete or even come into conflict with one another. We also found that, despite a prevalent discourse of saving 'for the future', there was comparatively little attention to the detail of that future – when it would come, what it would look like and who would be in it. We suggest that this makes it difficult for natural and cultural heritage management, as it is conventionally practised, to work on behalf of the future. Instead, most organisations imagine the future as a projection of the present. On the whole, this makes heritage practices conservative, in spite of the future-building capacities of heritage practices we have identified in this volume.

In the light of the growing acceptance of the inevitability of change – environmental, social, political – both within and outside of the heritage sector broadly conceived, such conservative approaches are no longer tenable and are indeed unsustainable. We have suggested that an alternative strategy, replacing tropes of risk and threats with more positive and creative engagements with change and transformation and accepting uncertainty as an opportunity rather than as something to be feared, might have significant implications for the sector. Such an alternative set of approaches, we suggest, can support the development of more sustainable and more selective conservation and preservation practices. As a result of our work, we see significant possibilities for a critical heritage practice oriented to instability and emergence, and suggest that, instead of focusing on loss and 'letting go', the sector might open itself to a more diverse repertoire of approaches which also acknowledges the possibilities generated by 'letting be' or 'letting become'. In this way of doing heritage otherwise, cultural remembrance is seen to work through change and disturbance, and destruction and renewal, as well as through preservation and perpetuation.

Such a model requires radically different ways of doing heritage, but opens up possibilities for developing new, more considered ways of collaborating and actively resourcing the future. This is complicated by certain 'fixed' aims and objectives: to fully contain radioactive waste; to save a species, or a language, from extinction; and to survive economically in a locality. Nonetheless, the long-term futures we have explored force an acceptance of change as inevitable. Accepting the inevitability of change means that the sector must find ways of engaging this change productively and actively. To do so, boundaries across natural and cultural heritage and strictly maintained domains of conservation practice need to be loosened and bridged, and new ways of caring, collecting, curating and communicating the values of heritage must be conceived.

It is important to note that while we see this book as providing a distinctive set of new pathways for heritage and for heritage studies – in terms of the direction the field of research might take, the new issues with which it might engage and the manner by which it might engage them – it is clear that these are not the only possible ways of thinking through heritage futures and future heritages, neither are they the only challenges that heritage studies might address, even in relation to preservation and conservation concerns. Instead, the present volume and its core themes should be understood as a direct product of the case studies it engages and the particular set of disciplinary interests – across anthropology, archaeology, creative practice, cultural geography, histories of science and material culture studies – which have catalysed as a result of the mix of researchers involved.

While the four themes of the research programme provide clear entry points into understanding how heritage practices broadly conceived can be compared with one another and rethought in relation to the distinctive futures each is engaged in resourcing and realising, there are other themes that have long been of interest to heritage studies that the book cannot address thoroughly. These concern, for example, the interrelations between heritage, conflict, violence and social unrest that represent another, considerable, challenge to thinking through the heritage futures in heritage studies (for example, see Tunbridge and Ashworth 1996; Breithoff 2020), as do questions of virtual and online heritage phenomena and practices (for example, see Harrison 2009; Geismar 2018). Nonetheless, we see the book and its themes as providing a starting point for initiating new ways of thinking and working that can be taken up by other researchers working in these and adjacent fields. In this sense, the book's four organising themes – Diversity, Profusion, Transformation and Uncertainty – while helpful as an organisational device in articulating the comparative analyses we wish to pursue, should not be seen as total or universal. While we aimed to make a radical new cut into heritage studies, we did so with the intention that it would open up, rather than close down, the possibility of other equally (or even more!) radical new ways of rethinking the direction of the field of research that might follow it.

Through the Heritage Futures research programme – and in this book about it – we have sought to develop new approaches to heritage and to critical heritage studies. We have breached the usual borders of what counts as heritage and have put the focus firmly on the future, rather than the past. At the same time, we have taken unconventional thematic areas as our starting point, while still attending closely to the actual practices performed by heritage and heritage-related fields of various kinds. This has allowed us to investigate natural and cultural preservation in significant depth, while also bringing our findings into comparative perspective with one another. Through this research, in which we have often worked closely with heritage practitioners, we have thus been able to identify how certain contemporary practices and assumptions actively realise and produce certain kinds of futures that may be problematic, conflicting or unanticipated. Recognition of the unsustainability of many forms of conventional heritage practices is no longer something that can be deferred. However, by attending to the often sophisticated and creative ideas and innovations that we have encountered in our research fields – and by thinking between and across them – we have sought to highlight where there is potential for thinking and doing heritage differently in the future. This is, we believe, a vital task, not only for heritage studies but for heritage itself. It is, moreover, vital for all of our futures.

Note

1. These comments can be read in full in context at https://heritage-futures.org/reflections-transforming-loss.

References

Abram, David. 1997. *The Spell of the Sensuous: Perception and Language in a More-Than-Human World*. New York: Vintage Books.

Adam, Barbara and Chris Groves. 2007. *Future Matters: Action, Knowledge, Ethics*. Leiden: Brill.

Adam, Barbara and Chris Groves. 2011. 'Futures Tended: Care and Future-Oriented Responsibility', *Bulletin of Science, Technology and Society* 31 (1): 17–27.

Adeney Thomas, Julia. 2016. 'Coda: Who is the "We" Endangered by Climate Change?'. In *Endangerment, Biodiversity and Culture*, edited by Fernando Vidal and Nélia Dias, 241–60. London: Routledge.

Agamben, Giorgio. 2009. *What is an Apparatus? and Other Essays*, translated by David Kishik and Stefan Pedatella. Stanford: Stanford University Press.

Agence France-Presse. 2017. 'Portugal: Interior Minister Resigns after Wildfires Kill 100', *The Guardian*, 19 October. Accessed 1 February 2020. www.theguardian.com/world/2017/oct/19/portugal-interior-minister-resigns-wild-fires-dead.

Agnew, Neville and Janet Bridgland, eds. 2006. *Of the Past, for the Future: Integrating Archaeology and Conservation: Proceedings of the Conservation Theme at the 5th World Archaeological Congress, Washington, DC, 22–26 June 2003*. Los Angeles: Getty Conservation Institute.

Ahlbom, Kaj, Timo Äikäs and Lars O. Ericsson. 1991. *SKB/TVO Ice Age Scenario* (Technical Report 91–32). Stockholm: Svensk kärnbränslehantering AB. Accessed 5 February 2020. www.skb.se/publication/5941/TR91-32webb.pdf.

Aikawa-Faure, Noriko. 2009. 'From the Proclamation of Masterpieces to the *Convention for the Safeguarding of Intangible Cultural Heritage*'. In *Intangible Heritage*, edited by Laurajane Smith and Natsuko Akagawa, 13–44. London: Routledge.

Alabaster, Olivia. 2015. 'Syrian Civil War: Svalbard "Doomsday" Seeds Transferred to Lebanon to Preserve Syria's Crop Heritage', *The Independent*, 10 October. Accessed 29 January 2020. www.independent.co.uk/news/world/middle-east/syrian-civil-war-svalbard-doomsday-seeds-transferred-to-lebanon-to-preserve-syrias-crop-heritage-a6689421.html.

Andrén, Mats. 2012. *Nuclear Waste Management and Legitimacy: Nihilism and Responsibility*. London: Routledge.

APG (Angiosperm Phylogeny Group) IV. 2016. 'An Update of the Angiosperm Phylogeny Group Classification for the Orders and Families of Flowering Plants: APG IV', *Botanical Journal of the Linnean Society* 181 (1): 1–20.

Appadurai, Arjun. 2006. *Fear of Small Numbers: An Essay on the Geography of Anger*. Durham, NC: Duke University Press.

Appadurai, Arjun. 2013. *The Future as Cultural Fact: Essays on the Global Condition*. London: Verso.

Appelgren, Staffan and Anna Bohlin. 2015a. 'Introduction: Circulating Stuff through Second-Hand, Vintage and Retro Markets', *Culture Unbound* 7: 3–11.

Appelgren, Staffan and Anna Bohlin. 2015b. 'Growing in Motion: The Circulation of Used Things on Second-Hand Markets', *Culture Unbound* 7: 143–68.

Arnold, Jeanne E., Anthony P. Graesch, Enzo Ragazzini and Elinor Ochs. 2012. *Life at Home in the Twenty-First Century: 32 Families Open Their Doors*. Los Angeles: Cotsen Institute of Archaeology Press.

Asdal, Åsmund, 2019, email communication to Rodney Harrison and Esther Breithoff, 27 February.

ATN (Associação Transumância e Natureza). 2015. *Nature Conservation Strategic Plan*. Figueira de Castelo Rodrigo: Associação Transumância e Natureza.

Baillie, Jonathan E.M., Craig Hilton-Taylor and Simon N. Stuart, eds. 2004. *2004 IUCN Red List of Threatened Species: A Global Species Assessment*. Cambridge: IUCN Publications. Accessed 5 February 2020. https://portals.iucn.org/library/node/9830.

Baird, Melissa F. 2017. *Critical Theory and the Anthropology of Heritage Landscapes*. Gainesville: University Press of Florida.

Bakewell, Lyndsey, Antonia Liguori and Michael Wilson. 2019. 'From Gallura to the Fens: Communities Performing Stories of Water'. In *Water, Creativity and Meaning: Multidisciplinary Understandings of Human–Water Relationships*, edited by Liz Roberts and Katherine Phillips, 70–84. London: Routledge.

Balzer, David. 2015. *Curationism: How Curating Took Over the Art World and Everything Else*. London: Pluto Press.

Barad, Karen. 2007. *Meeting the Universe Halfway: Quantum Physics and the Entanglement of Matter and Meaning*. Durham, NC: Duke University Press.

Baraitser, Lisa. 2014. 'Time and Again: Repetition, Maternity and the Non-Reproductive', *Studies in the Maternal* 6 (1): 1–7.

Baraitser, Lisa. 2015. 'Touching Time: Maintenance, Endurance, Care'. In *Psychosocial Imaginaries: Perspectives on Temporality, Subjectivities and Activism*, edited by Stephen Frosh, 21–47. Basingstoke: Palgrave Macmillan.

Barišić, Marko, Aida Murtić and Alisa Burzić, eds. 2017. *Mostarska Hurqualya: (Ne)Zaboravljeni grad*. Bihać: Grafičar.

Bartolini, Nadia. 2013. 'Rome's Pasts and the Creation of New Urban Spaces: Brecciation, Matter, and the Play of Surfaces and Depths', *Environment and Planning D: Society and Space* 31 (6): 1041–61.

Bartolini, Nadia and Caitlin DeSilvey. 2020a. 'Recording Loss: Film as Method and the Spirit of Orford Ness', *International Journal of Heritage Studies* 26 (1): 19–36.

Bartolini, Nadia and Caitlin DeSilvey. 2020b. 'Rewilding as Heritage-Making: New Natural Heritage and Renewed Memories in Portugal'. In *The Routledge Handbook of Memory and Place*, edited by Sarah De Nardi, Hilary Orange, Steven High and Eerika Koskinen-Koivisto, 305–14. London: Routledge.

Bastian, Michelle. 2014. 'Time and Community: A Scoping Study', *Time and Society* 23 (2): 137–66.

Bauman, Zygmunt. 2000. *Liquid Modernity*. Cambridge: Polity Press.

Baxter, Katherine, Gail Boyle and Lucy Creighton. 2018. *Guidance on the Rationalisation of Museum Archaeology Collections*. Swindon: Historic England. Accessed 5 February 2020. http://socmusarch.org.uk/projects/guidance-on-the-rationalisation-of-museum-archaeology-collections.

BBC News. 2018. 'Orfordness Lighthouse: Volunteers' Battle against the Sea', *BBC News*, 12 August. Accessed 29 January 2020. www.bbc.co.uk/news/av/uk-england-suffolk-45143431/orfordness-lighthouse-volunteers-battle-against-the-sea.

Beck, Petra. 2016. 'Restopia – Self-Storage as Urban Practice: "Like a Hotel – but for Things"'. In *Müll: Interdisziplinäre Perspektiven auf das Übrig-Gebliebene*, edited by Christiane Lewe, Tim Othold and Nicolas Oxen, 117–40. Bielefeld: Transcript Verlag.

Beck, Ulrich. 1992. *Risk Society: Towards a New Modernity*, translated by Mark Ritter. London: SAGE Publications.

Belk, Russell W., Melanie Wallendorf, John F. Sherry and Morris B. Holbrook. 1991. 'Collecting in a Consumer Culture'. In *Highways and Buyways: Naturalistic Research from the Consumer Behaviour Odyssey*, edited by Russell W. Belk, 178–215. Provo, UT: Association for Consumer Research.

Belk, Russell W., Joon Yong Seo and Eric Li. 2007. 'Dirty Little Secret: Home Chaos and Professional Organizers', *Consumption Markets and Culture* 10 (2): 133–40.

Bell, David and Joanne Hollows, eds. 2016. *Historicizing Lifestyle: Mediating Taste, Consumption and Identity from the 1900s to 1970s*. London: Routledge.

Bell, Mary Ellen and Susan E. Bell. 2012. 'What to Do with All This "Stuff"? Memory, Family, and Material Objects', *Storytelling, Self, Society* 8 (2): 63–84.

Bell, Susan E. 2013. 'Objects, Memory and Narrative'. Workshop presentation at Goldsmiths, University of London, 4 July 2013. Accessed 5 February 2020. http://eprints.ncrm.ac.uk/3176/1/NOVELLA_Objects_Memory_and_Narrative_to_post_2013_with_notes_added.pdf.

Benford, Gregory. 1999. *Deep Time: How Humanity Communicates across Millennia*. New York: Avon.

Benirschke, Kurt. 1984. 'The Frozen Zoo Concept', *Zoo Biology* 3 (4): 325–28.

Bennett, Jane. 2010. *Vibrant Matter: A Political Ecology of Things*. Durham, NC: Duke University Press.

Bennett, Tony. 1995. *The Birth of the Museum: History, Theory, Politics*. London: Routledge.

Bennett, Tony. 2013. *Making Culture, Changing Society*. London: Routledge.

Bennett, Tony. 2014. 'Liberal Government and the Practical History of Anthropology', *History and Anthropology* 25 (2): 150–70.

Bennett, Tony and Chris Healy. 2009. 'Introduction: Assembling Culture', *Journal of Cultural Economy* 2 (1/2): 3–10.

Bennett, Tony, Fiona Cameron, Nélia Dias, Ben Dibley, Rodney Harrison, Ira Jacknis and Conal McCarthy. 2017. *Collecting, Ordering, Governing: Anthropology, Museums, and Liberal Government.* Durham, NC: Duke University Press.

Bennett, Tony, Ben Dibley and Rodney Harrison. 2014. 'Introduction: Anthropology, Collecting and Colonial Governmentalities', *History and Anthropology* 25 (2): 137–49.

Benson, Etienne. 2010. *Wired Wilderness: Technologies of Tracking and the Making of Modern Wildlife.* Baltimore: Johns Hopkins University Press.

Berardi, Franco. 2017. *Futurability: The Age of Impotence and the Horizon of Possibility.* London: Verso.

Berger, John. 1972. *Ways of Seeing.* London: BBC and Penguin.

Bergson, Henri. [1888] 2007. *Essai sur les données immédiates de la conscience.* Paris: Presses universitaires de France.

Berman, Marshall. 1983. *All That is Solid Melts into Air: The Experience of Modernity.* London: Verso.

Bhaskar, Michael. 2016. *Curation: The Power of Selection in a World of Excess.* London: Piatkus.

Bieber, Florian. 2002. 'Nationalist Mobilization and Stories of Serb Suffering: The Kosovo Myth from 600th Anniversary to the Present', *Rethinking History* 6 (1): 95–110.

Binyon, Laurence. 1914. 'For the Fallen', *The Times,* 21 September, 9.

Bird Rose, Deborah. 2003. *Sharing Kinship with Nature: How Reconciliation is Transforming the NSW National Parks and Wildlife Service.* Sydney: NSW National Parks and Wildlife Service. Accessed 5 February 2020. www.environment.nsw.gov.au/resources/cultureheritage/SharingKinship.pdf.

Bird Rose, Deborah. 2011. *Wild Dog Dreaming: Love and Extinction.* Charlottesville: University of Virginia Press.

Bird Rose, Deborah, Thom van Dooren and Matthew Chrulew, eds. 2017. *Extinction Studies: Stories of Time, Death, and Generations.* New York: Columbia University Press.

Bohlin, Anna. 2019. '"It Will Keep Circulating": Loving and Letting Go of Things in Swedish Second-Hand Markets', *Worldwide Waste: Journal of Interdisciplinary Studies* 2 (1), Article 3: 1–11. Accessed 30 January 2020. http://doi.org/10.5334/wwwj.17.

Bonacchi, Chiara, Andrew Bevan, Daniel Pett, Adi Keinan-Schoonbaert, Rachael Sparks, Jennifer Wexler and Neil Wilkin. 2014. 'Crowd-Sourced Archaeological Research: The MicroPasts Project', *Archaeology International* 17: 61–68.

Bonacchi, Chiara, Mark Altaweel and Marta Krzyzanska. 2018. 'The Heritage of Brexit: Roles of the Past in the Construction of Political Identities through Social Media', *Journal of Social Archaeology* 18 (2): 174–92.

Bond, Steven, Caitlin DeSilvey and James R. Ryan. 2013. *Visible Mending: Everyday Repairs in the South West.* Axminster: Uniformbooks.

Borges, Jorge Luis. (2000 [1941]). 'The Library of Babel'. In *Fictions,* translated by Andrew Hurley, 65–74. London: Penguin.

Borowy, Iris. 2014. *Defining Sustainable Development for Our Common Future: A History of the World Commission on Environment and Development (Brundtland Commission).* London: Routledge.

Bourdieu, Pierre. 1984. *Distinction: A Social Critique of the Judgement of Taste,* translated by Richard Nice. London: Routledge and Kegan Paul.

Bowker, Geoffrey C. 2000. 'Biodiversity Datadiversity', *Social Studies of Science* 30 (5): 643–83.

Bowker, Geoffrey C. 2005a. *Memory Practices in the Sciences.* Cambridge, MA: MIT Press.

Bowker, Geoffrey C. 2005b. 'Time, Money, and Biodiversity'. In *Global Assemblages: Technology, Politics, and Ethics as Anthropological Problems,* edited by Aihwa Ong and Stephen J. Collier, 107–23. Malden, MA: Blackwell.

Bowker, Geoffrey C. and Susan Leigh Star. 2000. *Sorting Things Out: Classification and Its Consequences.* Cambridge, MA: MIT Press.

Bowkett, Andrew E. 2009. 'Recent Captive Breeding Proposals and the Return of the Ark Concept to Global Species Conservation', *Conservation Biology* 23 (3): 773–76.

Bråkenhielm, Carl Reinhold. 2015. 'Ethics and the Management of Spent Nuclear Fuel', *Journal of Risk Research* 18 (3): 392–405.

Brand, Stewart. 2008. *The Clock of the Long Now: Time and Responsibility: The Ideas behind the World's Slowest Computer.* New York: Basic Books.

Braun, Bruce. 2015. 'Futures: Imagining Socioecological Transformation: An Introduction', *Annals of the Association of American Geographers* 105 (2): 239–43.

Braverman, Irus. 2015. *Wild Life: The Institution of Nature*. Stanford: Stanford University Press.

Braverman, Irus. 2017. 'Anticipating Endangerment: The Biopolitics of Threatened Species Lists', *BioSocieties* 12 (1): 132–57.

Breithoff, Esther. 2020. *Conflict, Heritage and World-Making in the Chaco: War at the end of the Worlds?* London: UCL Press.

Breithoff, Esther and Rodney Harrison. 2020a. 'From Ark to Bank: Extinction, Proxies and Biocapitals in Ex-Situ Biodiversity Conservation Practices', *International Journal of Heritage Studies* 26 (1): 37–55.

Breithoff, Esther and Rodney Harrison. 2020b. 'Making Futures in End Times: Nature Conservation in the Anthropocene'. In *Deterritorializing the Future: Heritage in, of and after the Anthropocene*, edited by Rodney Harrison and Colin Sterling, 155–87. London: Open Humanities Press.

Brett, David. 1996. *The Construction of Heritage*. Cork: Cork University Press.

Bristow, Colin. 2007. 'Notes for a Guided Walk at Carclaze'. China Clay History Society. Unpublished.

Bristow, Colin. 2016. 'The Role of Carclaze Tin Mine in Eighteenth and Nineteenth Century Geotourism'. In *Appreciating Physical Landscapes: Three Hundred Years of Geotourism*, edited by T.A. Hose, 187–97. London: Geological Society of London.

Brophy, Kenneth. 2018. 'The Brexit Hypothesis and Prehistory', *Antiquity* 92 (366): 1650–58.

Brosius, J. Peter and Lisa M. Campbell. 2010. 'Collaborative Event Ethnography: Conservation and Development Trade-Offs at the Fourth World Conservation Congress', *Conservation and Society* 8 (4): 245–55.

Brown, Bill. 2015. *Other Things*. Chicago: University of Chicago Press.

Brown, Kate. 2019. *Manual for Survival: A Chernobyl Guide to the Future*. London: Allen Lane.

Brown, Sarah. 2019. 'Banishing Documentation Backlogs', Museums Galleries Scotland blog, 4 February. Accessed 23 February 2020. www.mgsblog.org/sector-stories/banishing-documentation-backlogs/.

Brumann, Christoph. 2014. 'Shifting Tides of World-Making in the UNESCO World Heritage Convention: Cosmopolitanisms Colliding', *Ethnic and Racial Studies* 37 (12): 2176–92.

Brumann, Christoph and David Berliner, eds. 2016. *World Heritage on the Ground: Ethnographic Perspectives*. New York: Berghahn Books.

Brundtland Commission. 1987. *Report of the World Commission on Environment and Development: Our Common Future*. Transmitted to the General Assembly as an Annex to Document A/42/427 – *Development and International Co-operation: Environment*. Accessed 5 February 2020. www.un-documents.net/wced-ocf.htm.

Brusius, Mirjam and Kavita Singh, eds. 2018. *Museum Storage and Meaning: Tales from the Crypt*. London: Routledge.

Buller, Henry. 2013. 'Animal Geographies I', *Progress in Human Geography* 38 (2): 308–18.

Buller, Henry. 2015. 'Animal Geographies II: Methods', *Progress in Human Geography* 39 (3): 374–84.

Buser, Marcos. 2016. *Rubbish Theory: The Heritage of Toxic Waste*. Amsterdam: Reinwardt Academy.

Butler, Alison. 2017. '13 Ways of Looking at a Lake'. In *The Long Take: Critical Approaches*, edited by John Gibbs and Douglas Pye, 177–91. London: Palgrave Macmillan.

Byrne, Denis. 2014. *Counterheritage: Critical Perspectives on Heritage Conservation in Asia*. New York: Routledge.

Callaghan, Des. 2014. 'Survey of Western Rustwort (Marsupella profunda) and other Bryophytes at Land at West Carclaze, Cornwall'. Cornwall Council, PA14-12186: Environmental Impact Vol.2 Appendices 9.2.

Callon, Michel, ed. 1998. *The Laws of the Markets*. Oxford: Blackwell.

Callon, Michel. 2005. 'Why Virtualism Paves the Way to Political Impotence: A Reply to Daniel Miller's Critique of *The Laws of the Markets*', *Economic Sociology: European Electronic Newsletter* 6 (2): 3–20.

Callon, Michel and Fabian Muniesa. 2005. 'Peripheral Vision: Economic Markets as Calculative Collective Devices', *Organization Studies* 26 (8): 1229–50.

Campbell, Colin. 1987. *The Romantic Ethic and the Spirit of Modern Consumerism*. Oxford: Blackwell.

Campbell, Colin. 2015. 'The Curse of the New: How the Accelerating Pursuit of the New is Driving Hyper-Consumption'. In *Waste Management and Sustainable Consumption: Reflections on Consumer Waste*, edited by Karin M. Ekström, 29–51. London: Routledge.

Carabelli, Giulia. 2018. *The Divided City and the Grassroots: The (Un)making of Ethnic Divisions in Mostar*. Singapore: Palgrave Macmillan.

CARMAH (Centre for Anthropological Research on Museums and Heritage). 2018. *Otherwise: Rethinking Museums and Heritage* (CARMAH Paper 1). Berlin: Centre for Anthropological

Research on Museums and Heritage. Accessed 5 February 2020. www.carmah.berlin/wp-content/uploads/2017/10/Carmah_Paper-1.pdf.

Caro, Tim. 2010. *Conservation by Proxy: Indicator, Umbrella, Keystone, Flagship, and Other Surrogate Species.* Washington, DC: Island Press.

Carrington, Damian. 2017. 'Arctic Stronghold of World's Seeds Flooded After Permafrost Melts', *The Guardian*, 19 May. Accessed 22 February 2020. www.theguardian.com/environment/2017/may/19/arctic-stronghold-of-worlds-seeds-flooded-after-permafrost-melts.

Carrington, Damian. 2018. 'Allow Nuclear Waste Disposal under National Parks, Say MPs', *The Guardian*, 31 July. Accessed 30 January 2020. www.theguardian.com/environment/2018/jul/31/allow-nuclear-waste-disposal-in-national-parks-say-mps.

Castañeda, Quetzil E. and Christopher N. Matthews, eds. 2008. *Ethnographic Archaeologies: Reflections on Stakeholders and Archaeological Practices.* Lanham, MD: AltaMira Press.

CBD (Convention on Biological Diversity). 2000. *Sustaining Life on Earth: How the Convention on Biological Diversity Promotes Nature and Human Well-Being.* Montreal: Secretariat of the Convention on Biological Diversity. Accessed 5 February 2020. www.cbd.int/doc/publications/cbd-sustain-en.pdf.

CBD (Convention on Biological Diversity). 2011. Nagoya Protocol on Access to Genetic Resources and the Fair and Equitable Sharing of Benefits Arising from their Utilization to the Convention on Biological Diversity. Montreal: Secretariat of the Convention on Biological Diversity. Accessed 5 February 2020. www.cbd.int/abs/doc/protocol/nagoya-protocol-en.pdf.

Chakrabarty, Dipesh. 2009. 'The Climate of History: Four Theses', *Critical Inquiry* 35 (2): 197–222.

Chapman, Arthur. 2018. 'Relativity, Historicity and Historical Studies', *Public History Weekly*, 15 March. Accessed 6 February 2020. https://public-history-weekly.degruyter.com/6-2018-9/relativity-historicity/.

Chase, Mark W., Douglas E. Soltis, Richard G. Olmstead, David Morgan, Donald H. Les, Brent D. Mishler, et al. 1993. 'Phylogenetics of Seed Plants: An Analysis of Nucleotide Sequences from the Plastid Gene *rbcL*', *Annals of the Missouri Botanical Garden* 80 (3): 528–80.

Chemnick, Leona G., Marlys L. Houck and Oliver A. Ryder. 2009. 'Banking of Genetic Resources: The Frozen Zoo at the San Diego Zoo'. In *Conservation Genetics in the Age of Genomics*, edited by George Amato, Oliver Ryder, Howard Rosenbaum and Rob DeSalle, 124–30. New York: Columbia University Press.

Chilvers, Jason. 2008. 'Environmental Risk, Uncertainty, and Participation: Mapping an Emergent Epistemic Community', *Environment and Planning A: Economy and Space* 40 (12): 2990–3008.

Chin, Elizabeth. 2016. *My Life with Things: The Consumer Diaries.* Durham, NC: Duke University Press.

Chrulew, Matthew. 2017. 'Freezing the Ark: The Cryopolitics of Endangered Species Preservation'. In *Cryopolitics: Frozen Life in a Melting World*, edited by Joanna Radin and Emma Kowal, 283–306. Cambridge, MA: MIT Press.

Cieraad, Irene. 2010. 'Homes from Home: Memories and Projections', *Home Cultures: The Journal of Architecture, Design and Domestic Space* 7 (1): 85–102.

CITiZAN (Coastal and Intertidal Zone Archaeological Network). n.d. 'G7 Police Lookout, Orford Ness (Formerly Orford Ness; East of England) (81581)'. Accessed 5 February 2020. https://citizan.org.uk/interactive-coastal-map/81581/.

Clark, Nigel. 2011. *Inhuman Nature: Sociable Life on a Dynamic Planet.* London: SAGE Publications.

Clarke, A.G. 2009. 'The Frozen Ark Project: The Role of Zoos and Aquariums in Preserving the Genetic Material of Threatened Animals', *International Zoo Yearbook* 43: 222–30.

Clarke, Bryan, James Murray and Michael S. Johnson. 1984. 'The Extinction of Endemic Species by a Program of Biological Control', *Pacific Science* 38 (2): 97–104.

ClayFutures. 2009. *Which Way for the Clay? Creative Community Engagement Project Report 2009.* Bodelva: Eden Project. Accessed 5 February 2020. www.edenproject.com/sites/default/files/documents/ClayFutures%20final%20report.pdf.

Clay Trails. n.d. 'Maps and Routes: Eden Project to Wheal Martyn'. Accessed 25 February 2020. www.claytrails.co.uk/eden-project-wheal-martyn.

Clemo, Jack. 1991. *Clay Cuts.* Church Hanborough: Previous Parrot Press.

Cockell, Charles and Gerda Horneck. 2004. 'A Planetary Park System for Mars', *Space Policy* 20 (4): 291–95.

Codée, Hans and Ewoud Verhoef. 2015. 'What's the Story? Using Art, Stories and Cultural Heritage to Preserve Knowledge and Memory'. In *Radioactive Waste Management and Constructing Memory for Future Generations: Proceedings of the International Conference and Debate, 15–17 September 2014, Verdun, France*, 53–56. Paris: Organisation for Economic Co-operation and Development. Accessed 6 February 2020. www.oecd-nea.org/rwm/pubs/2015/7259-constructing-memory-2015.pdf.

Collar, N.J. 1996. 'The Reasons for Red Data Books', *Oryx* 30 (2): 121–30.

Čolović, Ivan. 2011. *The Balkans: The Terror of Culture: Essays in Political Anthropology*. Baden-Baden: Nomos.

Conn, Barry J. 2012. 'Botanical Collecting'. In *The Oxford Handbook of Linguistic Fieldwork*, edited by Nicholas Thieberger, 250–80. Oxford: Oxford University Press.

Connerton, Paul. 1989. *How Societies Remember*. Cambridge: Cambridge University Press.

Connerton, Paul. 2008. 'Seven Types of Forgetting', *Memory Studies* 1 (1): 59–71.

Connerton, Paul. 2009. *How Modernity Forgets*. Cambridge: Cambridge University Press.

Connerton, Paul. 2011. *The Spirit of Mourning: History, Memory and the Body*. Cambridge: Cambridge University Press.

Cooper, Melinda. 2008. *Life as Surplus: Biotechnology and Capitalism in the Neoliberal Era*. Seattle: University of Washington Press.

Cooper, Melinda and Catherine Waldby. 2014. *Clinical Labor: Tissue Donors and Research Subjects in the Global Bioeconomy*. Durham, NC: Duke University Press.

Corley-Smith, Graham E. and Bruce P. Brandhorst. 1999. 'Preservation of Endangered Species and Populations: A Role for Genome Banking, Somatic Cell Cloning, and Androgenesis?', *Molecular Reproduction and Development* 53 (3): 363–67.

Corson, Catherine, Rebecca Gruby, Rebecca Witter, Shannon Hagerman, Daniel Suarez, Shannon Greenberg, Maggie Bourque, Noella Gray and Lisa M. Campbell. 2014. 'Everyone's Solution? Defining and Redefining Protected Areas at the Convention on Biological Diversity', *Conservation and Society* 12 (2): 190–202.

Costa, Mafalda and Michael W. Bruford. 2018. 'The Frozen Ark Project: Biobanking and Endangered Animal Samples for Conservation and Research', *Inside Ecology*, 12 January. Accessed 5 February 2020. https://insideecology.com/2018/01/12/the-frozen-ark-project-biobanking-endangered-animal-samples-for-conservation-and-research/.

Côté, Isabelle M. and Emily S. Darling. 2018. 'Scientists on Twitter: Preaching to the Choir or Singing from the Rooftops?', *Facets* 3: 682–94.

Cowell, Ben. 2008. *The Heritage Obsession: The Battle for England's Past*. Stroud: Tempus.

Crang, Mike and Penny S. Travlou. 2001. 'The City and Topologies of Memory', *Environment and Planning D: Society and Space* 19 (2): 161–77.

Crewe, Louise. 2011. 'Life Itemised: Lists, Loss, Unexpected Significance, and the Enduring Geographies of Discard', *Environment and Planning D: Society and Space* 29 (1): 27–46.

Crist, Eileen. 2016. 'On the Poverty of Our Nomenclature'. In *Anthropocene or Capitalocene? Nature, History, and the Crisis of Capitalism*, edited by Jason W. Moore, 14–33. Oakland, CA: PM Press.

Crop Trust. n.d. a. 'Svalbard Global Seed Vault'. Accessed 5 July 2019. www.croptrust.org/what-we-do/svalbard-global-seed-vault/.

Crop Trust. n.d. b. 'FAQ about the Seed Vault'. Accessed 5 July 2019. www.croptrust.org/what-we-do/svalbard-global-seed-vault/faq-about-the-vault/.

Cross, Sally and Helen Wilkinson. 2007. *Making Collections Effective*. London: Museums Association.

Csikszentmihalyi, Mihaly and Eugene Rochberg-Halton. 1981. *The Meaning of Things: Domestic Symbols and the Self*. Cambridge: Cambridge University Press.

Cwerner, Saulo B. and Alan Metcalfe. 2003. 'Storage and Clutter: Discourses and Practices of Order in the Domestic World', *Journal of Design History* 16 (3): 229–39.

Czarniawska, Barbara and Orvar Löfgren, eds. 2012. *Managing Overflow in Affluent Societies*. New York: Routledge.

Dames, Michael. 1992. *Mythic Ireland*. London: Thames and Hudson.

Das, Subhadra. 2015. 'Adventures in Disposal: Sawdust & Threads'. Museums and Collections blog. 17 February. Accessed 1 March 2020. https://blogs.ucl.ac.uk/museums/2015/02/17/adventures-in-disposal-sawdust-threads/.

Daston, Lorraine. 2012. 'The Sciences of the Archive', *Osiris* 27: 156–87.

Daston, Lorraine and Peter Galison. 2010. *Objectivity*. New York: Zone Books.

Daston, Lorraine and Elizabeth Lunbeck, eds. 2011. *Histories of Scientific Observation*. Chicago: University of Chicago Press.

Dawdy, Shannon Lee. 2016. *Patina: A Profane Archaeology*. Chicago: Chicago University Press.

Dawney, Leila Alexandra, Oliver J.T. Harris and Tim Flohr Sørensen. 2017. 'Future World: Anticipatory Archaeology, Materially Affective Capacities and the Late Human Legacy', *Journal of Contemporary Archaeology* 4 (1): 107–29.

De la Cadena, Marisol and Mario Blaser, eds. 2018. *A World of Many Worlds*. Durham, NC: Duke University Press.

DeLanda, Manuel. 2006. *A New Philosophy of Society: Assemblage Theory and Social Complexity*. London: Continuum.

Deleuze, Gilles and Félix Guattari. 1987. *A Thousand Plateaus: Capitalism and Schizophrenia*, translated by Brian Massumi. Minneapolis: University of Minnesota Press.

De Nardi, Sarah. 2017. 'Everyday Heritage Activism in Swat Valley: Ethnographic Reflections on a Politics of Hope', *Heritage and Society* 10 (3): 237–58.

Derrida, Jacques. 1994. *Specters of Marx: The State of the Debt, the Work of Mourning, and the New International*, translated by Peggy Kamuf. London: Routledge.

Derrida, Jacques. 1996. *Archive Fever: A Freudian Impression*, translated by Eric Prenowitz. Chicago: University of Chicago Press.

Descola, Philippe. 2013. *Beyond Nature and Culture*, translated by Janet Lloyd. Chicago: University of Chicago Press.

DeSilvey, Caitlin. 2012. 'Making Sense of Transience: An Anticipatory History'. *Cultural Geographies* 19 (1): 31–54.

DeSilvey, Caitlin. 2014. 'Palliative Curation: Art and Entropy on Orford Ness'. In *Ruin Memories: Materialities, Aesthetics and the Archaeology of the Recent Past*, edited by Bjørnar Olsen and Þóra Pétursdóttir, 79–91. London: Routledge.

DeSilvey, Caitlin. 2017. *Curated Decay: Heritage beyond Saving*. Minneapolis: University of Minnesota Press.

DeSilvey, Caitlin. 2019. 'Rewilding Time in the Vale do Côa'. In *Rethinking Historical Time: New Approaches to Presentism*, edited by Marek Tamm and Laurent Olivier, 193–206. London: Bloomsbury Academic.

DeSilvey, Caitlin. 2020. 'Ruderal Heritage'. In *Deterritorialising the Future: Heritage in, of and after the Anthropocene*, edited by Rodney Harrison and Colin Sterling, 289–310. London: Open Humanities Press.

DeSilvey, Caitlin and Nadia Bartolini. 2019. 'Where Horses Run Free? Autonomy, Temporality and Rewilding in the Côa Valley, Portugal', *Transactions of the Institute of British Geographers* 44 (1): 94–109.

DeSilvey, Caitlin and Rodney Harrison. 2020. 'Anticipating Loss: Rethinking Endangerment in Heritage Futures', *International Journal of Heritage Studies* 26 (1): 1–7.

DeSilvey, Caitlin, Simon Naylor and Colin Sackett, eds. 2011. *Anticipatory History*. Axminster: Uniform Books.

Devictor, Vincent and Bernadette Bensaude-Vincent. 2016. 'From Ecological Records to Big Data: The Invention of Global Biodiversity', *History and Philosophy of the Life Sciences* 38 (4), Article 13: 1–23. Accessed 1 February 2020. https://doi.org/10.1007/s40656-016-0113-2.

Dibley, Ben. 2012. '"The Shape of Things to Come": Seven Theses on the Anthropocene and Attachment', *Australian Humanities Review* 52: 139–53.

Dibley, Ben. 2015. 'Anthropocene: The Enigma of "the Geomorphic Fold"'. In *Animals in the Anthropocene: Critical Perspectives on Non-Human Futures*, edited by the Human Animal Research Network Editorial Collective, 19–32. Sydney: Sydney University Press.

Dicks, Bella. 2004. *Culture on Display: The Production of Contemporary Visitability*. Maidenhead: Open University Press.

Djokić, Dejan. 2009. 'Whose Myth? Which Nation? The Serbian Kosovo Myth Revisited'. In *Uses and Abuses of the Middle Ages. 19th–21st Century*, edited by János M. Bak, Jörg Jarnut, Pierre Monnet and Bernd Schneidmüller, 215–33. Munich: Wilhelm Fink Verlag.

Douglas, Mary. 1991. *Purity and Danger: An Analysis of the Concepts of Pollution and Taboo*. London: Routledge.

Douglas, Mary and Aaron Wildavsky. 1982. *Risk and Culture: An Essay on the Selection of Technical and Environmental Dangers*. Berkeley: University of California Press.

Douglas-Jones, Rachel, John J. Hughes, Siân Jones and Thomas Yarrow. 2016. 'Science, Value and Material Decay in the Conservation of Historic Environments', *Journal of Cultural Heritage* 21: 823–33.

Doyle, Richard. 1997. *On Beyond Living: Rhetorical Transformations of the Life Sciences*. Stanford: Stanford University Press.

Drazin, Adam and David Frohlich. 2007. 'Good Intentions: Remembering through Framing Photographs in English Homes', *Ethnos* 72 (1): 51–76.

Drozdzewski, Danielle, Sarah De Nardi and Emma Waterton. 2016. 'Geographies of Memory, Place and Identity: Intersections in Remembering War and Conflict', *Geography Compass* 10 (11): 447–56.

Dudley, Sandra H., ed. 2010. *Museum Materialities: Objects, Engagements, Interpretations*. London: Routledge.

Duijzings, Ger. 2000. *Religion and the Politics of Identity in Kosovo*. London: Hurst and Company.

Duijzings, Ger. 2007. 'Commemorating Srebrenica: Histories of Violence and the Politics of Memory in Eastern Bosnia'. In *The New Bosnian Mosaic: Identities, Memories and Moral Claims in a Post-War Society*, edited by Xavier Bougarel, Elissa Helms and Ger Duijzings, 141–66. Aldershot: Ashgate.

Edelman, Lee. 2004. *No Future: Queer Theory and the Death Drive*. Durham, NC: Duke University Press.

Edwards, Elizabeth. 2012. *The Camera as Historian: Amateur Photographers and Historical Imagination, 1885–1918*. Durham, NC: Duke University Press.

Ehrenfreund, P., N. Peter, K.U. Schrogl and J.M. Logsdon. 2010. 'Cross-Cultural Management Supporting Global Space Exploration', *Acta Astronautica* 66 (1/2): 245–56.

Eldrige, Devin. 2017. 'Self-Storage Innovations, Statistics, and Changes in 2017', *Medium*, 17 October. Accessed 6 February 2020. https://medium.com/@cpa_preneur/self-storage-innovations-statistics-and-changes-in-2017-25c0d7b81efe.

Elsner, John and Roger Cardinal, eds. 1994. *The Cultures of Collecting*. London: Reaktion Books.

Endres, Danielle. 2009. 'The Rhetoric of Nuclear Colonialism: Rhetorical Exclusion of American Indian Arguments in the Yucca Mountain Nuclear Waste Siting Decision', *Communication and Critical/Cultural Studies* 6 (1): 39–60.

English, Bonnie. 2013. *A Cultural History of Fashion in the 20th and 21st Centuries: From Catwalk to Sidewalk*. 2nd ed. London: Bloomsbury Academic.

ESA (European Space Agency). 2002. 'Rosetta Disk Goes Back to the Future'. Accessed 1 February 2020. http://sci.esa.int/rosetta/31242-rosetta-disk-goes-back-to-the-future/.

Escobar, Arturo. 2018. *Designs for the Pluriverse: Radical Interdependence, Autonomy, and the Making of Worlds*. Durham, NC: Duke University Press.

Fay, Michael F. 2011. 'Joseph Dalton Hooker (1817–1911) – A Great Linnean', *Botanical Journal of the Linnean Society* 167 (4): 353–56.

Federal Ministry of Justice and Consumer Protection. 2017. 'Gesetz zur Suche und Auswahl eines Standortes für ein Endlager für hochradioaktive Abfälle (Standortauswahlgesetz – StandAG)'. Accessed 24 February 2020. www.gesetze-im-internet.de/standag_2017/BJNR107410017.html.

FEDESSA (Federation of European Self Storage Associations). 2018. *European Self Storage Annual Survey*. Brussels: Federation of European Self Storage Associations. Accessed 5 February 2020. www.fedessa.org/publications/fedessa-european-annual-report.

Fenzi, Marianna and Christophe Bonneuil. 2016. 'From "Genetic Resources" to "Ecosystems Services": A Century of Science and Global Policies for Crop Diversity Conservation', *Culture, Agriculture, Food and Environment* 38 (2): 72–83.

Fincher, Ruth, John Barnett and Sonia Graham. 2015. 'Temporalities in Adaptation to Sea-Level Rise', *Annals of the Association of American Geographers* 105 (2): 263–73.

Fisk, Harold N. 1944. *Geological Investigation of the Alluvial Valley of the Lower Mississippi River*. Vicksburg, MS. US War Department Corps of Engineers.

Fitter, Richard and Maisie Fitter, eds. 1987. *The Road to Extinction: Problems of Categorizing the Status of Taxa Threatened with Extinction: Proceedings of a Symposium Held by the Species Survival Commission, Madrid, 7 and 9 November 1984*. Cambridge: IUCN Publications. Accessed 5 February 2020. https://portals.iucn.org/library/sites/library/files/documents/1987–001.pdf.

Fitzpatrick, Tony. 2004. 'Social Policy and Time', *Time and Society* 13 (2/3): 197–219.

Fletcher, Robert. 2014. 'Orchestrating Consent: Post-Politics and Intensification of Nature™ Inc. at the 2012 World Conservation Congress', *Conservation and Society* 12 (3): 329–42.

Fluck, Hannah. 2016. *Climate Change Adaptation Report* (Research Report 28). Swindon: Historic England. Accessed 5 February 2020. https://research.historicengland.org.uk/Report.aspx?i=15500.

Fluck, Hannah and Meredith Wiggins. 2017. 'Climate Change, Heritage Policy and Practice in England: Risks and Opportunities', *Archaeological Review from Cambridge* 32 (2): 159–81.

Forde, Susan. 2016. 'The Bridge on the Neretva: Stari Most as a Stage of Memory in Post-Conflict Mostar, Bosnia-Herzegovina', *Cooperation and Conflict* 51 (4): 467–83.

Forty, Adrian and Susanne Küchler, eds. 1999. *The Art of Forgetting*. Oxford: Berg.

Foster, Hal. 2004. 'An Archival Impulse', *October* 110: 3–22.

Foucault, Michel. 2008. *The Birth of Biopolitics: Lectures at the Collège de France, 1978–79*, edited by Michel Senellart; translated by Graham Burchell. Basingstoke: Palgrave Macmillan.

Foucault, Michel. 2009. *Security, Territory, Population: Lectures at the Collège de France, 1977–1978*, edited by Michel Senellart; translated by Graham Burchell. New York: Picador.

Fowler, Cary. 2008. *The Svalbard Global Seed Vault: Securing the Future of Agriculture*. Rome: Global Crop Diversity Trust. Accessed 6 February 2020. www.gov.uk/dfid-research-outputs/the-svalbard-global-seed-vault-securing-the-future-of-global-agriculture.

Franklin, Sarah. 2013. *Biological Relatives: IVF, Stem Cells, and the Future of Kinship*. Durham, NC: Duke University Press.

Fredheim, L. Harald and Manal Khalaf. 2016. 'The Significance of Values: Heritage Value Typologies Re-Examined', *International Journal of Heritage Studies* 22 (6): 466–81.

Fredheim, Harald, Sharon Macdonald and Jennie Morgan. 2018. *Profusion in Museums: A Report on Contemporary Collecting and Disposal*. Accessed 6 February 2020. https://heritage-futures.org/profusion-in-museums-report.

Friese, Carrie. 2013. *Cloning Wild Life: Zoos, Captivity, and the Future of Endangered Animals*. New York: New York University Press.

Frodeman, Robert. 2003. *Geo-Logic: Breaking Ground between Philosophy and the Earth Sciences*. Albany: State University of New York Press.

Frost, Randy O. and Gail Steketee. 2011. *Stuff: Compulsive Hoarding and the Meaning of Things*. Boston: Houghton Mifflin Harcourt.

Frozen Ark. 2020. 'The Frozen Ark Project'. Accessed 1 February 2020. www.frozenark.org.

Fuller, Steve. 2013. 'Beyond the Precautionary Principle', *The Guardian*, 10 July. Accessed 1 February 2020. www.theguardian.com/science/political-science/2013/jul/10/beyond-precautionary-principle.

Galison, Peter. 2015. 'On the Building, Crashing, and Thinking of Technologies and Selfhood: Peter Galison in Conversation with Etienne Turpin'. In *Art in the Anthropocene: Encounters among Aesthetics, Politics, Environments and Epistemologies*, edited by Heather Davis and Etienne Turpin, 181–90. London: Open Humanities Press.

Gault, Richard. 1995. 'In and out of Time', *Environmental Values* 4: 149–66.

Geismar, Haidy. 2015. 'Anthropology and Heritage Regimes', *Annual Review of Anthropology* 44: 71–85.

Geismar, Haidy. 2018. *Museum Object Lessons for the Digital Age*. London: UCL Press.

Geissler, Paul Wenzel, Guillaume Lachenal, John Manton and Noémi Tousignant, eds. 2016. *Traces of the Future: An Archaeology of Medical Science in Africa*. Chicago: University of Chicago Press.

Gell, Alfred. 1992. *The Anthropology of Time: Cultural Constructions of Temporal Maps and Images*. Oxford: Berg.

Gemeinholzer, Birgit, Gabriele Dröge, Holger Zetzsche, Gerhard Haszprunar, Hans-Peter Klenk, Anton Güntsch, Walter G. Berendsohn and Johann-Wolfgang Wägele. 2011. 'The DNA Bank Network: The Start from a German Initiative', *Biopreservation and Biobanking* 9 (1): 51–55.

Geppert, Alexander C.T. 2012. 'Rethinking the Space Age: Astroculture and Technoscience', *History and Technology* 28 (3): 219–23.

Gfeller, Aurélie Elisa. 2013. 'Negotiating the Meaning of Global Heritage: "Cultural Landscapes" in the UNESCO World Heritage Convention, 1972–92', *Journal of Global History* 8 (3): 483–503.

Giddens, Anthony. 1991. *Modernity and Self-Identity: Self and Society in the Late Modern Age*. Cambridge: Polity Press.

Ginn, Franklin, Michelle Bastian, David Farrier and Jeremy Kidwell. 2018. 'Introduction. Unexpected Encounters with Deep Time', *Environmental Humanities* 10 (1): 213–25.

Goldsmith, Donald. 1990. 'Who Will Speak for Earth? Possible Structures for Shaping a Response to a Signal Detected from an Extraterrestrial Civilization', *Acta Astronautica* 21 (2): 149–51.

Goldstein, Jason R. 1997. 'Deaccession: Not Such a Dirty Word', *Cardozo Arts and Entertainment Law Journal* 15 (1): 213–47.

González-Ruibal, Alfredo. 2008. 'Time to Destroy: An Archaeology of Supermodernity', *Current Anthropology* 49 (2): 247–79.

González-Ruibal, Alfredo. 2014. *An Archaeology of Resistance: Materiality and Time in an African Borderland*. Lanham, MD: Rowman and Littlefield.

González-Ruibal, Alfredo, Pablo Alonso González and Felipe Criado-Boado. 2018. 'Against Reactionary Populism: Towards a New Public Archaeology', *Antiquity* 92 (362): 507–15.

Gordillo, Gastón R. 2014. *Rubble: The Afterlife of Destruction*. Durham, NC: Duke University Press.

Gorman, Alice. 2009. 'The Archaeology of Space Exploration', *Sociological Review* 57 (Supplement 1): 132–45.

Gorman Alice. 2015. 'Robot Avatars: The Material Culture of Human Activity in Earth Orbit'. In *Archaeology and Heritage of the Human Movement into Space*, edited by Beth Laura O'Leary and P.J. Capelotti, 29–47. Cham: Springer.

Gorman, Alice. 2016. 'Culture on the Moon: Bodies in Time and Space', *Archaeologies* 12 (1): 110–28.

Gorman, Alice. 2018. 'A Sports Car and a Glitter Ball Are Now in Space – What Does That Say about Us as Humans?', *The Conversation*, 7 February. Accessed 1 February 2020. https://theconversation.com/a-sports-car-and-a-glitter-ball-are-now-in-space-what-does-that-say-about-us-as-humans-91156.

Goyder, David, Pat Griggs, Mark Nesbitt, Lynn Parker and Kiri Ross-Jones. 2012. 'Sir Joseph Hooker's Collections at the Royal Botanic Gardens, Kew', *Curtis's Botanical Magazine* 29 (1): 66–85.

Graber, Christoph Beat. 2006. 'The New UNESCO Convention on Cultural Diversity: A Counterbalance to the WTO?', *Journal of International Economic Law* 9 (3): 553–74.

Grange, Sophie, Patrick Duncan and Jean-Michel Gaillard. 2009. 'Poor Horse Traders: Large Mammals Trade Survival for Reproduction during the Process of Feralization', *Proceedings of the Royal Society B: Biological Sciences* 276: 1911–19.

Graves-Brown, Paul and Hilary Orange. 2017. '"The Stars Look Very Different Today": Celebrity Veneration, Grassroot Memorials and the Apotheosis of David Bowie', *Material Religion* 13 (1): 121–23.

Greene, Mark A. 2006. 'I've Deaccessioned and Lived to Tell about It: Confessions of an Unrepentant Reappraiser', *Archival Issues* 30 (1): 7–22.

Gregson, Nicky. 2011. *Living with Things: Ridding, Accommodation, Dwelling*. Wantage: Sean Kingston Publishing.

Gregson, Nicky, Alan Metcalfe and Louise Crewe. 2007a. 'Identity, Mobility, and the Throwaway Society', *Environment and Planning D: Society and Space* 25 (4): 682–700.

Gregson, Nicky, Alan Metcalfe and Louise Crewe. 2007b. 'Moving Things Along: The Conduits and Practices of Divestment in Consumption', *Transactions of the Institute of British Geographers* 32 (2): 187–200.

Gregson, Nicky, Alan Metcalfe and Louise Crewe. 2009. 'Practices of Object Maintenance and Repair: How Consumers Attend to Consumer Objects within the Home', *Journal of Consumer Culture* 9 (2): 248–72.

Griesser-Stermscheg, Martina. 2013. *Tabu Depot: Das Museumsdepot in Geschichte und Gegenwart*. Vienna: Böhlau Verlag.

Griffiths, Tom. 1996. *Hunters and Collectors: The Antiquarian Imagination in Australia*. Cambridge: Cambridge University Press.

Grodach, Carl. 2002. 'Reconstituting Identity and History in Post-War Mostar, Bosnia-Herzegovina', *City: Analysis of Urban Trends, Culture, Theory, Policy, Action* 6 (1): 61–82.

Groves, Christopher, Karen Henwood, Fiona Shirani and Catherine Butler. 2016. 'Invested in Unsustainability? On the Psychosocial Patterning of Engagement in Practices', *Environmental Values* 25 (3): 309–28.

Groves, Craig R., Deborah B. Jensen, Laura L. Valutis, Kent H. Redford, Mark L. Shaffer, J. Michael Scott, Jeffrey V. Baumgartner, Jonathan V. Higgins, Michael W. Beck and Mark G. Anderson. 2002. 'Planning for Biodiversity Conservation: Putting Conservation Science into Practice', *BioScience* 52 (6): 499–512.

Hackett, Amy. 2017. 'Trash or Treasure? Te Papa and the Collecting of Everyday Material Culture'. Master's thesis, Victoria University of Wellington.

Hacking, Ian. 1995. 'The Looping Effects of Human Kinds'. In *Causal Cognition: A Multidisciplinary Debate*, edited by Dan Sperber, David Premack and Ann James Premack, 351–83. Oxford: Clarendon Press.

Hage, Ghassan. 2003. *Against Paranoid Nationalism: Searching for Hope in a Shrinking Society*. Sydney: Pluto Press.

Hale, Ken, Michael Krauss, Lucille J. Watahomigie, Akira Y. Yamamoto, Colette Craig, LaVerne Masayesva Jeanne and Nora C. England. 1992. 'Endangered Languages', *Language* 68 (1): 1–42.

Hale, Thomas, David Held and Kevin Young. 2013. *Gridlock: Why Global Cooperation is Failing When We Need It Most*. Cambridge: Polity Press.

Hambrecht, George and Marcy Rockman. 2017. 'International Approaches to Climate Change and Cultural Heritage', *American Antiquity* 82 (4): 627–41.

Hamilakis, Yannis. 2011. 'Archaeological Ethnography: A Multitemporal Meeting Ground for Archaeology and Anthropology', *Annual Review of Anthropology* 40: 399–414.

Hamilakis, Yannis and Aris Anagnostopoulos. 2009. 'What is Archaeological Ethnography?', *Public Archaeology* 8 (2/3): 65–87.

Hand, Martin, Elizabeth Shove and Dale Southerton. 2005. 'Explaining Showering: A Discussion of the Material, Conventional, and Temporal Dimensions of Practice', *Sociological Research Online* 10 (2): 1–13. Accessed 1 February 2020. https://doi.org/10.5153/sro.1100.

Haraway, Donna J. 1991. *Simians, Cyborgs, and Women: The Reinvention of Nature.* London: Free Association.

Haraway, Donna. 2003. *The Companion Species Manifesto: Dogs, People, and Significant Otherness.* Chicago: Prickly Paradigm Press.

Haraway, Donna. 2004. *The Haraway Reader.* New York: Routledge.

Haraway, Donna. 2006. 'Encounters with Companion Species: Entangling Dogs, Baboons, Philosophers, and Biologists', *Configurations* 14 (1/2): 97–114.

Haraway, Donna J. 2008. *When Species Meet.* Minneapolis: University of Minnesota Press.

Haraway, Donna. 2011. 'Speculative Fabulations for Technoculture's Generations: Taking Care of Unexpected Country', *Australian Humanities Review* 50: 95–118.

Haraway, Donna. 2015. 'Anthropocene, Capitalocene, Plantationocene, Chthulucene: Making Kin', *Environmental Humanities* 6 (1): 159–65.

Haraway, Donna J. 2016. *Staying with the Trouble: Making Kin in the Chthulucene.* Durham, NC: Duke University Press.

Harmon, David. 2002. *In Light of Our Differences: How Diversity in Nature and Culture Makes Us Human.* Washington, DC: Smithsonian Institution Press.

Harrison, Colin J. 1979. 'Birds of the Cromer Forest Bed Series of the East Anglian Pleistocene', *Transactions of the Norfolk and Norwich Naturalists' Society* 25 (1): 277–86.

Harrison, Rodney. 2002. 'Archaeology and the Colonial Encounter: Kimberley Spearpoints, Cultural Identity and Masculinity in the North of Australia', *Journal of Social Archaeology* 2 (3): 352–77.

Harrison, Rodney. 2004. *Shared Landscapes: Archaeologies of Attachment and the Pastoral Industry in New South Wales.* Sydney: University of New South Wales Press.

Harrison, Rodney. 2009. 'Excavating Second Life: Cyber-Archaeologies, Heritage and Virtual Communities', *Journal of Material Culture* 14 (1): 75–106.

Harrison, Rodney. 2011. 'Surface Assemblages: Towards an Archaeology in and of the Present', *Archaeological Dialogues* 18 (2): 141–61.

Harrison, Rodney. 2013a. *Heritage: Critical Approaches.* London: Routledge.

Harrison, Rodney. 2013b. 'Forgetting to Remember, Remembering to Forget: Late Modern Heritage Practices, Sustainability and the "Crisis" of Accumulation of the Past', *International Journal of Heritage Studies* 19 (6): 579–95.

Harrison, Rodney. 2013c. 'Reassembling Ethnographic Museum Collections'. In *Reassembling the Collection: Ethnographic Museums and Indigenous Agency*, edited by Rodney Harrison, Sarah Byrne and Anne Clarke, 3–35. Santa Fe: School for Advanced Research Press.

Harrison, Rodney. 2014. 'Observing, Collecting and Governing "Ourselves" and "Others": Mass-Observation's Fieldwork Agencements', *History and Anthropology* 25 (2): 227–45.

Harrison, Rodney. 2015. 'Beyond "Natural" and "Cultural" Heritage: Toward an Ontological Politics of Heritage in the Age of Anthropocene', *Heritage and Society* 8 (1): 24–42.

Harrison, Rodney. 2016a. 'Archaeologies of Emergent Presents and Futures', *Historical Archaeology* 50 (3): 165–80.

Harrison, Rodney. 2016b. 'World Heritage Listing and the Globalization of the Endangerment Sensibility'. In *Endangerment, Biodiversity and Culture*, edited by Fernando Vidal and Nélia Dias, 195–217. London: Routledge.

Harrison, Rodney. 2017. 'Freezing Seeds and Making Futures: Endangerment, Hope, Security, and Time in Agrobiodiversity Conservation Practices', *Culture, Agriculture, Food and Environment* 39 (2): 80–89.

Harrison, Rodney. 2018. 'On Heritage Ontologies: Rethinking the Material Worlds of Heritage', *Anthropological Quarterly* 91 (4): 1365–83.

Harrison, Rodney and Colin Sterling, eds. 2020. *Deterritorializing the Future: Heritage in, of and after the Anthropocene.* London: Open Humanities Press.

Harrison, Rodney, Nadia Bartolini, Caitlin DeSilvey, Cornelius Holtorf, Antony Lyons, Sharon Macdonald, Sarah May, Jennie Morgan and Sefryn Penrose. 2016. 'Heritage Futures', *Archaeology International* 19: 68–72.

Harrison, Rodney, Hana Morel, Maja Maricevic and Sefryn Penrose. 2017. *Heritage and Data: Challenges and Opportunities for the Heritage Sector: Report of the Heritage Data Research Workshop*

Held Friday 23 June 2017 at the British Library, London. Accessed 6 February 2020. https://heritage-research.org/app/uploads/2017/11/Heritage-Data-Challenges-Opportunities-Report.pdf.

Harrison, Stephan, Steve Pile and Nigel Thrift, eds. 2004. *Patterned Ground: Entanglements of Nature and Culture*. London: Reaktion Books.

Hartog, François. 2016. *Regimes of Historicity: Presentism and Experiences of Time*, translated by Saskia Brown. New York: Columbia University Press.

Harvey, David. 1981. 'The Spatial Fix – Hegel, Von Thünen, and Marx', *Antipode* 13 (3): 1–12.

Harvey, David. 1996. *Justice, Nature and the Geography of Difference*. Oxford: Blackwell.

Harvey, David. 2001a. 'Globalization and the "Spatial Fix"', *Geographische Revue* 3 (2): 23–30.

Harvey, David C. 2001b. 'Heritage Pasts and Heritage Presents: Temporality, Meaning and the Scope of Heritage Studies', *International Journal of Heritage Studies* 7 (4): 319–38.

Harvey, David C. 2015. 'Heritage and Scale: Settings, Boundaries and Relations', *International Journal of Heritage Studies* 21 (6): 577–93.

Harvey, David C. and Jim Perry. 2015a. 'Heritage and Climate Change: The Future is Not the Past'. In *The Future of Heritage as Climates Change: Loss, Adaptation and Creativity*, edited by David C. Harvey and Jim Perry, 3–22. London: Routledge.

Harvey, David C. and Jim Perry, eds. 2015b. *The Future of Heritage as Climates Change: Loss, Adaptation and Creativity*. London: Routledge.

Hazir, Irmak Karademir. 2015. 'Cultural Omnivorousness'. *Oxford Bibliographies*. Accessed 6 February 2020. https://doi.org/10.1093/OBO/9780199756384–0134.

Heathcote, Jen, Hannah Fluck and Meredith Wiggins. 2017. 'Predicting and Adapting to Climate Change: Challenges for the Historic Environment', *Historic Environment: Policy and Practice* 8 (2): 89–100.

Heatherington, Tracey. 2012. 'From Ecocide to Genetic Rescue: Can Technoscience Save the Wild?'. In *The Anthropology of Extinction: Essays on Culture and Species Death*, edited by Genese Marie Sodikoff, 39–66. Bloomington: Indiana University Press.

Heazell, Paddy. 2010. *Most Secret: The Hidden History of Orford Ness*. Stroud: History Press.

Heinich, Nathalie. 2009. *La fabrique du patrimoine*. Paris: Éditions de la Maison des sciences de l'homme.

Heinich, Nathalie. 2011. 'The Making of Cultural Heritage', *The Nordic Journal of Aesthetics* 22 (40–41): 119–28.

Heise, Ursula K. 2016. *Imagining Extinction: The Cultural Meanings of Endangered Species*. Chicago: University of Chicago Press.

Helm, Dieter. 2015. *Natural Capital: Valuing Our Planet*. New Haven: Yale University Press.

Helmreich, Stefan. 2008. 'Species of Biocapital', *Science as Culture* 17 (4): 463–78.

Henderson, Jane. 2018. 'Managing Uncertainty for Preventive Conservation', *Studies in Conservation* 63 (Supplement 1): S108–12.

Herring, Scott. 2014. *The Hoarders: Material Deviance in Modern American Culture*. Chicago: University of Chicago Press.

Hertz, Ellen. 2000. 'Stock Markets as "Simulacra": Observation That Participates', *Tsantsa* 5: 40–50. Accessed 6 February 2020. www.tsantsa.ch/content/6-archiv/20-ausgabe-5/1-inhalt-5–1999/1-dossier/4-stock-markets-as-simulacra/4.stock-markets-as-simulacra-observation-that-participates-ellen-hertz.pdf.

Herzfeld, Michael. 2004. *The Body Impolitic: Artisans and Artifice in the Global Hierarchy of Value*. Chicago: University of Chicago Press.

Herzfeld, Michael. 2006. 'Spatial Cleansing: Monumental Vacuity and the Idea of the West', *Journal of Material Culture* 11 (1/2): 127–49.

Hetherington, Kevin, 2002. 'The Unsightly: Touching the Parthenon Frieze', *Theory, Culture and Society* 19 (5/6): 187–205.

Hetherington, Kevin. 2004. 'Secondhandedness: Consumption, Disposal, and Absent Presence', *Environment and Planning D: Society and Space* 22 (1): 157–73.

Hetherington, Kevin. 2005. 'Memories of Capitalism: Cities, Phantasmagoria and Arcades', *International Journal of Urban and Regional Research* 29 (1): 187–200.

Hetherington, Kevin. 2007. 'Manchester's Urbis: Urban Regeneration, Museums and Symbolic Economies', *Cultural Studies* 21 (4/5): 630–49.

Hewison, Robert. 1987. *The Heritage Industry: Britain in a Climate of Decline*. London: Methuen.

Heyd, David. 2010. 'Cultural Diversity and Biodiversity: A Tempting Analogy', *Critical Review of International Social and Political Philosophy* 13 (1): 159–79.

Himmelmann, Nikolaus P. 1998. 'Documentary and Descriptive Linguistics', *Linguistics* 36 (1): 161–95.

Himmelmann, Nikolaus P. 2008. 'Reproduction and Preservation of Linguistic Knowledge: Linguistics' Response to Language Endangerment', *Annual Review of Anthropology* 37: 337–50.

Hinchliffe, Steve. 2007. *Geographies of Nature: Societies, Environments, Ecologies*. London: SAGE Publications.

Hitchcock, Michael and Ken Teague, eds. 2000. *Souvenirs: The Material Culture of Tourism*. Aldershot: Ashgate.

Hobsbawm, Eric and Terence Ranger, eds. 1983. *The Invention of Tradition*. Cambridge: Cambridge University Press.

Hodder, Ian. 1999. *The Archaeological Process: An Introduction*. Oxford: Blackwell.

Hodgetts, Nick. 2011. 'A Revised Red List of Bryophytes in Britain', *Field Bryology* 103: 40–49.

Hogan, Susan and Sarah Pink. 2010. 'Routes to Interiorities: Art Therapy and Knowing in Anthropology', *Visual Anthropology* 23 (2): 158–74.

Högberg, Anders and Cornelius Holtorf. 2016. 'Långtidsförvaring av kärnavfall: Från samtidsarkeologi till framtidsarkeologi', *Primitive tider* 18: 285–95.

Högberg, Anders, Cornelius Holtorf, Sarah May and Gustav Wollentz. 2017. 'No Future in Archaeological Heritage Management?', *World Archaeology* 49 (5): 639–47.

Holbraad, Martin and Morten Axel Pedersen. 2017. *The Ontological Turn: An Anthropological Exposition*. Cambridge: Cambridge University Press.

Holbraad, Martin, Morten Axel Pedersen and Eduardo Viveiros de Castro. 2014. 'The Politics of Ontology: Anthropological Positions', *Fieldsights*, 13 January. Accessed 6 February 2020. www.culanth.org/fieldsights/462-the-politics-of-ontology-anthropological-positions.

Holdgate, Martin. 1999. *The Green Web: A Union for World Conservation*. London: Earthscan.

Holland, Alan and Kate Rawles. 1994. *The Ethics of Conservation: Report Prepared for, and Submitted to Countryside Council for Wales* (Thingmount Working Paper Series on the Philosophy of Conservation TWP 96–01). Lancaster: Lancaster University.

Holmes, Douglas R. and George E. Marcus. 2005. 'Cultures of Expertise and the Management of Globalization: Toward the Re-Functioning of Ethnography'. In *Global Assemblages: Technology, Politics, and Ethics as Anthropological Problems*, edited by Aihwa Ong and Stephen J. Collier, 235–52. Malden, MA: Blackwell.

Holmes, Douglas R. and George E. Marcus. 2006. 'Fast Capitalism: Para-Ethnography and the Rise of the Symbolic Analyst'. In *Frontiers of Capital: Ethnographic Reflections on the New Economy*, edited by Melissa S. Fisher and Greg Downey, 33–57. Durham, NC: Duke University Press.

Holmes, Douglas R. and George E. Marcus. 2008. 'Collaboration Today and the Re-Imagination of the Classic Scene of Fieldwork Encounter', *Collaborative Anthropologies* 1: 81–101.

Holtorf, Cornelius. 2010. 'Heritage Values in Contemporary Popular Culture'. In *Heritage Values in Contemporary Society*, edited by George S. Smith, Phyllis Mauch Messenger and Hilary A. Soderland, 43–54. Walnut Creek, CA: Left Coast Press.

Holtorf, Cornelius. 2012. 'The Heritage of Heritage', *Heritage and Society* 5 (2): 153–73.

Holtorf, Cornelius. 2015. 'Averting Loss Aversion in Cultural Heritage', *International Journal of Heritage Studies* 21 (4): 405–21.

Holtorf, Cornelius. 2018. 'Embracing Change: How Cultural Resilience is Increased through Cultural Heritage', *World Archaeology* 50 (4): 639–50.

Holtorf, Cornelius and Anders Högberg. 2013. 'Heritage Futures and the Future of Heritage'. In *Counterpoint: Essays in Archaeology and Heritage Studies in Honour of Professor Kristian Kristiansen* (BAR International Series 2508), edited by Sophie Bergerbrant and Serena Sabatini, 739–46. Oxford: Archaeopress.

Holtorf, Cornelius and Anders Högberg. 2014a. 'Communicating with Future Generations: What Are the Benefits of Preserving Cultural Heritage? Nuclear Power and Beyond', *European Journal of Post-Classical Archaeologies* 4: 343–58.

Holtorf, Cornelius and Anders Högberg. 2014b. 'Nuclear Waste as Cultural Heritage of the Future – 14361'. WM2014 Conference Proceedings, 2–6 March 2014, Phoenix Arizona. Accessed 20 February 2020. www.wmsym.org/archives/2014/papers/14361.pdf.

Holtorf, Cornelius and Anders Högberg. 2015a. 'Archaeology and the Future: Managing Nuclear Waste as a Living Heritage'. In *Radioactive Waste Management and Constructing Memory for Future Generations: Proceedings of the International Conference and Debate, 15–17 September 2014, Verdun, France*, 97–101. Paris: Organisation for Economic Co-operation and Development. Accessed 6 February 2020. www.oecd-nea.org/rwm/pubs/2015/7259-constructing-memory-2015.pdf.

Holtorf, Cornelius and Anders Högberg. 2015b. 'Contemporary Heritage and the Future'. In *The Palgrave Handbook of Contemporary Heritage Research*, edited by Emma Waterton and Steve Watson, 509–23. Basingstoke: Palgrave Macmillan.

Holtorf, Cornelius and Anders Högberg. 2016. 'The Contemporary Archaeology of Nuclear Waste: Communicating with the Future', *Arkæologisk Forum* 35: 31–37.

Holtorf, Cornelius and Anders Högberg, eds. Forthcoming a. *Cultural Heritage and the Future*. London and New York: Routledge.

Holtorf, Cornelius and Anders Högberg. Forthcoming b. 'Perceptions of the Future in Preservation Strategies'. In *Cultural Heritage and the Future*, edited by Cornelius Holtorf and Anders Högberg. London and New York: Routledge.

Holtorf, Cornelius and Anders Högberg. Forthcoming c. 'Nuclear Waste as Cultural Heritage of the Future'. In *Cultural Heritage and the Future*, edited by Cornelius Holtorf and Anders Högberg. London and New York: Routledge.

Holtorf, Cornelius and Toshiyuki Kono. 2015. 'Forum on Nara + 20: An Introduction'. *Heritage and Society* 8 (2): 139–43.

Hosey, Geoff, Vicky Melfi and Shelia Pankhurst. 2009. *Zoo Animals: Behaviour, Management, and Welfare*. Oxford: Oxford University Press.

Howard, JoGayle, Ann M. Donoghue, Mark A. Barone, Karen L. Goodrowe, Evan S. Blumer, Kelley Snodgrass, Doyle Starnes, Michael Tucker, Mitchell Bush and David E. Wildt. 1992. 'Successful Induction of Ovarian Activity and Laparoscopic Intrauterine Artificial Insemination in the Cheetah (*Acinonyx jubatus*)', *Journal of Zoo and Wildlife Medicine* 23 (3): 288–300.

Howard, J.G., C. Lynch, R.M. Santymire, P.E. Marinari and D.E. Wildt. 2016. 'Recovery of Gene Diversity Using Long-Term Cryopreserved Spermatozoa and Artificial Insemination in the Endangered Black-Footed Ferret', *Animal Conservation* 19 (2): 102–11.

Hummer, Kim E. 2015. 'In the Footsteps of Vavilov: Plant Diversity Then and Now', *HortScience* 50 (6): 784–88.

Huyssen, Andreas. 2003. *Present Pasts: Urban Palimpsests and the Politics of Memory*. Stanford: Stanford University Press.

IAEA. 2018. *Status and Trends in Spent Fuel and Radioactive Waste Management*. IAEA Nuclear Energy Series No. NW-T-1.14. Vienna: International Atomic Energy Agency.

ICCROM (International Centre for the Study of the Preservation and Restoration of Cultural Property) and UNESCO (United Nations Educational, Scientific and Cultural Organization). 2011. 'ICCROM-UNESCO International Storage Survey 2011: Summary of Results'. Accessed 29 February 2020. www.iccrom.org/wp-content/uploads/RE-ORG-StorageSurveyResults_English.pdf.

Ikin, Timothy. 2011. 'A Conservation Ethic and the Collecting of Animals by Institutions of Natural Heritage in the Twenty-First Century: Case Study of the Australian Museum', *Animals* 1 (1): 176–85.

Illich, Ivan. 1986. *H₂O and the Waters of Forgetfulness*. London: Marion Boyars.

Imerys. n.d. 'About Us'. Accessed 6 February 2020. https://imerys-kaolin.com/europe-middle-east/en/imerys-minerals-limited-news/.

Ingold, Tim. 2010a. 'The Textility of Making', *Cambridge Journal of Economics* 34 (1): 91–102.

Ingold, Tim. 2010b. *Bringing Things to Life: Creative Entanglements in a World of Materials* (NCRM Working Paper 05/10). Southampton: National Centre for Research Methods. Accessed 6 February 2020. http://eprints.ncrm.ac.uk/1306/1/0510_creative_entanglements.pdf.

Ingold, Tim. 2010c. 'Footprints Through the Weather-World: Walking, Breathing, Knowing', *Journal of the Royal Anthropological Institute* 16 (S1): S121–S139.

Ingold, Tim. 2013. *Making: Anthropology, Archaeology, Art and Architecture*. London: Routledge.

Ingold, Tim. 2015. *The Life of Lines*. London: Routledge.

IUCN (International Union for the Conservation of Nature). 2020. 'Protected Area Categories'. Accessed 19 February 2020. www.iucn.org/theme/protected-areas/about/protected-area-categories.

Jackson, Stephen T. and Richard J. Hobbs. 2009. 'Ecological Restoration in the Light of Ecological History', *Science* 325 (5940): 567–69.

Jameson, Fredric. 1991. *Postmodernism; or, The Cultural Logic of Late Capitalism*. Durham, NC: Duke University Press.

Jameson, Fredric. 2007. *Archaeologies of the Future: The Desire Called Utopia and Other Science Fictions*. London: Verso.

Jepson, Paul and Frans Schepers. 2016. *Making Space for Rewilding: Creating an Enabling Policy Environment* (Policy Brief). Nijmegen: Rewilding Europe.

Jones, Barclay G., ed. 1986. *Protecting Historic Architecture and Museum Collections from Natural Disasters*. Boston: Butterworths.

Jones, Kate E. 2014. 'From Dinosaurs to Dodos: Who Could and Should We De-Extinct', *Frontiers of Biogeography* 6 (1): 20–24.

Jones, Siân. 2010. 'Negotiating Authentic Objects and Selves: Beyond the Deconstruction of Authenticity', *Journal of Material Culture* 15 (2): 181–203.

Jones, Siân. 2017. 'Wrestling with the Social Value of Heritage: Problems, Dilemmas and Opportunities', *Journal of Community Archaeology and Heritage* 4 (1): 21–37.

Jørgensen, Dolly. 2013. 'Reintroduction and De-Extinction', *BioScience* 63 (9): 719–20.

Joung, Hyun-Mee. 2014. 'Fast-Fashion Consumers' Post-Purchase Behaviours', *International Journal of Retail and Distribution Management* 42 (8): 688–97.

Joyce, James. 1939. *Finnegans Wake*. London: Faber and Faber.

Joyce, Patrick. 1999. 'The Politics of the Liberal Archive', *History of the Human Sciences* 12 (2): 35–49.

Joyce, Rosemary A. 2000. 'Heirlooms and Houses: Materiality and Social Memory'. In *Beyond Kinship: Social and Material Reproduction in House Societies*, edited by Rosemary A. Joyce and Susan D. Gillespie, 189–212. Philadelphia: University of Pennsylvania Press.

Joyce, Rosemary A. 2016. 'Failure? An Archaeology of the Architecture of Nuclear Waste Containment'. In *Elements of Architecture: Assembling Archaeology, Atmosphere and the Performance of Building Spaces*, edited by Mikkel Bille and Tim Flohr Sørensen, 424–38. London: Routledge.

Kallow, Simon. 2014. *UK National Tree Seed Project Seed Collecting Manual*. Richmond: Royal Botanic Gardens, Kew.

Kaplan, Robert D. 2005. *Balkan Ghosts: A Journey through History*. New York: Picador.

Kew (Royal Botanic Gardens, Kew). 2018. *Science Collections Strategy 2018–2028*. Richmond: Royal Botanic Gardens, Kew. Accessed 6 February 2020. http://brahmsonline.kew.org/Content/Projects/msbp/resources/Training/Kew_Science_Collections_Strategy_2018–2028.pdf.

Kew (Royal Botanic Gardens, Kew). n.d. 'UK National Tree Seed Project'. Accessed 9 July 2019. www.kew.org/science/our-science/projects/uk-national-tree-seed-project.

Kiddey, Rachael. 2017. *Homeless Heritage: Collaborative Social Archaeology as Therapeutic Practice*. Oxford: Oxford University Press.

Kilroy-Marac, Katie. 2016. 'A Magical Reorientation of the Modern: Professional Ogranizers and Thingly Care in Contemporary North America', *Cultural Anthropology* 31 (3): 438–57.

Kilroy-Marac, Katie. 2018. 'An Order of Distinction (or, How to Tell a Collection from a Hoard)', *Journal of Material Culture* 23 (1): 20–38.

Kindersley, Tania. 2011. 'The Cupboard of Doom', *The Small Things: A Blog of Scotland, Horses, Dogs, Love and Trees*, 22 June. Accessed 24 February 2020. http://taniakindersley.blogspot.com/2011/06/cupboard-of-doom.html.

Kingshill, Sophia and Jennifer Westwood. 2012. *The Fabled Coast: Legends and Traditions from around the Shores of Britain and Ireland*. London: Random House.

Kirkham, Graeme. 2014. *United Kingdom China-Clay Bearing Grounds: Mineral Resource Archaeological Assessment*. Truro: Cornwall Archaeological Unit. Accessed 6 February 2020. https://doi.org/10.5284/1040157.

Kirshenblatt-Gimblett, Barbara. 1998. *Destination Culture: Tourism, Museums, and Heritage*. Berkeley: University of California Press.

Kirshenblatt-Gimblett, Barbara. 2006. 'World Heritage and Cultural Economics'. In *Museum Frictions: Public Cultures/Global Transformations*, edited by Ivan Karp, Corinne A. Kratz, Lynn Szwaja and Tomás Ybarra-Frausto, 161–202. Durham, NC: Duke University Press.

Kisić, Višnja. 2016. *Governing Heritage Dissonance: Promises and Realities of Selected Cultural Policies*. Amsterdam: European Cultural Foundation.

Kleist, Nauja and Stef Jansen. 2016. 'Introduction: Hope over Time – Crisis, Immobility and Future-Making', *History and Anthropology* 27 (4): 373–92.

Klug, Katharina. 2018. *Vom Nischentrend zum Lebensstil: Der Einfluss des Lebensgefühls auf das Konsumentenverhalten*. Wiesbaden: Springer.

Kobiałka, Dawid. 2018. '100 Years Later: The Dark Heritage of the Great War at a Prisoner-of-War Camp in Czersk, Poland', *Antiquity* 92 (363): 772–87.

Kohler, Robert E. 2006. *All Creatures: Naturalists, Collectors, and Biodiversity, 1850–1950*. Princeton: Princeton University Press.

Kohler, Robert E. 2007. 'Finders, Keepers: Collecting Sciences and Collecting Practice', *History of Science* 45 (4): 428–54.

Kohn, Eduardo. 2015. 'Anthropology of Ontologies', *Annual Review of Anthropology* 44: 311–27.

Kolstø, Pål. 2005. 'Introduction: Assessing the Role of Historical Myths in Modern Society'. In *Myths and Boundaries in South-Eastern Europe*, edited by Pål Kolstø, 1–34. London: Hurst and Company.

Kondo, Marie. 2014. *The Life-Changing Magic of Tidying Up: The Japanese Art of Decluttering and Organizing*, translated by Cathy Hirano. Berkeley: Ten Speed Press.

Koren, Marina. 2017. 'Why the Curiosity Rover Stopped Singing "Happy Birthday" to Itself', *The Atlantic*, 10 August. Accessed 3 February 2020. www.theatlantic.com/science/archive/2017/08/why-the-curiosity-rover-stopped-singing-happy-birthday-to-itself/536487.

Koselleck, Reinhardt. 2004. *Futures Past: On the Semantics of Historical Time*, translated by Keith Tribe. New York: Columbia University Press.

Koslov, Liz. 2016. 'The Case for Retreat', *Public Culture* 28 (2): 359–87.

Krauss, Michael. 1992. 'The World's Languages in Crisis', *Language* 68 (1): 4–10.

Kruse, Jamie and Peter L. Galison. 2011. 'Waste-Wilderness: A Conversation with Peter L. Galison', *Friends of the Pleistocene*, 31 March. Accessed 6 February 2020. https://fopnews.wordpress.com/2011/03/31/galison/.

Kunreuther, Howard, Douglas Easterling, William Desvousges and Paul Slovic. 1990. 'Public Attitudes toward Siting a High-Level Nuclear Waste Repository in Nevada', *Risk Analysis* 10 (4): 469–84.

Kurtović, Larisa and Azra Hromadžić. 2017. 'Cannibal States, Empty Bellies: Protest, History and Political Imagination in Post-Dayton Bosnia', *Critique of Anthropology* 37 (3): 262–96.

Langfield, Michele, William Logan and Máiréad Nic Craith, eds. 2010. *Cultural Diversity, Heritage, and Human Rights: Intersections in Theory and Practice*. London: Routledge.

Larsen, Anne. 1996. 'Equipment for the Field'. In *Cultures of Natural History*, edited by N. Jardine, J.A. Secord and E.C. Spary, 358–77. Cambridge: Cambridge University Press.

Larwood, Jonathan, Sarah France and Chris Mahon, eds. 2017. *Culturally Natural or Naturally Cultural? Exploring the Relationship between Nature and Culture through World Heritage*. Mold: IUCN National Committee UK.

Latour, Bruno. 1987. *Science in Action: How to Follow Scientists and Engineers through Society*. Cambridge, MA: Harvard University Press.

Latour, Bruno. 1993. *We Have Never Been Modern*, translated by Catherine Porter. Cambridge, MA: Harvard University Press.

Latour, Bruno. 1999. *Pandora's Hope: Essays on the Reality of Science Studies*. Cambridge, MA: Harvard University Press.

Latour, Bruno. 2004. *Politics of Nature: How to Bring the Sciences into Democracy*, translated by Catherine Porter. Cambridge, MA: Harvard University Press.

Latour, Bruno. 2005. *Reassembling the Social: An Introduction to Actor-Network-Theory*. Oxford: Oxford University Press.

Latour, Bruno. 2010. 'An Attempt at a "Compositionist Manifesto"', *New Literary History* 41 (3): 471–90.

Latour, Bruno. 2013. *An Inquiry into Modes of Existence: An Anthropology of the Moderns*, translated by Catherine Porter. Cambridge, MA: Harvard University Press.

Latour, Bruno. 2014. 'Another Way to Compose the Common World', *HAU: Journal of Ethnographic Theory* 4 (1): 301–7.

Latour, Bruno and Adam Lowe. 2011. 'The Migration of the Aura, or How to Explore the Original through Its Facsimiles'. In *Switching Codes: Thinking through Digital Technology in the Humanities and Arts*, edited by Thomas Bartscherer and Roderick Coover, 275–97. Chicago: University of Chicago Press.

Law, John. 2004. 'Enacting Naturecultures: A View from STS'. Accessed 6 February 2020. www.heterogeneities.net/publications/Law2004EnactingNaturecultures.pdf.

Law, John and John Urry. 2004. 'Enacting the Social', *Economy and Society* 33 (3): 390–410.

Lawton, John. 2010. *Making Space for Nature: A Review of England's Wildlife Sites and Ecological Network*. London: Department for Environment, Food and Rural Affairs. Accessed 6 February 2020. https://webarchive.nationalarchives.gov.uk/20130402170324/http:/archive.defra.gov.uk/environment/biodiversity/documents/201009space-for-nature.pdf.

LDNPP (Lake District National Park Partnership). n.d. 'Lake District Nomination'. Accessed 6 February 2020. www.lakedistrict.gov.uk/caringfor/policies/whs/lake-district-nomination.

Leach, James. 2007. 'Differentiation and Encompassment: A Critique of Alfred Gell's Theory of the Abduction of Creativity'. In *Thinking through Things: Theorising Artefacts Ethnographically*, edited by Amiria Henare, Martin Holbraad and Sari Wastell, 167–88. London: Routledge.

Lee-Crossett, Kyle. 2018. *Collecting Change/Changing Collections*. Heritage Futures. Accessed 9 July 2019. https://heritage-futures.org/app/uploads/2019/01/Collecting_Change_Changing_Collections_R.pdf.

Lee-Crossett, Kyle. 2019. 'Collecting Change/Changing Collections: Diversity and Friction in Contemporary Archive and Museum Collecting in London'. PhD thesis, University College London.

Lemke, Thomas. 2012. 'Second Nature: In the Age of Biobanks', translated by Ishbel Flett, *Yearbook of Comparative Literature* 58: 188–92.

Lentin, Alana. 2005. 'Replacing "Race", Historicizing "Culture" in Multiculturalism', *Patterns of Prejudice* 39 (4): 379–96.

Leuvenink, Annemiek. 2013. 'Facilitating Social Learning to Increase Levels of Local Involvement: The Case of Associação Transumância e Natureza in Portugal'. Master's thesis, Wageningen University. Accessed 6 February 2020. http://edepot.wur.nl/303040.

Lévi-Strauss, Claude. 1952. *Race and History*. Paris: United Nations Educational, Scientific and Cultural Organization.

Lewis, Simon L. and Mark A. Maslin. 2018. *The Human Planet: How We Created the Anthropocene*. London: Pelican Books.

Liakos, Antonis and Mitsos Bilalis. 2017. 'The Jurassic Park of Historical Culture'. In *Palgrave Handbook of Research in Historical Culture and Education*, edited by Mario Carretero, Stefan Berger and Maria Grever, 207–24. London: Palgrave Macmillan.

Lipe, William D. 1984. 'Value and Meaning in Cultural Resources'. In *Approaches to the Archaeological Heritage*, edited by Henry Cleere, 1–11. Cambridge: Cambridge University Press.

Löfgren, Orvar and Barbara Czarniawska. 2012. 'The Inherited Theories of Overflow and Their Challengers'. In *Managing Overflow in Affluent Societies*, edited by Barbara Czarniawska and Orvar Löfgren, 1–12. New York: Routledge.

Logan, William and Keir Reeves, eds. 2009. *Places of Pain and Shame: Dealing with "Difficult Heritage"*. London: Routledge.

Lomberg, Jon. 2018. 'Ashes and Small Change: The American-Made Nonmessage That New Horizons Offers the Cosmos', *Slate*, 27 December. Accessed 3 February 2020. https://slate.com/technology/2018/12/new-horizons-solar-system-message-aliens-extraterrestrials.html.

Lorimer, Jamie. 2015. *Wildlife in the Anthropocene: Conservation after Nature*. Minneapolis: University of Minnesota Press.

Lovatt, Melanie. 2015. 'Charity Shops and the Imagined Future of Objects: How Second-Hand Markets Influence Disposal Decisions when Emptying a Parent's House', *Culture Unbound* 7: 13–29.

Lowenthal, David. 1985. *The Past is a Foreign Country*. Cambridge: Cambridge University Press.

Lowenthal, David. 2015. *The Past is a Foreign Country: Revisited*. Cambridge: Cambridge University Press.

Lubar, Steven. 2017. *Inside the Lost Museum: Curating, Past and Present*. Cambridge, MA: Harvard University Press.

Lubar, Steven, Lukas Rieppel, Ann Daly and Kathrinne Duffy. 2017. 'Lost Museums', *Museum History Journal* 10 (1): 1–14.

Lucas, Gavin. 2002. 'Disposability and Dispossession in the Twentieth Century', *Journal of Material Culture* 7 (1): 5–22.

Luhmann, Niklas. 1976. 'The Future Cannot Begin: Temporal Structures in Modern Society', *Social Research* 43 (1): 130–52.

Luhmann, Niklas. 1993. *Risk: A Sociological Theory*. Berlin: Walter de Gruyter.

Luís, C., R. Juras, M.M. Oom and E.G. Cothran. 2007. 'Genetic Diversity and Relationships of Portuguese and Other Horse Breeds Based on Protein and Microsatellite Loci Variation', *Animal Genetics* 38 (1): 20–27.

Luís, Luís and Marcos García Díez. 2008. 'Same Tradition, Different Views. The Côa Valley Rock Art and Social Identity'. In *Archaeologies of Art: Time, Place, and Identity*, edited by Inés Domingo Sanz, Dánae Fiore and Sally K. May, 151–70. Walnut Creek, CA: Left Coast Press.

Lupton, Deborah. 1999. *Risk*. London: Routledge.

Lury, Celia and Nina Wakeford, eds. 2012. *Inventive Methods: The Happening of the Social*. London: Routlege.

Lyons, Antony. 2019. 'Sunless Waters of Forgetfulness (A Geopoetic Assemblage)'. *In Water, Creativity and Meaning: Multidisciplinary Understandings of Human–Water Relationships*, edited by Liz Roberts and Katherine Phillips, 54–69. London: Routledge.

Macdonald, Sharon. 2006a. 'Collecting Practices'. In *A Companion to Museum Studies*, edited by Sharon Macdonald, 81–97. Malden, MA: Blackwell.

Macdonald, Sharon. 2006b. 'Undesirable Heritage: Fascist Material Culture and Historical Consciousness in Nuremberg', *International Journal of Heritage Studies* 12 (1): 9–28.

Macdonald, Sharon. 2009. *Difficult Heritage: Negotiating the Nazi Past in Nuremberg and Beyond*. London: Routledge.

Macdonald, Sharon. 2013. *Memorylands: Heritage and Identity in Europe Today*. London: Routledge.

Macdonald, Sharon. 2016. 'Exhibiting Contentious and Difficult Histories: Ethics, Emotions and Reflexivity'. In *Museums, Ethics and Cultural Heritage*, edited by Bernice L. Murphy, 267–77. London: Routledge.

Macdonald, Sharon. 2020. 'Thing'. In *Dictionary of Now*, edited by Bernd Scherer, Olga von Schubert and Stefan Aue. Berlin: Matthes und Seitz Berlin.

Macdonald, Sharon and Paul Basu, eds. 2007. *Exhibition Experiments*. Malden, MA: Blackwell.

Macdonald, Sharon and Jennie Morgan. 2018a. 'What Not to Collect? Post-Connoisseurial Dystopia and the Profusion of Things'. In *Curatopia: Museums and the Future of Curatorship*, edited by Philipp Schorch and Conal McCarthy, 29–43. Manchester: Manchester University Press.

Macdonald, Sharon and Jennie Morgan. 2018b. '"How Can We Know the Future?": Uncertainty, Transformation and Magical Techniques of Significance Assessment in Museum Collecting'. In *Assessment of Significance: Deuten – Bedeuten – Umdeuten*, edited by Regine Falkenberg and Thomas Jander, 20–26. Berlin: Deutsches Historisches Museum.

Macfarlane, Allison M. and Rodney C. Ewing, eds. 2006. *Uncertainty Underground: Yucca Mountain and the Nation's High-Level Nuclear Waste*. Cambridge, MA: MIT Press.

Maffi, Luisa. 2005. 'Linguistic, Cultural, and Biological Diversity', *Annual Review of Anthropology* 34: 599–617.

Magrane, Eric. 2015. 'Situating Geopoetics', *GeoHumanities* 1 (1): 86–102.

Maho, Jouni Filip and Bonny Sands. 2002. *The Languages of Tanzania: A Bibliography*. Gothenburg: Acta Universitatis Gothoburgensis.

Makaš, Emily Gunzburger. 2007. 'Representing Competing Identities: Building and Rebuilding in Postwar Mostar, Bosnia-Hercegovina'. PhD thesis, Cornell University.

Maleuvre, Didier. 1999. *Museum Memories: History, Technology, Art*. Stanford: Stanford University Press.

Mandler, Peter. 1997. *The Fall and Rise of the Stately Home*. New Haven: Yale University Press.

Marcus, George E. 1995. 'Ethnography in/of the World System: The Emergence of Multi-Sited Ethnography', *Annual Review of Anthropology* 24: 95–117.

Marcus, George E. 2013. 'Experimental Forms for the Expression of Norms in the Ethnography of the Contemporary', *HAU: Journal of Ethnographic Theory* 3 (2): 197–217.

Marino, Mark C. 2014. 'Mobilizing Cities: Alternative Community Storytelling'. In *The Mobile Story: Narrative Practices with Locative Technologies*, edited by Jason Farman, 290–304. New York: Routledge.

Marris, Emma. 2013. *Rambunctious Garden: Saving Nature in a Post-Wild World*. New York: Bloomsbury.

Martin, Paul. 1999. *Popular Collecting and the Everyday Self: The Reinvention of Museums?* London: Leicester University Press.

Massey, Doreen. 2005. *For Space*. London: SAGE Publications.

Massey, Doreen. 2006. 'Landscape as a Provocation: Reflections on Moving Mountains', *Journal of Material Culture* 11 (1/2): 33–48.

Massumi, Brian. 2002. *Parables for the Virtual: Movement, Affect, Sensation*. Durham, NC: Duke University Press.

Mathur, Nayanika. 2016. *Paper Tiger: Law, Bureaucracy and the Developmental State in Himalayan India*. Delhi: Cambridge University Press.

Mauss, Marcel. 1990. *The Gift: The Form and Reason for Exchange in Archaic Societies*, translated by W.D. Halls. London: Routledge.

Maxwell, Robert. 2016. '"The Radium Water Worked Fine until His Jaw Came Off": The Changing Role of Radioactivity in the Twentieth Century'. In *That Was Then, This is Now: Contemporary Archaeology and Material Cultures in Australia*, edited by Ursula K. Frederick and Anne Clarke, 84–100. Newcastle upon Tyne: Cambridge Scholars Publishing.

May, Sarah. 2009. 'Then Tyger Fierce Took Life Away: The Contemporary Material Culture of Tigers'. In *Contemporary Archaeologies: Excavating Now*, edited by Cornelius Holtorf and Angela Piccini, 65–80. Frankfurt am Main: Peter Lang.

May, Sarah. 2013. 'The Contemporary Material Culture of the Cult of the Infant: Constructing Children as Desiring Subjects'. In *The Oxford Handbook of the Archaeology of the Contemporary World*, edited by Paul Graves-Brown, Rodney Harrison and Angela Piccini, 713–27. Oxford: Oxford University Press.

May, Sarah. 2020. 'Heritage, Endangerment and Participation: Alternative Futures in the Lake District', *International Journal of Heritage Studies* 26 (1): 71–86.

May, Sarah. Forthcoming. 'Heritage, Thrift and Our Children's Children'. In *Cultural Heritage and the Future*, edited by Cornelius Holtorf and Anders Högberg. London and New York: Routledge.

McAtackney, Laura and Russell Palmer. 2016. 'Colonial Institutions: Uses, Subversions, and Material Afterlives', *International Journal of Historical Archaeology* 20 (3): 471–76.

McDonald, Peter D. 2017. *Artefacts of Writing: Ideas of the State and Communities of Letters from Matthew Arnold to Xu Bing*. Oxford: Oxford University Press.

McFadyen, Mairi. 2018. 'Expressing the Earth: Personal Reflection', *Stravaig* 6: 4–16. Accessed 3 February 2020. www.geopoetics.org.uk/wp-content/uploads/2018/09/STRAVAIG6-3.pdf.

McKay, Don. 2011. *The Shell of the Tortoise: Four Essays and an Assemblage*. Kentville, NS: Gaspereau Press.

Mead, Margaret. 1970. *Culture and Commitment: A Study of the Generation Gap*. Garden City, NY: Natural History Press.

Meanwell, Andrea. 2016. *A Native Breed: Starting a Lake District Hill Farm*. Kendal: Hayloft Publishing.

Meanwell, Andrea. 2017. *In My Boots: A Year on a Lake District Farm*. Kendal: Hayloft Publishing.

Mehrhoff, Leslie J. 1997. 'Museums, Research Collections, and the Biodiversity Challenge'. In *Biodiversity II: Understanding and Protecting Our Biological Resources*, edited by Marjorie L. Reaka-Kudla, Don E. Wilson and Edward O. Wilson, 447–64. Washington, DC: Joseph Henry Press.

Mendoza, Neil. 2017. *The Mendoza Review: An Independent Review of Museums in England*. London: Department for Digital, Culture, Media and Sport. Accessed 6 February 2020. www.gov.uk/government/publications/the-mendoza-review-an-independent-review-of-museums-in-england.

Meskell, Lynn. 2002. 'Negative Heritage and Past Mastering in Archaeology', *Anthropological Quarterly* 75 (3): 557–74.

Meskell, Lynn, ed. 2005. *Archaeologies of Materiality*. Malden, MA: Blackwell.

Meskell, Lynn. 2009. 'Introduction: Cosmopolitan Heritage Ethics'. In *Cosmopolitan Archaeologies*, edited by Lynn Meskell, 1–27. Durham, NC: Duke University Press.

Meskell, Lynn. 2012a. 'Archaeological Ethnography: Materiality, Heritage, and Hybrid Methodologies'. In *Archaeology and Anthropology: Past, Present and Future*, edited by David Shankland, 133–44. London: Berg.

Meskell, Lynn. 2012b. *The Nature of Heritage: The New South Africa*. Malden, MA: Wiley-Blackwell.

Meskell, Lynn. 2013. 'UNESCO's World Heritage Convention at 40: Challenging the Economic and Political Order of International Heritage Conservation', *Current Anthropology* 54 (4): 483–94.

Meskell, Lynn. 2014. 'States of Conservation: Protection, Politics, and Pacting within UNESCO's World Heritage Committee', *Anthropological Quarterly* 87 (1): 217–43.

Meskell, Lynn, ed. 2015a. *Global Heritage: A Reader*. Chichester: Wiley-Blackwell.

Meskell, Lynn. 2015b. 'Gridlock: UNESCO, Global Conflict and Failed Ambitions', *World Archaeology* 47 (2): 225–38.

Meskell, Lynn. 2018. *A Future in Ruins: UNESCO, World Heritage, and the Dream of Peace*. New York: Oxford University Press.

Meskell, L., C. Liuzza, E. Bertacchini and D. Saccone. 2015. 'Multilateralism and UNESCO World Heritage: Decision-Making, States Parties and Political Processes', *International Journal of Heritage Studies* 21 (5): 423–40.

Metelerkamp, Peter. 2013. 'Photo Essay: Institutional Spaces'. In *The Oxford Handbook of the Archaeology of the Contemporary World*, edited by Paul Graves-Brown, Rodney Harrison and Angela Piccini, 522–48. Oxford: Oxford University Press.

MHCLG (Ministry of Housing, Communities and Local Government). 2019. *National Planning Policy Framework*. London: Ministry of Housing, Communities and Local Government. Accessed 6 February 2020. https://assets.publishing.service.gov.uk/government/uploads/system/uploads/attachment_data/file/779764/NPPF_Feb_2019_web.pdf.

Middleton, Guy D. 2017. 'Do Civilisations Collapse?', *Aeon*, 16 November. Accessed 6 February 2020. https://aeon.co/essays/what-the-idea-of-civilisational-collapse-says-about-history.

Miller, Daniel, ed. 2001. *Home Possessions: Material Culture behind Closed Doors*. Oxford: Berg.

Miller, Daniel. 2008. *The Comfort of Things*. Cambridge: Polity Press.

Miller, Riel. 2009. 'The Future of the Future: The Role of Anticipation in a Universe of Fundamental Indeterminacy'. Unpublished conference presentation at the Centre for Research in Futures and Innovation, University of South Wales.

Mirani, Leo. 2015. 'There Are Now More Than 24,000 different Android devices', *Quartz*, 5 August. Accessed 23 February 2020. https://qz.com/472767/there-are-now-more-than-24000-different-android-devices.

MLA (Museums, Libraries and Archives Council). 2004. *Accreditation Standard: The Accreditation Scheme for Museums in the United Kingdom*. London: Museums, Libraries and Archives Council.

Mol, Annemarie. 2008. *The Logic of Care: Health and the Problem of Patient Choice*. London: Routledge.

MOM (Memory of Mankind). 2013. Memory of Mankind information leaflet. Personal collection.

MOM (Memory of Mankind). 2017. 'Greatest Time Capsule of Humankind', *YouTube*, 17 October. Video. Accessed 2 March 2020. https://youtu.be/tm8o9w7X2XI.

MOM (Memory of Mankind). 2018. 'Memory of Mankind'. Accessed 3 February 2020. www.memory-of-mankind.com.

Monbiot, George. 2013. 'Sheepwrecked – How Britain Has Been Shagged by the White Plague', *The Spectator*, 30 May. Accessed 3 February 2020. www.monbiot.com/2013/05/30/sheepwrecked/.

Monbiot, George. 2017. 'Fell Purpose', *The Guardian*, 9 May. Accessed 3 February 2020. www.monbiot.com/2017/05/19/fell-purpose/.

Morgan, David. 2011. 'Thing', *Material Religion* 7 (1): 140–46.

Morgan, Jennie and Sharon Macdonald. 2020. 'De-Growing Museum Collections for New Heritage Futures', *International Journal of Heritage Studies* 26 (1): 56–70.

Morgan, Jennie and Sarah Pink. 2018. 'Researcher Safety? Ethnography in the Interdisciplinary World of Audit Cultures', *Cultural Studies ↔ Critical Methodologies* 18 (6): 400–9.

Morton, Timothy. 2009. *Ecology without Nature: Rethinking Environmental Aesthetics*. Cambridge, MA: Harvard University Press.

Morton, Timothy. 2011. 'Objects as Temporary Autonomous Zones', *Continent* 1 (3): 149–55.

Morton, Timothy. 2013a. *Hyperobjects: Philosophy and Ecology after the End of the World*. Minneapolis: University of Minnesota Press.

Morton, Timothy. 2013b. *Realist Magic: Objects, Ontology, Causality*. Ann Arbor, MI: Open Humanities Press.

Morton, Timothy. 2016. *Dark Ecology: For a Logic of Future Coexistence*. New York: Columbia University Press.

Morton, Timothy. 2017. *Humankind: Solidarity with Nonhuman People*. London: Verso.

Muniesa, Fabian. 2014. *The Provoked Economy: Economic Reality and the Performative Turn*. London: Routledge.

Muniesa, Fabian and Michel Callon. 2007. 'Economic Experiments and the Construction of Markets'. In *Do Economists Make Markets? On the Performativity of Economics*, edited by Donald MacKenzie, Fabian Muniesa and Lucia Siu, 163–89. Princeton: Princeton University Press.

Murtagh, William J. 2006. *Keeping Time: The History and Theory of Preservation in America*. 3rd ed. Hoboken, NJ: Wiley.

Murtić, Aida and Marko Barišić. 2019. 'Unruly Monument: Subverting the Topography of the Partisan Memorial Cemetery in Mostar'. *Paragrana*, 28 (1): 80–100.

Museums Association. 2007. *A Public Consultation on Museum Disposal*. London: FreshMinds.

Museums Association. 2012. *Effective Collections: Achievements and Legacy*. London: Museums Association.

Museums Association. 2014. 'Disposal Toolkit'. Accessed 6 February 2020. www.museumsassociation.org/collections/disposal-toolkit.

Museums Association. 2015. 'Code of Ethics for Museums'. Accessed 6 February 2020. www.museumsassociation.org/ethics/code-of-ethics.

Museums Association. 2018. *Museums Taskforce Report and Recommendations*. London: Museums Association.

NASA. 2017. 'NASA Beamed Your #MessageToVoyager'. Accessed 6 February 2020. https://voyager.jpl.nasa.gov/message/.

NASA Goddard. 2013. 'NASA | Happy Birthday, Curiosity!', *YouTube*, 5 August. Video. Accessed 6 February 2020. www.youtube.com/watch?v=uxVVgBAosqg.

Nash, Roderick. 1967. *Wilderness and the American Mind*. New Haven: Yale University Press.

National Assembly for Wales. 2015. 'Well-Being of Future Generations (Wales) Act 2015'. Accessed 6 February 2020. www.legislation.gov.uk/anaw/2015/2/contents/enacted.

The National Trust Acts 1907–1971, as Varied by a Parliamentary Scheme Implemented by the Charities (National Trust) Order 2005. Accessed 9 October 2019. https://nt.global.ssl.fastly.net/documents/download-national-trust-acts-1907–1971-post-order-2005.pdf.

National Trust. 2015. Spirit of Place Statement at Orford Ness. Unpublished.

National Trust. n.d. a. 'Behind the Scenes on Orford Ness'. Accessed 30 October 2018. www.national-trust.org.uk/orford-ness-national-nature-reserve/features/behind-the-scenes-on-orford-ness.

National Trust. n.d. b. 'Coastal Vegetated Shingle and Shingle Heath on Orford Ness'. Accessed 30 October 2018. www.nationaltrust.org.uk/orford-ness-national-nature-reserve/features/coastal-vegetated-shingle-and-shingle-heath-on-orford-ness.

National Trust and RSPB. 2014. *The Alde-Ore Estuary: Securing a Sustainable Future for Wildlife. The Layman Report*. Accessed 29 February 2020. http://ec.europa.eu/environment/life/project/Projects/index.cfm?fuseaction=home.showFile&rep=file&fil=LIFE08_NAT_UK_000199_LAYMAN.pdf.

Natural England. 2016. *Conservation 21: Natural England's Conservation Strategy for the 21st Century*. York: Natural England. Accessed 6 February 2020. https://assets.publishing.service.gov.uk/government/uploads/system/uploads/attachment_data/file/562046/conservation-21.pdf.

Natural Resources Wales. 2011. 'Ancient Woodland Inventory 2011'. Accessed 28 February 2020. https://data.gov.uk/dataset/345e5790-22aa-4f0a-9548-a806d81286f8/ancient-woodland-inventory-2011.

Navaro-Yashin, Yael. 2012. *The Make-Believe Space: Affective Geography in a Postwar Polity*. Durham, NC: Duke University Press.

Navarro, Laetitia M. and Henrique M. Pereira. 2012. 'Rewilding Abandoned Landscapes in Europe', *Ecosystems* 15 (6): 900–12.

Neimanis, Astrida. 2014. 'Alongside the Right to Water, a Posthumanist Feminist Imaginary', *Journal of Human Rights and the Environment* 5 (1): 5–24.

Nesbit, Rebecca. 2018. 'Time to Embrace the Anthropocene: An Interview with Chris Thomas', *British Ecological Society Bulletin* 49 (1): 40–43.

Newell, Sasha. 2014. 'The Matter of the Unfetish: Hoarding and the Spirit of Possessions', *HAU: Journal of Ethnographic Theory* 4 (3): 185–213.

Nicol, Danny. 2018. *Doctor Who: A British Alien?* Cham: Palgrave Macmillan.

Niedner-Kalthoff, Ulrike. 2015. *Producing Cultural Diversity: Hegemonic Knowledge in Global Governance Projects*. Frankfurt am Main: Campus Verlag.

NMDC (National Museum Directors' Conference). 2003. *Too Much Stuff? Disposal from Museums*. London: National Museum Directors' Conference.

Nordblad, Julia. Forthcoming. 'Concepts of Future Generations: Four Contemporary Examples'. In *The Oxford Handbook of the Future*. Oxford: Oxford University Press.

Norwegian Ministry of Agriculture and Food. 2015. 'Svalbard Global Seed Vault: More about the Physical Plant'. Accessed 23 February 2015. www.regjeringen.no/en/topics/food-fisheries-and-agriculture/landbruk/svalbard-global-seed-vault/mer-om-det-fysiske-anlegget/id2365142/.

O'Connor, M.R. 2015. *Resurrection Science: Conservation, De-Extinction and the Precarious Future of Wild Things*. New York: St. Martin's Press.

Oelschlaeger, Max. 1991. *The Idea of Wilderness: From Prehistory to the Age of Ecology*. New Haven: Yale University Press.

Office of Arts and Libraries. 1989. *The Cost of Collecting: Collection Management in UK Museums*. London: HMSO.

Okrent, David. 1999. 'On Intergenerational Equity and Its Clash with Intragenerational Equity and on the Need for Policies to Guide the Regulation of Disposal of Wastes and Other Activities Posing Very Long-Term Risks', *Risk Analysis* 19 (5): 877–901.

Olivier, Laurent. 2004. 'The Past of the Present: Archaeological Memory and Time', *Archaeological Dialogues* 10 (2): 204–13.

Olsen, Bjørnar and Þóra Pétursdóttir. 2016. 'Unruly Heritage: Tracing Legacies in the Anthropocene', *Arkæologisk Forum* 35: 38–45.

Olwig, Kenneth R. 2016. 'Virtual Enclosure, Ecosystem Services, Landscape's Character and the "Rewilding" of the Commons: The "Lake District" Case', *Landscape Research* 41 (2): 253–64.

O'Malley, Pat. 2015. 'Uncertainty Makes Us Free: Insurance and Liberal Rationality'. In *Modes of Uncertainty: Anthropological Cases*, edited by Limor Samimian-Darash and Paul Rabinow, 13–28. Chicago: University of Chicago Press.

Omura, Keiichi, Grant Jun Otsuki, Shiho Satsuka and Atsuro Morita, eds. 2019. *The World Multiple: The Quotidian Politics of Knowing and Generating Entangled Worlds*. London: Routledge.

Opitz, Sven and Ute Tellmann. 2015. 'Future Emergencies: Temporal Politics in Law and Economy', *Theory, Culture and Society* 32 (2): 107–29.

Orange, Hilary. 2015. 'Benders, Benches and Bunkers: Contestation, Commemoration and Myth-Making in the Recent Past'. In *Reanimating Industrial Spaces: Conducting Memory Work in Post-industrial Societies*, edited by Hilary Orange, 191–211. Walnut Creek, CA: Left Coast Press.

Orlove, Benjamin S. and Stephen B. Brush. 1996. 'Anthropology and the Conservation of Biodiversity', *Annual Review of Anthropology* 25: 329–52.

Osborne, Peter. 1995. *The Politics of Time: Modernity and Avante-Garde*. London: Verso.

Outram, Dorinda. 1997. 'Book Review – *Inventing Human Science: Eighteenth-Century Domains*, by Christopher Fox, Roy Porter and Robert Wokler', *English Historical Review* 112 (449): 1290–91.

Paglen, Trevor. 2013. 'Friends of Space, How Are You All? Have You Eaten Yet? Or, Why Talk to Aliens Even if We Can't', *Afterall: A Journal of Art, Context and Enquiry* 32: 8–19.

Pal, Sanchari. 2018. 'Freezing Future: Inside Chang La, India's Doomsday Vault in the Himalayas', *The Better India*, 1 March. Accessed 22 February 2020. www.thebetterindia.com/132661/chang-la-ladakh-doomsday-vault-india.

Park, Chris and Michael Allaby. 2013. *A Dictionary of Environment and Conservation*. 2nd ed. Oxford: Oxford University Press.

Parry, Bronwyn. 2004. *Trading the Genome: Investigating the Commodification of Bio-Information*. New York: Columbia University Press.

Pearce, Susan M. 1992. *Museums, Objects and Collections: A Cultural Study*. Leicester: Leicester University Press.

Pearce, Susan M., ed. 1994. *Interpreting Objects and Collections*. London: Routledge.

Pearce, Susan M. 1998. *Collecting in Contemporary Practice*. London: SAGE Publications.

Pearce, Susan M. 1999. *On Collecting: An Investigation into Collecting in the European Tradition*. London: Routledge.

Pels, Dick, Kevin Hetherington and Frédéric Vandenberghe. 2002. 'The Status of the Object: Performances, Mediations, and Techniques', *Theory, Culture and Society* 19 (5/6): 1–21.

Peltola, Taru and Johanna Tuomisaari. 2015. 'Making a Difference: Forest Biodiversity, Affective Capacities and the Micro-Politics of Expert Fieldwork', *Geoforum* 64: 1–11.

Peltola, Taru and Johanna Tuomisaari. 2016. 'Re-Inventing Forestry Expertise: Strategies for Coping with Biodiversity Protection in Finland', *Forest Policy and Economics* 62: 11–18.

Penny, H. Glenn. 2002. *Objects of Culture: Ethnology and Ethnographic Museums in Imperial Germany*. Chapel Hill: University of North Carolina Press.

Penrose, Sefryn. 2017. 'Creative Destruction and Neoliberal Landscapes: Post-Industrial Archaeologies beyond Ruins'. In *Contemporary Archaeology and the City: Creativity, Ruination, and Political Action*, edited by Laura McAtackney and Krysta Ryzewski, 171–89. Oxford: Oxford University Press.

Peres, Sara. 2016. 'Saving the Gene Pool for the Future: Seed Banks as Archives', *Studies in History and Philosophy of Biological and Biomedical Sciences* 55: 96–104.

Perrings, Charles, Carl Folke and Karl-Göran Mäler. 1992. 'The Ecology and Economics of Biodiversity Loss: The Research Agenda', *Ambio* 21 (3): 201–11.

Perry, Sara. 2019. 'The Enchantment of the Archaeological Record', *European Journal of Archaeology* 22 (3): 354–71.

Pescatore, Claudio. 2018. 'Information and Memory for Future Decision Making: Radioactive Waste and Beyond'. Accessed 6 February 2020. www.diva-portal.org/smash/get/diva2:1276461/FULLTEXT01.pdf.

Petrović, Tanja. 2013. 'Museums and Workers: Negotiating Industrial Heritage in the Former Yugoslavia', *Narodna umjetnost* 50 (1): 96–120.

Pétursdóttir, Þóra. 2013. 'Concrete Matters: Ruins of Modernity and the Things Called Heritage', *Journal of Social Archaeology* 13 (1): 31–53.

Pétursdóttir, Þóra. 2014. 'Things Out-of-Hand: The Aesthetics of Abandonment'. In *Ruin Memories: Materialities, Aesthetics and the Archaeology of the Recent Past*, edited by Bjørnar Olsen and Þóra Pétursdóttir, 335–64. London: Routledge.

Pétursdóttir, Þóra. 2017. 'Climate Change? Archaeology and Anthropocene', *Archaeological Dialogues* 24 (2): 175–205.

Pétursdóttir, Þóra. 2020. 'Anticipated Futures? Knowing the Heritage of Drift Matter', *International Journal of Heritage Studies* 26 (1): 87–103.

Pétursdóttir, Þóra and Bjørnar Olsen. 2014a. 'An Archaeology of Ruins'. In *Ruin Memories: Materialities, Aesthetics and the Archaeology of the Recent Past*, edited by Bjørnar Olsen and Þóra Pétursdóttir, 3–29. London: Routledge.

Pétursdóttir, Þóra and Bjørnar Olsen. 2014b. 'Imaging Modern Decay: The Aesthetics of Ruin Photography', *Journal of Contemporary Archaeology* 1 (1): 7–23.

Pilcher, Helen. 2016. *Bring Back the King: The New Science of De-Extinction*. London: Bloomsbury Sigma.

Pink, Sarah. 2009. *Doing Sensory Ethnography*. London: SAGE Publications.

Pink, Sarah. 2012. *Situating Everyday Life: Practices and Places*. London: SAGE Publications.

Pink, Sarah and Jennie Morgan. 2013. 'Short-Term Ethnography: Intense Routes to Knowing', *Symbolic Interaction* 36 (3): 351–61.

Pink, Sarah, Jennie Morgan and Andrew Dainty. 2014. 'The Safe Hand: Gels, Water, Gloves and the Materiality of Tactile Knowing', *Journal of Material Culture* 19 (4): 425–42.

Pistorius, Robin. 1997. *Scientists, Plants and Politics: A History of the Plant Genetic Resources Movement*. Rome: International Plant Genetic Resources Institute.

Pollock, Susan. 2016. 'Archaeology and Contemporary Warfare', *Annual Review of Anthropology* 45: 215–31.

Poulios, Ioannis. 2010. 'Moving beyond a Values-based Approach to Heritage Conservation', *Conservation and Management of Archaeological Sites* 12 (2): 170–85.

Povinelli, Elizabeth A. 2011a. 'The Woman on the Other Side of the Wall: Archiving the Otherwise in Postcolonial Digital Archives', *Differences* 22 (1): 146–71.

Povinelli, Elizabeth A. 2011b. 'Routes/Worlds', *e-flux Journal* 27: 1–12. Accessed 4 February 2020. http://worker01.e-flux.com/pdf/article_8888244.pdf.

Povinelli, Elizabeth A. 2012. 'The Will to Be Otherwise/The Effort of Endurance', *South Atlantic Quarterly* 111 (3): 453–75.

Povinelli, Elizabeth A. 2014. 'Geontologies of the Otherwise', *Fieldsights*, 13 January. Accessed 4 February 2020. https://culanth.org/fieldsights/geontologies-of-the-otherwise.

Povinelli, Elizabeth A. 2016. *Geontologies: A Requiem to Late Liberalism*. Durham, NC: Duke University Press.

Pratt, Mary Louise. 2017. 'Coda: Concept and Chronotope'. In *Arts of Living on a Damaged Planet: Ghosts and Monsters of the Anthropocene*, edited by Anna Lowenhaupt Tsing, Heather Anne Swanson, Elaine Gan and Nils Bubandt, 169–74. Minneapolis: University of Minnesota Press.

Pred, Allan. 2004. *The Past is Not Dead: Facts, Fictions, and Enduring Racial Stereotypes*. Minneapolis: University of Minnesota Press.

Puig de la Bellacasa, María. 2017. *Matters of Care: Speculative Ethics in More Than Human Worlds*. Minneapolis: University of Minnesota Press.

Pyykkönen, Miikka. 2012. 'UNESCO and Cultural Diversity: Democratisation, Commodification or Governmentalisation of Culture?', *International Journal of Cultural Policy* 18 (5): 545–62.

Quast, Paul E. 2018. 'A Profile of Humanity: The Cultural Signature of Earth's Inhabitants beyond the Atmosphere', *International Journal of Astrobiology* 1–21. Accessed 4 February 2020. https://doi.org/10.1017/S1473550418000290.

Rabinow, Paul. 1996. *Making PCR: A Story of Biotechnology*. Chicago: University of Chicago Press.

Rabinow, Paul. 1999. *French DNA: Trouble in Purgatory*. Chicago: University of Chicago Press.

Rabinow, Paul. 2003. *Anthropos Today: Reflections on Modern Equipment*. Princeton: Princeton University Press.

Rabinow, Paul. 2008. *Marking Time: On the Anthropology of the Contemporary*. Princeton: Princeton University Press.

Rabinow, Paul. 2011. *The Accompaniment: Assembling the Contemporary*. Chicago: University of Chicago Press.

Rabinow, Paul and Talia Dan-Cohen. 2005. *A Machine to Make a Future: Biotech Chronicles*. Princeton: Princeton University Press.

Rabinow, Paul, George E. Marcus, James D. Faubion and Tobias Rees. 2008. *Designs for an Anthropology of the Contemporary*. Durham, NC: Duke University Press.

Radin, Joanna. 2013. 'Latent Life: Concepts and Practices of Human Tissue Preservation in the International Biological Program', *Social Studies of Science* 43 (4): 484–508.

Radin, Joanna. 2015. 'Planned Hindsight: The Vital Valuations of Frozen Tissue at the Zoo and the Natural History Museum', *Journal of Cultural Economy* 8 (3): 361–78.

Radin, Joanna. 2016. 'Planning for the Past: Cryopreservation at the Farm, Zoo, and Museum'. In *Endangerment, Biodiversity and Culture*, edited by Fernando Vidal and Nélia Dias, 218–40. London: Routledge.

Radin, Joanna. 2017. *Life on Ice: A History of New Uses for Cold Blood*. Chicago: University of Chicago Press.

Radin, Joanna and Emma Kowal, eds. 2017. *Cryopolitics: Frozen Life in a Melting World*. Cambridge, MA: MIT Press.

Ramet, Sabrina P. 2006. 'Explaining the Yugoslav Meltdown, 1: "For a Charm of Pow'rful Trouble, Like a Hell-Broth Boil and Bubble": Theories about the Roots of the Yugoslav Troubles'. In *Conflict in South-Eastern Europe at the End of the Twentieth Century: A "Scholars' Initiative" Assesses Some of the Controversies*, edited by Thomas Emmert and Charles Ingrao, 5–37. London: Routledge.

Raxworthy, Robyn Alice. 2018 'Excavating the Archive: Heritage-Making Practices in Cornwall's Clay Country'. PhD thesis, University of Exeter.

Rebanks, James. 2009. *World Heritage Status: Is There Opportunity for Economic Gain?* Kendal: Lake District World Heritage Project. Accessed 6 February 2020. http://icomos.fa.utl.pt/documentos/2009/WHSTheEconomicGainFinalReport.pdf.

Rebanks, James. 2015. *The Shepherd's Life: A Tale of the Lake District*. London: Allen Lane.

Rebanks, James. 2019. *The Shepherd's View: Modern Photographs from an Ancient Landscape*. London: Penguin Books.

Reeves, Sarah. 2018. 'Storing a Collection of 500,000 Objects', *Inside the Collection*, 17 January. Accessed 6 February 2020. https://maas.museum/inside-the-collection/2018/01/17/storing-a-collection-of-500000-objects.

Reicher, Steve. 2014. 'Making a Past Fit for the Future: The Political and Ontological Dimensions of Historical Continuity'. In *Self Continuity: Individual and Collective Perspectives*, edited by Fabio Sani, 145–58. New York: Psychology Press.

Rendell, Jane. 2006. *Art and Architecture: A Place Between*. London: I.B. Tauris.

Rexhepi, Piro. 2018. 'The Politics of Postcolonial Erasure in Sarajevo', *Interventions: International Journal of Postcolonial Studies* 20 (6): 930–45.

Richardson, Lorna-Jane. 2014. 'Understanding Archaeological Authority in a Digital Context', *Internet Archaeology* 38. Accessed 4 February 2020. https://doi.org/10.11141/ia.38.1.

Richardson, Lorna-Jane and Simon Lindgren. 2017. 'Online Tribes and Digital Authority: What Can Social Theory Bring to Digital Archaeology?', *Open Archaeology* 3: 139–48.

Rico, Trinidad. 2008. 'Negative Heritage: The Place of Conflict in World Heritage', *Conservation and Management of Archaeological Sites* 10 (4): 344–52.

Rico, Trinidad. 2014a. 'The Limits of a "Heritage at Risk" Framework: The Construction of Post-Disaster Cultural Heritage in Banda Aceh, Indonesia', *Journal of Social Archaeology* 14 (2): 157–76.

Rico, Trinidad. 2014b. 'Islamic Values as Heritage Subjects', *Material Religion* 10 (4): 533–34.

Rico, Trinidad. 2015a. 'Heritage at Risk: The Authority and Autonomy of a Dominant Preservation Framework'. In *Heritage Keywords: Rhetoric and Redescription in Cultural Heritage*, edited by Kathryn Lafrenz Samuels and Trinidad Rico, 147–62. Boulder: University Press of Colorado.

Rico, Trinidad. 2015b. 'After Words: A De-Dichotomization in Heritage Discourse'. In *Heritage Keywords: Rhetoric and Redescription in Cultural Heritage*, edited by Kathryn Lafrenz Samuels and Trinidad Rico, 285–92. Boulder: University Press of Colorado.

Rico, Trinidad. 2016. *Constructing Destruction: Heritage Narratives in the Tsunami City*. New York: Routledge.

Riegl, Alois. 1982. 'The Modern Cult of Monuments: Its Character and Its Origins', translated by Kurt W. Forster and Diane Ghirardo, *Oppositions* 25: 21–51.

Rivers without Boundaries. 2019. *Heritage Dammed: Water Infrastructure Impacts on World Heritage Sites and Free Flowing Rivers: Civil Society Report to the UNESCO World Heritage Committee and Parties of the World Heritage Convention*. Moscow: Rivers without Boundaries and World Heritage Watch.

Roark, Tony. 2011. *Aristotle on Time: A Study of the Physics*. Cambridge University Press: Cambridge.

Robins, Robert H. and Eugenius M. Uhlenbeck, eds. 1991. *Endangered Languages*. Oxford: Berg.

Rocha, Filomena, Carlos Gaspar and Ana Maria Barata. 2017. 'The Legacy of Collecting Missions to the Valorisation of Agro-Biodiversity', *Poljoprivreda i Sumarstvo* 63 (2): 25–38.

Rockman, Marcy, Marissa Morgan, Sonya Ziaja, George Hambrecht and Alison Meadow. 2016. *Cultural Resources Climate Change Strategy*. Washington, DC: Cultural Resources, Partnerships, and Science Climate Change Response Program, National Parks Service.

Rodrigues, Ana S.L., John D. Pilgrim, John F. Lamoreux, Michael Hoffmann and Thomas M. Brooks. 2006. 'The Value of the IUCN Red List for Conservation', *Trends in Ecology and Evolution* 21 (2): 71–76.

Rose, Nikolas. 2007. *The Politics of Life Itself: Biomedicine, Power, and Subjectivity in the Twenty-First Century*. Princeton: Princeton University Press.

Rose, Nikolas. 2013. 'The Human Sciences in a Biological Age', *Theory, Culture and Society* 30 (1): 3–34.

Ruskin, John. 1849. *The Seven Lamps of Architecture*. London: Smith, Elder and Co.

Russell, Bertrand. 1950. *Unpopular Essays*. New York: Simon and Schuster.

Russell, Naomi. n.d. 'Perspectives on Disposal: Museum of London Review and Rationalisation Project', Collections Trust blog. Accessed 6 February 2020. https://collectionstrust.org.uk/blog/perspectives-on-disposal-museum-of-london-review-and-rationalisation-project.

Sagan, Carl, F.D. Drake, Ann Druyan, Timothy Ferris, Jon Lomberg and Linda Salzman Sagan. 1978. *Murmurs of Earth: The Voyager Interstellar Record*. New York: Random House.

Salazar, Juan Francisco, Sarah Pink, Andrew Irving and Johannes Sjöberg, eds. 2017. *Anthropologies and Futures: Researching Emerging and Uncertain Worlds*. London: Bloomsbury Academic.

Saldanha, Arun. 2017. *Space after Deleuze*. London: Bloomsbury Academic.

Samimian-Darash, Limor and Paul Rabinow, eds. 2015. *Modes of Uncertainty: Anthropological Cases*. Chicago: University of Chicago Press.

Samuel, Raphael. 1994. *Theatres of Memory, Volume 1: Past and Present in Contemporary Culture*. London: Verso.

Samuels, Joshua. 2015. 'Difficult Heritage: Coming "to Terms" with Sicily's Fascist Past'. In *Heritage Keywords: Rhetoric and Redescription in Cultural Heritage*, edited by Kathryn Lafrenz Samuels and Trinidad Rico, 111–28. Boulder: University Press of Colorado.

Sandford, Richard and May Cassar. Forthcoming. 'Heritages of Futures Thinking: Strategic Foresight and Critical Futures'. In *Cultural Heritage and the Future*, edited by Cornelius Holtorf and Anders Högberg. London and New York: Routledge.

San Diego Zoo Institute for Conservation Research. 2020. 'Frozen Zoo®'. Accessed 22 February 2020. https://institute.sandiegozoo.org/resources/frozen-zoo%C2%AE.

Sani, Fabio, Marina Herrera and Mhairi Bowe. 2009. 'Perceived Collective Continuity and Ingroup Identification as Defence against Death Awareness', *Journal of Experimental Social Psychology* 45 (1): 242–45.

Saramago, José. 1998. *Baltasar and Blimunda*, translated by Giovanni Pontiero. London: Harvill.

Saramago, José. 2010. *The Elephant's Journey*. Harmondsworth: Penguin.

Saramago, José. 2013. *Journey to Portugal: In Pursuit of Portugal's History and Culture*, translated by Amanda Hopkinson and Nick Caistor. London: Harvill.

Sarkar, Sahotra. 2002. 'Defining "Biodiversity"; Assessing Biodiversity', *The Monist* 85 (1): 131–55.

Savill, Richard. 2009. 'Recession-Hit Resort of Torquay is Dying, Residents Fear', *The Telegraph*, 5 March. Accessed 4 February 2020. www.telegraph.co.uk/finance/recession/4939389/Recession-hit-resort-of-Torquay-is-dying-residents-fear.html.

Savills. 2014. *West Carclaze Eco-Community Environmental Statement, Volume 3: Non Technical Summary*. Southampton: Savills. Accessed 6 February 2020. www.iema.net/assets/nts/Savills/West_Carclaze_Eco-Community_NTS_December_2014.pdf.

Schatzki, Theodore. 2010. 'Materiality and Social Life', *Nature and Culture* 5 (2): 123–49.

Schlanger, Nathan, Laurent Nespoulous and Jean-Paul Demoule. 2016. 'Year 5 at Fukushima: A "Disaster-Led" Archaeology of the Contemporary Future', *Antiquity* 90 (350): 409–24.

Schor, Juliet. 2008. 'Tackling Turbo Consumption', *Cultural Studies* 22 (5): 588–98.

Schröder, Jantine. 2019. *Preservation of Records, Knowledge and Memory (RK&M) across Generations: Final Report of the RK&M Initiative*. Paris: OECD Nuclear Energy Agency.

Schwenk, Theodor. 1996. *Sensitive Chaos: The Creation of Flowing Forms in Water and Air*. Forest Row: Rudolf Steiner Press.

Sebald, W.G. 2010. *The Emergence of Memory: Conversations with W.G. Sebald*, edited by Lynne Sharon Schwartz. New York: Seven Stories Press.

Seitsonen, Oula. 2018. 'Digging Hitler's Arctic War: Archaeologies and Heritage of the Second World War German Military Presence in Finnish Lapland'. PhD thesis, University of Helsinki.

Sellars, Richard West. 1997. *Preserving Nature in the National Parks: A History*. New Haven: Yale University Press.

Sepkoski, David. 2016. 'Extinction, Diversity, and Endangerment'. In *Endangerment, Biodiversity and Culture*, edited by Fernando Vidal and Nélia Dias, 62–86. London: Routledge.

Serres, Michel and Bruno Latour. 1995. *Conversations on Science, Culture, and Time*, translated by Roxanne Lapidus. Ann Arbor: University of Michigan Press.

Setamu, John, ed. 2015. *On Rock or Sand? Firm Foundations for Britain's Future*. London: Society for Promoting Christian Knowledge.

Ševčenko, Liz. 2010. 'Sites of Conscience: New Approaches to Conflicted Memory', *Museum International* 62 (1/2): 20–25.
Ševčenko, Liz. 2011. 'Sites of Conscience: Heritage of and for Human Rights'. In *Heritage, Memory and Identity*, edited by Helmut Anheier and Yudhishthir Raj Isar, 114–23. London: SAGE Publications.
Shamash, Jack. 2014. *The Sociology of Collecting*. Foxy Books.
Shanks, Michael. 2012. *"Let Me Tell You about Hadrian's Wall ... ": Heritage, Performance, Design*. Amsterdam: Reinwardt Academy.
Shapiro, Beth. 2015. *How to Clone a Mammoth: The Science of De-Extinction*. Princeton: Princeton University Press.
Sherkow, Jacob S. and Henry T. Greely. 2013. 'What if Extinction is Not Forever?', *Science* 340 (6128): 32–33.
Shukin, Nicole. 2009. *Animal Capital: Rendering Life in Biopolitical Times*. Minneapolis: University of Minnesota Press.
Simmons, John E. 2015. 'Collection Care and Management: History, Theory, and Practice'. In *The International Handbooks of Museum Studies, Volume 2: Museum Practice*, edited by Conal McCarthy, 221–47. Chichester: Wiley-Blackwell.
Sjöberg, Lennart and Britt-Marie Drottz-Sjöberg. 2001. 'Fairness, Risk and Risk Tolerance in the Siting of a Nuclear Waste Repositonry', *Journal of Risk Research* 4 (1): 75–101.
Sloterdijk, Peter. 2016. *Foams: Spheres III*, translated by Wieland Hoban. South Pasadena, CA: Semiotext(e).
Smith, Laurajane. 2006. *Uses of Heritage*. London: Routledge.
Sodikoff, Genese Marie, ed. 2012. *The Anthropology of Extinction: Essays on Culture and Species Death*. Bloomington: Indiana University Press.
Soleri, Daniela and Steven E. Smith. 1999. 'Conserving Folk Crop Varieties: Different Agricultures, Different Goals'. In *Ethnoecology: Situated Knowledge/Located Lives*, edited by Virginia D. Nazarea, 133–54. Tucson: University of Arizona Press.
Solli, Brit, Mats Burström, Ewa Domanska, Matt Edgeworth, Alfredo González-Ruibal, Cornelius Holtorf, Gavin Lucas, Terje Oestigaard, Laurajane Smith and Christopher Witmore. 2011. 'Some Reflections on Heritage and Archaeology in the Anthropocene', *Norwegian Archaeological Review* 44 (1): 40–88.
Sørensen, Marie Louise Stig and Dacia Viejo-Rose, eds. 2015. *War and Cultural Heritage: Biographies of Place*. New York: Cambridge University Press.
Soukup, Barbara. 2006. 'Language News in Review: UNESCO and the Quest for Cultural Diversity', *Language Policy* 5: 209–18.
SPAB (Society for the Protection of Ancient Buildings). 2017. 'The SPAB Manifesto'. Accessed 9 October 2019. www.spab.org.uk/about-us/spab-manifesto.
Spennemann, Dirk H.R. 2007a. 'The Futurist Stance of Historical Societies: An Analysis of Position Statements', *International Journal of Arts Management* 9 (2): 4–15.
Spennemann, Dirk H.R. 2007b. 'Futurist Rhetoric in US Historic Preservation: A Review of Current Practice', *International Review on Public and Non Profit Marketing* 4 (1/2): 91–99.
Springett, Selina. 2015. 'Going Deeper or Flatter: Connecting Deep Mapping, Flat Ontologies and the Democratizing of Knowledge', *Humanities* 4: 623–36.
SSAUK (Self Storage Association UK). 2018. *The Self Storage Association UK Annual Industry Report*. Nantwich: Self Storage Association UK. Accessed 6 February 2020. www.ssauk.com/publications/annual-industry-report.
SSAUK (Self Storage Association UK). 2019. *The Self Storage Association UK Annual Industry Report*. Nantwich: Self Storage Association UK. Accessed 6 February 2020. www.ssauk.com/publications/annual-industry-report.
Stainforth, Elizabeth and Helen Graham. 2017. 'Utopian Currents in Heritage', *Future Anterior* 14 (2): iii–vi.
Staniforth, Sarah, ed. 2013. *Historical Perspectives on Preventive Conservation* (Readings in Conservation). Los Angeles: Getty Conservation Institute.
Statsbygg. 2008. *Svalbard Global Seed Vault, Longyearbyen, Svalbard: New Construction*. Oslo: Statsbygg.
Stengers, Isabelle. 2000. *The Invention of Modern Science*, translated by Daniel W. Smith. Minneapolis: University of Minnesota Press.
Stengers, Isabelle. 2005. 'Introductory Notes on an Ecology of Practices', *Cultural Studies Review* 11 (1): 183–96.

Stengers, Isabelle. 2010. *Cosmopolitics I*, translated by Robert Bononno. Minneapolis: University of Minnesota Press.

Stengers, Isabelle. 2011. *Cosmopolitics II*, translated by Robert Bononno. Minneapolis: University of Minnesota Press.

Stephens, Simon. 2015. 'Q&A with Beverley Cook', *Museums Journal*, 23 September. Accessed 4 February 2020. www.museumsassociation.org/museums-journal/archive-search/23092015-q-and-a-with-beverley-cook.

Sterling, Colin. 2020. *Heritage, Photography, and the Affective Past*. Abingdon and New York: Routledge.

Stevens, Chris. 2018. 'A Virtual "Hop" Around the UK', *Inside Self-Storage* Fall: 25–6.

Stevens, Stan, ed. 2014. *Indigenous Peoples, National Parks, and Protected Areas: A New Paradigm Linking Conservation, Culture, and Rights*. Tucson: University of Arizona Press.

Stevenson, Alice. 2018. 'Lying in Wait: Inertia and Latency in the Collection'. In *Museum Storage and Meaning: Tales from the Crypt*, edited by Mirjam Brusius and Kavita Singh, 231–39. London: Routledge.

Stewart, Susan. 1993. *On Longing: Narratives of the Miniature, the Gigantic, the Souvenir, the Collection*. Durham NC: Duke University Press.

Stoetzer, Bettina. 2018. 'Ruderal Ecologies: Rethinking Nature, Migration, and the Urban Landscape in Berlin', *Cultural Anthropology* 33 (2): 295–323.

Stoler, Ann Laura. 2008. 'Imperial Debris: Reflections on Ruins and Ruination', *Cultural Anthropology* 23 (2): 191–219.

Stoler, Ann Laura. 2009. *Along the Archival Grain: Epistemic Anxieties and Colonial Common Sense*. Princeton: Princeton University Press.

Stoler, Ann Laura, ed. 2013. *Imperial Debris: On Ruins and Ruination*. Durham, NC: Duke University Press.

Storm, Anna. 2014. *Post-Industrial Landscape Scars*. New York: Palgrave Macmillan.

Storm, Anna. 2015. 'Heritage Messages of a Post-Nuclear Nature'. In *Radioactive Waste Management and Constructing Memory for Future Generations: Proceedings of the International Conference and Debate, 15–17 September 2014, Verdun, France*, 71–73. Paris: Organisation for Economic Co-operation and Development. Accessed 6 February 2020. www.oecd-nea.org/rwm/pubs/2015/7259-constructing-memory-2015.pdf.

Strasser, Susan. 1999. *Waste and Want: A Social History of Trash*. New York: Metropolitan Books.

Strasser, Susan. 2015. 'Rags, Bones, and Plastic Bags: Obsolescence, Trash, and American Consumer Culture'. In *Cultures of Obsolescence: History, Materialist, and the Digital Age*, edited by Babette B. Tischleder and Sarah Wasserman, 41–60. New York: Palgrave Macmillan.

Subcommission on Quaternary Stratigraphy Anthropocene Working Group. 2019. 'Results of binding vote by AWG: Released 21st May 2019'. Accessed 29 February 2020. http://quaternary.stratigraphy.org/working-groups/anthropocene/.

Sullivan, Graeme. 2009. 'Making Space: The Purpose and Place of Practice-Led Research'. In *Practice-Led Research, Research-Led Practice in the Creative Arts*, edited by Hazel Smith and Roger T. Dean, 41–65. Edinburgh: Edinburgh University Press.

Sunder Rajan, Kaushik. 2006. *Biocapital: The Constitution of Postgenomic Life*. Durham, NC: Duke University Press.

Sutton, Jenny, Elaine Taylor, Allan Bank and Marian Silvester. 2017. 'The Great Defender: Canon Hardwicke Rawnsley', *Views* 54: 10–12. Accessed 28 February 2020. www.nationaltrust.org.uk/documents/views-magazine-2017.pdf.

Svalbard Global Seed Vault. 2010. 'Seed Portal – Depositors and Material'. Accessed 6 February 2020. www.NordGen.org/sgsv/index.php?page=sgsv_information_sharing.

Swanson, Heather, John Law and Marianne E. Lien. 2018. 'Modes of Naturing: Or Stories of Salmon'. In *The SAGE Handbook of Nature, Volume 2*, edited by Terry Marsden, 868–90. London: SAGE Publications.

Swedish National Council for Nuclear Waste. 2019. Overview of eight countries – status April 2019. Stockholm. www.karnavfallsradet.se/sites/default/files/documents/report_2019_1.pdf.

Swenson, Astrid. 2014. *The Rise of Heritage: Preserving the Past in France, Germany and England, 1789–1914*. Cambridge: Cambridge University Press.

Swingland, Ian R. 2001. 'Biodiversity, Definition Of'. In *Encyclopedia of Biodiversity, Volume 1*, edited by Simon Asher Levin, 377–91. San Diego: Academic Press.

Takacs, David. 1996. *The Idea of Biodiversity: Philosophies of Paradise*. Baltimore: Johns Hopkins University Press.

Thacker, Eugene. 2005. *The Global Genome: Biotechnology, Politics, and Culture*. Cambridge, MS: MIT Press.

Thacker, Eugene. 2010. *After Life*. Chicago: University of Chicago Press.

The Telegraph. 2018. 'Twitter's Favourite Shepherd Quits Government Review of National Parks after Three Days Due to "Cretinous Attacks" from Environmentalists', *The Telegraph*, 24 June. Accessed 4 February 2020. www.telegraph.co.uk/news/2018/06/24/twitters-favourite-shepherd-quits-government-review-national/.

Thiemeyer, Thomas. 2018. *Das Depot als Versprechen: Warum unsere Museen die Lagerräume ihrer Dinge wiederentdecken*. Cologne: Böhlau Verlag.

Thomas, Chris D. 2017. *Inheritors of the Earth: How Nature is Thriving in an Age of Extinction*. New York: PublicAffairs.

Thompson, Ken. 2014. *Where Do Camels Belong? The Story and Science of Invasive Species*. London: Profile Books.

Thompson, Michael. 1979. *Rubbish Theory: The Creation and Destruction of Value*. Oxford: Oxford University Press.

Thoreau, Henry David. 1960. *Walden*, edited by Sherman Paul. Boston: Houghton Mifflin.

Thurlow, Charles. 2005. *China Clay from Cornwall and Devon: An Illustrated Account of the Modern China Clay Industry*. 4th ed. St Austell: Cornish Hillside Publications.

Tilley, Christopher and Kate Cameron-Daum. 2017. *An Anthropology of Landscape: The Extraordinary in the Ordinary*. London: UCL Press.

Tischleder, Babette B. and Sarah Wasserman, eds. 2015. *Cultures of Obsolescence: History, Materiality, and the Digital Age*. New York: Palgrave Macmillan.

Todorova, Maria. 1997. *Imagining the Balkans*. New York: Oxford University Press.

Tomlinson, John. 2007. *The Culture of Speed: The Coming of Immediacy*. London: SAGE Publications.

Tonkin, John. 2007. 'Walks along the Clay Trails with the China Clay History Society'. Unpublished notes.

Trouillot, Michel-Rolph. 1995. *Silencing the Past: Power and the Production of History*. Boston: Beacon Press.

Trower, Shelley. 2009. 'Clayscapes: Views of a Working Landscape, from Poetry to Oral History', *Cornish Studies* 17 (1): 17–33.

Tsing, Anna Lowenhaupt. 2005. *Friction: An Ethnography of Global Connection*. Princeton: Princeton University Press.

Tsing, Anna Lowenhaupt. 2015. *The Mushroom at the End of the World: On the Possibility of Life in Capitalist Ruins*. Princeton: Princeton University Press.

Tsing, Anna Lowenhaupt, Heather Anne Swanson, Elaine Gan and Nils Bubandt, eds. 2017. *Arts of Living on a Damaged Planet: Ghosts and Monsters of the Anthropocene*. Minneapolis: University of Minnesota Press.

Tunbridge, J.E. and G.J. Ashworth. 1996. *Dissonant Heritage: The Management of the Past as a Resource in Conflict*. Chichester: Wiley.

Tungate, Mark. 2007. *Adland: A Global History of Advertising*. London: Kogan Page.

Turner, Stephanie S. 2007. 'Open-Ended Stories: Extinction Narratives in Genome Time', *Literature and Medicine* 26 (1): 55–82.

Turner, Victor. 1982. *From Ritual to Theatre: The Human Seriousness of Play*. New York: Performing Arts Journal Publications.

Turow, Joseph and Matthew P. McAllister, eds. 2009. *The Advertising and Consumer Culture Reader*. New York: Routledge.

Tythacott, Louise and Kostas Arvanitis, eds. 2014. *Museums and Restitution: New Practices, New Approaches*. Farnham: Ashgate.

UNESCO (United Nations Educational, Scientific and Cultural Organization). 1950. *The Race Question*. Accessed 29 February 2020. https://unesdoc.unesco.org/ark:/48223/pf0000128291.

UNESCO (United Nations Educational, Scientific and Cultural Organization). 1966. Declaration of Principles of International Cultural Co-operation. Accessed 6 February 2020. www.un-documents.net/dpicc.htm.

UNESCO (United Nations Educational, Scientific and Cultural Organization). 1972. Convention Concerning the Protection of the World Cultural and Natural Heritage. Accessed 6 February 2020. https://whc.unesco.org/en/conventiontext/.

UNESCO (United Nations Educational, Scientific and Cultural Organization). 1989. Recommendation on the Safeguarding of Traditional Culture and Folklore. Accessed 6 February 2020. http://portal.unesco.org/en/ev.php-URL_ID=13141&URL_DO=DO_TOPIC&URL_SECTION=201.html.

UNESCO (United Nations Educational, Scientific and Cultural Organization). 1997. 'Hallstatt-Dachstein/Salzkammergut Cultural Landscape'. Accessed 25 February 2020. https://whc.unesco.org/en/list/806.

UNESCO (United Nations Educational, Scientific and Cultural Organization). 2001. Proclamation of Masterpieces of the Oral and Intangible Heritage of Humanity. Accessed 6 February 2020. http://unesdoc.unesco.org/images/0012/001246/124628eo.pdf.

UNESCO (United Nations Educational, Scientific and Cultural Organization). 2002. UNESCO Universal Declaration on Cultural Diversity, Adopted by the 31st Session of the General Conference of UNESCO, Paris, 2 November 2001. Accessed 6 February 2020. http://unesdoc.unesco.org/images/0012/001271/127160m.pdf.

UNESCO (United Nations Educational, Scientific and Cultural Organization). 2003. Convention for the Safeguarding of the Intangible Cultural Heritage. Accessed 6 February 2020. https://ich.unesco.org/en/convention.

UNESCO (United Nations Educational, Scientific and Cultural Organization). 2005. Convention on the Protection and Promotion of the Diversity of Cultural Expressions. Accessed 6 February 2020. https://unesdoc.unesco.org/ark:/48223/pf0000142919.

UNESCO (United Nations Educational, Scientific and Cultural Organization). 2017. The English Lake District. Accessed 24 February 2020. https://whc.unesco.org/en/list/422.

UNESCO Ad Hoc Expert Group on Endangered Languages. 2003. *Language Vitality and Endangerment: Document Submitted to the International Expert Meeting on UNESCO Programme Safeguarding of Endangered Languages, Paris, 10–12 March 2003*. Paris: United Nations Educational, Scientific and Cultural Organization. Accessed 6 February 2020. www.unesco.org/new/fileadmin/MULTIMEDIA/HQ/CLT/pdf/Language_vitality_and_endangerment_EN.pdf.

United Nations. 1992. Convention on Biological Diversity. New York: United Nations. Accessed 5 February 2020. www.cbd.int/convention/text/.

United Nations Conference on Environment and Development. 1992. The Rio Declaration on Environment and Development. Accessed 6 February 2020. https://www.cbd.int/doc/ref/rio-declaration.shtml.

United States Congress. 1916. Act to Establish a National Park Service (Organic Act), 1916: An Act to Establish a National Park Service, and for Other Purposes, Approved August 25, 1916 (39 Stat. 535). Accessed 5 February 2020. www.nps.gov/foun/learn/management/upload/1916%20ACT%20TO%20ESTABLISH%20A%20NATIONAL%20PARK%20SERVICE-5.pdf.

University of York. 2016. Holding on to the past: Why decluttering is such a dilemma', 25 April. Accessed 24 February 2020. www.york.ac.uk/research/themes/clutter-heritage/.

US NRC (United States Nuclear Regulatory Commission). 2009. 'Part 63: Disposal of High-Level Radioactive Wastes in a Geologic Repository at Yucca Mountain, Nevada'. Accessed 24 February 2020. www.nrc.gov/reading-rm/doc-collections/cfr/part063/full-text.html.

Urry, John. 2016. *What is the Future?* Cambridge: Polity Press.

Vakoch, Douglas A. 1998. 'The Dialogic Model: Representing Human Diversity in Messages to Extraterrestrials', *Acta Astronautica* 42 (10–12): 705–10.

Van der Veer, Peter. 2016. *The Value of Comparison*. Durham, NC: Duke University Press.

Van Dooren, Thom. 2007. 'Terminated Seed: Death, Proprietary Kinship and the Production of (Bio)Wealth', *Science as Culture* 16 (1): 71–93.

Van Dooren, Thom. 2009. 'Banking Seed: Use and Value in the Conservation of Agricultural Diversity', *Science as Culture* 18 (4): 373–95.

Van Dooren, Thom. 2014. *Flight Ways: Life and Loss at the Edge of Extinction*. New York: Columbia University Press.

Van Dooren, Thom. 2016. 'Authentic Crows: Identity, Captivity and Emergent Forms of Life', *Theory, Culture and Society* 33 (2): 29–52.

Van Dooren, Thom. 2017. 'Banking the Forest: Loss, Hope, and Care in Hawaiian Conservation'. In *Cryopolitics: Frozen Life in a Melting World*, edited by Joanna Radin and Emma Kowal, 259–82. Cambridge, MA: MIT Press.

Vecco, Marilena and Michele Piazzai. 2015. 'Deaccessioning of Museum Collections: What Do We Know and Where Do We Stand in Europe?', *Journal of Cultural Heritage* 16 (2): 221–27.

Vidal, Fernando and Nélia Dias. 2016a. 'Introduction: The Endangerment Sensibility'. In *Endangerment, Biodiversity and Culture*, edited by Fernando Vidal and Nélia Dias, 1–38. London: Routledge.

Vidal, Fernando and Nélia Dias, eds. 2016b. *Endangerment, Biodiversity and Culture*. London: Routledge.

Viejo-Rose, Dacia. 2011. *Reconstructing Spain: Cultural Heritage and Memory after Civil War*. Brighton: Sussex Academic.

Virilio, Paul. 1986. *Speed and Politics: An Essay on Dromology*. New York: Columbia University Press.

Von Droste zu Hülshoff, Bernd. 2006. 'A Gift from the Past to the Future: Natural and Cultural World Heritage'. In *Sixty Years of Science at UNESCO, 1945–2005*, edited by Patrick Petitjean, Vladimir Zharov, Gisbert Glaser, Jaques Richardson, Bruno de Padirac and Gail Archibald, 389–400. Paris: United Nations Educational, Scientific and Cultural Organization.

Wainwright, Angus. 2009. 'Orford Ness – A Landscape in Conflict?'. In *Europe's Deadly Century: Perspectives on 20th Century Conflict Heritage*, edited by Neil Forbes, Robin Page and Guillermo Pérez, 134–42. Swindon: English Heritage.

Wakefield, Stephanie. 2018. 'Inhabiting the Anthropocene Back Loop', *Resilience: International Politics, Practices and Discourses* 6 (2): 77–94.

Walasek, Helen, ed. 2016. *Bosnia and the Destruction of Cultural Heritage*. London: Routledge.

Waldby, Catherine and Robert Mitchell. 2006. *Tissue Economies: Blood, Organs, and Cell Lines in Late Capitalism*. Durham, NC: Duke University Press.

Walker, Lawrence R. and David A. Wardle. 2014. 'Plant Succession as an Integrator of Contrasting Ecological Time Scales', *Trends in Ecology and Evolution* 29 (9): 504–10.

Wallman, James. 2015. *Stuffocation: Living More with Less*. London: Penguin.

Walsh, Kevin. 1992. *The Representation of the Past: Museums and Heritage in the Post-Modern World*. London: Routledge.

Wang, Ning. 1999. 'Rethinking Authenticity in Tourism Experience', *Annals of Tourism Research* 26 (2): 349–70.

Waterman, Jonathan. 2010. *Running Dry: A Journey from Source to Sea Down the Dying Colorado River*. Washington, DC: National Geographic.

Waters, Richard D. and Jensen M. Williams. 2011. 'Squawking, Tweeting, Cooing, and Hooting: Analyzing the Communication Patterns of Government Agencies on Twitter', *Journal of Public Affairs* 11 (4): 353–63.

Watson, P.F. and W.V. Holt, eds. 2001. *Cryobanking the Genetic Resource: Wildlife Conservation for the Future?* London: Taylor and Francis.

Wearn, James A., Mark W. Chase, David J. Mabberley and Charlotte Couch. 2013. 'Utilizing a Phylogenetic Plant Classification for Systematic Arrangements in Botanic Gardens and Herbaria', *Botanical Journal of the Linnean Society* 172 (2): 127–41.

Westman, Clinton. 2013. 'Social Impact Assessment and the Anthropology of the Future in Canada's Tar Sands', *Human Organization* 72 (2): 111–20.

Whitbread-Abrutat, Peter. 2018. '"Landscapes in Limbo" – Cornish Claylands', *Future Terrains*. Accessed 5 February 2020. https://futureterrains.org/landscapes-in-limbo-cornish-claylands/.

White, Kenneth. 2003. *Geopoetics: Place, Culture, World*. Glasgow: Alba Editions.

Wijsmuller, Dieuwertje. 2017. *Deaccessioning and Disposal in Europe 2018–2017: A Research on Possibilities and Attitudes across the European Member States*. Museums and Deaccessioning in Europe. Accessed 5 February 2020. www.museumsanddeaccessioning.com.

Wikander, Ola. 2015a. 'Don't Push This Button: Phoenician Sarcophagi, "Atomic Priesthoods" and Nuclear Waste', *Årsbok*, 109–24.

Wikander, Ola. 2015b. 'Language, Nuclear Waste and Society: The Preservation of Knowledge over Vast Periods of Time and Its Relevance for Linguistics', *Lychnos*, 7–25.

Wildt, David E., William F. Rall, John K. Critser, Steven L. Monfort and Ulysses S. Seal. 1997. 'Genome Resource Banks: Living Collections for Biodiversity Conservation', *BioScience* 47 (10): 689–98.

WildWorks. 2014. 'Heart of Clay St Dennis Cornwall ECC', *YouTube*, 17 April. Video. Accessed 5 February 2020. www.youtube.com/watch?v=ujFmBZVmCCY.

Willetts, David. 2010. *The Pinch: How the Baby Boomers Took Their Children's Future – and Why They Should Give It Back*. London: Atlantic Books.

Willis, Fiona, Justin Moat and Alan Paton. 2003. 'Defining a Role for Herbarium Data in Red List Assessments: A Case Study of *Plectranthus* from Eastern and Southern Tropical Africa', *Biodiversity and Conservation* 12 (7): 1537–52.

Wilson, E.O., ed. 1988. *Biodiversity*. Washington, DC: National Academy Press.

Wilson, Elizabeth. 2003. *Adorned in Dreams: Fashion and Modernity*. London: I.B. Tauris.

Winter, Tim. 2014. 'Beyond Eurocentrism? Heritage Conservation and the Politics of Difference', *International Journal of Heritage Studies* 20 (2): 123–37.

Winter, Tim. 2015. 'Heritage Diplomacy', *International Journal of Heritage Studies* 21 (10): 997–1015.

Wisely, Samantha M., Oliver A. Ryder, Rachel M. Santymire, John F. Engelhardt and Ben J. No-vak. 2015. 'A Road Map for 21st Century Genetic Restoration: Gene Pool Enrichment of the Black-Footed Ferret', *Journal of Heredity* 106 (5): 581–92.

Withnall, Adam. 2019. 'Millions of Indigenous Forest-Dwelling Indians Face "World's Biggest Evic-tion" in the Name of Conservation', *The Independent*, 23 July. Accessed 5 February 2020. www.independent.co.uk/news/world/asia/india-indigenous-people-supreme-court-adivasis-tribals-eviction-fra-a9017961.html.

Wolfram, Stephen. 2018. 'How to Design Beacons for Humanity's Afterlife', *Wired*, 31 January. Accessed 5 February 2020. www.wired.com/story/how-to-design-beacons-for-humanitys-afterlife/.

Wollentz, Gustav. 2017a. 'Prehistoric Violence as Difficult Heritage: Sandby Borg – A Place of Avoidance and Belonging', *Current Swedish Archaeology* 25: 199–226.

Wollentz, Gustav. 2017b. 'Making a Home in Mostar: Heritage and the Temporalities of Belonging', *International Journal of Heritage Studies* 23 (10): 928–45.

Wollentz, Gustav. 2019. 'Conflicted Memorials and the Need to Look Forward: The Interplay be-tween Remembering and Forgetting in Mostar and on the Kosovo Field'. In *Memorials in the Aftermath of Armed Conflict: From History to Heritage*, edited by Marie Louise Stig Sørensen, Dacia Viejo-Rose and Paola Filippucci, 159–82. Cham: Palgrave Macmillan.

Wollentz, Gustav, Marko Barišić and Nourah Sammar. 2019. 'Youth Activism and Dignity in Post-War Mostar: Envisioning a Shared Future through Heritage', *Space and Polity* 23 (2): 197–215.

Woodham, Anna, Sara Penrhyn Jones, Bryony Onciul and Matthew Gordon-Clark. 2018. 'Enduring Connections: Heritage, Sustainable Development and Climate Change in Kiribati', *Journal of Museum Ethnography* 31: 199–211.

Woodward, Christopher. 2002. *In Ruins*. London: Vintage.

Woodward, Sophie. 2015. 'The Hidden Lives of Domestic Things: Accumulations in Cupboards, Lofts, and Shelves'. In *Intimacies, Critical Consumption and Diverse Economies*, edited by Emma Casey and Yvette Taylor, 216–31. Basingstoke: Palgrave Macmillan.

World Commission on Culture and Development. 1995. *Our Creative Diversity: Report of the World Commission on Culture and Development*. Paris: United Nations Educational, Scientific and Cultural Organization. Accessed 5 February 2020. https://unesdoc.unesco.org/ark:/48223/pf0000101651.

Worster, Donald. 1994. *Nature's Economy: A History of Ecological Ideas*. 2nd ed. Cambridge: Cam-bridge University Press.

Wurm, Stephen A., ed. 1996. *Atlas of the World's Languages in Danger of Disappearing*. Paris: UNESCO Publishing.

WWF (World Wide Fund for Nature). 2016. *Living Planet Report 2016: Risk and Resilience in a New Era*. Gland: WWF International. Accessed 5 February 2020. https://wwf.panda.org/wwf_news/?282370/Living-Planet-Report-2016.

Zeitlyn, David. 2012. 'Divinatory Logics: Diagnoses and Predictions Mediating Outcomes', *Current Anthropology* 53 (5): 525–46.

Zerner, Charles, ed. 1999. *People, Plants, and Justice: The Politics of Nature Conservation*. New York: Columbia University Press.

Zetterstrom-Sharp, Johanna. 2015. 'Heritage as Future-Making: Aspiration and Common Destiny in Sierra Leone', *International Journal of Heritage Studies* 21 (6): 609–27.

Zinn, Jens O., ed. 2008. *Social Theories of Risk and Uncertainty: An Introduction*. Malden, MA: Blackwell.

Index